THE WOMEN OF GR

✳ (REF 14245   ) £8.50

In print at £16.99

THE WOMEN OF GRUB STREET

Press, Politics, and Gender in the London Literary Marketplace 1678–1730

PAULA McDOWELL

CLARENDON PRESS · OXFORD
1998

Oxford University Press, Great Clarendon Street, Oxford OX2 6DP
Oxford New York
Athens Auckland Bangkok Bogota Bombay
Buenos Aires Calcutta Cape Town Dar es Salaam
Delhi Florence Hong Kong Istanbul Karachi
Kuala Lumpur Madras Madrid Melbourne
Mexico City Nairobi Paris Singapore
Taipei Tokyo Toronto Warsaw
and associated companies in
Berlin Ibadan

Oxford is a registered trade mark of Oxford University Press

Published in the United States by
Oxford University Press Inc., New York

British Library Cataloguing in Publication Data
Data available

Library of Congress Cataloging in Publication Data
McDowell, Paula.
The women of Grub Street : press, politics, and gender in the
London literary marketplace, 1678–1730 / Paula McDowell.
Includes bibliographical references (p.).
1. English prose literature—England—London—History and
criticism. 2. Women in the book industries and trade—England—
London—History—18th century. 3. Women in the book industries and
trade—England—London—History—17th century. 4. Women and
literature—England—London—History—18th century. 5. Women and
literature—England—London—History—17th century. 6. Manley, Mrs.
(Mary de la Rivière), 1663–1724—Political and social views.
7. Politics and literature—England—London—History. 8. Literature
publishing—England—London—History. 9. Women in journalism—
England—London—History. 10. Women in politics—England—London—
History. I. Title.
PR8476.M38 1997 820.9'9287'09032—dc21 97-44996

ISBN 0-19-818395-X
ISBN 0-19-818449-2 (pbk.)

1 3 5 7 9 10 8 6 4 2

Typeset by Best-set Typesetter Ltd., Hong Kong
Printed in Great Britain
on acid-free paper
by Biddles Ltd,
Guildford and King's Lynn

Acknowledgements

I FIRST became interested in eighteenth-century literature in 1979, when my freshman English teacher, Dr Lee Johnson of the University of British Columbia, Canada, assigned Henry Fielding's *Tom Jones*. Dr Johnson, it is only now that I am a teacher myself that I realize what courage good undergraduate teaching takes; to you and the other challenging teachers I had at UBC, I am grateful. At Stanford University, my interests were fostered by, and my projects supported by, exemplary scholar-teachers such as John Bender, W. B. Carnochan, Terry Castle, Barbara Gelpi, and Herbert Lindenberger. I was fortunate indeed to have had such models.

For financial assistance which enabled me to complete the dissertation and revise it as a book, I wish to acknowledge the Stanford English Department, the Mabelle McLeod Lewis Memorial Fund, the Thomas Killefer Dissertation Fellowship, the Woodrow Wilson National Fellowship Foundation, the Raymond Alden Dissertation Prize, the National Endowment for the Humanities Travel to Collections Award, the American Bibliographical Society, the Office of Graduate Studies and Research at the University of Maryland at College Park, and George Bridge.

My debts to the staff of diverse libraries and collections are at once broad and deep. I wish to acknowledge the London Public Record Office, the British Library and Museum, the former Sion College Library, the Dr Williams's Library of Nonconformism, the Library of the Society of Friends, the Bodleian Library, the Greater London Record Office, the Guildhall Library, the Corporation of London Record Office, the Huntington Library, the Lewis Walpole Library, the Stanford University Libraries, the Houghton Library, the Beinecke Rare Book and Manuscript Library, the McKeldin Library at the University of Maryland at College Park, and especially the Folger Shakespeare Library, whose educational outreach programmes are almost as splendid as its books.

A host of fellow eighteenth-century and book trade scholars have read portions of the book, or offered criticisms and suggestions. They are Elizabeth Bohls, Vincent Carretta, Mary Fissell, Sharon

Groves, Eleanor Shevlin, Calhoun Winton, and members of the Women in the Eighteenth Century Colloquium at the Folger Institute. Kristin Bailey, Sharon Groves, and Eleanor Shevlin provided ongoing research assistance and support, and shared their own scholarly work in progress. For exceeding all obligations of friendship and collegiality in reading closely the entire manuscript, I wish to express my deepest gratitude to Paula Backscheider, Carol Barash, Maureen Bell, J. Paul Hunter, Kathryn King, Susan Lanser, and two anonymous readers. Oxford University Press made my first experience of book publication a delight: special thanks to Jason Freeman, Sophie Goldsworthy, Janet Moth, and Jackie Pritchard, who have proven one thesis of this book, that authors are often greatly indebted to other 'makers' for shaping and strengthening their books. Thomas Moser Jr. has been a model of humanity; I feel fortunate to have known him.

My greatest debt is to George Bridge, whose laughter, labour, and love teaches me on a daily basis how to enjoy life to the fullest. This book is dedicated to him with love.

Contents

PART I. *'To Run One's Self Into Danger'*: *Women and the Politics of Opposition in the London Book Trade*

PART II. *'Telling the King His Faults'*: *Religio-Political Polemicism and Women's Public Expression*

PART III. *'I Take Truth With Me When I Can Get Her'*: *Delarivier Manley and the Reproduction of Political Intelligence*

Contents

List of Illustrations

Note on Primary Sources

Quotations from manuscripts have been reproduced exactly as they appear in the original, with the exception of 'ye' and 'yt' which have been replaced with their modern alternatives. *Sic* has been used sparingly. Conjectural readings of manuscript materials are indicated by square brackets, e.g. 'a letter to Mr. [Lorain] Thretning him with sword and pistol'. In citing State Papers from the London Public Record Office, diamond foliation numbers have been used, as was standard practice in 1986 when research for this portion of the book was undertaken.

Dates are given as they appear in the manuscripts except that 1 January is taken as the beginning of the year. I have altered the Quaker system of dating to conform to modern practice.

Due to lack of funding, Sion College Library closed permanently in July 1996. Rare books and manuscripts are currently being relocated to Lambeth Palace Library, where they will eventually be recatalogued and identified as the Sion College collection.

All pre-1900 imprints were published in London unless otherwise indicated.

Abbreviations

Add. MSS	Additional Manuscripts, British Library
BL	British Library
Bod.	Bodleian Library, Oxford
Boyer	Abel Boyer, *Political State of Great Britain*, 60 vols. (London, 1711–40)
CLRO	Corporation of London Record Office
CSPD	Public Record Office, *Calendar of State Papers, Domestic Series*
DNB	Leslie Stephens and Sidney Lee, eds., *Dictionary of National Biography*, 22 vols. (New York, 1885–1901)
Dr Wms	Doctor Williams's Library of Nonconformism, London
ECS	*Eighteenth-Century Studies*
Friends	Library of the Society of Friends, London
GL	Guildhall Library, London
HMC *Downshire MSS*	Historical Manuscripts Commission, *Report on the Manuscripts of the Marquess of Downshire*, 4 vols. in 5 (1924–40)
HMC *Portland MSS*	Historical Manuscripts Commission, *The Manuscripts of his Grace the Duke of Portland*, 10 vols. (1891–1931)
LEP	*London Evening Post*
Luttrell	Narcissus Luttrell, *A Brief Historical Relation of State Affairs from September 1678 to April 1714*, 6 vols. (Oxford UP, 1857)
MMM	Morning Meeting Minutes (Society of Friends)
MWJ	*Mist's Weekly Journal*
Nichols	John Nichols, *Literary Anecdotes of the Eighteenth Century*, 9 vols. (London, 1812–15)
PRO	Public Record Office, London
SP	State Papers (Domestic)
State Trials	T. B. Howell, comp., *A Complete Collection of State Trials*, 33 vols. (London, 1816–26)
Todd, *Dictionary*	Janet Todd, ed., *A Dictionary of British and American Women Writers 1660–1800* (Totowa, NJ: Rowman and Littlefield, 1987)

The next to your Habit is your Houses, which are deck'd with all manner of Curiosity, Richness and Delicacy, as your sinful Persons are: Your great spacious Lordly Houses, furnished with all manner of costly, rich and sumptuous Furniture, which would be too tedious, and fill up much Paper to insist upon; but your voluptuous Feeding, and excessive Feasting one another, in so much that you run out great Estates, both of your own and other Men's; but in your own Families, that is, among your Servants, many of you are very pinching and sparing, and to the Poor little or nothing, but what you are compell'd to in your Parish Duties; and your poor Neighbours, many hundreds in City and County, sits in their Houses with hungry Bellies, both of Weavers and others, that knows not which way to shift for Bread for their Children; some eating Bread sparingly, and drink Water, Others getting Garden stuff, as Cabbage, and such like for their Children to feed on; whilst you feed, *Dives* like, lying at your Ease, stretching your selves upon your rich Sattin Beds and Couches, wallowing in all your sinful Pleasures, not knowing what to Eat, Drink, or put on for Richness and Dainties; and others of you Hoards up Treasure as Sand, and are never satisfied, compassing Sea and Land to get Riches, adding House to House, and Land to Land, and all for Portions for our Children, say they; and thus the Fathers eat sowre Grapes, and the Childrens Teeth are set an edge.

(Joan Whitrowe, *The Widow Whiterow's* [sic] *Humble
Thanksgiving for the Kings Safe Return*, 1694)

Late, very late, Correctness grew our Care,
When the tir'd Nation breath'd from Civil War.

(Alexander Pope, 'The First Epistle of the
Second Book of Horace Imitated', wr. 1736)

Introduction
'Strange and Unheard of Revolutions'

In the spring of 1689, only weeks before he was rewarded with the bishopric of Salisbury for his support of William of Orange, the Reverend Doctor Gilbert Burnet approached the poet, dramatist, and novelist Aphra Behn, and offered the lifelong royalist court patronage in return for a poem celebrating the upcoming corona-tion of William and Mary.[1] Desperately in need of the money, Behn nevertheless rejected the offer, and instead published a declaration of her continued support for the now-exiled James II. Coyly (and wisely) veiled as *A Pindaric Poem To The Reverend Doctor Burnet, On The Honour he did me of Enquiring after me and my Muse*, Behn's personal political manifesto exemplifies a distrust expressed by many British women writers in the post-revolutionary period, of the motives of those responsible for the series of events Behn referred to as 'this Unpresidented Enterprise'.[2] The author of at least six separately published poems on Stuart royalty, including James II and Mary of Modena, their son James Francis Edward, and, most pointedly, James's daughter Queen Mary (as opposed to

[1] Burnet was not only William and Mary's personal chaplain, but also their policy adviser. The fact that Burnet was a high-ranking political strategist and experienced print propagandist makes his application to this 'low' woman writer remarkable—as does the fact that he had earlier referred to Behn in a letter to an aristocratic woman friend as 'so abominably vile a woman' (Gilbert Burnet to Anne Wharton, Dec. 1682, rpt. in James Granger, *Letters between J.G., and Many of the Most Eminent Literary Men of his Time . . .*, ed. J. P. Malcolm (1805), qtd. in *The Works of Aphra Behn*, ed. Janet Todd, vol. i: *Poetry* (Columbus: Ohio State UP, 1992), p. xxxiii, n. 38).

[2] Aphra Behn, *A Pindaric Poem To The Reverend Doctor Burnet, On The Honour he did me of Enquiring after me and my Muse* (1689), l. 93. Just as Behn referred to the Revolution of 1688 as this 'Unpresidented Enterprise', so most women writers of this period tended to refer to the events of these years in terms which suggest scorn or sadness rather than admiration. Delarivier Manley explicitly rejected the term 'Glorious Revolution' as propaganda (see Ch. 5). For this reason, despite the fact that the phrase 'Glorious Revolution' is by now so conven-tional as to have lost its original political bias, I have thought best to avoid it, as the majority of the women discussed here would have viewed it with suspicion or rejected it.

her husband William of Orange), Behn boldly declared that her
poetic Muse

> . . . would endeavour fain to glide
> With the fair prosperous Gale, and the full driving Tide
> But Loyalty Commands with pious Force,
>   That stops me in the thriving Course,
> The Brieze that wafts the Crowding Nations o're,
>   Leaves me unpity'd far behind
>   On the Forsaken Barren Shore,
> To Sigh with Echo, and the murmuring Wind;
>
> .   .   .   .
>
> Thus while the Chosen Seed possess the Promis'd Land,
>   I like the Excluded Prophet stand,
>   The Fruitful Happy Soil can only see,
>   But am forbid by Fates Decree
> To share the Triumph of the joyful Victory. (ll. 49–56, 61–5)

Behn represented herself as excluded from 'the thriving Course' by
virtue of her loyalty to her still-living King. In so doing, she implicitly contrasted her own unenviable position with that of Burnet,
whose fortunes were on the rise. Employing the persona of the
'Excluded Prophet', and thus drawing on the considerable strength
of the female prophetic tradition in seventeenth-century England,[3]
she deplored the changing political situation that rendered her, a
loyal royalist, 'Useless and Forlorn'—and paradoxically rendered
her royalist manifesto 'treasonous'.

More dangerously still, Behn went on to attribute the Revolution
of 1688 ('this Mighty Change') not to the merit of William of
Orange, the worthiness of the cause, or even the will of God, but
rather to Burnet's own 'wond'rous Pen' (l. 11):

> 'Tis to your Pen, Great Sir, the Nation owes
> For all the Good this Mighty Change has wrought;
> 'Twas that the wondrous Method did dispose,
> E're the vast Work was to Perfection brought. (ll. 66–9)[4]

---

[3] On the female prophetic tradition in 17th-cent. England, see Phyllis Mack,
Visionary Women: Ecstatic Prophecy in Seventeenth-Century England (Berkeley:
U. of California P., 1992), Elaine Hobby, *Virtue of Necessity: English Women's
Writing 1649–1688* (Ann Arbor: U. of Michigan P., 1989), ch. 1, and Dianne
Purkiss, 'Producing the Voice, Consuming the Body: Women Prophets of the Seven-
teenth Century', in Isobel Grundy and Susan Wiseman, eds., *Women, Writing,
History 1640–1740* (London: B. T. Batsford, 1992), 139–58.
[4] Burnet published eighteen pamphlets in 1689 alone and, as Behn points out, was
as much an agent as a chronicler of the political history of his time. At least one of

Alluding to Burnet's propagandistic services for William of Orange, Behn contemplated the extraordinary new power of the political press in her lifetime:

> Oh Strange effect of a Seraphick Quill!
>   That can by unperceptible degrees
> Change every Notion, every Principle
>   To any Form, its Great Dictator please:
> The Sword a Feeble Pow'r, compar'd to That,
>   And to the Nobler Pen subordinate;
> And of less use in *Bravest* turns of State. (ll. 70–6)

The 'Great Dictator' in Behn's poem was not James II, but rather polemicists such as Burnet—wielders of the new instrument of political power in England, the 'Nobler Pen'.[5] The Revolution did not liberate the English people from a 'Dictator', Behn suggested, but only potentially subjected them to a new one: the unstable tyranny of competing interest groups, whose battlefield was the propaganda press. The new ruler of British society was not 'public opinion' at all, but rather those few individuals who could manipulate this newly important discursive political construction through print. Concluding with the subtlest irony, Behn hinted that it was Burnet's propagandistic efforts for William of Orange, rather than William's supposed services or merit, that would make his name live: 'Your Pen shall more Immortalize his Name, | Than even his Own Renow[n]'d and Celebrated Fame' (ll. 102–3). Seven years earlier, a warrant had been issued for Behn's arrest for writing

Burnet's pamphlets justifying the Revolution, *An Enquiry into the Measures of Submission to the Supreme Authority; and of the Grounds upon which it may be lawful or necessary for Subjects to defend their Religion, Lives, and Liberties* (1688), was probably written even before William sailed. For this pamphlet, see Gilbert Burnet, *A Collection of Eighteen Papers* (1689), 120–4. For information regarding timing, see J. P. Kenyon, *Revolution Principles: The Politics of Party, 1689–1720* (1977; rpt. Cambridge UP, 1990), 13, who acknowledges H. C. Foxcroft, *A Life of Gilbert Burnet* (Cambridge, 1907), 538. For additional information on Burnet's propagandistic activities, see Martine Brownley, 'Bishop Gilbert Burnet and the Vagaries of Power', in Robert P. Maccubbin and Martha Hamilton-Phillips, eds., *The Age of William III and Mary II: Power, Politics, and Patronage 1688–1702* (Williamsburg, Va.: The College of William and Mary, 1989), 77–81.

[5] Whig propagandists routinely represented James II as 'tyrannick and arbitrary'. Behn turns this motif on its head here, suggesting that it is not James II who is the 'Great Dictator', but rather the ecclesiastic-cum-politician Burnet, who (mis)uses his 'Seraphick Quill' to 'Change every Notion, every Principle | To any Form, its Great Dictator please'.

'abusive reflections upon persons of Quality', and if she had lived to see her *Pindaric* printed she might well have found herself the object of another warrant.[6] But five days after Burnet preached the sermon at the coronation of William and Mary on 11 April 1689, the chronically ill Behn died. Aphra Behn's last known work, then, was both a political manifesto and a prophecy—a prophecy that not only models of political authority, but means of political power, were changing in England.

In the key period with which this book is concerned—roughly 1678 to 1730—the English press was undergoing some of the most important transformations in its history. The political upheaval of the Civil War period, combined with the collapse of press controls, had contributed to an explosion of the press in the 1640s, and the seventeenth-century growth in literacy[7] and emergence of a public sphere in print and politics were all faces of the same phenomenon. While there was some recovery of control after the Restoration with the Licensing or Printing Act of 1662, the English press would never again be as effectively censored as it had been prior to the 1640s. In 1695, the Licensing Act was allowed to lapse for good, ending official pre-publication censorship and government restrictions on the number of master printers throughout Britain. This

---

[6] On 12 Aug. 1682 a warrant was issued for Behn's arrest for having contributed an offending epilogue to the anonymous *Romulus and Hersilia; Or, The Sabine War* (PRO, Lord Chamberlain's Records, 5/191, f. 100). While Behn's epilogue was intended as an attack on the Whigs, it also criticized the Duke of Monmouth for having disobeyed his father Charles II, and so angered the King. To date, no archival evidence has been found that Behn was ever actually 'taken up'. She may have been let go with just a warning.

[7] What figures we have on early modern literacy remain far from definitive. Nearly all scholars agree, however, that literacy in England grew rapidly between 1600 and 1800, with the steepest acceleration occurring before 1675. Urban men and women were far more likely to be literate than their rural counterparts, and men were more likely to be literate than women. J. Paul Hunter's synthesis of studies of historical literacy estimates that female literacy in England rose from about 15–20% in 1600 to about 40% in 1750; his estimates are conservative ones. For concise overviews of studies of historical literacy, see Hunter, *Before Novels: The Cultural Contexts of Eighteenth-Century English Fiction* (New York: Norton, 1990), ch. 3, and Wyn Ford, 'The Problem of Literacy in Early Modern England', *History*, 78 (1993), 22–37. For an introduction to the historiographical controversy, see David Cressy, *Literacy and the Social Order: Reading and Writing in Tudor and Stuart England* (Cambridge UP, 1980), Keith Thomas, 'The Meaning of Literacy in Early Modern England', in Gerd Baumann, ed., *The Written Word: Literacy in Transition* (Oxford: Clarendon P., 1986), 97–131, and R. S. Schofield, 'The Measurement of Literacy in Pre-industrial England', in Jack Goody, ed., *Literacy in Traditional Societies* (Cambridge UP, 1968), 310–25.

event, combined with ongoing political turmoil, contributed to another major period of growth in the London book trades (see Part I). At the same time, the ongoing, gradual shift in the dominant mode of textual production in England—from courtly, manuscript literary culture to the print-based, market-centred system we know today—was giving rise to a recognizably modern literary market-place, and to the emerging professional literary subculture that by the late seventeenth century in England was already popularly referred to as 'Grub Street'.

This book argues that changing conditions of literary production and political expression in late seventeenth-century England, com-bined with increased literacy, enabled unprecedented female politi-cal involvement through print—that is, until transformations in sex roles and in English culture at large left eighteenth-century women increasingly depoliticized.[8] The birth of the modern literary market-place was concurrent with women's emergence in significant num-bers as publishing authors. At the same time, the survival of family industry in the book trades meant that women were still widely active as printers, publishers, hawkers, and ballad-singers as well. Working in *all* aspects of material literary production, and doing so for pay, the 'women of Grub Street' composed a series of heterogeneous collectivities, rather than a homogeneous 'subcul-ture'.[9] Divisions of rank and occupation within social orders, com-peting religious and political allegiances, and an array of other differences for the most part prevented these women from

[8] This depoliticization was largely a discursive effect, but it had real historical consequences. For book-length studies documenting the changing nature of 18th-cent. women's literary production, see Catherine Gallagher, *Nobody's Story: The Vanishing Acts of Women Writers in the Marketplace, 1670–1820* (Berkeley and Los Angeles: U. of California P., 1994), Jane Spencer, *The Rise of the Woman Novelist: From Aphra Behn to Jane Austen* (Oxford: Basil Blackwell, 1986), and Janet Todd, *The Sign of Angellica: Women, Writing and Fiction 1660–1800* (New York: Columbia UP, 1989). Also useful in this regard is Kathryn Shevelow, *Women and Print Culture: The Construction of Femininity in the Early Periodical* (London: Routledge, 1989).

[9] 'Subculture' is Pat Rogers's word in *Grub Street: Studies in a Subculture* (Lon-don: Methuen, 1972). To date, Rogers's is the only scholarly book-length study of the emergence in England of the concept and phenomenon of 'Grub Street'. Though our approaches are necessarily different ones, I am greatly indebted to Rogers's book, not least for inspiring my own. Brean S. Hammond's *Professional Imaginative Writing in England, 1670–1740: 'Hackney for Bread'* (Oxford: Clarendon Press, 1997) promises to further our understanding of Grub Street; my own book went to press before Hammond's was published.

understanding themselves as a group.[10] Yet if women writers, printers, and publishers did not typically understand themselves in collective terms, others did. Augustan political and cultural élites
recognized these women's joint access to their culture's most important mode of mass communication as a significant new threat to
the established order, and expended considerable energy working
to shut down their voices in print. In the period between the Popish
Plot and Exclusion Crisis (1678–83) and the consolidation of
Whig hegemony roughly fifty years later (1730)—combined with
the consolidation of the new literary marketplace, immortalized by
Alexander Pope in *The Dunciad* (1728)—decades of political unrest and an expanding press created new opportunities for diverse
oppositional communities. This book demonstrates that women
already at work in the London book trades were among the first to
seize those new opportunities for public political expression. At
this time of enduring significance in English political life, women of
the widest possible variety of socioeconomic backgrounds in fact
played so prominent a role in the production and transmission of
political and religio-political ideas through print as to belie simultaneous powerful claims that women had no place in civic life.

Meanwhile, this study registers a paradox. Over the course of
the period roughly 1678 to 1730, changing political conditions in
England were making possible new degrees of public political critique, and changing publishing conditions were enabling unprecedented communication of political ideas. Yet by the end of
this same period, Joseph Addison, Richard Steele, and others had
long since declared it their purpose to 'establish among us a Taste
of Polite Writing' (*Spectator*, no. 58, 7 May 1711), and writing
was increasingly evaluated according to new standards of polite
discourse.[11] While Addison and Steele explicitly addressed their

[10] As I suggest below, the group aspect here is a matter of socioeconomic and
cultural positioning rather than of an identity of interests. I am echoing Marx here
on the phenomenon of class (Karl Marx, *Capital: A Critique of Political Economy*,
vol. iii, trans. David Fernbach (Harmondsworth: Penguin, 1981), 1025–6).

[11] On the political uses of the new discourse of politeness see Lawrence E. Klein,
*Shaftesbury and the Culture of Politeness: Moral Discourse and Cultural Politics in
Early Eighteenth-Century England* (Cambridge UP, 1994), Paul Langford, *A Polite
and Commercial People: England 1727–1783* (Oxford UP, 1989), and J. G. A.
Pocock, *Virtue, Commerce and History: Essays on Political Thought and History,
Chiefly in the Eighteenth Century* (Cambridge UP, 1985). This point is discussed
further in the Conclusion.

popular periodicals to 'the Fair Sex', they also censured female 'Politicians . . . Free-Thinkers, and Disputants'. Warning their female readers that there was 'nothing so bad for the Face as Party-Zeal', they reminisced about a time when 'the most conspicuous woman . . . was only the best housewife' (*Tatler*, no. 42, 16 July 1709; *Spectator*, no. 57, 5 May 1711).

It is now well known that over the course of the late seventeenth and early eighteenth centuries in England state affairs became a matter of open daily discussion in new forums such as daily newspapers and city coffee-houses. It is also generally accepted that during this period something approximating 'public opinion' was established as a political force. Theorists of democracy and public discourse, most notably Jürgen Habermas, have categorized these developments as the crystallization of a new 'public sphere': a discursive realm embodied above all in the new political press, a space for critical political exchange wherein theoretically all persons who could divest themselves of particular interests could engage in the mutually beneficial task of monitoring the powers of the state.[12] By 1730, England saw the institutionalization of a critical political press that had been developing since at least the 1640s,[13] and political authority increasingly became a matter of competing public representations.

But as Habermas himself acknowledged, and as thirty years of scholarship have since confirmed, participation in what Habermas

---

[12] For a comprehensive bibliography of public sphere theory and related studies, see Arthur Strum, 'A Bibliography of the Concept *Öffentlichkeit*', *New German Critique*, 61 (1994), 161–202. Sources I have found especially valuable for this project include Craig Calhoun, ed., *Habermas and the Public Sphere* (Cambridge, Mass.: MIT Press, 1992), particularly the essays by Geoff Eley, Nancy Fraser, Jürgen Habermas, Mary Ryan, and David Zaret; Elizabeth C. Goldsmith and Dena Goodman, eds., *Going Public: Women and Publishing in Early Modern France* (Ithaca, NY: Cornell UP, 1995), especially the essay by Erica Harth; Margaret C. Jacob, 'The Mental Landscape of the Public Sphere: A European Perspective', *ECS* 28 (1994), 95–113; Klein, *Shaftesbury*, and articles listed in my bibliography; Greg Laugero, 'Publicity, Gender, and Genre: A Review Essay', *ECS* 28 (1995), 429–38; Steve Pincus, ' "Coffee Politicians Does Create": Coffeehouses and Restoration Political Culture', *Journal of Modern History*, 67 (1995), 807–34; and Shevelow, *Women and Print Culture*.

[13] By the 'institutionalization of a critical political press' I mean the increasing acceptance by those in power of daily newspapers, political essay journals, political broadsides, pamphlets, and so forth—'acceptance' being signalled by the institutionalization of government counter-propaganda (see Ch. 5) and by the Stamp Tax (see J. A. Downie, *Robert Harley and the Press: Propaganda and Public Opinion in the Age of Swift and Defoe* (Cambridge UP, 1979)).

designated the '*bourgeois* public sphere', while theoretically open to all, was from its inception delimited by factors of sex and rank: 'The fully developed bourgeois public sphere was based on the fictitious identity of the two roles assumed by the privatized individuals who came together to form a public: the role of property owners and the role of human beings pure and simple.'[14] While Habermas cautioned his readers that full participation in the bourgeois public was limited to substantially propertied males, early feminist critics of Habermas pointed to a more widespread exclusion of women, arguing that the bourgeois public was 'essentially, not just contingently masculinist'.[15] More recent feminist criticism has refined these early arguments, pointing out that some women were indeed included, even welcomed on certain terms. Eighteenth-century England may even have seen a 'normative enhancement of the feminine',[16] as the conversation of genteel women became valued as a civilizing influence in an increasingly profit-oriented (and still male-dominated) world. While feminists pointed to gender-based exclusions from public claims for rights, critics interested in class relations pointed to the exclusion of plebeian groups. The bourgeois public sphere Habermas theorized was never defined solely by the struggle against absolutism and traditional authority, but dealt with the problem of popular containment as well.[17] While many historians and theorists now understand the origins of 'the' public sphere as a matter of separate though overlapping 'publics', some still date the emergence of actually *competing* publics in England to the late eighteenth and early nineteenth centuries. Schol-

[14] Jürgen Habermas, *The Structural Transformation of the Public Sphere: An Inquiry into a Category of Bourgeois Society*, trans. Thomas Burger with the assistance of Frederick Lawrence, intro. Thomas McCarthy (Cambridge, Mass.: MIT Press, 1989), 56.

[15] Joan B. Landes, *Women and the Public Sphere in the Age of the French Revolution* (Ithaca, NY: Cornell UP, 1988), 7. Landes focuses on 'the era of the classical bourgeois public sphere' in France (1750 to 1850). For other important early feminist critiques and modifications see Strum, 'Bibliography'.

[16] Lawrence E. Klein, 'Gender, Conversation and the Public Sphere in Early Eighteenth-Century England', in Judith Still and Michael Worton, eds., *Textuality and Sexuality* (Manchester UP, 1993), 107.

[17] My language here echoes the essays by Eley and Fraser in Calhoun, ed., *Habermas*. In the preface, rather than the body, of *The Structural Transformation of the Public Sphere*, Habermas himself acknowledged that his investigation of the bourgeois public was limited to 'those features of a historical constellation that attained dominance' and left aside 'the plebeian public sphere as a variant that in a sense was suppressed' (p. xviii).

ars of the seventeenth century, by way of contrast, tend to link the emergence of a divided public sphere in print and politics to the collapse of press controls during the Civil War period,[18] and my own findings support arguments for a seventeenth-century emergence. What this book adds to these debates is a clear sense of women's involvement in seventeenth- and early eighteenth-century 'competing publics', particularly evidence that women were central to the development and institutionalization of a critical political press in Britain.

Focusing on middling and lower-class women's political activity through print, this book demonstrates that the public sphere in England was not always already masculine or bourgeois. But it also suggests that women's relationship to public politics through print changed by the mid-eighteenth century, and that in tracing women's shifting relationship to public discourse, gender and class must be read in tandem. In the preface, rather than the body, of *The Structural Transformation of the Public Sphere*, Habermas suggested but did not expand on the possibility that, from its inception, the idealized concept of 'the' (bourgeois) public actually functioned to contain, control, or otherwise delimit the activities of various other contemporary publics or forums for discussion. David Zaret has suggested that 'the liberal model of the public sphere emerged in England as an elite response to the radicalism and sectarianism that flourished during the [Civil War period]',[19] and my own investigation of middling and lower-class women's political activity through print has yielded considerable evidence to support such an argument. What one historian describes as the eighteenth-century 'construction of the public sphere as a polite zone'[20] should be emphasized as a *re*construction of something that existed earlier; a remodelling of competing publics into a new idealized 'community' to contend with fears of another Civil War in England. The point of this book is women's participation in, rather than exclusion from, a seventeenth- and early eighteenth-century public sphere in print and politics. But this book concludes by suggesting the implications, particularly for 'impolite' women, of the eighteenth-century consolidation of a polite public increasingly based on bourgeois

---

[18] See for instance Jacob, 'Mental Landscape', Pincus, ' "Coffee Politicians Does Create" ', and Zaret, 'Religion, Science, and Printing'.

[19] Zaret, 'Religion, Science, and Printing', 224.

[20] Klein, 'Gender, Conversation and the Public Sphere', 109.

individualism and secular reason. The 'civilized' public sphere Habermas described, in which a particular kind of female publicity was encouraged, functioned to contain other publics open to different female (and male) groups and constituted around different values. The eighteenth-century 'liberal model of the public sphere' —with its link to changing models of family and state, of political subjecthood and subjectivity, and of literary and cultural value— worked to shut down new opportunities for some even as it opened up opportunities for others.

In his valuable historical study of the emergence of the concept and phenomenon of 'Grub Street', Pat Rogers stressed the correlation for writers such as Jonathan Swift and Alexander Pope between the new pluralist literary marketplace and political, as well as literary, subversion. Emphasizing the prominence of events such as the Civil War and the Revolution of 1688 in the Augustans' collective memory, Rogers demonstrated that 'the vocabulary of Augustan satire . . . carries within itself a buried layer of allusion to civil unrest'.[21] 'Born in the century of revolution', writers such as Pope, Swift, Addison, and Steele witnessed 'big constitutional upheavals' and 'a steady undertow of popular disturbance', and saw the many forms of internal dissent which characterized their period as a 'genuine threat' (99). Rogers's study emphasizes 'Grub Street' as a 'constructive fiction of satire' in the works of Augustan cultural élites and as a mappable literary locus. My own study emphasizes the democratic possibilities inherent in the new literary marketplace and, especially, in the contemporary conjunction of print and politics. Rogers's study emphasizes 'Grub Street' as a noun; my own study emphasizes it as a rhetorical tool and as a form of social action. It is no accident that the earliest recorded uses of 'Grub Street' as a derogatory adjective date to periods of extreme political anxiety (1640s, 1680s). The particular response to the new literary marketplace that the label 'Grub Street' represents was part of an effort to establish peace in the world of letters after a century of political, as well as literary, upheaval. Alexander Pope explicitly acknowledged the link between literary and political anxieties when he wrote in 1736, 'Late, very late, correctness grew our care, | When the tir'd nation breath'd from civil war.'[22] Rogers's study

---

[21] *Grub Street*, 114.
[22] 'The First Epistle of the Second Book of Horace Imitated' (wr. 1736; pub. 1737), in *The Poems of Alexander Pope*, ed. John Butt (New Haven: Yale UP, 1963), 645, ll. 272–3.

emphasizes those who *expressed* anxieties concerning the newly pluralist literary marketplace; my own study emphasizes those who caused them. For among the newly vocal, competing political communities already in existence in revolutionary and post-revolutionary London was the heterogeneous 'community' of women printers, publishers, and authors this book links together as 'the women of Grub Street'.

The 'community' of women printworkers and propagandists in the late seventeenth- and early eighteenth-century London book trade was a matter of positioning rather than of an identity of interests. Their community was not yet grounded in a shared sense of gender identity; rather, community was made by their different but overlapping relationships to the new political print marketplace and to socioeconomic and cultural élites. Women in all three sections of this book were arrested for their involvement in the production and circulation of political ideas through print, and not only Augustan satire, but also records of the criminal justice system attest that the beneficiaries of the Revolution Settlement came to view these 'scandalous and reflecting', 'low indigent', 'seditious', 'fanatick', 'crackbrained', and otherwise impolite women as a genuine threat to an only tenuously re-established social order. In the late seventeenth and early eighteenth centuries in England, for the first time in history, a significant body of politically literate[23] women who were neither aristocratic nor genteel obtained access to the closest thing that their culture had to a 'mass medium': the press. That this event was unsettling enough to incite gentlemen as dissimilar as Prime Minister Robert Walpole and the Reverend Doctor Jonathan Swift to unite to 'contain the Revolution', so to speak, is one thesis of this book. Public sphere theorists have called for 'more historically specific, contextually specific analyses of social movements and possibilities and the arguments they make'.[24] This book helps to fill out Habermas's sociological model and in so doing challenges his framework. It is a contribution towards the history of public, though not necessarily 'polite', discourse.

While one goal of this study is to contribute towards the conceptual re-mapping of a key period in English political and literary history,

---

[23] My use of the phrase 'politically literate' here and throughout this book is intended to suggest a certain active involvement and acquisition of skills rather than a more passive-sounding political 'consciousness'.

[24] Stephen Leonard, contribution to 'Concluding Remarks', in Calhoun, ed., *Habermas*, 470–1.

another is to propose a new model for the study of the literary marketplace as a whole. Part of the task of rethinking the relationship between 'press, politics, and gender' in the early modern period is constructing a model that allows us to recognize ordinary women's (and men's) involvement. In investigating middling and lower-class participation in print culture, it is necessary to break down disciplinary and conceptual boundaries which separate the study of texts' ideological content and form (literary criticism) from the study of their physical production (publishing history). Authors who print their writings are not the only labourers involved in the production of their texts; nor can authors be understood in isolation from the publishing institutions within which they work. Twentieth-century literary critics' interest in bourgeois subjectivity and the rise of individualism has meant that dominant literary critical models emphasize individuals (especially authors). But traditional 'man-and-his-work' approaches, with their post-Romantic emphasis on individual authors, are not the most useful models for the study of non-élite men's and women's involvement in the print marketplace. This is especially true of literature in politically tumultuous periods, when authors, publishers, and other printworkers often worked closely together.[25]

Consider, for example, the case of one 'Mary Unknown', examined before Prime Minister Robert Walpole and Secretary of State Thomas Pelham Holles, Duke of Newcastle, for publishing a treasonable libel. 'Mary Baker alias Rowe' (who signed her letters to her co-workers 'Mary Unknown') confessed:

The paper now produced signed Thom Tell Truth, being part of the dedication to a Libel now produced intitled A Letter to a Member of

---

[25] A familiar case study here might be Jonathan Swift, who in producing his political writings worked closely with printer John Barber and employed a trade publisher, John Morphew, to serve as an extra layer of cover between himself and the law. As we will see in Ch. 5, Swift also employed Delarivier Manley as a sort of subcontractor—turning over to her certain polemical tasks which for various reasons he preferred not to complete himself. In studying the phenomenon of 'trade publishers', men and women who did not own copies but who allowed their names to be printed at the bottom of a work so as to serve as an extra layer of cover between the genuine publisher, the author, and the law, Michael Treadwell observes that 'periods which combined intense political activity with a high degree of uncertainty such as the Exclusion Crisis, the Glorious Revolution, almost the whole reign of Queen Anne, and even the South Sea Bubble are precisely the periods at which we find the largest number of trade publishers in London' ('London Trade Publishers 1675–1750', *Library*, 6th ser. 4 (1982), 99–134).

Parliament in the North, was by her carryd to the sd Walker, and was written by herself . . . it is not her own handwriting . . . the person that wrote it is named Brown . . . she dictated one part of it . . . this Brown is in the Country. She owns she wrote the Dedication; & . . . she wrote and carryd both That and the Letter to Walker; . . . she carryd the Letter first and he said there was not enough of it; Then she added the Dedication.[26]

According to Unknown's testimony here, at least three people played a role in the *first* stage of the production of the libel she had been trying to get printed. Unknown stated that the dedication to the libel was 'written by herself'—that is, that she was 'Thom Tell Truth'. Yet she also stated that it was 'not her own handwriting'. Unknown 'wrote' the text in the sense of invention, yet she did not write it in the technological sense of pen on paper. One Brown, now 'in the Country', may have written the bulk of the text, and served as a sort of scribe for Unknown's dictation of the rest. (Unknown may not have possessed the technology of writing, she may have had rheumatism in her hands, or she may simply have been lying about the 'dedication' not being in her own handwriting.) Unknown admitted to having carried a draft to one 'Walker the Bookseller' and, when he complained that 'there was not enough of it', to having added 'the Dedication'.

Compared to many such cases in the State Papers, the Prime Minister and Secretary of State's task here would actually have been relatively easy—especially if the web of production and dissemination had been this simple. The material form of the 'treasonable libel' in question here is straightforward: this is only a pamphlet-length manuscript. So far, only three individuals are implicated. But the examination of Unknown's cohort 'Plessen', an upholsterer with whom she had been living at an inn under the assumed name 'Rowe', and the discovery of *her* papers in *his* trunk, suggests the involvement of a fourth individual. To complicate matters further, 'Walker the Bookseller' may have been printer and newspaper proprietor Robert Walker, who was known for subcontracting out small jobs like this one.[27] It is possible, then, that even

---

[26] PRO SP 36/16, f. 151, 31 Dec. 1729. The ellipses in this passage are my own substitution for the repeated word 'that'. No other words have been deleted. A more detailed study of Mary Unknown will be published separately.

[27] Michael Harris, *London Newspapers in the Age of Walpole: A Study of the Origins of the Modern English Press* (London: Associated University Presses, 1987), 91–2.

in the case of this simple text not only multiple authors (with multiple aliases) but also multiple printing houses (with multiple workers in those houses) were involved in the attempt to move treasonous ideas into print.

In their effort to assign legal responsibility for a treasonable text to a punishable human body, Walpole and Newcastle began by committing Unknown to the Gatehouse prison at Westminster (PRO SP 44/82, 2 Jan. 1729/30). If we, in turn, were to attempt to assign authorial responsibility, we would have to study *all* stages of the text's collective production and distribution, as well as the perhaps widely varying motives of the individuals involved (economic, ideological, household family duty, and so on). Unknown stated that her purpose in meeting Walker was 'to get Mony from him'. What were her motives for her dangerous involvement in the production of this treasonous text? When Walker suggested that the paper be lengthened, was this a disinterested editorial judgement? Or was it the judgement of a cost-conscious printer, anticipating a wasteful use of paper and advising the 'author' to lengthen her text so that he could make the best possible use of each sheet? One Robert Walker, a printer, was known for specializing in opposition pamphlets. Was the Walker referred to here *Robert* Walker, and were his motives for agreeing to print this text ideological as well as economic ones? Did Walker, or any other 'producer' for that matter, simply not realize how dangerous this text was? To whom do we assign responsibility for the paper's literary effects, rhetorical strategies, overall success? To whom do we assign responsibility for its treasonous content?

Questions of authorship and intention in the production of political literature are more complicated than even post-Foucauldian literary theorists acknowledge. A shifted critical lens reveals that middling and lower-class women played a far greater role in the early modern literary marketplace than we have heretofore known, and of a different kind from that which we have attended to. This book's model for the study of 'press, politics, and gender' shifts the focus away from individual authors and authors as 'individuals'. Paying attention to *all* aspects of the material production and dissemination of texts, rather than to one person's role in that process, redirects a spotlight previously focused primarily on a small number of (typically) exceptionally well-educated, mostly male, post-Romantically conceived 'authors', and shines that searchlight on a whole class spectrum of men and women involved in the production and circulation of political ideas.

But in rethinking the relationship between print and politics in this period, and working to uncover women's involvement, feminist critics need to do more than broaden our notions of forms of involvement with printed texts. We need to scrutinize what *kinds* of texts we look at, and what kinds of questions we ask of women's textual involvement. While studies of Grub Street and the British book trade have until recently concentrated almost exclusively on male authors and textual workers, early feminist scholarship has sometimes also been exclusive. While twentieth-century literary critics have in general gravitated to ways of looking at texts centred on individual subjectivity, feminist critics have gravitated to expressions of gendered subjectivity, and the emphasis in feminist criticism has been on the establishment of the individualized (and gendered) female subject. While feminist critics have tended to concentrate on those women who wrote about gender, this book suggests that for the non-élite women considered here gender was not necessarily the first category of identity. A different angle of vision allows us to see the lingering power of older structures of feeling; other 'metaphors of being' not based in individual selfhood. This is especially important in studying women from the ranks of working tradespeople on down, who tended to find empowerment in more dispersed modes of being based in religio-political allegiances, trades or occupations, and other collective social identifications.

Early feminist literary criticism has also tended to follow highly respected traditional scholarship in employing what we are coming to recognize is an anachronistic, post-Romantic notion of the 'literary'. Feminist critics have concentrated not only on women writers to the exclusion of other printworkers, but also on those women writers who are most easily incorporated into current literary critical traditions of intelligibility and value. Valorizing creative and imaginative genres, and focusing attention on the novel, early feminist studies have risked marginalizing or even ignoring the dominant forms of women's textual production before 1730. For, contrary to the impression given by otherwise invaluable anthologies and studies of early women's writing, the overwhelming majority of British women's (and men's) published writings before 1730 consisted not of fiction or *belles-lettres* but of didactic and polemical materials and religio-political pamphlets and tracts.[28] This book is devoted to central textual genres of the seventeenth and early eighteenth centuries commonly neglected today (polemical, sectarian, and topical works). To take seriously such works is not to study 'marginal' literary forms or concerns, but rather the central print forms and concerns of the period. As part of this book's effort to uncover middling and lower-class women's political activity through print, each section points to the continuity of these religious and political textual forms with a still predominantly *oral* political culture. This book also posits a polemical explanation for these forms' eighteenth-century fall from favour: the emergence of a different set of literary values and agendas, a set of values that was not an inevitable shift but rather linked to particular class-based political and cultural agendas after 1688.

We are reminded frequently now that even our own most 'timeless' literary values have a history. And paradoxically, this book suggests, it is by venturing into the realm of what seems strange *to us* (the polemical, the didactic, the ungrammatical, the poorly printed) that we may come closer to understanding those apparently 'timeless' values' historical origins. As Robert Darnton suggests, 'by picking at the document where it is most opaque [to us] we may be able to unravel an alien system of meaning'.[29] By pursuing that which makes us uncomfortable in early modern print culture, as well as the pleasurably familiar, we may begin to understand not only our own literary values and agendas, but also (and most importantly for this project) those values' original socio-cultural functions and consequences.

To accommodate a methodology which strives to synthesize diverse areas of inquiry, this book is structured as a series of concentric circles rather than in a linear or chronological fashion.

---

[28] For general statistics see John Feather, 'British Publishing in the Eighteenth Century: A Preliminary Subject Analysis', *Library*, 6th ser. 8 (1986), 32–46 and James Raven, *A Chronological Check-List of Prose Fiction Printed in Britain and Ireland* (Newark: U. of Delaware P., 1987). On women, see Patricia Crawford, 'Women's Published Writings 1600–1700', in Mary Prior, ed., *Women in English Society, 1500–1800* (New York: Methuen, 1985), 211–82, Margaret J. M. Ezell, *Writing Women's Literary History* (Baltimore: Johns Hopkins UP, 1993), and Judith Phillips Stanton, 'Statistical Profile of Women's Writing in English from 1660 to 1800', in Frederick M. Keener and Susan E. Lorsch, eds., *Eighteenth-Century Women and the Arts* (Westport, Conn.: Greenwood Press, 1988), 247–54.

[29] Robert Darnton, *The Great Cat Massacre and Other Episodes in French Cultural History* (New York: Random House-Vintage, 1985), 5.

Part I examines the political activity of women workers in the London book trades, Part II focuses on the largest category of women's writing in this period (religious and religio-political works), and Part III explores in depth one woman's strategies as a political writer (Delarivier Manley). Part I turns first to women printers, publishers, booksellers, ballad-singers, hawkers, and other material producers and distributors of printed texts. The combination of phenomenal expansion and diminished institutional control was conducive to the participation of women at virtually every level of the press, and women workers, sometimes themselves illiterate, played a significant role in the production and dissemination of printed political literature in the revolutionary and post-revolutionary period. This section introduces women printers and publishers ranging from the leading Quaker printer Tace Sowle to those little-known, yet furthest-reaching links in the distributive networks of the London press: the hawkers who cried papers and sang ballads in the marketplace and street, at St Paul's churchyard, Temple Gate, and City coffee-houses. While providing basic information regarding women's institutional status and everyday commercial dealings in the book trade, the primary task of Part I is to investigate print as a new mode of association for women, and particularly as a vehicle for their political expression. On the basis of an examination of some fifty years of State Papers pertaining to press prosecutions, this section concludes that women workers in the book trade were anything but the passive distributors of *other* people's political ideas. A series of close-ups suggests the extraordinary range of female participation in the production and dissemination of political literature in this period—and its material and ideological consequences. To ask not only what measurable impact non-élite women had on traditionally defined spheres of politics, but what impact the political and religio-political debate which so colours print culture of their day had on *them*—how they supported themselves by it, suffered by it, situated themselves in relation to it, and sometimes significantly shaped it—is to witness these women workers actively negotiating public space for themselves and maximizing the agency available to them. The findings of this section suggest that working women experienced gender differently from their genteel counterparts, in this case aligning themselves with households, fellow workers, and occupations rather than with the category 'women', and going about their business little hampered by crystallizing ideologies of femininity. This section also illustrates the coalescence of oral and print culture, asserting in particular the power of 'oral publication': the oral adaptation of pamphlets and broadsides by ballad-singers and hawkers, who used their voices to politicize and commercialize printed texts.

Part II shifts the focus to the largest category of women's (and men's) writings in this period, religious and religio-political works. Underscoring the centrality of religious debates to the new literary marketplace and to the growth of a public sphere in print and politics, this section considers these debates as a prime forum for women's public expression. A profound sense of spiritual calling made public expression, both oral and printed, appear a *duty* for women of diverse socioeconomic backgrounds and ideological allegiances—women who claim that they would not otherwise have dared upbraid monarchs, advise parliaments, resist judicial authorities, and lambaste priests. Part II contrasts four middling women who held dramatically different religious and political beliefs: Elinor James, an Anglican monarchist; Anne Docwra, a Quaker; Joan Whitrowe, a one-time Quaker who may have been expelled from the movement for her dangerous radicalism; and Jane Lead, a theosophical visionary with an international following and her own London congregation. One cannot overemphasize the importance of religio-political debate to early modern literary, political, and cultural history, and the materials introduced here illuminate the role played by women of the middling and lower ranks in these debates. Chapter 3 concentrates on these women's material circumstances, and specifically the material production and circulation of their writings. Arguing that these women's printed texts must be understood as a supplement to a much larger, ongoing *oral* activism, this chapter shows that it is easier to understand early modern religious polemic if we set the printed texts in their oral environments. It also shows how modes of production and circulation influenced textual content, and how contemporary oral culture can be traced in the printed texts.

Despite their competing religio-political allegiances, the four women writers considered here all saw contemporary religious controversy as a summoning to public political activity. What were the particular psychological or ideological, as well as material, circumstances that encouraged these common women and others like them not only to print their works, but also to engage in oral activism in their communities? Chapter 4 furthers another argument of this book, concerning the persistence of older, 'collective' models of political subjecthood and subjectivity alongside new individualized and gendered models. A study of these women's 'metaphors of being', or notions of the self in society, and comparison of their ideological assumptions to those of their more privileged and (as I will argue) modern-thinking female contemporaries, reveals a close relationship between different metaphors of being and modes of female empowerment in this important transitional period, and links these competing assumptions to factors of occupation and class. While, by the late seventeenth and early eighteenth centuries, some aristocratic and genteel women were already beginning to perceive the self in recognizably modern ways as gendered, autonomous, and unique, middling and underclass women still tended to envision the self in more traditional ways as social, collective, and essentially unsexed. While early 'feminists' such as Margaret Cavendish or Mary Astell understood themselves primarily as *women* (and therefore as disempowered and detached from the world of public affairs), the four less privileged women considered here understood themselves less as 'women' than as 'Members of the Body of the Nation': part of an unbroken continuum with the state. Most important for this book's goal of tracing middling and lower-class women's political activity through print, different ways of envisioning the self led to different strategies for political action. Part II concludes by suggesting how changing ways of perceiving the self in eighteenth-century England changed what it was possible for particular female groups to be and to do.

In Part III, we see all of these forces come to bear on Delarivier Manley (c.1674–1724). Over the years that Manley was active as an author (roughly 1695–1720), the press became an accepted vehicle for political discussion in England, and ministerial 'propaganda machines' were set in place. Manley was among the first English authors self-consciously to devote herself to propaganda as a livelihood, and her political fiction in particular contributed to fundamental contemporary shifts in the *modus operandi* of British political life. The author of at least six volumes of political allegories, six political pamphlets, and as many as nine issues of the Tory *Examiner*, Manley exercised immediately acknowledged power as a political writer. She also provoked government action, as she was tried for seditious libel in 1710. This section reads Manley as an important transitional figure in the history of English women's political activity through print, mediating between an older, more polemical political culture and a new, increasingly secular and 'polite' one. Manley's political writings reflect a new model of political authority not as divinely instituted and protected (and corrected) by subjects, but rather as fundamentally open to contest via public representations. Her writings reflect a new self-consciousness about the *diverse* possibilities of propaganda, and the post-revolutionary shift to genres which would attain increasing prominence in the eighteenth century (party political journalism and especially the novel). Part III traces the means by which Manley attempted to legitimize her anomalous career as England's first avowed female political propagandist in the new age of 'public opinion', and suggests how her changing authorial self-representations over the period of her major political writings foreshadow the changing relationship of British women writers to the political press by the mid-eighteenth century.

Manley created a space for her innovative political fictions, I suggest, by representing herself as a female alternative intelligence agent of the private sphere—at precisely the same time that her one-time patron, Secretary of State Robert Harley, was secretly laying the foundations of the modern government 'intelligence agency' throughout England. The chief narrator of Manley's political allegory *Secret Memoirs and Manners of several Persons of Quality, of Both Sexes, from the New Atalantis, An Island in the Mediteranean* (1709), 'Lady Intelligence', is in fact a highly self-conscious portrait of Manley in her capacity as a propagandist. Manley's self-representation as a female intelligencer was an ingenious solution to her own doubly difficult situation as a female propagandist, but it had important implications for other writing women of her generation as well. For Manley's controversial work was not only an attempt to manipulate public opinion in the service of those politicians she called 'Tories'.[30] It was also a conscious demonstra-

---

[30] While, as a propagandist, Delarivier Manley did use the categories 'Whig' and 'Tory' as if they were a strong binary, these categories did not yet represent clearly demarcated political parties. Futhermore, as J. A. Downie notes, 'so long as they belonged to the privileged elite, there was a great deal of common ground between the vast majority of Whigs and Tories . . . most . . . were massively conservative and shared an ideology of order and hierarchy' (*To Settle the Succession of State: Literature and Politics 1678–1750* (New York: St Martin's P., 1994), 2).

tion of new opportunities for British women to transform 'private intelligence' into public political currency by means of their new access to print.

Manley drew on traditions of women's oral political exchange in shaping both the content and the form of her political fictions. Part III illustrates the coalescence of older oral traditions and new print possibilities in her fiction, particularly her recognition of the potential power of printed transformations of oral political 'gossip'. Reading Manley's work in the context of her contemporaries' heightened concern with issues of female power, Part III considers Manley's career-long obsession with an aristocratic woman, the thirty-year confidante of Princess and later Queen Anne: Sarah Jennings Churchill, First Duchess of Marlborough. While Manley depicted Churchill as a woman working to establish her own Whig propaganda or 'intelligence' network, Churchill's letters to the Queen concerning the *Atalantis* suggest that she in turn recognized her Tory attacker as a 'low indigent' commoner who had managed to transform 'gossip' into a powerful new mode of female agency by means of the political press. Significantly, while both Churchill and Manley, despite their diametrically opposite socioeconomic positions and party political allegiances, first learned to manipulate public opinion in the service of mainstream political causes,[31] both later turned to the press for the most personal of reasons: to defend their own transgressive conduct against their detractors. These

---

[31] The use of the word 'political' is a tricky issue for 18th-cent. scholars, particularly new historicists, with their interest in the discourse of power and its relations. On the one hand, it is clear that most 18th-cent. authors used the word 'politics' in a far more restricted fashion than we do today. On the other hand I agree with Paul Alkon that it would be counter-productive for 20th-cent. scholars of the period to restrict themselves to 'needlessly constraining definition[s] of politics'. Indeed, one of the conclusions I have come to in writing this book is that, in the course of writing about political issues in the traditional sense, 18th-cent. women came to understand a broader variety of issues as 'political'. I suspect that further study may reveal that women writers were among the first English authors to understand the implications of expanding their culture's notion of politics to include all parts of life. For clarity's sake, however, I have been conservative in my use of the word 'politics'. Unless otherwise indicated, when I state that a woman was interested in politics, I mean politics in the most common 18th-cent. understanding of that term, that is, 'the science of government: the art or practice of administring publick affairs' (Johnson, *Dictionary*). For further discussion of this issue and its implications, see Paul Alkon, 'Recent Studies in the Restoration and Eighteenth Century', *Studies in English Literature*, 29 (1989), 579–614; Felicity Nussbaum, 'Introduction: The Politics of Difference', *ECS* 23 (1990), 377; and Ruth Perry, 'Mary Astell and the Feminist Critique of Possessive Individualism', *ECS* 23 (1990), 444–57.

women's bold decision to defend themselves in print (or, as Churchill put it, to 'write and publish something in my own justification') may be seen as foreshadowing the increasing number of women who would deploy their culture's most powerful means of communication not so much in support of traditional religio-political causes or the new party politics, as in support of their own interests and those of their sex. For their sex was, this study concludes, an increasingly primary affiliation with which British women identified across boundaries of faith, party, occupation, geographical background, and even rank. Eighteenth-century women increasingly came to understand themselves as a group with shared interests and, potentially, shared strengths (as John Dunton put it, 'a Strong Party in the World'[32]). The origins of modern secular feminist discourse in England may be traced to this period, as women writers gradually turned from mainstream political writing to what we would call proto-feminist 'political' concerns. The increased availability of new technologies of communication, along with new kinds of strategic alignments, ensured that models of authority and means of political power were indeed being challenged in England. In the eighteenth century, English women began to understand a broader variety of concerns as 'political', and to take 'political representations' into their own hands.

---

[32] *Athenian Mercury* (1691–7), qtd. in Shevelow, *Women and Print Culture*, 34.

PART I

'To Run One's Self Into Danger'
Women and the Politics of Opposition
in the London Book Trade

Introduction

After much thought, author-bookseller John Dunton and other members of the Athenian Society resolved on a patron for 'this our *Eleventh Volume*' of the collected *Athenian Gazette: or, Casuistical Mercury* (1693). Innovators in search of 'something new and noisy', they addressed the volume not to a high-powered politician or aristocratic Maecenas, but to 'none other but the *Worshipfull Society of Mercury-Women* in and *about the City of* London'. A motley group of working women were unlikely patrons for Dunton and his fellow businessmen. There was, of course, no such 'Society', and indeed, along with the frequently illiterate and invariably impoverished hawkers and ballad-singers whose faces were familiar features of the urban landscape, there was no less organized body of persons in the increasingly intricate hierarchy of the early eighteenth-century book trade. But the Athenians were as shrewd as their periodical was long-lived. They had their reasons, and once they had piqued the reader's curiosity, they supplied the 'divers and sundry weighty Considerations' which moved them to dedicate their volume to the mercuries, in this passage addressed to the women themselves:

The first and strongest is *Interest*. . . . To be plain, we are sensible 'tis in your Power to Damn or Save a poor *Paper* at your Pleasure, Let *Bookseller* or *Author* do what they will: You are the *Messengers of Fate*, and a *Bloody Fight* it self won't do without your *Pains* and *Labour*—so much for *Interest*, now a little for *Gratitude*—We must own *Athens* had *fallen* long e're this, had not you (like *Minervas* as you are) strenuously supported it; not *Vander*'s self e're Walkt more dirty *Steps* than you on its *behalf*, nor with more Vigour declaims against its Rivals and *Enemies*.[1]

The *Athenian Gazette* (later *Mercury*) was the best known of all seventeenth-century literary periodicals, and its authors recognized the co-operation of various branches of the trade as an important

---

[1] *The Athenian Gazette: or, Casuistical Mercury*, vol. 11 (1693), preface. *The Athenian Gazette* (later *Mercury*) ran from 1691 to 1697, a long life by contemporary standards.

factor in its success. Dunton himself used the term 'mercury-women' loosely. While mercury-women were indeed responsible for the better part of local distribution of London newspapers and ephemera in this period, in this passage Dunton was referring to itinerant street-sellers usually known as hawkers, rather than to the more substantial pamphlet-shop keepers known as mercuries. Else-where, though, Dunton also extended his gratitude to mercury-women such as Elizabeth Nutt and Anne Dodd, whose cluster of shops at the Royal Exchange, Temple Bar, and other sites were among the most important wholesale outlets of the early eight-eenth-century press. Comparable tributes to any of these predomi-nantly female workers on the margins of the trade are rare, with the result that the furthest-reaching links in the distributive network of the urban press remain the least well known. If for a time we were to imitate Dunton and place the mercury-woman or hawker at the centre of the trade, as Hogarth placed the hawker in the centre of his crowd scene in *Industry and Idleness* 11 (Fig. 1), could we see the turn-of-the-century London press with the familiarity and acuteness of his eyes?

It should no longer be news that women have long played a significant role in the making and transmission of the printed word.[2] Even before the technology of print was widely developed,

---

[2] See Maureen Bell, 'A Dictionary of Women in the London Book Trade, 1540–1730', Masters of Library Studies diss., Loughborough U. of Technology, 1983, and 'Women Publishers of Puritan Literature in the Mid-seventeenth Century: Three Case Studies', Ph.D. diss., Loughborough U. of Technology, 1987; and articles listed in the bibliography; Natalie Zemon Davis, 'Women in the Crafts in Sixteenth-Century Lyon', *Feminist Studies*, 8 (1982), 46–90; Judith E. Gardner, 'Women in the Book Trade, 1641–1700: A Preliminary Survey', *Gutenberg-Jahrbuch* (Mainz: Verlag der Gutenberg-Gesellschaft, 1978), 343–6; Frances Hamill, 'Some Unconven-tional Women before 1800: Printers, Booksellers, and Collectors', *Papers of the Bibliographical Society of America*, 49 (1955), 300–14; Leona M. Hudak, *Early American Women Printers and Publishers 1639–1820* (Metuchen, NJ: Scarecrow Press, 1978); Felicity Hunt, 'The London Trade in the Printing and Binding of Books: An Experience in Exclusion, Dilution and De-skilling for Women Workers', *Women's Studies International Forum*, 6 (1983), 517–24, and 'Women in the Nineteenth Century Bookbinding and Printing Trades (1790–1914): With Special Reference to London', unpublished MA diss., University of Essex, 1979; Margaret Hunt, 'Hawkers, Bawlers, and Mercuries: Women and the London Press in the Early Enlightenment', *Women and History*, 9 (1984), 41–68; C. J. Mitchell, 'Women in the Eighteenth-Century Book Trades', in O. M. Brack, ed., *Writers, Books and Trade: An Eighteenth-Century English Miscellany for William B. Todd* (New York: AMS Press, 1994), 25–75; and Beverly Schneller, 'Using Newspaper Advertisements to Study the Book Trade: A Year in the Life of Mary Cooper', also in Brack, ed., *Writers, Books and Trade*, 123–44.

FIG. 1. William Hogarth, *Industry and Idleness*, plate 11. Reproduced by courtesy of the Lewis Walpole Library, Yale University

women worked as scribes, illuminators, and rubricators,[3] and within a few decades of the invention of printing several European women owned and ran printing firms. The presence of a significant number of female entrepreneurs in the early European book trade is attributable in part to what historian Rudolf Hirsch refers to as the 'free enterprise fashion' in which the new business of printing arose: 'Once the great variety of men (and sometimes women) had entered the field, it was too late to mold them into any type of closed corporation.' Guild power was past its zenith in Europe, and a relative absence of regulations allowed women of diverse backgrounds to enter the field.[4] The situation in early modern London, of course, was somewhat different. Technically, no commodity could be sold within City walls except by a freeman of a livery company, so membership in a livery company was still an important prerequisite of trade. And in 1557, more than a century after the invention of printing, the Worshipful Company of Stationers of the City of London would receive a royal charter, giving its extremely restricted membership the sole right in all of England to print, publish, or otherwise traffic in the printed word. But Dunton's 'Worshipfull Society of Mercury-Women' is a parody of a regulative body whose power had already substantially declined, and in the key period with which we are concerned here the English press would undergo some of the most important changes in its history.

Above all, the years 1680 to 1730 were for the English book trade a time of anarchic expansion. To begin to sense the implications of this unprecedented development, one has only to learn that while the Printing Act of 1662 (13 & 14 Charles II c. 33) had tried to limit the number of master printers in all of England to twenty-four, by 1705 there were between sixty-five and seventy printing houses in London alone.[5] Many gradual but pervasive transforma-

---

[3] We know, for example, of several notable female illustrators in late 13th-cent. Paris, such as Thomasse, who, rather like her 18th-cent. Grubbean counterparts, decorated manuscripts while simultaneously managing an inn (Christopher De Hamel, *A History of Illuminated Manuscripts* (Boston: David R. Godine, 1986), 130). In England, French Huguenot copyist Esther Ingles used her handwriting to secure patronage from late Elizabethan and early Jacobean royalty and aristocracy (Jonathan Goldberg, *Writing Matter: From the Hands of the English Renaissance* (Stanford, Calif.: Stanford UP, 1990), 146–53).

[4] Rudolf Hirsch, *Printing, Selling and Reading 1450–1550* (1967; 2nd printing Wiesbaden: Otto Harrassowitz, 1974), 27.

[5] Michael Treadwell, 'London Printers and Printing Houses in 1705', *Publishing History*, 7 (1980), 6.

tions in English society are pertinent here, but political developments are foremost among them. The birth of Whig opposition in
the 1670s, and development of party politics thereupon, was inte-
grally related to declining government and Company control.
Urban literacy, particularly female, increased dramatically over
the first three quarters of the seventeenth century, and a series of
unprecedented political events had fired an enlarged reading public's demand for written and printed news. At the same time, the
Revolution of 1688 had forced a new parliamentary monarchy to
redefine its relationship to the reading public. In the heated political
environment of late seventeenth-century London, what government
could afford to appear 'Tyrannick and Arbitrary'? Yet the failure of
those in power to renew the Printing or Licensing Act in 1695, thus
ending pre-publication censorship in England, was due not to modern ideas of the virtues of a free press, but rather to confusion and
oversight. It is no coincidence that the Triennial Act, requiring new
parliamentary elections every three years, had been passed less than
a year before the Licensing Act had been allowed to lapse. While
neither the Whigs nor the Tories supported an unbridled political
press (few Augustans did), neither party cared to have the other in
charge of pre-publication censorship, either. There were more general elections in the period 1695 to 1716 than in any other comparable period of British history, and the unique political situation
to which this new legislation gave rise was yet another spark that
helped to fire the explosion of the English press. The number of
master printers in London was no longer restricted by law, and
copyright protection was virtually non-existent. Until such fundamental attempts at the recovery of institutional control as the
Copyright Act of 1710 (8 Anne c. 21)[6] and the Stamp Tax in 1711
(9 Anne c. 23 and 10 Anne c. 19) there was a veritable Hobbesian
state of nature within the trade.

The combination of phenomenal growth and institutional chaos
was conducive to the participation of women at virtually every level
of the London press. In this period between the decline of effective
regulations and the consolidation of commercial controls and capital later in the century, women already working in the interstices of
the trade seized the opportunity to support themselves by means of

---

[6] While it is customary today to refer to 8 Anne c. 21 as the 'Copyright Act', the
actual title of the statute is 'An Act for the Encouragement of Learning by Vesting
the Copies of Printed Books in the Authors or Purchasers of Such Copies'. The word
copyright is not used.

a newly energized press they helped create. Not surprisingly, these
novel opportunities for women were not to be permanent ones.
Almost as soon as the Licensing Act had been allowed to lapse,
competition for commercial control of the publishing industry had
begun to intensify. Among other factors, the birth of the modern
literary marketplace was giving rise to a need for institutional
controls of a new kind, pertaining to new capitalist opportunities
within the trade. Printers and booksellers of substance began to
petition for legislation adequately protecting literary property, and
by the end of the legal year 1709 the first English Copyright Act
was passed. By mid-century, new laws protecting the investments
of major publishers had contributed to a consolidation of capital
within those publishers' hands. In time, this bookseller control
resulted in 'the corresponding disappearance of a whole range
of peripheral book trade activity'.[7] A substantial proportion of
'peripheral book trade activity' was the work of women. While a
small number of mid-century women in the trade were major copyowners who benefited from the general pattern of an increasing
concentration of wealth, generally speaking the mid- and later
eighteenth century saw the disappearance of women as significant
oppositional publishers and major printers.

If women workers' economic agency was relatively easy to control, though, the broader ideological implications of their increased
access to the press were not. For women writers, printers, and
publishers, access to the press was a vehicle of significant if limited
power. In pre- and post-revolutionary England, competition for the
control of public opinion grew to a previously unheard-of intensity,
and at every level of the production and distribution of print
women began to participate in this competition as never before.
The first part of this book focuses on the politically dissident or
'oppositional' activities of women in the London book trade. It is
the importance of those activities for the political and literary
history of ordinary women, for public sphere theory, and for feminism with which Part I is primarily concerned.

Chapter 1 provides an overview of women's daily commercial
activities in the book trade, surveying women's formal relations
with the Stationers' Company and general relations within the

---

[7] Michael Harris, 'Periodicals and the Book Trade', in Robin Myers and Michael
Harris, eds., *Development of the English Book Trade, 1700–1899* (Oxford Polytechnic Press/Publishing Pathways Series, 1981), 89.

trade, and then discussing representative women printers, booksellers, hawkers, and ballad-singers. Chapter 2 turns to the material which forms the basis for the central argument of Part I: that women in the book trade were not merely the producers and distributors of *other* people's political ideas. As makers and distributors of printed texts in a period of heightened political unrest, women workers in the book trade were commonly involved in the interrelated activities of making, tracing, and erasing 'seditious intentions'. Sketching the broad outlines of this involvement by means of a series of overlapping close-ups, Part I attempts to convince the reader—as Alexander Pope did his critics, albeit for different reasons—that the 'Meanness of offenders' should not render these small-time ideological 'criminals' beneath our attention ('A Letter to the Publisher. Occasioned by the Present Edition of the *Dunciad*' (1729)).[8] The inflammatory authors and scurrilous publishers whom Pope satirized in the *Dunciad*, and the women printers and publishers discussed here (sometimes overlapping groups), were united by a fear of the law. Observing the diverse efforts of female 'offenders', not only to participate in affairs of state, but also to take charge of their situations once they found themselves in conflict with the law, leads one to suspect that in England 'freedom of the press' was as much a product of administrative exhaustion as of enlightenment. Pope may have been more than half-serious when, accused of having written a satiric poem about 'persons . . . too obscure for Satyre', he compared the small-time subversives in his *Dunciad* to 'assassinates', 'insurrection[aries]', unruly mobs, and insubordinate servants, and argued that

Obscurity renders them more dangerous, as less thought of: Law can pronounce judgment only on open Facts, Morality alone can pass censure on Intentions of mischief: so that for secret calumny or the arrow flying in the dark, there is no publick punishment left, but what a good writer inflicts.[9]

But Pope's recognition here, that the 'Law can pronounce judgment only on open Facts', and corresponding call for 'good writer[s]' to step in to supply the deficiencies of the government, is equally important to this study of women's direct involvement in

[8] [Pope], 'To the Publisher', *The Dunciad Variorum*, in *Poems*, ed. Butt, 320.
[9] Ibid.

the political press, if only to suggest the ways in which Augustan authors such as Pope helped to determine its end-point. While the cultural work of authors such as Pope, Joseph Addison, Richard Steele, Jonathan Swift, and Samuel Richardson is not the primary subject here, such cultural work nevertheless casts a shadow over the intellectual and physical work of the women studied, and hints at ongoing economic, social, and ideological developments that were profoundly affecting their lives. By 1730, the predominant mode for political control of the press in England would shift from the pursuit of the ignis fatuus of efficient censorship to the more realistic goal of efficient counter-exploitation of the press. It was as if the British government had come to Pope's conclusion, that the most effective means of controlling seditious 'Intentions' was to counter them with orthodoxy—or as Pope put it, 'Morality' and the 'publick punishment[s]' that 'a good writer inflicts'. 'Moral' authors—including Samuel Richardson, a printer of substance and thus a doubly interested observer of these developments—would step in where the law had failed. And to a surprising extent, these talented authors would succeed in helping to contain the immediate consequences of marginal groups' new access to the powerful political tool of print.

Women in the London Book Trade

'I have been in the element of Printing above forty years, and I have a great love for it, and am a well-wisher to all that lawfully move therein, and especially to you that are masters.' So wrote printer-author Elinor James in her broadside *Mrs. James's Advice to All Printers in General* (*c.*1715), a broadside signed not once but three times with her own name. Elinor James saw herself as a printer with 'above forty years' experience, but this is not how book trade scholars have seen her. Rather, if Elinor James's half-century presence in the London book trade is noted at all, she is referred to as the *widow* of printer Thomas James—sometimes as many as twenty-one years before Thomas James was dead. Despite Elinor James's public participation in the trade, despite the knowledge of printing-house practices and tools she displays in the above broadside, despite the fact that Thomas James left her, and not his well-trained sons (or daughters), his printing house and equipment, Elinor James is assumed to have had a five-year rather than a fifty-year career as a printer (if she is assumed to have had a career as a printer at all). That is, it is assumed that if Elinor James did assist in the family printing business, it was as her husband's 'helpmeet'. In turn, Thomas James is assumed to have reported dutifully to his printing house every day for the length of his own fifty-year career—the practical as well as theoretical and legal 'head' of his family business.

The seventeenth- and early eighteenth-century London book trade consisted of a series of small family-owned and operated businesses passed down through families by intermarriage. And the dynamics of family life and economics, we are increasingly coming to see, are seldom this simple or predictable. In the eyes of the Stationers' Company—the livery company to which Thomas James was apprenticed, and of which he became a freeman in 1662,

the same year that he married 17-year-old Elinor Banckes—
Thomas James was the only 'Master Printer' in the James household.[1] And to a certain extent, this is a view that Elinor James
would have shared. ('Now to you journeymen,' she continues in
her *Advice to All Printers*, 'you are my brothers, for my husband
was a journeyman before he was a master, and therefore I wish
you well.') Elinor James referred to her husband as a 'master'—that
is, master of his household and master printer, master of his
journeymen and apprentices and the legal owner of his business.
But she also saw and referred to herself as a 'mistress'—that is,
mistress of a printing household; overseer of her journeymen
'brothers' and apprentices and a skilled tradeswoman with 'above
forty years' experience. James saw herself not as a passive observer
in her *husband*'s printing house nor even as a 'helpmeet' to her
husband while he was alive, but rather as a woman printer who
could state with pride in a broadside addressed to her peers, 'I have
been in the element of Printing above forty years, and I have a
great love for it, and am a well-wisher to all that lawfully move
therein.'

In early modern England, the nature and extent of a woman's
involvement in a given trade depended less on the trade's physical
demands than on whether or not it could be carried on within the
home. Home workshops made it possible for women to move back
and forth between different kinds of 'domestic' labour, and allowed
even women aspiring to genteel social status to do economically
important labour still within domestic space. John Dunton praised
Mrs Green, a printer's wife in Boston, for her versatility in moving
from one type of labour to another—first and most visibly from her
job as dutiful wife and mother, and second and more quietly to her
duties as unofficial partner in the family business:

[1] Marriage licence for Thomas James and Elinor Bank(e)s, 27 Oct. 1662, GL,
Registry of the Bishop of London, Book 27, MS 10,091/26. For information on the
Stationers' Company see Cyprian Blagden, *The Stationers' Company: A History,
1403–1959* (London: George Allen and Unwin, 1960), Graham Pollard, 'The Company of Stationers before 1557' and 'The Early Constitution of the Stationers'
Company', *Library*, 4th ser. 18 (1938), 1–38 and 235–60, as well as the introduc-
tions to W. W. Greg and E. Boswell, eds., *Records of the Court of the Stationers'
Company, 1576 to 1602, from Register B* (London: Bibliographical Society, 1930)
and William A. Jackson, ed., *Records of the Court of the Stationers' Company, 1602
to 1640* (London: Bibliographical Society, 1957).

Mrs. Green was not only a loving, faithful, and an obedient Wife, but an industrious Wife too; managing that part of his [Mr Green's] business which he had deputed to her, with so much application and dexterity as if she had never come into the House; and yet so managed her House as if she had never gone into the Warehouse.[2]

Home workshops gave women like Mrs Green crucial access to training, account books, and customers. While only a small proportion of women in the London book trade were ever formally apprenticed, any woman whose family allowed it could acquire skills, training, customers, and credit by watching, assisting, and sometimes taking over for relatives. While most women printers, booksellers, and binders in this period were in fact related to male or sometimes female members of the Stationers' Company, any woman could theoretically be admitted to the freedom of the Company in her own right by apprenticeship, patrimony, or redemption (purchase). The first woman to be formally apprenticed to the Company was Joanna Nye, daughter of an Essex parson, to Thomas Minshall, engraver, in 1666, and between 1666 and 1800 108 women were formally apprenticed to members of the stationery trades.[3]

It was fairly common for daughters to be trained in their parents' trade to carry on in the business after their death. The most important example of a woman admitted to the Stationers' Company by patrimony in this period was the Quaker printer Tace Sowle. The daughter of Andrew and Jane Sowle, Tace was made free of the Stationers' Company shortly after her father's death in 1695. Assisted by her mother and later her husband and then a foreman, she continued to manage the Sowle press for another fifty-four years. In

[2] *The Life and Errors of John Dunton Citizen of London* (1705), 2 vols. (rpt. New York: Burt Franklin, 1969), i. 105.

[3] This number is from Hunt, 'The London Trade', 518. While substantial, it represents less than 2% of the total number of apprentices during this period. Furthermore, until exhaustive studies of primary, as well as secondary, sources for the study of women in the book trade are completed such statistics must be viewed as provisional.

There is no record of Joanna Nye ever having been made free of the Company. To be admitted by redemption was to pay a fee for immediate membership, as when Sarah Andrews and Dorothy Sheldenslow were allowed to buy their way into the Company for £5 each in the 1680s booksellers' drive against stall-holders. In 1668, Elizabeth Latham, daughter of bookseller George Latham, became the first woman to be admitted by patrimony (Blagden, *The Stationers' Company*, 162).

a career spanning over half a century, she would become arguably the most important nonconformist printer of her generation.[4]

In 1705, John Dunton described Tace Sowle as

both a Printer as well as a Bookseller, and the Daughter of one; and understands her Trade very well, being a good Compositor herself. Her love and piety to her aged Mother is eminently remarkable; even to that degree, that she keeps herself unmarried for this reason (as I have been informed) that it may not be out of her power to let her Mother have always the chief command of her house. (*Life and Errors*, i. 222–3)

Tace Sowle did in fact marry the following year, but she nevertheless ensured that it would still 'not be out of her power to let her Mother have always the chief command of her house'. Seventy-five-year-old Jane Sowle became the nominal head of the Sowle press the same year that her daughter was married. Imprints after this date read 'J. Sowle', and for the next thirty years Tace Sowle's own name disappears.

Perhaps because she sensed the commercial value of an established name, Tace Sowle never gave up her name for that of her husband Thomas Raylton, but instead used the unusual compound 'Tace Sowle Raylton'. (Family pride may have played a role here also.) Thomas Raylton was not a member of the Stationers' Company, and there is no evidence that he ever had anything to do with the actual production of printed works in his wife's printing house. Unlike his new wife and mother-in-law, Raylton had no training or experience as a printer. His apprenticeship was as a blacksmith, and at the time of his marriage into the Sowle business he was working as a hosier. Records do show that Raylton helped with warehousing and accounting, and with dealing with distributors (customarily the wife's job in male-headed printing households). But records also show that Tace Sowle Raylton continued to oversee the production of publications as she had done for sixteen years before she was married, and as she would continue to do for another twenty-six years after she was widowed. When Tace's mother died in 1711 at the age of 80, imprints began showing

[4] In actuality Tace succeeded her father in 1691 and had probably assumed management of the printing house some time earlier. By 1690 Andrew Sowle was described as 'an old man' and nearly blind, and after this date his name no longer appears in imprints. For further information on the Sowle press and Quaker publishing see my article in James K. Bracken and Joel Silver, eds., *The British Literary Book Trade, 1475–1700* (Columbia, SC: Bruccoli Clark Layman, 1996), 249–57.

'assigns of J. Sowle'—that is, Tace Sowle Raylton. Thomas Raylton died in 1723 after a long illness, but Tace Sowle Raylton did not take on a foreman for another thirteen years. In 1736, she finally began employing Luke Hinde, a relative, as a foreman, and thirty years after her name disappeared from her own imprints it suddenly begins to reappear. Imprints begin showing 'T. Sowle Raylton and Luke Hinde' until Tace's own death another thirteen years later at 83 years of age.

While women running businesses are commonly assumed by modern historians to have been widows, the example of Tace and Jane Sowle will suggest that it was not impossible for women to be the legal and/or practical heads of family businesses even while a male relative was alive. As we will see in Chapter 2, women whose male relatives came into conflict with the law routinely managed family businesses while their husbands or brothers were in prison or in hiding. One exceptional woman printer, Jane Bradford, was accused of keeping her husband a prisoner in his own home. A government press spy described Bradford as 'the chief Orderer and Director in everything she undertakes, keeping her Husband, as a Prisoner, to protect her in ill Practices'.[5]

Bookseller-author John Dunton says a great deal about women in the book trade in his *Life and Errors*, and reveals the centrality of his own wife to his bookselling business. Although Dunton repeatedly stressed his wife's 'obedience', it is clear that Elizabeth Annesley Dunton had far more power in the family business than one or both of them cared to let on. 'Dear Iris', Dunton confessed, 'gave an early specimen of her prudence and diligence', and 'commenced Bookseller, Cash-keeper, managed all my Affairs for me, and left me entirely to my rambling and scribbling humours' (i. 79). Never fond of 'haggling behind a shop-board', Dunton left such

---

[5] Robert Clare, qtd. in Henry L. Snyder, 'The Reports of a Press Spy for Robert Harley: New Bibliographical Data for the Reign of Queen Anne', *Library*, 5th ser. 22 (1967), 326–45; 341. Mary Darly, the manager of an important London print shop and an etcher of political prints, appears to have had a similarly dominant role in the family business (Herbert M. Atherton, *Political Prints in the Age of Hogarth: A Study of the Ideographic Representation of Politics* (Oxford: Clarendon P., 1974), 18–21 and *passim*). Among those wives whose diligence John Dunton praised were Mrs Bilingsley, who took over the family business when bookseller Mr Bilingsley suffered from bouts of madness, and Abigail Baldwin, wife of Richard, who 'eased him of all his publishing work; and since she has been a Widow, might vie with all the women in Europe for accuracy and justice in keeping accompts: and the same I hear of her beautiful Daughter, Mrs. Mary Baldwin' (i. 230, 260).

drudgery to his wife, and set off for several journeys which took him out of London and even to North America for lengthy periods. Coming home after one extended absence, Dunton discovered that Iris had, as he put it, accomplished more in his warehouse in a month than he could have done in a year. This only made him feel comfortable departing once again—this time for more than a year. 'Plainly Mrs. Dunton had a finer head for business than her husband,' Dunton's biographer concludes.[6] Dunton would have been the first to agree, though he would also insist that it was he who 'always kept an eye over the main chance' (i. 79). Dunton's successes were Elizabeth Annesley's. After her death in 1697, his business never quite recuperated from the loss of her pragmatism and ability to inspire self-discipline in her husband.

A wife who assisted in the family business was for most book trade households in this period an economic necessity. But such a wife took on still greater economic importance when she was the widow or daughter of a member of the Stationers' Company. Marriage into the trade was a standard way for journeymen to acquire privileges, copyrights, equipment, connections, and customers. Samuel Richardson, for instance, twice married the daughters of former employers. The history of family interrelationships and passing down of copyrights in the book trade is exceedingly complex, but whenever possible copyrights were kept in the family through intermarriage. The best argument that Dunton's friend could come up with when trying to convince him to marry one Sarah Doolittle was to point out, 'You will have her Father's copies for nothing; and his Book on the Sacrament, you know, has sold to the twentieth edition, which would have been an estate for a Bookseller' (*Life and Errors*, i. 64).

The professional activity of married women is especially difficult to trace, for Stationers' Company records normally appeared in the husband's name.[7] Imprints must not be relied upon as a source of information as to who was in charge of a press on a daily basis. As we have seen, Tace Sowle was in charge of her family press for fifty-

---

[6] Stephen Parks, *John Dunton and the English Book Trade: A Study of his Career with a Checklist of his Publications* (New York: Garland, 1976), 20–37.

[7] Married women are, however, commonly found registering and freeing apprentices. See D. F. McKenzie, *Stationers' Company Apprentices 1641–1700* and *Stationers' Company Apprentices 1701–1800* (Oxford Bibliographical Society Publications, NS 17 (1974) and NS 19 (1978)).

eight years, yet her name appeared in her own imprints for only twenty-seven of those years. In the colonies, Rhode Island printer Ann Franklin (1696–1763) assumed management of her family printing business during her husband's long illness. When her husband died in 1735, she continued printing for another twenty-eight years. Judging solely by the imprints of the Franklin press, however, one would never guess that Ann Franklin outlived both her husband and then her son, and managed a successful printing business for 'almost as long as the two of them combined'.[8] Left with a worn press and type and four children of whom the eldest was only 9, Franklin trained her daughters as compositors and sent her son to his uncle Benjamin to learn printing. (She, in the meanwhile, served as the colony printer for Rhode Island and wrote and sold the *Rhode-Island Almanac*.) Eight years later, her son returned home as a journeyman printer, and from then on this proud mother ensured that every work she and her son printed appeared in his name. By 1758, Ann Franklin's name no longer appeared even on colony business—even when signs began appearing that her son 'missed her business acumen'. The printing for which her son was responsible appeared increasingly late, until eventually the Assembly Secretary charged him with indolence and laziness. Four years later, Franklin's son suddenly died—forcing her to come out of semi-retirement at the age of 66 and run the printing house, newspaper, and retail business once more. Only then, twenty-seven years after her husband's death, did she finally begin to use the solo imprint 'Ann Franklin'—rather than referring to herself (if she referred to herself at all) as the widow of her husband or the partner of her son. As the examples of Ann Franklin and Tace Sowle suggest, some women appear to have chosen to render their own labour invisible. Ann Franklin chose to have her son's name in imprints even when he was not doing the work, and when Tace Sowle continued to use the imprint 'assigns of J. Sowle' for thirteen years after the deaths of both her mother and her husband she was apparently *choosing* anonymity.

[8] For information on Franklin I am indebted to Margaret Lane Ford, 'A Widow's Work: Ann Franklin of Newport, Rhode Island', *Printing History*, 12 (1990), 15–25, Susan Henry, 'Ann Franklin: Rhode Island's Woman Printer', in Donovan H. Bond and W. Reynolds McLeod, eds., *Newsletters to Newspapers: Eighteenth-Century Journalism* (Morgantown, W. Va.: West Virginia U., The School of Journalism, 1977), 129–43, and Hudak, *Early American Women Printers*, esp. ch. 3. The quotation is from Henry, 'Ann Franklin', 138.

The women for whom we have most records of professional activity, then, are widows who did not remarry and who continued to print or publish in their own names. The wife of a freeman of the Stationers' Company automatically became a freewoman upon her husband's death. Providing that her husband was not in debt, she retained the family rights, equipment, and shares in the English stock.[9] Released from her legal status as a feme covert, she could sign contracts, be granted loans, and bind apprentices in her own name. Existing records show twenty-two widows carrying on their family businesses within a decade before or after 1705, averaging eleven years apiece as master printers.[10] When printer Ralph Holt died in 1688, his business was continued first by his widow Elizabeth, who continued to print for another fifteen years, and then by his daughter Sarah, who continued to print for another twenty-five years.[11] The Holts' printing house, then, was in independent female hands for over forty years—not to mention the years that Elizabeth

---

[9] The English stock was a monopoly on psalms, psalters, almanacs, and primers held jointly by members of the Company, and serving among other things as a source of provision for the Company poor. If a widow had no share, the Company might give her work by granting her the right to print some of the stock. While a widow did not lose her privileges as a freewoman by remarriage to a non-member, she did lose her stock, and, unlike her first husband, she could not pass her shares on.

[10] In 1705, press spy Robert Clare submitted a list of master printers in London and its environs to Robert Harley, then Secretary of State (rpt. in Snyder, 'The Reports of a Press Spy for Robert Harley', 326–45). Clare's list, when supplemented by the labours of Michael Treadwell ('A Further Report from Harley's Press Spy', *Library*, 6th ser. 2 (1980), 216–18 and 'London Printers and Printing Houses in 1705'), shows twenty-two widows carrying on their husband's business within a decade before or after 1705. These twenty-two widows continued to print for a total of 250 cumulative years, averaging over eleven years each. This figure, my own, includes only those women for whom approximate dates of termination of employment are known, and purposely excludes the most important of them all, Tace Sowle. Sowle did outlive and out-work her husband by another twenty-six years, but the business was hers initially.

One important bookselling widow was Abigail Baldwin, who continued as a publisher for fifteen years after the death of her husband Richard Baldwin in 1698. One of the most prolific 'trade publishers' of her day, Baldwin was a major distributor of political literature, including Whig journals such as the *Medley*. Baldwin was also a primary distributor of literary periodicals such as the *Spectator* and the *Female Tatler*, as well as several newspapers. She carried on the proprietorship of the popular *Postman* until 1700, when she sold it to Francis Leach, and in 1704 her idea of publishing the *Postman* in translation materialized into the first French-language paper for distribution in London and abroad. She was succeeded by her son-in-law James Roberts, who married her daughter Mary (see n. 5 above).

[11] Treadwell, 'London Printers and Printing Houses in 1705', 24.

Holt must have worked alongside her husband in order to acquire the skills that enabled her to continue the business successfully on her own.

At the same time, though, because marriage into the trade was a standard way for journeymen to acquire businesses, recent widows were a vulnerable group. A widow who was not intimately familiar with all aspects of a family business before her husband died could be at the mercy of her apprentices after her husband's death. As Daniel Defoe warned:

The only remedy she has here, is, if her husband had e'er a servant, or apprentice, who was so near out of his time as to be acquainted with the customers, and with the books, then she is forced to be beholden to him to settle the accounts for her, and endeavor to get in the debts; in return for which she is forced to give him his time and his freedom, and let him into the trade, make him master of all the business in the world, and, it may be, at last, with all her pride, lets the boy creep to bed to her; and when her friends upbraid her with it, that she should marry her prentice boy, when it may be she was old enough to be his mother: *Her answer is*, 'Why, what could I do? I see I must have been ruined else.'[12]

A recent widow who remarried out of a need for someone to oversee a family business she did not know how to run could be at the mercy even of her new husband. As Defoe prophesied grimly, 'it may be that the boy of a husband proves a brute to her, as many do, and as in such unequal matters indeed most such people do' (351). Operating a printing business meant more than overseeing press-work and distribution; it meant knowing how to obtain capital and credit and, above all, how to collect debts. A widow just setting up for herself in trade would have special difficulty in demanding repayment of loans—especially if she did not know who owed the family business money. Upon the death of printer Thomas Snowden, John Dunton reported, 'his widow follows the same

[12] Daniel Defoe, *Complete English Tradesman* (London, 1725–7), 350–1. Shortly after widow Dorothy Newcombe inherited her husband's interest in the patent of King's Printer, she was declared a 'lunatique', whereupon custody of her person and property was assigned to the manager of the King's Printing Office who had succeeded her husband. Six months later, she was suddenly declared to be of sound mind and memory once more, and, curiously, articles for a second marriage were executed shortly thereafter. Richard Hutchinson assumed control of her one-sixth interest in the King's Printing Office, valued at £200 annually, the day they were married (Robert L. Haig, 'New Light on the King's Printing Office, 1680–1730', *Studies in Bibliography*, 8 (1956), 161–3).

trade; and though I was pretty deeply indebted to her husband, yet she has not once asked me for it' (*Life and Errors*, i. 251). Dunton attributed Ann Snowden's financial negligence to her pleasant personality, but there may have been other factors at work here also. Tace Sowle, by way of contrast, knew exactly who owed her family business money. One of the first things that she did when she took over the Sowle press in 1691 was attempt to settle her father's outstanding accounts. At 25 years old, this young woman whose name means 'be quiet' in Latin attended the Quaker Morning Meeting to show this august body of 'antient Men Friends' 'several Accounts of Books sent to Barbados and Bristol some Years since and not paid for'.[13]

In the late seventeenth and early eighteenth centuries, the institutional position of the feme sole in the book trade was better than that of women in many other trades. Contrary to the practice of some other City livery companies, women in the Stationers' Company were neither barred from the more lucrative branches of the trade nor prohibited from carrying on a large business by restrictions on the number of journeymen they were allowed to employ. No book of prices or piece-rates excluded women printers or publishers from better-paying jobs in times of trade depression.[14] Of course the fact remains that no woman printer or publisher in this period, however experienced, ever had any direct institutional power in the Stationers' Company. While any (male) freeman of the Company who could afford to purchase the livery could become a liveryman, thus entitling him to vote in some elections within the Company as well as in mayoral and parliamentary elections, women were not allowed to purchase the Company livery, and so

---

[13] MMM, 13 Apr. 1691. 'Tace' is the imperative of the Latin *tacere*, 'to be quiet'.
[14] In the late 1760s and 1770s, by way of contrast, many trades began to legislate a sexual division of labour. In 1769, the silk weavers' book sought to exclude women from better-paid branches of the weaving trade except in wartime, and in 1779 journeymen bookbinders formed a union and excluded female sewers and folders (*A List of Prices in those Branches of the Weaving Manufactory called the Black Branch and the Fancy Branch . . .*, qtd. in M. Dorothy George, *London Life in the Eighteenth Century* (1925; Chicago: Academy Chicago Publishers, 1984), 183; Felicity Hunt, 'Opportunities Lost and Gained: Mechanization and Women's Work in the London Bookbinding and Printing Trades', in Angela V. John, ed., *Unequal Opportunities: Women's Employment in England, 1800–1918* (Oxford: Basil Blackwell, 1986), 74. See also Anna Clark, *The Struggle for the Breeches: Gender and the Making of the British Working Class* (Berkeley and Los Angeles: U. of California P., 1995), esp. ch. 7).

could not vote in Company elections. Because the livery was also the body from which the Court of Assistants, or Company government, was selected, women's inability to purchase the livery also prevented them from holding office within the Company. Although women were made free of the Stationers' Company as early as 1695, they did not earn the right to be elected to the livery until a merger granted it to them by accident in 1936.[15]

Ways to counter official and unofficial forms of sex-based institutional exclusion such as these did exist. As we will see, one important means of empowerment for women book trade workers was collective action. One type of collective action specific to this period was the conger, an association of copyright-sharing trade members whose combined strength allowed them to share the investment load of expensive printing tasks, and increased their ability to protect their property. From about 1690 to 1730, women joined and even formed wholesaling or printing congers. We know of several almost exclusively female congers, such as the one formed by Elizabeth Nutt, Ruth Charlton, M[ary] Cooke, Anne Dodd, and J. Read to produce the expensive *Annotations on the Holy Bible* in 1735.[16] According to one study, the leadership qualities and business acumen of Rebecca Bonwicke were responsible for bringing the important and innovative 'Printing Conger' into being.[17]

On a personal level, women's labour in the seventeenth- and early eighteenth-century book trade appears to have gone generally unremarked. Women printers and booksellers appear to have been mostly taken for granted; considered noteworthy only if they got caught breaking the law or if they were exceptionally skilled or unusual in some other way. When bookseller Thomas Malthus died leaving his widow Sarah to contend with a business in ruin, John Dunton assumed that Sarah Malthus would carry on in the business she had spent all her life in, and wished her well: 'Though Mr. Malthus was very unfortunate, yet I hope his Widow (our new *Publisher*) will have all the encouragement the Trade can give her;

[15] Blagden, *The Stationers' Company*, 278.

[16] Hunt, 'Hawkers', 49.

[17] Norma Hodgson and Cyprian Blagden, eds., *The Notebook of Thomas Bennet and Henry Clements (1686–1719): With Some Aspects of Book Trade Practice* (Oxford UP, 1956).

for she is not only a Bookseller's Widow, but a Bookseller's Daughter' (*Life and Errors*, i. 220).[18] As it happened, Dunton's goodwill towards Sarah Malthus would not in fact last long. Dunton employed Sarah Malthus to publish several of his books, and over the course of their working relationship he suffered bankruptcy. He came to the conclusion that Malthus's poor accounting skills had contributed to his financial collapse, and accordingly sought vengeance on her in *Dunton's Whipping-Post: or, a Satyr upon Every Body. . . . To Which is added . . . Dunton's Letter to his Few Creditors . . .* (1706). The table of contents of this work contains entries such as '*M[althu]s her haughty Character p. 33—A Poem writ to humble her p. 35*', and the series of public curses that follow are a Duntonesque hodgepodge of jestbook traditions and comic invective.[19] Between their lines, however, one discerns an aggressive female entrepreneur who (according to Dunton) spread oral and print rumours as to his financial insolvency throughout the trade. Malthus was a dangerous new kind of female gossip with access to the printing press—a 'Publisher of Lyes and Slander' who hired two of the authors whose papers she distributed to 'blast my Credit if possible' (13). *Dunton's Whipping-Post* begins with an address to Malthus and the authors of the *Moderator* and *Wandering Spy*:

How base was M[*althus*] and her Two Scoundrels to call me *Dunder-head—Simpleton—Fractur'd Bookseller—Whipping Spark* (that can't hold it) *Bankrupt, Jail Bird*; and to tell the World *I was starving, &c.*—when none of my Creditors even question'd their Money . . .

Had M[*althus*] call'd me *Sot*, or *Madman*, for trusting such a Hedge-Publisher, perhaps those that did not know me, might have believed her; but to call me *Bankrupt, Jail-Bird*, one that Writes to prevent Starving, is a malicious Falsehood. Nay, says another of M[*althus*]'s Hackneys (for she hir'd these Fellows to blast my Credit if possible) '*Wou'd I hang my self, no Chandler in Town wou'd trust me with a Penny Cord.*' (13)

If we are to believe Dunton, when he branded Sarah Malthus '*the Famous Publisher of Grub-street News*', one who '*Copies her*

---

[18] Thomas Malthus shared Dunton's penchant for fleeing the country and leaving the shop to his wife. On one of his overseas rambles, Dunton records crossing paths with Malthus, whose 'circumstances being something perplexed, he was making his way for Holland' (*Life and Errors*, i. 86).

[19] Witness for instance Dunton's opening address to Malthus and the authors of the papers she distributed: '*Rehearsal—Moderator—Spy*—down with your Breeches; and you Mrs. M[althus] off with your *Smicket*, for you have *Midwiv'd* so many Lyes into the World, as deserve Whipping till the Blood comes' (12).

Religion and Honesty from Hackney Authors' and who to please a customer will recommend '*Funeral Sermons* and *Wandering Spies &c.* with the same Breath' (33), he was following this woman publisher's own lead. He was fighting her in the public arena of print which *she* had already chosen—and on her own aggressive terms.

At the same time, though, even Dunton admitted of widow Malthus that 'all her Friends in Town, but my self, either had, or at least had endeavored to make a Prey of her' (37). Sarah Malthus's economic hardships serve to support Daniel Defoe's conviction of the difficulties that recent widows faced in carrying on family businesses.[20] Yet it is worth noting that in all his vitriolic attacks on Sarah Malthus, John Dunton never once suggested that this woman publisher's *sex* inherently disqualified her for successful independent business. Neither Dunton nor Defoe believed that the public sphere of commercial relations was or should be off limits to their female contemporaries on the basis of their sex. This fact serves to underline how profoundly economic and social transformations would influence assumptions about 'women's place' over the course of the eighteenth century—and so delimit their public activity.

INSIDE THE PRINTING HOUSE

The growth of the early eighteenth-century printing trade was the result of a proliferation of establishments rather than a significant increase in their size. Major mid-century printing houses like Samuel Richardson's or William Strahan's were exceptions,[21] and even at the end of the century two presses per printer and so four pressmen per shop was still closer to the norm. A typical establishment consisted of a master printer and his wife (or a widow and perhaps a manager), two pressmen per press, a compositor,

---

[20] 'As a just Judgment upon her', Dunton concluded, she 'has now neither Books nor *Moderators &c.* to Publish; and (after all her *Bounce*) can hardly pay 2 *s.* 6 *d.* i' th' Pound'. Dunton himself did not do much better. By 1714 he was deeply in debt, and working as a hireling to publishers such as Sarah Popping and Ann Dodd.

[21] By the 1750s, Richardson had forty employees at work in three different locations (Nichols, iv. 589, 591; William Merritt Sale, *Samuel Richardson: Master Printer* (Ithaca, NY: Cornell UP, 1950), 21) while Strahan had over fifty employees and a payroll of £40 to £50 a week (Alvin Kernan, *Samuel Johnson and the Impact of Print* (Princeton UP, 1989), 56).

apprentices, and assistants. Ideally there would be no task that the mistress of a printing house could not do. Among newspaper printers, where speedy distribution was of the first importance, wives tended to take charge of distribution while their husbands oversaw presswork. But women were by no means exempted from the most physically demanding tasks. Intensive, sustained presswork could be exhausting, but as D. F. McKenzie has shown, the maximally productive printing house where presses worked around the clock has existed only in historians' imaginations.[22] Secondary physical tasks like helping to remove sheets from the tympan of the press were certainly performed by girls as well as boys, a practice which provoked a set of younger printers to petition the Stationers' Company to pass a ruling against it in 1635.[23]

Perhaps because there were so many different types of work to be done in a printing house, and so many workers to deal with, women printers appear to have been a particularly tough group. Contemporaries acknowledge the forceful characters of women printers such as Jane Bradford and Elinor James, and the activities of three-time prison-inmate Elizabeth Powell will be discussed below. Reflecting upon his apprenticeship with printer Elizabeth Midwinter, Thomas Gent recalled that Mrs Midwinter, 'as her circumstances then were not so great as might be wished', often made him work nineteen-hour days, 'from five in the morning till twelve at night, and frequently without food from break-

---

[22] In attempting to reconstruct patterns of production within a shop, contemporary social conditions and attitudes towards regular work must be taken into consideration. A press might conceivably be in operation twelve hours a day, six days a week, but early 18th-cent. London was not yet a well-developed consumer society, and few journeymen had reason to keep up such a pace. Piece-rates were designed to protect employers from journeymen who might pick up and leave their jobs when conditions were gruelling (D. F. McKenzie, 'Printers of the Mind: Some Notes on Bibliographical Theories and Printing-House Practices', *Studies in Bibliography*, 22 (1969), 1–75). See also E. P. Thompson, 'Time, Work-Discipline and Industrial Capitalism', *Past and Present*, 38 (1967), 56–97.

[23] The ruling, which was intended to protect apprentices, stated that 'no Master Printer shall hereafter permit or suffer by themselves or their journeymen any Girles, Boyes, or others to take off anie sheets from the tinpin of the presse, but he that pulleth at the presse shall take off every sheete himself' (qtd. in Alice Clark, *Working Life of Women in the Seventeenth Century* (1919), intro. Amy Louise Erickson (London: Routledge, 1992), 166). Such rulings could not be efficiently policed, however, and it was still common for girls to assist at the press in the 18th cent. In Johnson's day, Boswell recorded that 'a certain respectable author' had married a printer's devil, 'a creature with a black face and in rags' (James Boswell, *Life of Johnson* (1791), ed. R. W. Chapman, intro. Pat Rogers (Oxford UP, 1983), 1141).

fast time till five or six in the evening, through our hurry with hawkers'.[24]

Printer Elinor James's own writings, especially her broadside *Mrs. James's Advice to All Printers in General* (*c.*1715), provide rare and important insight into the status and power that the mistress of a printing household could still have in this period, both in her own establishment and in the trade as a whole. James's solid footing in the commercial sphere—her public presence, if not authority—contributed to the confidence of her public voice. Her confidence in herself as a tradesperson went hand in hand with her confidence in what she was printing or speaking; the bravado with which (as we will see in Part II) she petitioned not only fellow printers, but also monarchs, members of parliament, City officials, and the citizens of London. James's confidence in her own judgement is also reflected in her handling of her husband's will. When Thomas James died in 1710, his will specified that his splendid inherited library be 'kept in some publick place or Library to be perused by all Gentlemen that shall resort thereunto who are to be entred and called the Jameson Society'.[25] While Thomas James left his wife his printing house and 'one Third part of my personal Estate . . . according to the Custom of the City of London', he also specified that she should receive this crucial legacy only on two harsh conditions: first, that she not touch his books ('no part of my Library of Books to be taken by my said Wife or deemed into her Third part'), and second, that she not 'molest my Executors in the Execution of this my Will'. But, as one might suspect, given these caveats written into Thomas James's will, Elinor James promptly disregarded both of these conditions upon her husband's death, and somehow managed to persuade his executors to hand over their job to herself. It was Elinor, not Thomas James, who chose to donate Thomas James's books to Sion College, a theological society for London clergymen which would become notable for its excellent library. In making her great bequest, one of the most important in the history of Sion College Library, she also donated portraits of her husband, Charles II, and, most strikingly, herself. The portrait

---

[24] Thomas Gent, *The Life of Mr. Thomas Gent, Printer, of York; Written by Himself* (1746; London, 1832), 9–10.
[25] Will of Thomas James, PRO Prob. 11/515/109, proved 9 May 1710. Thomas James was the grandson of Dr Thomas James, first keeper of the Bodleian Library. A more detailed study of the James family and library will be published separately.

FIG. 2. Elinor James (*c.*1645–1719), printer, author, and 'She-State-Politician'. Artist unknown. Reproduced by courtesy of the National Portrait Gallery

labelled 'Eleonora Conjux Thomae James' is an extraordinary document (Fig. 2). A printer, author, and (in the eighteenth-century sense) publisher in her own right, Mrs James is depicted in a gown of red silk, 'and her hands are crossed on a book, the binding of which is most minutely finished, and very splendid. On a table open before her is a pamphlet, intituled, "A Vindication of the Church of England, by Mrs. James: in Answer to a Pamphlet, intituled, A New Test of the Church of England's Loyalty" ' (Nichols, i. 308). Over the course of a thirty-five-year period from 1681 to 1716, Elinor James would write and publish at least fifty extant pamphlets and broadsides. In iconographical tradition, the book is a symbol of knowledge and power. James's donation to a theological society of which she could never be a full member, of a portrait of herself displaying a beautifully bound book and a controversial pamphlet that she wrote, printed or had printed, and distributed with her own hands, was the pointed gesture of an extraordinary individual. A politically literate, independent tradeswoman with a printing press immediately at her disposal, James was one of a striking number of Augustan women whose lives were profoundly affected by, even organized around, the new opportunities of print.

As the mistress of a printing house for nearly half a century, James witnessed profound changes in her trade, and by the end of her career she was deeply concerned for the fate of the economic 'family' as she had known it. In *Mrs. James's Advice to All Printers in General* she argued for a return to the strictly hierarchical organization of the live-in printing shop of her younger days—an establishment threatened by the capitalization of the printing business, and the increasing likelihood that workers would for ever be subordinates dependent on a wage. Her broadside documents the professionalization and industrialization of the book trade from one woman worker's point of view. It also provides rare insight into one not-so-benevolent site of pre-capitalist 'family' industry, and the central role that one woman printer saw herself as having in the training and discipline of her (mostly male) employees.

James began her *Advice to All Printers* by establishing her authority to speak—her forty years of experience, and emotional, as well as economic, solidarity with her trade ('I have been in the element of Printing above forty years . . .'). She urged London printers to prevent the 'great evil' of insubordination within the trade by refusing to employ other printers' workers—so that the printer who trained an apprentice might also have the benefit of the young man's labour once he had acquired some skills ('according to the will of God and good men'). James's firm sense of hierarchy within her printing house, and dictatorial, hands-on approach to controlling her apprentices, quickly removes any anachronistic hopes that a woman printer might be somewhat less ready to beat her 'servants'. More surprising to us, perhaps, is James's own sense of having been ill served by her apprentices when 'away he runs with great complaints, . . . [to] rail against and bely his master and mistress'.[26] However oppressive, James's political philosophy of passive obedience and the naturalness of a minutely graduated hierarchy was all of a piece, whether the contested site was White-hall or her own home.[27]

Significantly, though, just as James's apprentice craved 'liberty to go where he please[d]', and, refusing to acknowledge models of order he perceived as unjust, ran away, so James's own writings and actions show little evidence that she ever acknowledged gender as a valid factor in the organization of domestic government. It was her 'brother' journeymen whom she commended to mend their faults ('for what benefit have you in starving your wives and children and making yourselves sots only fit for hell?'). And it was her fellow printers whom she addressed as equals, instructing them to protect their own profits and their apprentices' futures by 'not . . . bind[ing] any boy except he be above the age of fourteen and the fewer the better'. James brought her broadside to a close by assuring her fellow masters that she was their 'sister and soul's well-

---

[26] This particular passage reads: 'You cannot be ignorant of the great charge in bringing up of servants in the art of printing; neither can you be insensible how remiss, provoking, and wasteful some servants are, especially when they are encouraged therein, by the unjust hope of getting away from their masters, and having over-work from other masters, that have not had the charge and trouble of bringing them up, which is too frequently practiced among you, to the ruin of the trade in general, and the spoiling of youth. For when a boy has served half his time, and has gained some experience in his trade, he presently begins to set up for conditions with his master; then he will not work unless he has so much for himself, and liberty to go where he pleases; which if his master denies, he then strives to vex his master, and waste his time and goods; and then when he beats him, away he runs with great complaints, when the master is all the while the sufferer; and it is no wonder to hear a boy that wants an honest principle to do his own duty, rail against and bely his master and mistress; for he thinks to excuse himself by blackening them' (*Advice to All Printers*).

[27] Women's attachment to these hierarchical political constructions is discussed in Ch. 4.

wisher'—and by fearlessly signing her name. We do not know how members of the Stationers' Company responded to James's broadside, which shows none of the emphasis on female weakness or incapacity which some twentieth-century critics have found to be characteristic of seventeenth- and eighteenth-century women's writings. James's own confident and authoritative tone, though, suggests that she at least assumed that her peers would read with interest her opinions and respect them.[28]

PUBLISHERS AND RETAILERS

In the eighteenth century, the word 'publisher' could refer to anyone involved in distributing printed materials. The usual way to refer to a person who performed a role similar to that of a modern publisher was simply as a bookseller—an umbrella term which covered a wide variety of functions. Terminological ambiguity is often a symptom of institutional change, and the division of labour within the Augustan book trade was indeed undergoing fundamental transformations.[29] Properly speaking, the mid-century bookseller of substance was not so much a seller of books, as a member of an increasingly professional organization designed to protect against the infringement of copyright. Major publishing booksellers such as Jacob Tonson paid their bills by manipulating copies rather than by 'haggling over a shop-counter', and combined with other

---

[28] Printing was not the only aspect of production in which women were employed. While quality paper-making was not yet a developed industry in England, women do figure as engravers, illustrators, and particularly, binders. Ellic Howe's list of binders from 1648 to 1815 shows at least thirty-eight women binders, of whom nine were at work from 1678 to 1730. There were probably more, for many entries are listed by their first initial only, in which case it is impossible to determine their sex. Of these nine, most had at least one apprentice, and the majority were widows and daughters of binders (*A List of London Bookbinders 1648–1815* (London: The Bibliographical Society, 1950)).

[29] Historians of the professions have seen the years 1680 to 1730 as an important transitional period, when several occupational groups first claimed the status of 'professions'—a distinction previously granted without dispute only to the church, the law, and medicine. The changing organization of the London book trade in this period was but one manifestation of a 'transition taking place ... across a whole sector of England's social structure'—a transition that would have measurable social and economic consequences for women (Geoffrey Holmes, *Augustan England: Professions, State and Society, 1680–1730* (London: George Allen and Unwin, 1982), 7).

publishers for their mutual protection. Major bookseller-publishers like these had the most to gain from new laws like the Copyright Act of 1710, and, not surprisingly, did the most to see them passed. Patterns of copy ownership, too, would become increasingly complex by mid-century, and the combined effect of these new systems of management and control was to widen existing barriers between 'elect' and 'peripheral' members of the trade.[30]

The large number of women who continued to work as booksellers of varying importance throughout the eighteenth century may be attributed in part to the fact that formal allegiance to the Stationers' Company was not a prerequisite of this aspect of the trade.[31] Several market-oriented female authors turned to bookselling after writing for pay proved too precarious a means of subsistence. It was the 'business' of authorship that first raised novelist and poet Elizabeth Boyd (fl. 1730–40) 'from almost the lowest Condition of Fortune, and a worse state of Health' to the relative security of her own pamphlet shop in St James. But significantly, it was retailing 'Papers, Pens, Ink, Wax, Wafers, Black Lead Pencils, Pocket-Books, Almanacks, Plays, Pamphlets, and all manner of Stationery Goods' that ultimately enabled this would-be professional woman writer to make a living.[32] (As Boyd's list of wares suggests, almost all booksellers retailed a wide variety of non-print items as well as books.) In one of her own works, *A Humorous Miscellany: or, Riddles for the Beaux* (1733), Boyd thematized the difficulties that she encountered as a bookseller. In her 'Verses on Captain D—s, who after subscribing to a certain *Pamphlet*, and keeping it upwards on nine *months*, both refused to pay for it, and returned it *Unsaleable*' (20), Boyd followed the example of several of her female contemporaries in turning to the

---

[30] Harris, 'Periodicals and the Book Trade', 89.

[31] In 1637, clause X of the Star Chamber 'Decree Concerning Printing' had attempted to end retail bookselling by anyone who had not served a seven-year apprenticeship to a member of the Stationers' Company, whether printer, binder, or bookseller, but books were retailed by such a wide variety of shopkeepers that this decree proved virtually impossible to enforce (Blagden, *The Stationers' Company*, 120). For examples of women booksellers later in the 18th cent., see James Raven, *Judging New Wealth: Popular Publishing and Responses to Commerce in England, 1750–1800* (Oxford: Clarendon P., 1992).

[32] Advertisement prefacing Boyd's *The Happy Unfortunate; or the Female Page: A Novel* (1732). Boyd began 'at a Cook's Shop, the Sign of the Leg of Pork and Sausages, in Leicester-street, by Swallow-street, St James', but by 1743 had moved up to 'the new Pamphlet-Shop over against the Crooked Billet in Leicester-street, near Burlington-Gardens'.

press to attack her delinquent customer in print. Like Boyd, memoirist Laetitia Pilkington (1712–50) for a time attempted to support herself by 'Nothing but Poetry' before supplementing her income by retailing prints and pamphlets. And of course, even bestselling novelist Eliza Haywood (1693–1756) had a brief spell as a publisher in Covent Garden 'at the sign of Fame'.[33] Bookseller-authors such as Elizabeth Boyd, Laetitia Pilkington, and Eliza Haywood are only a few relatively minor examples of a common overlap of authorship, publishing, and printing in this period. Several of the women writers discussed in Part II also 'published' (i.e. sold) their own works, and, as we will see in Part III, author Delarivier Manley lived with her printer John Barber. More famous examples include Alexander Pope, who in marketing his *Iliad* translation served as 'essentially his own publisher', and Samuel Richardson, who printed his own novels.[34] While printers in this period generally did not retail their own products, Tace Sowle was an important exception to this rule. In addition to serving as a printer for the Society of Friends, Sowle also served as a warehouser and distributing agent, and in the process acquired an expert knowledge of market demands. To stimulate readers' interests, Sowle bound trade lists into the backs of the books that she printed. In 1708, she printed the first Quaker bibliography, John Whiting's *A Catalogue of Friends Books; Written by Many of the People, Called Quakers*—a bibliography which also served as an effective sales catalogue for the products of her press. Like Elizabeth Boyd, and like most booksellers, Sowle also retailed a wide variety of non-book items having to do with writing. Along with dozens of Quaker works which reflect her particular religio-political allegiances, her list of stock includes 'Spelling-Books, books on physic, *A Diurnal Speculum, A New Discourse on Trade*'; 'Bibles, Testaments, Concordances, Spelling-Books, Primers, Horn-books; with Writing-Paper, Paper-Books, &c., and Marriage Certificates on Parchment, Stamp'd'.[35]

In addition to small-scale retailers and exceptional women publishers such as Tace Sowle, more specialized kinds of female

---

[33] See Thomas Lockwood, 'Eliza Haywood in 1749: *Dalinda, and her Pamphlet on the Pretender*', *Notes and Queries*, NS 234. 4 (1989), 475–7 and Catherine Ingrassia, *Paper Credit: Grub Street, Exchange Alley, and Feminization in the Culture of Eighteenth-Century England* (forthcoming).

[34] Maynard Mack, *Alexander Pope: A Life* (New York: Norton, 1985), 267.

[35] Sowle's list of stock typically followed her advertisements for books.

distributors included trade publishers, wholesaling mercury-women, and itinerants.[36] Of the five persons whom John Dunton referred to in his *Life and Errors* specifically as 'publishers' rather than as booksellers, two were in fact trade publishers—a historically specific subgroup of the Augustan press in which women figure prominently. In this period of enduring political tension, anonymity was often an important prerequisite for the expression of oppositional viewpoints in print. An additional middleman was needed; someone who could provide another layer of cover between authors and the law. When one Elizabeth Cape testified at the examination of retailer Sarah Popping (whose name appears in the *Dunciad Variorum* as publisher of several attacks on Alexander Pope) that although Popping's name was on the bottom of the pamphlet in question, she was not its 'onlie begetter', we may safely suspect that Popping was a trade publisher. 'Trade publishers' let their name be printed at the bottom of political or otherwise dangerous works for a small fee, and handled their distribution. As we will see in Part III, John Morphew served as a trade publisher for various political works co-produced by Delarivier Manley and Jonathan Swift, all of which were printed by John Barber. The period which saw the Exclusion Crisis, the Revolution of 1688, the tumultuous reign of Queen Anne, and the South Sea Bubble was the period in which the largest number of trade publishers were at work in London. Other women booksellers who acted as trade publishers in this period include Abigail Baldwin, Rebecca Burleigh, Sarah Malthus, and later Mary Cooper.[37]

[36] A small number of married women appear to have been employed as warehouse-keepers. Catherine Brett worked alongside her husband as warehouse-keeper to Nathaniel Mist, then after she was widowed set up as a bookseller. Examined regarding the publication of a seditious libel (*MWJ* nos. 177 and 178, 7 and 14 Sept. 1728), Brett explained that she helped to oversee stock, take care of financial transactions, and deal with the mercury-women to whom papers were distributed. When the mercury-women did not send round their servants to collect papers, she went after them herself, walking round to their various shops to see if they would take papers. She testified to having visited Anne Neville, an agent of mercury-woman Elizabeth Nutt, 'to ask her if she would have any of the Journals that week', along with several 'other Mercurys' (SP 36/8, ff. 152–3, 19 Sept. 1728). Brett continued to come into conflict with the law after she set up for herself as a bookseller. In 1743, 'Katherine Brett, parish of St Clement Danes near Temple Bar Bookseller' entered into a recognizance of £400 (SP 44/82, 19 Jan.).

[37] Treadwell, 'London Trade Publishers 1675–1750', 99–134. The day after Jacob Tonson the Elder announced publication of the official version of the Earl of Winton's trial for his role in the 1715 Jacobite rebellions, Sarah Popping's name

Another specialized kind of distributor in this period was the wholesaling mercury-woman. By the early eighteenth century, newspaper distribution was already more specialized than many other branches of bookselling. At least as early as 1661, one source made a clear wholesale/retail distinction, and acknowledged the importance of women in this aspect of the trade: 'Those people which go up and down the streets crying News-books, and selling them by retail, are also called Hawkers and those Women that sell them wholesale from the Press, are called Mercury Women.'[38] A 1728 source concurs, describing mercury-women as those who 'make a Trade of selling News papers and pamphlets, and retailing them out to the Hawkers' (SP 36/8, f. 154, 20 Sept. 1728). As Dunton's tribute to the '*Worshipfull Society of Mercury-Women*' suggests, though, the divisions of distributive labour were still blurred in actual practice. Dunton's own list of 'honest (Mercurial) Women' includes several women who are more usefully distinguished as trade publishers or simply as booksellers, and wholesaling mercury-women also retailed works.[39]

---

appeared on an 'unofficial' version of the paper. Three days later, she was taken into custody. Petitioning for her release, Popping claimed that 'being ill at the Time the said Paper came to her hands, her Sister, who is not acquainted with such Things, had published it before [she] knew anything of it'. She prayed that she be 'discharged without Fees; her Condition and the Profits she has by Publication not being able to bear it' (Ralph Straus, *The Unspeakable Curll* (New York: Robert M. McBride and Co., 1928), 66). In this particular case, Popping was working for publisher Edmund Curll, but she was clearly not averse to working against Curll either. Popping also served as a trade publisher for Pope's *A Full and True Account of a Horrid and Barbarous Revenge by Poison, on the Body of Mr. Edmund Curll*. The figure of the specialized trade publisher like Popping would disappear by mid-century—or, rather, merge with the 'regular' publisher. The important bookseller Mary Cooper (fl. 1743–61) did act as a trade publisher upon occasion, but she was far more prosperous and 'respectable' than Popping, and she did own copies.

Another trade publisher who worked for Curll was Rebecca Burleigh, widow of publisher Ferdinando Burleigh (d. 1714). When Pope advertised in the *Post Man*, 31 July 1716, that the pamphlet Burleigh had published for Curll as *Mr. Pope's Version of the First Psalm* was not genuine, she defied him, publicly challenging anyone who cared to consult the original manuscript to come to her shop (Strauss, *The Unspeakable Curll*).

[38] Blount's *Glossographia*, qtd. in D. F. McKenzie, *The London Book Trade in the Later Seventeenth Century* (Cambridge: Sandars Lectures, 1976), 25.

[39] Dunton's list of 'honest (Mercurial) Women' included 'Mrs. *Baldwin*, Mrs. *Nutt*, Mrs. *Curtis*, Mrs. *Mallet*, Mrs. *Croom*, Mrs. *Grover*, Mrs. *Barnes*, Mrs. *Winter*, Mrs. *Taylor*' (*Life and Errors*, i. 236). Even the servant of major wholesaling mercury Anne Dodd referred to her mistress as 'a Retailer of News papers and Pamphlets commonly called a Mercury' (SP 35/28/9, f. 18, 12 Aug. 1721). The fact

The most influential mercury-women in this period were the pamphlet-shop owners Elizabeth Nutt and Anne Dodd and their daughters. Elizabeth Nutt, the wife and later widow of printer John Nutt (d. 1716), who published Swift's *A Tale of a Tub*, oversaw a cluster of shops in the heart of the City near the Royal Exchange and served as the main newspaper supplier of City customers for almost half a century. In 1728, Nutt stated that 'it has been her Buisness for about Forty years to sell News Papers and Pamphlets at the Royal Exchange' (SP 36/9, f. 249, after 24 Aug. 1728). Nutt served as a primary distributor for leading newspapers such as the *Daily Post*, *Evening Post*, and *London Evening Post*, conveniently printed by her son Richard.[40] She was assisted in the management of her various outlets by her daughters Alice, Catherine, and Sarah. By 1740, Catherine, Sarah, and perhaps Alice were in charge of the important outlets around the Savoy and the Exchange.[41] Mrs Nutt, her daughters, and her agents received papers directly from certain printers or publishers as soon as they were ready, and accounted for them on a monthly basis.[42] From there, daughter Catherine Nutt explained, 'the Servants take them in the Morning, and distribute them to the people [hawkers and retail shopkeepers] who are to sell them' (SP 36/13, f. 109, 19 July 1729).

that this servant was sent to pick up 2,700 sheets (108 quires) of the *London Journal* from its printer every week, however, indicates that Dodd was serving as a wholesaler. No single outlet could retail this many copies of a single paper every week.

[40] Richard Nutt inherited a printing business by marrying Elizabeth Meere, only daughter of printers Cassandra and Hugh Meere. Cassandra Meere succeeded her husband as a printer when he died in 1723, but died herself only two years later.

[41] George Sampson Chadsey, a servant to 'Mrs. Nutt or her Daughters', testified that he was 'employed . . . to fetch on the Postnights from Mr. John Meres's in the Old Bailey'. On the date in question Chadsey picked up some fourteen or fifteen quires (350 to 375 sheets) of the *LEP* and delivered them 'as usual to Mrs. Catherine Nutt . . . at Mrs. Nutt's Shop at the Royal Exchange' (SP 36/50, f. 282, 8 Apr. 1740). When another daughter, 'Mrs. Sarah Nutt, of the Parish of St. John Baptist in the Savoy, Pamphlet Seller', was examined regarding the same issue (no. 1932, 1 Apr. 1740) 'bought at her Shop at the Royal Exchange', she stated that she was the one who sent Chadsey to the Mereses', and who 'accounts every Month with Meres himself for the sd Papers' (SP 36/50, f. 268, 5 Apr. 1740).

[42] Nutt dealt, for instance, with newspaper middleman John Peele, who was probably the first English 'publisher' in the modern sense of the word. Peele handled relations between the printers and retailers of the *Daily Post*, the *London Journal*, the *Free Briton*, and other papers.

Meanwhile, at Temple Bar and to the west, Anne Dodd Senior was distributing pamphlets and newspapers to Westminster customers. 'Anne Dodd Pamphlet Seller at the Peacock at Temple Bar' was a primary distributor of leading newspapers such as the *Daily Post*, the *London Journal*, and the *London Evening Post*, as well as of oppositional papers such as the *Craftsman* and *Common Sense* and the Jacobite *Mist's Weekly Journal*. In 1731, Dodd described herself as 'left an afflicted widow with a Large Young Family some years' (SP 36/23/134, 26 May 1731), and by 1739 her daughter Anne Dodd Junior had succeeded to her business. Along with her faithful employee Mary Dewe, who by 1739 had worked for 'Anne Dodd and her late mother about Fifteen or Sixteen years' (SP 36/48, f. 37, 2 July 1739), she parcelled out to smaller retailers enormous quantities of these and other papers. Known quantities include thirty quires (750 sheets) of *Common Sense* in 1739, seventy quires (1,750 sheets) of *Mist's Weekly Journal* in 1718, and a hefty 108 quires (2,700 sheets) of the *London Journal* in 1721 (SP 36/48, f. 37, 2 July 1739; SP 35/13/28, f. 57, 31 Oct. 1718; SP 35/28/9, f. 18, 12 Aug. 1721). Comparing the two quires (fifty sheets) of the *London Evening Post* received by retailer Robert Amey from Dodd (SP 36/50, f. 266, 5 Apr. 1740) with the 108 quires (2,700 sheets) of the *London Journal* received by Dodd herself helps to suggest the considerable scale of distribution in which wholesaling mercury-women such as Nutt and Dodd were engaged. Among the many smaller newspaper and pamphlet-sellers who would also qualify for Dunton's '*Worshipfull Society of Mercury-Women* in and *about the City of* London' was Mary Zierenberg, of Warwick Lane off Newgate Street, who dealt in large quantities of papers purchased from publisher John Peele. Examined regarding *London Journal* no. 107, 12 Aug. 1721, Zierenberg admitted that she sent her maid Susan Norman to Peele 'at divers times heretofore', and paid him 'from time to time' (SP 35/28/9, f. 22 [12 Aug. 1721]). Zierenberg took forty-two quires (about 1,050 sheets) of this particular issue, of which Peele himself claimed that currently circulating copies 'might amount to Ten Thousand in Number' (SP 35/28/9, f. 28 [12 Aug. 1721]). Other mercury-women included Laetitia Bartlett and her mother at the 'Corner of Swithin's Alley in Cornhill', who appear to have had an arrangement similar to Elizabeth Nutt and her daughters (SP 36/50, f. 274, 5 Apr. 1740), and 'Elizabeth Smith of the Parish of St. Anns Blackfryars Pamphletseller' (SP 36/13, f. 107, 19 July 1729).

HAWKERS AND BALLAD-SINGERS

Contrary to the impression conveyed by quaint lithographs in Victorian periodicals or the convivial set-pieces of Augustan journals, early eighteenth-century hawkers and criers of political ballads led desperate, vulnerable, and hazardous lives. Predominantly female, they were less socially moored than any other occupational group within the trade. They were often elderly, and frequently crippled or blind, and as Esther Haggett's address 'in the gravel pits in old So-hoe' suggests, they were commonly homeless too (CSPD 32/12, ff. 204–5, 29 Sept. 1701). Typically referred to in State Papers as 'those poor People', 'miserable Creatures', and in less compassionate terms, their own lives have too often been reconstructed in the terms of the 'pleasaunt histories' they hawked.

Octogenarian Elizabeth Scales was taken into custody in 1716 for publishing the anti-ministerial *The Shift Shifted*. Having no friend or relative capable of writing a petition on her behalf, she was forced to hire her gaol-keeper to write one for her. The document states that 'your poor Petitioner, aged about 80 Years, lives now very ill in the Gatehouse', where 'she is in a very distressed and deplorable Condition under her Confinement which Affliction she never before suffer'd'. It urges Secretary of State Charles, Viscount Townshend, to 'take so much Pity and Compassion on her unhappy Circumstances as to release her out of Goal, or otherwise she must inevitably starve and perish for want of Friends to support her'. Alone, destitute, and ill, this woman imprisoned for publishing a seditious libel could 'neither write nor read' (SP 35/67/60, f. 121 [*c*.1716]).

Septuagenarian Ellen Vickers, too, hawked papers 'purely for want of bread' (SP 35/11/14, f. 33, 25 Jan. 1717/18). Like many other widows in the trade, Mrs Vickers's daughter worked alongside her, and when her daughter's husband was disabled by military service he too was forced to rely on the labour of his wife and mother-in-law for support. When this mother–daughter team was taken into custody for crying seditious ballads, William Ogilbie wrote a petition on their behalf, explaining that his wife was 'helpfull to him to gett his and her bread in a Lawfull manner'. He also urged that Sarah Vickers Ogilbie—then in custody—was 'big with Child and [expecting] every hour when to be brought to bed of a Child having neither Linens or any [necessaries] for her Child or her self being in a poor condition' (SP 35/67/75, f. 150 [after 25 Jan. 1717/18]). (Sarah Ogilbie's mother, 'an old blind woman of 73 years of Age', seems equally ill-suited to the rigours of imprisonment.) When Vickers and Ogilbie were examined, both claimed not to have understood the nature of the papers they were selling, and both signed their name with a mark.

Unlettered and in this case also illiterate, Mrs Vickers nevertheless stated with some pride that 'she has used to cry papers about streets ever since the time of Dr. Sacheverell's Tryal' (SP 35/11/14, f. 35, 25 Jan. 1717/18). Mrs Vickers's habit of measuring time in her life by political events was common among hawkers and balladsingers, for a hawker's business was brisk in times of political turmoil. When John Dunton thanked the '*Worshipfull Society of Mercury-Women*', he wished them 'brave *roaring News* twice a Week for this seven Years next ensuing'. The particular event that Mrs Vickers remembered—the trial of Dr Henry Sacheverell for seditious libel in 1709—underlines the extraordinary degree to which Sacheverell's trial, and the intensification of party enmities thereupon, aroused vigorous participation among women and men far below the level of the electorate.

While many hawkers were impromptu 'employees' warding off starvation, others were at it for years. Some even carried trade lists like chapmen. Ellen Vickers's statement in 1718 that she had cried papers since Sacheverell's trial suggests that she had followed her trade for about a decade. Another hawker, 'Frances Carver, alias Blind Fanny', first appears in the State Papers in 1718 when she was taken into custody for singing 'the High Church Ballad' (SP 35/11/ 21, f. 59, 11 Feb. 1717/18) and reappears twenty-five years later when she was committed to Old Bridewell for selling unstamped newspapers.[43] Similarly Ann Mahoney, otherwise 'Irish Nan', was arrested and committed to a bridewell in 1744 for the seventh time—she too for selling unstamped newspapers.[44] Experienced

[43] 'Last Wednesday Frances Karver, alias Blind Fanny, was committed to Old Bridewell, by the Right Hon. the Lord Mayor, for hawking News-Papers, not being duly stamp'd, contrary to Act of Parliament' (*LEP* no. 2487, 18 Oct. 1743).
[44] See *LEP* no. 2540, 16–18 Feb. 1744 (qtd. below).

hawkers had regular routes that they travelled daily, first calling on printers' wives to see what papers were ready (the names of printing-house mistresses such as Mrs Bradford, Mrs Clifton, Mrs How(e), Mrs Hynes, Mrs Meeres, and Mrs Wilkins appear frequently) and then walking the streets of London selling the papers they had purchased at a discount. Hawker Esther Haggett of 'the gravel pits in old So-hoe' stated that 'On Friday last she went to Mr. Wilkins's printing-house in the White-Friars, to see what News papers or pamphlets came out that day'—as if she did it regularly (CSPD 32/12, ff. 204–5, 29 Sept. 1701). Messenger of the press Robert Stephens described Judith Jones as 'a hawker that serves the Amsterdam coffee-house', as if that well-known Whig gathering-spot were Jones's personal distributive territory (CSPD 29/436/44, 15 Jan. 1684). Nicknames such as 'Blind Fanny' and 'Lame Cassie' are reminders of hawkers' frequent physical disabilities and the poverty that so often went with disability in this period. Names such as these and 'Irish Nan' also suggest the familiarity of these women's persons and voices to ordinary citizens on London streets, and the possibility that these women served as reassuring human landmarks in an increasingly impersonal metropolis.

Hawkers such as Ellen Vickers and Frances Karver (or Carver) might be next to penniless for most of their lives, yet their labour was of real commercial importance. Booksellers saw competition from hawkers as a threat to their own business, and were constantly trying to suppress their activities. In 1664, the City Marshal's men voted 20 shillings a quarter for apprehending 'Hawkers, and Women crying bookes near the Exchange',[45] but such measures repeatedly proved impossible to enforce. Hawkers were indispensable, for they could actively seek out potential customers on London streets, and advertise freely with their voices. Dunton acknowledged both of these advantages when he observed of the '*Worshipfull Society of Mercury-Women* in and *about the City of* London' that 'not *Vander*'s self e're Walkt more dirty *Steps* . . . nor with more Vigour declaims against [his paper's] Rivals and *Enemies*'.

But hawkers could do more than seek out potential customers. They could also determine what type of news those customers were likely to buy. Their constant interaction with the public made these women, the least privileged in the trade, knowledgeable about what

---

[45] Qtd. in Blagden, *The Stationers' Company*, 164.

the average Londoner would pay for on the spot. As a result, it often happened that hawkers were the ones to initiate the printing or reprinting of a particularly hot, saleable text. When Under-Secretary of State Charles Delafaye received a seditious ballad along with the information that it was 'at this time printing at Cliftons in the Old Bayly up three pair of Staires in the Store garret' (SP 35/21/75, f. 205, 23 May 1720) he examined 'Catherine Clifton living in the Old Bailey in the City of London Printer'. Clifton admitted that she printed the ballad 'The Tory's Wholsome Advice'. But she also explained that 'it was done by a printed Copy which was delivered to her together with a written Copy of the same by one Ann a Ballad Singer whose Sirname she does not know, nor her Habitation, and gave her in Exchange a hundred other printed Ballads' (SP 35/21/77, f. 210, 25 May 1720). Catherine Clifton signed her name with a mark, and if 'Ann the ballad-singer' was hawker Anne Barnwell then she too was unable to write (and, perhaps, to read). But possible illiteracy did not prevent these two women, by themselves and of their own accord, from selecting and printing a highly seditious text in a matter of hours. In exchange for a provocative new text, Ann the ballad-singer received 100 printed ballads to sell. It would not have been difficult for an experienced ballad-singer to determine which printers might consider reprinting this dangerous text. Printers Catherine and Francis Clifton were Catholic, Jacobite, and dirt-poor—all factors which might encourage them to risk the underground production of a seventy-line ballad lamenting 'The Noble Hearts that dies, | For medling in [t]he State' (SP 35/21/77, f. 212, 25 May 1720).

Printers as notorious as the Cliftons could perhaps be avoided, but generally speaking, ballad-singers' circumstances must have forced them to sell what they could get. Political ballad-printing and distributing were hopelessly dangerous occupations, and the many women involved in distributing these materials endured a seemingly endless cycle of quick sales, quick arrests, and repeated periods of detention. A glut of urban working-class women looking for employment made a bad situation worse. Veteran Ellen Vickers stated that she

has often gone to Hynes the Printer, and to Clifton for papers to be . . . cryed. That she goes every day to those two places to enquire if they have anything to publish. That on Thursday she was told about places they would have something to publish next Day, and accordingly went again yesterday and found there above twenty other persons at one or other of those two Houses upon the same Errand. (SP 35/11/14, f. 35, 25 Jan. 1717/18)

With this kind of competition, it is not surprising that Ellen Vickers was caught crying seditious ballads like 'The Father's Letter to the Son, and the Son's Answer', obtained 'from the Wife of Andrew Hynes a Printer in Fleet lane', or the intriguing 'No Fence from Rogues, or turn in, turn out, turn up, turn down, turn which way you will, you cant save your Bacon' obtained 'from Mr. Clifton a Printer in black Horse alley in Fleetstreet' (SP 35/11/12, f. 31, 25 Jan. 1717/18). The printers in question here, the Hyneses and the Cliftons, did share political disaffections. But they also shared neighbourhoods (here, just off Fleet Street)—an important consideration for a 73-year-old who did most of her business on foot. Beyond the practice of renting out pamphlets for a fee, then returning them to the printer or mercury unsold (forbidden by law after 1782 (29 George III c. 50)), there was little that a hawker or ballad-crier could do to enhance her income on the comfortable side of the law. It is the other side of the law, then, to which we shall now turn.

2

Making, Tracing, and Erasing
Seditious Intentions

When Queen Mary Tudor granted the Stationers' Company a royal charter of incorporation in 1557, it was intended that the corporation would serve as the English government's most effective tool for control of the press. A self-regulating body, the corporation had the right to restrict the number of printers throughout England, and to search the premises of printers, booksellers, and binders for seditious, heretical, or otherwise illegal works in progress. After the Restoration, the offices of surveyor of the press and messenger of the press were created to help censor the press. Sir Roger L'Estrange became the first surveyor of the press, or chief censor, in 1663. Robert Stephens, a printer and member of the Stationers' Company much disliked by his fellow tradesmembers, became the first messenger of the press or assistant to the surveyor.

By the end of the seventeenth century, the British government was searching for new ways to supervise and control a rapidly expanding press. It had become clear that the government and the Stationers' Company had different (and sometimes competing) priorities. In 1689, the Revolution Settlement had made the contemporary shift in power from crown to parliament concrete, and the precise limits of acceptable political commentary were now unclear even to those in power. The growth of the party system, too, helped to make pre-publication censorship an administrative nightmare, for every time political power shifted so too did definitions of 'legal' and 'illegal'. It was a time of political, legal, economic, and social redefinition, and the English press was earning a name for itself as the most uncontrolled in Europe.

The primary means of government censorship in England after the lapse of the Licensing Act in 1695 was the law of libel.[1] Libel

---

[1] See Philip Hamburger, 'The Development of the Law of Seditious Libel and the Control of the Press', *Stanford Law Review*, 37 (1984/5), 661–765.

was a common-law offence, and extremely broadly defined. Of the
three main types of libel—blasphemous, obscene, and seditious—
the last was by far the most important to members of the revolutionary and post-revolutionary book trade, who frequently
encountered expressions of political and religious debate and dissent. Neither the government nor the trade had clear guidelines to
follow in determining or avoiding an expression that might be
considered libellous. Virtually the only area of mutual agreement
was that direct written or printed criticism of a monarch or his or
her ministers threatened the security of the state. Even in the years
1694 to 1716, when a new set of general elections every three years
inevitably helped to maintain an atmosphere of political turmoil,
any written or printed text with the potential to cause a breach of
the peace could be considered a seditious libel. In 1707, the Treason
Act (6 Anne c. 7) focused the disciplinary powers of the state
even more directly on the book trade, declaring it treasonous
to promote the idea in writing or in print that James Stuart or his
heirs had any claim to the throne.[2] Offences against property (such
as infringements of patent or copy, or evasion of the Stamp Tax)
were a concern for all women in the book trade. But the main
focus of what follows will be prosecutions for seditious libel and
treason, where women abound as producers, distributors, and
informants.

THE ECONOMY OF DISOBEDIENCE

Deciding where to position oneself in relation to a series of ill-
defined laws concerning printed materials was a daily concern for
members of the book trade, whether examinants under pressure to
inform, or producers and distributors faced with the decision
whether or not to become involved with a potentially profitable
work. Throughout the period 1678 to 1730, anyone who printed,
distributed, contrived, or procured a work could be prosecuted as
that work's 'publisher', and was subject to penalties the same as, or
greater than, the author. In the negotiation of risk consisted the
essential 'economy' of the trade: that functionally arranged system
whose elements were considerations of ideology and profit. In a

[2] As we will see, this law, which carried the penalty of death, was invoked only
once, against the 19-year-old journeyman printer John Matthews.

sense at once material and spiritual, one's business had to be carefully managed.

In a petition to Secretary of State Thomas Pelham-Holles, Duke of Newcastle, major wholesaling mercury Anne Dodd described the factors in her own economy thus:

> I have been left an afflicted widow with a Large Young Family some years, whose only Support has been that of Selling News papers, which, with as much Pains as my own ill State of Health would admit of, has by the Assistance of Heaven, Just enabled me to Feed my self, and helpless Children. I need not aquaint your Grace, that this Business sometimes Compells me to sell Papers that Give Offence, but I must Beg Leave to Declare Sincerely tis Greatly Against my Inclination when they are so; and, that what Papers I sell in Just Praise of Our Happy Government, far Exceede the Others in Number. Hard Case! that I must either Offend where I am shure I would not, or else starve my Poor Babes. (SP 36/23/134, 26 May 1731)

As a successful newspaper proprietor with a long-standing association with opposition weeklies, it was almost certainly more than the prerequisite of trade that Dodd 'sell Papers that Give Offence'. Dodd may have sold oppositional papers only 'Greatly Against [her] Inclination' (here, 'a Craftsman, a Paper that I neither Read, nor Understand'). But she clearly understood what she was dealing with, and decided that their potential benefits outweighed their inherent risks. In this attempt to be spared the expense and danger of prosecution—an experience with which she was completely familiar by 1731, as she 'need not aquaint [his] Grace'—she could only attempt to appease Newcastle with her calculation that the papers she sold 'in Just Praise of Our Happy Government, far Exceede the Others in Number'.

When calculating the risk involved in dealing with any given paper, the economic, emotional, and physical costs of every stage of prosecution had to be taken into account. The Secretary of State's office had the power to issue general warrants to search the home or workplace of anyone associated with the publication of a libel, and these searches were frequently carried out in the middle of the night.[3] Arrests were intimidating in themselves; messengers often

---

[3] By such a procedure, Robert Stephens discovered that Tace Sowle's father Andrew Sowle operated a secret press behind a trap door (Leona Rostenberg, *Literary, Political, Scientific, Religious and Legal Publishing, Printing, and Bookselling in England, 1551–1700: Twelve Studies* (New York: Burt Franklin, 1965), ii. 356).

entered by force and behaved brutally once inside. Equipment and supplies could be destroyed or confiscated, thus putting smaller suspects out of business without a trial, for type might account for two-thirds of a printer's initial capital investment, and paper was more expensive than labour. Three years after the prosecution of her son John, printer Philippa Redmayne was still petitioning Under-Secretary of State Charles Delafaye for the return of 'my printing materials that was taken from my son in the works of one Earberry near three years Since I having sold all my printing-house to that font of Letter. which is the humble petition of a poore Destressed widow' (SP 35/60/47, f. 109 [1725]). Francis Clifton lamented the destruction of his ballad formes 'wch the Messengers made my Wife brake before their ffaces'.[4]

Like most divisions of the civil service in early eighteenth-century England, the Secretary of State's office in charge of press control was understaffed. The initial stages of press prosecutions, as well as the trials themselves, were costly and time-consuming for everyone involved, and generally speaking it is true that the inadequacies of the late Stuart state administrative apparatus resulted in a period of 'freedom by default'.[5] But it is also true that in specific instances these same shortcomings resulted in nightmarish miscarriages of justice. Ann Herring's fate may be one example of what could happen in the course of the government's sometimes paranoic efforts to defuse 'seditious intentions' (SP 32/13/219–20 [Nov. 1696]). According to 'The Case of Robert Crosfield. Most Humbly Presented to the Consideration of the Lords Spiritual and Temporal, and Commons in Parliament Assembled', Ann Herring was a pawn in a larger conflict between Crosfield and the state—a conflict not even Crosfield claimed to have understood. Crosfield wrote from the Poultrey Compter, where he was in custody—ostensibly for his role in *A Dialogue between a Modern Courtier and an honest English Gentleman*, though he himself was convinced that other motives were involved. Crosfield openly confessed that he was the author of works such as *England's Glory Reviv'd* (1693)

---

[4] Infuriated that others were still printing and profiting from the said ballad at that very moment, Clifton had the boldness to add, 'but pardon me S^r I can't but think it a little hard . . . after I've paid for Coppies & have lost four or five Rheam without making half a Crown out of them' (SP 35/24/75, f. 221, 1720).

[5] John Feather, 'From Censorship to Copyright: Aspects of the Government's Role in the English Book Trade 1695–1775', in Kenneth E. Carpenter, ed., *Books and Society in History* (New York: R. R. Bowker Co., 1983).

on 'the ill Conduct and Management of Affairs' pertaining to the war, and explained how he obtained *A Dialogue*. He claimed to have been sent a parcel of books (pamphlets), and thinking that they 'tended to public good', hired several hawkers to sell them directly to members of parliament at the opening of session. Enquiries were made by the Secretary of State's office regarding the source of the pamphlets, but Crosfield never received orders to desist from publishing them. Instead, the messengers arrested hawker Ann Herring, and carried her before a justice 'who barely upon the Messenger's Report, that the book was Seditious, Committed the poor woman to the *Poultrey Compter*'. Crosfield went to the justice and urged him to discharge Herring, promising to take the matter upon himself. Accordingly, Crosfield was committed to the Poultrey, but although the justice promised 'to discharge the woman the next day without Fees', he 'since refuses to do it, though at the Secretaries Office she has said all she knows about the said book; and is miserably poor, and lies on the bare boards on the Common Side of the *Compter*, ready to perish; having also Two Children in the same starving Condition for want of her Labour to maintain them in this miserable time of Scarcity'. Crosfield wrote to the Secretary of State offering to reveal the author of the work for which he and Herring had been arrested, but was informed that 'a Prosecution wou'd be speedily ordered against us, which looks as if it was not desired to know the Author, but that the Design was rather to take Occasion from this Book, to Ruin me . . . and indeed this Close Expensive Prison . . . will e're long Ruin me, and my Family'. Crosfield sensed that 'there is a greater design to stop my mouth than to discover the author'; that is, that those in power did not *want* to set him free. Unfortunately, the same 'Close Expensive Prison' that would ruin Crosfield and his family would ruin a 'miserably poor' occupant of the common wards and her two 'starving' children even more quickly. By the peak of Walpole's career, the government would come to the modern realization that the most cost-effective way to control dissent is to produce masses of orthodoxy. But in the meantime, in its effort to silence individuals like Crosfield with or without a trial, the state arrested, detained, and ruined the health and trade of others—facelessly, through its makeshift instruments of control.

As we have seen in the Introduction in the case of Mary Unknown, the complexity of interaction between the various producers and distributors of any given work of political literature in this period sometimes made it difficult for the government to pinpoint 'seditious intentions'. Messengers' nets, then, had to be very widely spread. It was not uncommon for an entire household to be taken into custody at once. In 1728, in one of the government's attempts to crush Jacobite printer Nathaniel Mist, two sweeps of Mist's establishment were made, and everyone arrested who happened to be present at the time. In all, some two dozen persons were taken into custody, ostensibly for *Mist's Weekly Journal*, nos. 175 and 177, of 7 and 14 September. At least half of those arrested were women. Elizabeth Nutt and her daughter Alice, Mrs Wolf(e) the wife of Mist's printer, and Amy Walker, the Mists' household maid, were arrested for the first issue, and eight more women were taken up for the second issue. These included Catherine Nutt, who had shouldered her mother's and sister's workloads; Anne Neville, a mercury who worked for the Nutts; Mrs Smith, another mercury; Judith Salmon, her hawker; Catherine Brett, along with her husband, warehouse-keeper to Mist; Mary Carter and her daughter Elizabeth, caretakers of Mist's house in his absence; and poor Mrs Birnie, a neighbour trying to send Mist's imprisoned employees some clothes.

After suspects were taken up, they were examined at length. Preliminary examinations, like arrests, were intimidating in themselves. Even an experienced offender like Nathaniel Mist, the government hoped, might be 'frighten[ed] . . . into' discovering the author of another offending issue of his paper by 'an Examination by the Lords' (SP 35/13/28, f. 79, [31] Oct. 1718). Regardless of their seniority or lack thereof, everyone taken into custody could be examined at length. A frightened printer's devil was at least as likely to leak information as a hardened offender like Mist.

In theory, prisons and compters were intended to serve as holding-places rather than as penal instruments. In practice, however, poorer offenders who could not find someone to sign for bail for them, provide sureties for keeping the peace, or pay their gaol-fees sometimes remained there for weeks and even months. Conditions, as is well known, were worst for the poor. As the following memo regarding the release of the aforementioned Mrs Wolf(e) reminds us, though, conditions for the working poor were not much better outside:

wife of John Wolf—Discharge—there is nothing to charge her with and turning her loose will probably be the severer punishment being very poor. (SP 36/8, f. 64 [24 Aug. 1728])[6]

Like pre-trial imprisonment, bail, fees, and fines were not supposed to serve as penal instruments, but in actual fact inevitably did so. In the 1730s, bail amounts of £100 seem to have been about average. Combined with the economic losses sustained as a consequence of arrest, imprisonment, fines, fees, and disruption of business, the difficulty of finding someone to sign for bail amounts like this could silence smaller offenders for good. Such was the intention, surely, behind the staggeringly high bail levied upon the members of Nathaniel Mist's printing household in the aforementioned prosecutions. Bail for Amy Walker, Mist's maid, was levied at £300—the same amount that was levied for his head pressman and compositor (SP 36/8, f. 248, 26 Oct. 1728).[7] Bail for repeat offenders was a still more formidable prospect. In 1739, Anne Dodd's servant Mary Dewe was levied a bail fee of £50 for her involvement in the anti-ministerial *Common Sense*, no. 125, of 23 June 1739. Nine months later, she was levied another bail fee of £100 for her role in the *London Evening Post*, no. 1932, 1 Apr. 1740. High bail amounts set for servants may have been intended to induce them to inform on their masters. As in the case of Mist's servant, above, bail for Dodd's servant Mary Dewe was set as high as for several others who might appear to us to have played a greater role in the publication of the libel. At £100, Dewe's bail was as high as for any of the 'pamphletsellers' involved (SP 44/82, 22 Apr. 1740).

---

[6] John Wolf(e) had followed Mist into hiding.

[7] When Walker was finally brought to trial in the spring, the sentence was equally severe. For her involvement in the newspaper, presumably in her capacity as Mist's servant, Walker was sentenced to six months' hard labour. This was as severe a punishment as anyone else in the printing house received, and far more severe than the punishment meted out to Mist's apprentice pressman. The *LEP* no. 226, 20 May 1729, records that 'Yesterday the Court of King's Bench at Westminster, gave Judgment on the four Persons convicted for printing and publishing Mist's Journal of the 24th of August last, viz. John Clark, the Press-man, for printing and publishing, was sentenced to stand three Times in the Pillory, viz. at Charing Cross, Temple Bar, and the Royal Exchange, and to suffer six Months Imprisonment; Robert Knell, the Compositor, to stand twice in the Pillory, once at Charing Cross, and once at the Royal Exchange; and also to suffer six Months Imprisonment; Joseph Carter (the Apprentice, and a Press-man) to walk round the four Courts in Westminster-Hall, with a Paper on his Forehead, denoting his Offence, and to suffer one Month's Imprisonment.' For Amy Walker's sentence, see below.

Obviously, few shop servants like Mary Dewe could have signed for bail amounts of £150. Women workers' bail was usually signed for, or fines and fees paid for, by their employers and fellow tradespeople and sometimes their neighbours and relatives. Henry Cook, bookseller, entered into a recognizance of £100 for his wife Elizabeth in 1732, but the recognizance of mercury-woman 'Anne the Wife of Samuel Neville' in the same case was entered into by her co-workers Richard Nutt and Daniel Brown (SP44/82, 24 Apr. 1732).[8]

It was the frequency and seriousness of the offence that determined a tradeswoman's bail, rather than her sex, her status in the trade, or any other factor. Bail amounts levied for Elizabeth Nutt—matriarch of the London pamphlet trade, and a repeated offender—were almost always higher than for everyone else involved in a given publication. By the time that she had reached her seventies, Elizabeth Nutt had come into conflict with the authorities many times. Accordingly, 'for publishing an infamous libel, intitled, *The Divine Catastrophe of the Kingly Family of the House of Stuarts, Or a Short History of the Rise Reigne and Ruine thereof*', Mrs Nutt was required to sign for a bail amount of £100—twice as much as her son Richard Nutt, who printed the paper, or Daniel Brown, who sold it (SP 44/82, 2 Jan. 1729/30; my emphasis). In 1732, Elizabeth Nutt and her daughter Alice were levied bail amounts of £200 each. Meanwhile Richard Nutt, who printed the paper, was levied a fee of half that amount—the same amount as bookseller Daniel Brown (SP 44/82, 4 Apr.).[9] The bail fees levied for various persons performing similar jobs was not necessarily the same. In 1737, 'Anne Parker of St. Giles Cripplegate, Printer' was levied a bail fee of £200, while 'Walter Baker, printer' was levied a fee of only half that amount for his involvement in the same case (SP 44/82, 21 Oct.).

---

[8] In the *Daily Post* and *Evening Post* prosecutions of 17 July 1729 for nos. 3065 and 3119 respectively, the bail of 'Catherine Nutt Spinster' and 'Rich. Nutt, Printer' was signed for by fellow tradesmembers 'Robert Gosling, bookseller in Fleetstreet' and 'Mr. Tho. Stagg, Bookseller in Westminster Hall'. Gosling also signed for part of the bail of mercury-woman Elizabeth Smith, and the rest was signed for by 'Edward Colson sword cutter at Charing Cross'. Mary Dewe's bail was signed for by neighbours 'Robert Jeeves of St. Clement Danes Victualler and Robert Winberley Turner of St. Clement Danes' (SP 36/13, ff. 114–17, 19 July 1729).

[9] As repeat offenders, however, mother, daughter, and son were all levied bail fees of twice the amount that they had been required to sign for two years earlier.

To see fellow tradesmembers standing bail for one another, or even, as in the case of the Nutt family, taking on additional chores when one or more of their co-workers was in custody, is to sense the guild-like solidarity of these interdependent workers, and the efficient redistribution of human resources that took place in response to disruption from 'outside'. When one member of an economic family was arrested, the others swung into action to recoup their loss—a phenomenon which caused the government to carry out frequent mass arrests in the hopes of shutting down production completely and/or identifying the author.

As prosecutors well knew, the spouse of a prisoner formed an especially strong connection to the outside. Women not only supplied food and money to their imprisoned husbands, but also wrote petitions for them and served as go-betweens for materials produced inside prison.[10] Several women printers and publishers are known to have continued producing the papers for which their husbands were then imprisoned or in hiding—*without* modifying those papers' oppositional content. In 1682, a warrant was issued for the arrest of Mrs Nathaniel Thompson, for 'publishing an *Intelligence*, when her husband was in gaol' (CSPD 29/2/61, 16 Nov.). The same year, Jane Curtis continued to publish the *True Protestant Mercury* for several months after her husband Langley Curtis went into hiding. Only when Jane Curtis was arrested in lieu of her husband did the paper finally stop (28 Oct. 1682).[11] Wives of newspaper writers brought their imprisoned husbands blank paper, and came back a few days later to take away the next week's copy. Accordingly, book trade wives preferred prisons with convenient locations. It may have been the 'distance motive', as much as her husband's ill health, which motivated Alice Applebee to petition Lord Townshend in 1715 against confining her husband in King's Bench in Southwark, a long walk from the centre of the book trade. Since being taken into custody by a messenger, Mrs Applebee

---

[10] I have not yet found any instances of men supplying food to their imprisoned wives. In the several cases I have found where married women were imprisoned while their husbands were still alive, the husbands were usually in exile or in hiding (Jane Curtis and Elizabeth Powell for instance). For an example of a husband working to free his imprisoned wife and mother-in-law, see the case of William Ogilbie, Sarah Vickers Ogilbie, and Ellen Vickers above.

[11] For further information on Jane Curtis see Maureen Bell, 'Women and the Opposition Press after the Restoration', in John Lucas, ed., *Writing and Radicalism* (London: Longman, 1996), 39–60.

wrote, John Applebee had 'contracted a Violent Fitt of Sickness' and was 'reduced to a very weak condition'. She was fearful lest he be moved at the height of his illness, and requested that he be allowed to remain in the messengers' hands. John Applebee may have been in poor health, but with Alice Applebee's substantial assistance his newspaper *The Original Weekly Journal* never missed an issue during the period of his confinement. In her petition to Lord Townshend, Alice Applebee did not mention that it was more convenient for her to remain in contact with her husband while he was in the custody of a messenger, than if he were to be taken to Southwark and confined in King's Bench (SP 35/2/10, f. 30 [1715]).

When author George Flint was imprisoned for his *Weekly Remarks* in Jan. 1716, his wife Mary Flint continued to work for their political cause—until she too was arrested for her role in distributing a sequel to this paper, the 'vile and treasonable' *The Shift Shifted: or, Weekly Remarks* (SP 44/80, 22 July 1716). Later that year Mary Flint would be caught smuggling 'treasonable Letters and Papers, being Materials for the said Paper' to her husband in prison 'under pretence of bringing him a Pudding' (*Weekly Journal*, 15 Sept. 1716). Still later the same year she would be sentenced to a year's imprisonment and a £20 fine for another similar offence (*Evening Post*, 11 Dec. 1716). Even her own imprisonment could not defeat Mary Flint's efforts, however. In April 1717 she helped her husband escape for good.[12]

Theoretically, according to the law of coverture, a married woman could not be sent to prison if her husband was alive. But as we have seen above in the case of Jane Curtis, this was (once again) not necessarily the case in actual fact. Langley Curtis was alive and in hiding, but this did not stop Lord Chief Justice Sir William Scroggs from imprisoning Mrs Curtis and bringing her to trial for publishing a broadside criticizing himself. According to *An impartial account of the tryal of Francis Smith. . . . as also of Jane Curtis* (1680) Scroggs simply accepted the 'offer of two witnesses to make affidavit that Langley Curtis was dead'.[13]

---

[12] W. J. Sheehan, 'Finding Solace in Eighteenth-Century Newgate', in J. S. Cockburn, ed., *Crime in England 1550–1800* (Princeton UP, 1977), 236.

[13] Timothy Crist, 'Government Control of the Press after the Expiration of the Printing Act in 1679', *Publishing History*, 5 (1979), 49–77, 58. See also *State Trials*, vii. 959 for her Guildhall trial 7 Feb. 1680.

In addition to the losses suffered during prosecution, post-trial punishment might include fines, penalties, or penal sentences. Mary Dalton's sentence of twelve months' imprisonment and a £20 fine was harsh, and in this case signals a repeat offender. Equally severe penalties imposed on Mist's employees in 1728 indicate a desire to crush Mist's activities once and for all. As we have seen, servant Amy Walker was levied a bail amount of £300. She was also punished as severely as Mist's apprentice pressman and compositor. 'For publishing the said paper', *LEP* no. 226 reports, Walker was 'to be sent to the House of Correction for six Months, there to be kept to hard Labour, and to be stript down to her Waist, and receive the Correction of the House' (20 May 1729).

Hawkers could be arrested at any time for 'vagrancy' and committed to a bridewell for ten days on the order of a justice of the peace. Because these women often had no other way of making a living, notices of their frequent arrests are sprinkled throughout contemporary newspapers. In the autumn of 1743, hawker Ann Mahoney was arrested and sentenced to three months' hard labour:

Committed. Anne Mahony, to Tothill-Fields Bridewell, for three Months to hard Labour, by James Frazier, Esq: for vending unstamp'd News Papers, upwards of 400 being found upon her. (*The Country Journal: Or, the Craftsman*, no. 893, 6 Aug. 1743)

A few months after her release, she was arrested again, and sentenced to another three months' hard labour:

Last Thursday Anne Mahony, otherwise Irish Nan, was committed to Clerkenwell Bridewell, for three Months to hard Labour, by James Fraser, Esq.; for selling unstamp'd Newspapers. This is the seventh Time of her being committed for Offences of the like Nature. (*LEP* no. 2540, 16–18 Feb. 1744)[14]

Given punishments for poverty such as these, it is not surprising that one 'Sarah Turbat, a Hawker' was sentenced 'to stand on the Pillory at Bow-Lane End, Cheapside, and suffer six Months Imprisonment'—not for selling unstamped newspapers, but 'for cursing the King' (*The Weekly Journal: or, British Gazeteer*, 20 Oct. 1722).

[14] Similarly Susannah Wilcox was arrested and committed for selling unstamped papers: 'On Friday last two Officers belonging to the Stamp Duties, seiz'd Susannah Wilcox in Ratcliff-Highway, with near 300 unstamp'd News-Papers upon her; she was carried before Justice Jones of Shadwell, who committed her to Clerkenwell-Bridewell to hard Labour' (*LEP* no. 2487, 18 Oct. 1743).

After the imposition of the Stamp Tax in 1712, the decision whether or not to distribute unstamped papers was yet another factor in each hawker's individual daily calculation of risks. By the 1740s, new penalties were directed squarely against the hawkers and criers. From 1 May 1743, the sale of unstamped papers became punishable by three months' imprisonment (16 George II c. 2). The very desperateness of hawkers' material circumstances, though, ensured that no penalty, however harsh, could ever wholly check their illegal activities.

WOMEN AND THE *VOX POPULI* PROSECUTIONS

Of all the workers in the London book trade whom one might logically consider as candidates for charges of treason in this period, it is surely both ludicrous and tragic that the British government should have focused its full disciplinary powers on 19-year-old journeyman printer John Matthews. The Treason Act of 1707 was invoked only once in its history, to hang Matthews for his role in publishing the inflammatory Jacobite pamphlet *Ex Ore Tuo Te Judico. Vox Populi, Vox Dei* (1719). But if this series of press prosecutions centred on John Matthews, they neither began nor ended with him. Indeed, part of the horror of this young man's fate springs from the fact that he was neither the most important nor the most interesting of the wide cast of characters involved. More than two dozen women in the book trade were intimately concerned in the making, tracing, and erasing of *Vox Populi*'s seditious intentions, whether as co-printers, publishers, distributors, journalists, family members, or informants. To trace their involvement is to suggest the diversity of female participation in the production and control of political print in this period—and its material and ideological consequences.[15]

In the summer of 1719, a hawker named Anne Barnwell delivered to the wife of messenger Girling a bundle of papers that she (Barnwell) may have been unable to read.[16] Examined shortly there-

---

[15] I am indebted to R. J. Goulden's 'Vox Populi, Vox Dei: Charles Delafaye's Paperchase', *Book Collector*, 28 (1979), 368–90 for first provoking my own interest in the women of the *Vox Populi* prosecutions.

[16] Barnwell signed her name with a mark, suggesting that, like most hawkers, she was unable to write (and perhaps to read).

after by Charles Delafaye, Anne Barnwell explained that the bundle of political ballads and pamphlets in her possession 'were bought by her of a Woman who keeps a Shop in the Strand within two or three doors of Essex Street, where Pamphlets are sold, one half of it being put to that use, and the other a Toy Shop, and that she believes that there are large quantitys of the s^d Pamphlets to be publickly vended there' (SP 35/16/119, f. 298, 13 June 1719). Two days later, 'Thomas Gawen of the Parish of St. Clements, Pamphletseller' was examined, and admitted that the pamphlets were sold in his shop (SP 35/16/127, f. 314, 15 June).[17] Gawen stated that he had obtained the materials in question from 'one John, journeyman of one Jermingham', a goldsmith, and soon John Lowden was taken up. On 7 July, messengers searched the house of printer Mary Matthews, and found copies of *Vox Populi, Vox Dei* in the bedroom of her son John.

Meanwhile, printer Elizabeth Powell was watching closely. An author-printer like Elinor James, Elizabeth Powell was the widow of Edmund Powell, a Jacobite who had been charged with treasonous publication in July 1715 and forced into hiding until he died fifteen months later in October 1716. While her husband was in exile, Mrs Powell had written, printed, and published what she had *intended* to be two weekly newspapers. Both of these newspapers, however, were so offensive to the government as to cause her to be arrested and thrown into Newgate for seditious libel on the very first issue. The first and only issue of the first paper, pointedly titled the *Orphan*, includes this portrait of herself and her family as the political victims of an authoritarian state:

an Afflicted Woman struggling for Bread for herself, her Children, and her Distressed Husband, is Banished, stript of his Subsistence, and his Wife and Children left Poor and Bare to shift for themselves, by his having Unfortunately fallen under the Displeasure of the Government. (no. 1, 21 Mar. 1716)[18]

---

[17] The woman from whom Barnwell purchased the materials was probably Anne Gawen. Messenger Girling was speaking of either Gawen or Barnwell when he wrote to Delafaye later that day: 'I must Submite to better Judgm^t. than my own, whether the Woman who deliver'd those Pamphlets to my Spouse; and received the Money for them, ought not to have been taken in Custody as well as her Husband' (SP 35/16/126, f. 312, 15 June 1719).

[18] The *Flying Post*, no. 3779, 24 Mar. 1716, reports that: 'Last Thursday Night Mrs. Powel, wife of Edmund Powel, Printer in Black Fryars, was committed to Newgate by Lord Townshend's Warrant, for printing an Impudent and scandalous

Undeterred by a brief spell in Newgate, Elizabeth Powell promptly began a second newspaper, the *Charitable Mercury and Female Intelligence*, within days of her release.[19] Alluding to her recent imprisonment—and so making use of the economic and psychological hardships it caused, by transforming those hardships into publicity—Powell repeated her claim to be the target of a repressive regime: 'It is well enough known to the Publick, that I intended lately to entertain 'em with a Paper under another Title; and I need not tell by what means I am prevented from pursuing my Design' (no. 1, 7 Apr. 1716). Powell promised that the *Charitable Mercury and Female Intelligence* would contain nothing in it 'which may give Offence to any Reasonable Person'. And she hoped that 'if any Unguarded Expression should drop, it will be taken in the best Sense'. But by asking her readers to interpret her expressions in a benign manner ('in the best Sense') she actually underlined for them the fact that there was more than one sense in which those expressions could be taken. Similarly, in assuring the government that she and the 'Gentlemen . . . offering their Assistance' in the paper would 'take Particular Care not to fall under the Displeasure of the State . . . for we all allow that *A Burnt Child may dread the Fire*', she can only have alarmed those in power by assuring them, not that she would refrain from printing seditious libels, but rather that she would do everything in her power to avoid being '*Burnt*'! Even more boldly, Mrs Powell 'plac'd an old *Italian Proverb* at the Head of [the] Paper, as a Cautionary Maxim' by which she would 'regulate [her] future Performance'. Whatever safety or concession there may have been in printing this seditious maxim in Italian, Powell undermined it completely when she then went on to translate the maxim into English, 'for the Benefit of my own Sex, and others that may not understand Italian'. Rejecting the élitism of unnecessary foreign quotations, and throwing all caution to the winds, Elizabeth Powell translated her newspaper's motto as 'To speak ill of Grandees, is to run ones self into Danger; but

Libel against the Government, entitul'd, the *Orphan*. Note, her Husband has absconded for some time, for printing another scandalous and seditious Pamphlet, entitul'd, *A Letter to Sir Richard Steele*, and for which 100L. Reward has been offer'd by the Government for apprehending him.'

[19] The full title of the paper was the *Charitable Mercury and Female Intelligence. Being a Weekly Collection of All the Material News, Foreign and Domestick: with some Notes on the Same.*

whoever will speak well of 'em must tell Many a Lye.' Among other remarks of a similarly outrageous nature, Elizabeth Powell concluded the inaugural issue of her newspaper with a manifesto of her political beliefs, declaring that in matters pertaining to the Church of England, she would grant 'those inveterate Enemies of her and her Professors, the Fanat[i]ks of all Sorts' (the Whigs) her toleration—though such toleration was 'more than they ever practis'd when they were in Power'. None of this was likely to convince the Secretary of State's office that it had made the right decision in releasing Mrs Powell on a promise of good behaviour. As with the first issue of the *Orphan*, so with the *Charitable Mercury* the first issue caused Powell to be taken into custody. She was released on bail two months later—and for a while, she kept quiet.

In 1719, however, Elizabeth Powell came into conflict with the law once more. That year, Powell had begun a third newspaper, the title of which made it immediately clear that she was still harbouring a deep personal and political antagonism towards the state. A less openly antagonistic paper, the *Orphan Reviv'd: or, POWELL's Weekly Journal* (1719–20) was primarily concerned with domestic and foreign political, military, and economic news. But on 12 September 1719 the paper reported the committal of young John Matthews to Newgate on a bill of High Treason, and on 24 October it called for 'the Clemency of the Government'. On 7 November, the day after Matthews was hanged, it provided 'an Account of young Mr. Matthews the Printer's Behaviour on the Day of his Death and at the Place of Execution'. The following week, 'more Particulars being since come to Hand', it described the behaviour of Matthews's mother and other circumstances of his death in detail. By depicting the remorseful condemned whispering a last request to the executioner 'that his heart might be preserved from the Flames', and adorning the event with a last-minute reprieve that came too late, Powell's *Orphan Reviv'd* joined in the underground popular political protest already under way, which eventually made young John Matthews a favourite in-house martyr of the eighteenth-century London press.

But it was not, in fact, Elizabeth Powell's Jacobite and High Church sympathies that provoked this apparent concern for John Matthews. It was her fear that she might share his fate. Less than two weeks after Matthews was publicly hanged, Under-Secretary of State Charles Delafaye learned from William Hornigold, periwig-maker, that two of Powell's journeymen—Edward Holloway and a 'little man wearing a brown bob wig'—had printed *Vox Populi* at her printing house on 14 and 15 November (SP 35/18/105, f. 206, 19 Nov. 1719).[20]

Elizabeth Powell's workers were quickly taken into custody, but on 23 November journeyman Edward Holloway wrote to Justice Samuel Buckley laying the blame firmly on Powell herself. Holloway admitted that he had shown a copy of *Vox Populi, Vox Dei* to his mistress at one time, which he claimed to have been given by Hornigold, and that 'she spoke to me about printing of it'. But he stressed that he did not print the treasonous text until

about the time of Matthews's being Hanged Mrs. Powell ask'd me again about it, but I told her that I had parted with it, *yet she told me that if I could get it, it would go off very well at that time, but I answer'd her 'twas dangerous*, and she said that was not the only thing that was found against Mr. Matthews . . . and therefore told me if I would do it she would give me half what she got by them, and I, (having been lame in the Rheumatism almost a whole Month, and not able to do a days Work, was not willing to disoblige her) complied to do it. (SP 35/18/122, f. 248, 26 Nov. 1719; my emphasis)

According to Holloway and other sources, only a few days after Matthews's execution, Elizabeth Powell actively searched out and reprinted the very text for which Matthews had been hanged. A businesswoman as well as a Jacobite, Mrs Powell knew that the explosive atmosphere surrounding Matthews's trial made *Vox Populi* a certain bestseller: a text that 'would go off very well at that time'. Indeed, Mrs Powell did more than coerce her cautious journeyman into printing the treasonous pamphlet in the middle of the night. She also gave him explicit instructions to cover up her own involvement:

On Saturday Night November 14th when she paid me, she ask'd me [whether] I had done any of it, and bid me come on Sunday to do it, but I did not for which she was angry, but I told her I would do it at Night . . . I ask'd her whether I should ask Mr. Hoyle another Journey Man to help me, she said I might but bid me tell him the Job was mine, because he should not know that she was concerned in it . . . between 4 and 5 a Clock in the Morning Mr. Hornigold came up and saw us at Work, and took a dozen of them. (SP 35/18/122, f. 248, 26 Nov. 1719)

---

[20] Not surprisingly, five weeks later Powell's *Orphan Reviv'd*, no. 58, 26 Dec., described William Hornigold as 'Mrs. Powell's *late* Lodger' (my emphasis).

Journeyman John Hoyle concurred with this version of the story:

About Eleven at night, Mrs. Powell . . . came up into the work room that night when they were printing said paper finding them at work asked what they were doing, to which Holloway answered they were upon a job for himself, she reply'd then she must be paid for the use of her Tools & they . . . desired her to send up a Peck of Coals & a pound of Candles which she did accordingly . . . & the Examin^t. did not see her again til the next day at noon after they had done printing said paper. (SP 35/18/125, f. 257, 28 Nov. 1719)

Mrs Powell's printing house was searched, but Powell herself was already in hiding. Nevertheless, as the editor and author as well as the printer of a newspaper, Elizabeth Powell was still able to fight back in print against the government. Accordingly, she railed against those who had 'made free with the searching of Mrs. Powell's House, and insinuated to the Publick, as if She was guilty of the Fact her Journeymen and Lodger stand accused of'. She blamed her 'late Lodger' informant Hornigold for introducing the treasonous pamphlets into her house. And she claimed that despite all appearances, she was 'altogether a Stranger either to the Printing and Publication thereof, which will be made to appear when her Circumstances will permit her to clear herself before her Superiors, from Whom she only absconds, for the present, for Fear of Misrepresentations'.[21] Still in hiding a week later, Powell reported the arrest of another printer of *Vox Populi* in her *Orphan Reviv'd* of 5 December. At this point she began working—albeit in her own bold manner—to improve her 'public relations' with the state. She

---

[21] The *Orphan Reviv'd*, 28 Nov. 1719. A few days earlier, Powell's informing lodger William Hornigold confessed that he was the person initially responsible for introducing *Vox Populi* to Powell's journeyman. The rest of Powell's claims here are fiction. Hornigold testified that he had obtained a copy of the pamphlet from Claudius Bonner, a working aquaintance of Powell's, who had printed it at the printing house of the Widow Rumbold (SP 35/18/105, f. 206, 19 Nov.). Bonner was later examined and claimed that he found a printed copy of *Vox Populi* in a woman's purse in the street. Upon further examination, he revealed that James Alexander, another working aquaintance of Powell's, proposed to him that they print the pamphlet as far back as the previous April. Accordingly, Bonner and Alexander went to the printing house of Mrs Rumbold, where Bonner had served his apprenticeship, and printed the paper (SP 35/19/9, f. 29, 10 Dec. 1719; SP 35/19/15, ff. 43–4, 16 Dec. 1719).

Hornigold's version of Bonner's involvement is slightly different. He claims that in approximately June Alexander came to him and asked him to get the paper Bonner was printing for him, and that shortly thereafter Bonner delivered about six (SP 35/19/21, ff. 57–8, 21 Dec. 1719).

assured those in power that she would 'write nothing that shall give Offence to any Branch of the Ministry, while I enjoy the benign influence of the Government'.

Meanwhile, the wife of Elizabeth Powell's journeyman Edward Holloway was providing Under-Secretary Delafaye with detailed information regarding Mrs Powell's role in the reprinting of *Vox Populi*. Mary Holloway swore that Mistress Powell did 'frequently solicite her said Husband to print a Libel intituled Vox populi Vox Dei, and to procure a Copy of the said Libel in order to print the same, with a promise that the said Powell would publish the said Libel, and give him the said Printer, as a reward, one half of what should be gained by sale thereof'. Mary Holloway, as well as her husband, appears to have experienced Elizabeth Powell's forceful character, for Powell also tried to convince her 'to persuade her Husband to print the Libel'. It was she herself, Mary Holloway admitted, who first obtained a copy of the treasonous pamphlet from the informant William Hornigold (SP 35/19/10, f. 31, 11 Dec. 1719).

Meanwhile, Mrs Powell was still watching from 'afar'. In her *Orphan Reviv'd*, no. 58, 26 December 1719, she updated her readers on the ongoing *Vox Populi* prosecutions. About one month later, she reported that in the middle of the night

Mrs. Powell's House was again visited by Mr. John Kent Messenger of the Press assisted by a Constable, a Person belonging to an Adjacent Tavern, and a Person that keep'[s] an Ale-house, while three several Detachments of the Watch form'd the Blockade there of Those within had it in Command to Surrender, at Discretion, but the Maid being no[t] well vers'd in that matter was willing first to have her young Mistress's Opinion [Powell's daughter], her Mother having been out of the way for some Time, upon which the Shop Window was immediately broken, and an Entry forcibly made under a Pretence of a Third Edition of Vox Populi being at the Press. But when they came to look more narrowly in the Matter, nothing like it appear'd; so far to the Contrary the Men were all fast asleep, and so had the young Gentlewoman and her Maid too had not they been unseasonably awak'd. (*Orphan Reviv'd*, no. 62, 23 Jan. 1720)

Although Mrs Powell had been 'out of the way for some Time' (several months in fact) her paper had not missed an issue. The Secretary of State's office, furthermore, had been reduced to listening to the advice of the by-then desperate Edward Holloway as to how this elusive offender might be taken. Holloway suggested that if they took Elizabeth Powell's daughter into custody, Powell herself would come out of hiding and 'certainly surrender, because her Daughter shall not be kept confined'. Mrs Powell's fierce protection of her daughter was matched by her daughter's concern for her. As Holloway explained, Elizabeth Powell's daughter had earlier carried a 'bundle of Treasonous Papers' to his wife Mary Holloway, and asked Mrs Holloway to help protect her mother by hiding them (SP 35/20/57, f. 136, 1 Feb. 1719/20).

The next issue of the *Orphan Reviv'd*, no. 66, 20 February 1720, shows the new imprint 'Printed and sold by Eliz. Powell, at Mr. Clifton's in the Old Bailey'. Powell had been arrested again on 5 February,[22] but she had still not given up the public platform of her newspapers. In July she was once more discharged without bail, probably 'in Commiseration to the extream Poverty of her and her numerous Family'.[23]

Unfortunately for the government, though, Mrs Powell was by no means the only woman printer with an intense personal interest in John Matthews's case. Shortly after Elizabeth Powell was finally taken up, Charles Delafaye received a ballad 'much cryed about . . . taken upon one Cowling who saith she hath given you some information abt Clifton the Printer, and pretends to meritt some favour from you, and Mr. Ellis, however I have putt her into the Workhouse till I knew yo' pleasure' (SP 35/24/87, f. 216, 28 Feb. 1720). For the second time, an entire series of investigations was initiated on the basis of information received from a ballad-singer—this time, one who got herself thrown into the workhouse despite having co-operated with the state.

On 23 May, Delafaye received another ballad, 'The Tory's Wholsome Advice', along with the information that it was then being printed at the Cliftons' (SP 35/21/75, f. 205). Two days later, 'Catherine Clifton living in the Old Baily in the City of London Printer' was examined, and, as we have seen, confessed that the ballad was brought her by 'Ann a Ballad Singer' (SP 35/21/77, f. 210, 25 May 1720). 'The Tory's Advice' concerned 'The Noble Hearts that dies, | For medling in [t]he State':

---

[22] 'Yesterday Morning the Widow Powell, who had absconded some Months, for reprinting the Pamphlet call'd *Vox Populi, Vox Dei*, was apprehended by the King's Messengers, at a House in Aldersgate-Street, and carry'd to Westminster, where she is close confin'd' (*Original Weekly Journal*, 6 Feb. 1720).

[23] This was the explanation given for Powell's release from Newgate four years earlier (*Weekly Journal*, 31 Mar. 1716).

> ... the next the truth to tell, a charming Youth there fell
> John Matthews was his Name
> before his Morning Sun arose i[t] did go down
> And set before 'twas Noon
> He was treacherously betray'd by Servants false 'tis said
> For Gain 'tis true, their Master slew,
> A trap for his Life they laid. (SP 35/21/77, f. 212, 25 May 1720)

In six months the cocky teenager who had admitted to printing *Vox Populi* at his mother's press solely to make some pocket money, and who was informed upon by his mother's journeyman and apprentice only when they themselves were put under impossible pressure, had been transformed by popular sentiment into a noble young master betrayed by his own scheming servants and the overwhelming forces of an oppressive state. The ballad concludes by advising its audience to 'be merry and wise, the Crew despise, | And keep out of their Net' (SP 35/21/77, f. 212, 25 May 1720).

This particular ballad was only one of several political works confiscated from the Cliftons' shop, including the likes of 'Sir James King's KEY to Sir George Horn's Padlock' on the Pretender's access to King George's 'padlocked puss' (SP 35/24/75, f. 241, n.d.). John Matthews and James Francis Edward Stuart might seem incongruously paired in the Cliftons' repertory, but along with Charles I, James II, Dr Henry Sacheverell, and James Sheppard they were among the favoured martyrs of the early eighteenth-century popular press. This process of popular transformation, whereby heterogeneous political, religious, and underworld figures like these ones became the heroes of common people ranging from illiterate balladsingers to small tradespeople concerned with issues of the freedom of the press, is worth a close look. For in their own way, the fiction-making skills exercised by hawkers on those most public of early modern stages, London streets, are a model for Augustan popular literary life.

'YOU MAY SING IT *BUT I DARE NOT*': ORAL PUBLICATION AND THE LAW

The medling with Hawkers and Ballad-Singers may be thought a Trifle; but it ceases to be so, when we consider that the Crying and Singing such Stuff, as vile as it is, makes the Government familiar, and consequently contemptible to the People, warms the Minds of the Rabble, who are more capable

of Action than Speculation, and are animated by Noise and Nonsense. . . .
The greatest Mischief arises from these small Papers, and their being nois'd
about the Streets: 'Tis the quickest and surest way Sedition has to take.
(Anon., *Some Reflections on the License of the Pulpit and Press* (Dublin,
1714), 31–2)[24]

The importance of oral public discourse to popular political
culture in London can scarcely be overestimated. If ordinary Londoners could conceivably avoid sermons, they could scarcely avoid
the conversations, arguments, and oral advertising of the coffee-
house, marketplace, or street. And for the illiterate majority in
England, these modes of communication were in fact the most
regular source of news. While printed texts could be confiscated
and censored, however, oral political culture was almost impossible
to control.

Thus, as the anonymous author above advised the Hanoverian
government in 1714, not only the weightier pamphlet but also the
modest broadside ballad had to be taken seriously as a vehicle of
popular political thought. Precisely because ballads were less sub-
stantive in form and content than pamphlets, they were dangerously quick and inexpensive to produce. Ballads' anonymity, too,
made them difficult to trace. Pamphlets were often unsigned also,
but as this author pointed out, 'the Publishers of 'em are to be come
at' (32). Pamphlets were sold by mercury-women and retail shopkeepers, whose locations could be determined and premises
searched. Furthermore, because the early eighteenth-century pamphlet press was eminently dialogic, 'the Operation of one Pamphlet
[was] often spoil'd by that of another' (32). Political ballads, by
way of contrast, were a form of verbal play. No matter how
polemically effective, ballad arguments were typically expressed at
a level of generality and sportiveness that might encourage counter-
ballads but did not encourage detailed point-by-point response.

Most important, as this author understood, the unique 'Mischief'
of political ballads lay not so much in the precise printed contents
of 'these small Papers' as in 'their being nois'd about the Streets'.
Like stage plays or sermons, political ballads were an innately
public form, whose richest communicative or strategic power was

---

[24] P. B. J. Hyland attributes this pamphlet to Daniel Defoe, but unfortunately does
not cite his evidence for this attribution ('Liberty and Libel: Government and the
Press during the Succession Crisis in Britain, 1712–1716', *English Historical Review*, 101 (1986), 863–88).

realized only orally. The ballad-singer's stage was the street, and she was a street-artist whose expertise was demonstrated by her ability to draw a large crowd. The oral publication of a ballad, then, had a geography: spatial circumstances whose description no detailed arrest report could be without. In 1723, messenger of the press Richard Watts wrote to Charles Delafaye about a ballad-singer whom he had arrested for crying the libellous 'Dialogue between an ancient Citizen's Horse and a Country Plowman as they met together in Old-Street Square'.[25] In his letter, the messenger was careful to include these details of the scene of the crime: 'Such Scandallis Libells as the Inclosed was cryed thorow our Streets and Sung in every Corner, which caused great Lafter and many people gatherd togather and the person that publisht it I apprehended and caryed it with the person to a Justiss of peace who bound her to the assizes held att Kingson' (SP 35/43/50, f. 147, 22 May 1723). It did not matter to this ballad-singer's audience that this anti-Hanoverian dialogue between 'King Charles's black Nag' and 'a strange beast up in Hanover Square' whose rider 'look'd like a clown but was dress'd like a *King*' anachronistically merged the 'reins' of two kings who may have competed for English men and women's loyalties but could never have done so in person. On the ballad-singer's stage, the street, logic was no match for humour when it came to quick sales. Humour also often overtakes logic in persuasive power, especially when an audience is *hearing* a text rather than reading it. The ballad-singer's imaginative oral delivery could do more than draw a crowd. It could also make a hastily produced ballad's incongruities and exaggerations, spelling errors and typographical shortcuts irrelevant to either its rhetorical or its commercial success.

It was the hawker or ballad-singer's ability to 'rewrite' a text orally—and so, potentially, to transform the original author's 'intentions'—that the editor of the *Grub-Street Journal* acknowledged somewhat nervously in this tribute to hawker 'Phillis':[26]

---

[25] For an earlier variant on this theme see 'A Dialogue between the Two Horses' (1676), reprinted in George de F. Lord et al., eds., *Poems on Affairs of State*, i: *1660–1678* (New Haven: Yale UP, 1963), 274–83. In this version two marble and bronze horse statues debate the faults of their masters Charles I and Charles II.

[26] The similarity of names, dates, and favoured retailing locations suggests that the hawker immortalized in the *Grub-Street Journal* was Phillis Leveridge, who worked for major wholesaling mercury Anne Dodd. Examined regarding a seditious

PHILLIS, who has long had the honour to be itinerant Bookseller, vulgarly called Hawker, to our Society, is very well known to all who frequent Coffeehouses, especially those about Temple bar. . . . PHILLIS has a peculiar happiness of misnaming, wrestling, and commenting upon almost every thing she carries; which raises a curiousity not to be satisfied under the expence of six pence. Thus has many an author, who might otherwise have perish'd unobserv'd, been recommended, by the industry of PHILLIS, to the custom of a Coffee-house, and made the subject of one whole day's conversation. Of many instances of this kind which I have observ'd, I need mention but one, which happen'd last week. (no. 86, 26 Aug. 1731)

The *Grub-Street Journal* editor goes on to tell how he was passing time at the Grecian as usual, when '2 or 3 of those criers of wit and politicks came in' and attempted to sell their pamphlets and papers. But no one would buy until Phillis made her customary rounds, and 'after a turn or 2 (as is her manner) cry'd Noble Captain, won't you buy?—Her[e]'s a Sermon against religion'. Hawker Phillis is depicted as having the ability to promote 'undeserving' Grub Street authors. More threateningly, she is also depicted as having the ability, by 'misnaming, wrestling, and commenting upon . . . every thing she carries', to politicize a text of her own accord: to make someone else's printed words serve her *own* intentions.[27]

The already difficult task of pinning down 'seditious intentions' became next to impossible when the seditious 'text' in question was solely an oral one. In January 1717/18, less than three years after

libel, Leveridge stated that 'she usually sits at the Temple Gate to sell such Books, and often goes to Coffee houses to sell them; particularly most Coffee Houses above Temple Barr' (SP 36/5, f. 178, 10 Mar. 1728). Leveridge's pattern of distribution was so regular, in fact, that key evidence was obtained from an apple-seller whose stall was located at Temple Gate.

[27] By 1731 the hawker's free public circulation of her body also made her the object of sexual puns and innuendoes. The passage excised from the above quote is: 'Whether her name only might have first recommended PHILLIS to our kindness; or whether she has otherwise merited of some particular Members, in whose songs she is so often celebrated, I shall not determine. This is certain, that no body can deserve the employment better than her: for (not to mention her wonderful facility in turning, and the frequency of her doing so) . . .' A female shopkeeper's reputation for virtue might be protected by the fact that if she dealt with the public, she nevertheless did so out of a domestic space. But the most effective stage for the hawker's skills was the most exposed one, and as the ignominious term 'streetwalker' suggests, this most 'public' of women was considered to be publishing herself along with her texts. Allowing herself to be debilitated by the tag, however, was a luxury unavailable to an impoverished hawker like Phillis. Her only option was to use it, if she chose, to promote her trade.

the Jacobite invasion of Scotland, Charles Delafaye set about attempting to prosecute two women's seditious voices. Three witnesses had testified that 'they heard Eleanour Vickars and Sarah Ogleby, in a publick place called Dean's Yard . . . cry a paper by the Title of a Letter from the King to the Prince and the prince's Answer'. The paper that these women cried, however, was simply 'printed with the Title of the Father's Letter to the Son and the Son's Answer' (SP 35/11/14, f. 37, 27 Jan. 1717/18). Both women claimed that 'they knew not there was any Hurt in . . . these papers' (SP 35/11/14, f. 33, 27 Jan. 1717/18). Yet Ellen Vickers admitted that she had had no directions from the printer or his wife to cry the paper by a new title, but rather 'did it of her own head supposing it to be so' (SP 35/11/14, f. 35, 25 Jan. 1717/18). While neither Ellen Vickers nor Sarah Ogilbie could sign their names, and both may have been illiterate, this mother–daughter team appear to have imaginatively politicized (and commercialized) the text that they were selling of their own accord. These two women, who may have been unable to read the paper in question, retitled it in this explicitly seditious manner. (The 'Letter' is about cuckoldry, and any personal attack on a monarch or his ministers could be considered a seditious libel.) Vickers's and Ogilbie's oral transformation of the printed letter's generic 'father' into an identifiable though carefully unspecified 'king', then, was as crucial to the text's communicative and commercial success as its formal (traceable) contents. Makers in their own right, ballad-singers like Ellen Vickers and Sarah Ogilbie are another more ubiquitous example of the overlap of production and distribution in the London literary marketplace in this period. In order to assign legal responsibility for the 'seditious intentions' of these women's oral cries, the Secretary of State's office had first to determine what part of the treasonous sum total of authorship, publication, and 'rewriting' was theirs.

And, in fact, the Under-Secretary of State was so unsure as to how he could legally prosecute this particular case of oral seditious publication that he wrote to the Attorney-General for advice. He enclosed the examinations of the two offenders 'yet in Custody for crying a foolish, ridiculous paper, but containing villanous, seditious, and traiterous innuendos which were made the stronger by the manner of their crying it'. At a loss for a solution, he questioned whether 'these women and all offending in the like kind' might simply be sent to the 'House of Correction' as 'loose, idle, disorderly persons' (SP 35/11/14, f. 29, 27 Jan. 1717/18). They could be, and these women were.

One month later, the government was once again faced with a series of prosecutions involving the on-the-spot making and erasing of a text's seditious intentions. The Secretary of State's office had received a sheet of verse headed 'Honour and Glory, or a Poem On her late Majesty Queen Ann's Birth-day'. More alarmingly, the government had also been informed that the ballad had been orally advertised by the seductive title 'the High Church Ballad you may sing it but I dare not' (SP 35/11/21, f. 57, 11 Feb. 1717/18). Two women, Susan Shrewsbury and Mary Prior, were immediately committed to a bridewell, and three more female ballad-singers were examined. The manner in which these women cried the ballad in question was as crucial to record as their names:

Hester Wats Cryed the High Church Ballad
Elizabeth Robartson cryed you may sing it but i dare not
Francies Carver for crying Queen Ann Poem
(SP 35/11/21, f. 59, 11 Feb. 1717/18)

Hawker Hester Watts rechristened 'A New song Commemorating the birthday of her late Majesty Queen Ann of ever blessed Memory', with a refrain of 'Then in spite of her Enimies, malice and Spleen, | We'll drink to the memory of *Ann* our good Queen', with the somewhat incongruous new title 'The high Church Ballad'. 'Confessing it', she was sent to 'the House of Correction'. Elizabeth Robartson, also confessing that she retitled the verses 'The new Ballad you may sing it but I dare not', shared Watts's fate. But hawker Frances Karver (or Carver) wisely denied any 'Intentions of Mischief' or desire to 'rewrite' the text orally as she published it. Declaring that 'she did not intend to cry it by any false Title', she was discharged.

The title 'you may sing it but I dare not' is both provocative and cryptic, and was probably chosen with a view to increasing sales and avoiding arrest at the same time. This strategic ambiguity is characteristic of early eighteenth-century political ballads, and underlines their relationship to rich seventeenth- and early eighteenth-century traditions of oral prophecy. As we will see in Part II, as a subgenre religio-political prophecy had strong associations with underground loyalties and with women. It has been estimated that well over half of women's published writings between 1649 and

1688 were prophecies, many of which addressed the major national political issues of their day, including the call for religious tolerance, the abolition of tithes, and specific elements of doctrine influencing affairs of state.[28] From the female prophets of the Civil War period, Interregnum, and Restoration, through early eighteenth-century Behmenist mystics like Jane Lead and Quakers like Margaret Askew Fell Fox, women were foremost among those who saw in the ideology of divine inspiration a shadowy but glorious vision of the eventual overthrow of the hierarchies of the national church. One of the most entertaining of seventeenth-century prophets was the sibylline Mother Shipton, whose prophecies were published at least twenty times between 1641 and 1700 and continued in popularity throughout the eighteenth century.[29] Mother Shipton's prophecies were associated with popular radicalism, and similarly the partisan predictions of almanac-maker Sarah Jinner (fl. 1658–64) were among the most radical of their day.[30]

Prophecies remained prominent in political literature of the Popish Plot and Exclusion Crisis, and were used to justify the Revolution of 1688. They could be used to sanction a new regime, as when William III was represented as a long-awaited deliverer, but at least as frequently they were used to sanction resistance to established authority. In the eighteenth century, the Jacobites were foremost among those who employed the magical, incantatory quality of verse (especially the ballad refrain) in the service of political prophecy.[31] Shortly after the birth in 1720 of Charles Edward Stuart, the 'New Pretender', one Elizabeth Smith was committed to Bridewell for singing Jacobite ballads including 'The Highland Lasses Wish'.[32] The oral traditions of prophecy, ballad-singing, and underground political loyalties all merge in this treasonous exaltation of an exiled prince, and celebratory anticipation of his restoration. A contemporary reader or listener familiar with Jacobite ballads would immediately recognize the subject of this ballad as James Francis Edward Stuart, the Old Pretender, whose birth to James II

[28] Hobby, *Virtue of Necessity*, 26. See also Mack, *Visionary Women* and Keith Thomas, *Religion and the Decline of Magic* (New York: Scribners, 1971).

[29] Thomas, *Religion and the Decline of Magic*, 393 n. 1, 414, and ch. 13 *passim*.

[30] Bernard Capp, *Astrology and the Popular Press: English Almanacs 1500–1800* (London: Faber and Faber, 1979), 87.

[31] On Jacobite verse and political culture more generally, see Paul Kleber Monod, *Jacobitism and the English People 1688–1788* (Cambridge UP, 1989), esp. ch. 2.

[32] Also 'The Old T—p M—'s Letter to his Son, concerning the Choice of a New P[arliamen]t. With his Son's Answer' (SP 35/29/60, f. 268 [1721]).

and Mary of Modena in 1688 set off the Revolution. In 'The Highland Lasses Wish', young 'J—my' is celebrated as the rightful heir to the British throne. Still more immediately threatening, he is represented as about to come into his own:

II.
He is the Lord of the Heyland Clan,
The Sprightly Son of a Noble Man,
Then call him a Bastard or all that you can,
For J—my is Brisk and Lordly.

IV.
He shall lig in a Lordly Bed,
With Lordly Diet he shall be fed,
He'll be a great Man when his Grand-sir is dead,
For he is brisk and Lordly. (SP 35/29/60, f. 270, n.d.)

'Altho' he was brought in a Frying-Pan' (a reference to the warming-pan scandal, entertained by Queen Anne herself in order to cast doubt on the legitimacy of James Francis Edward's birth) and although he now resides in the highlands, this charismatic hero, the ballad refrain reminds us, is a true-born Englishman and a prince. The reference to 'J—my's' 'Grand-sir' is ambiguous; James Francis Edward's grandfather and father were already dead. 'Grandsir' could be used in this period to signify any old man of an age befitting a grandfather, and, as with most potentially treasonous political ballads, this one should most likely be read according to a hermeneutics of censorship.[33] (The grandsir whose death 'J—my' awaits in 1720 then may be King George I.) In the terms of a popular literary and political tradition that delighted in riddles, too, 'J—my' may also have been intended to represent the thriving

[33] This phrase is Annabel Patterson's in *Censorship and Interpretation: The Conditions of Writing and Reading in Early Modern England* (Madison: Wisconsin UP, 1984). Patterson is concerned with the development of new codes of communication under conditions of censorship in 17th-cent. England, but her arguments are suggestive for the 18th cent. as well. In illustrating the development of 'a system of communication in which ambiguity becomes a creative and necessary instrument, a social and cultural force of considerable consequence' (11), Patterson concerns herself 'less with genre than with a whole range of smaller strategies and conventions' constituting what she calls a 'hermeneutics of censorship' (8–9). This 'cultural bargain' between writers, political leaders, and readers in general determined how 'interpretation in fact worked, how it could be carried out in any given sociopolitical situation' (7), and thus enabled a 'functional ambiguity, in which the indeterminacy inveterate to language was fully and knowingly exploited by authors and readers alike' (18).

underground allegiance to the Jacobite cause, as well as James Francis Edward himself. 'J—my' is a generic young fellow to please almost all—a lusty, virile prince and noble clan leader all in one. Indeed, in the character of 'J—my' may be seen the origins of 'Bonny Prince Charlie', the romantic popular hero pledged to restore liberty.

But it is worth noting that the prophesied ruler of 'The Highland Lasses Wish' is something different from his romantic descendants, for he is represented not so much as a hero who will restore liberty to the poor and oppressed, as one who will recover his *own* rightful power and wealth. The central image here is not of ruling well, but of living well—lying in bed and eating without having to work for it, in a magical economic order where food is plentiful and needs only to be passively received to be enjoyed. There is an odd sense of potential identification here, between the ballad's popular audience and its hero—an innately noble man called a bastard and much else ('all that you can') and stripped of his goods—and a sense of communal wish-fulfilment in his being raised to wealth. But the pent-up resentments of a lifetime of material deprivation from which this text's most powerful image appears to have sprung are released not in a vision of a classless society, but rather in a nearly comic prophecy of a restored and leisured king. While clearly treasonous under contemporary law, this ballad is not necessarily the expression of an insurrectionary voice. As strategic political action it succeeds best in consolidating the already-converted, and in helping to diffuse political intelligence to the sheerer density and hence greater pervasiveness of cultural myth.

DANGEROUS ACQUAINTANCES: FEMALE TRADE INFORMANTS

As the three different witnesses ready to testify against Ellen Vickers and Sarah Ogilbie will attest, the Secretary of State's office received many tips as to the seditious intentions of its citizens from merchants and other onlookers on London streets. One William Davis, merchant, sent a letter to messenger Thomas Hopkins, informing him of 'news' of which he was already well aware: 'The City of London to the great grief of its Inhabitants is Daily Anoy'd, with Numerous and odiously Scandalous Pamphlets, against the late House of Commons, thereby rendering some of its worthy Members ridiculous and hateful to the People, and Monstorous to the World' (SP 32/12, f. 267, 29 Nov. 1701).[34] Another merchant, William Pickett of Vine Street, St Giles', was more helpful. When he heard hawkers crying *The French King's reasons for owning the pretended Prince of Wales king of England, Scotland, and Ireland* he asked where it was published, hurried to Mrs Bradford's printing house in Little Britain, and purchased three quires (seventy-five sheets) of the treasonous publication. He then turned the papers over to messenger Hopkins to use as evidence against her (CSPD 32/12, ff. 198–9, 26 Sept. 1701).

The most useful inside information, however, came from tradesmembers themselves—and sometimes, from their servants, lodgers, and relatives. After the lapse of the Licensing Act in 1679, the government sought to encourage tradesmembers to inform on one another by offering a reward. Journeyman Richard Crowder may have sought this reward when he informed on his master and mistress Langley and Jane Curtis. Crowder told the state of a variety of seditious literature being printed at the Curtises' establishment, including *A Song on the Downfall of the Whigs*, which Jane Curtis 'sang with [him] by her fireside'.[35]

An increasingly institutionalized means for tracing seditious intentions in the eighteenth century was the regular payment of trade informants. The press spy most familiar to students of literature is Daniel Defoe, but the government had many others in its pay, and among these were a number of women.[36] By 1716, Secretary of

---

[34] Of more value was Davis's information that the publisher of a recent libel against the House of Commons was Elizabeth Cooper at the Crooked Billet. 'From time to time', Davis noted, Mrs Cooper and one Thrusterum Savage 'publish all things that tend to treason, faction, and Rebellion'. The worst of these, once again, was a pamphlet printed by the Bradfords. Evidence to support his claims, Davis assured the government, could be obtained from 'Michael Hastings at the Crooked Billet aforesaid, William Bird, a Hawker and several others; or any Hawker in the Street' (SP 32/12, f. 267, 29 Nov. 1701).

[35] Leona Rostenberg, 'Robert Stephens, Messenger of the Press: An Episode in 17th-Century Censorship', *Papers of the Bibliographical Society of America*, 49 (1955), 141.

[36] The activities of male informants have been discussed by others. Particularly important press spies were Robert Clare, whose weekly reports included 'an Alphabetical List of the Names and Places of Abode of the Several Master Printers, &c. in and About London' (1705) listing nine women printers, and Samuel Negus, who submitted 'A compleat and private List of all Printing-houses in and about the Cities of London and Westminster' (1723). Negus, who classified printers according to

State Charles Townshend was paying the wives of several printers
a regular salary of 28 shillings a week, ostensibly for their husbands' services in 'detecting the Printers and Publishers of Libells
against the Government'.[37] But there is no reason to assume that
women in the trade were any less willing or able than men to
inform on their fellow tradesmembers. At least one woman who
appears to have been in Charles Delafaye's employ was Martha
Hubart, who wrote to the Under-Secretary of State in 1719 asking
for a warrant to arrest 'R. Oven and his daughter' for treason:

ther has been all menes yuse to take thees pepele but to no efectt. I have
some thing more to aquant Honer wich if your Honer pleas to give me leve
may be more efectlull ther being a pason consarne who [S'] John think must
be takein by Honers warnt. I shall be redy to when your Honer please to
a send with all dute and respek

Your Honers
Humbell Savant
Martha Hubart.
(SP 35/18/123, f. 252, 26 Nov. 1719)

Another female informant, widow Elizabeth Brown, expected to be
rewarded with a pension for her services as an informant to the
government. Like many other informants, however, Mrs Brown
was to find that co-operating with the state did not always pay.

   When Elizabeth Brown learned from 'Anne the Wife of Mr.
Seneca' that Anne's son John Semple 'was concerned with Mathews
in printing the Traytorous Libel Vox Populi Vox Dei', and from
lodgers in the same house that 'Mr. Seneca is in great pain for fear
he should be in trouble on their account', she betrayed the confi-
dences of this mother regarding her son and denounced John
Semple to the authorities (SP 35/32/88, f. 215, 6 Aug. 1722).

---

their political and religious affiliations, recorded thirty-four men and women 'said to
be High Flyers', thirty-four 'known to be well affected to King George', three nonjurors, and four Roman Catholics—and earned himself a place in the Post Office in
return (Snyder, 'The Reports of a Press Spy for Robert Harley', Treadwell, 'A
Further Note from Harley's Press Spy', and Nichols, i. 288–312). A two-party
system of government made for a ready supply of politically motivated informants.
In a memo on libellers, Treasury Solicitor Anthony Cracherode confidently assured
Gazetteer Samuel Buckley 'I don't doubt but that our Journalists & other news-
writers will quickly furnish us with matter for Indictments, on w[ch] it will not be
difficult to convict them' (SP 35/13/6, f. 12, 2 Oct. 1718).

[37] Townshend to A[nthony] Cracherode, SP 44/118, 4 Aug. and 1 Nov. [1716].

Townshend did offer Mrs Brown a substantial reward for her services on this and other occasions. As the following letter to Prime Minister Robert Walpole reveals, however, more than a year later she was still trying to get paid:

Having had an Opportunity to Detect the Traiterous Practices of Mr. Semple, who about a Year ago was Secured and Examined as is well known to Your Excellency, my Lord Townshend was pleas'd to Order that fifty Pounds Should be given, and to Promise that I should be put upon the Civil List for a Pension . . . But this Promise not being as yet Effected, and having Suffer'd Very much for having Served the Government upon this as well as Former Occasions, I humbly beg the Favour off Your Excellency to Order that I may Receive Fifty Pounds towards Paying off my Pressing Creditors (who are incensed against me upon my Service in regard to Semple) and towards the Subsistence off my Self and my Distressed Family, till Such time as it please your Excellency to put me upon the Civil List.[38]

Unlike male informers, female informants could not be provided with minor government jobs, and so were reliant on gifts and pensions. Like Mrs Brown's place 'upon the Civil List for a Pension' and 'Fifty Pounds towards Paying off my Pressing Creditors', however, these rewards appear to have been slow in coming if they came at all.

Another factor to be taken into consideration when deciding whether or not to inform was the relentless psychological and sometimes physical abuse to which informants were subjected by their fellow tradesmembers. Mary Holloway's willingness to co-operate with the government in prosecuting printer Elizabeth Powell caused her and her husband to be reviled as traitors, and eventually to be exiled from their working communities. Months after Mary Holloway had informed on Elizabeth Powell, both she and Edward Holloway were still being hounded by their co-workers. Or rather *ex*-co-workers, for Holloway could no longer find employment of any kind, and as a result wrote to Delafaye 'in Distress and great Want'. Holloway had not, he claimed,

---

[38] SP 35/45/40, f. 106, 16 Sept. 1723. As we shall see in Ch. 5, Delarivier Manley wrote a similar letter to Chancellor of the Exchequer Robert Harley in 1711. For her services to the government as a propagandist, Manley asked Harley to 'reward my good endeavours, whether by some small pension . . . or some other effect of your bounty' (19 July 1711, HMC *Portland MSS*, v. 55). Harley later sent Manley £50, the same amount that Mrs Brown requests here for her services as government informant.

a farthing in the World to support himself and Wife, being also in a Manner without Cloaths, and am likewise Insulted by those of the Printing Trade, because I made my self an Evidence for the King, and [more] because my Wife was the Instrument of taking of Mrs. Powell, of which your Honour is very well acquainted with. (SP 35/19/48, f. 129, n.d.)

In another letter, Holloway reported how his wife was being abused by tradesmembers and neighbours:

My Wife, because she was the occasion of taking Dr. Pittis and Mrs. Powell, is [——?], and call'd the basest and Treacherous Woman in the World, both by Mr. Hornigold and his Wife; and likewise say before other people, (on purpose to make us look odious) that my Wife is only fit for a Bailiffs follower, or to betray or get People, which neither he or his Wife (he says) would do for a Thousand Pound. . . . Besides, I am treated with the most scurrilous Billingsgate Language that can be Invented. (SP 35/20/106, f. 262, 26 Mar. 1720)

Finally, in a third letter, Mrs Powell's one-time journeyman wrote to Delafaye again, reminding him of the abuse that his wife was still suffering. He begged the Under-Secretary that he

not let my Wife Perish for want of Money to buy her Necessaries for now she does, and is forced to leave her Lodging. She has tried all the Friends that she has till they will do no more for her, and now she is forced to apply her self to your Honour for Relief. (SP 35/24/58, f. 178, n.d.)

Informing was easy for women in the trade, but living with the consequences of their actions clearly was not. At the very least, an informant's character was likely to be defamed in return for having defamed that of others. When one J. Lightbody learned that printer Mrs Collins was working with messenger Shaw 'to do me a prejudice', he wrote to Shaw stating his hope that he would 'not through the Caprice of an ill Woman, be brought to do injustice to one who has done you or any other Wrong [*sic*]', and threatening that he would not 'if he can help it patiently suffer such as she to asperse my Character and ruin my Business' (SP 35/49/74, f. 270, 27 May 1724).

WOMEN'S MODES OF SELF-DEFENCE WITHIN THE TRADE

The abuse to which Mary and Edward Holloway were subjected by their co-workers should serve to caution us against idealizing collective modes of action within the trade. The early eighteenth-century book trade, while small and family-based by modern standards, was by no means a harmonious 'community'. At the same time, though, the London book trade may be seen as a series of interlocking collectivities that sometimes shared specific interests. The ability of 'those of the Printing Trade' to put Edward Holloway out of business and to reduce Mary Holloway to 'Distress and great Want' over the course of one winter suggests the power of these collectivities when working together to protect their mutual interests. As we will see, solidarity was an important tool for women in the trade. Women workers could not yet organize for their mutual protection and advancement on an institutional level, but they could and did do so in private, and the effects of these sometimes all-female 'mutual protection networks' were felt by the Secretary of State.

Whether women in the book trade saw themselves as part of a group, or whether they believed themselves to be chillingly alone, their tool of choice for survival was the word. In the course of their daily business, women printers, booksellers, and hawkers gained a heightened awareness of the strategic powers of the spoken, written, and printed word, and, not surprisingly, turned to these resources as a means of self-defence, survival, and, sometimes, redress. Occasionally, more physical means of self-defence were employed. These were hard-working, practical women after all, for whom the demands of middle-class decorum were unlikely to outweigh the benefits of freedom gained by escaping out of a shop window or bashing a messenger of the press on the head. For the most part, though, when women in the book trade were forced to devise for themselves a means of maintaining or regaining their freedom to work, it was the evasive oral testimony, carefully crafted written petition, or printed newspaper advertisement that they employed.

Strategies for self-defence began with avoidance of arrest. As we have seen in the case of Elizabeth Powell, more experienced members of the book trade were adept at 'abscond[ing] for the present'—whether by escaping to France (Edmund Powell), slipping into the anonymity of the London crowds (Elizabeth Powell), or adopting an alias (Mary Unknown). If one could not always abscond, however, one could always resist arrest. When in 1693 messenger of the press Robert Stephens attempted to arrest

journeyman printer William Anderton on suspicion of High Treason, he first had to fight off Anderton's wife and mother-in-law.
Only when Stephens obtained the assistance of two other men did
he finally manage to arrest Anderton, and even then 'not without a
great deal of trouble':

He saw the prisoner's mother in the yard, and she well knowing Mr.
Stephens, she immediately cried out Thieves, and came up to him, (her
daughter, the prisoner's wife, being with her) fell upon him, and tore his
hair off his head, crying out Murder; at which time the prisoner came out
of the house, and fell upon him, and abused him in a very uncivil manner,
telling him, he scorned to be a subject to Hook-Nose [William III]. (*State
Trials*, xii. 1246–7)

Similarly, when Secretary of State Robert Harley's messengers attempted to arrest printer Jane Bradford on suspicion of producing
a seditious libel in 1705, they encountered physical, as well as
strategic, resistance:

Being come to her House, the Doors were again shut upon us; but we got in
at the Shop-Windows, and after a small Scuffle, seiz'd Mrs. Bradford, and
search'd the House throughout for the Papers, but could find none of them.
For Mr. Stevens and Mr. Chapman alarming her before we came, had, no
doubt, made her secure all things worthy our Notice out of the way.[39]

When messengers arrived at printer Laurence Howell's establishment to investigate charges against him, Mrs Howell made them sit
on the doorstep all night until they were forced to go away and
obtain a proper warrant.[40]

   If more physical means of self-defence failed in the earliest stages
of prosecution, they might help at a later stage, such as when
pilloried friends or relatives faced the mob. When author Daniel
Defoe faced the pillory, he wrote and published his famous *Hymn
to the Pillory* (1703) to 'prepare' the crowds for his favourable
reception. When publisher Elizabeth Harris's husband Benjamin
was pilloried, she stood in front of him and shielded him from
stones—'like a kind Rib', as John Dunton put it (*Life and Errors*, i.
217). As in Daniel Defoe's case, the London crowd could upon
occasion be more supportive than destructive. On at least one

---

[39] Robert Clare, qtd. in Snyder, 'The Reports of a Press Spy for Robert Harley',
342.
[40] Laurence Hanson, *Government and the Press 1695–1763* (Oxford: Clarendon
P., 1936), 41.

occasion, two impoverished female hawkers pilloried for singing Jacobite ballads drew a sympathetic audience who gathered a collection of £4.[41]

Ideally, though, one would not proceed to this dangerous stage of prosecution, and many women avoided doing so by their wits and words alone. Once a suspect had been arrested, she was examined by the appropriate authorities, in this case the Secretary of State's office in charge of press control. The examination process could be terrifying, but for those able to keep their calm there was room to manœuvre. Testimonies could be 'shaped' without being falsified, and falsified when artistry failed. Two particularly impressive examples follow of young women literally talking their way out of possible prison sentences and fines.

In eighteenth-century England, as E. P. Thompson has shown, the anonymous, threatening letter was for the poor and disenfranchised an important tool of social protest and political activism.[42] In 1718, three years after the Jacobite uprisings, one 'J.S.' wrote to Justice Samuel Buckley, informing him that one Ann Barnham Junior was the author of one such anonymous letter—in this case, 'a Letter to M^r [Lorain] Thretning him with sword and pistol' (SP 35/11/82, f. 196, 10 Apr. 1718). Ann Barnham's use of anonymous words to deploy threats of violence against a male enemy is intriguing in itself. But the revelation of a veritable library of Jacobite papers in Barnham's possession constituted grounds for an immediate warrant to search:

S^r

permit me y^r Honour to acquaint you that Ann Barnham Junr Living in pelican Court in Little Brittain is the Author of a Letter to M^r [Lorain] Thretning him with sword and pistol and has Despersed several of Shephards speechs and has a number of Them in little Table under the Window up one pair of Staire were you will find the Bed Tester plot the prophecy on the 10 of June a goldin mine opened for the Dutch with other Treasonable papers. (SP 35/11/82, f. 196, 10 Apr. 1718)

J.S. must have known Ann Barnham well (a servant, perhaps?) for the following day the 'Dying Speech of James Shepheard' was

---

[41] *Dormer's Newsletter*, 21 Jan. 1716, qtd. in Hyland, 'Liberty and Libel', 886.
[42] See E. P. Thompson, 'The Crime of Anonymity', in Douglas Hay et al., eds., *Albion's Fatal Tree: Crime and Society in Eighteenth-Century England* (New York: Random House-Pantheon, 1975), 255–344.

indeed 'taken out of the drawer in Ms Ann Barnhams Rooms' (SP 35/11/84, f. 200, 11 Apr. 1718). James Sheppard had been hanged at Tyburn less than three weeks earlier, and 'dying speeches' representing him as the martyr of a corrupt government were already flooding the underground press. The version taken out of Ann Barnham's drawer was openly treasonous, and to make matters even more serious, Sheppard's 'Dying Speech' was only one of several incendiary papers in Barnham's possession. Another printed sheet 'taken out of Ms Ann Barnhams pocket' urged greater female political involvement in the Jacobite cause, and prophesied that only 'When Dames of *Britain* shall espouse | The Royal Cause . . . Then, not till then the injur'd nation | May hope to see a R[estora]tion' (SP 35/11/85, f. 201, 11 Apr. 1718).

Barnham, a bookbinder living with her father (probably Robert Barnham) in Little Britain, was taken into custody and examined. As the victim of an informant who apparently knew her well, Barnham was in an especially difficult position. Treasonable papers had been found in her table drawer and on her person, and she simply could not plead ignorance. Mustering considerable self-composure, then, this young woman instead pleaded 'Curiosity':

> She says that some Evening last Week as she was passing in Little Britain she observed several people taking papers from off a Ledge of a Window, asked what they were, which being told she went on to a Chandler's Shop where she had some Business & in her return home seeing some of those papers still remaining, she took one of 'em which is the same now produced to her. (SP 35/11/86, f. 202, 11 Apr. 1718)

Piling circumstantial detail upon detail, Barnham added that 'the Place where she found the paper abovementioned Entitled The Dying Speech of James Shepheard was on the Ledge of a Barber's Shop Window on the outside of the Shutters after the Window being shut up, whose Name is Ward living in little Britain' (SP 35/11/86, f. 202, 11 Apr. 1718). Barnham's testimony that she just happened to be walking by Ward's barber-shop in the course of her daily business is believable, for he was a close neighbour. And her claim that she took the paper 'purely out of Curiosity, as several other persons had before done' is not out of the question either. What literate young woman would not avail herself of so rare a luxury as a printed sheet evidently laid out for passers-by to look at or borrow for free? But Barnham's elaborate details as to how and where she obtained this particular speech seem intended to hide more than they reveal—or at least, to distract attention from more dangerous questions that could be asked. For the nature of Barnham's 'Curiosity' set her apart from other casual readers of this text. It was an informed interest to say the least. In the course of her examination, Barnham commented with respect to 'The Dying Speech of James Shepheard; Who Suffer'd Death at Tyburn, March the 17th, 1717/18. Deliver'd by him to the Sheriff, at the Place of Execution' that she

believed it to be genuine by reason of some passages contained therein which she had before been told were in the Speech delivered by James Shepheard to the Person who officiated for the Sheriffs at the place of Execution, & which she had heard repeated by a person who said he had seen the sd James Shepheard in Custody, particularly in the 5th Paragraph therein. (SP 35/11/86, f. 202, 11 Apr. 1718)

'Where, but in my own Country . . . has a publick National Price been twice set on the Head of its Lawful Sovereign? And this by the Protestant Invaders of his, and his Subject's undoubted Rights[?]' demands the martyred Sheppard in his 'Dying Speech'. Barnham had already analysed this openly treasonous text paragraph by paragraph, compared it with other versions she had nearly memorized, and added it to a substantial personal collection of Jacobite pamphlets and newspapers. As the aforementioned ballad's appeal to the 'Dames of *Britain*' suggests, many of Barnham's female contemporaries saw in what they perceived as the noble martyrdoms of Charles I, James II, 'James III', John Matthews, or James Sheppard a reflection of their own collective situation as women. Barnham's radical Jacobite activism appears to have been more than what the government apparently took it for: the feminine foible of a young lady placed by her father's line of business too close to an onslaught of dangerous books.

When another young woman, Katherine Higden, living with her father and brother or husband 'John Hidgen at the Star in Milk Street near Cheapside Linnen-Draper', was examined for the same treasonous paper, she employed similar tactics of evasion. Unlike Ann Barnham, Katherine Higden could not claim to have been exposed to dangerous printed materials in the course of her daily work. When in the line of business was a linen-draper likely to be faced with 'a Stitched Pamphlet consisting of several pieces, entituled, To Robert Walpole Esq., To the Army and People of England, To Mr. William Thomas, & To a thing they call the Prince of Wales'? Like Ann Barnham, however, Katherine Higden could and did plead 'Curiosity'. John Higden denied 'the said Stitched Book or Pamphlet to be his, or that he knew there was any such in any part of his House' (SP 35/11/109, f. 244, 19 Apr. 1718). The burden of explanation thus fell upon Katherine, who could not deny that a copy of Sheppard's speech had been discovered in her closet. But the Secretary of State's office could not argue with, or much benefit from, Katherine Higden's simple explanation that she

bought it of a Hawker a woman, who sold her at the same time a Newspaper, after which she offered this to the Exam^r: who bought it out of Curiosity, but has no knowledge of the said Hawker's person her name or Dwelling, That it is above a week ago, but exactly how long the Exam^r: can't tell.

Katherine Higden
(SP 35/11/110, f. 246, 19 Apr. 1718)

At a time when a decent wage for a small tradesperson would have been less than £1 a week, there could have been few sisters or wives of linen-drapers for whom the experience of buying newspapers and pamphlets was so habitual that it was not worth remembering one week later. While Katherine Higden might have been sent out to buy the newspaper for someone else, she purchased Sheppard's speech on her own initiative, and for herself. Furthermore, even if her 'Curiosity' and simple-minded forgetfulness were not part of an act, it is extremely unlikely that in 1718 she would not have sensed the danger of hiding on her premises this violently Jacobite text with its attack on William 'the Usurper's . . . Tyranny'. A third linen-draper was examined regarding a copy of the speech found in his own house. His claim that he too 'did not know (as he says) that it was there or how he came by it' seems evidence of a larger plot (SP 35/11/116, f. 259, 21 Apr. 1718).

Ann Barnham and Katherine Higden kept their calm, and revealed virtually no information that could be used against them, even as they represented themselves as willing to co-operate with the state. On a larger scale, this procedure was employed collectively by a number of largely female mutual protection networks within the trade. The endurance of mother–daughter teams like

Jane and Tace Sowle, Elizabeth Nutt and her daughters Alice, Catherine, and Sarah, the Anne Dodds Senior and Junior (assisted by the faithful Mary Dewe), and, to a lesser extent, Ellen Vickers and Sarah Ogilbie, attests to the importance of solidarity in female-headed book trade households, and to the practical as well as psychological advantages that group action could have when one or more members of an interlocking cell of workers came into conflict with the law.

The various female members of the Nutt and Dodd establishments were well trained by frequent experience to take over for one another when one or more of them was in custody. These women were also well trained to protect their mutual interests during examinations. In 1729, both the Nutt and Dodd establishments were implicated in the publication of a libel in the *Daily Post*, no. 3065, 17 July, and thereafter in the *Evening Post*, no. 3119, of the same date. Their methods of self-defence in this case were tellingly similar. When Catherine Nutt was examined, she employed all the Nutt women's usual strategies of polite but evasive oral testimony—strategies with which government authorities in charge of press control were by then familiar:

Being asked whether she did not sell that Paper, she answers, that she does not know that she sold that Paper, or any Papers entitled the Daily Post of that Date; Being asked whether she usually sells the paper that comes out daily entitled the Daily Post, she says she has sometimes sold it, but cannot say she has constantly done so, for that she is not always at her Shop; Being asked whether that Paper, as often as it comes out, is not taken in by her or her Mother or her Mother's Servants in order to its being exposed to Sale; she says the Servants take them in the Morning, and distribute them to the people who are to sell them.

Asked the same questions with respect to the *Evening Post*, Catherine Nutt responded equally evasively. She admitted that 'those papers as they come out are sent to her Mother or her Servants, she knows not by whom', and protected her mother by adding that Mrs Nutt 'is at the Bath, that she set out for the Bath last Monday [——?] sennight, and, as she believes, will be absent a fortnight or three weeks to come'. Asked by a sceptical Charles Delafaye who looked after the 'Shop and Trade' while her mother visited the Bath, Catherine Nutt answered the Under-Secretary that 'she and her sister Alice have that trust' (SP 36/13, f. 110, 19 July 1729). If it can be frustrating to read one such round-about testimony, it must have been infuriating to listen to several of them. Delafaye heard an almost identical explanation from Anne Dodd's servant Mary Dewe, who was as loyal to her employer as Catherine Nutt was to her mother:

She does not sell Pamphlets for her own Account, but for her s^d Mistress Anne Dodd; She says that her said Mistress is out of Town, and ill, and has been so most part of this Summer, and gave no directions for the selling of this individual paper, but only in General for selling the Daily Post with other Papers when they should come out. (SP 36/13, f. 120, 21 July 1729)

Mary Dewe did admit that Anne Dodd paid publisher John Peele for the paper. When Peele was examined, however, he too claimed that although he had been distributing the *Daily Post* for years, when the issue in question was published, he was 'out of Town' for ten days (SP 36/13, f. 118, 21 July 1729).

Another woman, Phillis Leveridge, worked for Anne Dodd in some capacity, though whether as a shopkeeper or hawker is difficult to determine, for her *modus operandi* seems designedly ambiguous. Examined before Under-Secretary Charles Delafaye and Justice George Vaughan in 1728 regarding political pamphlets and ballads, Leveridge referred to Dodd as her mistress. Yet she described herself not in the usual manner as 'servant to Anne Dodd', but rather as 'above six years a Seller of Pamphlets and Books'. Leveridge frankly stated the printers that she knew, and what she obtained from them. She had 'been frequently sent by . . . Dodd . . . to . . . Watts for [votes], to Mr. Baske[t] for King's Speeches and proclamations, [and] to Mr. Read for the St. James's Evening Post'. But she also made a curious point of adding of her own accord that 'she does not deal with Clifton who is a printer of sham papers'. When asked where she obtained the two books and one half-sheet of political ballads taken upon her (*A New Miscellany of Court Songs*, parts I and II, and *Two New Ballads*, including 'The L—d's Address to King George II' and 'The K—g's Answer', and 'A New Ballad'), she explained:

She had them of a Woman named Ann Bowes who plys in the Temple and carrys them under her Riding hood: That the said Woman gave the Examinant several Dozen of them to sell. That she has often met the said Woman at the Temple Gate to receive such Books of her to sell; The Examinant says she usually sits at the Temple Gate to sell such Books and often goes to Coffee-houses to sell them; particularly those Coffee-houses above Temple Barr; The Examinant denys that she knows where Ann Bowes lives;—says she pays Ann Bowes for the Books after she has sold them, but not beforehand. (SP 36/5, f. 178, 10 Mar. 1728)

Leveridge denied that she knew anything about Bowes but her name, and where she usually met her to make a pick-up. An anonymous informant writing to Delafaye some three weeks later may have cleared up the mystery—or simply complicated it—when he wrote that

It is probable from what the Applewoman confess'd in relation to Phillis, that one Woman constantly brought all those Papers to her, who pretended to come from Southwark Side: It is indeed more than probable that Person must be a Woman who has liv'd as an upper Servant with Mrs. Dodd many years. She commonly goes by the Name of Nurse, but her true Name may soon be learnt, if requisite. (SP 36/5, f. 251, 29 Mar. 1728)

This information that one of Anne Dodd's own employees was regularly distributing political ballads and other printed materials to another of Dodd's employees in a pre-appointed location outside of Dodd's shops, and doing so in such a way as to veil her own connection with Dodd, may serve to suggest the complexity of (here, all-female) distributive networks when political materials were involved, and the sophistication of a major mercury-woman's diverse relationships with her various employees.

When evasive oral testimonies did not serve their purpose, the senior members of the Nutt and Dodd households were also adept at fashioning written petitions. Women who possessed the technology of writing could pen petitions for themselves (or for their husbands and sons). Illiterate and unlettered women were dependent on lawyers, gaol-keepers, or friends. Hundreds of such petitions survive, and many offer excellent opportunities to study the ways that women publishers of illegal political materials represented their political and publishing activities in relation to their businesses, their families, and the state.

When a warrant was issued against Anne Dodd for her involvement in the libellous *MWJ* no. 175, 24 Aug. 1728, Dodd wrote to Newcastle stating that she 'hath been long confined to her Chamber, in the Country, thro' a violent and dangerous Indisposition, and still continues in a very ill State of Health'. Speaking of herself in the third person, as was customary in formal petitions, Dodd

stated that she was 'notwithstanding her Weak Condition, willing
to Come to Town, hoping upon a Surrender of her Person, your
Grace will be pleased to admit her to Bail, without any Confinement, for should she be Imprisoned, her life would be inevitably
endangered' (SP 36/8, f. 238, 17 Oct. 1728). By 1728, however, this
experienced offender had long since exhausted the sympathy of the
state. Despite her 'dangerous Indisposition', Dodd was immediately
committed to Newgate (SP 44/82, 8 Nov. 1728). A few years later,
Dodd was forced to try her petition-writing skills once again—this
time from prison, and in a shaky hand. She was to be tried for her
involvement in the oppositional *Craftsman*, and, as we have seen,
asked Thomas Pelham Holles, Duke of Newcastle, to have sympathy for her position as 'an afflicted widow with a Large Young
Family', who was 'sometimes compell[ed] . . . to sell Papers that
Give Offence' (SP 36/23/134, 26 May 1731). This time, Dodd
spoke in the first person, without all the usual formulae of petitions,
in a tone of dignified self-awareness, and of familiarity with the
Secretary of State ('I need not Acquaint Your Grace . . .'). As a
major figure in the London newspaper trade Dodd defined herself
as much by her business as by her sex.[43] While she made several
references to her family ('let my Children Plead with your Grace to
Put a Stop to the Procedings', 'starve my Poor Babes', 'the Fatherless', and so on), pathetic references to dependants were standard in
petitions by both women and men, and Dodd did not rely solely on
her status as a mother to obtain a pardon. Dodd's petition is
deferent, but in early modern England deference must never be
confused with subservience (let alone with 'feminine modesty'). It is
more like a personal letter than a legal document. Most importantly, it appears to have been successful.[44]

[43] The strategies of women workers in the London book trade strike me as
different from those of the 16th-cent. French female supplicants whom Natalie
Zemon Davis describes in *Fiction in the Archives: Pardon Tales and their Tellers in
Sixteenth-Century France* (Stanford, Calif.: Stanford UP, 1987). Davis writes that
'the women's supplications do not cohere as often as do the men's around a scenario
of occupation or estate. . . . a gender role constitutes the woman's estate, and her
account sweeps the facts of work and place into a narrative carried by themes of
family, sexual honor, and inheritance. . . . these are tales in which wifeliness and/or
women's sexual honor are at stake' (87–9). Petitions written by women in the 17th-
and early 18th-cent. London book trade, by way of contrast, tend to cohere around
occupation as much as gender, and do not emphasize their families any more than
men's petitions do. See Ch. 4 for a discussion of middling and lower-class women's
'metaphors of being' in this period, and in particular an argument that working
women experienced gender differently from their genteel contemporaries.
[44] Hunt, 'Hawkers', 58.

Anne Dodd dwelt on the legal and economic ramifications of working in her particular trade, rather than on some essentially 'female' condition. She wrote of being ill, widowed, and the head of a large economic family—not of some imagined gender trait, such as the newly popular 'femininity'. When Elizabeth Nutt was taken into custody for the same issue of *Mist's Weekly Journal* that Anne Dodd was in 1728, she employed a similar approach, but hired a lawyer or gaol-keeper who set down her request for a *nolle prosequi* in a meticulously neat hand:

> The humble Petition of Elizabeth Nutt Widow.
> Most humbly Sheweth,
> That she is an Antient Woman, near Seventy years of Age, has a large Family, and many Children unprovided for.
> That it has been her Buisness for about Forty years to sell News Papers and Pamphlets at the Royal Exchange.
> That she has not only at all times to the best of her knowledge avoided giving Offence to the Government, but has always been ready to give all the Information she could of the Authors, Printers, or Publishers of any Papers whatever that have offended the State. . . .
> That this Prosecution, if carry'd on to the utmost Rigour of the Law, must inevitably end in the utter Ruin of herself and Numerous Family:
> Therefore she, with the most profound Submission, presumes to throw herself at Your Most Sacred Majesty's Feet, most humbly imploring Your Majesty's Royal Compassion and Forgiveness; And that Your Majesty would be Graciously Pleas'd to Order a Nolle Prosequi to Issue, to stop the Proceedings against her. (SP 36/9, f. 249 [after 24 Aug. 1728])

Like printer Elinor James, Elizabeth Nutt was proud of her forty years' experience, and tried to use it to her advantage. Perhaps mistakenly, Nutt emphasized her role as a matriarch of the London pamphlet trade. As those in charge of press control were already well aware, many tradespeople were dependent on her cluster of outlets around the Royal Exchange. Nutt's lawyer (or whoever drafted this petition) dressed her essential dignity in all the appropriate formulae, addressing the petition 'To the King's Most Excellent Majesty' and emphasizing Nutt's status as a loyal subject of the King. Nutt took care to note that she did not have the least knowledge of the libellous issue in question, but she never used the word 'ignorance' (a familiar buzzword of petitions written for wives by their husbands). In Elizabeth Nutt's case claiming *naïveté* was not an option.

The sex of the author was in fact a key factor in the shaping of these petitions, for men and women tended to represent female subjectivity differently in these papers, and conceived of women's relation to the state in different terms. Many women had petitions written by their lettered husbands, and the sex of the petition writers made a difference in the representation of women workers' agency and rational decision-making ability, as well as the nature of women's involvement in the trade. Husbands typically represented their wives as troublesome helpmeets who had (temporarily) slipped out from under their own control. When William Ogilbie petitioned Charles Delafaye for the release of his pregnant wife Sarah Ogilbie and 73-year-old mother-in-law Ellen Vickers, he began by reasserting his (in this case theoretical) role as head of his household. Mentioning his military service, he pointed out that he was now 'a pensioner in Chelsea hospital having spent his blood in the [service] of the Crown'. He referred to the wife whose labour supported him as 'a Young Woman . . . ignorant', and blamed his mother-in-law (SP 35/67/75, f. 150 [after 25 Jan. 1717/18]). When Francis Clifton was taken into custody for his wife Catherine Clifton's role in printing 'The Tory's Wholsome Advice', he bombarded the Secretary of State's office with petitions and letters, each one making a different kind of appeal characteristic of male book trade workers writing on behalf of their imprisoned wives. Representing his own wife as a troublesome helpmeet, Clifton urged Under-Secretary Delafaye to consider 'the distressed State that I and my whole Family . . . Labour under' 'thro' the inanimadvertency of my Wife'. He hoped that Delafaye would 'commiserate my deplorable Condition, a wife lame & at down lying, my self weak & Consumptive & involv'd in debt so far that I scarce dare to show my Head' (SP 35/24/75, f. 225 [1720]). And he complained of the ultimate insult, that other printers were simultaneously printing 'The Tory's Wholsome Advice' 'even tho' they heard my Wife suffer'd for it'. Probably referring to confiscated equipment and supplies, he asked Delafaye to 'let my Wife have hers again' (SP 35/24/75, f. 221 [1720]). In another letter, he stressed that 'I was not privy to the Printing that Ball^d but my Wife only' (SP 35/24/75, f. 231 [1720]). In a fourth letter, he apologized that his wife 'shou'd in my absence do any thing to incurr the Displeasure of the Governm^t. and be troublesome to you' (SP 35/24/75, f. 235 [1720]). Even if Catherine Clifton was solely responsible for printing 'The Tory's Wholsome Advice'—and she may well have been, for as we have seen Mrs Clifton was fully capable of selecting and printing politically dangerous materials by herself—it is illuminating to see her infamous husband representing his 'troublesome' wife as having 'inadvertently' printed a seditious text that *he* would never have condoned.[45]

Gender differences in male- vs. female-authored representations of women book trade workers may be seen clearly by comparing the petition of printer Mary Dalton to Secretary of State James Craggs with her brother Isaac Dalton's description in his newspaper of her prosecution for another offence. There is an important difference of genre here which must be acknowledged. While Mary Dalton's petition is a legal document written to a powerful government official, her brother Isaac Dalton's newspaper is political propaganda seeking to appeal to a broad audience. But both are strategic action representing female subjectivity and citizenship, and the disparity between them is enormous. Mary Dalton signed her petition and appears to have written it herself. Simply stated, her petition

Humbly sheweth,

That she is under very great Concern for having incurred the Displeasure of the Government by printing the List seized in her House which Mistake she was led into by its being publickly cryed about the Streets.

That she does sincerely promise to be very careful for the Future not to offend again in the like Kind; and to behave her self on all Occasions as becomes loyal and dutiful Subject to his Majesty King George.

She humbly prays that your Honour will be pleased to overlook any Mistake she may have been Guilty of, and to give Orders that she may be enlarged.

Mary Dalton
(SP 35/78/95, f. 95 [before 1721])

In the post-revolutionary period, the boundaries of acceptable political commentary were in a state of flux. For this and other reasons, it was not uncommon for printers such as Mary Dalton to protect themselves by observing what kind of political materials were being 'publickly cryed about the Streets'. A printer such as Dalton would observe her fellow tradesmembers' fates, then make her own decisions about what to print accordingly. Mary Dalton used the word 'Mistake' twice, yet she never once referred to herself as 'ignorant' or suggested that she was incapable in any way. On

---

[45] Frances Clifton himself was described by the Treasury Solicitor as 'so obstinate an offender', among other epithets (SP 35/24/75, f. 229, 6 Mar. 1720).

the contrary, she described herself as 'under very great Concern' for her error, and promised to be 'very careful for the Future'. The existence of literally hundreds of petitions like this one, written by female tradesmembers to some of the most politically and economically powerful men in the country, suggests that working women of a broad spectrum of social ranks saw themselves as capable of exercising a modicum of control over their own lives, and of taking responsibility for their own actions. While it would be easy for us to see a woman like 80-year-old hawker Elizabeth Scales—in 1716 ill, impoverished, and imprisoned for selling a newspaper that she could not read—as the powerless victim of a sociopolitical and legal system beyond her control, the very existence of 'The most humble Petition of Elizabeth Scales' to Lord Townshend (SP 35/67/60, f. 121 [1716]) should remind us that this is not necessarily the way that these women saw themselves.

If printer Mary Dalton conceived of herself as an independent tradeswoman who made her own decisions and as a 'loyal and dutiful Subject to his Majesty King George', however, her brother Isaac Dalton represented her as a sentimental heroine in the merciless clutches of an oppressive ministry. Isaac Dalton had been imprisoned earlier that year for printing a seditious libel in his anti-Walpole weekly *Robin's Last Shift* (*Weekly Journal*, 31 Mar. 1716). In his sequel newspaper, *The Shift Shifted*, Dalton transformed the efforts of Prime Minister Robert Walpole and Secretary of State Charles Viscount Townshend to suppress his political papers into a crime far worse than his own:

To imprison a man [i.e. Dalton himself] for a Fancy, tho' he be thereby ruin'd, we have that as a Trifle, a Nothing to Moloch. But to take his young Maiden Sister only for happening to receive a little Money for him; for this, I say, to cram her into a Messenger's, and thence bring her directly to the Bar, all over-whelmed with Tears and Confusion, without a Moment's Preparation for her Tryal, and there after a Fine of 30 Marks, appoint the beautiful young modest Maiden to remain confin'd for a Twelvemonth in a loathsome Gaol, conversing with the Strums of Newgate. Suppose she have innocently assisted her Brother in his Distress, does that (call it a Crime) come up to this Punishment? Was ever such a Virgin ever so unmercifully expos'd for such a Crime. (*The Shift Shifted*, 18 Aug. 1716)

Whereas Mary Dalton represented herself as a concerned citizen willing to take responsibility for her actions, her brother portrayed her as a 'young Maiden', a 'beautiful young modest Maiden', a

'Virgin', and in relation to himself, as his sister. While Mary Dalton represented herself as the person responsible for 'printing the List seized in her House', Isaac Dalton represented her as a genteel young lady who 'innocently assisted her Brother in his Distress'. Emphasizing his sister's sexualized female body, and constructing a dichotomy of virtuous and vicious women, he placed her in opposition to other sexualized female bodies ('the Strums of Newgate'). He did not call her ignorant, as so many book trade husbands called their wives, but he represented her as helplessly dissolving into 'Tears and Confusion' when she was prosecuted—a sharp contrast with the self-possessed young woman who wrote her own dignified petition directly to the Secretary of State. Isaac Dalton's exploitative representation of his sister as an innocent helpmeet who became a martyr to the government was not atypical. Political journalist Abel Boyer represented Mrs Treganey in a similar vein, as martyr to the vindictive press prosecutions of Henry St John, First Viscount Bolingbroke:

His *Barbarities* in such Prosecutions is notorious—Among the rest, a harmless Woman that kept a Pamphlet-Shop without *Temple-Bar*, for selling the *Hanover* Ballad, and Publishing the *Protestant Post Boy* (Written by Mr. *Philip Horneck* and Mr. *A. Boyer*, the Editor of this *Political State*) was by him committed to *Newgate*, where she died with hard Usage. (Boyer, xxxiii. 155, Feb. 1727)

Abel Boyer, Isaac Dalton, and many other male (and sometimes female) political writers knew that martyr-making hurt the government. If a female martyr could be found, the jab would have an extra piquancy for the reading public.

If petition- and propaganda-writing husbands and brothers represented their female relatives as ignorant and misguided, did petition- and propaganda-writing women represent their male relatives in the same manner? As we have seen, in her 1715 petition to Lord Townshend concerning her husband, Alice Applebee represented John Applebee as having been 'reduced to a very weak condition' by being taken into custody. Alice emphasized that she and her husband were 'in very Poor and Mean Circumstances', and went so far as to suggest to the Secretary of State that he 'admit your Petitioners Husband to put in Bail or to be discharged by such other Means as to your Lordships great Wisdom shall seem meet'. While Alice did claim that her husband 'was drawn in by the Author' to reprint the paper for which he was in custody, she did not press the point. John Applebee already had a reputation as a 'High Flyer', and few persons would have believed that he did not understand the subversive implications of the letter that High Church advocate Charles Leslie had supposedly 'drawn [him] in' to reprint (SP 35/2/ 10, f. 30 [1715]). Among instances of petition- and propaganda-writing wives, printer Elizabeth Powell's defence of her husband Edmund in her newspaper *The Orphan* probably comes closest to Isaac Dalton's propagandistic representation of his sister. Mrs Powell represented her 'Distressed Husband' as 'Banished, stript of his Subsistence, and his Wife and Children left Poor and Bare to shift for themselves' (no. 1, 21 Mar. 1716). Powell's defence of her husband in her own Jacobite newspaper, however, was ultimately doubly threatening to the status quo. For Powell's female propaganda was not only critical of the state, but also a radical usurpation of masculine sociolinguistic privilege.

As the example of Elizabeth Powell and her newspapers suggests, the most public option for self-defence and strategic action by women in the book trade, and an important new tool for English women in general, was the newly available forum of print. A wide variety of flourishing weeklies eager to sell space to the public meant that, increasingly, any woman with a small amount of cash and a large amount of courage could speak for herself to a broad audience.[46] When pamphlet-shop keeper Elizabeth Rayner found it necessary to defend herself in public against what she perceived to be the unlawfulness and brutality of the state, she inserted into the *Daily Journal* the following threatening notice to the authorities:

Whereas two certain Gentlemen came Yesterday to my Shop, next Door to the George Tavern at Charing-Cross, and pretended to have an Authority for seizing a Pamphlet lately publish'd by me, call'd Iago display'd, &c. and did forcibly carry away with them a great Number of the said Pamphlets, together with the Prints belonging to the same, alledging that they were scandalous Libels; This is therefore to give Notice, That if the said two Gentlemen will apply themselves to me, they may be inform'd of the

---

[46] The cost of a one-inch-long advertisement in a newspaper such as *The Daily Advertiser* in the mid-18th cent. was about 2s. (Schneller, 'Using Newspaper Advertisements to Study the Book Trade: A Year in the Life of Mary Cooper', 125). See also James Raven, 'Serial Advertisement in 18th-Century Britain and Ireland', in Robin Myers and Michael Harris, eds., *Serials and their Readers 1620–1914* (Winchester: St Paul's Bibliographies, 1993), 103–24.

Author, who will appear and answer to the Contents of the said Pamphlet. And I do hereby declare, that if the Authority they took upon them was not legal, I will pursue them with the utmost Severity, as the Law directs in those Cases.

E. Rayner[47]

(*Daily Journal*, no. 3165, 26 Feb. 1731)

Mrs Rayner's aggressive public challenge to the 'Authority' of messengers of the press who did not identify themselves prior to the execution of a search seems curiously akin to what in modern terms might be viewed as an assertion of her civil rights. This bold declaration is followed by an even bolder advertisement for the second edition of *Iago Display'd*, 'to be had, notwithstanding the means made use of for suppressing the same' (*Daily Journal*, no. 3165, 26 Feb. 1731).

While Elizabeth Rayner threatened recourse to the law if the two gentlemen who confiscated her stock of *Iago Display'd* did not co-operate with her, publisher and newspaper proprietor Elizabeth Mallet could only appeal to bookseller solidarity against the piracy of a pamphlet in which she held a share. Accordingly, her advertisement stated that

Whereas a certain Person has pirated *The Danger of Priestcraft to Religion and Government*, to the apparent prejudice of the Booksellers who gave a considerable Price for the Copy: 'Tis hop'd that all Booksellers, who have any regard to Property, and that consequently it may come to be their own Case, will discountenance the sham Edition, which is printed in a Sheet and a half of a small letter, and publish'd by *Brag* in *Avemary lane*.

Recourse to the courts against copyright infringement was still highly impractical for all but the most powerful booksellers. Elizabeth Mallet's only option was to appeal to the good faith and self-interest of her co-workers, warning them that her misfortune 'may come to be their own Case', and informing them that 'the true

---

[47] As the phrase 'my Shop' suggests, Elizabeth Rayner, and not her husband printer William Rayner, managed the pamphlet shop at Charing Cross. Two years earlier, in 1729, William had been involved in a libel case, and four months after Elizabeth inserted the above advertisement in the *Daily Journal* he would be arrested once more for an anti-Walpole broadside, *Robin's Reign or Seven's the Main* (SP 44/82, 5 July 1731). He was imprisoned for two years, during which time Elizabeth kept both the printing business and pamphlet shop in full operation. For further information on the Rayners see Michael Harris, 'London Printers and Newspaper Production during the First Half of the Eighteenth Century', *Printing Historical Society Journal*, 12 (1977–8), 33–51.

Edition . . . is now only to be had of Mrs. *Mallet* near *Fleetbridg Price 4d.*' (BL Harley 5995/95, n.d.).[48]

Women printers and newspaper proprietors did not have to pay for the public space of the press, for they had ready-made vehicles, tools, and audiences of their own. As we have seen, printer-author Elizabeth Powell used whatever newspaper she happened to be writing and printing at the time as an arena for public political activity and personal redress. According to John Dunton, too, publisher Sarah Malthus hired two of the authors whose newspapers she distributed to do battle in print with her trade enemies. Whenever printer-author Elinor James disagreed with the actions of monarchs, ministers, or other public political bodies she simply composed, printed, and distributed broadsides telling them so (and, of course, informing the rest of her audience at the same time). The fact that at least one of James's critiques caused her to be committed to Newgate suggests that, in the politically volatile atmosphere of the post-revolutionary period, the British government, like Alexander Pope in his 'Letter to the Publisher Occasioned by the Present Edition of the *Dunciad*', did not see 'Mean . . . offenders' such as Elinor James as we tend to do: as being without consequence.

The years 1678 to 1730 were a distinct period of economic transformation, both in the structure of the London press and in English society as a whole. In the London book trade, as Michael Harris and others have shown, the period marked the increasingly capitalist organization of production and the corresponding build-up of bookseller control. As Harris observes, 'the real profits to be made by London booksellers lay less in the retail business . . . than in the ownership of copies. Between about 1680 and 1730 this predominant fact of life provided the main stimulus to change within the

---

[48] Another form of piracy affecting publishers was the notorious practice of printing false 'postscripts' to tri-weekly newspapers. Before the 1720s, when evening newspapers had become common, separately printed postscripts were employed to add important additional news to a paper that had already been run off. Until the practice of postscripts began to drop off by about 1713 (James Sutherland, *The Restoration Newspaper and its Development* (New York: Cambridge UP, 1986), 28–9), newspaper proprietors such as Mrs Snowden had virtually no effective means for suppressing counterfeits, and could only return to the press, warning their readers as Snowden did hers 'to take care of being imposed upon by a Counterfeit Paper, For the *True Postscript* to the *Flying-Post* is printed only by *Ann Snowden*, in *Great Carter-Lane*, near *Doctors Commons*' (BL Harley 5995/137, 15 Aug. 1704).

upper levels of the book trade.'[49] By the 1730s, more complicated forms of management had evolved, and by 1750, a very large concentration of resources lay in a very few hands. An increasingly complex shareholding investment system hastened the subordination of the majority of men and women in the trade to major copyowners, as did strict new copyright laws (however difficult to enforce). 'The gradual build-up by the "respectable" booksellers of a rather daunting control', Harris observes, resulted not only in 'the disappearance of a whole range of peripheral book trade activity' (89) but also in delimited opportunities for those workers who did remain.[50] As in other trades, the professionalization and capitalization of the book trade was contributing to a profound transformation in the distribution of economic and social power in England.

The years 1680 to 1730 were also a watershed in the history of English women. In her *Working Life of Women in the Seventeenth Century*, pioneering economic historian Alice Clark categorized different types of female labour in the economically productive patriarchal household of feudal-agricultural England under the headings of 'domestic', 'family', and 'capitalist' industry. Clark then linked changing modes of production with shifting social structures and (implicitly) gender relations. In Clark's terms, 'family industry' was distinct from capitalist industry in that it united capital and labour under one roof. The economic family unit, which included male and female relatives as well as servants and apprentices, was the unit of production of goods to be exchanged. The workshop was the home, and upon the death of the father the mother became the head of the family business. Clark saw capitalist industry as having already substantially replaced family industry by the eighteenth century, and saw the erosion of family industry as contributing to a decline in women's status. Since Clark's book was

---

[49] Harris, 'Periodicals and the Book Trade', 68. See also Harris, *London Newspapers in the Age of Walpole*.

[50] One example of the effects on smaller tradespeople of major copyright owners combining to protect their mutual interests is the fate of printer Mary Say. Say and two other members of her family printed the *Daily Gazetteer* for nearly fifty years without restrictions. In 1775, however, a contract between Say and the owners of the paper prohibited Say from printing any other papers except the *Craftsman* and *General Evening Post*. The major copyright owners thus made Say more dependent on their own goodwill—and increased their own already considerable bargaining power (R. L. Haig, *The Gazetteer: 1735–1797* (Carbondale: Southern Illinois UP, 1960), 276–80).

first published nearly eighty years ago, much work has been done in women's history, and Clark's thesis has been challenged by a 'myriad . . . of . . . individual case studies' and 'a barrage of statistical data analysis'.[51] Historians have become alert to the problem of 'golden-ageing' in women's history, and have questioned Clark's assumptions regarding the alienation of women from capitalized labour.[52] Yet Clark's work has not been fully superseded, and her findings, one recent historian concludes, 'are as regularly confirmed as they are disputed'.[53]

It is too early to know what the effects of capitalization and professionalization were on women in the London book trade. We still lack case studies of the particular job duties, trade and social status, and independent economic power of all except a very few women printers and publishers, or a general survey of women's broad involvement in print culture in the mid- and later eighteenth century. We know that there were women who participated in publishing partnerships throughout the eighteenth century, yet we know little about these women's day-to-day involvement in trade, or how typical they were of women in book trade families. We know that a few women benefited greatly from the increasing concentration of wealth in the trade by inheriting patents and copies, yet we also know that these women typically chose not to work in the trade. While Tace Sowle carried on her father's printing business, and Anne Dodd Junior her mother's pamphlet shops, Catherine Lintot inherited her father's £30,000 law patent, and within three years had largely sold her way out of the business. For women like Catherine Lintot, the inheritance of patents and copies rather than of equipment and skills may have marked their disenfranchisement from family businesses even as it marked their family's arrival at genteel status.

[51] Amy Louise Erickson, intro. to Alice Clark, *Working Life of Women in the Seventeenth Century* (1919; London: Routledge, 1992), p. viii.
[52] For a summary and bibliography of scholarship on early modern women's work and status since Clark, see Erickson's excellent introduction. Erickson agrees that 'a pre-existing hierarchical conception of women's and men's work was undoubtedly exacerbated when men's work was separated from the home by the long-term development of a cash economy'. But she also concludes strikingly that 'a comparison of medieval circumstances with those that prevail today reveals more continuity than change in the important features of women's working lives' ('Introduction', pp. xx, xviii).
[53] Ibid., p. viii.

Of course working-class women have never stopped working, and the small-time female retailer or poorly paid female engraver or colourist never disappears. During the seventy-year period from 1800 to 1870, some eighty women worked as booksellers or printers in London for periods ranging from one to thirty years.[54] But in general, even when home and workshop were not yet divorced (as was the situation of printer Samuel Richardson for most of his life), the economic efficiency of book trade wives became less crucial to the success of family businesses over the course of the eighteenth century. Changing economic conditions gave rise to new ideological notions about women and 'women's work', and the idea that a prosperous tradesman 'kept' his wife eventually prevailed.[55] Middle-class women's separation from paid economic activity— their 'domestication' as it is somewhat oddly called, as if women were ever not also primarily responsible for domestic labour—was increasingly made to appear 'natural' (that is, arising out of women's essential nature). Narrowing notions of acceptable female behaviour heightened the challenges already faced by those women who attempted to enter into or carry on small businesses in the trade. With a few important exceptions (the mid-century newspaper proprietor and publisher Mary Cooper, for instance, or the

---

[54] Philip A. H. Brown, *London Publishers and Printers c.1800 to 1870* (London: British Library, 1982). In the course of the government campaign to silence radical printers at the accession of George IV, a few women carrying on in their female ancestors' tradition of oppositional publishing were arrested. Among these were Jane and Mary Anne Carlile, the wife and sister-in-law of Richard Carlile, the author of the *Republican*. When Richard was imprisoned in 1819 for publishing a blasphemous libel, Jane Carlile assumed control of the business, until she too was prosecuted for libel. When Richard was arrested and sentenced to two years' imprisonment for publishing *The Age of Reason*, Jane took over the publishing and bookselling business, issuing an account of Richard's trial with reprinted passages from the book for which he had been prosecuted. Although she too was brought to trial and found guilty in 1820, she was later released on a technicality—and promptly took over the publication of the *Republican*, until she was tried yet again in 1821. When she too was sentenced to two years' imprisonment, it appeared that the *Republican* might have seen its final days—until Mary Anne stepped in and took over for her imprisoned relatives. Mary Anne in turn was tried and imprisoned in 1821 for publishing a paper attacking government corruption, *A New Year's Address to the Reformers of Great Britain* (Donald Thomas, *A Long Time Burning: The History of Literary Censorship in England* (New York: A. Praeger, Publishers, 1969), 203).
[55] The example of printer Samuel Richardson and his wife is discussed in the Conclusion to this book.

important printseller Mary Darly) women at work in the London book trade in the later eighteenth century tended to be retail booksellers of relatively minor economic importance—not major nonconformist printers like Tace Sowle or important oppositional publishers like the Anne Dodds.

Alice Clark's view of middle-class women's exit from paid economic activity by the eighteenth century is in agreement with the following complaint by one of our women workers' most observant contemporaries:

In former times tradesmens widows valued themselves upon the shop and trade, or the warehouses and trade that was left them; and, at least, if they did not carry on the trade in their own names, they would keep it up till they put it off to advantage. . . . And I may venture to say, that where there is one widow that keeps on the trade now, after a husband's decease, there were ten, if not twenty, that did it then. (Daniel Defoe, *Complete English Tradesman*, i. 352)

Daniel Defoe lived nearly all of his life in St Giles, Cripplegate, a few minutes' walk from the centre of the book trade. In his *Complete English Tradesman* (1725–7), Defoe chastised not only proud 'ladies of this age' who would not learn their family business, but also foolish and vain husbands who would not share their business know-how with their wives. Defoe recognized that not only economic transformations, but also corresponding ideological ones, were profoundly affecting the economic, social, and political opportunities of women of his generation. The mid-eighteenth-century assumption that she would quietly close up shop and wait for her Stationers' Company pension upon the death of her husband infuriated the widow James (not Elinor James).[56] Accordingly, in approximately 1736, she issued the following circular throughout the trade:

Advertisement.
The death of Mr. Thomas James, in Bartholemew-close, letter-founder, having been industriously published in the newspapers, without the least mention of any person to succeed in his business, it is become necessary for

---

[56] This 'widow James' cannot be Elinor James (d. 1715) but may be her daughter-in-law. Elinor James's son Thomas was a 'letter-founder' (typefounder) who worked in Bartholemew-close. If either the *DNB* errs in dating Thomas James's death in 1738 or C. H. Timperley errs in dating this advertisement 1736, then this deceased typefounder could be Elinor James's son Thomas—making this irate widowed typefounder her daughter-in-law.

the widow JAMES to give as public notice, that she carries on the business of letter-founding, to as great exactness as formerly, by her son JOHN JAMES.[57]

Similarly, the Widow de Beaulieu, bookseller, found it necessary to have the following notice inserted in the newspapers—apparently to counter the public's assumption that the death of her husband also meant the death of the family business:

The Widow of John de Beaulieu, Bookseller over against St Martins Church in St Martins-lane, continues to sell the Books of her late Husband at very reasonable rates, even cheaper than at first. (*Post-Man*, no. 1076, 16 Jan. 1703)

Towards the end of the eighteenth century, bookseller James Lackington regarded his second wife's attachment to books as close to miraculous—'a very fortunate circumstance' which 'tended to promote [his] trade'. Running on at some length, Lackington enthused that his wife's tastes 'made her delight to be in the shop, so that she soon became perfectly acquainted with every part of it'. Lackington noted that his wife oversaw the business whenever he was away, and credited her with increasing his customers.[58] That Lackington considered himself extraordinarily blessed suggests that his wife's hands-on involvement in the family business was not typical for middle-class women of the 1790s. One hundred years earlier, Dorcas Lackington's assistance in her husband's retail business would have been taken for granted (as was Elizabeth Dunton's at the beginning of the century).

The primary goal of Part I has been to demonstrate opportunities for political activity through print by women in the London book trade at a time of political unrest. As with working women's economic and social status, so with middling women's political activism only detailed studies of later periods will confirm or disprove what this study of the period 1678 to 1730 suggests: that as women lost their once-central role in the making and distributing of printed texts, they also lost their immediate, unsupervised access to one of their most powerful political tools (the press).

---

[57] Qtd. in C. H. Timperley, *A Dictionary of Printers and Printing, with the Progress of Literature, Ancient and Modern* (London, 1839), 655.

[58] James Lackington, *Memoirs of the First Forty-Five Years of the Life of James Lackington, The present Bookseller in Chiswell-street, Moorfields, London* (London, 1792), 326.

For some, to ask how women exercised their influence in state affairs, or contributed to a sense of popular pressure at Westminster or St James's, is to come to the deadening conclusion that 'the single most essential truth about women's political influence and involvement in eighteenth-century England is that their political activity must nearly always be measured through the achievements or failures of men'.[59] For others, such an impasse is reached only because the political history of women has been wrongly conceived as a mere through-way back to the history of men. A new angle of vision provokes new questions, and reveals new resources. The history of women in the book trade is a history of ideas as well as commodities, and in the study of women's role in the production and distribution of print a particularly rich set of resources for further study is to be found. For despite significant restraints on their activities, when women emerged as significant producers and distributors of print in seventeenth- and early eighteenth-century England, they opened up new channels of communication which have never been entirely closed since. It would be irresponsible to assume that these women of Mary Astell's generation were any more intimately engaged in the ongoing, would-be 'dialogue' of politics in English society than their grandmothers. But print gave new permanence to their half of the 'dialogue', and made it possible for some eighteenth-century women to share in their own, newly collective faith that 'if one web be destroyed, a few hours work will spin another, stronger and better than before'.[60]

[59] Karl von den Steinen, 'The Discovery of Women in Eighteenth-Century Political Life', in Barbara Kanner, ed., *The Women of England from Anglo-Saxon Times to the Present* (Hamden, Conn.: Archon Books, 1979), 229.
[60] *The Republican*, 27 Oct. 1820, qtd. in Thomas, *A Long Time Burning*, 203.

PART II

'Telling the King His Faults':
Religio-Political Polemicism and Women's
Public Expression

Introduction

On 11 December 1689, Elinor James was 'committed to Newgate for dispersing scandalous and reflecting papers'.[1] The papers in question were addressed to William of Orange, and in fact, Mrs James not only 'dispersed', but also wrote and printed or oversaw their printing herself. In view of contemporary restraints on women's public political expression, the papers were something of a scandal in themselves, but it was their seditious content that alarmed the government. For if James's ostensible purpose was to thank William of Orange for vindicating the Church of England by landing at Torbay, her underlying message was that protecting the church was William's *only* purpose in England. Now it was time for him to pray for King James's conversion from Catholicism, then go home. 'The whole Nation rejoyced at your coming, as a Reconciler,' she explained. But 'not half the Nation thought You would have accepted of the Crown, as long as the King your Father was alive'.[2]

In modern capitalist societies, Fredric Jameson has remarked, religion is 'a mere private hobby and one ideological subcode among many others'. But

in a presecular and prescientific world, one in which commerce is itself a limited and interstitial phenomenon, religion is the cultural dominant; it is the master-code in which issues are conceived and debated. . . . Religious and theological debate is the form, in precapitalist societies, in which groups become aware of their political differences and fight them out.[3]

---

[1] Luttrell, i. 617. James's arrest is also recorded in GL, CLRO, Newgate Sessions Book, SM60. She was fined 13s. 4d.

[2] Elinor James, *This being Your Majesty's Birth-Day, I thought no time more proper than this, to return you Thanks . . . for declaring, that the Church of England is one of the greatest supports of the Protestant Religion* (c.1689). 'The King your Father': James II was William's father-in-law; the paper is also implicitly addressed to Mary, James II's daughter.

[3] Fredric Jameson, 'Religion and Ideology', in Francis Barker et al., eds., *1642: Literature and Power in the Seventeenth Century*, Proceedings of the Essex Conference on the Sociology of Literature July 1980 (U. of Essex, 1981), 317–18.

The centrality of religious debate to early modern British political and literary culture has long been accepted. Only recently, however, have public sphere theorists recognized the importance of the growth of a public sphere in religious life in seventeenth-century England: 'a public sphere in religion that cultivated nearly the same critical, rational habits of thought that Habermas locates in the public spheres of politics and letters'.[4] Only recently, too, have feminist critics become aware of the extent to which one heterogeneous group first became aware of its own mutual political interests in the terms and spaces of this debate. The heated religio-political debate-in-print of the seventeenth and early eighteenth centuries was a prime forum for English women's public expression. Undaunted by her arrest, Elinor James went on to publish more than *fifty* broadsides and pamphlets over the course of a fifty-year career as a polemicist and oral activist. The same London audience that could scarcely avoid James's printed papers and opinions might also encounter the texts and voices of the Quaker Anne Docwra, the religious and political radical Joan Whitrowe, or the theosophical visionary Jane Lead. At a time when women's virtues were increasingly understood to 'open fairest in the shade',[5] a profound sense of religious calling made public expression, both oral and printed, appear a 'duty' to women of diverse ideological allegiances and socioeconomic backgrounds.

Religious and religio-political works formed by far the largest category of printed materials available to seventeenth- and early eighteenth-century British readers, and religious, religio-political, and didactic works formed the bulk of British men and women's literary production as well. At a time when the number of separately published items appearing in Britain averaged about 600 items annually, more than 200 religious works were published every year.[6] The writings of late Stuart and early Hanoverian

---

[4] David Zaret, 'Religion, Science, and Printing in the Public Spheres in Seventeenth-Century England', in Calhoun, ed., *Habermas*, 221.

[5] 'But grant, in Public Men sometimes are shown, | A Woman's seen in Private life alone: | Our bolder Talents in full light display'd, | Your Virtues open fairest in the shade' (Alexander Pope, *Moral Essays*, 'Epistle II: To a Lady', *Poems*, ed. Butt, 567, ll. 199–202).

[6] On the average annual output of separately published items in England between 1660 and 1780, see Pat Rogers, 'Books, Readers, and Patrons', in Boris Ford, ed., *From Dryden to Johnson*, vol. iv of *The New Pelican Guide to English Literature* (Harmondsworth: Penguin-Pelican, 1982), 215. For the period 1701–99, see

women of all ranks demonstrate an intense familiarity not only with the Bible, but also with sermons, prayer books, biblical commentaries and reference works, manuals of piety and devotion, and religio-political pamphlets and tracts. What evidence we have suggests that the overwhelming majority of women's published writings before 1730 were also religious or religio-political in nature.[7]

Meaning, as Tony Bennett has pointed out, 'is not a *thing* that texts can *have*, but is something that can only be produced'. All 'texts, in the course of their histories, are constantly re-written into a variety of material, social, institutional, and ideological contexts'.[8] When early modern women read the Bible or listened to a sermon, they were not the passive recipients of ideology. Like any text, Scripture could be 'productively activated' in a number of ways. It was for this reason, of course, that Henry VIII passed the Act of 1543, making it illegal for 'women, artificers, apprentices, journeymen, yeomen, husbandmen, and laborers' to read the Bible, and forbidding all unlicensed persons to read or expound Scripture in public.[9] Religion works by symbolic expression as much as by explicit statement, and its political importance for early modern women was intimately related to this inherent figural ambiguity. As print placed bibles in new hands, an older hegemonic code could be appropriated for new possibilities. Women of all orders saw biblical exegesis and theological controversy as a welcome 'summoning

Feather, 'British Publishing in the Eighteenth Century', 32–46 and Kernan, *Samuel Johnson and the Impact of Print*, 61. On the importance of religious works to early 18th-cent. readers and publishing institutions, see Terry Belanger, 'Publishers and Writers in Eighteenth-Century England' and Thomas R. Preston, 'Biblical Criticism, Literature, and the Eighteenth-Century Reader', both in Isabel Rivers, ed., *Books and their Readers in Eighteenth-Century England* (Leicester UP and St Martin's P., 1982), 5–25 and 97–126. The data here regarding the annual output of sermons and other popular religious works are from Preston, 'Biblical Criticism', 98–9.

[7] See Crawford, 'Women's Published Writings 1600–1700', 211–82; Ezell, *Writing Women's Literary History*, esp. ch. 7; Hilda L. Smith and Susan Cardinale, comps., *Women and the Literature of the Seventeenth Century: An Annotated Bibliography Based on Wing's Short-Title Catalogue* (New York: Greenwood Press, 1990); and Stanton, 'Statistical Profile of Women's Writing in English from 1660 to 1800', 247–54.

[8] Tony Bennett, 'Texts, Readers, Reading Formations', *Bulletin of the Midwest Modern Language Association*, 16 (1983), 8, 14.

[9] Elizabeth L. Eisenstein, *The Printing Revolution in Early Modern Europe* (Cambridge UP, 1983), 159.

to intellectual activity'.[10] Chapters 3 and 4 show how, for four untutored women of the middling and lower-middling orders, it served as a summoning to public political activity as well.

The four women religious writers considered here wrote and spoke from a broad spectrum of viewpoints and from varying socioeconomic levels within the middling ranks. It is no coincidence, however, that each of these women had relatively easy access to the contemporary publishing institutions discussed in Part I. For it was access to print more than anything else that allowed these particular women to leave a substantial body of writings, and so to present an insistent threat to social norms. As the mistress of a printing house, Elinor James had a printing press at her disposal at almost any time. As Quakers (at least, for a time) Anne Docwra and Joan Whitrowe had access to a highly organized, regularly financed system for the production and distribution of printed materials. And as the spiritual leader of her own nonconformist sect, and a respected visionary whose works were eagerly translated into German and Dutch, the sometime blind and destitute Jane Lead had not only supporters willing to print her works, but also a personal scribe with an Oxford education.[11]

Chapter 3 considers these women's material circumstances and access to print: their relation to the world of the London book trade discussed in Part I. In particular, Chapter 3 argues that these women's printed texts, however numerous or substantial, must be understood as but a supplement to an equally important, ongoing *oral* activism. The late seventeenth- and early eighteenth-century literary marketplace was one in which a residual oral culture and a still new print culture were coalescing. The printed news and public

[10] This phrase is from Natalie Zemon Davis, 'City Women and Religious Change', in *Society and Culture in Early Modern France* (Stanford, Calif.: Stanford UP, 1975), 65–95, 80.

[11] While the four women considered here span a broad spectrum of beliefs and allegiances, that spectrum should not be misunderstood as all-inclusive. Part II does not, for instance, consider Catholic women, in part because Catholic women are now receiving detailed attention from other scholars, and because evidence for political activity by Catholic women of the middling and lower ranks is extremely scarce. On Catholic women and print in London in this period see Frances E. Dolan, *Whores of Babylon: Catholicism, Gender, and the Law from the Gunpowder Plot to the Popish Plot*, forthcoming; Kathryn King, *Jane Barker's Imagined Communities: Religion, Politics, Medicine, and the Literary Tradition*, forthcoming; as well as recent work on Elizabeth Cellier, a woman of relatively high social status, by Rachel Weil and others cited in my bibliography.

debate of the new 'Journals, Medleys, Merc'ries' was inseparable from an older oral culture in which news and opinions were still spread primarily by conversation and gossip in the marketplace, coffee-house, and street. The oral contexts of early polemicists' literary production can never be fully recovered, of course, but those contexts must nevertheless be stressed, for it would not be too much to say that for the four women considered here print was but one phase in an ongoing *oral* religio-political dialogue. Furthermore, as Chapter 3 will show, contemporary oral culture left its visible and audible traces in these women's printed texts—influencing not only textual content (the stories these women tell of their oral encounters) but also material production and modes of circulation and use.

While Chapter 3 considers material circumstances, Chapter 4 considers psychological or ideological ones, asking what world views and notions of the self in society enabled four radically disempowered, late Stuart women of the middling and lower-middling ranks to see themselves as active participants in state affairs. Chapter 4 examines what I call these women's 'metaphors of being': the ideological ways that they perceived themselves, and their relation to the society in which they lived. While several of these women's aristocratic and genteel female contemporaries were already beginning to perceive the self in recognizably modern ways as gendered, autonomous, and unique, the four non-élite women considered here all envisioned the self in more traditional ways as collective, social, and essentially unsexed. Accordingly, these women saw themselves as part of an unbroken continuum with the state—rather than as part of a separate, complementary, and fundamentally apolitical 'private sphere'. While the late seventeenth and eighteenth centuries saw the emergence of a recognizably modern secular feminism based on new models of gendered subjectivity (a model we will see crystallizing in the political fiction of Delarivier Manley), the four religio-political authors considered here seldom wrote about themselves as 'women' in their works. Gender is the unsaid of their texts, and modern notions of the gendered subject, like that of the individual self, can only be anachronistically applied. The famous declaration of Margaret Cavendish, Duchess of Newcastle, that 'We Women . . . are no subjects' is evidence of a more intense awareness of women's disenfranchised status in patriarchal society than James, Docwra, Whitrowe, or Lead ever expressed. It is evidence of a sense of isolation and alienation from the public political sphere that these women apparently never experienced—a sense that women's world was detached from political history, and that women's voices bore no 'Authority therein':

> As for the matter of Governments, we Women understand them not; yet if we did, we are excluded from meddling therewith, and almost from being subject thereto; we are not tied, not bound to State and Crown; we are free, not Sworn to Allegiance, nor do we take the Oath of Supremacy: we are not Citizens of the Commonwealth, we hold no Offices, nor bear we any Authority therein; we are accounted neither Useful in Peace, nor Serviceable in War; and if we be not Citizens in the Commonwealth, I know no reason why we should be Subjects in the Commonwealth: And the truth is, we are no Subjects.[12]

Between them, James, Docwra, Whitrowe, and Lead published several thousand pages of writing consciously aimed at transforming personal and political history in the public sphere, and it is difficult to imagine any one of them having felt so dispossessed. An expanding press opened up previously unimaginable opportunities for a woman of wealth, leisure, and creative daring such as Margaret Cavendish. Yet paradoxically, modern notions of the self as gendered, autonomous, and unique not only served to delimit Cavendish's own participation in the public political sphere, but also contributed to an apparent depoliticization of English women over the course of the eighteenth century. Changing notions of 'the female self', that is, served partially to contain the more immediately threatening consequences of women's new access to the political press.

Metaphors of selfhood are neither true nor false. Each presents a version of real relations, and enables a different mode of subjection—and resistance. The class-specific dreams of personal autonomy and subjective self-construction of aristocratic and genteel women writers such as Margaret Cavendish and Mary Astell were empowering for them (as indeed they have been for almost three centuries of women since). But they must nevertheless be problematized as a *universal* mode of feminist resistance. For they were not, in fact, the only models of subjectivity and modes of empowerment available to women even within these women's own

---

[12] Margaret Cavendish, *CCXI. sociable letters, written by the thrice noble, illustrious, and excellent princess, the Lady Marchioness of Newcastle* (1664), 27.

time. Indeed, modern notions of subjectivity associated with liberal individualism and the Enlightenment may actually have worked to reduce less privileged women's conviction of their own involvement and agency in public politics—even as those notions enabled these women's aristocratic and genteel contemporaries to imagine new forms of political activity based in gender identity, and new worlds, where women had 'Authority therein'.[13]

---

[13] See for instance Margaret Cavendish, *The Description of a New World, Called The Blazing-World. Written By the Thrice Noble, Illustrious, and Excellent Princesse, The Duchess of Newcastle* (1668) or Mary Astell, *A Serious Proposal To the Ladies, For the Advancement of their true and greatest Interest. By a Lover of Her Sex* (1694).

3

Oral Religio-Political Activism and Textual Production

> For all my Labours and Travels, this Paper will not contain them.
>
> (Elinor James, *Mrs. JAME's* [sic] *Apology because of Unbelievers*, c.1694)

What did print mean to early female polemicists and preachers, and especially to those women whose lack of access to printed texts— or lack of time to read them—ensured that they remained rooted in a still fundamentally oral world? 'I wish well to the Readers, whoever they be,' Elinor James declared at the head of one of her earliest broadsides. James's headnote sounds a tone of regret, as if she recognized that to print her ideas was to lose control over how her audience would respond to them. '*I have given so many, that I can give no more*,' she lamented, '*and therefore through the earnest desires of some, I have yielded to Publish them, contrary to my Intentions.*' Unable to chastise her addressees in person, or to correct their mistaken interpretations, she could only ask God to 'bless this Paper, that the Reader may be the better'. Even with God's help, print could be a strangely distancing mode of communication.[1]

In turning to the newly available tool of print to supplement their ongoing oral efforts to influence public opinion, Elinor James, Anne Docwra, Joan Whitrowe, and Jane Lead were not trying to avoid more public polemical encounters. These women used print not to 'cover' themselves but rather to expand the public oral audience that they already had. These women typically signed their papers

---

[1] Elinor James, *Mrs. JAMES's Vindication of the Church of England, In An Answer to a Pamphlet Entituled, A New Test of the Church of England's Loyalty* (1687), 1, and *Mrs. James Prayer for the Queen and Parliament, and Kingdom too* (1710). After each broadside is cited once, all further references are cited parenthetically in the text.

and books, and provided readers and hearers with their own personal addresses.[2] They did this to 'authenticate' their works and of course to maximize the sales of their texts. But they also provided their personal addresses so that readers and hearers who disagreed with their opinions could come and debate issues further with them in person. In one paper, Elinor James challenged anyone who said that 'King *Charles* the *First* . . . was a wicked Man' to 'come to me, I live in *Mincing-lane*, and I will pull his Eyes out'.[3] ('Not his Temporal Eyes, but his Spiritual Eyes', she explained, perhaps lest potential disputants be frightened off.) Even septuagenarian Jane Lead included her own name and address in imprints so that persons who disagreed (or agreed) with her could 'Orally confer with' her.[4] 'If any one be dissatisfied in any Point handled in this Book,' Lead assured the readers and hearers of her printed texts, 'the Author is ready to give answer thereunto, while she is yet Living.'[5] As we will see, Jane Lead cultivated an international, as well as local, audience. But most of all she cultivated 'Inquiring Minds': persons who wished to debate spiritual and religio-political issues with her in person, and who shared her ongoing, burning desire to know. The broadsides, pamphlets, and books written by these polemicists must be read as the products—and agents—of oral discussion and debate: voicings of specific speech communities which may be inferred by listening between the lines of the texts themselves. They are utterances responding to specific other utterances, and in them, their authors' anticipation of readers' rejoinders can be heard.

In order to appreciate these works, then, any consideration of their aesthetic or literary qualities must be informed by an awareness of their oral contexts. There may be a vast difference between our own expectations, as for the most part professional readers of printed texts, and the expectations of the bulk of these women's audience, people who were neither socioeconomic nor cultural

---

[2] Joan Whitrowe was an exception to this rule. While she did typically sign her works, her later pamphlets were too outspoken to show either her own address or a publisher's name or address in imprints.

[3] Elinor James, *November the 17th, 1714. This day ought never to be forgotten, being the Proclamation Day for Queen Elizabeth* (1714).

[4] *The Wonders of God's Creation Manifested, In the Variety of Eight Worlds: As they were made known Experimentally to the Author* (1695), A3ᵛ.

[5] Jane Lead, *The Enochian Walks with God, Found out by a Spiritual-Traveller* (1694), postscript.

élites. One modern scholar's well-intentioned comparison of tradeswoman Elinor James to the genteel Mary Astell, and statement that, unlike Astell, 'Mrs. James was not an intellectual, and did not reach for historical precedent . . . to justify her attitudes', may be misleading.[6] Different histories are available to different social orders and cultural groups, and in seventeenth-century England, the text-based history available to a learned and leisured woman such as Astell was not available to a working woman like James, who played an active role in her printing household while raising five children in her spare time. As we will see, the 'historical precedent' for which Elinor James did in fact reach was the personal and collective history of oral transmission and memory. Her arguments are frequently supported by 'historical' examples, signalled by the phrase 'I remember when . . .'. In late seventeenth- and early eighteenth-century London, the religio-political culture of ordinary women was still fundamentally an oral culture. Furthermore, this chapter will show, this oral polemical culture informed not only the content, but also the format and other aspects of the material production and circulation of these women's printed texts. A consideration of these four authors' diverse modes of publishing their religious and political ideas, of their intended audiences, and of the ways that these conditions of publication influenced the external format and internal characteristics of their texts will help to reduce the opaqueness of these women's writings for the modern reader, and enable us to move on to a consideration of their religious and political world views and ideas.

According to her own account, Elinor James had no formal education and had taught herself to read: 'God Almighty established me in his Worship when I was very Young, and not any body taught me to Read, but God Almighty taught my Heart, and my Heart taught me my Book; and I can give a large Account of my Faith, as any one in three Kingdoms.'[7] As we have seen, Elinor James worked alongside her husband in the family printing house until his death, then carried on the business on her own. Mrs James appears to have

[6] Ruth Perry, *The Celebrated Mary Astell: An Early English Feminist* (Chicago: U. of Chicago P., 1986), 183.
[7] Elinor James, *Mrs. James's Reasons Humbly Presented to the Lords Spiritual and Temporal. Shewing Why She is not willing, that at this time there should be any Impeachments* (1715).

been the more outspoken partner in her forty-eight-year marriage; John Dunton described Mr James as competent and well read, but added that he was 'something the better known for being husband to that *She-State Politician* Mrs. *Elianor James*'.[8] Available evidence suggests that Thomas James was a quiet man who preferred to spend his leisure hours in his splendid inherited library.[9] While Thomas James never printed any of his own writings, he did fill five manuscript volumes with notes towards a theological project. He also filled a tiny commonplace book with proverbs and sayings such as, 'Ill thrives the hapless ffamily, that shows | A Cock that's silent, and a Hen that crows.'[10] What evidence we have suggests that in the early years of their marriage Thomas James oversaw the family press while Elinor James raised their five children. As Mrs James stated in one early broadside describing her religio-political activism to the King, 'I have had many Children, and have Nurs'd them all my self, and I have had Three and Four Children Young and no Maid, and none to help me neither in Sickness or Health, and yet I have found Opportunity to come to *White-hall*.'[11] Thomas James appears to have helped his 'She-State Politician' wife to get one of her first and most cautious broadsides into print, for one of her earliest known papers, *The Case between a Father and his Children*, shows his name in the imprint: 'Printed by Tho. James at the Printing-Press in Mincing-Lane. 1682.' The bulk of James's papers, however, show her own name in the imprints, a typical imprint being 'Printed for me *Elinor James*. 1687'. 'Printed for' usually means that someone else did the printing, and in this case we do not know who that someone was. It may have been Thomas James, it may have been Elinor or her sons and daughters (three of whom were trained in the business), or it may have been an apprentice or journeyman. At any rate, as we have seen in Part I, Elinor James displayed a thorough familiarity with the equipment and challenges of a printing house, and she almost certainly oversaw the printing of her papers even if she did not physically print them. As we will see, this fact will have implications not only for their textual

---

[8] *Life and Errors*, i. 252–3.

[9] On this library see Ch. 1, 'Inside the Printing House'.

[10] 'Mr. Thomas James's Common Place Book', n.d. For the current whereabouts of books and manuscripts held at Sion College Library until 1996, see Note on Primary Sources.

[11] Elinor James, *May it please Your Most Sacred Majesty, Seriously to Consider my great Zeal and Love* (1685 or 1686).

content, but also for their material form and modes of circulation and use.

James routinely published her opinions on the major national events of her day, including the Exclusion Crisis, the Revolution of 1688, the Act of Union, and the impeachment of Dr Henry Sacheverell (to name a few). Like her contemporary tradesman-author Daniel Defoe, she was intensely interested in government policy and the details of commerce; among other issues, she commented at length on the East India and South Sea Companies, the economic *dis*advantages of a free press, and labour relations in London printing houses. She warned Charles II against 'Sins of the Flesh', James II against 'promoting Popery', and, as we have seen, William of Orange against taking his 'Father's' crown. And she advised City of London government, as well as national political leaders, on issues ranging from mayoral elections to the training of magistrates to the enforcement of City by-laws. Satirized in her own time as 'London City Godmother', she has been dismissed by critics and historians since as 'a very extraordinary character, a mixture of benevolence and madness' (Nichols, i. 306). According to her own account, however, this self-educated tradeswoman nevertheless managed to obtain audiences with Charles II, James II, and William III, and, as she put it, to find 'Favour in the Eys of all sorts of people' (a phrase which will become more meaningful in a moment). By the time that she was in her seventies, Mrs James could declare with some pride that 'I have made Application for above this forty years to Kings, Queens, and Princes.'[12]

As the mistress of a printing house, James was quick to use her family press as a tool of both political activism and personal redress. The practical experience, knowledge of current affairs, and respect among her peers that she acquired as a successful tradesperson contributed to the authority of her public voice. James demanded respect from her peers, and when she did not get it, she returned to her press once more. When an anonymous dissenter attacked her *Mrs. JAMES's Vindication of the Church of England* (1687), she immediately printed a response to her opponent's 'canting address'. She criticized the printer of the paper in particular, for she was deeply offended that a fellow tradesmember would

---

[12] Elinor James, *November the 5th, 1715. Mrs. James's Thanks to the Lords and Commons for their Sincerity to King George* (1715).

work against what she imagined to be Stationers' Company solidarity. She attempted to shame printer George Larkin by suggesting that he had shown himself to be less principled than her Catholic enemies, pointing out that despite the flood of papers she had printed against the Catholics, they had refrained from publishing *ad feminam* attacks upon herself. Her fellow printer, on the other hand (a nonconformist), had printed a response gratuitously mocking her—in her eyes for motives of profit alone:

I am very sorry that you should Print such a Scurrilous Paper against me, because I never did you any Injury in Thought, Word, or Deed, and it seems to be Unkind (you being a *Printer*) for I have always had a Tender Regard for *Printers* (for my Husbands sake) but now you well reward me.... The *Roman Catholicks* boast, That they would not Abuse me in any Thing, for all I have Printed so many Papers against them: I must needs say, The most part of them hath been very Civil; therefore you are worse than they.[13]

Elinor James did learn something about business from George Larkin, however. While she stated in her original *Vindication* that *'It is not Interest that moves me to this, for I never made Gain of any thing that ever I did, nor none I do desire; for it was nothing but the Fear of Gods Judgments that hath been the sole Cause of all my Actions for above these Twenty years'* (1), her next pamphlet contains the new headnote, 'I have been blam'd for giving so much, and therefore Price 1d.' And in a remark directed at government press licensers, as well as George Larkin, she added, '*I find those that Vilifies the* CHURCH *Prints with* Allowance *and without, therefore I that Vindicate Her need not any*' (*Mrs. James's Defence*, 1).

James's broadsides were explicitly addressed to three monarchs, the Houses of Lords and Commons, the Lord Mayor, aldermen, and citizens of London, and others, and wherever possible she preferred to distribute them in person. Seventeenth- and early eighteenth-century petitioners often tried to gain a physical audience with the recipients of their political papers; delivering manuscripts into the monarch's own hands on his or her way to chapel was a standard social practice. James printed her broadsides to distribute in person, as a political activist might hand out flyers today. The conditions of authorship and publication of James's

[13] Elinor James, *Mrs. James's Defence of the Church of England, in a Short Answer to the Canting Address, &c.* (1687), 2.

texts register themselves at the level of material production and also at the level of content. As popular political argument rather than high art, timely production was more important than aesthetics, both in the rhetorical construction of James's arguments and in the material production of her texts. These hastily produced papers reflect the heated debates of street and shop, and James's conversations with fellow community members ranging from prominent dissenting leaders to London's labouring poor. They are not polished, 'written' texts; indeed they may never have been 'written' at all, but rather composed directly with a compositor's stick. The 'endings' of James's papers are not pre-planned conclusions to carefully developed arguments but rather simply a matter of coming to the end of the sheet. In several of James's broadsides she actually switches to smaller type three-quarters of the way down— as if she realized that she still had a lot to say and was running out of space. Other physical characteristics include changing type sizes, varied fonts, and makeshift type composition. The most striking consequence of the fact that this confident woman either printed or oversaw the printing of her broadsides herself, however, is the delightful type size, placement, and repetition of her own name (Fig. 3). James typically titled her works *Mrs. James's Advice*, *Mrs. JAMES's Vindication*, and the like, and often printed her name in huge letters at the top of her texts. She also customarily signed her broadsides, sometimes more than once, in large or otherwise distinctive letters. And as we have seen, she concluded her papers with her familiar (and, for a woman, pointed) imprint, 'Printed for me, *Elinor James*'. James's oral 'publication' of her printed texts also registers itself in her rhetorical style and in the stories she tells of her oral encounters. Despite having at least five children, as well as a business to attend to, James managed to spend a good portion of her days outside her home and workplace, delivering her papers and discussing politics and religion with her neighbours. 'For all my Labours and Travels, this Paper will not contain them,' she declared.[14] Her printed papers offer a substantial record of this ongoing oral activism, for she frequently recycled her most notable oral (and sometimes physical) encounters in print. As we will see, James's printed papers also describe her oral audiences with various monarchs, which she recounts for her listeners in loving (and often comic) detail.

[14] Elinor James, *Mrs. JAME's Apology because of Unbelievers* (before 1694).

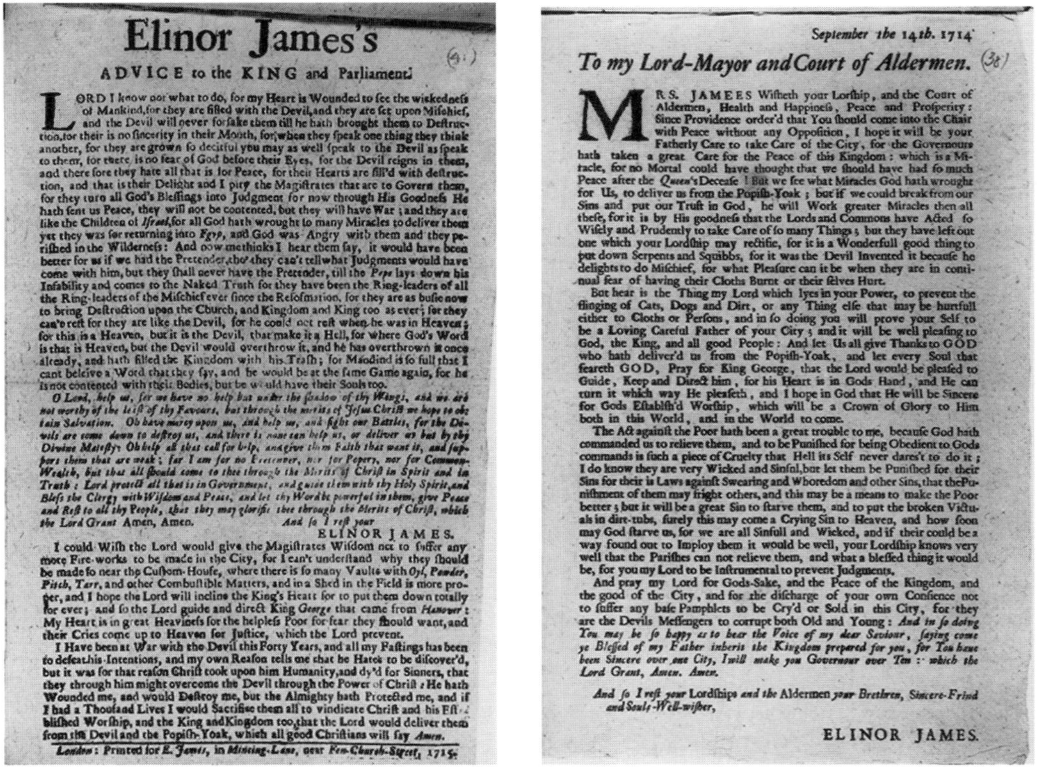

FIG. 3. Typical broadsides by Elinor James. Reproduced by courtesy of the Bodleian Library, Oxford

Writing on the threshold of print culture, at a time when most English men and women could not read,[15] James sometimes felt the need to communicate news to her fellow Londoners orally as well as in print. In one address to the 'gentlemen of the City', she informed City of London leaders that a recent by-law 'against Making, Buying, Selling, or Flinging, of Squibs' (firecrackers) was not being adequately enforced. She suggested that local beadles were to blame, for they had not gone from house to house throughout their wards, informing citizens of the new order. And she volunteered to take matters into her own hands. Appointing herself as a deputy to the city's elected officials, she offered to travel door to door throughout the town, informing her fellow citizens of the law: 'I have inquired, and find but here and there one that has had notice, and therefore, I am resolv'd to be very diligent in this matter my self, for I have great hopes of the Young-Men . . . for they will carry themselves very civilly towards me.'[16] James's dozens of extant broadsides must have played a significant role in informing ordinary Londoners of political and topical news between 1681 and 1716, and, to some extent, her extraordinary offer to communicate the news in person was a logical extension of this role. The fact that she believed she would be taken seriously by her fellow citizens supports the possibility that not all Londoners considered her to be eccentric, 'mad', or merely amusing.[17] And of course, the fact that she was arrested for her 'scandalous and reflecting papers' suggests that the government considered some of her efforts to influence public opinion to be dangerous.

For most later eighteenth-century women writers—and indeed most of her contemporaries—James's willingness to publish her body along with her texts would have been unthinkable. But there is every indication that James actually relished her diverse public activities in her community—that she enjoyed debating political and religious issues in public and was proud of her ability to hold her own in an argument. We have seen how in one paper James

---

[15] See the note on literacy in the Introduction.

[16] Elinor James, *Sir, My Lord Mayor and the Aldermen his Brethren, upon Serious Consideration for the good of the City . . .* (*c.*1690).

[17] What little contemporary commentary there is on Elinor James is by élites and polemical opponents, and therefore does not provide a balanced picture of her contemporary reception. Contemporary commentators include, in addition to the author of the Larkin pamphlet discussed above, John Dryden and Robert Spencer, Earl of Sunderland (see below).

challenged anyone who said that 'King Charles the First was a wicked Man' to come to her printing house to discuss matters further in person. But there is evidence to suggest that James did more than encourage those who disagreed with her to confront her personally. She also sought out face-to-face encounters with her prominent contemporaries. James's printed papers allude to her oral activism at sites of popular political activity such as Westminster, Whitehall, Guildhall, and the halls of major City livery companies, and her own claims are supported by contemporaries' observations and a variety of archival evidence.[18] In November 1687, for instance, James physically disrupted a meeting at Grocers Hall where a nonconformist minister was preaching before the Lord Mayor and caused such a commotion that Secretary of State Robert Spencer, Earl of Sunderland, saw fit to record the incident in a newsletter to a fellow peer. (Significantly, Sunderland assumed that his fellow peer was already familiar with Elinor James.[19]) Another of James's broadsides is titled *Mrs. Elianor James's Speech to the Citizens of London, at Guild-Hall* (1705). Was this woman who loved public confrontation using the word 'Speech' here metaphorically, or were these printed papers an extension of oral electioneering James did at Guildhall?

Several of James's papers recount her public debates with prominent dissenters. They describe her physical, as well as verbal, confrontations with Quaker leader William Penn, in whom she had been gravely disappointed. In an address to Quakers and other 'unbelievers' she explained, 'I have been told, *That you were Subtle Dissemblers*, but I would not believe it; but when I came to speak to your *Great Dons*, I found I was Deceiv'd! Though I do not doubt but there are Thousands of *Innocent Souls*; but it is not You, Mr. *Penn*.'[20] In another pamphlet warning James II against his Popish councillors, Elinor James informed her Catholic King of her own

[18] James's public oral (and sometimes physical) encounters with prominent contemporaries ranging from Popish Plot fabricator Titus Oates to two Lord Mayors of London to the Rector and Wardens of St Bennet's Church will be detailed in a separate publication.

[19] HMC *Downshire MSS*, vol. i, pt. 1, 276: Robert Spencer, Earl of Sunderland, to Sir William Trumbull, 11 Nov. 1687, qtd. in Lois G. Schwoerer, 'Women and the Glorious Revolution', *Albion*, 18 (1986), 201.

[20] Elinor James, *Mrs. JAMES's Defence of the Church of England, in a Short Answer to the Canting Address, &c.*, pt. 2, 'A Word or Two to the *Quakers Good Advice* to the Church of England, *Roman Catholick*, and *Protestant Dissenter*' (1687), 8.

personal battle against local Catholics.[21] In an address to the Lords and Commons in 1705, she recalled these encounters with local Catholics once more: 'The Priests and Jesuits for Ten Weeks were endeavoring to pervert me, but King Charles delivered me, and the Lord kept me, else they might have made a Prey upon me.'[22] Implicitly offering herself as a model of strength, she advised the members of parliament to remain loyal to the established church.

Like so many religious polemicists of her day, Elinor James deployed well-publicized bodily fasts as a form of activism. A private fast became a public sign and rhetorical tool when it was 'published to the World', and James took care to describe her fasting procedures in detail. She explained that the Devil 'has been the sole cause of my Fastings, that I may weaken and prevail over him, and that my Fourteen Days and Nights, and thirteen, and three times twelve, and all the rest that I have published to the World, have been sincerely perform'd without the taste or relish of any thing in this World'. She advertised the fact that when she walked to and from Windsor Castle, she 'went fasting and returned fasting without the taste or relish of any thing' (*Mrs. JAME's* [sic] *Apology because of Unbelievers* (*c*.1694)). And she recorded that upon the impeachment of Dr Henry Sacheverell in 1709, she fasted fourteen days and nights to divert God's judgements from the House of Commons. All the while, she prayed for the members of parliament that God would 'pardon their ignorance' (*Mrs. James* [sic] *Prayer for the Queen and Parliament* (*c*.1710)).

According to her own scattered autobiographical remarks, James managed to acquire a considerable public reputation as a petitioner. In one broadside, James claimed that during Charles II's reign a number of the King's courtiers came to visit her. The purpose of their 1684 visit was to enlist her aid in petitioning Charles II to pardon a dissenting minister who had been condemned to death for treason. Thomas Rosewell, a dissenting minister, was tried at King's Bench for High Treason on 18 November 1684. He eventually pleaded the King's pardon and was discharged. James's account of these events is as follows:

[21] Elinor James, *Most Dear Soveraign, I Cannot but Love and Admire You* (*c*.1686).
[22] Elinor James, *Mrs. James's Consideration to the Lords and Commons . . . Dec. the 15th 1705* (1705).

I remember in King *Charles*'s Time there was one *Roswell* a Dissenting Minister, they had inform'd the King that he had preach'd Treason and he was taken up and put into Prison, and the King was resolv'd he should die, but his Friends made such Interest that the whole Court was against it, and the Duke of *York* and the Duke of *Monmouth* begg'd his Pardon, and the most part of all the Lords, but the King was very angry with them, and would not hearken to any of them, and when they had try'd all Things, at last they came to me, and I went to Prison to him, and he did confess that he did not say the Words that they alledg'd to his charge; so I went to the King at Night, for I think the next day he was to die, and when I came the King was in his Bed-Chamber, and a Lord went to tell him, that Mrs. *James* was come to beg *Roswell*'s Life, and I heard him say, *Does* Mrs. James *come to beg* Roswell's *Life, then she shall have it,* and yet I did not know the Man: And if I did it for a Discenting Minister, you cannot blame me for doing it for an Angel of the Church of God's Establish'd Worship. (*Mrs. James* [sic] *Prayer*)

How are we to understand James's extraordinary style and self-representation in this passage ('when they had try'd all Things, at last they came to me'), and the role of such a passage in a 1710 broadside titled *Mrs. James Prayer for the Queen and Parliament, and Kingdom too*? Like all such narrative set-pieces of her oral encounters, James's account of her 1684 visit to Charles II in a 1710 broadside must be read with the broadside's potential audience and circumstances of publication in mind. Despite the grand title of the paper, James's primary goal in narrating this story of her visit to King Charles II was neither to impress her most powerful contemporaries nor to provide an accurate transcription of 'what really happened'. (James was, after all, telling this story twenty-five years after the fact.) Rather, her goal in telling her story and in so witty a fashion was to impress her popular audience with her credentials as a petitioner. By so doing, she aimed to generate support for High Church Tory Henry Sacheverell, the main subject of the 1710 broadside, then being tried for treason like Rosewell but in her opinion 'an Angel of the Church of God's Establish'd Worship'.

The sociocultural environment of the popular broadside, like the political ballad, was the street. Political or 'news' broadsides were commonly read aloud in public places, and this mode of publication played a key role in shaping their style of presentation. Broadsides, like street ballads (and indeed like many forms of religio-political debate in this period), may be said to be 'a conversion of showmanship into the literary medium'.[23] We have seen in Part I how hawkers and criers of political ballads used their voices to draw a crowd. While James explicitly addressed her texts to prominent public persons and political bodies ('the Queen and Parliament, and Kingdom too'), she distributed them primarily to ordinary people on London streets (persons who were neither socioeconomic nor cultural élites). One polemical opponent sarcastically thanked James, for instance, for having 'Edified the *Tripe-Women* and Convinc'd the *Porters*'—members of the urban working classes. While this opponent's remark is obviously intended to be insulting, it may provide a clue as to who made up part of James's audience. James's proud observation that she had managed to find 'Favour in the Eys of all sorts of people' may provide another such clue, and suggests that her audience was diverse.

As products of a typographic culture, we demand the characteristics of 'written' style: clear expression, linear development, and objectivity (especially in political news). As products of a fundamentally oral religio-political culture, however, James's audience may have been accustomed to political commentary and story-telling characterized by digression, repetition, personal subjective intrusions, and the speaker's insistent testimonial 'I'. James typically advanced her political arguments by telling stories—comic and dramatic stories such as this one of her apparent audience with Charles II, in which she was always, no matter how humble, the centre of attention. Her personal 'intrusions' into her political arguments, and engaging narratives of her own verbal and physical encounters, served important functions, such as to place the narrator in the thick of her tale and to testify to her 'eye-witness' status.[24] And instead of being a 'flaw' in the eyes of *all* members of her audience, James's reliance on story-telling skills and personal subjective argument rather than text-based modes of argument may have inspired trust in some members of her audience (especially those members who were hearing her texts rather than reading them). Certainly her witty tale-telling, self-dramatization, and jest-book dialogue, all so heavily indebted to the oral world all around her, would have gone further than a scholarly point-by-point argu-

[23] Natascha Wurzbach, *The Rise of the English Street Ballad, 1550–1650* (1981), trans. Gayna Walls (Cambridge UP, 1990), 228.
[24] On such strategies see ibid., as well as John Beverly, 'The Margin at the Center: On *Testimonio* (Testimonial Narrative)', *Modern Fiction Studies*, 35 (1989), 11–28.

ment to hold the attention of an oral audience. The early modern popular broadside, street ballad, satirical political song, or public political speech worked as effectively through the skills of the showman as through reasoned argumentation. A good joke might work as well as careful analysis to hold a crowd. For those members of her audience who *could* read her broadsides, James drew additional attention to narrative set-pieces such as this one by composing them in smaller type and setting them apart from the main body of her text.

But the encounters that James narrated most lovingly in her printed papers were undoubtedly her apparent audiences with various monarchs. When her beloved King Charles II was rumoured to have died, 'the first thing' that she 'desired of King James' was to 'go to Church, and the second thing was to satisfie me of his Brothers Death' (*Mrs. James Prayer for the Queen and Parliament* (1710)). At a later date, religious conviction and 'want of exercise' caused her to seek an audience with James II, as she had apparently sought an audience with his brother. This time, however, her goal was neither to 'tell the king his Faults' nor to obtain a pardon for a dissenting minister. Rather, she intended to ask her Catholic monarch's blessing on an extended journey that she was planning. Like many of her contemporaries, Elinor James was convinced that James II would be a good Protestant if only his Popish councillors would leave him alone. Unlike many of her contemporaries, Mrs James planned to travel to Rome to tell the Pope so:

I was very unwilling that King *James* should give his Supremacy to the *Pope*, and I told [King James] that I had a great Faith, and that I wanted Exercise, and I desired him that I might go to the *Pope*, if his Majesty would be pleas'd to give me leave . . . but he was in a Passion, and charg'd me that *I should not go, for if I did, he would send an Express and fetch me back again*, and I did hear some Gentleman that stood by, say, *Who would think the King should mind this Woman, let her go, and the Devil go with her, for she will never return back again*; but after the King was gone, they said, *You must not expect to find so much Favour in the Pope's Court as you do in this*; and I said, *Surely I shall find a great deal more, for you tell me that he is Christ's Vice-gerent.* (*Mrs. James's Reasons Humbly Presented to the Lords* (1715), 5)

Characteristically reporting back the oral objections of her onlookers ('I did hear some Gentleman that stood by, say, *Who would think the King should mind this Woman, let her go, and the*

Devil go with her'), James explained how upon angering (embarrassing?) James II with her travel plans she settled upon the quieter expedient of sending the Pope one of her broadsides or 'letters':

> But my Lord *Grandison* being there, I told him I would fain send the Pope a Letter, but I could not tell who to send it by, and he told me that his Cousin was going an Ambassador to the *Pope* (which was Lord *Castlemain*) and if I did go to him in his Name, and if he promised upon his Honour that he would deliver it, that I might believe him, and I did so do, and when I brought it he said that the Pope did not understand *English*, and with much ado I got it translated into *Latin*, and I shew'd it to Dean *Stillingfleet*, and he told me that he never read any thing better translated. (*Mrs. James's Reasons*, 5–6)

According to James, the King was better pleased with this option of her sending a broadside to the Pope, and even managed to joke with his courtiers about this determined Protestant petitioner:

> But [as] for that in *English* I shew'd it the King, and he did go in, and heard it read, and the King seemed very well pleas'd with it, . . . and after Dinner when he went a walking, he said, *My Lords, I will tell you News, Mrs.* James *a-going to Convert the Pope*, which made them all laugh; but the *Roman-Catholicks* which heard it, was highly displeased. In *Monmouth*'s Rebellion, I would a gone to have made Peace, but the King would not let me. (*Mrs. James's Reasons*, 5–6)

James's account of her audience with James II foregrounds the different responses of various courtiers to her request to be allowed to travel to Rome to petition the Pope. While the Protestant lords laugh at the King's joke that '*Mrs.* James *a-going to Convert the Pope*', the '*Roman-Catholicks* which heard it, was highly displeased'. Not only James's oral activism, but also her printed texts may have evoked different responses from various sectors of her London audience. What evidence we have suggests that socioeconomic and cultural élites tended to view her papers as a joke, a nuisance, or a threat, depending upon how particular papers intersected with or undermined their own interests. Catholic John Dryden, for instance, considered Elinor James to be all three of these (see below). The very fact that James's educated and genteel contemporaries bothered to record or respond to her papers and actions at all, however, suggests that they believed that she had an audience—and, more worrying, an ability to influence public opinion. The very fact that James's élite contemporaries had middle-class, female-authored political pamphlets to mock suggests that the nature of contemporary political and literary life was changing, and that more voices, however 'low', were being heard. For every educated or élite reader who scorned Mrs James's ambitious plans, cheaply produced papers, and bad grammar, another more ordinary Londoner may well have admired her audacity in addressing City leaders, members of parliament, and even kings.

After recounting her missions to Charles II and James II, Mrs James recorded a still more serious mission to William III—to tell the real 'Pretender' what she thought of him. The substance of her overall message for William of Orange may be surmised from her concluding reflection: 'Has not God done great things for me, for the first time that I came to the King it was to tell him of his Faults, and how kindly did he receive me, that the whole Court [took] notice of it' (*Mrs. James Prayer for the Queen and Parliament* (1710)). As we have seen, Elinor James was violently opposed to the removal of James II from the throne. She published more papers on the Revolution of 1688 than on any other issue and, like so many of her female writing contemporaries, deeply questioned the motives of those responsible for the forced abdication of a monarch. She urged parliament to 'take not any thing away from the King', warned them that it was not God's will that their minds should 'run upon another King', and prophesied that 'If the King falls, his Fall will be our RUIN.' And of William of Orange's propagandistic representation as a saviour of the established church, she warned:

if he really does this and has no By-ends, I'll say he will be a Glorious Prince: But if he has any By-ends to lesson the King and promote Himself, his End will be miserable. . . . For ther's not any weary of the king, but only desires to be Free'd from *Popery*: If his Highness don't do that, he had better have stay'd in his own Countrey.[25]

Throughout her writings, as in this dangerous passage, Elinor James continued to refer to the exiled James II as 'the King'. William III was only 'his Highness' or 'the Prince', and while she

[25] Elinor James, *My Lords, You can't but be sensible of the* great Zeal *I have had for King and Kingdom* (c.1688), *To the Right Honourable Convention. Gentlemen, Though you have a New Name* (c.1688), and *My Lords, I can assure your Lordships, that you are infinitely admir'd* (c.1688). Only a few months later, as we have seen, Aphra Behn would write her *Pindaric Poem To The Reverend Doctor Burnet*, critiquing Burnet for similar propagandistic representations of 'Nassau'.

did eventually honour William with the same title as his predecessor, in her own mind there was always a hierarchical, patriarchal
relationship between the two (James II being William's 'Father').
We have seen how, in the 'scandalous and reflecting papers' which
caused her to be committed to Newgate, Elinor James addressed
her remarks to William III but continued to refer to the exiled
James II as '*the King* your Father' (my emphasis). A standard
metaphor of patriarchalism thus becomes subversive in this context. In the same paper, James advised William to 'Pray for the King
your Father, *That God would Convert and Convince him, and
establish him in his Truth, that he may be qualified for his Kingdom*; and when he is so qualified to resign . . . freely.'[26] In another
address, this time to the citizens of London, James compared her
fellow citizens' paying allegiance to William of Orange to the
children of Israel worshipping a golden calf. She urged her fellow
citizens to remain loyal to their exiled lord James II—for 'although
the King is gone, yet GOD remains'.[27]

In the heat of events in 1688, James had entreated the House of
Lords 'seriously to consider the Mighty Occasion that calls you
hither (the like has not been known for these many Ages)'. Six years
later, she looked back on the Revolution of 1688 as the most
momentous and troubling event to date in her life, and reflected on
her own 'scandalous' responses to it. Unusually melancholy in tone,
her *Mrs. JAME's Apology because of Unbelievers* (*c*.1694) explains
her motives for petitioning three different kings:

I have not desired any thing but what has been for the good of all: for the
sole cause of all my Actions was to divert his Judgments, and implore his
Mercies, and my Application to King CHARLES was that he should appease
His Anger by mending his ways: And as for King JAMES all his Reign, God
bears me witness of the sincerity of my heart towards his Truth, and how
Manfully I fought under his Banner against all Opposers; and yet at the
same time I lov'd him dearly. I did not do any thing out of Spight, but out
of pure sincerity, knowing that it would be his overthrow. . . . I was not
willing the Prince [of Orange] should take the Crown, because I knew it
was more for his glory to let it alone.

Another eight years later, in 1702, James consoled herself with the
knowledge that while Charles II, James II, and William III were all

----

[26] Elinor James, *This being Your Majesty's* Birth-Day, *I thought no time
more proper than this, to return you Thanks* (*c*.1689).

[27] Elinor James, *Mrs. James's Advice to the Citizens of London* (*c*.1688).

hopelessly flawed, 'as for Queen Anne, in Her centers all the Vertues that will (by the Blessing of God) make Her and Her People Happy'.[28] Thirteen years later still, she looked back on her fifty-year career as a polemicist and oral activist. Demanding of her audience, 'was it not a great Thing of me to go to King *Charles the Second* to tell him his Faults[?]', she then answered her own rhetorical question: 'the same Power can make me to rectifie a Kingdom' (*Mrs. James's Reasons Humbly Presented to the Lords* (1715), 4).

While Elinor James had access to her own personal publishing institution, Quaker Anne Docwra (*c.*1624–1710) had access to a remarkably sophisticated alternative publishing formation: a network and support system designed to spread the Word, and lend the Society of Friends crucial coherence from within. As their name 'Publishers of Truth' suggests, early Quakers made extensive use of the power of the printed word to shape public opinion and foment sociopolitical change. Quaker commitment to the use of the press may be inferred from the fact that in the years 1659 and 1660 the Friends published about 10 per cent of the total extant titles published in England, despite comprising less than 1 per cent of the population.[29] According to one historian of Quakerism, between the beginnings of the movement in the early 1650s and the appearance of the first Quaker bibliography in 1708, 440 Quaker writers printed 2,678 different publications.[30] At this time of harsh prosecution and strict press licensing, this illegal nonconformist sect produced not less than two and a quarter million books and tracts.[31]

For Quaker women in particular the practical and psychological

---

[28] Elinor James, *May it please Your Lordships, Seriously to Consider what Great Things God has done for You* (1702).

[29] Thomas O'Malley, ' "Defying the Powers and Tempering the Spirit": A Review of Quaker Control over their Publications 1672–1689', *Journal of Ecclesiastical History*, 33 (1982), 74. The word 'extant' here is important. After 1672, the Quakers had a very thorough policy for collecting their own works; thus proportionately more of their publications survive.

[30] Nathan Kite, *Antiquarian Researches among the Early Printers and Publishers of Friends' Books* (Manchester: John Harrison, 1844), 60–1.

[31] Luella M. Wright, *The Literary Life of the Early Friends 1650–1725* (New York: Columbia UP, 1932), 8. See also William C. Braithwaite, *The Beginnings of Quakerism* (1912), 2nd edn. rev. Henry J. Cadbury (York: William Sessions, 1981) and *The Second Period of Quakerism* (1919), 2nd edn. prep. Henry J. Cadbury (York: William Sessions, 1979), and my 'Tace Sowle'.

benefits of access to this publishing support system may be surmised from the fact that seventeenth-century Quaker women produced twice as many extant printed editions as any other female
group.[32] Anne Docwra published at least seven tracts between 1682
and 1700, and was an ardent polemicist for religious toleration, the
separation of church and state, and women's right to prophesy and
testify in public.[33] The benefits of the Quaker publishing system
may also be surmised from the many jealous observations of
Docwra's chief polemical opponent, apostate Quaker Francis Bugg.
Bugg remarked, for instance, that Docwra's books were printed
and 'Sold by *Tacy Sowle*, the Quakers Bookseller, as a Sign both of
their Approbation, and Unity'.[34] As we have seen in Part I, Tace
Sowle served as primary printer and publisher for the Friends, and
her press was the primary channel through which Quaker works
were issued. In addition to Anne Docwra's pamphlets, Tace Sowle
printed books and tracts by more than a dozen women writers.
These women, not all of them Quakers, include Elizabeth Bathurst,
Sarah Cheevers, Elizabeth Chester, Mary Edwards, Alice Ellis,
Katharine Evans, Jane Fearon, Alice Hayes, Elizabeth Jacob, Jane
Lead, Mary Mollineaux, Elizabeth Stirredge, Jane Truswell, and
the 'mother of Quakerism' Margaret Askew Fell Fox.

From its beginnings, then, Quakerism was a religion of the book.
As part of her ongoing efforts to educate the public as to who
Quakers were and what they believed, Anne Docwra engaged in
an ongoing battle-in-print with apostate Quaker Francis Bugg.
In addition to their other religio-political writings Docwra and
Bugg produced a total of at least one dozen works slandering
each other's beliefs, backgrounds, and personal characters. Their

---

[32] Crawford, 'Women's Published Writings 1600–1700'.

[33] According to her own account, Docwra was 'the eldest daughter of William
Waldegrave, of Buers, in the County of Suffolk' (*An Apostate-Conscience Exposed*
(1699), 64). In about 1647, she married James Docwra of Fulborne near Cambridge,
and in about 1664 she became a Quaker. Her husband died in 1672, and after about
1681 she dwelt in Cambridge. For further biographical information on Docwra,
possibly of mixed value, see her works, as well as the many biographical claims
made by Francis Bugg in his *Jezebel Withstood, and Her Daughter Anne Docwra,
Publickly Reprov'd; For Her Lies and Lightness in Her Book, stiled, An Apostate
Conscience, &c.* (1699) and *A Seasonable Caveat Against the Prevalency of
Quakerism* (1701), 57.

[34] Francis Bugg, *William Penn, the Pretended Quaker, Discovered to hold a
Correspondence with the Jesuite's* [sic] . . . *To which is Added, A Winding-Sheet for
Ann Dockwra* (1700), 3.

exceedingly public dispute is worth considering in detail for the insights it provides into the character and rhetorical and commercial strategies of early modern popular religio-political print culture.[35]

Remembering that theological discourse was in fact the 'bestselling' form of print material in the early modern literary marketplace does much to help decode the 'otherness' for twentieth-century readers of debates such as Docwra and Bugg's. As a Quaker, Docwra did not need to concern herself with printing costs as much as Bugg did; Quaker central organization did this for her.[36] Quaker texts also had a ready-made readership. Quaker Monthly Meetings throughout Great Britain and Ireland were required to take copies of all Quaker books authorized and published by central organization. Bugg, by way of contrast, had to rely on a general audience to purchase his books for their educational and entertainment value. To some extent, the extraordinary mudslinging of his exchange with Docwra can be explained by this simple fact. In the increasingly competitive literary marketplace in which these authors wrote, even religious books had to entertain as well as edify. Then as now, there were potential 'sales advantages in calculated eccentricity'.[37] The outrageous rudeness of these religious-tracts-cum-jestbooks is to some degree the textual equivalent of 'going naked as a sign.' The taunting jests, breathless rant, and verbal jousting to be found there are a form of rhetorical entrepreneurism. Theological arguments and gossipy, personal squabbling interanimate one another, and satisfy a public need for 'news' as well as intellectual debate.[38] In addition, while from their beginnings the 'Publishers of Truth' were a well-organized 'religion of the book', at the same time the traces of contemporary oral culture are everywhere evident in their writings. The magnificent series of insults bandied back and forth between Docwra and Bugg,

[35] This kind of virulent personal-public debate is an understudied though central aspect of 17th-cent. popular religious controversy. For a study of nonconformist literary culture which touches on some aspects of these debates see N. H. Keeble's *The Literary Culture of Nonconformity in Later Seventeenth-Century England* (Athens: U. of Georgia P., 1987).

[36] On Quaker central organization see McDowell, 'Tace Sowle'.

[37] Christopher Hill, *The World Turned Upside Down: Radical Ideas during the English Revolution* (1972; Harmondsworth: Penguin-Peregrine, 1985), 17.

[38] At almost the same time that Docwra and Bugg were attacking one another in print, Delarivier Manley was publishing her gossipy political allegories, satisfying a similar public desire for entertainment, 'news', and edifying intellectual debate.

and the statement and rebuttal form of their pamphlets, are the textual equivalents of a verbal street fight. Criticism, no matter how outrageous, is responded to point by point, and name-calling and derogatory remarks are standard (rather like the verbal phenomenon oral theorists refer to as 'flyting').

Francis Bugg's concern with expenses is certainly one unrelenting reminder that religious books are commodities as well as vehicles of ideas. Bugg frequently complained of the expense of engaging in public debate with Docwra, and this is not surprising, for while indebted to contemporary oral culture, theirs was a text-based, as well as text-focused, confrontation. Docwra and Bugg fought against one another's books, responded to each other's printed texts with more printed texts, and referred to printed texts as evidence for their charges. Bugg printed Docwra's letters and concerned himself largely with what Docwra had or had not written. Docwra repeatedly referred to 'my book' and provided her readers with specific page numbers and citations. Nor, as Docwra herself pointed out, was Bugg the only polemical opponent to find her threatening enough to attack by name in print. As she explained, one of her papers which Bugg had tried to use against her was itself written in response to 'a Book that came out in Print, written against me, printed 1685'.[39] As with Docwra's pamphlets, so Bugg's were published by a woman: 'Mrs. *Janeway*, Bookbinder, in *London*-house Yard, next door to *Child's Coffee-House* in St. Paul's churchyard.' By 1701, Bugg claimed to have published '17800 Books, Small and Great', and to be 'indebted for Paper, Printing, and Binding, near 100 pounds'. Bugg also provides us with the information that his *Jezebel Withstood, and Her Daughter Anne Docwra, Publickly Reprov'd* (1699) was printed in a substantial edition of 1,000 copies, while his *A Winding-Sheet for Ann Dockwra* was printed in an edition of 500.[40] There is a strong sense of the materiality of literary production throughout Bugg's religious writings, for he constantly lamented print's expense. He claimed to have irrefutable evidence against Docwra's claims in his

---

[39] Anne Docwra, *The Second Part of an Apostate-Conscience Exposed: Being an Answer to a Scurrilous Pamphlet . . . Written and Published, by F. Bugg, intituled, Jezebel withstood, and her Daughter Ann Docwra reproved for her Lies and Lightness, in her Book, stiled, An Apostate-Conscience Exposed, Etc.* (1700), 29.

[40] Advertisement for Francis Bugg, *News from New Rome, occasioned by the Quakers challenging of Francis Bugg, whereby their errors are farther exposed* (1701), 13, 17, 15, 16.

possession, but that to print these materials would be to 'fill another Half Sheet'. This expense was too much to 'bestow . . . upon this craz'd old piece which is now creeping into the Unity of the Quakers' (*Jezebel Withstood* (1699), 4).

While Bugg jealously noted Docwra's indebtedness to the Quaker system of textual financing, Docwra argued that Bugg was a Grub Street hack writing in the pay of the established church. Docwra's works represent the Anglican church as a propaganda machine: a state-sponsored publishing system which encouraged malcontents like Bugg to slander dissenters for pay. Bugg was a 'Mercenary Agent, belonging to such of the Clergy, as are uneasie under the Liberty granted to Protestant Dissenters' (*Second Part of an Apostate-Conscience Exposed* (1700), 3). He turned to religious hackwork due to his 'Seared Conscience', his 'Shatter'd Head', and above all his 'Desperate Fortunes' (*Second Part of an Apostate-Conscience Exposed* (1700), 7). His pious tracts were in fact nothing but 'Lyes and Deceit', written 'to cheat the *Clergy* of their Money' (*Second Part of an Apostate-Conscience Exposed* (1700), 40 (*sic*; *recte* 16)). We have seen how, in the *Dunciad*, Alexander Pope pronounced that 'Law can pronounce judgment only on open Facts' and called for 'good writer[s]' to step in to supply the deficiencies of the government. In her own writings, Anne Docwra also recognized the power of writers to influence public opinion, but she also recognized government-sponsored print propaganda as a powerful new form of 'positive censorship' in her society. She argued that the legal slander of nonconformists was in fact an increasingly central form of state persecution of oppositional voices: 'F. Bugg, and his Abettors of the Clergy, have raised a New Persecution, with Tongue and Pen' (*Second Part of an Apostate-Conscience Exposed* (1700), 5). A propagandist such as Bugg might publish 'Lyes and Deceit', but once those 'Lyes and Deceit' were printed they were powerful weapons. Playing on the meaning of 'magazine' as a place where ammunition is stored, she observed, 'I perceive by [Bugg's] Writing, that he hath prepared a large *Magazine of Forgery* against me, if his Clergy will pay for printing it' (*Second Part of an Apostate-Conscience Exposed* (1700), 33).

Bugg rallied back against Docwra's charges that he was in the pay of the established church. He declared, 'I never Wrot for Money, nor was I ever a Beggar, nor have I wanted a sufficient support to this Day.' But he contradicted his claim that he 'never

Wrot for Money' when he then went on to admit to having accepted support for his writing from the church, and sought to justify his financial strategies by comparing them to what appeared to him the well-funded publishing programme of the Quakers. 'If I have Applyld my self to the Clergy,' he explained, 'that thereby, I might be Inabled to Defend my Christian Profession, against the Powerful Fund of the Quakers; it is no more than *Fox, Whitehead*, and others of the Quakers have done, who at first were not able to Print a Book at their own Charge' (*William Penn, the Pretended Quaker* (1700), 15). In *An Apostate-Conscience Exposed, And The Miserable Consequences thereof Disclosed, For Information and Caution* (1699), Docwra attacked Bugg's services as a 'Mercenary Agent', and attempted to counter his church-subsidized propaganda. In *Jezebel Withstood, and Her Daughter Anne Docwra, Publickly Reprov'd; For Her Lies and Lightness in Her Book, stiled, An Apostate Conscience &c.* (1699) Bugg responded to Docwra's charges, systematically quoting each one of Docwra's 'Lies' and printing replies. In *The Second Part of an Apostate-Conscience Exposed* (1700) Docwra responded to Bugg's response, and provided further evidence for her own case against him. Referring to the Act of Toleration granting freedom of worship to Protestant subjects, she accused her opponent of being 'uneasie under the Liberty granted to Protestant Dissenters' (3).

In opposition to the rising tide of Augustan polemics against religious enthusiasm, Docwra appended to this pamphlet a defence of inspiration, a 'Treatise concerning Enthusiasm' by 'A. D.' By the eighteenth century, religious enthusiasm was associated with the political upheaval of the Civil War period, and increasingly became 'the bugbear . . . of polite and scholarly . . . society'.[41] Jonathan Swift's satire *A Tale of a Tub* (wr. 1696; pub. 1704), written and published during the same years that Anne Docwra was publishing her works, exposes 'Enthusiasts and Phanaticks among us' and specifically links religious enthusiasm to women.[42] Section VIII is devoted to 'the Learned *Æolists*' ('All Pretenders to Inspiration whatsoever' (95 n.)) and notes that the practices of 'our *Modern Æolists*' are encouraged in '*Female* Priests . . . who are agreed to

---

[41] Hill, *The World Turned Upside Down*, 355.

[42] Jonathan Swift, *A Tale of a Tub with Other Early Works 1696–1707*, ed. Herbert Davis (Oxford: Basil Blackwell, 1965), vol. i of *The Prose Works of Jonathan Swift*, 124 n.

receive their Inspiration . . . like their Ancestors, the *Sybils'* (99). ('*Female* Priests' is glossed 'Quakers who suffer their Women to preach and pray' (99 n.).) Docwra, by way of contrast, argued that the motives of those who would represent marginalized and persecuted religious groups as 'fanaticks' were fundamentally political ones. She worked to 'shew the Legerdemain that hath been used in this Nation, by some of the Learned, concerning this strange word *Enthusiasm*, which they have frighted the Ignorant People with, making them believe that there is dangerous matter contained in it' (*Second Part*, 39). (Swift for instance specifically links religious enthusiasm with 'revolutions of government'.) By means of her word choice 'Legerdemain', Docwra suggested that the leaders of the Church of England, rather than the dissenters, were the purveyors of deception and 'black arts'. In the case of enthusiasm, Docwra argued, it was in fact the 'Learned' rather than the simple folk who were 'superstitious' and 'irrational'. She pointed out that 'the strange word *Enthusiasm*, is from a Greek word, and signifies in *English, Inspiration*' (*Second Part*, 39) and noted that English dictionaries confused '*Divine Motions* with *Poetical Fury*'. She concluded her treatise by emphasizing that in all such matters, it was not ordinary folks but 'learned Men [who] are most subject to Error' (*Second Part*, 46).

Docwra came to believe that the new public forum of print was in fact the safest place to do battle with one's enemies. Oral debates could be misrepresented to those who did not hear them, and manuscript letters could be misquoted or forged. Docwra claimed to have received personal letters from Bugg full of 'Clamour and Threats, if I will not Retract my Book, which I do not intend' (*Second Part of an Apostate-Conscience Exposed* (1700), preface, 31). She claimed too that her opponent had 'forged letters, as from me to him, and printed them with my name to them'. Docwra believed that she was no longer 'free to answer F. Bugg, or any of his Cabal, but in Print, least they should put false Constructions of them, or add some Forgery to them' (*Second Part*, 9, 31). While Docwra increasingly saw print as one of the safest places to conduct an argument, Francis Bugg fundamentally distrusted this new mode of communication. Despite a John Dunton-like obsession with print, Bugg still appears to have felt most comfortable with oral modes of debate. In his *Seasonable Caveat Against the Prevalency of Quakerism* (1701) Bugg questioned why 'this Ann Docwra, whose Books they [the Quakers] sell, disperse, and spread for the Service of Truth . . . does she not come forth and prove what she says' (75). In *William Penn, the Pretended Quaker, Discovered to hold a Correspondence with the Jesuite's* [sic] *at Rome. To which is Added, A Winding-Sheet for Ann Dockwra* (1700), he went further, actually challenging Docwra to a public trial. He listed the names of four people—including a son—who would witness that he was not as Docwra claimed 'distracted'. He dared Docwra to abandon the 'shelter' of print and dispute religio-political matters with him in person. He suggested that she choose six men to serve on an ad hoc 'jury', along with six men of his own choice. And he added that if this supposedly neutral jury could not decide who made the better argument, he was willing to stand before two more supposedly neutral judges, the Vice-Chancellor and Mayor of Cambridge. In the 1640s, the Brownist pamphleteer and preacher Katherine Chidley carried on a pamphlet war with Thomas Edwards, and challenged her opponent to an oral parley much like this one that Bugg proposed to Docwra. Each opponent was to choose six persons who, in the presence of an impartial moderator, would listen to the details of the oral debate, then decide upon a verbal 'victor'.[43] In stylistic terms, as well as in actuality, oral parleys such as the Chidley–Edwards and Docwra–Bugg debates are at the heart of early modern religio-political print polemic. They are another example of the fundamentally oral underpinnings of late Stuart and early Hanoverian literary life.

Obsessed with print and yet afraid of it, Francis Bugg complained of his polemical opponent that the Friends 'now cry her up, *Oh, a brave Woman!* and she cries up them, *Oh G.* Whitehead *is a Gentleman Quaker*' (*Seasonable Caveat*, 62–3). Bugg dedicated his career as a polemicist-hack to alerting the nation to the powerful new combination of dissent and print, and to pointing out the dangerous 'Effects such Books have amongst . . . credulous People' (71).

Other than Francis Bugg, what were some of Anne Docwra's most pressing concerns as a Quaker? Docwra's first publication, *A Looking-Glass for the Recorder and Justices of the Peace, And Grand Juries for the Town and County of Cambridge* (1682), was

---

[43] On Katherine Chidley, see Ethyn Morgan Williams, 'Women Preachers in the Civil War', *Journal of Modern History*, 1 (1929), 561–9.

written in response to the intensified persecution of dissenters during the Popish Plot and Exclusion Crisis (1678–83). In December 1681, the Privy Council had attempted to enforce the Clarendon Code to the fullest. Local magistrates had been ordered to enforce the Corporation Act of 1661, excluding Quakers and other nonconformists from any share in government or administration, and subjecting them to disabling fines and imprisonment. Docwra's *Looking-Glass* was written to chastise what she saw as a corrupt local government. Two of her other pamphlets of the 1680s were also responses to intensified persecution: *An Epistle of Love and Good Advice to My Old Friends and Fellow-Sufferers in the Late Times, The Old Royalists And their Posterity* (1683) and *Spiritual Community, vindicated amongst people of different perswasions in some things* (1687). These pamphlets, however, are directed not to corrupt magistrates and governors but to 'Old Friends and Fellow-Sufferers', and are aimed primarily at enhancing internal cohesion among the Quaker movement.

In her address to local magistrates in *A Looking-Glass for the Recorder* (1682), Docwra used unwritten collective oral memory, written and printed texts, and a subtext of prophetic threat to condemn the hypocrisy and corruption of local governments. Demonstrating typical Quaker familiarity with English statute law,[44] she pointed to specific laws pertaining to dissent. More generally, she boldly demanded that justices and juries might 'understand so much of Religion as is declared in the Laws and Statutes of this Land, and that the Oyer of the Law may be observed and allowed in all points, which is no more than the undoubted Right of every Free-Born Subject of this Nation' (1). Barely disguising her contempt for local magistrates and clergymen, she pointed out that these spiritual and political leaders were paid to uphold the law, not abuse it by fining dissenters and confiscating their property for their own gain. 'I pray let us have Law for our Money, ye are paid for it before-hand,' Docwra wrote. 'It is hard to find in the Histories of former Ages such a Money-Trade made of Religion, as

---

[44] See Craig W. Horle, *The Quakers and the English Legal System 1660–1688* (Philadelphia: U. of Pennsylvania P., 1988). Docwra cites Michael Dalton's *The Countrey Justice, Conteyning The Practise of the Justices of the Peace out of their Sessions* (London, 1618), a standard lawbook consulted by the Quakers throughout the 17th cent. She also claims that her father bid her read 'the great Statute Book', saying that 'it was as proper for a Woman as a Man to understand the Laws' (*An Apostate-Conscience Exposed* (1699), 24–5).

hath been made in *England* within this two and Forty Years'
(*Looking-Glass*, 2).

Docwra believed that the ideological notion of a national Church
of which all British subjects were members was a pernicious myth
likely to cause England's downfall if left unchallenged. At the very
least, those who did not choose to participate in Church of England
services should be left to the censure of the parish church, rather
than be punished by secular authorities. Relying on personal
memory as well as on the collective oral memory of her audience,
she illustrated the evils of forced conformity, warning that the
persecution of dissenters would bring on another civil war:

Force makes Hypocrites, which is the same Spirit that appeared in many of
those that were concerned in the War against King *Charles* the first, which
were the conforming Party mostly: *I very well remember that* [my empha-
sis], and the Bishops Severity also; they were very Officious in their Offices,
to make them Church-men with their Church-Policy, so called, which
proved to be the same nature in effect with that of the *Spaniards* with the
West-Indians. (*Looking-Glass*, 3–4)

She argued that recent Acts of Parliament were directed primarily
against Catholics, not Protestant dissenters. And she pointed out
that if the justices of the peace were genuinely concerned that
Quakers harboured Catholic affiliations, there was a Test Act in
force which made it easy for those in power to determine who was
Catholic. She herself, she claimed, had nearly been made subject to
the penalties of 'the 32nd and 29th of *Elizabeth*', but was later
discharged—presumably the best evidence that she was not a Pap-
ist. Employing the 'I was there' mode of argument of a residual oral
culture even as she referred to printed statute law, she referred to a
document that she herself had signed as evidence of her fundamental harmony with the government: 'I my self, with several others,
subscribed to the Declaration contained in the said Act, before
Judge *Montegue*, a Record thereof is in the Exchequer, and a Copy
of it in the Sheriffs hand, whereby we are discharged of the Penalties of the Statutes of the 32nd and 29th of *Elizabeth*, aforesaid'
(*Looking-Glass*, 6). Notwithstanding her subscription to this act,
she and fellow Quakers had been robbed of their goods, though
'restored again upon Complaint' (6). This was illegal, for 'there is
no Law to compel People to Conform, if they can shew a lawful or

reasonable excuse' (7). The Scriptures provided examples of ordinary people like herself who dissented not against the faith but against the corruption of clergymen and princes (5). Finally, Docwra argued, imprisoning the people of England in filthy gaols and confiscating their property was not an effective way to promote Christ's gospel.

For Docwra, as for so many early religio-political polemicists, the notion of historical inevitability served as a crucial enabling presupposition. The 'legal Tyranny' of those in power would certainly bring on another civil war, for the 'poor People' of England could endure their wretched circumstances no longer. 'Vipers' might flourish now, Docwra warned,

> But Storms will come to make them Creep
> Into their Holes, in hopes of Sleep;
> Instead of Rest, with Sorrow Weep
> This is the Portion that will be
> Due to so great Hypocrisie.
>   Anne Docwra. (*Looking-Glass*, 10)

Recalling the 'late Experience' of the Civil War, as well as the continuing instability of recent years, Docwra deployed unwritten oral memories to support her political prophecies for the future: 'There is nothing but Truth and Righteousness will stand in this Land of our Nativity, all things else stand but as a tottering Wall in *England*, as late Experience hath shown, whether they be Laws against Dissenters, flattering Addresses, Abhorrences, forced Oaths, contrived Covenants and Engagements for or against this or that Government' (*Looking-Glass*, 7). As an appendix to her argument for religious freedom, she affixed an advertisement informing those in power that the warrants they had had drawn up against local dissenters were unlawful and unlikely to be profitable: 'Those People that the warrants are out against are mostly poor People, and but few, if any at all (that I can hear of) that can or will provide the Money for to pay such an illegal Debt.' As in the body of her pamphlet, so in the appended advertisement she concluded her appeal with a prophetic curse: 'Disappointment will be the portion of all those that carry on such Designs as this: The Lord God Everlasting hasten the Confirmation of it that men may see where they are, and what they are doing. A.D.' (*Looking-Glass*, 11). If nothing else could authorize her public political critique of the government, the end of the world made it not only possible, but urgent for her to write.

Polemicist and preacher Joan Whitrowe published at least eight tracts over a period of twenty years from 1677 to 1697.[45] Most active in the immediate post-revolutionary period, she addressed most of her pamphlets specifically to William and Mary, expressing a sense of disillusionment that these professed saviours of the church had not lived up to her own and the nation's expectations. Whitrowe's relentless threats and advices are distinctive in their tone and in the specificity of their demands for social change. More than any of the other women political writers considered here, Whitrowe was motivated to write by her anger at the indifference of the propertied classes to the ubiquitous suffering of the poor. Concerned with immediate social problems rather than abstract constitutional issues, her pamphlets are rich in social observation, and her critique of property is sustained. Her papers are informed by an intensive, primary concern with what we might call class relationships, and serve as a reminder of the importance of class hostilities to seventeenth-century religious and political upheaval. They should also serve to caution those modern scholars who see sectarian radicals as having been 'reduced to silence and inertia' after the Restoration.[46]

Initially united with the Quakers but later separated from them, Joan Whitrowe may have been one casualty of the Quakers' own intensified internal press controls during the later years of the Restoration. Mysterious references to Whitrowe in Francis Bugg's polemics against Anne Docwra suggest that at one point the Society of Friends tried to put an end to Whitrowe's radical (and exceptionally dangerous) writings by withdrawing support for their publication. In denigrating Anne Docwra, Francis Bugg made a vague and chilling allusion to Joan Whitrowe's books being 'stopt'. Anne Docwra's books, Francis Bugg complained, were still 'sold by [the

---

[45] She refers to more which apparently have not survived. Her tombstone refers to 'several pious Books', probably her pamphlets (BL Add. MS 5841, 'Epitaph of Joan Whitrowe').

[46] Even Elaine Hobby writes that 'After the Restoration, as persecution of radicals increased under the workings of the Clarendon Code, sectaries were gradually reduced to silence and inertia' (*Virtue of Necessity*, 26).

Quakers], and not stopt, as *Joan Whitrow's*'. Bugg implied that Joan Whitrowe was 'rebuked as an Incendiary', and suffered pre-publication censorship of her writings not by the government but rather by her own persecuted group. Joan Whitrowe's censorship by her peers, and difficulty in publishing her 'too-radical' writings, presents an interesting case study of one woman political writer's access to the means of material literary production. It should also serve to caution twentieth-century readers against idealizing the mutual support systems and collaborative publishing programmes of early sectarian groups.

Early Quakers suffered relentless persecution from dominant religious institutions, and it is not surprising that the leaders of the movement sought to minimize divisive criticism from within. After 1672, Quaker central organization acted in the capacity of a modern 'publisher', financing production, supplying printers with copy, and overseeing national and international distribution. But the executive bodies of 'antient men Friends' which made up Quaker central organization also served as a complex board of review for all Quaker publications. The Morning Meeting read over even the works of their founder George Fox line by line with meticulous care, and decided which passages must be altered or omitted. Like any alternative social formation for which survival is dependent on internal cohesion, the embattled Quaker community of the late seventeenth and early eighteenth centuries was a powerful force for internal censorship. By the 1700s, the Quaker press was 'characterised by caution and extreme political sensitivity, which had been absent in the 1650s'.[47]

Minutes of the meetings of Quaker central organization reveal that Joan Whitrowe's writings were censored by the Friends on at least one occasion. On 23 July 1677, meeting minutes record Quaker leaders' concern that Whitrowe had not yet submitted a book that she was writing to the Morning Meeting for approval. Rebecca Travers, a prominent Quaker at whose house meetings were held, was nominated by the group to speak to Whitrowe about submitting her manuscript 'book' for pre-publication review:

Rebecca Travers is desired to speake or write to Joane Whitrow that shee submit the book (conteyning A Relation of what her daughter spoke at the time of her death) to friends as others doe that send books that friends may

---

[47] O'Malley, ' "Defying the Powers and Tempering the Spirit" ', 85.

Leave out what they see not of service to the Truth, which friends are dissatisfied with. (MMM, vol. i (1673–92))

One week later, meeting minutes record that Whitrowe did submit this particular book to Quaker leaders as requested. The appropriate reviewers, however, found certain passages to be unacceptable: 'the book brought by Joane Whitrow [to] be left to J. Claypoole and Rebecca Travers to consider and Tis desired by this meeting that what is chiefly to her owne praise be left out' (MMM, vol. i (1673–92), 30 July 1677). The manuscript 'book' in question was *The Work of God in a dying Maid, being a short account of the dealings of the Lord with one Susanna Whitrow about the age of fifteen years and daughter of Robert Whitrow inhabiting in Coventgarden in the county of Middlesex; together with her experimental confessions to the power and work of the Lord God both in his judgments and mercy to her soul*. The first of her books that the Quakers censored, then, was Joan Whitrowe's too-personal account of the death of her daughter Susanna.[48]

By 1689, Joan Whitrowe wrote, 'I walk alone as a Woman forsaken.'[49] A marginal figure even within the Quaker movement, Whitrowe's far more radical writings after the Revolution of 1688 may have been considered too dangerous to publish. Whitrowe's post-revolutionary polemics are extremely aggressive. She had specific suggestions for social change and argued at length for a more just distribution of available resources. By 1692, she signed herself *'one that is of no Sect or gathered People'*, suggesting that by this time she no longer saw herself as part of the Quaker community or any other.[50] And by 1694, her outspoken criticism of the disparities of wealth and poverty in her society was addressed to dissenters as well as to members of the Church of England. If Whitrowe's writings were 'stopt' by the Quakers, she was effectively silenced. After a flurry of activity, her publications ceased abruptly in

[48] For further details of *The Work of God in a Dying Maid* (1677) see Ch. 4. The work also records the recent death of her 6-year-old son Jason.

[49] Joan Whitrowe, *The Humble Address of the Widow Whitrow to King William: With a Faithful Warning to the Inhabitants of England, To Haste and Prepare by True Repentance, and Deep Humiliation, to meet the Lord, Before His Indignation burns like Fire, and breaks forth into a mighty Flame, so that none can quench it* (1689), 13.

[50] Joan Whitrowe, *To King William and Queen Mary, Grace and Peace. The Widow Whitrow's Humble Thanksgiving . . . for the King's safe Return to England* (1692), 7.

1697.[51] For many female polemicists, the Quaker press was the only practical avenue to print. How many women (and men) must have been silenced by the movement's understandable 'concern with uniformity and caution'?[52]

Whitrowe's printed books and papers were but a small part of her public activism. Both before and after her separation from the Quakers, she travelled enormous distances on foot, praying, preaching, and displaying her abused body as a sign of God's wrath. Just before the Great Plague, the Lord commanded her to go to Bristol. Accordingly, she undertook one of her first major journeys. With 'a Sack-Cloth on my Body, and Ashes on my Head', she travelled to Bristol to deliver her call to repentance, then returned home to London

where I came to my Husband and Family in ten Days time, or the tenth Day of my parting from them, leaving a young Child of a Year old that suck'd at my Breast,[53] and found all things well, my-self also, so well as if I had not gon one Mile, although a weak Woman of Body, and not able to go two Miles without Pain, yet in the strength of the LORD I went almost two hundred Miles a Foot. (*Humble Address*, 9)

Shortly thereafter, the plague began, and she was once again 'commanded to go out of my own House Sack-cloth and Ashes, and proclaim the terrible Day of the LORD' (*Humble Address*, 10). Herself gravely ill, she prayed to God to remove her own burden. But the Lord explained:

It is the burden of the Iniquities of the Nation I have laid upon thee, and thou must bear my Indignation, for thou art their Sign of the Repentance and Humiliation I require of them: then I knew what the Prophet *Habakkuk* meant when his Lips quivered, his Belly trembled, and rottenness had entered his Bones. (10)

---

[51] It is not yet known how Whitrowe got her works into print after she left the Quakers. Only three of her works show printers' or publishers' names in imprints. The imprint of *The Widow Whitrow's Humble Thanksgiving*, which was apparently licensed, reads: '*Printed by* D. Edwards *in* Nevel's Alley in Fetter-Lane, for J. B. 1694.' Two other works, *Faithful Warnings* and 'To the King and Both Houses of Parliament', show Elizabeth Whitlock's name in imprints. *Faithful Warnings* shows: 'Printed, and are to be Sold by E. Whitlock, in *Stationers-Court* near *Stationers-Hall*. 1697.'

[52] O'Malley, '"Defying the Powers and Tempering the Spirit"', 84.

[53] The 'young Child of a Year old' was probably Whitrowe's daughter Susanna, who died in 1677 at the age of 15.

Whitrowe saw her physical body as 'a sign to the Multitude' (12), and the illnesses to which it was liable as marks of God's wrath. Sustained fasting, sackcloth and ashes, and the discomforts of long-distance foot travel were in themselves modes of religio-political activism. They were part of a signifying system of the body, aimed at encouraging all who saw her to 'humble themselves in the dust'. When the Lord commanded Whitrowe 'to wear Sackcloth three years', she did, 'till after the death of King *Charles*' (12). And when he told her to 'depart from the Multitude . . . to give up Name and Fame, and whatsoever was dear to me in this Life', she did that too—to the point where she eventually came to see herself as 'one that is of no Sect or gathered People whatsoever' (*To King William and Queen Mary*, 16).

Upon the death of Queen Mary in 1694, God commanded Whitrowe to travel to the City of London from Putney. ('I knew not for what, for I had been there a little before, therefore had no Business of my own.'[54]) Once she had arrived in the City, the Lord commanded her to call the people of London to fasting. Caught up in a crowd somewhere between Cheapside and Cornhill, Whitrowe 'opened [her] Mouth to them, and said, *The Lord calls for Fasting, and you go to Feasting*'. She moved with the crowd through the streets, 'declaring the Word of the Lord throughout *Cornhill*, and part of the next Street'. Once she had delivered her public testimony to her own (and the Lord's) satisfaction, she 'left them, and Returned that Day to *Putney*' ('To the King', 109–10).

On another occasion, Whitrowe received a similar call to oral activism immediately after dropping off a book manuscript at the printer's:

as I was going from the Printers, conversing with the Lord, and contemplating of his Glorious Power, being fill'd with Harmonious Praises in Melodious Sounds; yet as it were in deep Conflict of Spirit; and this going on till I came about the middle of *Pater-noster-Row*, where I stood still and beheld; and, as I *looked* with Admiration, these Words, in great Power, spoke aloud in my Ears, *This is* London, *the City of Abomination, this is the Abominable City*: And these words were Repeated over and over, till I came about the middle of *Cheapside*. ('To the King', 187–8)

[54] Joan Whitrowe, 'To the King, and Both Houses of Parliament', Prefatory Epistle to *Faithful Warnings, Expostulations and Exhortations, To The several Professors of Christianity in England, as well as those of the Highest as the Lowest Quality* (1697), 109.

She continued walking through this central commercial area of London until she came to Bishopsgate, where, filled with a sense of despair for the 'Abominable City', she fell on her knees and prostrated herself before the Lord—as well as, no doubt, before many onlookers in this busy part of working London.

Whitrowe's writing and publishing, then, should be understood as an extension of an ongoing mode of religio-political activism which was oral and 'bodily'. As Phyllis Mack has pointed out, 'the acts of writing and public prophecy were actually more similar than one might suppose; writing involved public confrontation as well, since works were hawked by their authors on street corners or in front of taverns, or handed to magistrates like a modern summons'.[55] As we have seen, Elinor James preferred to distribute her printed papers to their powerful addressees in person. Whitrowe, too, was willing to endure a long journey on foot and a long wait for a fleeting opportunity to hand over her papers to the King. One of her pamphlets is signed '*Putney April* the 11th, 1696. This I delivered into the King's Own Hands, the 11th Instant. *Jone Whitrow*'—as if even the touch of a king she disapproved of gave a powerful talismanic quality to other copies of the paper.[56]

Like James, too—and indeed like all of the polemicists discussed here—Whitrowe appears to have found print a challenging and sometimes awkward mode of communication. Whitrowe's printed texts paint a portrait of a zealous activist plagued not only by material hardships and loneliness, but also by the mental and material struggles of authorship. Whitrowe wrote of her depression and frustration when work was not going fast enough, and of her desire to start new projects before current ones were in press. Most poignantly, she expressed a sense of despair that she could not address all the injustices of her society at once. By 1694 she thought that she 'could write a Volume of Sights, Visions and Revelations which she hath had above for these thirty Years'. But it was not that easy. 'Had it stood with my will,' she explained,

I had never been concern'd more with this Generation, after having delivered the three first books to the King and Queen, but having delivered the

[55] Phyllis Mack, 'Gender and Spirituality in Early English Quakerism, 1650–1665', in Elisabeth Potts Brown and Susan Mosher Stuard, eds., *Witnesses for Change: Quaker Women over Three Centuries* (New Brunswick, NJ: Rutgers UP, 1989), 59 n. 31. See also Mack, *Visionary Women*.
[56] Joan Whitrowe, *To the King, And Both Houses of Parliament* (1696).

last of the three, Titled to Queen *Mary* . . . a strong powerful Voice Said, *Arise and thrash, Oh Daughter of Sion.* . . . Then after this I wrote another Printed-book to the King and Queen, and four Papers in writing at several times, which I delivered into their own hands; and then after I had delivered those Writings, I wrote another Book, which I had almost finished, but this coming so forceable upon me, I laid that by, and this hath been longer in hand than I expected when I begun it, for indeed all things looking so dark and dismal, I rather expected some dreadful Judgment would break forth before this Book would be finished.[57]

Lying in her bed feeling low in spirits, Whitrowe threw her book manuscript out of her hand, 'as Moses threw the Tables of Stone'. But 'a powerful voice' charged her with neglecting her duty, and told her to '*Write down thy Poverty*, which I immediately did'. And 'now', Whitrowe concluded of her latest publication, 'I have given you an Account why it was not committed to the Press before now' (*Widow Whiterow's Humble Thanksgiving*, 35–7).

    In this instance, Whitrowe related how she experienced a particularly dreadful form of writing-induced melancholy and 'writer's block'—a strong sense of impending 'Judgment' preventing her from putting quill to paper. On another occasion, Whitrowe was prevented not from completing a manuscript, but rather from taking it to a printer. Despite her strong dislike of William III's personal behaviour and political policies, Whitrowe claimed to have held back one of her manuscripts out of concern lest she add to the King's grief upon the death of his wife. She had originally, she claimed, written a paper to the Queen, 'telling her therein, that the Sword of the Lord was drawn and Furbished, two-Edged, yea three Edged, and only wants Commission'. But in this same paper, she had also prophesied Queen Mary's death—a prediction whose fulfilment put her on guard against printing the paper: 'And so [I] went on, declaring to [the Queen] the very thing that came to pass to my unspeakable Grief, which Paper I had Printed at this time, but for fear of renewing the *King*'s Sorrows' ('To the King, and Both Houses of Parliament', Prefatory Epistle to *Faithful Warnings* (1697), 188).

    Despite her apparent concern for William's feelings upon the death of his wife, Whitrowe was in fact deeply disturbed by William and Mary, and addressed the majority of her pamphlets

---

[57] Joan Whitrowe, *The Widow Whiterow's Humble Thanksgiving for the Kings Safe Return* (1694), 33.

explicitly to them. As for so many late Stuart women writers, the Revolution of 1688 was for her a momentous occasion: a series of events of enduring spiritual and political importance. The bloodless coup was irrefutable evidence of divine intervention in state affairs: the strength of 'the Lord's own Arm which HE made bare in the sight of all' (*Humble Address of the Widow Whitrow to King William* (1689), 4). The new King and Queen were irredeemably indebted to God for their earthly crown, yet they gravely endangered their already precarious positions as heads of state by flouting God's will. Whitrowe spent the better part of her career as a polemicist and preacher urging William and Mary to fulfil their promises as professed champions of the Protestant faith, and advising the 'Church and People of *England*' to 'put into practice what you have promised the Lord' (*Humble Address*, 14). Among many other requirements, William III was to 'visit the Widow and Fatherless in their Afflictions', give up his hunting, and stop playing with his dogs in church:

I saw thee upon *East-Sheen-Common*, where thou wast taking thy pleasure in Hunting: I was much grieved to see the King spending his precious time in such a vain Exercise, in such a day as this, when the Nation lies bleeding. . . . Oh King! is this a day for Pleasure . . .? I beseech thee consider the end of the LORD, in bringing thee into the Nation, was it to do thy own Will, or the Will of Him that sent thee? . . . thou, O King, art a witness, that it was not thy Sword, nor thy Might that brought thee hither, but the Lord's own Arm which HE made bare in the sight of all. And now I beseech thee consider how highly thou art ingaged to the LORD for all his Goodness; and what thou wilt return to the KING of Eternal Glory. (*Humble Address*, 4–5).

Queen Mary was to abandon her vain and worldly pursuits, while the people of England were to reflect:

What did you send for King *William* out of his own Country, and turn out King *James*? You said it was to set up the *Christian Religion*, and to Establish it: why is it not done? . . . put into practice what you have promised the Lord; but if you will not, then it will appear to all the World, that you did not all this to set up the *Christian Religion*, but to set up your selves.[58]

---

[58] *To Queen Mary: The Humble Salutation and Faithful Greeting of the Widow Whitrowe. With a Warning to the Rulers of the Earth* (1690) and *The Humble Address of the Widow Whitrowe to King William* (1689), 13–14.

Whitrowe repeatedly warned the King to bow down before the Lord, for 'without Him you can do nothing'.[59] Many religious polemicists of the post-revolutionary period appear to have taken special pleasure in reminding William III what little power he had in comparison to his predecessors, and in pointing out that even that mite was given to him by the Lord (and so could be taken away again). Whitrowe urged William and Mary to remember that they were God's 'Vice-Gerents here on Earth', and prayed that they would 'joyn unanimously together in Heart and Soul to humble themselves in the dust before Thee the Almighty GOD'.[60] Whitrowe's radically levelling image of the King and Queen humbling themselves in the dust was a personal favourite. She repeatedly warned William and Mary to 'come down from your Thrones, and humble yourselves in the dust by Fastings and Prayers, and deep Humiliation, crying mightily to GOD the Father' (*Widow Whiterow's* [sic] *Humble Thanksgiving*, 5). She also exercised considerable aggression by means of the ostensibly dutiful act of biblical quotation. In the headnote to her *Humble Thanksgiving* (1694) she highlighted Jeremiah 13: 18: 'Say unto the KING and to the QUEEN humble your Selves, sit down.'

Religious conviction afforded women such as Whitrowe an outlet for aggression in the form of a desire for millenarian 'revenge'. As in Anne Docwra's polemics, so in Joan Whitrowe's pamphlets there is a powerful subtext of prophetic threat. These women's writings, and also Jane Lead's, contain powerful subversive 'visions' characteristic of millenarian writings. In these futuristic fictions, existing social hierarchies are dissolved, and widows and children have enough to eat. (And, of course, rulers like William and Mary are 'humbled in the dust'.) Like these millenarian visions, the curse-poem was another important subgenre in women's religio-political polemicism. Whitrowe prophesied that neither force nor the rule of law could prevent the eventual inevitable destruction of the 'great ones': 'There's neither Strength nor Policy shall stand, | Against what GOD's a bringing on this Land. | The Youth shall howl, the Aged shall weep sore, | Yet there's glad tidings for the Meek and Poor' (*Widow Whiterow's Humble Thanksgiving*, 4). In another pamphlet Whitrowe expressed her gratitude for King William's safe return from the battle at La

[59] Joan Whitrowe, *To the King, and Both Houses of Parliament* (1696).
[60] Joan Whitrowe, *To King William and Queen Mary* (1692), 7 and *Widow Whiterow's Humble Thanksgiving* (1694), 4.

Hogue, but recorded her disgust at the wood wasted in bonfires to celebrate his victory:

How many poor destressed Families both in City and Country would be glad and rejoyce to have that Firing to warm and refresh them and theirs in cold and bitter Weather; that was spent in waste when the KING came home to gratifie the humors of an ungodly Crew, who one day cries *Hosana, Hosana*; and the next day with a louder vote, *Crucifie, Crucifie*. (*To King William and Queen Mary* (1692), 6)

Whitrowe's critique of the conspicuous consumption and waste of state rituals is in fact more subversive than it might initially appear. While directed ostensibly not at William III but at those 'Judges, Justices, and Officers of all sorts, that do not fulfill the Will of GOD' (5), her complaint was graphically illustrated with a powerful image of mob violence. In 1692, the image of a crowd chanting '*Crucifie, Crucifie*' would immediately bring to mind the execution of Charles I and the recent forced abdication of James II. By implicitly reminding William III of England's willingness to 'crucifie' his predecessors, Whitrowe effectively hinted that this professed saviour of the church was no more secure than they.

Whitrowe's critique of conspicuous consumption was characteristic of her increasing solidarity not with any particular faith but rather with the working poor: 'many hundreds in City and Coun-ty, [that] sits in their Houses with hungry Bellies, both of Wea-vers and others, that knows not which way to shift for Bread for their Children' (*Widow Whiterow's Humble Thanksgiving*, 21). Whitrowe was intensely aware of what the aristocracy and gentry did and did not do with their money; almost without exception, her writings contrast the subsistence level existence of the labouring poor with the privileged lives of the propertied classes. She criticized the upper ranks' excessive attention to things of the flesh, especially fine food and apparel, and she consistently referred to élites rather than to working people as 'the drunkards, the feasters, the swearers, gamesters, whoremongers, the proud'.[61] She attacked colonialism and rapacious overseas trade, the amassing of excess wealth and estates, and especially disregard for the poor. Above all, she argued that the endless accumulation of capital in the hands of a few must be curbed:

---

[61] Joan Whitrowe, *To Queen Mary: The Humble Salutation and Faithful Greeting of the Widow Whitrowe* (14 Dec. 1690), 18.

The next to your Habit is your Houses, which are deck'd with all manner of Curiosity, Richness and Delicacy, as your sinful Persons are: Your great spacious Lordly Houses, furnished with all manner of costly, rich and sumptuous Furniture, which would be too tedious, and fill up much Paper to insist upon; but your voluptuous Feeding, and excessive Feasting one another, in so much that you run out great Estates, both of your own and other Men's; but in your own Families, that is, among your Servants, many of you are very pinching and sparing, and to the Poor little or nothing, but what you are compell'd to in your Parish Duties; and your poor Neighbours, many hundreds in City and County, sits in their Houses with hungry Bellies, both of Weavers and others, that knows not which way to shift for Bread for their Children; some eating Bread sparingly, and drink Water, Others getting Garden stuff, as Cabbage, and such like for their Children to feed on; whilst you feed, *Dives* like, lying at your Ease, stretching your selves upon your rich Sattin Beds and Couches, wallowing in all your sinful Pleasures, not knowing what to Eat, Drink, or put on for Richness and Dainties; and others of you Hoards up Treasure as Sand, and are never satisfied, compelling Sea and Land to get Riches, adding House to House, and Land to Land, and all for Portions for our Children, say they; and thus the Fathers eat sowre Grapes, and the Childrens Teeth are set an edge. (*Widow Whiterow's Humble Thanksgiving*, 21-2)

It was the immediate duty of the substantially propertied of all faiths to make 'plentiful Provision, not only for them of your own Judgment, but for all sorts, that the Widow, Fatherless, and Strangers may have no want' (*Widow Whiterow's Humble Thanksgiving*, 23). Such stop-gap solutions to desperate poverty, however, were only the first step on the agenda for social change. Petty charity 'compell'd . . . [by] Parish Duties' was a sop to the poor rather than a commitment to social justice. For the problem of inequality was inherent in the mode of production and distribution itself:

But you Covetous, Earthly minded Professors of all sorts, your niggardly pinching the Poor, your giving five, ten, twenty or forty Shillings, nay five, ten, twenty Pounds; (though who is so liberal) will not excuse you that have Hundreds, and Thousands, and many Thousands lying by a year will not excuse you . . . when His Majesty calls you to an account what you have done with his Treasure . . . will you say, we hoarded it up by us; or will you say, we gave it our Children for their Portions, to live in Pride and Luxury. (*Widow Whiterow's Humble Thanksgiving* (1694), 23)

Not only the landowners and capitalists but also the 'Teachers and Rulers of this Generation' were hypocritical and covetous, concerned only 'for their Self-Interest in one kind or other; some for yearly maintenance, others for Name and Fame, or to be highly esteemed for their Gifts and Parts' (*Widow Whiterow's Humble Thanksgiving* (1694), 12). The 'Professors of Religion' in fact 'outstrip the Prophane', striving for 'Honours and Preferments into great Places' (*Humble Address*, 6). Given insights into the relation of religion, politics, and property in this period such as these, it is perhaps not surprising that by 1689 Whitrowe declared: 'I walk alone as a Woman forsaken; I have fellowship with them that lived in Caves, and in Dens, and desolate places of the Earth, of whom the World was not worthy' (*Humble Address*, 13). For by that time, her sweeping social critique was directed at members of the Church of England and dissenters alike.

Protestant mystic and spiritual autobiographer Jane Lead (1623–1704) was born into an Anglican family in Norfolk.[62] At about 16 years of age, she committed herself to a lifelong search for spiritual knowledge or 'Divine Philosophy'. (When she died in 1704 at 81, her son-in-law described her as being in 'the sixty-fifth year of her vocation to the inward and divine life'.[63]) At 18 she travelled to London, ostensibly to visit her brother, a merchant. In London during the tumultuous Civil War period (from roughly 1642 to 1643) she spent time among various dissenting conventicles. But this independent activity ceased in 1644, when she was required by her parents to marry a distant relative, William Lead. She was married for twenty-six years, during which time she raised two daughters to adulthood but did not write.[64]

---

[62] The chief biographical sources on Lead are Bod. MS Rawlinson D. 832–3; Dr Wms MS 186.18 (1) a–c; Christopher Walton, *Notes and Materials for an Adequate Biography of the Celebrated Divine and Theosopher William Law* (1854); Catherine F. Smith, 'Jane Lead's Wisdom: Women and Prophecy in Seventeenth-Century England', in Jan Wojcik and Raymond-Jean Frontain, eds., *Poetic Prophecy in Western Literature* (Rutherford, NJ: Fairleigh Dickinson UP, 1984), 55–63 and other articles listed in the bibliography; Joanne Magnani Sperle, 'God's Healing Angel: A Biography of Jane Ward Lead', diss., Kent State U., 1985; and D. P. Walker, *The Decline of Hell: Seventeenth-Century Discussions of Eternal Torment* (Chicago: U. of Chicago P., 1964), ch. 13.

[63] Dr Wms MS 186.18 (1) c.

[64] Only one of these two daughters, Barbara Lead Walton Lee, outlived her. Two additional daughters died in infancy.

In 1663 or 1664, Lead became acquainted with John Pordage (1607–81), an Anglican minister whom Richard Baxter described as being 'much against property, and against relations of magistrates, subjects, husbands, wives, masters, servants, etc.'[65] A theological and political radical, Pordage had since 1649 been the head of a communal household which Ranter Abiezer Coppe described as a 'family communion', the members 'aspiring after the highest spiritual state' through 'visible communion with angels'. In 1651 Pordage was charged with heresy, though later acquitted. By 1664, when Lead became acquainted with them, John Pordage and his wife Mary (d. 1668) were leading a small London sect. Despite the harsh penalties of the Conventicle Act, and despite her own family's strong disapproval, Lead joined the Pordage 'communion'.

John Pordage was one of the first English commentators on the philosophy of German Jacob Boehme (1575–1624). Viewed by Georg Wilhelm Friedrich Hegel and others as 'the first German philosopher', Boehme was a shoemaker by trade, who called himself the *Philosophus der Einfältigen* ('philosopher of the simple folk'). At the age of 25, he experienced a powerful spiritual revelation, and thereafter produced an unceasing stream of mystical writings until his death twenty-four years later. His writings were circulated in manuscript and print throughout Germany, England, Holland, France, Russia, and (later) America. During the Civil War period and Interregnum they were translated into English, and became influential among intellectuals, dissenters, and poets (eventually including William Blake). Among other challenges to Anglican doctrine, Boehme's philosophy of the 'Inner Light' offered John and Mary Pordage and their followers a radical alternative tradition to the academic divinity of English ruling-class universities. Like the Pordages, Jane Lead became an ardent disciple of Boehme.[66]

In 1670 William Lead died and, after twenty-six years of marriage, Jane Lead was thrown into sudden poverty. Considerations of personal security almost certainly played a role in her decision to

[65] *Reliquiae Baxterianae*, i. 77–8, qtd. in Hill, *The World Turned Upside Down*, 225.
[66] For additional information on Boehme, see Andrew Weeks, *Boehme: An Intellectual Biography of the Seventeenth-Century Philosopher and Mystic* (Albany: State U. of New York P., 1991).

move into John Pordage's communal household four years later; still, despite the fact that she was then nearly 50, Lead's brother ordered her to leave the Pordage household at once or forfeit all hope of family assistance. Lead's brother ordered her to come and live with him instead, and there 'abide during his Life, where all things should be provided, and need not to have any other dependance'.[67] According to Lead's diary, this plan was approved by her family and 'pressed upon me with many Arguments': 'They rolled upon me many great and heavy Weights, which would have pressed down my Faith, seeing many Archers drawing up against me, with out-stretched Bows' (*Fountain*, i. 328–9). Despite enormous pressure to accept this more conventional plan (her own daughter in particular 'laying much to my Charge, for slighting such Providences'), Lead refused to leave the spiritual community and home of her choice. She and John Pordage became co-seekers and co-leaders of an alternative communal congregation, and their close friendship and spiritual partnership would last seventeen years.

The same year that Lead's husband died, she began keeping a diary of her spiritual revelations and attainments. Written over a period of sixteen years from 1670 to 1686, with gaps of weeks and sometimes months, the diary chronicles the progress of her inward life. One of Lead's spiritual fellows described the diary as consisting of 'loose papers, like the Sibylline leaves . . . penned for her own private memory and recollection' (Walton, *Notes*, 508). Lead's disciple credited Pordage with saving these scraps of paper, stating that Lead herself would not have done so (Walton, *Notes*, 202–3). While Lead's friends collected this material for nearly thirty years without publishing it, the diary was eventually published between 1696 and 1701 as *A Fountain of Gardens, Watered by the Rivers of Divine Pleasure and Springing Up in All the Variety of Spiritual Plants*. Consisting of three volumes, with volume three in two parts, this little-studied text totals more than 2,500 printed pages.

While John Pordage helped to collect and transcribe Jane Lead's spiritual diary, Lead helped to see Pordage's manuscripts into print. When Pordage died in 1681, Lead edited and published his *Theologia Mystica, or, The Mystic Divinite of the Aeternal*

[67] *A Fountain of Gardens, Watered by the Rivers of Divine Pleasure and Springing Up in All the Variety of Spiritual Plants*, vol. i (1696), 328.

Invisibles (1683). In a nine-page preface to this work, she provided a brief biography of Pordage and represented herself as the expert in his doctrine. Also after Pordage's death, Lead assumed leadership of their congregation and immediately began publishing her own works. From her earliest published work, a signed tract of forty pages titled *The Heavenly Cloud Now Breaking. The Lord Christ's Ascension Ladder sent down; to shew the way to reach the Ascension, Glorification, through the Death and Resurrection* (1681), Lead saw herself as spiritually privileged and as a leader. Her persona here and throughout her prolific writings is that of a 'Heavenly Spy', whose heavenly mandate it was 'to make report of those substantial, high, and worthy precious things, which I have seen and found in the Love-deep, and unmeasurable space of Eternity' (*Heavenly Cloud*, 39). For Lead, as for so many seventeenth-century prophets, the gift of vision was an indication of election, 'an injunction to the prophetic individual to accept responsibility for the public articulation of the divine *logos*, as part of a missionary or revolutionary programme'.[68] Having lived through the unprecedented upheaval of the Civil War period and Interregnum, Lead saw herself as an active observer and participant in a vast spiritual and political drama being played out on a national scale. Throughout her works, there is a sense of her revelations as a duty which she must discharge.

Between the publication of Lead's 1683 *The Revelation of Revelations, Particularly as an Essay Towards the Unsealing, Opening and Discovering The Seven Seals, the Seven Thunders, and the New-Jerusalem State* and her 'discovery' ten years later in a House of Charity in Stepney, little is known about her activities or whereabouts. In 1694, a fellow follower of Jacob Boehme, Loth Fischer of Utrecht, translated Lead's *Heavenly Cloud* into German, and from that point there was no looking back. At the age of 71, this elderly, nearly blind, 'Simple, and Unletter'd'[69] woman then living in an almshouse was catapulted into sudden fame. Her publications earned her a following among thriving theosophical movements on the Continent, and within three years she would find herself at the

---

[68] Christine Berg and Philippa Berry, 'Spiritual Whoredom: An Essay on Female Prophets in the Seventeenth Century', in Barker et al., eds., *1642: Literature and Power in the Seventeenth Century*, 37–54, 41.
[69] 'A Prefatory Epistle of the Editor', *A Revelation of the . . . Gospel-Message* (1697), a3^r.

centre of an international and local spiritual community called the Philadelphian Society.

After John Pordage, Lead's most important spiritual partner was Francis Lee (1661–1719), an Oxford theologian and non-juror who had left England to study medicine in the Netherlands. Lee first learned about Lead when he was in the Netherlands by reading her works in German. Urged by two separate sources to seek her out, he returned home to England in 1694, and discovered her living in Stepney, 'her cell lying at a little distance in the country, and in a House of Charity' (Walton, *Notes*, 226). This was the beginning of a new spiritual alliance for Lead and, crucially for her access to contemporary publishing institutions, the beginnings of a strong institutional base. Lee would inform his Oxford schoolfellow rector Richard Roach about Lead, and the two of them would become leading exponents of Lead's philosophy. For the next ten years, until her death in 1704, Lead would have two Oxford-educated scholars to help transcribe her visions, answer her growing correspondence, and see her prolific visions into print. In 1696, Francis Lee would even marry Lead's widowed daughter Barbara Walton, after this convenient idea was suggested to Lead in a vision.

During this period, Lead's 'friends multiplied on all sides, her low estate was turned as in a dream, and an invisible hand brought in supplies continually' (Walton, *Notes*, 509). Shortly after Lead's *Heavenly Cloud* was translated into German, one Baron Kniphausen, an administrator at the court of Frederick III, Elector of Brandenburg, read the work. Dazzled by her prophetic gift, Kniphausen sent money to enable Lead to move out of the House of Charity, and she and her daughter Barbara Walton took a little house in Hoxton Square in Shoreditch (Walton, *Notes*, 226). Kniphausen also paid Loth Fischer to translate Lead's other works as soon as they appeared, and from this point on her prolific writings were translated into German and Dutch almost as soon as they were published in English.[70] Together, Lead and her new friends would organize the Philadelphian Society (fl. 1694–1703). At the age of 71 this woman of 'low estate' became the spiritual leader of an illegal nonconformist sect.

---

[70] On the German Philadelphians, see Nils Thune, *The Behmenists and the Philadelphians* (Uppsala: Almquist and Wiksells, 1948) and Walker, *The Decline of Hell*.

In 1697 the Philadelphian Society decided to 'go public', imple-
menting a full-scale programme to impart Lead's mystical knowledge to a growing audience. Lead was already holding private
meetings in her house at Hoxton and becoming well known
abroad, but the Society decided to heighten these developments by
consciously cultivating what we might call multiple media publics.
By means of public meetings, manuscript correspondence, and a
steady stream of print publications, the Philadelphians sought to
consolidate and expand the membership of their sect. The
Philadelphians met privately at first, both at Lead's house in
Hoxton and at another private house in Baldwin's Gardens. But
according to Richard Roach, these meetings became so crowded
that the Society was forced to move to a bigger location. In particular, the 1697 publication of the inaugural issue of the Society's
journal *Theosophical Transactions* gave such an 'Alarm to the
world . . . that their Meeting at Baldwin's Gardens began to be
crowded with such Numbers that they were constrained to become
more Public' (Bod. MS Rawlinson D. 833, f. 83). The Society began
holding regular meetings at locations such as Hungerford Market,
Westmoreland House, and Lorimer's Hall.[71] These public meetings
drew a large audience of observers and participants, ranging from
'a sober sort of Company very attentive and inquisitive' to 'Boys
and . . . rude fellows' (Bod. MS Rawlinson D. 833, f. 53). Eventually, though, the open public meetings had to stop due to 'great
Opposition and Violence from ye rude Multitude' (Bod. MS
Rawlinson D. 833, ff. 65–6 and Roach, *Great Crisis* (1725), 36). As
she became older, Lead eventually became too ill to cope with large
crowds, and the group returned to small private meetings at Lead's
home ('afterwards settled at *Hoxton*, and finish'd their Public Testimony to the Kingdom there' (Roach, *Great Crisis*, 99)). Lead's
printed texts, then, were attempts not to 'cover herself' but rather
to communicate her already public speaking to a wider local and
international audience. And of course, as we have seen, Lead's
printed texts promised that 'Whoever . . . shall desire further Satisfaction in this Subject, the Author will readily Answer to such
Inquiring Minds, and Orally confer with them.'[72]

---

[71] [Richard Roach], *The Great Crisis: Or, The Mystery of the Times and Seasons
Unfolded* (1725), 99 and Bod. MS Rawlinson D. 833.
[72] *The Wonders of God's Creation Manifested, In the Variety of Eight Worlds: As
they were made known Experimentally to the Author* (1695), A3ᵛ.

Lead and Lee also worked to expand the Philadelphian Society by means of a steady stream of manuscript correspondence. The printed publications of the Society frequently refer to 'Letters continually coming from Forreign Parts', and observe that Lead had 'an Established Correspondency in most parts of Europe, relating to the Affairs of Religion'.[73] *Theosophical Transactions* also contains extracts from international manuscript letters. Indeed so heavy was Lead's correspondence that Lee's chief complaint concerning her 'cell' in the almshouse in Stepney was not that she was materially deprived but rather that the 'cell's' location made it 'altogether inconvenient for her constant correspondence abroad' (Walton, *Notes*, 226).

The third medium of Jane Lead's public preaching was print. In 1697, the Society published a series of keynote publications, beginning with their in-house journal *Theosophical Transactions By the Philadelphian Society, Consisting of Memoirs, Conferences, Letters, Dissertations, Inquiries, &c. For the Advancement of Piety and Divine Philosophy*. Between March and November, five issues of this serial were published, of which the first was seventy-two pages long. Anticipating the practice of some eighteenth-century journals, one of the chief purposes of *Theosophical Transactions* was to advertise Jane Lead's books. The journal provided a list of publications to date and announced forthcoming publications of interest to the journal's readers. Readers were made to feel part of a community even as they were cultivated as potential consumers. Other contents of specific journal issues range from extracts from contemporary publications (including Mary Astell's *Serious Proposal to the Ladies* (1694)) and letters from foreign correspondents to discussions of Jane Lead's diary and the Jewish cabbala. Like the Quakers, the Philadelphians consciously cultivated an international sectarian community by means of print. According to the editors of *Theosophical Transactions*, 'our design is to Publish many *Secret Memoirs* of the greatest Consequence' (1: 2).

In 1696, the Philadelphian Society undertook the major project of publishing Lead's sixteen-year diary of her spiritual attainments. The first of three volumes was printed in 1696, and five years later,

---

[73] *Wonders of God's Creation Manifested* (1695), a2ᵛ; *Theosophical Transactions*, 1: 1.

in 1701, the printing of the 2,500-page diary was complete. In the preface to the diary, Lead suggests that a private donor was responsible for financing this major project. She observed with some pride that a certain 'Worthy Person' had read some of her works and, 'having had a savour and Relish' of them, 'did make a generous offer, to have the Bank and Stock of what the Holy Unction had dropped in, brought forth into Manifestation' (*Fountain*, i. 3–4). Lead's diary would become the single most important text of the Philadelphian movement, discussed at length by local and international followers both in letters and in other printed publications. Also during this formative period, a series of three *Message[s] to the Philadelphian Society* by Lead were published (1696–8).

Despite the many hours she spent in the 'Heavenly Sphere', then, Jane Lead was not without a certain business acumen. The Philadelphians used each of their public media as a means of advertising; every new meeting, manuscript letter, or printed publication advertised past publications and those in progress. The printed records of Lead's oral communications were marketed locally and internationally—advertised in *Theosophical Transactions*, introduced by editorial prefaces, and puffed by devoted followers. The Society used Lead's name as a marketing tool, and so did Lead herself. Like a modern book jacket, the title page of Lead's early work *Revelation of Revelations* (1683) added to the work's prestige by providing the information that it was 'Published by *J. L.* the Author of the *Heavenly Cloud*, made mention of, particularly in the *Preparatory Epistle* to that late Theosophick Piece, Entituled, *Theologia Mystica*' (a work also edited by Lead). The title page of *Revelation* also proclaimed that there was a genuine need for the publication, as the biblical Revelation of St John had 'not hitherto so far been brought forth to light (except by the Spiritual Discerner [Lead]) to any degree of Satisfaction, as to the understanding of the grand Mystery'. The local distribution of this work was typical of the thoroughness with which even Lead's earliest works were marketed. The work was sold by Tace Sowle's father Andrew in Shoreditch, at the 'Book-sellers in *London* and *Westminster*', and by Lead herself 'at the Carpenters in *Bartholomew-Close*'.

As soon as Lead had built up a name for herself, she used it, even cross-referencing her publications in her own works. Indeed, by a certain point in her career Lead's name had acquired so much cultural capital that one entrepreneurial contemporary started to use it on works she did not write. Accordingly, the preface to Lead's 1696 *Message to the Philadelphian Society* states, 'Whereas some Things have been Scandalously set forth, and Printed under the Name of this Author to the Reproach of Truth, and the Dishonour of that which is Holy, it is thought fit for the putting a Stop to such Impostures, and the Evil which might thence ensue, to give a Catalogue of the *Books* which the Author hath hitherto Published.' From this point on, an increasingly lengthy annotated list of 'Books Written by J. Lead' was printed to accompany Lead's writings—establishing a form of proto-copyright over them and at the same time enabling them to be collected by the loyal.

To be most successfully marketed, though, Lead's theosophical mysticism had to be made palatable to the common reader. Several of Lead's communications were prefaced by editorial matter which attempted to explain, defend, and 'authorize' each work. The 'Subordinate Author' or scribe of *The Wonders of God's Creation Manifested, In the Variety of Eight Worlds; As they were made known Experimentally to the Author* (1695) assured readers that he was well aware that 'What is contained in this Treatise . . . will appear more than ordinarily Strange, to the greatest part of those who shall look upon it'. But if the Dutch and Germans were sending letters (and money) to the English author, the 'Subordinate Author' pointed out, surely the English should learn to appreciate Jane Lead's visions too:

The Acceptation which the former Books, that have through this Instrument been brought forth to the Light, have found Abroad in other Nations, since the setting forth of the *Heavenly Cloud*, and of the *Revelation of Revelations* in the High Dutch Tongue, is certainly greater than can have proceeded from any Dead, or Lifeless Testimony. To Relate how God has blessed them, and doth daily Bless them, as it appears from Letters continually coming from Forreign parts, would be to write an History. And if a Prophet be so much Esteemed in his own, as in another Country; this is no new thing. (*Wonders of God's Creation*, A2ᵛ)

As this passage suggests, the Society especially liked to advertise its international acclaim—as a means of enlarging its audience still further. In the preface to Lead's next work, *The Ark of Faith: or, A Supplement to the Tree of Faith, etc. For the Further Confirmation of the same. Together with A Discovery of the New World* (1696), the 'Subordinate Author' was similarly ambitious and cautious at the same time: 'It is hoped that this little Treatise, as well as the foregoing one, of which this is a Continuation, will not give Offence to any; but will afford matter of Joy and Comfort to very many, both in This, *and in several other Nations to whom they shall come*' (my emphasis). The editor added that 'it cannot but be reasonably expected that [God] will do Right to one [Lead] that is such an Eminent Asserter of [the Faith]'. And he promised that when 'the Great Diary of this Author, or as much as can be recovered of it, shall come to be Published', the progress of this life of faith and details of 'whatever else may conduce to its growth' would be infinitely more clear. The first volume of Lead's 'Great Diary' would be published the following year.

Through oral communications, manuscript correspondence, and a steady stream of print publications, the Philadelphian Society worked to consolidate their group across international, as well as local, boundaries. Partly as a result of these aggressive marketing strategies, Lead was one of precious few late Stuart women who could write with the knowledge that she was addressing an international audience. It must have been exhilarating to direct her visionary wisdom and advice 'to whomsoever this Treatise may come, whether, in this Nation, or in any more remote Places, where God is pleased to have it Published',[74] or to title another work *A Message to the Philadelphian Society, Whithersoever dispersed over the Whole Earth* (1696).

In assessing the social and political implications of prophetic writings such as Lead's, it is crucial to remember that our distinction between personal and public history is not one that Lead's seventeenth-century contemporaries would have understood. Michel Foucault has suggested that 'religious beliefs prepare a kind of landscape of images, an illusory milieu favorable to every hallucination and every delirium'.[75] Removed from their historical political contexts, the 'spiritual travels' of Jane Lead's nightly dreams may indeed seem like landscapes of madness or hallucination, or the unmediated products of unconscious drives. But visionary writings like Lead's are better understood as the product of a different mode of reading—the product of a different way of conceptualizing

---

[74] *Wonders of God's Creation Manifested* (1695), 95 (*sic; recte* 65).
[75] Michel Foucault, *Madness and Civilization: A History of Insanity in the Age of Reason*, trans. Richard Howard (New York: Random House-Vintage, 1988), 215.

the relationship between biblical, contemporary, and personal spiritual history. Like many ordinary men and women of her day, Lead read the Bible as a hermeneutic tool: a key to the events of her time. She 'read' her own nightly visions this way too, and published transcriptions of them as tools for her readers' interpretation of their own personal and collective spiritual and political lives.

For nonconformists such as the Philadelphians or the Quakers, especially, issues of spirituality were not private, personal matters, but public matters of urgent national importance, inseparable from problems of institutions and power. After the Restoration, the millenarian sects and radical reformists that Lead had encountered in her youth had been forced underground (although not silenced, as we have seen). Millenarian excitement had been tempered by fear, and the 'Holy People' of England, as Lead put it, had been 'scatter[ed] and divide[d]' by years of heightened persecution. Now, near the end of Lead's lifetime, the godly were 'scared and affrighted away from each other, upon poor, low, and worldly Circumstances; so as no Body of Saints can yet get together'.[76] Not surprisingly, having seen the outcome of the Civil War first hand, Lead concluded as her contemporary John Milton had done (and as William Blake would do 100 years later) that the most effective revolutions would be psychically based: 'great and wonderful Revolutions relating to the accomplishment of a full and perfect Redeemed State among Mortals' (*Tree of Faith*, 3–4).

But when Lead urged her readers to 'Dive into your own Celestiality, and see with what manner of spirits you are endued: for in them the powers do entirely lie for Transformation' (*Fountain*, ii. 170), she was not substituting psychology for politics, in keeping with the larger rejection of millenarianism for private salvation in her culture. When Lead's contemporary Mary Astell advised women to look within for sources of transformation, it was to a private, individual interiority different from Lead's collective one, and there is a sense in which Astell's empowering advice ultimately served to direct both her own and later women religious writers' focus away from public politics. After having published her own religio-political opinions for over a decade, Astell abandoned political writing in 1709, and for the last twenty years of her life

---

[76] *The Tree of Faith: or, The Tree of Life, Springing up in the Paradise of God* (1696), 7.

did not publish any new works.[77] As we will see in Chapter 4, in contrast to the more privatized and unified notion of the self already held by some of her contemporaries, Lead's interior 'Celestiality' was a 'Divine Chaos': a site bombarded with drives over which she had neither authority nor control. When Lead urged her readers to look within for sources of social transformation, she echoed traditional mystic wisdom and anticipated twentieth-century thinkers who have pointed to the role of the unconscious in historical change.

More simply, too, it is important to remember that Lead's activity as a spiritual authority in the public sphere—as the respected leader of a nonconformist sect, with two learned male scribes, a congregation of some 100 followers, and a continental, as well as local, audience—was itself a challenge to traditional modes of order (what we might call an inherently political act). At the end of Lead's 'Great Diary', Christ appears and prophesies of the Philadelphians, 'though the Beginning of this Gathering be few, and of those that are dispisable, poor, and indigent; yet of such shall be made the Jewels, which I will wear upon my Crown' (*A Fountain of Gardens*, vol. iii, pt. 2, 276). Lead was concerned with 'all Ranks, Orders, and Degrees of Persons, from the highest to the lowest' ('Epistle to the Reader', vol. iii, pt. 1, A2ʳ) and she herself had experienced what it meant to be 'dispisable, poor, and indigent'. With respect to her lack of formal education, even her loving son-in-law Francis Lee described her as 'a Person of no extraordinary Capacity or Learning . . . so far from being Extraordinary in the Eye of the World, as not to be at all Considerable . . . one that is Simple, and Unletter'd' ('A Prefatory Epistle of the Editor', *A Revelation of the . . . Gospel-Message* (1697), a3ʳ). In an age in which there was no strict separation between church and state, and the English monarch was also the head of the national church, the proposition that there was a mystical, as well as literal interpretation of Scripture, and that this was currently being revealed to an elderly woman living in an almshouse in Stepney, was threatening. Lead endured 'Opposition and Violence' not only from 'ye rude Multitude' and her own family, but also from eminent theologians. Yet despite the risks of her doctrines and lifestyle, she published her

---

[77] Astell did write a new preface to her *Bart'lemy Fair: Or An Inquiry after Wit* (1709) which was reprinted in 1722 (Ruth Perry, 'Mary Astell', in Todd, *Dictionary*, 33).

visions and dictates regularly for twenty years, even retailing her works herself at a time when many authors employed trade publishers to place an extra layer of 'cover' between themselves and the law. Lead's spiritual convictions enabled herself and some 'dispisable, poor, and indigent' men and women like her to reject the passive roles assigned to them by their society and to engage in purposeful activity on behalf of a revolution they believed they would finally win. In this sense, they had material force.

4

Metaphors of Being and Modes of Empowerment

From a twentieth-century perspective, the single most consistently startling aspect of late Stuart women's religio-political polemicism may well be these women's habit of addressing public political authorities in personal terms. Twenty-five years after the death of Charles II, Elinor James still remembered her infinite social superior as if he were her beloved friend. 'The King had a Divine Soul, for he never deny'd me any thing,' she recalled.[1] Elaine Hobby has attributed female polemicists' use of personal forms of address to a 'desire to dispense with class differences'.[2] This hypothesis works well in some cases, but it cannot explain the use of the same personal forms of address by women writers who were political conservatives. For a woman like Elinor James, 'a desire to dispense with class differences' was tantamount to questioning the will of God.

Despite their competing religio-political allegiances, Elinor James, Joan Whitrowe, Anne Docwra, and Jane Lead all shared a sense of collectivity and fundamental unity of purpose with the king and kingdom of England, and, paradoxically, saw this imagined 'unity' as authorizing their own oppositional, nonconformist, and otherwise subversive public voices. Political radical Joan Whitrowe despised many aspects of William and Mary's personal behaviour, and looked forward to the day when all 'the Priests and Rulers of this Generation' would be 'humbled in the dust'. Yet when Whitrowe saw King William in person, she exuded not so much a sceptical 'deference', as a strange sort of transporting *love*:

Another time, as I was going by Water, I met thee going to land at *Whitehall*, and our Boat standing still, I felt the power of GOD's Love so to thee, that it transported my Spirit into a Heavenly Joy; I was drawn forth

---

[1] Elinor James, *Mrs. James Prayer for the Queen and Parliament, and Kingdom too* (c.1710).
[2] Hobby, *Virtue of Necessity*, 41.

into Prayer, and these were some of the Words. . . . And so I departed in this holy Extasie, making my request to God for thee.[3]

While women such as Joan Whitrowe conceived of human interiority as social and essentially unsexed, several of their female contemporaries had already begun to see the self in distinctly more modern ways. Changing modes for the discursive representation of human interiority must not be confused with material social history, but in the following pages I would like to explore what I take to be their mutually constitutive relationship. In particular, I posit a distinct connection between what has been celebrated as the establishment of the gendered female subject in print by roughly 1700, and women's eventual disappearance as sources of spiritual authority in the public sphere. Focusing on these four female polemicists' notion of human identity as collective and essentially unsexed, I will outline ways in which these women's particular 'psychological circumstances' both enabled and shaped their literary production. Finally, I will suggest how changing ways of perceiving the female self in the eighteenth century changed what it was possible for different female groups to be and to do.

In seventeenth-century England, the individual was neither a pronounced political nor psychological reality. The family, rather than the individual, was the essential unit of government in church and state, and human beings were defined as much by their place in a network of social dependencies as by their own particular qualities of mind. As the individual was not a political concern, so neither was individual self-expression a paramount aesthetic concern. Quaker authors often wrote and published works collaboratively, and even their most personal autobiographical writings may be understood as having been 'collaboratively' produced, in that they followed highly formulaic patterns of expression shared by an entire community. Early female polemicists' sense of collective social being is mirrored in the form of their texts. While many of their public addresses are epistolary in nature (having clearly stated senders and addressees, and anticipating their readers' implicit rejoinders) 'sender' and 'addressee' are not 'self' and 'other' in the familiar modern sense. Rather, as I will show, they are aspects of

---

[3] Joan Whitrowe, *The Humble Address of the Widow Whitrow to King William: With a Faithful Warning to the Inhabitants of England* (1689), 4.

one collective self—members of one 'Body, and all the Members makes the Whole'.[4]

Though infinitely distant upon the chain of being, then, a woman like Joan Whitrowe conceived of herself as existing on the same subjective continuum as William and Mary. Her fundamental sense of unity even with sovereigns she disapproved of gave her the authority to address them in print, for she was speaking to other aspects of her social self—benevolently encouraging her fellow sinners to uphold their part of their larger mutual spiritual and social contract with God. 'And now, O KING, I am required to visit thee, and to lay before thee what the LORD requires of thee,' she explained in one 'humble address', as if she were about to present the King with a warrant. 'Seeing I intend nothing but what is good for the King and his People, I desire to have Liberty to ease my self of the burden which hath lain upon me many years, before thou camest into this Nation' (*Humble Address* (1689), 12, 9).

Jürgen Habermas and others have explained how Renaissance monarchy and lordship was constituted through 'representative publicness'—the habitual display of supposedly inherent spiritual power and dignity.[5] Kingship was something publicly represented through state rituals like the costly bonfires to which Whitrowe objected, or other public displays like the one she travelled far out of her way to attend. Somewhat less successfully than his predecessors, perhaps, William III attempted to represent himself as the embodiment of a higher power, and as inseparably 'connected' with his people. (Queen Anne's figural self-representation as a mother to her people springs to mind here as well.) Whitrowe was intensely sensitive to the vast inequalities within her society, yet she nevertheless went out of her way to deliver her pamphlets into the King's own hands. As we have seen, she recorded at least one face-to-face encounter as if the King's touch had endowed her papers with the authority of divine grace. This sense of essential unity of purpose with her sovereign despite the vast social disparity between them was a product of her notion of social and spiritual being. That

---

[4] Elinor James, *Mrs. JAMES's Vindication of the Church of England, In An Answer to a Pamphlet Entituled, A New Test of the Church of England's Loyalty* (1687), 5.

[5] See *The Structural Transformation of the Public Sphere*. For a study of royal spectacle and the theatrics of power in this period, see Paula R. Backscheider, *Spectacular Politics: Theatrical Power and Mass Culture in Early Modern England* (Baltimore: Johns Hopkins UP, 1993).

ideological notion, in turn, was in part a product of her rulers' conscious cultivation of representative publicness.

To an even greater degree than Joan Whitrowe, printer-author Elinor James saw herself as subject to the state and on a continuum with all the other elements of the kingdom. Her social identity was not a matter of choice; indeed it was not founded in subjectivity at all. James saw herself as born into a network of dependencies, and did not consciously differentiate herself from the other elements of that web. Her representation of the economic family in her *Mrs. James's Advice to all Printers in General* (*c*.1715) was a microcosmic version of her notion of the state. As we have seen in Chapter 1, however, James's idea of a well-ordered printing 'family' was anything but what *we* would call benevolent or paternalistic. Her relations with the members of her economic family emphasized above all 'the Excellency of Obedience'. What, then, are we to make of James's various outpourings to public figures and bodies of state, which can often be described as loving or 'motherly' in tone?

Upon the occasion of the impeachment of Dr Henry Sacheverell in 1709, James assured the 'Queen and Parliament, and Kingdom too' (and especially the gentlemen of the House of Commons) that 'my love to you has been sincere God knows, for no Mother could be more indulgent over her own Children than I have been over you: Nor any Mother Fasted and Prayed for her Natural Children as I have done for you; but now your Actions has wounded me' (*Mrs. James Prayer*). Addressing her vast social superiors, James nevertheless adopted a familar tone ('my love to you has been sincere') and intimate terms of address ('no Mother could be more indulgent over her own Children'). This is precisely the 'emotional cosiness' that E. P. Thompson so rightly warns us *against* assuming as a norm in later eighteenth-century society. James's representations of her visits to court do indeed suggest 'human warmth in a mutually assenting relationship' and 'a circle of loved, familiar faces'.[6] Her inset stories or 'set-pieces' of her visits to kings are in fact the most vivid, warmly depicted, and sometimes comic scenes in all of her works. James exuded an abstract but very real love for public figures such as Charles II, James II, and Henry Sacheverell

---

[6] E. P. Thompson, 'Eighteenth-Century English Society: Class Struggle without Class?', *Social History*, 3 (1978), 136. The phrase 'a circle of loved, familiar faces' is Thompson's quotation of Peter Laslett, *The World We Have Lost* (London: Methuen, 1965), 21.

('an Angel of the Church of God's Establish'd Worship'). And paradoxically, I suggest, it was precisely this lived emotion that gave her, a disenfranchised seventeenth-century tradeswoman, the psychological platform that she needed to *challenge* patriarchal models of order by participating in public affairs.[7]

As her passionate support for Dr Henry Sacheverell suggests, Elinor James routinely identified with the Church of England as well as the state. While she typically referred to the church with the feminine pronoun 'she', James also expressed her hope that the church would be 'more than a Conqueror' (*Mrs. JAMES's Vindication* (1687), 7). Her envisioning of the church as androgynous—at once a feminine 'she', and a masculine 'Conqueror'—was also, we will see, the way that she managed to think about herself. Like the other female polemicists considered here, James wrote about political issues at length, but did not explicitly include her own subordination under that heading. The vast bulk of these women's writings is in fact silent on the issue of sexual hierarchies and sex-based inequities of power. To quote their few scattered protofeminist remarks out of context is to risk misleading twentieth-century readers as to the overall nature of their works. To a significant extent, this chapter will show, James managed to cope with the increasingly formularized gender ideologies of her day by sheer figural avoidance. Representing herself in abstract symbolic terms as a mother or sister, she nevertheless rejected notions of gendered interiority—notions of feminine selfhood that would mean that she could not also identify with symbols of patriarchal authority or aggression. And until the end of their days, I suggest, James and other women like her actually freed themselves to act by their fluidly sexed 'metaphors of being'. To a limited extent, that is, they escaped the cage of gender without ever leaving it.

In her analysis of what she terms seventeenth-century 'Tory feminists'' 'ideology of the absolute self', Catherine Gallagher uses the writings of Margaret Cavendish and Mary Astell to illustrate her thesis that in late Stuart England, 'Toryism and feminism converge because the ideology of absolute monarchy provides, in particular historical situations, a transition to the ideology of the

---

[7] On 'the paradox of a rebellious traditional culture' (what I call subversive conservatism) see E. P. Thompson, *Customs in Common: Studies in Traditional Popular Culture* (New York: The New Press, 1993).

absolute self.'[8] Gallagher argues that Cavendish and Astell, the aristocratic and genteel contemporaries of the four women considered here, envisioned the female subject as 'isolated and complete unto herself' (27). Gallagher is one of many feminist critics who now hold up Mary Astell's protofeminist works as a prototype of the eighteenth-century 'feminization of the writing subject' (27). For late Stuart women such as Cavendish and Astell, 'the monarch becomes a figure for the self-enclosed, autonomous nature of any person' (26). Paradoxically 'what first appears to be an absolutism that would merely lead to the subjection of all individuals except the monarch' is for 'Tory feminists' 'the foundation for a subjectivity that would make its own absolute claims' (27).

Gallagher focuses solely on the writings of two élite or genteel women, and her thesis cannot explain the dramatically different beliefs of these women's more ordinary female contemporaries. Mary Astell, who never married, lived most of her adult life in genteel poverty, yet she was nevertheless the daughter of a wealthy coal merchant with connections to the landed gentry on both sides of her family. (She also had aristocratic friends.) The Duchess of Newcastle, meanwhile, spent many of her leisured days in circumstances so isolated and unencumbered that she 'began writing poetry to console herself'.[9] Our metaphors of consciousness are determined in part by our social being. While neither Astell nor Cavendish had any children, James, Whitrowe, and Lead all had children to care for—perhaps making them less likely to envision the self as autonomous and unique. If the Duchess of Newcastle envisioned every woman as 'isolated and complete unto herself', women like James, Docwra, Whitrowe, and Lead were less free of the network of dependencies—domestic, familial, and economic—that contributed to their own understanding of identity as social. If Cavendish conceived of herself as 'an absolute monarch without a country', Elinor James saw herself as a 'God Mother' to the City of London, a self-appointed diplomat for her kingdom, an adviser to

[8] Catherine Gallagher, 'Embracing the Absolute: The Politics of the Female Subject in Seventeenth-Century England', *Genders*, 1 (1988), 25. Gallagher's *Nobody's Story* considers the rhetoric of gendered feminine authorship in selected novels by five women writers (including Manley).

[9] Nancy Cotton, 'Margaret Cavendish, Duchess of Newcastle,' in Todd, *Dictionary*, 231.

her King, and as the 'sister and soul's well-wisher' of her journey-men 'brothers'. James's writings are rich in diverse modes of female political being—all imaginary, of course, but, like all metaphors, capable of structuring thought and action nevertheless. Had a woman like James ever been confronted with the 'ideology of the absolute self', such a model of subjectivity and political being would have entailed for her a devastating loss of a sense of socio-political connectedness and wholeness.

Mary Astell and Elinor James shared almost exactly the same religious and political allegiances and wrote at almost exactly the same time about many of the same issues, yet they had strikingly different concepts of self. Astell imagined the self as autonomous and unique and granted gender a far more central place in her thinking about human identity than did James—or Whitrowe, Docwra, or Lead.[10] While Astell wrote extensively about personal autonomy and subjective self-construction for women, Elinor James's writings are not gender-driven, and she appears to have identified with the Church of England and with members of the Stationers' Company rather than primarily with members of her sex. James wrote, 'Now journeymen, you are my brothers,' yet she never wrote, 'Now ladies, you are my sisters' (as Astell did in effect) or 'We Women' (as Cavendish did). Like Catherine Gallagher, Catherine Belsey has seen Mary Astell's works as a watershed example of changing notions of human identity. Astell's *Some Reflections upon Marriage* (1700) marks 'a change in the discursive position of women'. While the first edition of Astell's *Reflections* was published anonymously, and the voice in the text is ostensibly masculine, tell-tale third-person pronouns ('He wants one to man-age his family . . . one whom he can entirely govern') invite the reader to take up a new subject position not previously offered in discourse—a perspective that is 'feminine—and feminist'.[11]

Over the course of the eighteenth century in England, models of subjectivity and political subjecthood shifted, and notions of sexual difference were increasingly codified, dispersed through print, and

---

[10] This is not to say that Astell would have supported our modern 'individualism'. On the relationship between personal and political autonomy and social obligation in Astell, see Perry, 'Mary Astell and the Feminist Critique of Possessive Individualism'.

[11] Catherine Belsey, *The Subject of Tragedy: Identity and Difference in Renaissance Drama* (London: Methuen, 1985), 215–21. Specific quotes are from pp. 220 and 215–16.

consolidated across social boundaries. The term 'women' would become an increasingly homogenized construct: a new imaginary 'unity', like our polemicists' 'king and kingdom at large', and its meaning or implications increasingly consolidated across boundaries of religion, occupation, regional background, and even rank. A new identity was conferred upon women as a group, and one which came to appear 'natural', if not always freely chosen. In embracing and helping to shape the newly homogeneous identity and social roles conferred upon them by periodicals, conduct books, religious materials, novels, and other literary and cultural forms, eighteenth-century women conceded certain possibilities. The eighteenth-century acceptance and even encouragement of certain kinds of female public speech was predicated on new models of the self and of the relation between the family and the state: models that figuratively positioned women outside the realm of paid economic activity and political affairs. To complicate our picture of the more immediate consequences for eighteenth-century women, of their coming to a new sense of themselves not as 'Members of the Body of the Nation' but rather as gendered individuals in an increasingly secular society, let us consider these four female polemicists' own notions of the self as social, collective, and essentially unsexed, and the ways that their own different metaphors of being helped to shape their participation in public politics.

Exiled or apostate Quaker Joan Whitrowe was far more aggressively isolated from various networks of social dependencies than any of the other female polemicists to be considered here. Yet even she felt a sense of collectivity with 'the Church and People of England', and addressed them in the second person, as she did the King and Queen. Declaring herself to be 'in the Universal Love of GOD to all Mankind, without Respect to Persons, Sects or Opinions', Whitrowe informed 'all sorts and Sects' how heavily her physical body bore the weight of *their* sins: 'I am to acquaint you, that the last Lord Mayors Day I bore a heavy burden for your *Feasting*.'[12] When the social body was collective, the righteous bore the burden of the nation's infirmities, and fasted for the people's collective salvation. 'Thus far I am clear of your Blood by performing my Service to GOD, and my Duty to my Neighbors, whom I

[12] Joan Whitrowe, *Faithful Warnings*, Preface, a1ʳ; *Humble Address* (1689), 14.

desire the welfare of as my own soul,' Whitrowe explained with a certain magnanimity of spirit. She signed this particular address to the kingdom 'Your Friend, ready to serve you to the utmost of my Power according to the Will of GOD. | J. Whitrowe' (*Humble Address*, 14).

Whitrowe realized that those who were guilty of the abuses she advertised would 'cast a Stone at me, as they did at the faithful Servants of the LORD of old'. But she resolved that 'I must take my Lot among those blessed Ones, though unworthy; but I will get me into the secret of His Pavilion, under the Shadow of the Almighty, where I shall be hid from the strife of Tongues' (*Humble Address* (1689), 8–9). Given what we know about the widespread public persecution of Quakers and other nonconformists, it is possible that Whitrowe's 'cast a Stone at me' is not entirely figurative. Whitrowe's sense of collectivity or kinship with historical and biblical communities, then, is all the more remarkable. What were some of the material and political implications of this way of conceiving self and society for this marginalized and increasingly isolated woman? Among others, modern individualism and the ethics of property were a contagious infection, spread throughout the 'body' of the nation by the ruling classes. For 'what can be expected when the Priests and Rulers of Nations or Kingdoms are so corrupted with By-Ends and Self-Respects, but that the People should be infected with the same pestilential Disease[?]' (*Widow Whiterows Humble Thanksgiving* (1694), 12).

Whitrowe outlived her husband and children, and became a preacher and polemicist after their deaths. She tried to go about 'doing Good, visiting the Sick, and relieving the Poor' while she still had a family to care for, but it was obviously difficult for her, and there is evidence to suggest that her husband did not approve of her activities. While the majority of Whitrowe's pamphlets focus on national political issues, one early co-authored pamphlet provides a glimpse of a difficult family life. Collectively written by Joan Whitrowe and other Quaker women, and including a brief preface signed by Whitrowe's husband Robert, *The Work of God in a Dying Maid: Being a short Account of the Dealings of the Lord with one Susannah Whitrow* (1677) reconstructs Whitrowe's daughter's deathbed performance as an alliance between mother and daughter. Susannah Whitrowe's deathbed 'dealings' include much praise for her mother, noting in particular the suffering caused her by her 'Evil' father:

'Oh, my bowed down and broken-hearted Mother! What has been thy Sufferings in this Family! Oh! how has thou been oppressed with our Iniquities? . . . how often has thou told my Father, The Lord would visit him with sore and grievous Judgment if he did not Repent, and turn from the Evil of his Ways?' (16–17)

As we have seen in Chapter 3, Quaker leaders disapproved of what they saw as Joan Whitrowe's excessive sense of self in this pamphlet, and ordered that 'what is chiefly to her own praise be left out' (MMM, vol. i, 30 July 1677). Twelve years later, in another pamphlet written after she had separated from the Quakers, Whitrowe recalled God's grace in saving her family during the devastation of the Great Plague—only to take her 'dear Children' and 'evil' husband to himself a few years later. More than a decade after the deaths of her children, Joan Whitrowe still blamed those deaths on her husband Robert Whitrowe's sins:

It pleased the LORD to preserve me and mine, at that Time, and for many years after, until it pleased Him to prepare my dear Children for Himself, and then he took them out of all the Snares and Temptations of this sinful Life. . . . Then I enquired of the LORD why He took them away in their youth; and He said, *Because* of their Father's evil Life.

The death of Robert Whitrowe, Joan Whitrowe believed, freed her to pursue salvation unencumbered by wifely duties. God took away her sinful husband in order to deliver her to his own calling: 'in order for my deliverance to the Work he had called me to' (*Humble Address* (1689), 11). Whitrowe did not mention the 'evil' father of her children ever again in all of her extant works.

    With the exception of this early co-authored pamphlet, Whitrowe only rarely alluded to her subjected status as a woman, and even then only when addressing a monarch. She advised William III to 'take this counsel, though from a Woman (the Lord is no respector of Persons)'.[13] Whitrowe saw herself as an Old Testament prophet-scourge and was more likely to compare herself to Moses, Habakkuk, Isaiah, or other patriarchs than to early female supporters of the church. In her *Faithful Warnings, Expostulations and Exhortations, To The several Professors of Christianity in England, as well as those of the Highest as the Lowest Quality* (1697) she modelled herself after the biblical David— farmer's son, boy hero, and military leader who eventually became

[13] Joan Whitrowe, *The Humble Salutation and Faithful Greeting of the Widow Whitrowe to King William* (1690), 14.

king of all Israel. As David eventually won King Saul's trust and was taken into his court, so Whitrowe prayed of her religio-political polemicism and preaching, 'Oh! that I might be so happy to prevail with the King and his Parliament, to try this way of winning the People of this Land.' While Whitrowe did address one pamphlet specifically to Queen Mary, this pamphlet differs little from the papers she addressed to King William or to William and Mary as joint monarchs. Whitrowe addressed Queen Mary as a sovereign rather than as a fellow woman, and demonstrated no great solidarity with Mary or any other aristocratic lady when she commanded them, 'ye Women that are of Ease, be astonished, pluck off your Gorgious Attire, put on Sackcloth, and cover your Head with Ashes, and sit on the Ground; and from thence, take up a deep and heavy Lamentation for the miseries that are coming upon you'.[14]

On one occasion, Whitrowe did find it necessary to scour her memory for female, rather than male, models of religio-political activism. Like all of the female polemicists discussed here, Whitrowe was forced to defend her authorship against the accusations of persons unable to believe that a woman could 'write these Books' without the assistance of a man. Accordingly, she recalled '*Mary Magdalen*, and the other *Mary*', '*Lidia*', '*Deborah* the Prophetess', '*Jael*', and '*Huldah*, the Prophetess' and several other biblical examples of women's public speaking, and proclaimed:

> Whereas it is thought by some that are strangers to me and my Writings, that a Woman did not write these Books which I have put forth, but, at least say, that I have the help of some Man, give GOD the Glory, *Jone Whitrow* writ every Word, I poor nothing unworthy Creature wrote it, I cannot say whether a Word might be mispelt and mended, but otherways my Hands writ them (and can produce many Witnesses that saw me write them) and I had no help, but the help of the LORD. (*Widow Whiterow's Humble Thanksgiving* (1694), 37)

In the same year as Elinor James, Joan Whitrowe also used the biblical example of Balaam's ass to justify her own untutored speaking. As James had urged her own sceptical readers to 'Let me be like Balaam's Ass, to turn away a Curse' (*Mrs. JAME's Apology* (*c*.1694)), so Whitrowe queried 'why should it be thought incredible for a Woman to write truth, any more than a Man? . . . Is not

---

[14] Joan Whitrowe, *To Queen Mary: The Humble Salutation, and Faithful Greeting of the Widow Whitrowe. With a Warning to the Rulers of the Earth* (1690), 9.

he [God] able to open the Mouth of an Ass?' (38). If the Lord could use a donkey to mediate his divine messages, why could he not also use a woman? By citing this humble example of biblical precedent for miracles, and offering to provide witnesses who could swear that she possessed the technology of writing, Joan Whitrowe sought to assure her readers that the Lord frequently 'made use of Women, as well as Men' (38). Whitrowe thought of herself in masculine and feminine terms interchangeably. In the majority of her pamphlets she managed largely to ignore her subjected status as a woman—at least until one of her opponents used her sex against her as a weapon.

As Phyllis Mack and others have suggested, for Quakers such as Anne Docwra the 'ideology of the absolute self' would have been absolute anathema. Quaker writings were collaboratively published and even authored, and, as we have seen in the case of Joan Whitrowe, too much 'self' in these writings was subject to internal censorship by the Friends. For Docwra, 'Community' was first the fellowship of the Quakers, but, beyond that, this vocal social critic was empowered by a sense of mutual welfare even with her fellow sinners in the English government. Docwra believed that it was her obligation to chastise political and religious leaders in print: 'It is a Duty incumbent with every true *Christian*, to show those that they love, their Mistakes.'[15] While Docwra rejected the notion of a national church of which all English subjects were automatically members, she nevertheless claimed a deeper, extra-political unity even with those public officials who had distrained her goods. 'I have no Enmity in my Heart against any of them, but do desire well for them: Gods love is Universal to Mankind . . . I heartily wish that they would understand and practise this, it would soon put an end to Differences in Religion' (*Looking-Glass*, 8). She repeatedly warned religio-political leaders that moral choices would have sociopolitical consequences—consequences which would affect 'this Land of our Nativity' as a collective body. Haunting her readers with the still-vivid spectre of the civil wars, she threatened, 'They that have true love to King and his Government, must mannage his business in Truth and Righteousness, for if they do otherwise . . .

[15] Anne Docwra, *A Looking-Glass for the Recorder and Justices of the Peace, and Grand Juries for the Town and County of Cambridge* (1682), 8.

there is a Fire kindled in this Nation that burns secretly, which will break forth into Flames' (8). Religious oppression would ultimately affect everyone in England regardless of religio-political views: 'make all things run on heaps again, as it hath done formerly, so that all Parties may be Sufferers for a Time' (8–9).

Unlike Whitrowe, Lead, or James, Anne Docwra did argue explicitly against restrictions on women's public preaching and prophecy. In *An Epistle of Love and Good Advice to My Old Friends and Fellow-Sufferers in the Late Times* (1683) she stressed that the 'Light, Power and Spirit of the Lord God is tendred to all Mankind, as well Women as Men', and pointed to specific women who worked in support of the early church. Challenging the injunctions of St Paul, she argued that those Scriptures which enjoined silence upon women referred to temporary, local conditions, and furthermore, that God had specifically declared that he would make use of women's speech.[16] She aggressively quoted several passages of Scripture favoured by early modern women writers, such as Galatians 3: 28 ('There is neither Jew nor Greek, there is neither bond nor free, there is neither male nor female: for ye are all one in Christ Jesus'). And she concluded as we will, that 'Much more might be said in this case which I do forbear, this being sufficient' (3).

Docwra did not conceive of human consciousness as fundamentally gendered. She did not distinguish herself from her male opponents on the basis of her sex, and, more surprisingly, for the most part neither did they. Francis Bugg did not assume that Anne Docwra's sex was inherently a stroke against her, invalidating her authority in the public sphere. No matter how violent Bugg's detractions, only rarely are they gender-exclusive. By comparing the rhetorical strategies available to Francis Bugg in the 1690s with those available to critics of women's political writing in the 1790s, one quickly detects fundamental eighteenth-century transformations in assumptions about 'women's nature'—and begins to sense the implications of those transformations for women who continued to work publicly for political and social reform.

---

[16] Like so many other female polemicists and preachers, Docwra quoted Acts 2: 17–18 by heart: '17. And it shall come to pass in the last days, saith God, I will pour out of my Spirit upon all flesh: and your sons and your daughters shall prophesy, and your young men shall see visions, and your old men shall dream dreams: 18. And on my servants and on my handmaidens I will pour out in those days of my Spirit; and they shall prophesy.'

Bugg did not routinely invoke absolute categories pertaining to sex to delimit Anne Docwra's activities, condemning women's public speech as inherently 'unwomanly'. In fact, Bugg was not particularly hostile to women's religio-political polemicism and preaching as such. He agreed that there was divine sanction for women's public activity in support of the church, and in one instance held up the biblical example of Esther as a positive example of 'Boldness' in a woman: 'But as to Boldness, it is sometimes commendable, and sometimes not; there is a modest Boldness, and an impudent Boldness. Esther was a bold courageous Woman, a Woman that did venture her Life for the Church's sake. . . . But there is a Boldness which the Wicked are too much affected with.'[17] Bugg attacked Anne Docwra as a lying *Quaker*. He called her crackbrained, crazy, dishonest, and old, but these charges are not gender-specific—and in fact, Docwra had employed many of these same insults against Bugg first. Bugg remarked, for example, that 'I cannot but take notice how frequent it is with this old Woman to expose me as distracted, shatter-brain'd' (*Seasonable Caveat*, 60). Incensed by the fact that Docwra had represented him as 'a poor indigent Person',[18] he set out to prove that it was a 'grand Lie' (*Jezebel Withstood*, 1). Furthermore, Docwra was at least as capable of defending herself against Bugg as he was against her. In response to Bugg's denigration of her as 'this crazy old piece, which is now creeping into Unity with the Quakers', this 76-year-old woman defiantly declared:

I have not only been in Unity, but in Community with them, above thirty-six Years, even those *F. Bugg* calls *G. Fox*'s Party, which are the most stedfast and real Quakers, so called, and am not so crazy as he reports me: Although I am entred into the seventy-six Year of my Age, yet, through Mercy, I can walk the Streets to visit the Sick, and my Friends and Relations also, and can see without Spectacles still, to read *F. Bugg*'s Lyes and Deceit, he hath used to cheat the *Clergy* of their Money. (*Second Part of an Apostate-Conscience Exposed*, 40 (*recte* 16))

Bugg, on the other hand, rather feebly responded to Docwra's charges by providing the names of persons who could testify that he was not 'distracted'.

---

[17] Francis Bugg, *A Seasonable Caveat Against the Prevalency of Quakerism* (1701), 58.

[18] Francis Bugg, *Jezebel Withstood, and Her Daughter Anne Docwra, Publickly Reprov'd; For Her Lies and Lightness in Her Book, stiled An Apostate Conscience &c.* (1699), 1.

To modern readers, Bugg's *Jezebel Withstood, and Her Daughter Anne Docwra, Publickly Reprov'd* might appear to be a gender-specific, *ad feminam* attack on Docwra as a woman writer. In the context of seventeenth-century Quaker debate, however, this is not necessarily the case. Quakers referred to male as well as female enemies of the faith as 'Jezebels', and so did apostate Quaker Francis Bugg. Another of Bugg's books, for example, castigated the entire Quaker community as *The Painted Harlot Stript and Whipt*. As Phyllis Mack explains, 'Quakers lived and proselytized in a society where the language of social roles and moral values was completely gendered. . . . In such an atmosphere, speaking and writing in a culture where one strove to be at least partially at home, it would have been impossible to communicate . . . and avoid using the language of masculine and feminine.'[19] As members of a persecuted nonconformist group proselytizing in a culture where 'Womanhood' was popularly understood to be a negative abstraction, Quaker women actually used this seemingly disabling world view in their own interests (and in so doing, one suspects, partially deflected its power over themselves). Quaker women held on to the popular, negative meaning of the abstract concept 'woman' and used it against their enemies—while simultaneously rejecting the concept's individual descriptive implications for themselves. Bugg's linking of Docwra to the powerful Jezebel, queen of Israel, was more likely to have been intended to place her and the whole Quaker cabal in a polemical tradition as enemies to the Protestant faith, than to have slandered Docwra in particular as a whore, or to have argued against women's right to speak in public. Similarly, when Bugg urged Quaker leader George Whitehead to 'turn this She-goat out of their Heard, unless she'll bear a Faggot, &c' (*Jezebel Withstood*, 8) he was not necessarily drawing on the popular association of goats and lechery—and so suggesting that Docwra herself was sexually 'monstrous', as Horace Walpole would do later in the eighteenth century when he referred to Mary Wollstonecraft as a 'hyena in petticoats'. Rather, the goat was also associated with the devil, and Bugg was implying that Quakers were members of the devil's party. The following year, for example, Bugg commented on one of Docwra's own statements, 'Here the Cloven Foot appears, though Disguised; for Malice and Hypocrisy

---

[19] See Phyllis Mack, 'Gender and Spirituality in Early English Quakerism, 1650–1665', 39. See also Mack, *Visionary Women*.

walk Hand in Hand, under a Quaker-Bonnet' (*William Penn, The Pretended Quaker*, 15).

Francis Bugg could not simply condemn Anne Docwra as unwomanly and expect to win his case, for the implications of the term were not yet fixed—not yet consolidated across boundaries of faith and class. Accordingly he was forced to defame his female polemical opponent in several more trivial and ultimately less effective ways. Docwra wrote most of her works when she was in her seventies, and, not too surprisingly, Bugg frequently tried to invalidate her arguments on the basis of her age. He declared that he would first reveal Docwra's lies, 'then leave the old Woman with her incoherent Fables' (*Jezebel Withstood*, 1). And he concluded after another particularly venomous set of insults, 'But to the matter, else I shall exceed my Half Sheet, which I am willing to winde up this old Woman in' (*Jezebel Withstood*, 4). He routinely referred to Docwra as 'a notorious Liar' (*Jezebel Withstood*, 4) or as 'this old Dissembling Hypocrite, *Ann Docwra*'. And in one instance he appealed to the reader: 'Now, Reader, Had not this Woman a ---- Forehead well Enlaid with Impudence, how dare she appear in Print with such bare Fac'd Lyes?' (*William Penn, The Pretended Quaker*, 10). Both Bugg and Docwra sought to discredit one another's birth and background. Bugg claimed of Docwra that her grandfather was 'fed in his Tenants Barn' (*Seasonable Caveat*, 57–8) and mocked, 'Oh, Cousin *Docwra*, for shame Cover thy Face; wear a Vail, and sit down and mourn for thy Sins . . . Remember *Cherry-Hynton*, thy former place of Abode' (*William Penn, The Pretended Quaker*, 11). He called her 'Proud', 'Haughty', 'Envious', 'Venomous', 'Infamous', 'Crazy', 'Crack-brained', and more. And when all of these failed, he descended to the merely disgusting: 'I thought I had done, when I shewed in *Jezebel Withstood* how this Woman wheels about; and to creep in their Unity, is become Scandalous, in her now writing, and with them turns and licks up her old Vomit, which she spued forth many years since, and when a *Quaker* too.'[20]

One hundred years later in England, opponents of women's public expression would be able to invoke widely disseminated, absolute categories of femininity and masculinity to advance their arguments. When the Reverend Richard Polwhele wished to

---

[20] Francis Bugg, *The Christian Ministry . . . Distinguished* (1699), 6.

invalidate Mary Wollstonecraft's political polemicism in 1798, for instance, he had only to represent her as a freak of nature—and did so to popular applause in his attack on women political writers in *The Unsex'd Females*.[21] If Anne Docwra had written in the 1790s rather than the 1690s, Francis Bugg might have used the newly crystallized ideology of middle-class motherhood against her— warning her to mind her domestic responsibilities if she were a mother, or hinting that her barrenness was a function of her freak- ish 'unwomanliness' if she were not. The Reverend Polwhele im- plied that Mary Wollstonecraft's 'unwomanliness' was responsible for her difficulties in childbirth, and represented her death shortly thereafter as a meaningful emblem in which he detected the 'Hand of Providence'. In the late seventeenth century, by way of contrast, it never occurred to Docwra's harshest critic that her reproductive status was relevant to her religio-political arguments. No matter how outrageously rude (and imaginative) his insults, Bugg never once implied that Docwra was a bad wife or mother, or that by not being a mother she had failed in her essential duty as a woman. Similarly, while Polwhele immortalized Wollstonecraft as 'the Arch-Priestess of female libertinism', and attacked her on the basis of her sexuality as much as her politics (*Unsex'd Females*, 29 n., 20 n.), Docwra escaped this gendered line of attack with only an occasional conventional comparison to Jezebel. Mary Wollstonecraft's political polemics were far more eloquently and powerfully argued than Anne Docwra's. Ironically, however, be- cause notions of subjectivity had shifted and conventions of accept- able female behaviour had narrowed by the 1790s, Mary Wollstonecraft's opponents did not have to work nearly as hard as Docwra's opponents did to invalidate her arguments in the eyes of her contemporaries.

Like most seventeenth-century prophets, Jane Lead considered her- self to be a mere physical bodily channel for the communication of divine understanding.[22] The Apocalyptic Virgin Wisdom, God's mediator, would communicate with her by means of unconscious drives, 'the which Command for Publication I must obey, and all her Rules and Methods observe':

[21] Richard Polwhele, *The Unsex'd Females: A Poem*, 1798, rpt. ed. and intro. Gina Luria (New York: Garland, 1974).
[22] See above, p. 2 n. 3.

I did not know when I published my two last Treatises, that of the *Enochian Life* [1694], and the other of the *Paradisical Laws* [1695], that my God would ever have had made use of me any more in this kind; the Day of my Life being so far spent, and growing to its evening Rest. But my Lord doth still follow me with fresh Revelations, and Inkindlings from his own immense Deep, which runs as a Fiery Stream through me, so that I find there is no resisting this all-driving Power; by which hidden and unknown Worlds must be made manifest in this Last Age of Times. (*Wonders of God's Creation* (1695), 30–1, 7–8)

Lead viewed her mortal body as a 'rotten sack, or sack of corruption'.[23] She did not like to be referred to as a 'prophetess', for 'God was wont to be very jealous of his glory', and the term was 'by no means safe'. Yet she clearly considered her mortal body to be the sacred site of divine happenings, and according to a fellow member of the Philadelphian Society 'was deeply grieved when any came to her with undue reverence'.[24]

While liberal humanism proclaims the existence of a unified self, 'the inalienable and unalterable property of the individual',[25] Jane Lead saw human interiority as fluid and unfixed. As a prophet, she was not a liberal humanist subject, an 'author' of meaning and action. Rather, she was a configuration of states of being—a space across which psychic impulses flowed, 'Inkindlings' from an immense deep. She was part of a social and spiritual collectivity which could only be expressed symbolically, and her understanding of human interiority as collective and essentially unsexed was reflected in the fluidity of her imagery. Traversed by unconscious drives—'fiery streams' of Wisdom's brightness—she dreamed of unmeasured spaces, waters, fountains, and an alternative spiritual community to be achieved in part by her own call to 'Philadelphians all over the Earth'. Lead's language of the body was a call to psychic action—the product of a philosophy which held that the first step in obtaining power was learning to envision it. As Wisdom commands:

Behold! I am at hand to do as great and mighty Works as ye are able to receive. So will I imprint not only the Image of Purity, but of Power upon you, that so ye may full out be made Partakers of my Profession. . . . For in my Calling it is [not] only requisite to have Light and Understanding

---

[23] Dr Wms MS 186.18 (1) c.
[24] Ibid.
[25] Belsey, *The Subject of Tragedy*, 34.

. . . but Strength and Might. . . . Now before ye can Proficients and Practitioners in all things answerable to your President herein be; ye must come to be strong, and find ability to turn about that which moveth the Creating Word by which all lost dominion may be renewed.[26]

Lead's visionary philosophy might seem millenarian or idealist today, but there is no question that to her mind it had material consequences. Attended by an 'Illustrious Troop of Heroins Divine I Celestial Amazons; untaught to yield',[27] Lead's 'Eternal Virgin Wisdom' was the self-contained mother and mate of Christ—who in turn gave Lead the 'Munition-strength' to print her works for an international audience: 'I should not have rendred my self publick: *For every Woman [that prayeth or prophesieth with her head uncovered] dishonoureth her Head. I Cor. 11. 5.* But Christ being my Head-covering I have both Commission, and Munition-strength, upon which I shall proceed, and go forward.'[28]

Francis Lee explained how his spiritual adviser (Lead) first came into contact with the female spiritual principle she called 'my Tuteress the Supream Wisdom': 'To a certain Person, that for many Years had been led wonderfully in the Ways of God, it came to pass that one day upon a deep Contemplation of the Paradisical World, there appear'd in the midst of a most bright Cloud, a Woman of a most Sweet and Majestick Countenance.'[29] As in so much Christian and Jewish thought, so in Lead's philosophy, Wisdom or 'Sophia' is a figure of great power, complexity, and importance. Lead's model is indebted not only to biblical precedents such as the personification of Wisdom in Proverbs and the 'woman clothed with the sun'

---

[26] Jane Lead, *The Ark of Faith: or, A Supplement to the Tree of Faith. Together with a Discovery of the New World* (1696), 23–4.

[27] [Richard Roach], 'Solomon's Porch', prefatory poem to Jane Lead's *Fountain of Gardens* (1697), vol. i, n.p.

[28] Jane Lead, *The Enochian Walks with God, Found out by a Spiritual-Traveller* (1694), 'An Introduction,' A2–A3.

[29] Jane Lead, *The Tree of Faith: or, The Tree of Life, Springing up in the Paradise of God; From which All the Wonders of the New Creation, in the Virgin Church of the First-Born of Wisdom must proceed* (1696), 79; Francis Lee, preface to Jane Lead, *The Laws of Pardise, Given forth by Wisdom to a Translated Spirit* (1695). In her 'Great Diary', Lead represented her first encounter with Wisdom as taking place two months after her husband's death. William Lead died in February 1670, and by April Jane Lead had entered into a new phase of spiritual accomplishment. For the next thirty-four years she produced an almost unceasing stream of mystical writings. Married for nearly thirty years, she referred to her husband only a few times in these writings, once as 'that First Husband who so long hindered my Marriage with the Lamb' (*Fountain of Gardens*, i. 71).

in Revelation, but also to the theosophy of Jacob Boehme. Boehme ascribed to the divinity fluid and interchangeable attributes of masculine and feminine, and in his works drew no clear dividing line between Wisdom and God. By insisting on the androgynous nature of the deity, Boehme 'made himself vulnerable to charges of heresy', and similarly Lead's Wisdom is 'dangerously near to push-ing her way into the Trinity'.[30] In the writings of both authors Sophia plays a greater role than does Jesus Christ.

In contrast with what Catherine Gallagher calls seventeenth-century 'Tory feminists'' 'ideology of the absolute self', Jane Lead urged her followers to enter 'into a Self-Annihilation, so as a Nothing to be, with reference to the Creaturely Being, that the All-Deistick Unction may arise as an overflowing Tide' (*Fountain of Gardens*, 1: 14). While the Philadelphians were currently 'Scatter'd and dispers'd throughout all Kingdoms and Nations', they would ultimately be 'gathr'd into one Unity of Spirit, as Baptized into the Fiery Pool of Love' (*Living Funeral Testimony* (1702), sig. A1). Lead's emphasis on the collective had material personal, as well as political implications, and it also represented a challenge to Church of England doctrine. Her desire for spiritual community may have influenced her style of living, for from the time that she moved into the Pordage household in the 1670s all of her domestic arrange-ments were communal. John and Mary Pordages' own mentor, Abiezer Coppe (1619–72), was known for his insistence upon the extinction of private property, and the Philadelphians agreed that there 'must be no Self-Appropriation; the very Root of Self must be removed: for the Blessings of the Kingdom are not to be enjoyed in Propriety, but in Community' (Jane Lead, *Signs of the Times*, Prefatory Epistle). The Philadelphian temple would be built up not by private property and material gain, but 'by LOVE . . . to God, and to each other; as *true Members of the same Body*' (*Signs of the Times* (1699), A2r; my emphasis).

While Lead did not see her doctrine or practices as a social or political threat of any kind, she and her supporters were forced to defend themselves against accusations of political radicalism. The Philadelphians insisted that they were not 'for turning the World

---

[30] Andrew Weeks, *Boehme: An Intellectual Biography of the Seventeenth-Century Philosopher and Mystic* (Albany: State U. of New York P., 1991), 121; D. P. Walker, *The Decline of Hell: Seventeenth-Century Discussions of Eternal Torment* (U. of Chicago P., 1964), 229.

upside down, as some have Represented 'em', and stressed that they were 'not Enemies to the Civil or Ecclesiastical Rights of Any' (*State of the Philadelphian Society* (1697), 8–9). But in insisting that they believed in 'Civil or Ecclesiastical Rights' for all, the Philadelphians actually supported the arguments of those who would see them as a threat. At a time when the church and state were not distinct institutions, and an English monarch was removed from his throne ostensibly on the basis of his Catholicism, English subjects were not supposed to believe in total freedom of worship.

In general, the Philadelphians saw the established church as one in which 'all the Extraordinary Stirrings of the Divine Spirit are too generally Slighted' (*Wars of David*, sig. A3ʳ). Like the Quakers, they rejected formal worship and a rigorous reliance on Scripture as injurious to the growth of wisdom and the inner light. While several of Lead's beliefs provoked objections from eminent theologians ('Persons . . . not set quite free from the Traditions of Men' (*Wars of David* (1700), A3)), the most threatening of those beliefs appears to have been her doctrine of universal salvation. Francis Lee was forced to defend Lead at length against scholar and theologian Henry Dodwell, who was especially alarmed by her 'pernicious' notions concerning hell.[31] Lead was convinced that hell torments were not eternal, and that even the 'Final Restitution of the [bad] Angels is not Impossible to God'.[32] Dodwell and others held the notion of universal redemption to be a dangerous doctrine in a 'licentious age'.[33] Paradoxically, if the Philadelphians were theological 'radicals' in anything, to some of their contemporaries it was in their doctrine of limitless divine power and love.

The emphases on androgyny and collectivity in the Philadelphian philosophy may help to explain Lead's anomalous status as the acknowledged leader of a London sect, and, more generally, as a female spiritual authority in the public sphere. These emphases appear to have encouraged broadly 'feminist' attitudes among her followers; Lead's most ardent supporters included men like John Pordage, Francis Lee, and Richard Roach, and the in-house journal of the Philadelphian Society contains what must be one of the first

[31] Walton, *Notes and Materials*, 193.
[32] *A Revelation of the Everlasting Gospel-Message* (1697), Table of Contents p. A3ʳ, description of contents of ch. 19. See also *The Enochian* (1694). Lead's doctrine of universal salvation was one of the key points where her philosophy differed from Jacob Boehme's.
[33] Walton, *Notes and Materials*, 193.

reviews of Mary Astell's protofeminist pamphlet *A Serious Proposal to the Ladies* (1694). Of Astell's proposal for a women's community or college, the editor of *Theosophical Transactions* uncompromisingly declares: 'Among all the Designs for the Publick Good that have been Propos'd these many Years, there is . . . none of them All [that is] of such an Absolute *Necessity* to the Well-Being of a State.' But we can be sure that the visionary Jane Lead—for whom all the raw materials for social transformation lay within the human unconscious, waiting to be tapped—would have disagreed with this earthbound reviewer, who realistically concluded of Astell's protofeminist 'vision' that 'Great Designs must expect always great Oppositions: and how well soever they may hereafter succeed, 'tis odds but that for some while they must be censur'd by the generality as Romantick'.[34]

Only a few years after her committal to Newgate prison, Anglican Elinor James explained: 'God knows how dearly I love the good and welfare of this City, and I love that Magistrates should be respected, but my sole desire is that they should be all of a Unity' (*Mrs. Jame's* [sic] *Apology* (c.1694)). Whether or not Elinor James realized that, in the eyes of her rulers, achieving a homogeneous 'unity' meant silencing dangerously outspoken voices like hers, it is nevertheless certain that she was empowered rather than silenced by her sense of social collectivity not only with the common people of England, but also with the 'Priests and Rulers of this Generation'. By remembering that the same political convictions and lived emotions that may strike us today as debilitating or oppressive in fact moved many disempowered seventeenth-century women to subversive public expression, we gain access to middling and lower-class women's participation in the major national political debates of their time.

Through print, Elinor James sought to be an immeasurably public being—an uncontainable public voice. Print enabled James to

---

[34] *Theosophical Transactions By the Philadelphian Society, Consisting of Memoirs, Conferences, Letters, Dissertations, Inquiries, &c.* (1697), 1: 60. The Philadelphian Society was carried on after Lead's death in 1704 under the leadership of Richard Roach. In his own writings, Roach paid far more attention to gender issues than Lead ever did. The fact that he found it necessary to address the issue of female participation in the Philadelphian Society suggests that by the 1720s, female involvement and leadership in sectarian movements could no longer be taken for granted.

connect with the other parts of her social self, and her various figural self-representations reflect this sense of collective identity. James saw herself as a lover of the King, a sister to her fellow members of the Stationers' Company, a godmother to the City of London, and more. Her symbolic self-imaginings allowed her to address public political bodies in print:

I made Applications to my late Soveraign Lord the King (whom my Soul Loved) *That he would be pleas'd to let me Undertake for the City, and to make me a God Mother*, to which the King Answered, *It would be too great an Undertaking for me*, but I replied, *That if it might not be for all, that it might be for some*, and the King granted my desire, and I ask'd His Majesty whether He would not wish Well to it, and the King Replied, *Ay, with all my Heart and Soul*. (Mrs. JAMES's *Vindication* (1687), 3)

James's opponents in the popular press sneered at her would-be political participation through figural self-representation. In particular, they mocked her desire to be a 'God Mother' 'for the City', assuring her that 'though you could not (as you Gravely tell us) obtain to be the *City*'s, you shall have our Vote to be the Churches God Mother'.[35] But the very fact that in 1687 James's opponents had female-authored political pamphlets to mock suggests that this tradeswoman's symbolic self-imaginings nevertheless had material force.

What little feminist critical attention has been paid to Elinor James has focused almost exclusively on brief, scattered remarks in which she demonstrates an awareness of her disenfranchised status as a woman. But more extensive study of James's dozens of extant broadsides and pamphlets suggests that these statements have been taken out of context, and that, as a result, their strikingly minor place in her writings has been distorted. James's writings do not generally reflect a belief that gender was a fundamental epistemological category, let alone a valid factor in the organization of everyday life. James discussed her subjected status as a woman in patriarchal society only when a polemical opponent confronted her with it. Her writings do not reflect any sustained concern with the sex-based inequities of power all around her.

[35] Anon., *An Address of Thanks, On Behalf of The Church of England, to Mris* [sic] *James, For her Worthy Vindication of That Church* (Printed by George Larkin, 1687).

When we situate the brief, scattered passages in which James does pay attention to gender hierarchies within the larger political arguments in which those passages are embedded, however, we discover a radical discursive discontinuity which is in fact more illuminating than the remarks themselves. James's thoughts on gender were sudden irruptions: outbursts which pointed to gaps or contradictions in the ideology she lived by, and revealed her fragmented, unstable position as a female polemicist. For early modern women, identity was a matter of context. A woman's legal position shifted according to her changing relationships with different men (daughter, wife, widow, and so on) and accordingly, early women writers had no single, unified position from which to speak.[36] As the mistress of a printing house, James occupied a position of considerable authority, but at the same time she was also a subjected wife. As loyal subject, civic adviser, mistress of a printing household, would-be dutiful wife, and more, James wrote from different, sometimes incompatible, subject-positions. Consequently, the contradictions between these subject-positions are constantly foregrounded, and her discourse at times appears radically discontinuous.

For Elinor James, the family was a unit of economic production and government on a continuum with the state. There is no indication that she ever seriously imagined that any other form of family unit could exist, and indeed in over thirty years of religio-political polemicism she specifically alluded to the family only twice: once to discuss what she took to be ideal hierarchical relationships in the households of master printers, and once when she used the family metaphorically as an analogue to the state. James's conception of the family as an economic unit, and rigorous notions of ideal 'family' life in her *Mrs. James's Advice to All Printers in General* (c.1715), have been discussed in Chapter 1. Her second allusion to what we might call the politics of the family will be considered now.

Like her *Mrs. James's Advice to All Printers*, James's early *The Case between a Father and his Children. Humbly represented to the Honourable Lord Mayor and Court of Aldermen* (1682) depicts the early modern economic family not as a harmonious site of

[36] My language in this paragraph echoes Belsey, *The Subject of Tragedy*, 149–50.

productive labour and mutual affection, but rather as a deeply troubled social space darkened by 'disobedience', 'rebellion', insubordination, and distrust. In *The Case between a Father and his Children*, James employed a parable of supposedly 'unnatural' family relations to mirror contemporary divisions within the larger 'family' of the state. Drawing at once on the conventional family/state analogy and on her personal experience and knowledge as a 'Mother of Children', she addressed the Lord Mayor and Court of Aldermen:

I beseech your Lordship to pardon me in giving you this trouble, it is the great love I bear to Unity, and the consideration that I am a Mother of Children, and some part am sensible of the Excellency of Obedience, and how it prevails over the hearts of Parents; so that thereby they are instrumental to obtain the Blessing of God Spiritual and Temperal; but what a lamentable case it is when Children are disobedient and rebellious, it provokes the Wrath of God and Man, and makes them miserable in this World and the World to come, without Repentance. The serious consideration of this, hath caused me to present to your Lordship, and the Aldermen your Brethren, a Case between a Father and his Children.

Like so many of James's pamphlets and broadsides, this one is epistolary in form. It is addressed to particular public officials, and signed with her characteristic tag 'Your Humble Servant and Souls Well-wisher, ELINOR JAMES'. But by representing her own role in this genial epistolary exchange as that of one parent imparting advice to others, Elinor James actually veiled her inversion of social hierarchies of address. And by constructing a model of epistolary relations between sender and addressee whereby she was 'a Mother of Children' and the Lord Mayor 'a Father to this City', she figuratively equalized the radically disparate discursive positions of tradeswoman and City official.

But there is yet another sense in which the disparate positions of sender and addressee in James's pamphlet were not just 'equalized', but inverted. After these preliminary remarks, James went on to narrate her personal political parable of 'a certain Friend of mine that lives near me'—an indulgent and loving father whose wicked children took advantage of him precisely when he was most in need: 'The Children finding their Father in necessity, they dealt subtilly, and said amongst themselves, We will deal by him as we please, and he shall condescend to our Proposals ... we are resolved to humble our Father, to comply with our desires, or to make him miserable, in not Ministring to his necessities.' The father was patient with his rebellious children, and asked them the reason for their cruel behaviour:

> But when the Father propos'd this Question, though it was with mildness and sweetness, they were so far from acknowledging their Faults, that they would make themselves as though they had received an injury to be questioned, and therefore they would Right themselves by Law; and though they would not assist their Father in his necessity, yet they could find Kash to incourage the Lawyers.

'I'll appeal to your Lordship and your Brethren', James asked the Lord Mayor and aldermen, 'Whether these Children are not unkind and ungrateful?' With apparent humility, James then begged the Lord Mayor and aldermen not to despise her endeavours, for her parable was the message of one 'who longs for a Unity between the Father and his Children, but cannot be so happy without your Lordship and the Aldermen your Brethrens Assistance'. In the terms of James's parable, however, the mistreated 'father' was the King of England, and the evil children his subjects—especially, the Lord Mayor and aldermen. James reinforced this representation of the City's leaders as childish siblings by referring to the aldermen and Lord Mayor as 'brethren'. Where then was James herself represented in the parable? She was not figured as one of the children, for, as we have seen, it was her authority as a mother of children that helped her to write. Nor was she represented in the parable as the subjected wife of the poor father, for in fact there is no mention of a wife or mother at all. Inevitably, to have depicted the missing wife and mother in the parable would have been to draw a parallel between the figural female and herself, the female author. By choosing not to represent the mother, James managed to remain outside the figural hierarchy of the parable, as the authoritative author of the text. She was therefore figuratively parallel not with the rebellious children (the Lord Mayor and aldermen) but with the *King*— who was in turn paralleled with the divine 'father', or God. It was from this elevated psychological and rhetorical platform of her own making, then, that James could pronounce her severe verdict on the disobedient aldermen and Lord Mayor, essentially declaring them to be guilty of treason: 'it is seldom known that an unkind Child to a temporal Father, was ever counted an Obedient Servant to God, if not Obedient then Rebellious.'

James published her best-known pamphlet, *Mrs. JAMES's Vindication of the Church of England, In An Answer to a Pamphlet Entituled, A New Test of the Church of England's Loyalty* upon the occasion of James II's 1687 Declaration of Indulgence.[37] While she herself, she admitted, was 'not so much for Liberty of Conscience', she was also 'naturally Inclin'd to Love Kingly Authority'. She therefore found it necessary to defend her Catholic King against his detractors. The bulk of *Mrs. JAMES's Vindication* was addressed to the author of the pamphlet *A New Test*, and was dialogic in nature, reacting to the earlier pamphlet, and anticipating further polemical debate.

In one part of this pamphlet, James addressed members of the Church of England, and warned religious authorities especially to 'return the King Thanks'. She chastised recent Catholic convert John Dryden for belittling her in his preface to *The Hind and the Panther. A Poem, In Three Parts* (1687). Dryden had refused to answer the challenge of one of his own polemical opponents, Edward Stillingfleet, then Dean of St Paul's. In his preface, he explained that 'because I would not take up this ridiculous Challenge, he tells the world I cannot argue: but he may as well infer that a Catholick can not fast, because he will not take up the Cudgels against Mrs. *James*, to confute the Protestant Religion'.[38] James responded by representing Dryden as a religious turncoat, and as an enemy to the Church of England:

> As for Mr. *Dryden*, though some blame him for using my Name I do not; because he hath used it civilly. Indeed I do not know him, nor never read his Book, but am told he doth Abuse the CHURCH of ENGLAND, for which I blame him: For I count it not Wisdom for a Wit, to reflect on that he so lately own'd. (*Mrs. JAMES's Vindication*, 2)

As this passage suggests, Elinor James does not appear to have been particularly bothered by John Dryden's satiric use of her name in his own religio-political polemic. Dryden was after all a learned and famous man, and she was used to less genteel treatment from her polemical opponents. But then suddenly, in the middle of her

---

[37] This is the pamphlet on display in Elinor James's portrait (Fig. 2).

[38] John Dryden, *The Hind and the Panther. A Poem, In Three Parts* (1687), *The Works of John Dryden*, vol. iii, ed. Earl Miner and Vinton A. Dearing (Berkeley: U. of California P., 1969), 122. The editors of this volume describe Elinor James as 'the widow of a London printer'. In actual fact Thomas James lived for another twenty-three years.

most impassioned religio-political polemic, she exclaimed: 'O that I were but a Man, I would study Night and Day, and I do not doubt but that I should be more than a Conquerer, and so I hope to be nevertheless.'[39] James's brief personal outburst is buried in the midst of an engaged discussion of national politics, and to come upon it suddenly is extremely startling. The shock value of this momentary irruption of desire cannot be conveyed out of context, but it must nevertheless be stressed, for it is one of the most intriguing—and revealing—aspects of James's generally unselfconscious style. 'The ideological, all the while claiming to project a coherent vision, is always contradictory, always structurally incoherent,' Fredric Jameson has remarked.[40] The scattered and momentary irruptions of a gendered consciousness in Elinor James's texts point to ideological contradictions. They are one example of what Catherine Belsey has called the particular 'discursive discontinuity' of seventeenth-century women's public writings. In her own mind, James was a 'Loyal Subject' of the King, a citizen of the City of London, and a member of a City livery company. At the same time, though, she was also a woman—and accordingly, in the eyes of many (especially her opponents) the subject of her husband and 'head', not free to conscript herself in the public service of her King as she chose. (As Margaret Cavendish would have advised her, 'We [Women] are no Subjects.') As a result, while she tried to live—and disseminate—patriarchal ideology as if it were both natural and just, she unintentionally exposed its gaps whenever she wrote.

James believed in passive obedience and the naturalness of a minutely gradated social hierarchy. Yet she remained virtually silent about her own position on this chain of dependency and subordination. By refusing to acknowledge at least some of the socially constructed meanings of gender in her society, she managed to negotiate a realm of apparent freedom. But freedom can normally only occur within the limits defined by the dominant group, and gender remained conveniently 'unsaid' in James's texts only until one of her opponents used it against her, forcing her to confront it as a 'truth'. When James was writing in accordance with the goals of those in power, she was free to do as she pleased— including to write and to print her opinions on state affairs. But

[39] Elinor James, *Mrs. JAMES's Vindication* (1687), 2. James's envy of her husband's scholarly life and splendid personal library may be apparent in this quotation.
[40] Fredric Jameson, 'Religion and Ideology', 326.

when she was working in opposition to hegemonic culture, she recognized, the construct of gender was a powerful weapon, increasingly deployed against her: 'I know you will say *I am a Woman, and why should I trouble myself?* Why was I not always so, when I pleaded with the Parliament about the *Right of Succession*, and with *Shaftsbury* [*sic*], and *Monmouth*, and at *Guild-Hall*, and elsewhere[?]' (*Mrs. JAMES's Vindication* (1687), 3). Like her 'O that I were but a Man' outburst above, this sudden moment of textual swerve is completely discontinuous with its contexts. It is a brief, mirror-like scene of 'recognition', in which James suddenly confronted the full ramifications of an ideology in which she otherwise proudly participated. James lived the better part of her working days as if her sex was irrelevant. And for the most part, she managed to move in and out of difference as it suited her.[41] Not surprisingly, there were times when her opponents would not allow her this luxury, and resorted to joking about her self-identification as 'City God Mother' and status as edifier of the 'Tripe Women'. Even then, though, James could see that these polemicists were her religio-political opponents—and that gender was a construct they used against her only when it was in their own interests to do so ('for [Interest] is the God of this World' (*Mrs. JAMES's Vindication*, 3)). James's firm sense of gender as a polemical weapon or rhetorical tool rather than as an inherent essence allowed her vocally to reject the gendered interiority assigned to her—and to point out that her sex was being deployed against her for interested personal and political ends.

James's *Vindication* attracted considerable attention, and at least one anonymous author published an extended response. As we have seen, the anonymous author of the ironic *An Address of Thanks, On Behalf of the Church of England, to Mris. James* (1687) remarked in particular how 'wonderously' James had 'Edified the *Tripe Women*, and Convinc'd the *Porters*' 'that *our*

---

[41] Three hundred years later, feminist lawyers are still trying to construct a legal model which would allow for different degrees of gender identification. In her analysis of the historic sex discrimination suit brought against Sears by the Equal Employment Opportunities Commission in 1979, ultimately determined against the plaintiff, historian Joan W. Scott concludes that we still need 'a simple model that would at once acknowledge difference *and* refuse it as an acceptable explanation for [oppression and discrimination]' ('Deconstructing Equality-Versus-Difference: Or, the Uses of Post-Structuralist Theory for Feminism', *Feminist Studies*, 14 (1988), 42).

Church is the only Church for Loyalty; and that you your self (how light soever) *can Weigh down all the rest*, in that excellent Qualification'. James took the phrase 'how light soever' to be a sexual innuendo, and in a third pamphlet responded to her dissenting opponent: 'You talk of my Lightness, but I never was so Light as to Dishonour my Husband, or Defile my Bed; and in this Excellent Qualification, I may Weigh all such as you Down.'[42] Her bold rejoinder is significant for two reasons. First, as in the works of Joan Whitrowe and Jane Lead, there are only a very few instances in all of Elinor James's prolific writings where she refers to her husband, and this is one of them. (James quite strikingly omitted Thomas James from an important list of allegiances when she declared, 'I will be True to my God, my King, and my Countrey' (*Vindication*, 6).) Second, this is one of even fewer allusions in James's writings to her female body. James made reference to her sexuality here only because an opponent had slandered her in this regard. Furthermore, she refused to see conjugal fidelity as most of her contemporaries did: as a gendered virtue, necessarily specific only to women. In a later pamphlet, James held up as exemplary the relationship of Queen Anne and Prince George who 'live like Turtle-Doves together', and advised members of parliament to work harder to imitate their monarch's companionate marriage.[43] Comparing her own marital fidelity to that of her polemical opponent, she found her opponent gravely wanting, and concluded: 'So I would intreat you to be Quiet, and keep your Addresses unto your self, and let me alone, for I do not Love to be Disturb'd with Controversies, but Wish you the *Grace of Repentance*. So I rest, ELINOR JAMES' (3). On a par with chastity, silence was considered to be *women's* greatest ornament. By telling her male opponent to 'be Quiet, and keep your Addresses unto your self', Elinor James dramatically underlined her refusal to concede to the increasingly rigid dichotomy of sexual difference of her day.

James recognized the feminine as a position of marginality and subordination in her society, but she did not identify with it. She used it as a symbolic category, only—in parables and other figural representations, to depict what she perceived to be right relations in

[42] Elinor James, *Mrs. JAMES's Defence of the Church of England, in a short answer to the canting address* (1687), 3.
[43] Elinor James, *May it please Your Lordships, Seriously to Consider what Great Things God has done for You* (1702).

church and state. In a pamphlet to the Convention Parliament, she urged the Lords to remain loyal to King James, despite his 'flirtation' with Catholicism. 'Though there may be many things said against the King,' she wrote, 'yet . . . consider that *he* has been *misled* by *strangers*, as many *Men* has been *misled* by *strange Women*, yet they are not willing their *Wives* should turn *them* out of *doors* and take other *Husbands*, tho' *they* might do it by the *Law*, yet People would think such to be *Bad Women*.'[44] James's logic here is similar to her contemporary Mary Astell's when Astell demanded, 'If Absolute Sovereignty be not necessary in a State, how comes it to be so in a Family?'[45] Both women are suspicious of double standards for fidelity and obedience in public and private, especially on the part of Whig gentlemen. Recognizing though not approving the sexual double standards imposed on women, she pointed out that the least the Lords could do was to give King James II the same liberties that they gave themselves. To deny their monarch special 'liberties'—freedom to explore, if not to partake of alternatives, in this case the Catholic faith—would be to feminize him. It would be to put him in the woman's position, which did not allow for steps off the straight and narrow track. Any speaker, male or female, could use the category of the 'feminine' as James did here. This was not the installation of a 'feminine—and feminist' perspective in discourse, but rather a much older use of the feminine as a symbolic category in political debate. Similarly, James's various self-representations as 'God Mother' to the City of London are not evidence of 'the establishment of the gendered female subject in discourse', but rather the rhetorical tool of a woman writing, who happened to recognize that she was female. They are evidence of a common-sense awareness of sex, rather than of a modern sense of gendered consciousness.

In one rare instance, Elinor James did for a moment appear to express an ideological gender dichotomy of her own, implying that some human character traits are exclusively feminine. In her address to the Lord Mayor and aldermen regarding the new by-law prohibiting squibs, she complained that despite the prohibition, the women of London were still hurling firecrackers at one another:

---

[44] Elinor James, *To the Right Hon. Convention. Gentlemen, though you have a new name* (c.1688).
[45] Mary Astell, *Reflections Upon Marriage. The Third Edition. To which is Added a Preface, in Answer to some Objections* (1706), [10].

As the City is made now, I can compare it to nothing but Hell: your Windows taken down, and Men tuck'd up flinging Serpents one at another, as if they would destroy each other; . . . But that which grieves me worst of all is, that you have corrupted Women-kind, for they should be Innocent, Severe, and Modest, and Tender-Hearted, and afraid to do anything that is injurious; and I am sorry their Natures should be chang'd.[46]

While James appears to have expressed an ideological assumption here about 'Women-kind's' 'Tender-Hearted' nature, however, in actual fact she admitted only that this was the way women should be, not the way they inherently are. Furthermore, she consistently cautioned men too to be 'afraid to do anything injurious'. In recommending to the House of Lords in late 1688 or early 1689 that they remain loyal to King James, she advised the members of parliament to work 'to Reclaim him by Fine and Gentle Means', and stressed that 'this must not be done in a hurry'.[47] Most importantly, James's desire for female 'modesty' might restrict women's firecracker throwing, but it did not preclude her own vocal participation in state affairs.

James was empowered by a sense of her own civic leadership, and frequently represented herself as a martyr or hero through self-sacrificing service to the state. She informed King James that 'to Serve Your Majesty, I could venture my Life, if I had a Hundred Lives I would Sacrifice them all to do You Good', and as we have seen, she valiantly declared to his detractors, 'My Resolution is, That I will be True to my God, my King, and my Countrey, and I am resolv'd . . . never to change if I were to suffer a Thousand Deaths'.[48] She demanded of her audience, 'Was it not a great Thing of me to go to King *Charles* the Second to tell him his Faults[?]'[49] And she declared with enabling conviction that 'God has preserv'd me and fought my Battle, and made me more than a Conqueror, and I don't fear all the Powers of Hell, for I stand upon an Infallible Rock my Blessed Saviour.' It was one thing for a man to boast that 'though I met with Opposition, yet my Faith did not fail;

---

[46] Elinor James, *Sir, My Lord Mayor and the Aldermen his Brethren, upon Serious Consideration for the good of the City* (c.1690).

[47] Elinor James, *My Lords, I can assure your Lordships, that you are infinitely admir'd* (1688 or 1689).

[48] Elinor James, *Most Dear Soveraign, I Cannot but Love and Admire You* (c.1686), and *Mrs. JAMES's Vindication* (1687), 6.

[49] Elinor James, *Mrs. JAMES's Reasons Humbly Presented to the Lords Spiritual and Temporal* (1715), 4.

for I always told my Opposers, I should have the conquering Game'.[50] But it was quite another for a tradeswoman, especially a tradeswoman with a printing press. When eighteenth-century middling female voices as confident and aggressive as this one were printed and distributed across England's largest city, they represented a threat to the established order. 'A lived hegemony is always a process,' Raymond Williams has remarked. 'It does not passively exist as a form of dominance.'

If hegemony is 'continually resisted, limited, altered, challenged by pressures not at all its own', however, it is also continually 'renewed, recreated, defended, and modified'.[51] Elinor James lived to see the emergence of new opportunities, and she also lived to see some of them disappear. To a remarkable extent, she had managed to ignore the socially imposed limitations of her sex, and to live as if she 'were but a Man'. But as she was well aware, sexual ideology was increasingly becoming a weapon that she could not simply disregard. One anonymous opponent picked up immediately, for instance, on her extraordinary self-representation as a civic hero. The author of *An Address of Thanks . . . to Mrs. James* referred to 'all these your Great and Heroick Atchievements', and thanked James for her 'Brave Efforts'. Even more significantly, however, whereas James had always represented herself as a conquering hero, her opponent transformed her into an Amazonian heroine. Comparing her to Joan of Arc, a female military leader and cross-dresser of sorts, her opponent consistently foregrounded her sex where she did not do so herself: 'In this Extremity, you, Madam! are the *Pucelle de Dieu*, that *Joan of Arque*, who stept in to Retrieve our Forlorn Affairs, and bouy up our Sinking Reputation; You are the brave *Semiramis* that must Rebuild the Walls of our *Babel*.' James's opponents insisted that she see herself as a woman before any other identity. As gender ideologies were increasingly consolidated and disseminated through print, differences among women were increasingly reconceptualized as 'difference', and the actual diversity of female voices was homogenized as what some twentieth-century scholars still refer to as 'the feminine voice'. Gender had become a 'truth'.

[50] Elinor James, *May it please Your Lordships* (1702) and *Mrs. James Prayer for the Queen and Parliament, and Kingdom too* (1710).

[51] Raymond Williams, *Marxism and Literature* (Oxford: Oxford UP, 1977), 112.

Like so many women writers of the revolutionary and post-revolutionary period in England, James saw herself as a prophet whom no one would heed. She had spent forty years of her life, she believed, trying to convince British monarchs to live godly lives, and so divert God's judgements from the kingdom. But they had disregarded her warnings, 'and so brought evil upon themselves, which I would a prevented, but I could not, being that I was a Woman: *O! That I had been a Man it would have been the same Thing*.' As usual, James decided in this passage that her sex was not really the determining factor in her public reception after all. But as if she finally recognized that, regardless of her own opinion, her opponents would remind her of her sex, she decided at last to take advantage of her sex for whatever it was worth. She went on to conclude in a wholly different vein: 'Well now as I am a Woman hearken to me now, after above forty Years speaking.'[52]

Historian Phyllis Mack has concluded that 'women as sources of any spiritual authority—whether divine or demonic—had virtually disappeared from the public arena by 1700'.[53] Other feminist critics have agreed that this period also witnessed the emergence of the gendered female subject in print. Chapter 4 has tried to suggest a connection between these two events so central to the historical development of English women, and to sound a note of caution amidst admittedly more encouraging celebrations of the emergence of the 'feminine self'. The transition from seventeenth- and early eighteenth-century female polemicists' notion of human interiority as collective, social, and essentially unsexed to the autonomous gendered self of modern liberal individualism did not bring freedom or equality. Yet the establishment of women as gendered subjects in discourse did help some eighteenth-century women to see their mutual interests across social boundaries. And as Catherine Belsey suggests:

To have a subject-position . . . is to occupy a place in discourse, to be able to speak. . . . To be a subject is to be able to claim rights, to protest, and to

---

[52] Elinor James, *November the 5th, 1715. Mrs. James's Thanks to the Lords and Commons for their Sincerity to King George* (1715).
[53] Phyllis Mack, 'Women as Prophets during the English Civil War', *Feminist Studies*, 8 (1982), 34. My own research suggests that this date is slightly too early.

be capable of devising a [more effective] mode of resistance than witchcraft or prophecy. It is to be in a position to identify and analyze the nature of women's oppression. (220–1)

The same texts which mark a 'change in the discursive position of women' also mark the origins of an explicitly feminist discourse. As we will see in Chapter 5 in the case of Delarivier Manley, women writers' increasing identification with gendered subject-positions helped them to see women as an oppressed 'group' in themselves— and much later, to organize a political movement centring on their own particular needs. This study of the historical construction of metaphors of human interiority has affirmed a close relationship between different metaphors of being and modes of female empowerment in a single historical period. Perhaps it has also suggested the possibility of change.

PART III

'I Take Truth With Me When I Can Get Her'
Delarivier Manley and the Reproduction of
Political Intelligence

Introduction

For every kind of beasts, and of birds, and of serpents, and of things in the sea, is tamed, and hath been tamed of mankind:
But the tongue can no man tame; it is an unruly evil, full of deadly poison.

(James 3: 7–8)

In 1711, the editor of the *Examiner* publicly announced retirement. Exulting that 'supported by the goodness of the Cause, I have waded through Seas of Scurrility, without being Polluted by any of that Filth they have incessantly cast at me', the author of one of the first political essay journals in English and the most prominent Tory organ of its time had nevertheless decided to forgo 'the Fatigue of Politicks and State-Reflections, till some more urgent Occasion again calls forth my Endeavours'. It is a familiar posture, this last stand of the disgruntled Augustan artist in the face of Grub Street. At first, one hears in this elevated leave-taking the declamatory tones of a frustrated Jonathan Swift substituting self-aggrandizement for the advancement that he had still not received from his patrons. This particular lament and leave-taking, though, belonged not to Swift but to his co-editor Delarivier Manley (1672–1724).[1]

As Swift, Alexander Pope, Joseph Addison, Richard Steele, and other members of the Augustan cultural élite would show themselves well aware, the career of the first avowed female political propagandist in English in the 'never dying War of Pen and

[1] The *Examiner* (1st ser.) ran from 9 Aug. 1710 to 26 July 1711. Manley took over the editorship from Swift, completing no. 46, 7 June 1711, and continuing the paper until the conclusion of the first series with no. 52, which is quoted here. The *Examiner* was printed by John Barber at his printing house at Lambeth-Hill. Manley was then living with Barber, and may have had a more ongoing relationship with the paper than has been recognized. On possible earlier contributions by Manley, see Gwendolyn B. Needham, 'Mary de la Rivière Manley, Tory Defender', *Huntington Library Quarterly*, 12 (1948–9), 253–88.

Tongue'[2] was the sign of a new age. It was an age in which, as Aphra Behn had observed in 1689, 'The Sword [had become] a Feeble Pow'r, . . . | . . . to the Nobler Pen subordinate; | And of less use in *Bravest* turns of State.'[3] Institutional and political developments had given rise to a new state of affairs for English writers— a state of affairs to which Pope would give apocalyptic resonance in the *Dunciad* (1728), and one which directly enabled Manley's career. By 1728, the press would become an accepted arena for the public discussion of political affairs—a discursive battlefield on which, as we have seen, women printers, publishers, and polemicists had fought. This is the world of writing as work in which Manley attempted to make a living after bad luck and bad choices ('Youth, Misfortunes, and Love') combined to undo many of the benefits of her birth.[4] By 1714, the year in which she pretended publicly to renounce politics as 'not the business of a Woman', she was the author of at least six volumes of political allegories totalling some 1,500 pages in quarto, six political pamphlets, and as many as nine issues of the Tory *Examiner*. At a time when, as we

---

[2] Delarivier Manley, *Memoirs of Europe, Towards the Close of the Eighth Century, Written by Eginardus, Secretary and Favourite to Charlemagne; And done into English by the Translator of the New Atalantis* (1710), i. 189; rpt. in Patricia Köster, ed., *The Novels of Mary Delariviere Manley 1705–14*, 2 vols. (Gainesville, Fla.: Scholars' Facsimiles and Reprints, 1971). With the exception of the *New Atalantis*, all subsequent references to Manley's novels are to this facsimile edition and will be cited parenthetically by each novel's original title, volume, and page number.

[3] *A Pindaric Poem To The Reverend Doctor Burnet, On The Honour he did me of Enquiring after me and my Muse* (1689).

[4] Manley, *The Adventures of Rivella; or, the History of the Author of the Atalantis. With Secret Memoirs and Characters of several considerable Persons her Cotemporaries* (1714), 12. Manley's socioeconomic position is not easily categorized. While the daughter of a gentleman, she was orphaned as a teenager, and according to her own account tricked into a bigamous marriage which left her with at least one illegitimate child. Without the independent means to preserve her status, she was viewed by most members of polite society as sexually infamous and socially marginal. In defining the 18th-cent. 'middling sort', historian Margaret R. Hunt estimates that an urban householder needed at the bare minimum £50 'to sustain a lifestyle and a level of "independence" commensurate with middling status' (*The Middling Sort: Commerce, Gender, and the Family in England, 1680–1780* (Berkeley and Los Angeles: U. of California P., 1996), 15). While Manley had a privileged education and insisted on representing herself as a gentlewoman, it is certain that she had no assurance of such an income for most of her life.
    A scholarly biography of Manley is much needed. For further biographical information see Dolores Diane Clarke Duff, 'Materials toward a Biography of Mary Delariviere Manley' (diss., U. of Indiana, 1965) and Fidelis Morgan, *A Woman of No Character: An Autobiography of Mrs. Manley* (London: Faber and Faber, 1986).

have seen, circulating any stories about those in power could be dangerous, Manley's allegorical fictions in particular encouraged reflection on the behaviour and actions of prominent persons and public authorities. Among the first English authors to recognize and exploit the new centrality of print propaganda in post-revolutionary society, her political fictions and journalism played an important early role in helping fundamentally to shift the *modus operandi* of British political life.

Thanks to critics such as John J. Richetti, Ros Ballaster, and others, Delarivier Manley's contribution to the development of the English novel is now well known. Feminist critics, in particular, have explored issues of gender and genre, outlining Manley's experiments with gendered narrative voice and tracing the development of a 'feminocentric' literary tradition in her work.[5] The lens of Manley as a novelist and a feminist has been invaluable in incorporating her firmly into current literary critical traditions of intelligibility and value; indeed, Manley is the one 'woman of Grub Street' in this book who has received substantial critical attention precisely because her life and works can be made to fit such models. But the lens of gender and genre is only one way to look at Manley's legacy, even the legacy of her fiction, and another lens or model will be employed here.

While today Manley's best-known work, *Secret Memoirs and Manners of several Persons of Quality, of Both Sexes, from the New Atalantis, An Island in the Mediteranean* (1709), is read chiefly as a scandal chronicle, in her own time it was taken seriously enough as a political intervention to cause the printer's, publisher's, and author's arrest. Manley's requests that her political fiction be read for the 'Design' rather than the 'Performance' are instructions that this reading will follow. To read Manley for her instrumentality rather than her execution is to restore her to her particular political and cultural moment—and particularly, her position as

---

[5] On Manley's contribution to the novel and to a 'feminocentric' literary tradition, see Ros Ballaster, *Seductive Forms: Women's Amatory Fiction from 1684 to 1740* (Oxford: Clarendon P., 1992), Gallagher, *Nobody's Story*, John J. Richetti, *Popular Fiction before Richardson: Narrative Patterns 1700–1739* (Oxford: Clarendon P., 1969; rpt. 1992), Spencer, *The Rise of the Woman Novelist*, and Todd, *The Sign of Angellica*. I am grateful to Ros Ballaster for sharing with me in 1989 her then-unpublished dissertation chapters on Manley and Behn; Catherine Gallagher and others read my own 100-page dissertation chapter on Manley in 1987.

part of a vast network of politically literate women in the print trades: women whose lives were fundamentally affected by the contemporary conjunction of print and politics. To read Manley as a woman writing about politics for pay is to show how the world of writing as *labour*—the (under)world of London printing, publishing, and polemicism detailed in Parts I and II—informed her writings and sense of self. It is no mere coincidence that Manley created the satiric political narratives that she did, when she did, specifically because of her place in a larger world of work and politics.

Manley shared many concerns and experiences with the women printers, publishers, and polemicists already discussed here, yet she also differed from them in many ways. Her writings exemplify shifts taking place across post-revolutionary British political and literary culture, as well as shifts in women's writing and models for female authorship. Chapter 5 reads Manley as a key transitional figure in the history of middling women's political activism through print, mediating between the female political culture of the seventeenth century and the 'new wave' of women's writing and self-representation in the eighteenth century.[6] As we have seen in Chapter 4, new models of political authority and political subjecthood worked in tandem with new models of gendered and individualized personal identity, and Manley exemplified new ideas of the subject being developed in this period alongside older models. Unlike the other women political writers and workers discussed in this book, Manley's writings are characterized by a high degree of self-consciousness not only as political participant but as *author*. This is apparent not only in her 'literary autobiography', *The Adventures of Rivella; or, The History of the Author of the Atalantis* (1714), but also in what Chapter 5 will argue was her satiric self-portrait as woman party writer in the *New Atalantis*. Manley's most influential work is structured as a conversation among three female spies who, recalling Manley's politically active female contemporaries, hover around urban public sites in search of political news. The leader of this female narrative trio is 'Lady Intelligence', whom Chapter 5 reads as the most important of

---

[6] On this new wave see Spencer, *The Rise of the Woman Novelist*, Todd, *The Sign of Angellica*, and Jeslyn Medoff, 'The Daughters of Behn and the Problem of Reputation', in Grundy and Wiseman, eds., *Women, Writing, History 1640–1740*, 33–54.

Manley's many experiments with authorial self-representation as a propagandist. Manley created a space for her innovative fictions by representing herself as a female 'alternative intelligence' agent of the private sphere. Informer, newsmonger, and political gossip, 'Intelligence' is a new kind of counter-publicity agent, employed by 'the omnipotent Princess Fame, of whom all the monarchs on the earth stand in awe' (13). And particularly British monarchs after 1649 and 1688, one might add, for Manley's self-representation as female intelligence agent was simultaneous with the institutionalization in Britain of a recognizably modern critical political press. Whereas those in power had long used the tool of print to disseminate positive 'publicity' about themselves, an increasingly pluralist literary marketplace meant that a new kind of 'intelligence agent' (propagandist) such as Manley might now also disseminate negative counter-publicity ('secret intelligence') with similar ease. Manley's self-representation as Intelligence was also simultaneous with the founding of a recognizably modern government intelligence agency. Under the leadership of Secretary of State Robert Harley—to whom Manley sent a volume of the *New Atalantis*, and from whom she once received payment—the foundations of a government intelligence network were laid—not only to collect information, as today, but also to disseminate it as part of the ministry's ongoing attempt to influence public opinion. Like Harley, and like Manley herself, Manley's 'Intelligence' recognizes that the distinction between what is and is not 'news' is ideological and can be manipulated to political ends.

The task of the early eighteenth-century political journalist was not so much to report previously unknown 'news' as to participate in the ongoing interpretation of an occurrence or rumour of which one's public was already partly aware. Political essay journals such as the Tory *Examiner* or Whig *Medley* did not so much *produce* news, as *re*-produce it, in an ongoing attempt to influence public opinion. In shaping the form as well as the content of her political fictions, Manley drew not only on aristocratic French fiction and the work of English predecessors such as Aphra Behn, but also on popular oral culture. Empowered rather than silenced by stereotypes of women's 'perpetual Talk',[7] this self-conscious

---

[7] This phrase is from Jonathan Swift's representation of 'Miss Faction' in his *Examiner*, no. 32, 8 Mar. 1711 (discussed below).

propagandist represented her political fiction as the reproduction of old stories—a phrase which also helps to explain the presence of a topos of biological generation in the *New Atalantis*, a work intended as an intervention in mainstream politics. For in fact, Manley actually managed to constitute her authority as woman party writer and as a 'literary labourer' in general by publicly foregrounding her damning status as unwed mother, then rewriting contemporary cultural associations between textual and biological generation to suit her own personal and political needs. She managed to transform both her institutional liabilities as a female propagandist, or teller of tales, and her personal liabilities as the mother of an illegitimate child, into an innovative perspective on contemporary political affairs via the figure of the 'gossip': today, more often than not, a person who spreads anonymous or damaging talk, but etymologically and historically a companion who attended a woman at a lying-in.

Manley's self-representation as female intelligencer was an ingenious solution to her own doubly difficult situation as woman party writer. But as her contemporaries realized, it also had implications for other politically literate women of her generation. The *New Atalantis* has been called 'the publication that did most harm to the Ministry [in 1709]'.[8] But Manley's greatest threat in her own time, this chapter argues, lay not so much in the particular stories she told, as in the extent to which she realized that, by means of print, 'private intelligence' could be public political currency. Manley's political allegories have been recognized as a contribution to the history of the novel and as innovative and effective works of mainstream propaganda. In what follows, however, I would like to suggest that they should also be seen as what Swift, Addison, Steele, and other leading figures of the Augustan periodical press recognized as a demonstration of the potential political instrumentality of women's 'perpetual Talk'. As a woman whose reputation was irreparably damaged by the circulation of scandal, Manley recognized the profound power of anonymous talk. As a pioneering political writer, she discerned the new force of public opinion in her society, and the new power of printed texts to influence it. The female narrative trio of the *New Atalantis* is no mere 'frame device'.

[8] George Macaulay Trevelyan, *England under Queen Anne*, vol. iii: *The Peace and the Protestant Succession* (London: Longmans, Green and Co., 1934), 38.

Rather, it is a putting-into-print of Manley's politically minded, print-oriented female contemporaries, and a transforming lens for the work's newly *gender-driven* political concerns. Others have discussed Manley's specifically female identity in her writings, and it is not my goal to discuss her role in the construction of models of gendered selfhood for women *per se*. Rather, this chapter asks what happens in post-revolutionary British culture when old and new traditions conjoin in Manley: traditions of political print activism by middling women, new models of gendered subjectivity, and a new degree of self-consciousness about the diverse possibilities of propaganda.

To see Manley's political fictions as a site where traditions conjoin—the highly gender-conscious but still largely aristocratic tradition of seventeenth-century fiction and the broader tradition of middling and lower-class women's political activity through print—is to begin to understand just how *doubly* important—and threatening—she was. The implications of Manley's gendered political writings for women of her generation were, Chapter 5 concludes, at once recognized and countered by her male political writing contemporaries. This examination of Manley's personal and political strategies as a political writer concludes by examining what I take to be the polemical responses of Addison, Steele, Swift, and others to her works. Comments made by leading male figures of the Augustan political press on the subject of women and party during the years 1709–11 were reactions not only to the new 'She-State-Politician' of the post-revolutionary period, but also specifically to Manley. Contrary to current assumptions, it was not Manley's sexual themes and behaviour which provoked these authors' polemics, or even her blatant privileging of political over what we might call 'aesthetic' concerns in her works. These gentlemen's attacks were satirical; in Steele's case they were also motivated by personal enmity towards Manley. But they nevertheless betray a real anxiety on the part of these men and the divided society in which they lived, concerning what they perceived to be women's dramatically increased participation in politics, propaganda, and the manipulation of 'public opinion'. Manley's self-representation as 'Lady Intelligence' was simultaneous with the coming of age of a generation of politically minded, vocally critical women: women in the London (under)world of printing and publishing who had lived through 'strange and unheard of

Revolutions'[9] and who also had immediate unsupervised access to print.

These gentlemen responded to Manley as the epitome of a larger phenomenon, and their responses affected her writings and self-representations and those of her female contemporaries. Manley's late-career writings show a shift in her strategies for authorial self-representation, and her public (pretended) exit from political involvement. Her paradoxically public retirement from the 'Fatigue of Politicks and State-Reflections' foreshadows the changing relationship of British women to the political press by the mid-eighteenth century: their turn away from explicit polemic and public activism towards more 'polite' textual practices and literary forms.

[9] Manley, *The Secret History of Queen Zarah and the Zarazians; Being a Looking-glass for —— in the Kingdom of Albigion* (1705), i. 59.

5

Delarivier Manley's Public Representations

According to her own account written twenty-six years after the fact, the flight of Mary of Modena to France in 1688 put an end to Delarivier Manley's youthful hopes of 'going to Court'. At the same time, her father's grief over 'the Misfortunes of his Royal Master [James II] sunk so deep into his Thoughts, that he dy'd soon after, in mortal Apprehension of what would befall his unhappy Country'.[1] Left parentless, seduced by her Whig cousin John Manley, and robbed of all chance of a respectable marriage, Manley was, she implied, *forced* to write for pay as a means of supporting herself. The Whigs' overthrow of their rightful sovereign was to blame for her anomalous career. As these examples suggest, Manley freely used her own family history for propagandistic purposes and represented the Revolution of 1688 as responsible for her personal misfortunes. She also represented her political allegiances as having been for ever established in her youth. Alluding to her own political ancestry frequently in her fictions, she declared herself 'a perfect *Bigot* from a long untainted Descent of loyal Ancestors, and consequently immoveable'.[2]

In her *Pindaric Poem to the Reverend Doctor Burnet* (1689), Aphra Behn had represented the Revolution of 1688 as 'this Mighty Change' and 'this Unpresidented Enterprise' (67, 97). Sixteen years later, Manley added her voice to what was by now an entire chorus of anti-Whig women's voices. Attempting to defamiliarize events now too familiar, Manley referred to the events of 1688 as 'strange

[1] *Rivella*, 28–9. In actual fact Sir Roger Manley died before the Revolution in Mar. 1687.

[2] *Rivella*, 116. See also *Rivella*, 12, 14–15, 19–29; *Memoirs of Europe*, i, preface; and *Secret Memoirs and Manners of several Persons of Quality, of Both Sexes, from the New Atalantis, An Island in the Mediteranean*, ed. Rosalind Ballaster (Penguin, 1992), 222–3. All further references to the *New Atalantis* are to the Penguin edition and will be cited parenthetically in the text.

and unheard of Revolutions', and characterized the 'Utopians' as a people who 'change monarchs, with the same ease that they shift their linen'.[3] As Behn had referred to 'this Unpresidented Enterprise', so Manley rejected the epithet 'Glorious' as propaganda. Of her detested cousin John Manley, she wrote: 'he joined Henriquez [William of Orange] with the Count de Grand Monde, securing the strongest citadel of the kingdom, against the reigning prince, and naming it the Glorious Cause' (*New Atalantis*, 224–5). Like Behn writing to Burnet, she scorned propagandistic representations of William of Orange as a 'deliverer' of the Church of England from Catholic tyranny. She particularly expressed scepticism of those high-ranking political strategists who veiled political ambition in piety, making 'Religion the highest Point of their Politicks', while their pious *sententiae* were but 'Precious Stones to embellish their Designs, and dress up their Secret Mysteries in such a pleasant Garb'.[4] In writing about the so-called 'Glorious Revolution' from a point of view other than that of the victors, however, Manley came to understand the 'bloodless' Revolution as above all a revolutionary *fiction*: an ideological representation of historical events.[5] As a revolution achieved by the pen, it was a fiction with which she, as woman party writer, could compete.

Manley was enormously indebted to Behn's writings, even borrowing characters' names from her works. But there are important differences, as well as similarities, between their political writings, and some of those will become clear in what follows.[6] Whereas Behn represented the events of 1688 as having shut down opportunities for her, a loyal royalist, as a political writer, Manley

[3] *Queen Zarah*, i. 59; *New Atalantis*, 190. In the specific context of Manley's encoded narrative, the 'Utopians' are the Scottish, as well as implicitly the English.

[4] *Queen Zarah*, ii. 91. As a propagandist, Manley was not above making the same strategic use of religious discourse that she critiqued in her Whig enemies. She sounds like a satirical version of Elinor James, for instance, when she complains of Church of England doctrine being 'wrested' by the Whigs, 'to speak the Language of Ruin to the Hierarchy and Sovereignty, an odious Explanation, by way of Limitation, being lately brought in, to introduce Rebellion and Prophaneness' (*Memoirs of Europe*, ii. 286–7).

[5] On the Revolution of 1688–9 as in essence an 'intensive propaganda campaign', see Lois G. Schwoerer, 'Propaganda in the Revolution of 1688–89', *American Historical Review*, 82 (1977), 843–74.

[6] For Manley's debt to Behn see Spencer, Todd, Ballaster, Gallagher, and others cited in the Bibliography. Nearly every feminist literary study of Manley of the past decade has framed her as Behn's successor.

represented these 'strange and unheard of Revolutions' as having propelled her into a career that she would not otherwise have chosen: a career as a party writer in the new age of 'public opinion'. Jürgen Habermas posits a key distinction between two different forms of political representation in late Stuart England: one characteristic of the dying social order and the other of the new social order just then being born. Habermas's model, which may be schematized as a distinction between 'representative publicness' and public representations, is useful in beginning to understand the subtle but important differences between Manley and Behn as political writers, despite their loosely similar ideological allegiances and writing careers. As befitting a monarch whose ideological underpinning was the notion of divine right, political authority before the Revolution was a matter of representative publicness. Lordship was constituted in the act of publicity, 'the display of inherent spiritual power or dignity before an audience'.[7] Behn's Restoration political writing, and especially her formal political poetry, epitomizes representative publicness in action. Behn contributed to the ongoing constitution of lordly authority by representing Charles II, James II, Mary of Modena, and the infant Pretender as mythical or divine, and their births, successions, and deaths as cosmic events.[8] During Manley's lifetime, even women political writers who critiqued monarchs or their ministers often saw themselves as ultimately serving the monarchy. We have seen, for instance, how printer-author Elinor James saw herself as upholding church and crown even when she was arrested for her 'scandalous and reflecting papers'. In clash with the assumptions of absolutist society, on the other hand, during this same period 'the emergent bourgeoisie gradually replaced a public sphere in which the ruler's power was merely represented *before* the people with a sphere in which state authority was publicly monitored through informed critical discourse by the people'.[9] In contrast with Behn,

---

[7] Habermas, *The Structural Transformation of the Public Sphere*, translator's note, p. xv.

[8] See her poems listed in the Bibliography, now conveniently reprinted in Germaine Greer, ed., *The Uncollected Verse of Aphra Behn* (Stump Cross: Stump Cross Books, 1989) and Janet Todd, ed., *The Works of Aphra Behn*, i: *Poetry* (Columbus: Ohio State UP, 1992).

[9] McCarthy, intro. to Habermas, *The Structural Transformation of the Public Sphere*, p. xi.

and despite her own (different) royalist sympathies, Delarivier Manley's post-revolutionary political writing did not serve the monarchy to any great extent, but rather specific party political interests.[10] Her writings register a shift in British culture from a model of political authority as originating in divine right and representative publicness, to a model of authority as arising in the people's needs and contested via public representations. Unlike the women religio-political writers discussed in Part II, Manley's political writings during the same years were neither religious nor monarch-centred nor addressed to public political bodies. Manley's political appeal was not to monarchs, ministers, or government officials, but rather to those private persons who monitored their authority. Her writings bypass public figures except in attempts to gain patronage from them, and function as party political propaganda consciously aimed at manipulating 'public opinion'.

And in fact, Manley's political fictions may indirectly have functioned to challenge the assumptions of lordship altogether by popularizing competing 'public representations' of those in power. At a time when the aristocracy were still regarded by many with a sort of quasi-religious awe,[11] and the printed word commanded greater epistemological authority than it does today, Manley presented even monarchs *en déshabillé*. Whereas Aphra Behn represented Charles II and James II 'not simply as rulers but as sacred majesties, god-kings on earth, whose private failings in no way detracted from their high office',[12] Manley felt no qualms about representing

---

[10] While critics now routinely speak of Behn as a 'Tory propagandist', the meanings of such a phrase shift significantly between the period of Behn's political writings and the period of Manley's. I see Behn, who died in 1689, first and foremost as a royalist: a supporter not so much of any clearly defined political 'party' as of 'the side loyal to the succession of James II to the throne' (Backscheider, *Spectacular Politics*, 109). For this and other reasons I am inclined to agree with John L. Sutton that it was Manley who first fully exploited the potential of the scandal chronicle as a 'weapon of party politics' ('The Source of Mrs. Manley's Preface to *Queen Zarah*', *Modern Philology*, 82 (1984), 171). For discussions of *Love-Letters* as propaganda see Backscheider, *Spectacular Politics*, Ballaster, *Seductive Forms*, and Todd, *The Sign of Angellica*, as well as Todd's introduction to the new Penguin edn. (1996).

[11] I am thinking here of a woman like Joan Whitrowe, who clearly recognized the relationship between the poverty all around her and the leisured lives of the ruling class, yet travelled on foot miles out of her way to stand in the King's 'aura', bless and pray for him, and demonstrate her troubled yet very real deference. See Part II above for a discussion of the complex relationship between deference and social protest in early women's religio-political polemicism.

[12] Todd, *The Sign of Angellica*, 73.

Charles II and James II as fools when it suited her propagandistic purposes. Whereas a polemicist like Elinor James was empowered by her self-image as subject-protector of Stuart monarchy, Manley represented Charles II as a hedonist 'steadfast in nothing', James II as 'indiscreet and bigoted', and human nature as corrupt and self-interested across all social ranks. While suspicious of all political master-narratives, the chief master-narrative Manley critiqued in her writings was the Whig narrative of 1688 as liberating the nation from tyranny.[13] When Manley depicted her favourite satirical targets, John and Sarah Churchill, First Duke and Duchess of Marlborough, as a scheming couple 'big with the coming hopes of being at the head of the empire' (*New Atalantis*, 14), her negative counter-publicity was intended to expose *Whig* corruption and duplicity. Yet when taken as a whole—and despite her glowing portraits of Tory leaders—the overall effect of her several bestselling volumes is to undermine the ideology of aristocracy. Manley was prosecuted, ostensibly, for the *particular* stories she told, but she might just as well have been prosecuted for telling any stories about those in power. The circulation of any such stories potentially threatened the primacy of the state's own representations. Whether or not she actually changed anyone's opinion of the Duke and Duchess of Marlborough, Manley underlined for her readers the extent to which all public persons' media images were constructs. If lordship, like kingship, was a matter of representations, the mere existence of alternative genealogies could undermine the authority of any statesman's, politician's, or even monarch's authorized fictions of self. Expressing this insight in characteristically amatory terms, Manley hinted that in the bedroom, a king stripped of his royal robes is just a man. And at that point, significantly, he is open like any other man to the political and sexual manipulations of women:

Such is the Fortune of Monarchs in Love, when they are with their Mistresses they commonly lay aside that Majesty with [*sic*] dazles the Eyes and affects the Hearts of Mankind; they go undress'd into their Chambers, and make themselves so familiar with their Mistresses, they afterwards use them as other Men. (*Queen Zarah*, i. 8–9)

[13] In the 18th cent. the *New Atalantis* was understood as 'a representation of the characters of some of those, who had effected the Revolution' (Theophilus Cibber [Robert Shiels], *The Lives of the Poets of Great Britain and Ireland, to the Time of Dean Swift* (1753), 5 vols. (Hildesheim: Georg Olms Verlagsbuchhandlung, 1968), iv. 15).

Kingship was a matter of signification, not essence. Accordingly, it could be challenged by competing (and here female-authored) representations—whether the designedly instrumental remarks of a royal mistress at court or the public 'secret histories' of a woman party writer in the political press.

For John Milton, writing the *Areopagitica* at the outbreak of the Civil War, truth was ultimately self-evident to all reasonable beings.[14] For Delarivier Manley writing in the first age of party, truth was a luxury available to few, and the majority forced at all times to choose among a multiplicity of competing substitutes or 'representations'. At one level, Manley made in her political writing the conventional truth claim of Augustan propagandists, that her 'secret intelligence' was truthful, 'from the best sources'. But at another level, Manley also advanced an ongoing satiric critique of such claims. She hinted repeatedly that political representation was inherently ideological and openly signalled her intention to make use of this fact. She referred to her first political allegory, *Queen Zarah*, as a 'Little History'. Yet she simultaneously hinted much when she added that while 'he that composes a History' was 'obliged to Write nothing that is improbable', it was 'nevertheless allowable that an Historian shows the Elevation of his Genius, when advancing Improbable Actions, he gives them Colours and Appearances capable of Perswading'.[15] Coming as it does, in the

[14] While admitting that truth 'might have more shapes than one', John Milton nevertheless urged parliament to 'see the ingenuity of Truth, who, when she gets a free and willing hand, opens herself faster than the pace of method and discourse can overtake her' (*Areopagitica; a Speech of Mr. John Milton for the Liberty of Unlicenc'd Printing, to the Parliament of England* (London, 1644)). After 1688, Jonathan Swift (like Delarivier Manley) was considerably less optimistic. In Swift's works it is the mad Gulliver who most closely echoes Milton's confidence in asserting that 'the truth immediately strikes every reader with conviction' (*Gulliver's Travels and Other Writings*, ed. Louis A. Landa (Boston: Houghton Mifflin Co., 1960), 5).

[15] *Queen Zarah*, i, 'To the Reader', A2^r, A4^v. Sutton's 'The Source of Mrs. Manley's Preface to *Queen Zarah*' has revealed that Manley's critically acclaimed preface is in fact a 'translation of an essay on prose fiction contained in a French "courtesy book" published in 1702—the Abbé de Morvan de Bellegarde's *Lettres curieuses de littérature et de morale*' (171). Bellegarde's essay, in turn, is 'a paraphrase of the second part of the sieur du Plaisir's *Sentimens sur les lettres et sur l'histoire* published in 1683' (167). The fact that the preface to *Queen Zarah* was not Manley's original work does not diminish the striking nature of such a statement in a work designed as propaganda. Furthermore, Sutton's discovery supports the attribution of *Queen Zarah* to Manley, about which there has been some doubt. For details, see Sutton, 'The Source of Mrs. Manley's Preface to *Queen Zarah*', and Köster's edn.

preface to her first political allegory, this remark should be read as more than a casual acknowledgement on Manley's part of the fictionality of history. It should be read as a manifesto: a tough-minded acknowledgement of her contemporaries' deployment of 'history' for propagandistic purposes, and a scarcely veiled declaration of her intention to do the same.

LADY INTELLIGENCE VS. ASTREA

Motivated to write by a combination of economic necessity and political conviction, Delarivier Manley was a literary chameleon of sorts, capable of modifying her self-representations to suit her readers' tastes and her own changing ideological needs. Her provisional identities were a function of her historical moment as well as her sex. Caught between changing systems of textual financing, and doubly disadvantaged as a woman party writer in a late patronal mode of production, her authorial identities are at once a barometer of her shifting status in the literary marketplace and a rich record of her encounters with patrons, publishers, and fellow writers for pay. To trace Manley's textual representations of her achievements—the postures of her increasing notoriety—is to watch an increasingly shrewd businesswoman learn to advertise her success even as she parodied it, and make capital even out of her own ambivalence towards her pursuits. It is also to watch a late Stuart Englishwoman who wrote about politics and got paid for it satirize emerging 'polite' models of female authorial self-representation—and construct new, more effective models for herself as a woman party writer instead.

Manley began her career as an avowed propagandist with the publication of *The Secret History of Queen Zarah and the Zarazians* (1705). Part 1 was timed to grace the important parliamentary elections of that year, and 'the Kind Reception the first Part met with' resulted in the publication of a second part in November.[16] As its title suggests, the subject of *Queen Zarah* was

---

[16] *Queen Zarah*, ii, preface, A2^r. The 'Avis au Lecteur' of a 1711 French edition of *Queen Zarah* claims that the work had already sold 15,000 copies in English (Köster's edn., p. xiii). Manley almost certainly sold her copy to a publisher for a lump sum, and was unlikely to have benefited from the book's sales. There is no evidence that she received Tory patronage for the book. For the timing of Part 2, see Edward Arber, ed., *The Term Catalogues, 1668–1709* (London, 1906), iii. 481.

Sarah Jennings Churchill and the leading Whigs upon whom she was believed to have considerable influence. In 1709, Manley published a more complex fictional achievement in the same allegorical mode, for which she was indicted for seditious libel in October.[17] Like *Queen Zarah*, Manley's *New Atalantis* was timed to do maximum damage to the Whigs. The first volume was published in May, just before the opening of the 1709 parliamentary session, and proved so successful that it was already in its third edition by the time that the second volume was brought out six months later. Despite its length, the *New Atalantis* went through six editions in its first ten years, making it the bestselling novelistic fiction of the decade. The public reception of Manley's works would be an important factor in her increasingly focused and daring authorial self-representations.

With the emergence of women into the literary marketplace in significant numbers in Manley's lifetime, new models for female authorship were being constructed, models that Manley confronted as a political writer. In Manley's youth, two different models were available to women writers: the witty but scandalous Aphra Behn (*c.*1640–1689) and the poet and dramatist Katherine Philips (1632–64) who was marketed for 'her Verses and her Vertues both'.[18] By the time that Manley published her first political fiction in 1705, however, the origins of a national literary history had given rise to a new ideological spectrum of female literary virtue and vice.[19] Whereas before 1700 Behn and Philips had *both* been positive exemplars, by the eighteenth century Behn was quickly becoming an anti-model for the new 'literary lady', who would not 'urge [her] pen to prostitution'.[20] Manley demonstrated an

---

[17] The publishers and printer of the *New Atalantis* were taken into custody immediately after the publication of vol. ii on 20 Oct. 1709. A warrant was sent out for Manley's arrest, and, according to her own account, she turned herself in to protect her co-workers. She was in custody from 29 Oct. to 5 Nov., when she was admitted to bail. She was tried for libel at Queen's Bench on 11 Feb. 1710, and, for reasons which remain open to speculation, was discharged without sentence (Luttrell, vi. 505–8, 546). She went on to publish a sequel to the *New Atalantis* almost immediately, thinly disguised as *Memoirs of Europe*.

[18] Sir Charles Cotterell, preface to *Poems By the most deservedly Admired Mrs. Katherine Philips The matchless Orinda* (1667).

[19] On the implications for English women of the origins of a national literary history, see Ezell, *Writing Women's Literary History* and my 'Consuming Women: The Life of the "Literary Lady" as Popular Culture in Eighteenth-Century England', *Genre*, 26 (1993), 219–52.

[20] Elizabeth Inchbald, preface to *A Simple Story* (1791; Oxford UP, The World's Classics, 1988), 2.

awareness of contemporary models for female authorial self-representation, and she also demonstrated an awareness of contemporary shifts. Her 1695 poem 'To the Author of *Agnes de Castro*' represents Catherine Trotter Cockburn as a successor to Behn and Philips, and presents the latter as two equally exemplary female literary predecessors. Fourteen years later, however, she scorned what she viewed as Trotter Cockburn's hypocritical mid-career switch in self-representation from one 'pole' to the other of the new ideological spectrum of female literary virtue. In Manley's eyes, Trotter Cockburn had succumbed to oppressive new models of female authorship, renouncing a promising career in the playhouse and 'fitt[ing] her self with an excellent mask called religion' (*New Atalantis*, 160). Neither 'Aphra' nor 'Orinda' were appropriate models for Manley as a post-revolutionary woman party writer. Accordingly, she ultimately rejected both models in the *New Atalantis*—and created a new, more empowering one instead.[21]

Set in the context of post-revolutionary women's political activity, it seems fitting that Manley should frame the *New Atalantis* as a conversation between three politically literate female narrators. The one male narrator, a gentleman 'well fashioned, talkative, and vain', gets only two out of 800 pages in the original edition, and in those two pages is made the butt of a joke.[22] The first female frame character, the goddess Astrea, has just returned to corrupted earth, where she encounters her bedraggled fellow goddess 'Mother Virtue'. Astrea must prepare herself to serve as tutor to the next ruler of Atalantis, and in order to instruct her pupil she must spy on the political and amatory affairs of persons eminent in high life. As goddesses, Astrea and Virtue are possessed with the gift of invisibility, enabling them to hover round assemblies, courts, and public parks without making spectacles of themselves at the same time. This divine duo then runs into the more earthy character 'Lady Intelligence', who serves as their urban tour guide and as the main narrator of affairs.

---

[21] In the *New Atalantis*, Manley does quote one of her admirers to the effect that 'Nor Afra, nor Orinda knew so well, | Scarce Grecian Sappho, Delia to excel' (53), but this is a male enthusiast in a tavern speaking.

[22] The typesetting of the Penguin edition makes this joke somewhat less apparent (see pp. 85–6). The gentleman does not really 'narrate' in the sense of telling a story. He simply provides the answer to one of Astrea's questions. Astrea does not want the gentleman's company; she simply wants to know who a certain person is. But this male gossip makes himself more of a nuisance than his intelligence is worth. Accordingly, the divinities play a trick on him, and disappear.

The fact that Aphra Behn used the pseudonym 'Astraea' in her writings has convinced several modern readers that Manley's character Astrea should be read as a reincarnation of or tribute to Aphra Behn.[23] But Manley's high-minded and sententious deity arguably has nothing in common with Behn save her name. In her own lifetime, Behn was the respected author of bestselling fiction, poetry, and plays, and six years after her death the young Manley could still hold Behn up as a positive model of female authorship. But by the time of the *New Atalantis*, twenty years after Behn's death, the moral climate of the nation had changed, and Behn's already controversial reputation was under heightened attack. Augustan re-presentations of Behn had already begun the long process of literary history, whereby this complex and prolific author was reduced to the caricature of herself which appears in later eighteenth- and nineteenth-century literary histories as 'so unsexed a writer as Mrs. Aphra Behn'.[24] We cannot know what Manley thought of Behn in private. We can and do know, though, how Manley constructed her own literary career in relation to Behn's in public. And despite her own debt to Behn, in her own writings after 1700 Manley's allusions to her female literary predecessor are in fact distressingly derogatory.[25] In print, at least, the mature Manley largely rejected Behn as a workable model for her own female authorial self-representation.

Several of Manley's contemporaries employed the name 'Astraea' as a marketing ploy rather than as a tribute, and it is possible that Manley was doing something similar.[26] The following section

[23] Among classical and European authors who drew on the myth of Astraea, classical goddess of justice and traditional harbinger of the golden age, were Ovid, Virgil, Ariosto, Spencer, and their imitators, as well as panegyrists of Elizabeth in England and Henry IV in France. (Among the latter was Honoré d'Urfé in *L'Astrée*, one of the most influential European literary works of the 17th cent.) By the 18th cent. the use of the name 'Astraea' was in fact so conventional in polite literary circles that one of the speakers in a dialogue poem reprinted in the *New Atalantis* is named 'Astrea' (55–60). For further information on the use of the name 'Astraea' see Frances A. Yates, *Astraea: The Imperial Theme in the Sixteenth Century* (London: Routledge and Kegan Paul, 1975).

[24] Eric Robertson, *English Poetesses: A Series of Critical Biographies, with Illustrative Extracts* (London: Cassell and Co., 1883), 9.

[25] Manley attacks Behn on moral grounds in her *Memoirs of Europe* (i. 289). What seems like a 'gratuitous slap' at Behn is in fact not gratuitous, but rather part of her mature attempt to distance herself from her problematic literary predecessor.

[26] Susanna Centlivre's letters, for instance, were written and published under the pseudonym Astrea, and admirers addressed poetry to her by this name (John Wilson Bowyer, *The Celebrated Mrs. Centlivre* (Durham, NC: Duke UP, 1952)).

argues, however, that in the carefully distinguished personalities of the three female narrators of the *New Atalantis* Manley's contemporaries would have detected a sophisticated satire on emerging models of 'polite' female authorial self-representation. Manley's female narrators have distinct personalities, personalities that reflect increasingly rigid ideological divisions of sexual virtue among eighteenth-century women. Far from recalling the scandalous and witty Aphra Behn, Manley's goddess Astrea is in fact a type of the new ideal woman writer in her most socially acceptable forms. Chaste and virtuous, and claiming to prefer privacy and retirement, she is in fact reminiscent of Katherine Philips—or rather posthumous representations of Philips, which foregrounded her domestic and spiritual concerns above her scathing royalist verses.[27] Astrea's professed contentment 'to pass unknown and unregarded among the crowd of mortals' (13) echoes Philips's much-professed choice of 'A Countery Life'—the title of one of her most frequently reprinted poems. And certainly Manley's virtuous goddess, who shuns publicity to the point of rendering herself invisible, seems the polar opposite of the prolific female dramatist who declared of her pursuit of public fame, 'I am not content to write for a Third day only. I value Fame as much as if I had been born a *Hero*.'[28] Manley's Astrea is also given to constant moralizing and is particularly fond of *sententiae*. As she once abandoned earth 'in a Disgust', so now her comments serve, like contemporary 'Societies for the Reformation of Manners', to 'recommend virtue and discountenance vice'. She is

---

[27] On Philips and Behn as 'ideologically constructed identities often differing markedly from contemporary historical and biographical descriptions', see Backscheider, *Spectacular Politics*, esp. 73–81, as well as my 'Consuming Women' and the works cited there.

Manley's *The Lost Lover; Or, The Jealous Husband: A Comedy* (1696) contains a character 'Orinda, an Affected Poetess', whom some critics identify with Katherine Philips. Like Philips, Manley's 'Orinda' is a polite poet who expresses a preference for country retirement. But Manley's Orinda also has a Scottish accent, and other critics hold that Manley was satirizing not Philips, who had been dead for thirty years, but a contemporary woman writer whom she also satirized elsewhere, Catherine Trotter Cockburn (who was of Scottish descent). In support of the Trotter hypothesis, Manley's Orinda also talks incessantly about her suitors—something that the chaste Philips decidedly did *not* do. I read Manley's Orinda as I do her 'Astrea' in the *New Atalantis*: as a satirical composite of the contemporary women writers (or rather their self-representations) Manley did not like. Regardless of how we are to interpret Manley's 'Orinda' character, however, the character is further evidence of her concern with issues of female authorial self-representation.

[28] Preface to *The Lucky Chance; Or, The Alderman's Bargain* (1687).

capable, upon occasion, of self-righteousness and even cruelty; when Intelligence narrates the story of the seduction of the young and innocent 'Charlot' by her guardian, Astrea coldly points out the 'Morals' of the story as soon as it is finished, without expressing any sympathy for the young woman, the rest of whose 'life was one continued scene of horror, sorrow, and repentance' (45). (The disembodied voice of a fourth narrator, who does not appear as a character in the story, drily responds to the two sententious goddesses at this point: 'Having done moralising upon that story, they followed the Lady Intelligence into the palace' (45).) Manley tended to place herself in opposition to didacts such as her character Astrea in her writings, and she frequently portrayed contemporary moralists as hypocrites. We have seen her depict fellow female dramatist Catherine Trotter Cockburn in this manner, as 'fitt[ing] her self with an excellent mask called religion'.

But Manley did more than reject emerging models of genteel female authorial self-representation as oppressive. She also fictionalized her polite contemporaries' condemnation of her personal behaviour. Weaving into her text the story of her own seduction and betrayal by John Manley, she also took care to depict her two virtuous female narrators harshly condemning her autobiographical character 'Delia'. Astrea's sole response to Delia's tragic story of her social and economic ruin is to declare with a chilling ennui that she is 'weary of being entertained with the fopperies of the fair' (228). According to Astrea, by the loss of their chastity women like Delia are 'reduced to be the despicablest part of the creation' (228). In addition to a distinct personality, each of Manley's female narrators has a distinct social rank. While Astrea and Virtue are divinities, Lady Intelligence is of a lower social order. Even her name reflects her less exalted social position; while the names 'Astrea' and 'Virtue' are taken from literary traditions transmitted primarily by élites, the name 'Intelligence' was taken from the popular press and was a term that might be heard daily by anyone who had access to hawkers' voices crying 'intelligences' on London streets.

Intelligence refers to the two goddesses as 'Your Excellencies' and recognizes them as her superiors in social rank. Yet she also regards them as decorous to the point of folly and explicitly rejects their philosophy of life. When the female narrative trio happens upon another group of women who 'have neither the spleen nor

[the] vapours', 'laugh loud and incessantly', and are wholly 'at their ease', Astrea remarks, 'sure these seem to unknow that there is a certain portion of misery and disappointments allotted to all men. . . . The very consideration is sufficient . . . to put a damp upon the serenest . . . joy' (153–4). Intelligence responds to Astrea's gloomy didacticism with a comment much like the Duchess of Cleveland's reputed advice to Manley after she had been seduced. Since a woman's lost reputation could never be recovered, why not go on living regardless? Intelligence argues scandalously that for these laughing women to 'put a damp upon' their pleasures would be 'afflicting themselves unprofitably'—and moves on (154).

Intelligence lacks patience for the goddesses' edifying discourse, and is herself devoid of the desire to moralize. Manley parodied her own lack of interest in the didactic when after one long moralistic exchange between the goddesses Intelligence interrupts: 'Your Eminences are declaiming a length beyond my understanding, give me leave to get what information I can of that new adventure before us' (136).[29] In an earlier political allegory Manley had remarked that 'an Historian that amuses himself by Moralizing or Describing, discourages an Impatient Reader, who is in haste to see the End of Intrigues'.[30] Satirizing her newly proper contemporaries, Manley has Intelligence pause before one story to remark, 'But (ladies) in the pursuit of my story, perhaps there may be some things that are not very proper for so nice an ear as Virtue; and 'till I receive your commands in that point . . . I am at a loss how to behave my self' (18). Equally revealing is the fact that while Virtue and Astrea cannot sympathize with the ruined 'Delia', Intelligence pities the young woman and rails against her seducer. She feels for Delia because she *is* Delia. That is, both 'Intelligence' and 'Delia' are representations of Manley.

Like Manley, Intelligence *works* for a living—and works out of London, the political and literary centre of England. In Manley's day, most English news was printed in London, and with the exception of foreign and military affairs London was also the centre of journalistic attention. Accordingly, Intelligence is almost wholly

---

[29] Todd also recognizes 'the satiric point in [the] juxtapositions of different voices' (*The Sign of Angellica*, 87).

[30] See *Queen Zarah*, preface, a5^r, where she also writes that 'Moral Reflexions, Maxims and Sentences, are more proper in Discourses for Instructions than in Historical Novels, whose chief End is to please' (a4^v).

concerned with London news. 'See, my dear Astrea,' Virtue observes, 'as we approach the capitol, how busy Intelligence appears, like a courtier new in office! She bustles up and down, and has a world of business upon her hands' (13). Intelligence prefers bustling public places to rural retirement and solitude, and drags Astrea and Virtue from one public pleasure ground to another until Astrea marks her difference from this vulgar woman by remarking, 'My Lady Intelligence judges of us by herself, that we likewise find diversions among the most company' (90). When the group wanders to a rural area, they must rely upon a 'loquacious country-woman' to guide them, and Manley's own writing degenerates into a half-hearted attempt at the pastoral ('She set before 'em curds new-pressed, cream fresh from the cow[31] . . . strawberries just gathered . . .' (84)). As this passage will suggest, Manley too was an urban creature who spent time in the country only when forced to do so by debt or scandal. None of Manley's fictional characters idealizes rural retirement or longs for 'A Countery Life'; even Virtue concludes of her search for a worthy place on earth that 'Quite exploded from courts and cities, I was reputed to have refuged among the villagers, but alas! they knew less of me there, than in the cabinets of princes' (6).

Whenever the issue of authorship is raised, Intelligence functions as a mouthpiece for Manley's own economic circumstances and views. Intelligence views writing for pay as work, and literary texts as commodities as well as vehicles of ideas. Not coincidentally, Intelligence carries around with her in her satchel copies of Manley's own poems. At one point, she shares the poems with the two deities, 'just warm from the muse, finished but yesterday and newly communicated to me, to be distributed abroad' (54–5). Before sharing one poem, however, she complains of Manley's misfortunes as a literary 'labourer':

we don't pretend so much merit for this piece, I'll only tell you, that a certain poet,[32] who had formerly wrote some things with success but, either shrunk in his genius or grown very lazy, procured another brother of Parnassus [Manley] to write this elegy for him and promised to divide the

---

[31] While the Penguin edn. of the *New Atalantis* gives this word as 'bowl', I believe the correct reading is 'cow', as in the Köster facsimile edn.

[32] Paul Bunyan Anderson suggests that the 'poet . . . shrunk in his genius' is Manley's one-time friend dramatist Mary Pix (1666–1709) ('Mistress Delariviere Manley's Biography', *Modern Philology*, 33 (1936), 272).

profit. The reward being considerable and sweet, he defrauded the poor labourer of his hire. (48)

'Justly incensed against the treachery of his friend', Intelligence explains, the 'poor labourer' resolved to turn to the press, and 'print this piece in the next miscellanea' (48). Manley effectively did just this when she incorporated the poem into the *New Atalantis*. Through Intelligence, Manley also expressed her envy of her more privileged female contemporaries' superior material conditions for aesthetic achievement. When Intelligence shares with the goddesses another poem by Anne Finch, later Countess of Winchelsea (1661–1720), Astrea accounts for the poem's superior artistry by surmising that the author must be 'one of the happy few that write out of pleasure and not necessity. By that means it's her own fault, if she publish any thing but what's good' (93). Intelligence also complains of Manley's doubly disadvantaged situation as a woman party writer, comparing her unenviable economic circumstances even as an experienced propagandist with the patronage showered on young Richard Steele as an inexperienced poet:

I remember him almost t'other day but a wretched common trooper. He had the luck to write a small poem and dedicates it to a person whom he never saw, a Lord that's since dead, who . . . encouraged his performance, took him into his family, and gave him a standard in his regiment. . . . fortune did more for him in his adversity, than would have lain in her way in prosperity. (102–4)[33]

But the single most important clue to Manley's self-representation as 'Intelligence' lies in Intelligence's employment as 'first Lady of the Bedchamber' and 'Groom of the Stole' to a powerful princess (13). Throughout her political writings, Manley's primary female satirical target was Sarah Jennings Churchill, First Duchess of Marlborough, who served as First Lady of the Bedchamber and Groom of the Stole to Princess and later Queen Anne. By an odd twist, then—an explanation of which will be posited below—Manley's emblematic self-representation borrows the official job title of her favourite female political target.

In Manley's day, as we have seen, the term 'intelligence' would first bring to mind not wisdom but news. Seven years after the *New*

---

[33] Elsewhere Manley referred to Steele in his capacity as a party writer as 'a Bread-Writer, a sorry half Sesterce Fellow' and as a 'commodious useful Hireling' (*Memoirs of Europe*, i. 236–8).

Atalantis was published, printer-author Elizabeth Powell published
her own newspaper, the *Charitable Mercury and Female Intelligence* (1716). Official 'intelligences' were news reports whose com-
pilation was supervised by the Secretary of State and whose
function it was to provide not only 'extraordinary information
concerning enemy countries or domestic plotters, but also a regular,
settled supply of every kind of news from at home or abroad'.[34]
Until 1688, the Secretary of State's office held a monopoly of all
licensed news and collected the latter by means of a network of post
office interceptors, correspondents, and spies. Manley frequently
used the word 'intelligence' in this sense, to signify secret communication and correspondence. She observed the importance of 'due
intelligence, without which it was not possible to take right measures' (*New Atalantis*, 207) and that 'Indispensable of War, good
Intelligence' (*Memoirs of Europe*, ii. 268). She noted the importance of good intelligence to politicians' careers, observing of Lord
Treasurer Sidney, First Earl of Godolphin, that 'the Count wanted
not any requisite of a profound statesman, especially that one of
spies and good intelligence'. She also depicted Godolphin gaining
intelligence about powerful women at court by bribing their female
servants: 'Biron [Godolphin] had intelligence from Madam de
Caria's favourite woman' (*New Atalantis*, 195).[35] In the *New
Atalantis*, Manley represents even the goddesses Justice (Astrea)
and Virtue as unable to function without good intelligence. The
two goddesses command Intelligence to serve them and encourage
her to proceed even with her 'improper' stories. To judge wisely in
public political matters, Astrea explains, even goddesses must be
'thoroughly instructed' and 'informed of the most minute particular' (18–19).

Most importantly, though, the powerful princess whom Intelligence serves is neither Justice, Virtue, nor even Queen Anne,
but rather 'the omnipotent Princess Fame, of whom all the

---

[34] Peter Fraser, *The Intelligence of the Secretaries of State and their Monopoly of
Licensed News 1660–1688* (Cambridge UP, 1956), 1.

[35] Manley also used the word 'intelligence' in the sense of secret communication
when she recounted the story of her examination by the Secretary of State's office:
'They us'd several Arguments to make her discover who were the Persons concern'd
with her in writing her Books; or at least from whom she had receiv'd Information
of some special Facts, which they thought were above her own Intelligence' (*Rivella*,
113).

monarchs on the earth stand in awe' (13).[36] The new ruler of post-revolutionary British society, Manley suggests, was neither the monarch nor parliament but Public Opinion. Manley was writing at a time when 'public opinion' was beginning to matter in politics, and opportunities for manipulation of public opinion through print were first being recognized and exploited by a small number of leading statesmen. In 1702 Robert Harley wrote his famous letter to Godolphin envisaging the usefulness of an in-house propagandist, and in 1704 Daniel Defoe published the first issue of his periodical *A Weekly Review of the Affairs of France*, which one historian has described as an 'unofficial ministerial press organ'.[37] By 1714, '*both* parties had fairly sophisticated means of producing and disseminating propaganda at their disposal for the first time'.[38]

But Manley's self-representation as a female 'intelligence agent' actually *preceded* the establishment of an effective intelligence system in England. During the same decade that Manley was writing her political allegories, from 1705 to 1714, Robert Harley was working to establish the foundations of a ministerial intelligence network—not only to collect information, but also to disseminate 'political views held by the ministers in an attempt to influence public opinion in the widest sense'.[39] Defoe's circuits of Great Britain in Harley's service, substantially for the purpose of establishing a government intelligence network, took place between 1705 and 1708. The *New Atalantis* was published the following year (1709).

Manley recognized the importance of carefully managed 'public representations' to politicians' careers in the new age of 'public

---

[36] Having seen her father lose his throne in 1688, Queen Anne was particularly concerned with gaining the affection of her subjects and did so by a variety of methods. One of her first actions upon succeeding to the throne was to issue a proclamation 'for restraining the spreading [of] false news, and printing and publishing of irreligious and seditious papers and libels' (28 Mar. 1702; qtd. in Downie, *Robert Harley and the Press*, 57).

[37] For details see Downie, *Robert Harley and the Press*, esp. ch. 3; for a different view see Paula R. Backscheider, *Daniel Defoe: His Life* (Baltimore: Johns Hopkins UP, 1989), 151–8. From the first issue of 19 Feb. 1704, Defoe's *Review* contained '*an Entertaining Part in Every Sheet, Being Advice, from the Scandal Club . . . in Answer to Letters sent Them for That Purpose*'. Manley published her first political scandal novel in 1705.

[38] Downie, *Robert Harley and the Press*, 181.

[39] Ibid. 2.

opinion' and followed the activities of Whig propagandists with some care. In one of her own propagandistic fictions she outlined what she took to be the similar duties of Richard Steele.[40] Cataline (Lord Wharton) praises Stelico's talents as a literary mercenary and demands:

Where shou'd we then meet such another diligent, obsequious, trembling, dutiful, Mercenary? Many indeed are willing, but how few are found able? *Stelico* shall make it his Care to daub and misrepresent even the brightest and greatest Characters, to threaten and stigmatize with his Pen, those whom we fear and disapprove; he shall prepare Mens Minds for a favourable Approbation of our Proceedings, vilifie to the Life those of our Enemies, and when we have done our parts, applaud us for the well Performance.[41]

In the *New Atalantis*, Astrea agrees with Intelligence concerning the new power of political representations. Even monarchs were subject to representation's seductions: ''Tis impossible a prince can come to the knowledge of things but by representation, and they are always represented according to the sense of the representator' (110). Yet Astrea also defines herself as morally superior to those who deal in them. Whereas Intelligence makes public representations her business, Astrea laments the power of female favourites at court who 'represent . . . things through their false, mischievous, or flattering glass, appropriating the royal ear and favour that should be open and shine diffusively as does the sun' (211).

  In her letters to Robert Harley over a period of four years, Manley offered, like her character Intelligence, to serve as a new kind of counter-publicity agent whose weapon was 'representations'. 'I have attempted some faint representations, some imperfect pieces of painting, of the heads of that party who have misled thousands', she wrote by way of introduction to her vast social superior, consciously offering not 'truths' but superior fictions.[42] Four years later, Manley's last known letter to Harley offered once

---

[40] On the vicissitudes of Manley's relationship with Steele, see Morgan, *A Woman of No Character*, esp. 106–20.

[41] *Memoirs of Europe*, i. 237–8. Manley felt strongly (and wrongly) that the Tories were behind the Whigs, both in exploiting the new political press and in rewarding their own propagandists. In looking back on her career as a Tory supporter in 1714 she observed, 'she had chose to declare her self of a Party most Supine, and forgetful of such who served them' (*Rivella*, 110).

[42] 12 May 1710, HMC *Portland MSS* iv. 541.

again to 'represent' him more fairly: 'Your actions, always aiming at the good and glory of the nation, ought to be fairly represented to set those men right who only condemn for want of information.'[43] As Daniel Defoe put it in one of his own letters to Harley, 'A Man Can Never be Great That is Not Popular, Especially in England.'[44] Only a tiny proportion of the English people, Manley understood, had direct, unmediated access to goings-on at court. All the rest relied on reproduced intelligence as she did. Accordingly, there was a chance that she too 'might make myself a little serviceable'.[45]

Manley's complaints about her works being read for the 'Performance' rather than the 'Design' are reminders that her goal was to produce politically instrumental fictions, not enduring aesthetic achievements. In her letters to Harley, Manley repeatedly stressed her 'service to the cause' and what she took to be her writings' demonstrable *results*:

Though the performances were very indifferent, yet they were reckoned to do some service, having been the first public attempt made against those designs and that Ministry, which have been since so happily changed. (19 July 1711)

. . . several things which I had writ which . . . were then thought to have done the first public service to the present cause. (3 June 1714)

. . . several little pamphlets and papers of which, if I am rightly informed, some have not been disapproved by your Lordship, and the world. (ibid.)

Eventually Harley sent Manley £50, for which she expressed deep thanks. As she later informed him, though, that was 'all I ever

---

[43] 30 Aug. 1714, ibid. v. 491.

[44] July to Aug. 1704, *The Letters of Daniel Defoe*, ed. George Harris Healey (1955; Oxford: Clarendon P., 1969), 33. This entire letter, which outlines 'A Scheme of General Intelligence', bears comparison to Manley's self-representation as intelligencer.

[45] 2 Oct. 1711, HMC *Portland MSS* v. 95. Downie makes the important point that one of Harley's strengths as an organizer of propaganda was his ability to see that the many different audiences for propaganda in this period required many different kinds of propagandists. Many ordinary readers of propaganda were unlikely to be moved by the 'erudition of a Dr. Swift' (*Robert Harley and the Press*, 134).

Swift echoed Manley's language of 'service to the cause' in writing about her in his *Journal*: 'Lord Peterborough desired to see me this morning at nine. . . . I met Mrs. Manley there, who was soliciting him to get some pension or reward for her service in the cause, by writing her *Atalantis*, and prosecution, &c. upon it. I seconded her, and hope they will do something for the poor woman' (*Journal to Stella*, ed. Harold Williams (Oxford: Clarendon P., 1948), i. 306).

received from the public for what some esteem good service to the cause'.[46] Looking back on her career as a supporter of the Tory party, she concluded that 'the most severe Criticks upon *Tory* Writings, were *Tories* themselves, who never considering the Design or honest Intention of the Author, would examin the Performance only, and that too with as much Severity as they would an Enemy's' (*Rivella*, 110–11).

At one level, Manley's persona Intelligence believes in her job as exposer of 'pretenders to Vertue' and takes her duties most seriously. 'I have yet very much to show and to inform you of,' Intelligence bows to her divine companions. 'Called to so eminent a station, I shall endeavour to discharge my self as I ought of an employment honourable and distinguishing' (60).[47] At another level, however, Intelligence exemplifies Manley's own ambivalence towards her propagandistic endeavours and is part of her characteristic satire on her own methods. For even as Manley represented herself as 'Intelligence', she also distanced herself—*from* herself—by making her persona a comic figure. Astrea and Virtue mock Intelligence throughout the *New Atalantis*. When this business-like woman is eager to investigate the shrieks of a woman at night in an 'obscure Quarter' of St James's Park, Virtue smilingly asks her daughter, 'Do you think, my dear Astrea, that 'twould be difficult to decide whether my Lady Intelligence be agitated by a principle of curiosity or charity?' (162). The invisible 'fourth narrator', too, mocks Intelligence's jealousy when others attempt to usurp her authority as informant. When the 'gentleman talkative and vain' intrudes into the ladies' conversation, the fourth narrator states that Intelligence 'neither bore him, nor the countrywoman any great good will for usurping upon her province and forcing her to a long and painful silence' (86). Most often, though, Intelligence

---

[46] 30 Aug. 1714, HMC *Portland MSS* v. 491. In the same letter Manley described herself as having 'nothing but a starving scene before me'. When Harley sent Manley £50, she thanked him profusely. When Harley sent Swift this same amount of money for similar services during the same period, Swift was much vexed and sent it back. He was playing for the much higher stakes of a bishopric and could afford to be offended by monetary gifts.

[47] Manley's own self-valorizing, proto-professional identification in her political writing as a guardian of the public welfare was a conventional topos, a marketing strategy, and a psychological strategy for coping with material want. Only three months after her trial, her health 'very much disordered by my fears and the hardships I received', she was drumming up support for equally libellous projects, and announcing her motives in a similarly grand manner.

parodies herself. A voyeur and a spy, she knows that her news is unofficial, unlicensed. She recognizes that different people have different ideas of what is 'news', and she accepts the fact that her divine companions are sometimes scornful of the low 'gossip' she finds worth reporting. Manley's penchant for self-satire was to some extent an Augustan trait, shared by contemporaries such as Alexander Pope and Jonathan Swift. But it was also a function of her insight into and ambivalence towards the nature and long-term implications of the new propaganda press. The disturbing and exhilarating importance of symbolic manipulation in her society, and inescapably ideological nature of that manipulation, is an underlying theme of her works. The changing nature of political authority as increasingly a function of representations and the potential availability of print as a mass medium of manipulation were a combination she simultaneously exploited and warned her readers against.

While Manley's most careful critics have invariably been at pains to prove that the 'substratum of truth [in Manley's political allegories] has been overlooked',[48] assessing her fictions' 'truth value' may not ultimately be the best way to understand their power. Manley was writing propaganda, and the power of propaganda, like the power of 'gossip', cannot be measured in terms of its quantifiable 'truth'. In *Queen Zarah*, Manley demonstrated this insight for her readers by depicting her protagonist Sarah Churchill successfully deploying false rumours to accomplish her political goals. Simply by hinting to Albanio (James II) that his daughter (Princess Anne) has warm feelings for Mulgarvius (Buckinghamshire), the evil Zarah manages to get the latter expelled from court (i. 40–52). False rumours, Manley's female politician knows, could work as well as true ones to advance or undermine political agendas and careers. Like Manley admitting to Harley that 'I have endeavoured to make myself a little serviceable; had I either instructions or encouragement I might succeed better', Manley's persona Intelligence frankly admits that factual knowledge of court affairs is a luxury seldom available to her. Accordingly, she must sometimes perform her job without it. 'It is not my principle to run away with appearances. I love to be minutely informed. . . . My business is

---

[48] Needham, 'Mary de la Rivière Manley, Tory Defender', 260. See also Köster edn., pp. xvii–xix, et al.

indeed to give intelligence of all things, but I take Truth with me when I can get her' (162). Manley knew that people thirst for news of any kind and generally trust their own ability to judge whether or not what they read or hear is 'true'. In her own case, it was the 'truth' of popular sentiment that she sought to capture and use: the unconscious prejudices and predilections of her audience that she strove to personify, magnify, and raise to the level of cultural myth. In order to take advantage of an already fermenting popular distrust of '*Zarah and Volpone*'s Reign', Manley coloured the working relationship of Sidney Godolphin and the Duchess of Marlborough with the overtones of an amour. 'It is well known Volpone pays more Court to *Zarah's Couchee* than *Albania's* [Queen Anne's] *Levee*,' her narrator remarks.[49] In 1710, the Duchess of Marlborough's correspondent Arthur Maynwaring would attempt to assuage her worries about the *New Atalantis* by informing her that the stories about her in Manley's book were nothing to 'trouble or concern yourself' about, ''tis all old and incredible stuff of extortion and affairs'.[50] As we will see, however, Sarah Churchill knew as well as her 'low indigent' attacker that Maynwaring was missing the point. Rumours could be political currency—whether they were 'old and incredible' or not.

And of course, Manley attempted to defend herself during her 1709 examination for libel by claiming that the *New Atalantis* was mere gossip: nothing but 'old Stories that all the World had long since reported' (*Rivella*, 110). Like an oral tale-teller, Manley *did* reproduce 'old stories'. She even recycled particularly useful ones several times. She also thematized the fact that she was retelling— and retailing—stories that 'everybody already knows'. In the *New Atalantis*, Intelligence's divine audience can foretell the outcome of her story of John Churchill's role in the Revolution. Like Manley's own readers, Intelligence's listeners experience this story with a suspenseful foreboding, and perhaps also a secret pleasure at being in the know: 'Methinks I shudder with the dread or apprehension of the Count's [Churchill's] Ingratitude! How do I foresee that he

---

[49] *Queen Zarah*, i. 105; ii. 22. Jonathan Swift made the same distortion in claiming that Godolphin's 'Passion for the Duchess . . . dragged him into a Party, whose Principles he naturally disliked' (*The History of the Four Last Years of the Queen* in *The Prose Works of Jonathan Swift*, ed. H. J. Davis et al., 16 vols. (Oxford: Blackwell, 1939–74), vii. 9).

[50] Sarah Churchill (Duchess of Marlborough), *Private Correspondence*, 2 vols. (London: Henry Colburn, 1838), i. 236.

deserved not that distinction [heaped upon him by James II]? Put me out of pain; has he not been ungrateful to the royal bounty?' (16). Astrea and Virtue listen to Intelligence's account not to learn a *new* story, but rather to re-hear a story that they already know. In this way, like her character Lady Intelligence, Manley combined news and novelty with repetition and familiarity—and so supplied different kinds of pleasure to her audience at once.[51]

LADY INTELLIGENCE VS. MRS NIGHTWORK

Understanding Manley's representation of her political writing as the reproduction of intelligence—the 'tak[ing] up [of] old Stories that all the World had long since reported'—may help to explain the extraordinary occurrence of a topos of childbirth in a work designed to function as mainstream propaganda. The *New Atalantis*'s cast of shady midwives and abandoned bastards, and graphically depicted scenes of childbirth and infanticide, may well be unparalleled in eighteenth-century fiction. At the same time, in the *New Atalantis* and elsewhere, Manley also made more conventional use of childbearing metaphors as models for the creative process. Manley's metaphors of the author as parent, the text as infant, or the act of publication as 'giving birth' would not in themselves strike her contemporaries as unusual. When read in conjunction with her extremely unconventional representation of the actual birth process, however, these metaphors suddenly take on striking new resonances.

For women writers, the association of artistic and biological 'creation' has always held special difficulties. For an eighteenth-

---

[51] In analysing Behn's *Love-Letters*, Judith Kegan Gardiner discusses the function of repetition with variation in fiction by early women writers, interpreting this phenomenon as characteristic of 'women's erotic formula fiction' ('The First English Novel: Aphra Behn's *Love Letters*, the Canon, and Women's Tastes', *Tulsa Studies in Women's Literature*, 8 (1989), 201–22). But many writings by male as well as female authors in this period are also characterized by repetition with variation, and this phenomenon may simply be traceable to these authors' socioeconomic position and historic moment in print culture. Behn, Manley, John Dunton, Charles Gildon, Daniel Defoe, and other writers of this period whose fiction is characterized by a high level of repetition were all 'Grub Street' authors writing for a nascent literary marketplace, and repeating oneself is a quick way of filling up a page. In addition, these particular authors, none of whom was classically trained, were highly indebted to a residual oral culture in which repetition with variation was a commonplace structuring device.

century woman writer who was also known to be the mother of at least one illegitimate child, however, the association should have been utterly debilitating. As Manley's autobiographical character 'Delia' sighs, 'My wretched son, whenever I cast my eyes upon him, was a mortal wound to my repose; the errors of his birth glared full upon my imagination' (*New Atalantis*, 226).[52] Confronted with her readers' inevitable association of textual and biological generation, Manley devised an ingenious solution, and one that was far-reaching in its implications. By means of her politicization of the figure of the 'gossip', Manley managed to transform both her institutional liabilities as a female propagandist, or teller of tales, and her personal liabilities as the mother of an illegitimate child, into an innovative narrative perspective that allowed her to comment authoritatively on political and sexual affairs at the same time. Instead of vainly trying to write around her public reputation, that is, Manley wrote *through* it—and so made her personal notoriety serve her political ends. Manley's frank and unsentimental depictions of childbirth in a work otherwise intended as political propaganda are in fact an integral part of her effort to come to terms with her anomalous status as woman party writer, literary labourer, and mother of an illegitimate child. A consideration of Manley's attempt to transform social liabilities into marketplace assets will help to account for the seemingly extrinsic topos of childbirth in the *New Atalantis*. It will also help twentieth-century readers accustomed to more linear narratives to make sense of the work's much-criticized but in fact highly innovative form.

The term 'gossip' originally designated a godmother or god-father, and came to mean any close friend. A dominant meaning of 'gossip' in seventeenth-century England was 'a woman's female friends invited to be present at a birth' (*OED*).[53] Manley used the term 'gossip' in this sense when, in writing of her political opponent

---

[52] Manley also alluded to the birth of her son in her fictionalized autobiography. The narrator states, 'I must refer you to her own Story, under the Name of *Delia*, in the *Atalantis*, for the next Four miserable Years of her Life' (*Rivella*, 29)

[53] Hobby, *Virtue of Necessity*, 10. Samuel Johnson recalls this sense when he defines 'gossip' in his *Dictionary* as 'one who runs about tattling like women at a lying-in'. Patricia Meyer Spacks sees Johnson as the first to connect 'gossip unambiguously and officially with women' (*Gossip* (Chicago: U. of Chicago P., 1986), 26). But the association of women and gossip was present long before Johnson's day, as the example of Mrs Noah in the medieval Chester plays will suggest.

Richard Steele, she mentioned the 'merry up-sitting of the gossips' at the birth of one of his illegitimate children (*New Atalantis*, 103).[54] In her representation of the midwife Mrs Nightwork, who serves as a fourth female narrator in the *New Atalantis*, Manley drew on a long-standing association of 'gossips', midwives, and female talk. One thinks of Shakespeare's midwife Mistress 'Taleporter',[55] or Christopher Smart's gossipy 'Mother Midnight' in *The Midwife*, a periodical which explicitly acknowledges Delarivier Manley (Fig. 4).[56]

The notion of the poet as biological parent, inspired creator of immortal offspring, may be traced back at least as far as Plato's *Symposium*. The related metaphor of publishing as 'giving birth to' a work, with its contingent implications of a 'tearing asunder' or 'abandonment', may be traced through classical, medieval, and Renaissance texts.[57] As Robert Escarpit notes, the Romans described publishing by the root of the verb *edere*, which means 'to

---

[54] Manley mentions Steele's illegitimate children more than once. In one instance she claims that she recommended her own midwife to Steele, but that he failed to pay the woman: 'Being informed of the narrowness of his circumstances, she gave him credit to her midwife, for assistance to one of his damsels, that had sworn an unborn child to him. The woman was maintained till her lying-in was over, and the infant taken off his hands, *par la sage femme*, for such and such considerations upon paper. He had no money to give . . . his credit was stretched to the utmost' (*New Atalantis*, 102–3; see also *Memoirs of Europe*, ii. 309).

[55] *The Winter's Tale*, IV. iv. 268–9.

[56] Christopher Smart's periodical *The Midwife, Or The Old Woman's Magazine* appeared monthly from 16 Oct. 1750 to late 1752 or early 1753. The periodical's chief persona, 'Mrs. Mary Midnight', echoes Manley's Mrs Nightwork in name, personality, and trade (midwifery, gossip, and politics). Most issues conclude with a section titled 'The Midwife's Politicks: Or, Gossip's Chronicle of the Affairs of Europe', which echoes the title, concerns, and style of *Memoirs of Europe*. The caption to the periodical's frontispiece, 'De la Riviere Invt.' ('De la Riviere invented it'), explicitly alludes to Manley. The frontispiece depicts two elderly women ('gossips') sitting before a fireplace in run-down lodgings, surrounded by pen and ink and sheets of paper and what appear to be periodical issues or pamphlets. Despite the run-down lodgings there are books on the mantelpiece. Like the female frame characters in the *New Atalantis*, Smart's Mrs Midnight goes on rambles through the town in search of 'news', travelling at night so that she too can 'see without being seen'. Many other aspects of this periodical and its 'Mary Midnight' persona also recall Manley's career and writings.

[57] See Ernst Robert Curtius, *European Latin Literature and the Latin Middle Ages* (1952; Princeton UP, Bollingen Series XXXVI, 1973), esp. 132–4. On the association of reproductive and poetic labour in the long 18th cent., see Terry J. Castle, 'Lab'ring Bards: Birth Topoi and English Poetics 1660–1820', *Journal of English and Germanic Philology*, 78 (1979), 193–208.

FIG. 4. 'De la Riviere Invenit': tribute to Delarivier Manley in the frontispiece to Christopher Smart's *The Midwife, Or The Old Woman's Magazine* (1750–2). Reproduced by courtesy of the Beinecke Rare Book and Manuscript Library, Yale University

put into the world', 'to give birth to'. The word 'publish' descends from the Latin *publicare*, 'to make public'.[58] The same year that the *New Atalantis* was delivered to the world, the first English copyright law was passed, making authors the primary proprietors of their works and reinforcing the notion of texts as infants authored by their parents. In the eyes of the government, of course, the chief advantage of the Copyright Act of 1710 was that it made literary 'paternity suits' possible—assisting prosecutors in their efforts to hold individuals responsible for the consequences of their writings.

In the nascent literary marketplace in which Manley worked, though, the publication of most literary texts was less likely to resemble a property investment than an abandonment of one's progeny to its fate. From the literary 'Labourer's' point of view, texts were less likely to resemble immortal offspring than ephemeral '*Mushrooms* of a Night, or *Abortives* under the Mother-Pangs' that leave 'their unhappy Parent the *Mortification* of seeing 'em *expire* as soon as they began to *Be*' (*Memoirs of Europe*, i. 1). Manley's unenviable economic circumstances ensured that, for her, authorship was not inspired 'creation' but rather material work. Accordingly, she had little patience for those who would represent their literary endeavours as 'inspired' and mocked the idea at key moments in her texts. In retelling the story of her examination by the Secretary of State's office, she claimed that when she was asked 'from whom she had receiv'd Information of some special Facts', her answer was that 'it must be *Inspiration*, because knowing her own Innocence she could account for it no other Way' (*Rivella*, 113).

Among the many variations of the metaphor of the author as parent and text as offspring that Manley deployed was the notion of the text as still-born, aborted, or monstrous birth. Like contemporaries such as John Dryden and Alexander Pope, Manley deployed these metaphors against her enemies, or had them deployed against her by the same. In her ironic political pamphlet *The Duke of* M[arlboroug]h's *Vindication: In Answer to a Pamphlet Lately Publish'd call'd* [Bouchain, *or a Dialogue between the* Medley *and the* Examiner], she compared the writings of her Whig competitors to still-born and monstrous births, then condemned them as aban-

[58] Robert Escarpit, *The Sociology of Literature* (1958), trans. Ernest Pick (Painesville, Oh.: Lake Erie College Press, 1965), 46.

doned bastards for good measure. To quote from the Whig papers that would prove her argument would be 'giving life to . . . still-born, shapeless Births, which but just appear'd and perish'd'. Refer-ring to their anonymous publication, she then added, 'Nor do I remember any Person to have so far Glory'd in those monstrous Productions, as to own being a Parent to them' (12).

When in 1696 one 'J. H.' sought to capitalize on Manley's debut as a playwright by publishing an unauthorized collection of her letters, he also sought to capitalize on her reputation as the mother of a bastard by representing himself as a man-midwife eager to 'deliver' her genius to the world (and the town, in turn, as 'big to see what a Genius so proportionate can produce').[59] Thirty years later, when Edmund Curll sought to capitalize on Manley's death by republishing her works, he used the same metaphor, suggesting that her suppression of a 1705 edition of her letters was a form of infanticide—a crime that he would right by bringing the text back to life.[60] Meanwhile, Alexander Pope was drafting his *Dunciad* (wr. 1719–28; pub. 1728) in which he would represent Manley's fellow female writer for pay, Eliza Haywood, with 'two babes of love clinging to her waste'—emblems of her scandalous memoirs, il-legitimate literary forms dropped like unwanted infants on the London literary marketplace. Contemporary printers and publish-ers often represented one another as midwives who 'delivered' literary works to the public. John Dunton drew on the same asso-ciation of publishing, midwifery, and gossip when he accused pub-lisher Sarah Malthus of having 'Midwiv'd so many Lyes into the World' that she 'deserve[d] Whipping till the Blood comes'. Dunton warned Malthus that if he had not given her her break as a pub-lisher, 'Thou'dst else in the forgotten Crowd | Of *Common Mid-wives* liv'd unknown'.[61] In Manley's youth, a spate of books on midwifery were published, including some by women midwives.[62]

---

[59] *Letters Written by Mrs. Manley* (1696), preface, A2ʳ⁻ᵛ.

[60] Curll, who reprinted Manley's letters in 1725, claimed that she had given him a copy in 1705 with a 'positive injunction that it should never more see the light of day till the thread of her life was cut' (*A Stagecoach Journey to Exeter* (London, 1725), n.p.).

[61] *Dunton's Whipping-Post: or, a Satyr upon Every Body* (London, 1706), 12, 35.

[62] See Robert A. Erickson, ' "The Books of Generation": Some Observations on the Style of the British Midwife Books, 1671–1764', in Paul-Gabriel Boucé, ed., *Sexuality in Eighteenth-Century Britain* (Manchester UP, 1982), 74–94, and *Mother Midnight: Birth, Sex, and Fate in Eighteenth-Century Fiction (Defoe, Richardson, and Sterne)* (New York: AMS Press, 1986).

In the 1680s, the enormous notoriety of Catholic midwife-author Elizabeth Cellier, the so-called 'Popish Midwife', contributed to a nexus of associations in this period between women, publishing, midwifery, and politics. The same associations may be seen in 1688 in the so-called 'warming-pan scandal', when allegations ('gossip') began circulating that the son born to Mary of Modena on 10 June was not a real Prince of Wales but an impostor smuggled into the Queen's bedchamber in a warming-pan. Childbirth became a political event of national importance and the subject of endless rumours and 'gossip', and the oral testimony of midwives was enrolled in Chancery and published by royal authority.[63]

In telling the story in the *New Atalantis* of her own seduction and betrayal by her cousin, Manley suggested that her status as a 'fallen woman' was directly linked to the fact that she was left 'motherless' as a girl. Like her character 'Charlot', Manley's mother died when she was young, leaving her to be seduced by an older male relative. Manley's apparent feelings of 'motherlessness' may also be reflected in the relations among her three female narrators in the *New Atalantis*. While the goddesses Astrea and Virtue are an affectionate mother–daughter team, Manley's persona Intelligence is an apparently motherless outsider. Several of Manley's best-known female characters in the *New Atalantis*, the 'Ladies of the New Cabal', have the economic means to avoid unwanted children entirely. These ladies explicitly reject the social role that is imposed upon them and, like Mary Astell, deeply regret 'the custom of the world, that has made it convenient (nay, almost indispensable) for all ladies once to marry' (156). Economically privileged, they banish 'the troublesome sex' from their circle and form an all-female community so appealing that even the virtuous Astrea is forced to admit that women were not placed on earth solely 'to propagate the kind' (161). For those women like herself who could not avoid unwanted pregnancies, Manley made clear, there were often inconvenient or tragic consequences. Venturing to the margins of the city, the *New Atalantis*'s narrative trio come upon a crowd eager to see 'a woman nailed to the gibbet' (82) for murdering her bastard child. A country-woman explains that a division of soldiers has recently marched through the community, leaving 'I know not how

[63] See Rachel J. Weil, 'The Politics of Legitimacy: Women and the Warming-Pan Scandal', in Lois G. Schwoerer, ed., *The Revolution of 1688–1689: Changing Perspectives* (Cambridge UP, 1992), 65–82.

many unborn bastards behind 'em' (83). She recounts how the young woman whose body is now nailed up as a ghoulish moral emblem gave birth all alone in her chamber: 'She told her brother she was tormented with the toothache and wanted to go to bed. . . . to't she goes. Pain after pain, tear after tear, cry after cry. . . . after a few more labour pains, she is delivered all alone by her self of a brave boy. Lest he should cry, she tore out his bowels in the birth' (83).

Wandering through another 'remote Place' by moonlight, the trio is surprised once more, this time by the sight of a pregnant woman being lifted from a coach. The woman, they are shocked to discern, is about to give birth any moment—her horrendous muffled cries give her away. Racked with pain, she 'groans in a terrible manner', and urges her gentleman companion to 'haste and fetch the midwife. I'm surrounded with horror, the rack of nature is upon me, and no kind assisting hand to relieve me' (136). The responses of Manley's narrators are telling. Astrea exclaims, 'O Lucina, be propitious! Well did the unhappy fair term it the rack of nature! Can any thing be more exquisite? Oh! how piercing are her cries,' while Virtue asks her daughter, 'Shall we not appear and offer her our assistance in her misery?' (137). But Manley's persona Intelligence wants nothing to do with the woman about to give birth. She is interested in childbirth only in so far as it is potential news, preferring to hide and gather 'intelligence'.

Intelligence then recognizes the midwife 'Mrs Nightwork', and the trio stand by as she assists at the delivery in the dead of night. It is here, in Manley's careful differentiation between her characters Lady Intelligence and Mrs Nightwork, and her depiction of their testy relationship, that her simultaneous deployment and rejection of the figure of the gossip—and, by extension, the oral political culture to which her fictions are indebted—becomes most clear. Manley recognized that strict distinctions between 'gossip', 'intelligence', and 'news' were ideological rather than objective ones, and she made this recognition a foundation of her political writing career. At the same time, however, Manley took care to define herself *against* traditional representations of the gossip as a mere chatterer—a retailer of stories for their own sake. By including in the *New Atalantis* a dramatic face-to-face encounter between a traditional gossip and her own politicized brand of 'female intelligencer', she attempted at once to draw on female oral politi-

cal traditions and to define herself away from those traditions
deemed unrelated to or beneath the concerns of 'high' politics.

Once again, the social rank of Manley's narrators is pointedly
differentiated; Mrs Nightwork is of a distinctly lower social order
than 'Lady Intelligence', who as we have seen is of a lower social
order than the two female divinities. While Manley, in her self-
representation as Intelligence, emphasized her disadvantaged position in relation to 'polite' women like Astrea and Virtue, she also
represented herself as superior to women like Mrs Nightwork.
A commoner rather than a goddess or a 'Lady', Mrs Nightwork
addresses Intelligence as 'Your Ladyship'. Loquacious and undigni-
fied, she is a disturbingly unethical figure. While bowing to Lady
Intelligence's superior news, Mrs Nightwork also suggests boldly
that 'we [midwives] are a kind of rearguard to the Princess you have
the honour to serve' (138). This remark only serves to intensify
Intelligence's distrust, for everyone knows that a midwife is supposed to keep secrets, not spread them by serving 'Princess Fame'.[64]
But Manley's 'Mrs Nightwork' rambles on with stories of illegitimate children she has delivered (and disposed of?) until Intelligence
interrupts sarcastically, 'You are admirable company, Mrs. Nightwork. I'm afraid you are taking my province from me, and engross-
ing all the scandal to your self' (138). Offended by Nightwork's
suggestion that she too served 'Fame', Intelligence sneers, 'Is not
that something against conscience? I thought, Mrs. Nightwork, you
had been sworn to secrecy' (138). 'Directly, but not indirectly,' Mrs
Nightwork responds shadily, and her answer is provocative, for she
has just confessed to techniques of communication identical to
Manley's own. Manley's 'secret histories' were written in a series of
overlapping codes, some of which were so complex that even her
most politically *au courant* contemporaries needed separately published 'keys' to decipher their meanings with any degree of
certainty. Like her gossipy Mrs Nightwork, Manley employed
allusions, innuendoes, allegory, and other circuitous devices to
protect herself and communicate at the same time. She symbolized

---

[64] A midwife's employment was dependent upon the reliability of her word.
Licensed by a bishop and required to 'swear an oath which bound [her] to ensure
that no false charges of paternity were brought, no babies swapped, hidden or killed
and not to assist at secret confinements', the midwife was traditionally associated
with secrets (Hobby, *Virtue of Necessity*, 183, 9). See also Erickson, *Mother
Midnight*.

this necessary strategy of indirection in the form of Intelligence's elaborate garments, which, as Astrea observed, are 'all hieroglyphics' (13).

Mrs Nightwork refers to the communicative strategy that she shares with her creator as speaking 'under the rose'. Like Intelligence, and like Manley herself, she sees scandal as an important part of her job: 'without this indirect liberty, we should be but ill company to most of our ladies, who love to be amused with the failings of others' (139). But if Mrs Nightwork's methods are similar to Lady Intelligence's, the ends to which she puts her news are different. The traditional gossip's stories are malicious and told merely to entertain. The female 'intelligencer', by way of contrast, does not circulate titillating stories for their own sake, but rather deploys them for worthy political ends. Like the oral depositions of the midwives present at the birth of the Prince of Wales in 1688, printed and circulated nation-wide by royal authority, Mrs Nightwork does once wander out of her usual territory into the more high-stakes realm of political commentary. She describes Charles II as 'steadfast in nothing during the course of his whole reign but in adhering to his brother in a case that has since cost the empire so much blood and treasure' (140). Annoyed by Nightwork's usurpation of her own territory of politics, Intelligence warns her off, threatening, 'You are a politician, I find, Madam, as well as a midwife.' Mrs Nightwork promptly apologizes for her oral wandering into the realm of politics: 'I beg your Ladyship's ten thousand pardons for repeating what you must be much better informed of than I can pretend, but 'tis our way, when once we set in, we talk on, whatever it is about' (140).

Manley distances herself from the traditional gossip figure in early modern culture in many ways. Characteristically, though, her most certain clue that the reader is supposed to reject Mrs Nightwork's code of ethics is a political one. Mrs Nightwork casually remarks that she is 'extremely tender of an oath, and would not break it for any thing but interest' (139). In the economy of late Stuart royalist, Jacobite, and Tory women's fiction, oath-breakers are almost always Whigs (and therefore despicable). Earlier in the *New Atalantis*, Whig John Churchill is critiqued as a man who betrayed James II for personal interests: 'The Count had a tender conscience, and could not act to the prejudice of his interest; he left an indulgent master, and went to Henriquez' (25). Upon hearing Nightwork's politically encoded statement of her ethics,

Intelligence sarcastically asserts her own social and moral superiority: 'You are improving as well as diverting company, Mrs. Nightwork' (139). Mrs Nightwork eventually takes her leave with the new-born infant tucked under her petticoat (possibly suggesting its murder by smothering, the most common form of infanticide in this period). A creepy figure who anticipates Moll Flanders' 'governess', Mrs Nightwork is only one of many shady midwives in Manley's fiction, and the unwanted infant only one of dozens. An understanding of Manley's attempt to transform personal liabilities into marketplace assets by means of her simultaneous deployment and rejection of the figure of the 'gossip' helps to account for this unusual aspect of the content of the *Atalantis*. At once drawing on and rejecting long-standing female oral political traditions, Manley simultaneously created a space for her own politically encoded writings and valorized her party political propaganda as something superior to mere 'female talk'.

J. Paul Hunter has stressed the 'tendency of the novel to associate itself with gossip and with oral discourse' and has argued that late seventeenth- and early eighteenth-century English fiction served as a supplement to, or substitute for, the oral exchange of the coffeehouse. Women, in particular, 'came quickly to relate to the deep cultural phenomenon'.[65] By insisting that Manley's fiction be placed in its historical contexts, as part of a fundamentally oral culture in which 'pamphlets, periodicals, and informal talk fed each other in an ever-intensifying attention to the latest news or pseudo news',[66] we come closer to understanding how her books were read— and why it did not occur to her contemporaries to criticize their *structure*.

Until recently, modern critics of Manley (almost all of them novel scholars) have seen the lack of unified 'plots' in her fictions as a flaw. In 1946 B. G. MacCarthy described the construction of the *New Atalantis* as 'execrable', while in 1969 John J. Richetti declared that 'works such as the *New Atalantis* ... possess none of the unity of theme or characterization that makes a narrative meaningful to us today'.[67] But when Manley's political allegories are read

[65] J. Paul Hunter, ' "News, and new Things": Contemporaneity and the Early English Novel', *Critical Inquiry*, 14 (1988), 504 n. 23.

[66] Ibid. 499.

[67] B. G. MacCarthy, *Women Writers: Their Contribution to the English Novel 1621–1744* (Oxford: B. H. Blackwell, 1946), 218, and Richetti, *Popular Fiction before Richardson*, 121. I am indebted to Richetti's book for first sparking my own interest in Manley.

as her contemporaries read them—not through the lens of later developments in the history of the novel, but rather as part of a contemporary conversation about state affairs—such criticisms are at once historicized and largely invalidated. Manley's political fictions do not have unified linear plots. Conversations seldom do. Her books were not read for the plot, but devoured for information, like contemporary newspapers. When Arthur Maynwaring reported on the *New Atalantis* to Sarah Churchill, he provided not a 'plot summary' but rather a series of extracts illustrating the manner in which the Duchess and persons important to her were represented. He read the book, that is, as a blatantly biased, politically encoded 'reference book' of current scandal.

In his sociological model of the emergence and transformation of the bourgeois public, Jürgen Habermas designated the public sphere as (in Nancy Fraser's words) 'an arena in modern societies in which political participation is enacted through the medium of talk'.[68] If the distinguishing characteristic of the post-revolutionary public sphere in England was the organization of dialogue as a political mode, then Manley's 'coffee-house conversations in print' created a public sphere in which literate women could participate. They created a virtual 'public', in which political participation by fictional characters was enacted through the medium of talk, and political participation by readers was enacted through voyeuristic private participation in that conversation. Both the *New Atalantis* and its sequel *Memoirs of Europe* are structured as a series of conversations, in which the usual fare of the marketplace, street, or alehouse, 'news mongering and . . . gossip about current topics', is discussed in the privacy of a small group.[69] In his study of the competing voices or discourses which make up the eighteenth-century novel, J. Paul Hunter pays special attention to what he sees as a cultural redefinition of news. While readers continued to demand news of state affairs, they also developed 'an interest in

---

[68] Nancy Fraser, 'Rethinking the Public Sphere: A Contribution to the Critique of Actually Existing Democracy', in Calhoun, ed., *Habermas*, 110.

[69] Hunter, ' "News, and new Things" ', 501; see also *Before Novels*. It is worth recalling here Walter J. Ong's observation that 'non-rhetorical styles congenial to women writers helped make the novel what it is: more like a conversation than a platform performance' (*Orality and Literacy: The Technologizing of the Word* (London: Methuen, 1982), 160). MacCarthy is in fact quite accurate when she goes on to describe the *New Atalantis* as 'consist[ing] of endless conversations' (*Women Writers*, 218).

lesser, more private, and personal events. Everyday and domestic events began to appear more and more frequently in print, both in periodicals and separate titles.'[70] Manley was among the first English authors to exploit the new market for 'private news' for party political ends. Her politicized 'Secret Histories', like Aphra Behn's politicized 'Love-Letters', played a role in the redefinition of news that Hunter outlines, while at the same time participating in contemporary shifts in the *modus operandi* of political life. Manley drew on traditions of women's oral exchange in shaping the form, as well as the content, of her innovative fictions. Her combination of what Hunter calls the 'news-function' and modes of female talk was among her most important contributions, not only to the history of the English novel, but also to the history of women's political writing and ultimately to the history of feminism.

POLITICS, ALLEGORY, AGENCY: 'TO TURN OUR SEXES WEAKER DESTINY'

> She is first Lady of the Bedchamber to the Princess
> Fame, her garments are all hieroglyphics. (*New Atalantis*, 13)

> I have attempted some faint representations, some imperfect pieces of painting, of the heads of that party who have misled thousands. If anything moves your curiosity I will explain what you desire.
>
> (Manley to Harley, 12 May 1710)[71]

> *Astrea.* Can your poets here below speak truth?
> *Intelligence.* Metaphorically, or by way of allegory.
>
> (*New Atalantis*, 60)

In tracing the development of new codes of communication under conditions of censorship in Stuart England, Annabel Patterson describes what she calls a 'hermeneutics of censorship': a cultural pact between the state and the governed, which allowed various forms of allegorical subterfuge to flourish even in a time of political repression.[72] Writers developed new strategies for communicating political ideas indirectly, whether by employing encoded forms of

---

[70] Hunter, ' "News, and new Things" ', 507.
[71] 'Mrs. Dela Manley to [the Earl of Oxford]', 12 May 1710, HMC *Portland MSS* iv. 541.
[72] Patterson, *Censorship and Interpretation*, 8–9.

expression such as allegory, irony, and mock dialogues, or by transforming genres not usually associated with oppositional expression into political tools. In tracing the generic evolution of the romance, Patterson suggests that 'from being an attractive but untrustworthy alternative to the serious, romance itself came to be redefined as serious, a way of perceiving history and even a means of influencing it' (160). Ambiguity became 'a creative and necessary instrument', and fictionality 'a means of mediating historical fact' (11).

John J. Richetti has argued that popular fiction of Manley's day depended for its success upon the exploitation of 'a body of assumptions and attitudes which commands immediate, emotional, and inarticulate assent, as opposed to a set of ideas which requires self-conscious and deliberate intellectual formulation'. 'To read these popular narratives', Richetti suggests, 'was, at least for the moment of belief and participation that even the most inept narrator can induce, to submit to an ideology, a neatly comprehensible as well as comprehensive pattern of reality.'[73] Manley's *Queen Zarah* 'depends for its effects upon a carefully established and almost stylized "scene" of aristocratic elegance, gallantry, intrigue, and corruption' (127). Manley's political allegories do work by means of the pleasurable manipulation of surface texture, but not because their author was incapable of 'deliberate intellectual formulation'. Rather, they work this way because they are propaganda, and propaganda art has a distinct set of strategies of its own. As we have seen, Manley was intensely aware that her fictions were 'very indifferent' from an aesthetic standpoint, yet she also exulted that they were 'thought to have done the first public service to the present cause'.[74] Theorists of political propaganda allegory point out that this subgenre's essence is the design of provoking a certain pattern of behaviour from the audience. Political allegory is most successful as propaganda when it functions as a form of mind control:

The victim of propaganda is allowed no other course but to empathize with scenes that are cast in highly organized, systematized, bureaucratic molds. Since this kind of order is often the aim of the political propagandist, he

---

[73] Richetti, *Popular Fiction before Richardson*, 11.
[74] 'Mrs. Dela Manley to [the Earl of Oxford]', 19 July 1711, HMC *Portland MSS* v. 55 and 3 June 1714, ibid. 453.

needs only to get his audience interested in the surface texture of the conformist action. By involving the audience in a syllogistic action, the propagandist gets a corresponding pattern of behavior from the audience. . . . At least this is what he hopes will happen. In getting this attention to the total action he depends . . . on imagery. The imagery of allegory is often glittering and excitingly rich, even wondrous.[75]

Instead of disguising her propagandistic methods, Manley actually foregrounded them. She employed multiple, competing, and some-times obviously untrustworthy narrators; she told the same story twice in different ways and even 'cross-referenced' the different accounts; and she frequently foregrounded her awareness that political truths were a matter of representation.[76] Her remarkable willingness to advertise her political writing as propaganda func-tions to give hasty readers the impression that she is judiciously leaving matters of interpretation up to them. This is not, however, a possibility. Rather it is precisely the way that political propa-ganda art works.

The report of Whig MP Arthur Maynwaring to Sarah Churchill concerning the *New Atalantis* is a reminder of just how seductive Manley's glittering, stylized scenes could be. For even Maynwaring, the Duchess's confidant, found himself charmed by the work—despite the fact that his benefactor was one of its chief satirical victims.[77] Partly, no doubt, out of politeness to Churchill, Maynwaring described the *New Atalantis* as 'that vile book', 'the nauseous book', 'this trifling book', and 'this stupid book' (*Priv. Corr.* 236–8). But he also let slip the adjective 'delightful'—and so gave away his initial pleasure. Initially, Maynwaring appears to have found even Manley's portrait of the Duchess being set upon by the 'rabble' amusing. 'There is one scene which I think you could hardly help laughing at,' Maynwaring wrote, 'which is, when 240 [the Duchess] is going to be pulled to pieces by the mob, for all

[75] Angus Fletcher, *Allegory: The Theory of a Symbolic Mode* (1964; Ithaca, NY: Cornell UP, 1986), 68.

[76] For an example of an obviously untrustworthy narrator, see the narrator of Manley's autobiography, who begins his 'Impartial Histor[y]' by admitting that he has spent his life as her unrequited admirer. For an example of intertextual cross-referencing, see the same text, where Manley refers the reader to another version of Rivella's 'Story, under the name of *Delia*, in the *Atalantis*' (*Rivella*, 53, 29).

[77] On the relationship of Arthur Maynwaring and Sarah Churchill see Frances Harris, *A Passion for Government: The Life of Sarah, Duchess of Marlborough* (Oxford: Clarendon P., 1991), esp. chs. 10–12.

manner of ill done to 42 [the Queen], and to England, generous
Hilaria [Masham] sends a troop of guards to rescue her. . . . I hope
[it] will make you laugh as it did me' (236–8).[78] 'The whole point
of allegory', theorists have suggested, 'is that it does not *need* to be
read exegetically; it often has a literal level that makes good enough
sense all by itself.'[79] As Maynwaring's comments on, and the continued popularity of, the *New Atalantis* suggest, Manley's allegories were not only effective interventions in a particular political
crisis. They were also successful narratives, eminently entertaining
in themselves.

Allegory has been theorized as a 'symbolic mode': a specific
literary device in one of its manifestations, but also more fundamentally a 'process of encoding our speech'. The etymology of
allegory, a term stemming from '*allos+agoreuein* (*other+speak
openly, speak in the assembly or market*)', suggests that the relationship between censorship, marginalization, and 'devious, ironi-
cal ways of speaking' may be inherent in the mode itself, and, as
theorists suggest, 'the political overtones of the verb *agoreuein* need
always to be emphasized'.[80] If allegory is inherently the mode of
those who cannot speak openly in the marketplace, it begins
to make sense why in seventeenth- and early eighteenth-century
France and England the political *roman à clef* was to a striking
extent a gendered phenomenon, practised notably by women.[81]
Like cant languages or other forms of encoded speech, allegory is
for the politically disenfranchised not so much a cultivated aesthetic
practice as a daily linguistic strategy. It is a way of speaking
'otherwise', in order to speak at all.

Manley's debt to seventeenth-century aristocratic French fiction
is now well known.[82] Her political allegories fall squarely into the

---

[78] For this scene see *New Atalantis*, 209.

[79] Fletcher, *Allegory*, 7. Catherine Gallagher also makes this point ('Political
Crimes and Fictional Alibis: The Case of Delarivier Manley', *ECS* 23 (1990), 511),
as do I in 'The Women of Grub Street' (diss., Stanford U., 1991).

[80] Fletcher, *Allegory*, 3, 2 n. 1.

[81] For compelling evidence that by the end of the 17th cent. the 'politico-sexual
intrigue' had been 'established . . . as a narrative realm in which the woman writer
had a privileged authority and interest' see Ballaster, *Seductive Forms*, 125 and Joan
DeJean, *Tender Geographies: Women and the Origins of the Novel in France* (New
York: Columbia UP, 1991).

[82] This is largely thanks to Ballaster, *Seductive Forms*, as well as indirectly to
Robert Adams Day, *Told in Letters: Epistolary Fiction before Richardson* (Ann
Arbor: U. of Michigan P., 1966). From the multi-volume heroic romance to the more
tightly constructed and realistic 'nouvelle', 'histoire', or 'petite histoire', translations
of French fiction flooded the English literary marketplace in Manley's lifetime.

French category of the *chronique scandaleuse,* social satires which sometimes had 'a directly political and . . . incendiary purpose'.[83] Manley owed a special debt to Marie-Catherine le Jumel de Barneville, comtesse d'Aulnoy, whose fiction she mentions in her work.[84] She may also have known Lady Mary Wroth's *The Countess of Montgomeries Urania* (1621) or John Barclay's *Argenis* (1621), examples of the French heroic romance form used by English authors 'to comment on contemporary figures and their scandalous activities'.[85] Like most of the fiction-reading public in her day, she almost certainly knew Aphra Behn's *Love-Letters between a Nobleman and his Sister* (1684–7), which combines current politics with a new kind of reading pleasure.[86] Continuing in a direction that Behn was moving when she died, Manley played a major role in the evolution of the scandal chronicle as a political instrument. In doing so, however, she retained the scandal chronicle's deeply gendered concerns, and in this way she helped to turn a tide in British women's political writing. In Manley's political fiction two traditions are conjoined: the largely aristocratic French tradition of 'feminocentric' fiction used as a tool of social and political satire, and the long-standing tradition of middling British women's polemical political activism through print.

As politically disenfranchised persons increasingly expected to distinguish themselves 'as tender Mothers and faithful Wives, rather than as furious Partizans', eighteenth-century Englishwomen increasingly communicated their political convictions as Manley's Mrs Nightwork did her secrets: 'indirectly'.[87] Political allegory may be said to be a form of narrative invisibility, for it aims to make the exact intentions of the author at once obvious and impossible to trace. It is significant that both of Manley's two most important literary predecessors in her capacity as a fiction writer are known to have served as government spies. While Marie d'Aulnoy served as an agent for the French government, Aphra Behn served as a spy for

---

[83] Ballaster, *Seductive Forms,* 56.

[84] Manley mentions d'Aulnoy's *Mémoires de la cour d'Espagne* (1679–81) in her *Letters Written by Mrs. Manley* (1696). In 1707, her *Lady's Pacquet of Letters* was published along with a translation of d'Aulnoy's *Mémoires de la cour d'Angleterre* (1695).

[85] Todd, *The Sign of Angellica,* 47.

[86] As Paula R. Backscheider writes, 'since at least the 1640s English readers had been bombarded with political tracts, but Behn created a pleasure vehicle to carry her propaganda' (*Spectacular Politics,* 110).

[87] *Spectator,* 81, 2 June 1711; *New Atalantis,* 139.

Charles II during the Second Anglo-Dutch War.[88] Instead of serving as a spy herself, however, Manley transformed her predecessors' voyeuristic activities into a narrative strategy: a narrative strategy that was also a form of cultural power. The narrators of the *New Atalantis* are themselves female 'spies' who possess the ability to 'make us garments of the ambient air, and be invisible, or otherways, as we shall see convenient' (9).[89] Their ability to 'pass unknown and unregarded among the crowd of mortals' (13) makes them examples of feminine modesty, but it also gives them a distinct strategic advantage.[90] Like her intelligence-gathering spies, Manley pointed out, women could use their own marginality in political life to serve their interests. And, with their new access to the political press in England, women could now also disseminate their 'secret intelligence' to a sizeable public audience—silently transforming themselves into active participants in state affairs.

Anonymous gossip is the discursive equivalent of physical invisibility. Its source cannot be identified, nor its consequences controlled. 'The anxiety aroused by gossip', observes Patricia Meyer Spacks, 'derives partly from its incalculable scope.'[91] The power of Manley's fictions stems largely from their deployment of popular gossip: a paradoxically authoritative mode of communication, precisely because it is impossible to trace. At one point in her book

[88] For information about d'Aulnoy's spying activities, see Morgan, *A Woman of No Character*, and Glenda K. McLeod, 'Madame, d'Aulnoy, Writer of Fantasy', in Katharina M. Wilson and Frank J. Warnke. eds., *Women Writers of the Seventeenth Century* (Athens, Ga.: U. of Georgia P., 1989), 91–118. For an interpretation of known information about Behn's spying activities, see Angeline Goreau, *Reconstructing Aphra: A Social Biography of Aphra Behn* (New York: Dial, 1980), and Janet Todd, *The Secret Life of Aphra Behn* (Rutgers, NJ: Rutgers UP, 1997). Behn's 'code name' as a spy was 'Astraea', and it is tempting to speculate that if Manley did invoke Behn in her character 'Astrea', it was in Behn's capacity as a female spy.
[89] Manley's travelling personifications-in-a-cloud anticipate the later 18th-cent. literary technique of omniscient narration, as well as writers' deployment of near-invisible female voices as a narrative strategy. Critics of Jane Austen have stressed the importance of gossip in her novels, and its relationship to narrative technique, particularly her use of *style indirect libre*. As in Austen's novels, so in Manley's *Atalantis* female gossip 'naturaliz[es] and "femininiz[es]" the voice of authority by subtly disseminating it into a chattering cacophony of voices' (Casey Finch and Peter Bowen, 'The "Tittle-Tattle of Highbury": Gossip and the Free Indirect Style in *Emma*', *Representations*, 31 (1990), 3).
[90] As Ballaster observes, 'the enforced invisibility of women in the world of politics is now presented through the figure of Astrea as a supernatural gift' (*Seductive Forms*, 115).
[91] Spacks, *Gossip*, 6.

on gossip, Spacks remarks, 'I have called it "a private mode," but the matter is not so simple. . . . Gossip belongs to the realm of private . . . discourse . . . but it incorporates the possibility that people utterly lacking in public power may affect the views of figures who make things happen in the public sphere' (6–7). Drawing on traditional allegorical representations of 'Rumour' or 'Fama' as a woman, as well as on the larger traditions of women's oral discourse from which those stereotypes originated, Manley re-appropriated a debilitating label for her own purposes. 'Rumour' and 'gossip' were the 'news' of the politically disenfranchised; she would show how they could also be the tools.

Manley's interest in new possibilities for female political agency was to some extent a consequence of the historical moment in which she lived. Late seventeenth- and early eighteenth-century print culture reflects a widespread concern with issues of illicit female power, and textual genres ranging from the most popular to the most privileged are filled with examples of powerful women culled from the Bible, mythology, history, and literature. Biblical leaders and progenitors such as Deborah, Judith, Esther, Jezebel, and Eve, as well as classical characters such as Semiramis, Juno, Dido, and Hippolyta and her fellow Amazons, compete for attention with figures from history and popular culture such as Boadicea, Queen Elizabeth, Mary Queen of Scots, and Pope Joan. And all of these literary and historical characters compete for attention with those seemingly omnipresent royal mistresses—the same powerful women who provoked Pope's complaint that in Charles II's reign 'Jilts rul'd the State'.[92] After the Revolution of 1688, the passing of the English crown through the female line in the persons of Mary II and Anne brought to a head long-standing debates concerning female political influence.[93] A female monarch's closest personal servants were also female, and older fears of royal mistresses were supplanted by new anxieties concerning 'She-Court Favorites'. John Dunton marked Queen Anne's accession with *Petticoat Government. In a Letter to the Court Ladies* (1702) and

---

[92] Pope, *An Essay on Criticism*, in *Poems*, ed. Butt, 160, l. 538.

[93] While William and Mary were joint regnant monarchs, with executive power lodged in William alone, it was widely believed that Mary was truly a regnant queen, and women writers certainly saw her as an important emblem of female power. See Carol Barash, *English Women's Poetry, 1649–1714: Politics, Community, and Linguistic Authority* (Oxford: Clarendon P., 1996) and W. A. Speck, 'William—and Mary?', in Schwoerer, ed., *The Revolution of 1688–1689*, 131–46.

probably the corresponding *Prerogative of the Breeches, in a Letter to the Sons of Men*. Once the crown was safely back in male hands in 1714, Dunton marked the event with a pamphlet exploring the theme of female leadership as seduction, *King Abigail: or, The Secret Reign of the She-Favourite, Detected, and Applied; In a Sermon Upon these Words*, And Women rule over them, *Isa. 3. 12* (1715).

Manley's own interest in possibilities for female political agency through public representations may be traced back to her earliest known works. Her first known publication, the encomium to Catherine Trotter Cockburn, praised Trotter Cockburn's *Agnes de Castro* (1695), concluding, 'Fired by the bold example, I would try | To turn our sexes weaker destiny. | Oh, how I long in the poetic race, | To loose the reins, and give the glory chase; | For, thus encouraged and thus led by you, | Methinks we might more crowns than theirs subdue.'[94] From the beginning of her career as a published author, Manley represented successful female authorship as a contest not only for the bays, but also potentially for political power. Led by Trotter, and inspired by Mary II and Princess Anne, women writers could pursue more than just a crown of laurel.[95] In 1696, Manley's sensational drama of incestuous and adulterous passion, *The Royal Mischief. A Tragedy*, explored in depth issues of illicit female power. Focusing on the political and sexual intrigues of the Persian queen 'Homais', the play was loosely based on the relationship of Charles II and his mistress Barbara Villiers Palmer, Countess of Castlemaine and Duchess of Cleveland (1641–1707), who was popularly suspected to have had considerable influence over the King. Manley's exploration of Cleveland's supposed influence over Charles II anticipated her later, more enduring fascination with the Duchess of Marlborough who was popularly feared to have comparable power over Queen Anne.[96] By the time that Manley's *Queen Zarah* (1705) was published, the friendship between Anne and her most threatening 'She-Favorite' had grown strained. In 1705, though, Sarah Churchill's declining favour was

---

[94] Delarivier Manley, 'To the Author of Agnes de Castro' (1695).
[95] On contemporary women writers' use of Mary II and Anne to usurp 'linguistic and political authority', see Barash, *English Women's Poetry*.
[96] Manley stayed with the Duchess of Cleveland for six months in 1694. Twenty years later she described herself as having 'reign'd six months in Hilaria's [Cleveland's] Favour' (*Rivella*, 33).

still obscured from the eyes of the people by Anne's continued reliance on Sidney Godolphin and John Churchill, over whom the Duchess still retained considerable sway.

The manipulation of her society's hatred for 'She-Court Favorites'[97] was central to Manley's propagandistic methods from the beginning. It was like Manley to sense that 'the people who, with no indulgent eyes, examine into the actions of favourites, had always rather rail than applaud, and hate that grandeur they cannot share in' (*New Atalantis*, 204). Manley also knew that she was most likely to tap sensitive cultural nerves by focusing on a female favourite. Acknowledging the very distrust of female favourites that she was exploiting, she observed that Sarah Churchill's political machinations at court in the reign of Queen Anne were baulked by the 'ungovernable Spirit of the *Albigionois* [the English]', already made wise to the power of female favourites in 'the Female Reign of *Rolando* [Charles II]' (*Queen Zarah*, i. 110). Churchill would become the title villain of Manley's first political allegory, *Queen Zarah*, as well as a primary satirical victim of both the *New Atalantis* and *Memoirs of Europe*.[98] Manley attacked Churchill in her penultimate *Examiner* issue, no. 51, 19 July 1711, as well as in her ironic political pamphlet *The Duke of* M[arlboroug]h's *Vindication* (1711). By drawing on her contemporaries' simultaneous fascination with and distrust of politically influential women, Manley could appeal to them on unconscious as well as conscious levels.

But there were other, more deep-seated reasons for Manley's career-long fascination with Sarah Churchill. When Manley pointed out that even monarchs 'come to the knowledge of things but by representation, and [things] are always represented according to the sense of the representator' (*New Atalantis*, 110), she was not only referring to the Duchess's propagandistic activities, she was learning from them as well. For above all, Sarah Churchill is represented in Manley's fictions as a female 'intelligencer' or

---

[97] John Dunton, *King Abigail: or, The Secret Reign of the She-Favourite* (1715), 11.

[98] Sarah Jennings (1660–1744) married John Churchill in 1678, and for twenty-five years served as foremost female friend, First Lady of the Bedchamber, and Groom of the Stole to Princess and later Queen Anne. When Anne ascended the throne in 1702, she promptly made Sarah and John Churchill Duchess and Duke of Marlborough, and, along with Sidney Godolphin, paid considerable heed to their advice.

propagandist. Throughout Manley's fictions Churchill is depicted as a master of representations: a woman aware of the power of fictions, and, as we have seen, adept at achieving her goals by circulating 'intelligence'. Manley represented Sarah Churchill as the master-mind behind two key political 'desertions': John Churchill's decision to become 'a treacherous Villain to his Master, and a Traytor to his King' by going over to William of Orange in 1688, and Princess Anne's decision to consent to the forced abdication of her father (*Queen Zarah*, i. 65, 67, 63). In short, 'Zarah's' life was 'one continued Scene of politick Intrigue' (*Queen Zarah*, i. 41).

Shortly after the publication of the second volume of the *New Atalantis* in November 1709, Arthur Maynwaring wrote to Sarah Churchill about Manley's 'vile book'. As we have seen, he attempted to assuage Churchill's concerns, primarily by assuring her that Manley's printed gossip was 'all old and incredible stuff of extortion and affairs' (*Priv. Corr.* i. 236). In his next letter, Maynwaring urged Churchill not to worry herself about 'the nauseous book', as there was 'not a word in it relating to 240 [the Duchess], but very old, false, and incredible scandal' (237). Churchill's own letters, however, suggest that, like Manley, she knew that false 'gossip' was potentially as damaging as true. Rumours could be politically effective, whether they were 'old and incredible' or not.

Maynwaring commented on the expanding power of the political press and on the difficulty of controlling the anonymous gossip that Manley had circulated:

The license of the press is too great, and I hope some proper way may be found to restrain it this winter; but I would not have the rise taken from this trifling book, which, as you observe truly, would only make it spread more. . . . I am afraid it will be very difficult quite to cure the mischief; for so long as people will buy such books, there will always be vile printers ready to publish them: and low indigent writers will never be wanting for such a work. (237, 239)

The lust of the literate for printed news, the growing horde of entrepreneurs in the book trade eager to cater to this expanding group, and the breakdown in press controls marked by the lapse of the Licensing Act in 1695 were an explosive set of phenomena that many women of Manley's generation sought to exploit—including Sarah Churchill herself. Sarah Churchill's electioneering activities have been well documented.[99] Her involvement with the propaganda press in 1705, however, is of special relevance to Manley's own. That year, the Duchess sent Daniel Defoe an anonymous gift of money in return for his services to Whig members of the ministry. In her payment to Defoe, Sarah Churchill acted independently of her husband, and almost certainly without his knowledge. (At that time, both John Churchill and Sidney Godolphin, then Lord Treasurer, were popularly believed to be Tories.[100]) In a letter dated 15 May 1705, Charles Montagu, Lord Halifax, complimented Churchill on her generosity, and agreed that 'a little money can not be better placed by those who are in Power, then in obliging and engaging those who have Wit, and Storys, that may be turned on them, or the Enemy'.[101] Somehow, Manley must have heard about the Duchess's encouragement of Defoe, for in her own witty 'Story' published the same year, she represented the Duchess not only as a woman working to set up a secret propaganda or 'intelligence' network, but also specifically as an employer of Defoe. 'To establish a firm and lasting Interest in the Senate of *Albigion*', the Duchess 'sent Circular Letters with Secret Instructions' to the 'Petty States and Provinces', and set to work '*Foeski* [Defoe], a seditious *Zarazian*, and a virulent Pamphleteer' (*Queen Zarah*, ii. 75, 51, 76).

One year before Manley's *New Atalantis* was published, Sarah Churchill and Arthur Maynwaring had designed and executed one of the most important pieces of campaign literature of the 1708 elections.[102] In a letter to Churchill concerning the *Advice to the Electors of Great Britain; Occasioned by the Intended Invasion from France,* Maynwaring observed, 'I took the hint of it from one of the letters with which your Grace honoured me, wherein you mention the usefulness of raising a Cry upon the Jacobites.'[103]

---

[99] See in particular Henry L. Snyder, 'Daniel Defoe, the Duchess of Marlborough, and the *Advice to the Electors of Great Britain*', *Huntington Library Quarterly*, 29 (1965–6), 53–62 and Frances Harris, 'The Electioneering of Sarah, Duchess of Marlborough', *Parliamentary History*, 2 (1983), 71–92 and *A Passion for Government.*

[100] Snyder, 'Daniel Defoe', 56.

[101] Blenheim MSS, E36, qtd. ibid. 57.

[102] Snyder, 'Daniel Defoe', 58. Downie calls the *Advice to the Electors* 'the most effective piece of printed literature' of the elections (*Robert Harley and the Press*, 104).

[103] Letter dated 3 Apr. 1708, Blenheim MSS, E28, qtd. in Snyder, 'Daniel Defoe', 60.

Looking back upon their propagandistic endeavour one year later, in November 1709—the same month that Manley was gaoled for the *New Atalantis*—Maynwaring advised the Duchess that the two of them 'must always be upon the watch, and even write books together, as was done before the last elections' (*Priv. Corr.* i. 277). In 1708 and 1709, then, two of the most important works of political propaganda, respectively Whig and Tory, were either instigated or written by women. Along similar lines, while in 1711 Manley would assume editorship of the Tory *Examiner*, Maynwaring and the Duchess of Marlborough were, according to one critic, the most likely source for the idea of setting up the Whig *Medley* in response.[104] If Sarah Churchill was involved in helping to set up the Whig *Medley*, then it may be said of two of the most prominent political essay journals of Queen Anne's reign that for a time, one was edited by a woman while the other was co-instigated by another woman and published by a third woman, the Whig Abigail Baldwin, who served as a primary distributor for the *Medley*.

Sarah Churchill's letters to Queen Anne concerning the *New Atalantis* and related publications are evidence that, like Manley, she was ahead of her time in recognizing the 'public' as an increasingly important conceptual entity in British political life. Immediately after the publication of the second volume of the *New Atalantis*, Churchill wrote to the Queen not to deny the book's claims, but rather to use those claims as evidence for her own argument concerning public opinion.[105] Stressing the new importance of paying lip service to the 'will of the people', the Duchess warned the Queen that her subjects were beginning to suspect that her (Tory) bedchamber woman Abigail Masham was capable of influencing her royal decisions. 'I think you are influenced by this favorite to do things that are directly against your own interest and safety,' Churchill wrote. 'And you seem to think that there is nothing in all this' (*Priv. Corr.* i. 242). Attempting to support her claim, the Duchess threatened to appeal neither to the Queen's

---

[104] Frank Ellis, ed. and intro., *Swift vs. Mainwaring: The Examiner and The Medley* (Oxford: Clarendon P., 1985), p. liii.

[105] In writing about the *New Atalantis*, Churchill relied solely on Maynwaring's synopsis, and sometimes confused Manley's work with the anonymous *The Rival Duchess: or, Court Incendiary. In a Dialogue between Madam Maintenon and Madam M[asham]* (1708).

councillors nor to a fellow peer, but rather to the 'first ordinary man' on the street: 'To shew you that I am not alone of this opinion, if I should ask the first ordinary man that I met, what had caused so great a change in you, he would say that the reason was because you were grown very fond of Mrs. Masham, and were governed by those that govern her' (243). Finally, as 'definitive evidence' for her claim concerning the new importance of attending to public gossip, she turned to Manley's *New Atalantis*. 'I had almost forgot to tell you of a new book that is come out,' she remarked. (Her air of casualness here is feigned, as there is more than one extant draft of this letter.) Relying on Maynwaring's synopsis, she stated of Manley's book that 'the subject is ridiculous, and the book not well written' (244). Demonstrating characteristic political savvy, however, she then added, 'but that looks so much the worse, for it shews that the notion is extensively spread among all sorts of people' (244). Churchill used Manley's 'ridiculous book' to defend herself against accusations of personal and political transgressions. 'My only crime, at least that you are pleased to tell me of, is that I think you [the Queen] have an intimacy with her [Masham]. Therefore, to show you that I am not singular in that opinion, I will transcribe a few passages out of a book that is lately printed' (240). Summarizing her argument, she concluded:

Now, since the people find ... this lady is your favorite, and that the Tories, in such simple books as they can get written and published, proclaim this great favourite to all the world; I hope you will no longer think it a crime in me—what you have formerly imputed for one—that I believed your Majesty allowed her great liberties ... since all that matter is now in print, and, notwithstanding the prosecution, I suppose sold at every shop. (246)

In the case of the *New Atalantis*, Churchill recognized that 'vile printers' and a 'low indigent' common woman had managed to transform 'gossip' into a new mode of female political agency. It is interesting to speculate that Churchill's recognition of this fact may in some indirect way have contributed to her own later manipulation of public opinion not only for mainstream political purposes, but also for the 'factious', feminist purpose of defending herself. After decades of suffering through the adverse representations of 'such simple books as they can get written and published', the

Duchess finally decided that an equally public *self*-representation would be the most effective antidote. Accordingly, in the preface to her *Account of the Conduct of the Dowager Duchess of Marlborough* (1742) she declared: 'The calumnies against me were so gross; and yet so greedily devoured by the credulity of party rage, that I thought it became me to write and publish something in my own justification' (274). In her own autobiographical *Adventures of Rivella*, Manley too combined partisan political representations with the more personal 'political' agenda of representing herself. She anticipated this move in the *New Atalantis*, where her persona Delia begs the Duke of Beaufort's chaplain to 'Represent me through your charitable glass, with that persuasive enchanting eloquence, to the two shining Princesses of Adario [Ormonde] and Beaumond [Beaufort]' (227).

In responding to gossip, slander, and libel by means of the nascent subgenre of female apology, Churchill and Manley became forerunners of an increasingly large body of eighteenth-century women who would deploy their culture's most powerful means of communication not only in support of traditional political or religious causes, but also in support of their own interests and those of their sex. As we have seen, a number of gradual historical and ideological transformations made this choice possible. A dramatic rise in urban female literacy in the first three-quarters of the seventeenth century, along with the seventeenth-century explosion of the press to some degree as a consequence of this new market, were among the more measurable developments, and these transformations in patterns of literacy and communication gave rise to more subtle ideological permutations. The Duchess's understanding of the 'public' as a conceptual entity of increasing political importance after 1688 was a crucial prerequisite for her turn to the press as a worthwhile 'court of appeal'. In mainstream politics, in lifestyle, and in rank, Sarah Churchill and Delarivier Manley had nothing in common. In turning to the press to defend their 'feminine transgressions', however, they suddenly did. In the eighteenth century, a significant number of British women would 'write and publish something in my own justification'. In Manley and Churchill's lifetime, that is, women began to understand a broader variety of concerns as 'political' and to take political representations into their own hands.

CONCLUSION: THE EROTICIZATION OF INTELLIGENCE

Joseph Addison, Richard Steele, Jonathan Swift, and other leading figures of the Augustan periodical press all wrote about what they perceived to be an alarming increase in women's political involvement in their lifetimes, and represented that involvement as emblematic of a larger breakdown in social control. Manley's career as a political writer, well known to each of these authors, provides a stark contrast to these gentlemen's satirical female politicians of the playhouse, parlour, and street. This final section will argue that Addison, Steele, and Swift's anxieties concerning female 'Disputants' were in fact brought to conscious expression in the years 1709 to 1711 by their personal knowledge of Manley's propagandistic activities. Contrary to received opinion, it was not so much Manley's verbal or sexual outrageousness that provoked these men's printed objections to her writings, as her demonstration of new possibilities for female political agency through print in 'a Country [already] torn with so many unnatural Divisions' (*Spectator*, no. 81, 2 June 1711). Writing to women (as well as men) on political subjects in the traditional sense, Manley threatened to encourage a new understanding of the 'political' in the process. The same propagandistic talents that Manley exhibited as a political writer could be—and later *were*—used for the personal political purpose of defending her own conduct and manipulating the new force of public opinion to feminist ends.

When Jonathan Swift satirized contemporary political divisions in the *Examiner*, he created an allegorical genealogy of party in which he represented 'faction' as a woman (no. 32, 8 Mar. 1711). 'Miss Faction', the youngest daughter of Liberty, is a new politicized version of the female gossip. Like Manley's character Lady Intelligence, and real-life counterparts such as polemicist and activist Elinor James, Miss Faction hovers round sites of popular political activity, threatening to upset the status quo by means of her 'perpetual Talk':

She intruded into all Companies at the most unseasonable Times, mixt at Balls, Assemblies, and other Parties of Pleasure; haunted every Coffeehouse and Booksellers Shop, and by her perpetual Talking filled all Places with Disturbance and Confusion. She buzzed about the Merchant *in the* Exchange, *the* Divine *in his Pulpit, and the* Shopkeeper *behind his*

Counter. Above all, she frequented Publick Assemblies, *where she sate in the shape of an* obscene, ominous Bird, *ready to prompt her* Friends *as they spoke.*

Miss Faction frequents coffee-houses, bookshops, the Royal Exchange, and other key locations for the public circulation of political ideas, and her physical freedom mirrors the liberties she takes with her tongue. A powerful force for the dissemination of political news in a society where nearly half the adult population could not read, her seemingly 'idle gossip' in fact threatens the order of things.

To a certain extent, when Swift feminized political faction and represented popular political participation as a woman speaking out of place, he was drawing on standard Renaissance types of the gossip and scold. He was also drawing on their antecedent, the classical disorderly woman (especially Fama, the teller of tales). But Swift's contribution to the literary tradition of disorderly women in this issue of the *Examiner* is nevertheless strikingly personalized. In a curious passage reminiscent of Manley's *New Atalantis*, Swift traced the origins of political faction to the nursery, and depicted his own disruptive female figure's problematic birth. Miss Faction's character, he informs us, was influenced by a malevolent goddess-midwife at delivery: 'Juno, *doing the Office of the Midwife, distorted* [*the infant*] *in its Birth, out of Envy to the Mother, from whence it derived its* Peevishness *and* Sickly Constitution.' Crippled by the haughty goddess, and endowed with her temper, Miss Faction grew up to be '*so Termagant and Froward, that there was no enduring Her any longer in* Heaven'. Thereupon she was expelled from Heaven and sent to torment men on earth—an ominous inversion of Manley's virtuous goddess Astrea, 'who had long since abandoned this world . . . in a disgust' (*New Atalantis*, 4).

It is no coincidence, I suggest, that, two months before publishing his sketch of Miss Faction, Swift had met Delarivier Manley for the first time. Nor is it a coincidence that Swift's association of political faction, gossiping women, problematic births, and malevolent midwives closely echoes the pattern of imagery we have traced in Manley's *New Atalantis*—which Swift had just read.[106] The same

---

[106] In a letter to Addison dated 22 Aug. 1710, Swift recorded that he had read Addison's 'character in Mrs. Manley's noble Memoirs of Europe' (*Works*, ed. Sir Walter Scott (London, 1884), xix. 265).

FIG. 5. 'The French Assassin Guiscard' (1711), sold by Edward Lewis. Delarivier Manley wrote her own pamphlet on the Guiscard assassination attempt, *A True Narrative of What Pass'd at the Examination of the Marquis de Guiscard* (1711), at the request of Jonathan Swift. Reproduced by courtesy of the Trustees of the British Museum

pattern of imagery and associations recurs yet again in Swift's poem about Manley, which Harold Williams speculates was written the same year.[107] Finally, the same *Examiner* issue by Swift begins with a discussion of Aristophanes' speech on androgyny in the *Symposium*, which recalls Manley's gender-bending status as female party writer. (Manley herself expressed frustration at having to pass herself off as a man in her political journalism when she remarked in her own *Examiner* issue a few months later, 'How many Fathers has this paper of mine been ascribed to?' (no. 52, 26 July 1711).)

From the time that Swift published his genealogy of Miss Faction on 8 March 1711, until October the same year, he would in fact work closely with Delarivier Manley. He commissioned her to write at least three political pamphlets during this period, including the politically sensitive *A True Narrative of What Pass'd at the Examination of the Marquis de Guiscard, at the Cock-Pit, the 8th of March*, 1710–11 (Fig. 5), and he turned over to her the editorship of the *Examiner* in June (eleven weeks after 'Miss Faction'). And while Swift clearly appreciated Manley's talents as a propagandist, he appears to have found them disturbing as well. In his disturbing poem 'Corinna', a poem which has struck more than one of his modern editors as 'difficult to explain', Swift represented Manley as a woman party writer whose erotico-political satires made the *beau monde* 'feel her scratch and bite':

> This Day, (the Year I dare not tell,)
>   *Apollo* play'd the Midwife's Part,
> Into the World *Corinna* fell,
>   And he endow'd her with his Art.
>
> But *Cupid* with a *Satyr* comes;
>   Both softly to the Cradle creep:
> Both stroke her Hands, and rub her Gums,
>   While the poor Child lay fast asleep.

---

[107] Harold Williams, ed., *The Poems of Jonathan Swift*, 2nd edn. (Oxford: Clarendon P., 1958), i. 148–50. On Swift's Corinna as Manley, see Williams's edn., as well as Pat Rogers, ed., *Jonathan Swift: The Complete Poems* (New Haven: Yale UP, 1983), 650, and Anne McWhir, 'Elizabeth Thomas and the Two Corinnas: Giving the Woman Writer a Bad Name', *English Literary History*, 62 (1995), 105–19. The first editor to identify Swift's Corinna as Manley was Hawkesworth in 1755. While most critics now agree that Corinna is probably a composite type of the new 'woman of Grub Street', most also agree with Rogers that Manley 'remains the best [specific] candidate'.

Then *Cupid* thus: This little Maid
　Of Love shall always speak and write;
And I pronounce, (the Satyr said)
　The World shall feel her scratch and bite. (ll. 1–12)[108]

The infant Corinna is delivered by Apollo, a male deity performing a traditionally female role ('the Midwife's Part'). Corinna is then visited at birth by Cupid and a Satyr, who together prophesy that she, in turn, will play a theoretically masculine part: politically instrumental 'speak[ing] and writ[ing]' in 'the World' at large. For Corinna, paradoxically, trouble in the nursery results in public power. As we have seen, just a few months before, Manley's *New Atalantis* had explored the same associations between childbirth, midwifery, and female political agency at length.

While Jonathan Swift figured contemporary political faction as a woman, Joseph Addison endeavoured in the *Spectator* 'to expose . . . Party-Rage in Women' (no. 81, 2 June 1711). Urging his female contemporaries to 'distinguish themselves as tender Mothers and faithful Wives, rather than furious Partizans', he implicitly acknowledged women's power to influence mainstream politics. Commenting on the fashion of female theatre-goers to transform their faces into political signifying systems of the body by placing patches in certain parts of their faces, he argued that even 'Women of honour who patch out of principle and with an eye to the interest of their country' were forces not for civic awareness and order, but for civic sabotage and even civil war. These politically active

---

[108] The poem concludes:

> At twelve, a Wit and a Coquette;
> 　Marries for Love, half Whore, half Wife;
> Cuckolds, elopes, and runs into Debt;
> 　Turns Auth'ress, and is *Curll*'s for Life.
>
> Her Common-Place-Book all gallant is,
> 　Of Scandal now a *Cornucopia*;
> She pours it out in *Atalantis*,
> 　Or *Memoirs* of the *New Utopia*. (ll. 25–32)

Harold Williams is the critic who describes 'Corinna' as 'difficult to explain' in his edition of *The Poems of Jonathan Swift*, 149. Swift's reference to '*Memoirs* of the *New Utopia*' in this poem is not necessarily a reference to Eliza Haywood's *Memoirs of a Certain Island Adjacent to the Kingdom of Utopia* (1725). There were many other 'memoirs' and 'utopias' in circulation in the London literary marketplace long before Haywood's attempt to capitalize on a trend. Swift is more likely referring to vols. iii and iv of Manley's *Atalantis*, published under the title *Memoirs of Europe* (1710).

women served not only 'to aggravate the hatreds and animosities that reign among men', but also to challenge the existing sexual order. They were 'Amazons' 'deprived of those peculiar charms with which nature has endowed them'—a significant force for disorder in 'a Country . . . torn with so many unnatural Divisions'. At so turbulent a historical moment, Addison implied, anything other than the most general female patriotism—expressed silently, through the cash nexus by donations—was dangerous to all men regardless of party. To date, critics have failed to notice that *the same week* that Joseph Addison published his lament regarding women's involvement in party politics, a woman was taking over the editorship of the leading propaganda organ of the Tory party. Manley's first issue of the *Examiner* as editor was published on 7 June 1711—only *five days* after Addison's *Spectator* issue above.

As Joseph Addison urged his female contemporaries to 'think it [their] greatest Commendation not to be talked of one way or other', so Richard Steele called for the return of an imaginary patriarchal golden age when 'the most conspicuous Woman . . . was only the best housewife' (*Tatler*, no. 42, 16 July 1709). We know that Steele was not passing the judgement of a historian when he suggested that in England's past, 'There were not then among the Ladies . . . Politicians, Virtuosae, Free-Thinkers, and Disputants; nay there was then hardly such a Creature ev'n as a Coquet.' Rather, he was contributing to the consolidation of new polite norms of female behaviour by projecting notions of domestic, apolitical womanhood into an imagined past. And he was doing so, this study suggests, at least in part because he was disturbed by what he perceived to be an excess of female 'Disputants' immediately around him. 'Stelico' was at this time also engaged in a virulent political as well as personal battle with Delarivier Manley—a battle fought publicly for nearly twenty years by means of the vehicle of the press.[109] Steele's comments on female 'Politicians' here were published only *three days* before the first volume of Manley's *New Atalantis* went into a second edition on 19 July 1709. Manley's political allegory had been published in May and was so popular that a second edition was called for immediately. At the same time that Steele was satirizing female 'Virtuosae',

---

[109] For details of this battle see Morgan, *A Woman of No Character*, 106–20.

Manley was working to supply her new-found fans with a second volume.

Shortly before that second volume was released in October, Steele attacked Manley once more, this time explicitly in the *Spectator*. Depicting her as 'Epicene', tutor in the arts of war at 'Madonella's' (Mary Astell's) college for women, Steele represented Manley's printed gossip as a powerful weapon. Alluding to the biblical injunction against the 'deadly poisons' of the tongue, he warned that uncontrolled poison could be dangerous: 'Of these military performances, the direction is undertaken by Epicene, the writer of Memoirs from the Mediterranean, who, by the help of some artificial poisons conveyed by smells, has within these few weeks brought many persons of both sexes to an untimely fate' (*Tatler*, no. 63, 3 Sept. 1709). In referring to Manley's politically instrumental fictions as 'artificial poisons', Steele sounded a note that Samuel Richardson would echo at mid-century in denigrating 'the Behn's, the Manley's, and the Heywood's'. In a letter to a female friend, herself a polite author, Richardson called for the 'virtuous' women writers of his own time to counter the dangerous force of their female literary predecessors and so supply 'the Antidote to these Women's Poison'.[110] In 1729, Alexander Pope declared, 'Law can pronounce judgment only on open Facts, Morality alone can pass censure on Intentions of mischief: so that for secret calumny or the arrow flying in the dark, there is *no publick punishment left, but what a good writer inflicts.*'[111] At mid-century, the author of *Pamela* and *Clarissa* implicitly appeared to agree, calling for 'good writer[s]' to supply newer, quieter models of female authorial self-representation to displace those of their more unruly sisters.

In late October 1711, Manley published two anti-Whig, anti-war pamphlets praised by Swift, the ironic *The Duke of M——h's Vindication: In Answer to a Pamphlet Lately Publish'd call'd* [Bouchain] and *A Learned Comment on Dr. Hare's Excellent Sermon Preach'd before the Duke of Marlborough, on the Surrender of Bouchain.*[112] Less than three weeks later, the *Spectator* came out

---

[110] Richardson to Mrs Chapone, 6 Dec. 1750, qtd. in John Carroll, ed., *Selected Letters of Samuel Richardson* (Oxford: Clarendon P., 1964), 173 n. 68.

[111] [Pope], 'To the Publisher,' *The Dunciad Variorum*, in *Poems*, ed. Butt, 320; my emphasis.

[112] For Swift's praise, see his letter to Stella of 22 Oct. 1711.

with a weird paper depicting a 'Club of She-Romps' who 'take each a Hackney-Coach, and meet once a week in a large upper Chamber, which [they] hire by the Year for that purpose'. Of course the 'She-Romps' are only one of many plotting collectivities of women who lurk through the pages of the *Tatler*, *Spectator*, and Swift's writings. But in the portrait's overtones of female erotic play and its message of a new female alliance openly hostile to men, the 'Club of She-Romps' seems an ominous satiric counterpart to Manley's 'Ladies of the new Cabal':

We are no sooner come together than we throw off all that Modesty and Reservedness with which our Sex are obliged to disguise themselves in publick Places. I am not able to express the Pleasure we enjoy from ten at Night till four in the Morning, in being as rude as you Men can be. . . . As our Play runs high the Room is immediately filled with . . . torn Petticoats . . . Flounces, Furbelows, Garters, and Working-Aprons. . . . besides the Coaches we come in our selves, there is one which stands always empty to carry off our dead Men, for so we call all those Fragments and Tatters with which the Room is strewed. (*Spectator*, no. 217, 8 Nov. 1711)

The eerie scene that follows, in which the She-Romps 'demolish a Prude' by ripping off her clothes, anticipates Samuel Richardson's depiction of the role played by Mrs Sinclair and her female fellows in the rape of Clarissa. Like Swift warning that 'a Knot of Ladies, got together by themselves, is a very School of Impertinence and Detraction, *and it is well if those be the worst*',[113] Mr Spectator's depiction of a Club of deadly She-Romps expresses an awareness that gossip is a means of solidarity and illicit social power for the subordinated; that 'the relationship . . . gossip expresses and sustains matters [as much as] the information it promulgates'.[114] Characteristically, Manley both recognized and parodied her male contemporaries' concern regarding what appeared to be a new nexus of female intimacy, gossip, and political activism. In her sequel to the *New Atalantis*, one male character complains that the ladies now talk about nothing but politics, 'to the Exclusion of their formerly adorr'd Topicks, Scandal, Cloaths and Gallantry'. Another laments, 'These are no longer the Days of Passion. . . . Either

[113] Swift, *Letter to a Young Lady on Her Marriage* (1723), 88, my emphasis. Manley was gravely ill in 1723 and died the following year.
[114] Spacks, *Gossip*, 5–6.

the handsome Women are taken up with *Parties*, buried in *Politicks*, or compound for something more gross' (*Memoirs of Europe*, i. 259, ii. 321–2). The same year that Manley published *Memoirs of Europe*, Daniel Defoe echoed her male characters' concerns when he complained in the *Review* that 'All Manner of Discourse among the Women, runs now upon State Affairs, War, and Government; Tattling Nonsense and Slander is Transposed to the Males, and adjourned from the *Toilet*, to the *Coffee-Houses*' (*A Review of The Affairs of France*, vol. 7, 9 May 1710). It is possible that Manley understood the *Spectator*'s 'She-Romps' issue as being hostile to her own activities. Three weeks later she came out with another anti-Whig pamphlet, *A True Relation of the Several Facts and Circumstances of the Intended Riot and Tumult on Queen Elizabeth's Birth-day* (1711), in which she gratuitously attacked Richard Steele.

There are female communities and scenes of women discussing politics in all of Manley's allegorical fictions except one. Manley's fictionalized autobiography, *The Adventures of Rivella; or, the History of the Author of the Atalantis* (1714), is structured as a conversation between two men—and, not coincidentally, marks her pretended public renunciation of her career as a political writer. The main narrator of Rivella's story, Sir Charles 'Lovemore', claims that he has 'brought her to be asham'd of her Writings' and that 'henceforward her Business should be to write of Pleasure and Entertainment only, wherein *Party* should no longer mingle. . . . She now agrees with me, that Politicks is not the Business of a Woman' (*Rivella*, 116–17).[115] To understand Manley's dramatically changed authorial self-representation in her last major fiction, it is crucial to note that she actually had no genuine intention of giving up party writing when she published *Rivella*. Rather, she was plotting to 'go underground', by publicly adopting a more 'feminine' authorial persona. To date, critics have failed to notice that on

---

[115] One year after Manley's death, Mary Davys published her *Familiar Letters, Betwixt a Gentleman and a Lady* (1725), in which the male protagonist, losing a political argument with the female protagonist, begs her to 'put a stop to this sort of Correspondence; and let your Letters for the future, be fill'd with the innocent Diversions of the Town: tis a pity Berina's Temper should be ruffled with Politicks' (278). Berina agrees to cease discussing politics, but laments that her male correspondent has 'laid such strict Injunctions on my Pen [he has] robb'd me of my darling Pleasure' (280). She then resolves, 'since you will not let me be a Politician, to invoke the Muses, and turn Poetess' (283).

precisely the same day that Manley dated the 'Translator's Preface' to *Rivella*, 3 June 1714, she also dated another letter to Robert Harley—offering her services as a propagandist and sketching her plans for another full-length political allegory along the lines of the *New Atalantis*.[116] Manley's changing authorial self-representation in *Rivella* was precisely that—a change in representations (and no more). Her dramatic public renunciation of her party writing was a symbolic gesture to placate increasingly vocal eighteenth-century critics. It was an updating of female authorial self-representations, not an abandonment of political 'representations' altogether.[117]

So, consciously rejecting her previous modes of authorial self-representation as a female intelligencer, Manley elevated herself at last to a new position as her generation's successor to Aphra Behn and the Ovidian erotic tradition. Structuring her last allegorical fiction as a conversation between two men who are more interested in her female sexual body than her political writings, she instigates the story of her life by having one gentleman inquire, 'Do Her Eyes love as well as Her Pen?' (8). The narrator of her story, Sir Charles Lovemore, begins by admitting that he has been her lifelong admirer, while the second frame character, the Chevalier D'Aumont, records the tavern gallantry of another Manley enthusiast, 'Quote *Ovid* now no more ye amorous Swains, | *Delia* than *Ovid* has more moving Strains' (43). Meaning to be complimentary, Lovemore contrasts Rivella with the famous French classicist Anne Lefebvre Dacier—who was, to be sure, 'an admirable Scholar, a judicious Critick, but what has that to do with the Heart?' (3). The two gentlemen then go on to provide for the reader an explicit blazon of Rivella's body parts—from her 'publickly celebrated' hands and arms to her 'Neck and Breasts' of 'establish'd Reputation for Beauty and Color' (10). Depicting herself as the parodic object of desire, Manley forced the reader to adopt the position that she suspected some readers to have taken all along: as the voyeuristic observer of her female sexual body, of the woman political writer 'making a spectacle of herself'.

---

[116] 3 June 1714, HMC *Portland MSS* v. 453.

[117] Manley's relatively late-career self-representation as literary seductress is so striking that some critics have read her entire career retrospectively through its lens. By the time that Manley represented herself in this pointedly satirical manner, however, she had been writing for pay for nearly twenty years, representing herself in a variety of manners, including public political heroine.

After a decade as a propagandist and nearly two decades as a publishing author, 'the AUTHOR of the *ATALANTIS*' publicly exchanged the empowering self-image of the author as spokesperson for the public welfare for her own variant of one more familiar to 'Grub Street' authors: the author as whore. Manley made her own body, rather than her 'secret intelligence', the new starring attraction of her text. It must be emphasized, however, that Manley's late-career self-representation in *Rivella* is satiric—the culmination of a long-standing habit of self-satire. For while Manley depicts Lovemore praising specific body parts, she also depicts herself as sorely lacking in the conventional requirements of feminine beauty. Despite her 'publickly celebrated' hands and arms, she is nevertheless 'a Lady, who is no longer young, and was never a Beauty'. 'Neither tall nor short', and 'inclin'd to Fat', her face is so scarred from 'the Disaster of her having the Small-pox in such an injurious manner' that 'few, who have only beheld her in Publick, could be brought to like her' (5–8). A few pages later we are reminded yet again of the 'Want of Beauty in her Face' (12). Whereas Manley's predecessor Aphra Behn successfully represented herself as an object of erotic fascination in her texts,[118] Manley represented herself twenty-five years after Behn's death as an ageing woman writer faced with dramatically narrowed options for support and self-representation. 'Poor, plain, middle-aged, alone, disreputable', as well as in such poor health that Swift described her in 1712 as 'poor Mrs. Manley . . . she cannot live long',[119] Manley depicted herself not so much as Behn did, as a woman successfully manipulating the construct 'femininity', but rather as one angrily giving in to it when confronted with diminished alternatives. Whereas Behn represented herself as having the power over her readers, Manley represented her two male narrators as having the power over *her*—celebrating her renunciation of politics and imaginatively placing her in the feminine private space of the boudoir. In her writings from 1705 to 1715, Manley's allegiances and identities had been multiple: royalist daughter, Tory supporter, ruined woman, party writer. After 1714, she suggested, her new allegiance in her writing must be to her gender: to her femaleness and to 'feminine' writing ('Pleasure and Entertainment only, wherein *Party* should no longer mingle').

[118] Ballaster, *Seductive Forms*, ch. 3 *passim*.
[119] MacCarthy, *Women Writers*, 231; Jonathan Swift, *Journal to Stella*, 28 Jan. 1711/12.

Still, while Manley's deliberately foregrounded femininity in 1714 may be seen as a sign of survival strategies for women writers to come, her putting-on of femininity with a vengeance suggests that she still retained the power of putting it off. In her last allegorical work, Manley dramatized the taming of her own political tongue. But she also signalled that in mid- and later eighteenth-century Britain, women's political activity through print would not cease, but take on new, more subtle forms.

Conclusion
'The Antidote to these Women's Poison'?

In the Introduction to this book I suggested that the idealized
'community' of the bourgeois public Habermas theorized was in
fact constructed in opposition to a multiplicity of competing
publics already in existence in revolutionary and post-revolutionary
London. What Habermas identified as 'the fiction of the one public'[1] functioned after 1688 not so much to 'contain absolutism'
as to delimit democracy—and in so doing, to contend with fears
of another civil war in England. The containment of 'factious',
sometimes female, religio-political groups was not a secondary
consequence but a primary factor in the articulation of the new
(bourgeois) public. An emergent élite negotiated a historic alliance
with an older aristocratic élite by positing that not landed wealth or
title, but rather 'reason' and 'virtue' (read property and the forms of
distinction it can buy), justified the authority of some Englishmen
over others, and legitimized substantially propertied but untitled
gentlemen's rise to power.

Despite recent valuable work on the competing publics of revolutionary and post-revolutionary England, critics too often fall
under the spell of the bourgeois public's own fictions. Most still see
the struggle against absolutism as primary, and many still follow
the bourgeois public's own lead in assuming that there was only
one new public sphere in this period (rather than a whole host of
overlapping publics, some of which had to be shut down to maintain the established order). After 1688, a desire to stabilize the
nation in its post-revolutionary phase may have made 'the fiction of
the one public' easier to tolerate. But the willingness of Terry
Eagleton and others to concede that the institutions of the bourgeois public were 'born . . . of political consensus' marks even
Marxist literary critics as occasional unwitting captives of the very

---

[1] Habermas, *The Structural Transformation of the Public Sphere*, 56.

'fiction' they seek to interpret.[2] With respect to the situation in post-revolutionary London, one might more accurately describe the bourgeois public as having been engineered out of political turmoil than 'born of political consensus'. Yet many literary critics still restrict the sources for their judgements to writings by élite or genteel authors, while many public sphere theorists still date the origins of actually competing publics in England to the period of the American and French Revolutions. Terry Eagleton, for instance, rightly critiques as 'belated' Habermas's mid-nineteenth-century dating for the 'structural transformation of the bourgeois public' ('the irruption into it of social and political interests in palpable conflict with its own "universal" rational norms'). But he then goes on to re-date these transformations to the 1790s:

For what is emerging in the England of the late-eighteenth and early-nineteenth centuries, in that whole epoch of intensive class struggle charted in E. P. Thompson's *The Making of the English Working Class*, is already nothing less than a 'counter-public sphere'. In the Corresponding Societies, the radical press, Owenism, Cobbett's *Political Register* and Paine's *Rights of Man*, feminism and the dissenting churches, a whole oppositional network of journals, clubs, pamphlets, debates and institutions invades the dominant consensus, threatening to fragment it from within.[3]

Eagleton is not atypical of contemporary cultural critics in assuming that because E. P. Thompson's magisterial study begins in the 1780s, therefore class struggle that was genuinely a threat must not have existed in England until the final decades of the eighteenth century. But as this study of non-élite women's political activity 1678–1730 has shown, versions of the multiple publics Eagleton describes ('feminism and the dissenting churches, a whole oppositional network of journals, clubs, pamphlets, debates and institutions invad[ing] the dominant consensus, threatening to fragment it

---

[2] Terry Eagleton, *The Function of Criticism: From* The Spectator *to Post-structuralism* (1984; London: New Left Books-Verso, 1987), 12. Eagleton does note that 'the bourgeois public sphere was consolidated more in the wake of political absolutism than as a resistance to it from within'. Rather than pursuing this key insight, however, he quickly smooths over this contradiction in his theory of the emancipatory origins of the bourgeois public, in this instance by ascribing it to 'the peculiarities of the English' (10). Like Eagleton's 'born', Joan B. Landes's 'incarnation' dematerializes and mystifies the historical processes by which the bourgeois public was constructed, in both early 18th-cent. England and late 18th-cent. France (*Women and the Public Sphere in the Age of the French Revolution*, 7).

[3] Eagleton, *The Function of Criticism*, 35–6.

from within') were present in England 100 years earlier than Eagleton suggests (and in some cases even earlier). Most important for the goal of this book, of tracing middling and lower-class women's political activity through print, non-élite women as well as men were central to these earlier competing publics. The Quakers, with their female printer and polemicists and national and even international distribution of nonconformist texts by 1700; the Philadelphian Society, with its leader Jane Lead, and aggressive pursuit of a multiple-media public via oral, manuscript, and print communications; the women book trade workers and propagandists studied here, whose involvement in contemporary political culture, while little known today, was considered dangerous enough in their own time to necessitate their sometimes repeated arrest—all of these, and the 'alternative publics' of which these groups and individuals were a part, were present in London in the 1680s, rather than the 1780s—and in some cases to an even greater extent than 100 years later.

It was the threat of persons like 'Mary Unknown', this book concludes—members of politically disenfranchised groups with new access to tools of mass communication—that caused the *bourgeois* public Habermas theorized to be constructed on the particular founding principles that it was. More than 100 years before the 'structural transformation of the bourgeois public' Habermas talks about, gradual but major shifts in English culture were modifying the nature and function of the public sphere in England. New models of political authority and political subjecthood, of the relation between the family and the state, and of appropriate discourse were central to the project of bourgeois hegemony. The eighteenth century saw an epistemological division of labour whereby 'the family was increasingly distinguished from the state, while the component members of the family were increasingly distinguished from each other'.[4] Whereas the female polemicists and activists studied here, however critical of particular monarchs, tended to see themselves as authorized to speak out on state affairs because of their status as subjects ('Members of the Body of the Nation'), the new model of the bourgeois family as a counterpart to or safe haven from the state rather than a subordinate unit of it was disabling.

---

[4] Michael McKeon, 'Historicizing Patriarchy: The Emergence of Gender Difference in England, 1660–1760', *ECS* 28 (1995), 298.

The century's increasing emphasis on the individual, formed in the 'haven' of the family, and on individual rights and self-improvement was disorienting for many working women, whose modes of empowerment had traditionally been based on more collective modes of being and social identification. Just as state, family, and individual underwent a new demarcation in this period, so too the previously inseparable discursive realms of literature, religion, and politics underwent a 'delimiting scrutiny'.[5] Religio-political literature like the pamphlets and broadsides studied here was increasingly satirized as fanatic or 'enthusiastic'—in contrast with the seventeenth century, when 'religious discourse was a, if not the, predominant means by which individuals defined and debated issues in [the public] sphere'.[6] As Jonathan Swift satirized contemporary religious sects in *A Tale of a Tub*, and specifically linked enthusiasm with women, so Joseph Addison and Richard Steele satirized religious sects in the *Spectator* and *Tatler*, and in one issue specifically satirized Jane Lead's Philadelphian Society. *Tatler*, no. 257, 30 Nov. 1710 describes a travelling waxwork show exhibiting all the sects of England, particularly one sect with a high membership of 'both sexes' who 'called themselves the Philadelphians, or the Family of Love'. At a time when the vast bulk of English literature was religious or political, what some scholars have called an increasingly 'aestheticized' notion of literature began to spread. Augustan literary anxieties were linked to political ones, and the same period that saw the explosion of the political press, the crystallization of the public sphere, and the popularization of the designation 'Grub Street' also saw narrowing notions of 'worthwhile writing'.[7] Eighteenth-century shifts in notions of the 'literary'

[5] Michael McKeon, 'Politics of Discourses and the Rise of the Aesthetic in Seventeenth-Century England', in Kevin Sharpe and Steven N. Zwicker, eds., *Politics of Discourse: The Literature and History of Seventeenth-Century England* (Berkeley and Los Angeles: U. of California P., 1987), 36. On the shifting place of the polemical in 18th-cent. literary culture, see McKeon, as well as Steven N. Zwicker, 'Lines of Authority: Politics and Literary Culture in the Restoration', in Sharpe and Zwicker, eds., *Politics of Discourse*, 230–70.

[6] David Zaret, 'Religion, Science, and Printing in the Public Spheres in Seventeenth-Century England', in Calhoun, ed., *Habermas*, 213.

[7] For an introduction to critical debates concerning the historical formation of the concept of 'literature', see Williams, *Marxism and Literature*, 45–54 and *Keywords*, 1976 (rev. edn. New York: Oxford UP, 1985), 183–8; René Wellek, 'What is Literature?', in *What is Literature?*, ed. Paul Hernadi (Bloomington: Indiana UP, 1978), 16–23; Douglas Patey, 'The Eighteenth Century Invents the Canon', *Modern Language Studies*, 18 (1988), 17–37; Alvin Kernan, *Samuel Johnson and the Impact of Print* (Princeton UP, 1989); Trevor Ross, 'The Emergence of "Literature": Making

were at once class-based and class-biased, and had specific political, as well as cultural, consequences: 'These forms of the concepts of literature and criticism are, in the perspective of historical social development, forms of a class specialization and control of a general social practice, and of a class limitation of the questions which it might raise.'[8] The battle to control cultural consumption by the social body was in essence a battle to control the social body.

More generally, new bourgeois models for discursive behaviour ensured that 'what counts as rationality is precisely the capacity to articulate within [the bourgeois public's] constraints'.[9] 'Gentlemen of taste' countered 'scandalous and reflecting', 'low indigent', 'seditious', 'crackbrained', and otherwise impolite participants in the new pluralistic literary culture of their time with principles of 'polite exchange' and 'tasteful discussion' (with Habermasian vs. Hobbesian models of communicative exchange, so to speak). Writing was increasingly evaluated according to new standards of polite discourse, and polite conversation was institutionalized as the grounding of bourgeois society in new periodicals like the *Tatler*. As early as 1700, Jane Lead's son-in-law and editor worried that the 'stile and manner' of her passionate, mystical writings would not be 'suitable to the Genius of this Polite Age'.[10] A polemicist like Joan Whitrowe, with her openly hostile tone, her disregard for aesthetics, and her constant foregrounding of competing interests, could not even have articulated her concerns under the constraints of the new bourgeois rules of discourse. Even today, our first response to Whitrowe's radically 'impolite' and grammatically incorrect writings (as in the epigraph to this book) might be to wonder whether she was a madwoman. Instead, this book has tried to show, we should recognize her simply as a *mad woman*: an angry, non-élite person who managed to communicate her radical views perfectly effectively within the constraints of an older political culture.[11]

and Reading the English Canon in the Eighteenth Century', *English Literary History*, 63 (1996), 397–422; and the forum on 'Literature, Aesthetics, and Canonicity in the Eighteenth Century', in *Eighteenth-Century Life*, 21 (1997), 80–107.

[8] Williams, *Marxism and Literature*, 49.
[9] Eagleton, *The Function of Criticism*, 15.
[10] [Francis Lee], preface to Jane Lead, *The Wars of David, and the Peaceable Reign of Solomon . . . Set Forth in Two Treatises* (1700), A4.
[11] In the 18th cent., even plebeian authors increasingly aspired to genteel literary status. Witness mid-century poet Ann Yearsley, whom Donna Landry discusses in a chapter appropriately subtitled 'Working-Class Writer, Bourgeois Subject?' (*The*

Thus for early modern persons who saw print primarily as an arena for religio-political, rather than imaginative, activity, the eighteenth century's increasing emphasis on propriety and on polite and secular genres had serious short- and long-term consequences. In any culture, certain writers or speakers are enabled by valorized literary modes and forms, while others find their expression delimited by them. In writing about nineteenth-century working-class writers and the novel Raymond Williams observes:

> though they had marvelous material that could go into the novel very few of them managed to write good or even any novels. Instead they wrote marvelous autobiographies. Why? Because the form coming down through the religious tradition was of the witness confessing the story of his life, or there was the defense speech at the trial when a man tells the judge who he is and what he has done. . . . These oral forms were more accessible, forms centered on 'I', on the single person. The novel with its quite different narrative forms was virtually impenetrable to working-class writers for three or four generations, and there are still many problems in using the received forms for what is, in the end, very different material. Indeed the forms of working-class consciousness are bound to be different from the literary forms of another class, and it is a long struggle to find new and adequate forms.[12]

In the eighteenth century, as well as the nineteenth, increasingly prominent and highly skilled genres like the novel were less immediately available to untutored authors and audiences than less decorous forms like pamphlets and broadsides. Paradoxically, an expanding literary marketplace with its broad variety of polite, 'secular' genres may have done as much as we have seen Walpole or Newcastle try to do to shut down a more polemical literary culture.

For late seventeenth- and early eighteenth-century women, access to the press at all its many interdependent levels was a vehicle of

---

Muses of Resistance: Laboring-Class Women's Poetry in Britain, 1739–1796 (Cambridge UP, 1990)). As Paul Langford and others have suggested, 'politeness was primarily about the social control of the individual at a time of intense enthusiasm for individual rights and responsibilities' (*A Polite and Commercial People: England 1727–1783* (Oxford UP, 1992) 5).

[12] Raymond Williams, 'The Writer: Commitment and Alignment', *Marxism Today* (June 1980), 25. The research done in this book has led to similar conclusions concerning the continuing importance of oral culture to non-élite involvement with print.

significant if limited power. When subcultural, oppositional, and otherwise socially subversive female voices such as the ones considered here were printed and distributed across the nation's largest city (and sometimes beyond) those voices were a significant force for social change. This book has helped to uncover a legacy of female religio-political activity through print that existed long before the better-known political activity of English women in the 1790s. Watching the development of traditions of female political activism suggests that it is no accident that the same period which saw women's significant participation at *all* levels of the political press also saw 'the first sizable wave of British secular feminist protest in history'.[13] Just as the written word allows for the 'decontextualization of discourse',[14] so print intermittently enabled the oppressed to move from an awareness of their particular instance towards the recognition of a general condition. What had once been 'felt individually as personal insecurity' came to be 'viewed collectively as structural inconsistency'.[15] Mass-distributed texts addressed invisible publics from afar, generating new collective identities and silent adherents to a cause. And even with sharp restrictions on women's participation in public political affairs through print, it may be said that print allowed for a more polyphonic engagement of individuals in controversy.

But print also enables the spread of official doctrine, and in the eighteenth century print also helped to consolidate and disseminate new genteel notions of femininity. Print made it easier for notions of appropriate female behaviour to be codified and dispersed across social and geographic boundaries, and barriers between 'modest' and 'immodest' women came to seem as absolute as older divisions of faith, political allegiance, occupation, economic position, and even rank. Eighteenth-century women increasingly encountered works addressing them not as royalists or Williamites, Protestants or Catholics, or members of one kinship group or another, but as women (Pamela, Shamela, Clarissa, Evelina, Belinda, Helen, Emmeline, Emma, and so on). The term itself would become an

[13] Moira Ferguson, ed., *First Feminists: British Women Writers, 1578–1799* (Bloomington: Indiana UP, 1985), 15.
[14] Jack Goody, intro., *Literacy in Traditional Societies* (Cambridge UP, 1968). See also Ong, *Orality and Literacy*.
[15] Clifford Geertz, 'Ideology as a Cultural System', in *The Interpretation of Cultures: Selected Essays* (New York: Basic Books, 1973), 232.

increasingly homogenized construct, and one of the new collective identities furthered by print was gender.[16]

At almost the same time that a broad class spectrum of British women were gaining access to their culture's most powerful tool of communication, the press, the social, intellectual, and political roles available to women were being circumscribed, and women writers' subject-matter was being restricted. While the eighteenth century saw the acceptance and even encouragement of certain kinds of female publicity, this acceptance was predicated on women's acceptance of new subject-positions that distanced them from immediate participation in state affairs. While innovative literary forms like periodicals broke new ground by addressing women as women, the same forms often fiercely satirized other female social identifications such as Whig or Tory, royalist or Williamite, and so on. Periodicals like the *Tatler* and *Spectator* contributed to the conceptual reconsignment of 'the Fair Sex' either to a polite public or to a private sphere reconceptualized as a safe haven from the realm of state affairs and especially the new party politics. While many male writers at mid-century, despite the changing relationship between literature and politics, continued to be involved in party political writing (Henry Fielding for instance), women writers were expected to direct their talents to more 'feminine' literary subjects than politics and polemics. While none of the women discussed in this book participated in the construction of new genteel models of femininity (except in so far as Delarivier Manley may be said to have publicized such models by parodying them) many eighteenth-century women did contribute to a gradual transformation of British women's collective identity. Dominant institutions reproduce themselves by engendering in their subjects 'a collusion which is the very condition of their survival'.[17] Women writers became active participants in the new project of bourgeois class hegemony, even as that project's ideology sought drastically to circumscribe their activity in the public political sphere. The eighteenth-century emergence of the category 'woman' as the paramount social marker of

---

[16] The findings of this book support claims made by Nancy Armstrong and others that in 18th-cent. England 'gender came to mark the most important difference among individuals' (Nancy Armstrong, *Desire and Domestic Fiction: A Political History of the Novel* (New York: Oxford UP, 1987), 4).

[17] Terry Eagleton, *The Rape of Clarissa: Writing, Sexuality and Class Struggle in Samuel Richardson* (Minneapolis: U. of Minnesota P., 1982), 82.

a self gave a necessary grounding to modern secular feminism. At the time of its construction, however, it was yoked to restrictive notions of genteel female behaviour and to a sexual division of literary labour. While the gendered subjectivity of an Astell or a Cavendish became an important base for a new kind of proto-feminist 'political' writing, modern notions of the self as gendered and unique may have worked to reduce less privileged women's conviction of their own agency and involvement in national and local politics.

Of course 'a lived hegemony is always a process . . . it does not just passively exist as a form of dominance'.[18] Englishwomen have never stayed wholly out of public politics, and it is well known that the French Revolution, in particular, gave rise to a vigorous (if relatively brief) period of female polemical activity. But mid- and later eighteenth-century women writers were increasingly forced to find new, *gender-based* ways of authorizing their public political expression: drawing on their supposed 'moral authority', for instance, to address issues of national concern.[19] The origins of a national literary history, and the mass marketing of the new 'literary lady' in consumer items such as miscellanies and collections, helped to erase the religio-political and polemical origins of British women's active entry into print culture by disseminating new genteel norms for female literary activity.[20] A dramatic, disproportionate depoliticization of English women was achieved largely through print: the very medium which had recently given women new opportunities for political association. By the 1790s, the young Mary Wollstonecraft could have no idea that she had female liter-

[18] Williams, *Marxism and Literature*, 112.

[19] For book-length discussions of women writers' shifting strategies, see Gallagher, *Nobody's Story*, Spencer, *The Rise of the Woman Novelist*, and Todd, *The Sign of Angellica*. As Eliza Haywood hinted of her fellow women in 1722, 'what she dares not attempt in publick, she will be sure to do in private; she then works underground like a Mole' (*Letters from a Lady of Quality to a Chevalier, Translated from the French*, appendix: 'A Discourse Concerning Writings of this Nature', 18). The theme of women going 'underground like moles' would in fact become a literary topos by mid-century. At the peak of Lovelace's frustration in *Clarissa*, when Clarissa and Anna Howe have outplotted him, Lovelace swears, 'Plot, contrivance, intrigue, stratagem!—Underground moles these ladies.' He then vows to 'bind, gag, strip, rob, and do anything but murder' to intercept their letters (Samuel Richardson, *Clarissa or The History of a Young Lady* (1747–8), ed. Angus Ross (Penguin, 1988), 851).

[20] On this erasure see Ezell, *Writing Women's Literary History*, as well as my 'Consuming Women'.

ary forebears who devoted their lives to political activity through print just as she would do, for that substantial part of the British 'female literary tradition' had been erased.

The 'success story' of printer-author Samuel Richardson's serving-maid heroine Pamela—Pamela's spectacular transformation from wage-earning *worker* to supported *wife*—may be seen as a symbolic reflection of and attempt to validate ongoing socioeconomic as well as cultural transformations. The capitalization and professionalization of Richardson's own print trade led to the disempowerment of many workers both male and female, and for many women in book trade families (including Richardson's own wife) displacement from the realm of paid economic activity altogether. As Part I has stressed, much very basic scholarship on women's status and roles in the later eighteenth-century book trade still remains to be done. But major structural changes were in place in the London book trade by 1730, and we have begun to see how these changes affected women. With the decline of family industry,[21] fewer wives, daughters, and sisters stood a chance of being able to learn anything of their relatives' trade. We have seen Daniel Defoe warn proud tradesmen's wives to learn the family business thoroughly before they were left to fend for themselves, and we have seen printer-author Elinor James lament the undermining of the domestic economy which had enabled her own acquisition of skills. As the mistress of a printing house for half a century, James witnessed in her own home what we may recognize as the early side-effects of capitalism (in this case, apprentices walking out on their masters and mistresses, easily able to hire themselves out for a wage). By the end of her lifetime, James was deeply concerned for the fate of the 'economic family' as she had known it. In her broadside to her fellow printers, she argued for a return to the strictly hierarchical, live-in printing shop of her younger days. The same developments that James was lamenting from her own relatively secure position as a printer were simultaneously undermining the opportunities of women in other book trade families. While

---

[21] Alice Clark's term, now common among historians, describes an intermediary stage in the history of work in England between 'domestic industry' and 'capitalist industry'. In 'family industry', 'some members of the family worked for wages but that work, like domestic production, was still carried out mainly within the household, so work was still visibly shared by both spouses' (Erickson, intro. to Clark, *The Working Life of Women in the Seventeenth Century* pp. viii–ix).

male workers increasingly faced the likelihood that they would
never own their own shops but rather become perpetually dependent on a wage, wives and daughters of those workers who never
owned their own shops were unlikely to learn anything of their
husband's or father's business. Most important for our purposes of
tracing women's political activity through print, along with older
organizational structures in the book trades went some women's
immediate, unregulated access to the press.

The eighteenth-century gendered separation of paid and unpaid
labour, and corresponding privatization and feminization of the
home, may be illustrated in the successive establishments of Samuel
Richardson, while the effects of these developments on middle-class
tradesmen's wives may be seen in the comparative occupations of
Richardson's mother-in-law and his wife. Very late in his career, in
1755, Richardson finally separated dwelling house and printing
establishment for the first time. He was extremely proud of this
separation of home and workshop, signalling as it did the culmination of his long rise from apprentice to master to the 'arrived' status
of a gentleman. In letters to Lady Bradshaigh, he puffed his new
'intirely separate' dwelling house:

the new [dwelling house] will be a comfortable Dwelling; and as it will,
tho' connected with the Business Part, be intirely separate from it, and no
Part of the Business done in it, my Family will have more Convenience,
than it had before; because a great Part of the other larger House (and yet
the new one is 45 feet deep) was taken up in the Business.[22]

Yet Richardson also noted that his wife Elizabeth was extremely
unhappy with these new arrangements—even though her own new
'quarters' would be substantially larger than the 'Dwelling-Part' of
the printing establishment that she had lived in before. Elizabeth
Leake Richardson was in fact so averse to the new separate dwelling house that she refused to move immediately when the house
was ready—provoking Samuel Richardson to describe himself
as 'like a Man setting out on a needful Journey, & arrested when
he had got within Sight of ye End of it'.[23] So great was Mrs
Richardson's 'perverse' stubbornness in this matter that Mr

[22] Richardson to Lady Bradshaigh, 17 Dec. 1755, Forster MS, XI, f. 163, qtd. in
T. C. Duncan Eaves and Ben D. Kimpel, 'Samuel Richardson's London Houses',
Studies in Bibliography, 15 (1962), 146. See also Sale, *Samuel Richardson, Master
Printer*, 7–17.
[23] Richardson to Lady Bradshaigh, 9 Feb. 1756, Forster MS, XI, f. 167, qtd. in
Eaves and Kimpel, 'Samuel Richardson's London Houses', 147.

Richardson—the eighteenth-century novel's vocal promoter of the new bourgeois 'companionate' marriage—was provoked to lament: 'I have a very good Wife. I am sure you think I have: But the Man who has passed all his Days single, is not always and in every thing, a Loser.'[24]

Why was Elizabeth Leake Richardson so resistant to moving to a newly renovated house which would provide her with more spacious and elegant living quarters than she had had before? Many factors were no doubt involved here, but one of those factors may well have been her sense of her increasing disenfranchisement from her family's business. To be sure, Mrs Richardson would inherit most of her husband's valuable copyrights after his death. But Elizabeth Leake Richardson's mother Elizabeth Leake had worked alongside her own husband John Leake in the family printing house, and had taken over management of the family business after her husband's death. And Elizabeth Leake Richardson's beloved brother James Leake was a prominent bookseller in Bath. (It was of course James Leake's decision to move to Bath that allowed Samuel Richardson, by marrying Elizabeth Leake, to set up business in *her* family's shop in the first place.[25]) If Elizabeth Leake Richardson, on the other hand, played no active role in her eminently successful husband's printing house, that does not mean that the business she grew up in was not of great significance to her—linking her to the memory of her parents and to her brother as well as her husband, and providing an important sense of continuity and purpose in her life. As eighteenth-century women such as Elizabeth Leake Richardson lost their once-central role in the economy of the skilled trades, they also lost an important daily link to the public world with which that economy was continuous—and so gradually redirected their energies to more private and personal concerns.

Our lack of knowledge about the political and literary lives of non-élite women has been thought to be a consequence of this kind of work not being 'doable'. But it is not so much the 'constraints of the archive' which are to blame for our lack of knowledge, this study suggests, as exclusionary critical practices and the constraints (and

---

[24] Richardson to Thomas Edwards, 29 Mar. 1756, Forster MS, XII, 1, f. 158, qtd. in Eaves and Kimpel, 'Samuel Richardson's London Houses', 147–8.

[25] Eaves and Kimpel, 'Samuel Richardson's London Houses'.

comforts) of the professional institutions within which many of us work. Critical traditions of intelligibility and value can prevent us from seeing what lies right before us; convenient or unexamined assumptions can function to foreclose certain types of scholarship before it starts. A current textbook on 'England in the Eighteenth Century' informs us that 'Slightly over half the nation was female. Yet, compared with men, we know little about what women felt, thought, and did. It was men who left most of the records behind— a fact that speaks all too eloquently of *how muted women had to be*.'[26] That some eighteenth-century women in the print trades would be 'muted' was indeed the sometime wish of government officials in charge of press control. But of course eighteenth-century women were never 'muted', and we need to get past the prescriptive literature to the broad variety of records that are indeed available for a more complete picture of ordinary women's convictions and lived experiences.

Eighteenth-century shifts in the relation of politics, religion, and literature had immediate consequences for a then-flourishing tradition of women's political activity, and those same shifts may have continuing consequences for us today. Augustan authors rejected previously widespread discursive modes and cultural concerns as immoderate, dull, or vulgar, and twentieth-century scholars have often followed suit without questioning the assumptions and ideologies at work. Disciplinary boundaries, cultural biases, and, at best, professional exigencies which cause us to rope off certain literary forms, practices, and concerns as 'not literary' and therefore 'not what we do' actually parallel post-revolutionary gestures of containment. Dominant literary critical models may be one indirect legacy of the post-revolutionary political and cultural developments outlined here.

If the goal for *some* of us is to understand the political and literary lives of men and women across a broad class and ideological spectrum, then we need to take greater risks than we have done in working to develop new methodologies. Despite inroads made by new historicism, we still need to work harder to examine the full range of texts in our period, rather than clinging to the most easily assimilated genres and to an anachronistic notion of the 'literary'.

---

[26] Roy Porter, *English Society in the Eighteenth Century* (Penguin-Pelican, 1982; rev. edn. 1990), 21–2; my emphasis.

If 'class [and might I add gender?] is defined by men [and might I add women?] as they live their own history, and in the end, this is the only definition', then literary critics who sympathize with the large goals of Marxism need to work to learn more about the lived experiences and convictions of persons who may well have *not* been the most 'literate' spokespersons of their society. We need to look beyond those forms of involvement with printed texts and kinds of texts valorized today, to the broader variety of sources available for a more complete view of less studied groups' 'lived history'. For the modern academic literary critic, of course, projecting one's manifesto in support of non-élites through the lens of analyses of élite authors is more expeditious than finding ways to reconstruct directly the lives and opinions of the so-called 'inarticulate'.[27] But it should not really surprise us that 'the energetic resistance to the dominant culture [E. P.] Thompson finds in a plebeian counter- or subculture is in effect missing or neutralized' in most eighteenth-century novels;[28] nor should it surprise us that working-class writers did not generally flourish using bourgeois literary forms. A more

[27] Similarly E. P. Thompson notes professional historians' strategies for circum-navigating 'the exceedingly difficult business of attempting to find out what was the actual consciousness of the inarticulate labouring poor' (*Customs in Common*, 20). Today even Marxist literary critics can carve out distinguished academic careers without descending lower on the social ladder in their writings than the 'bourgeois'. Terry Eagleton's witty condemnations of bourgeois cultural institutions, agendas, and aesthetics are academic bestsellers, and this prominent Marxist critic never descends lower on the social ladder in his writings on the 18th cent. than Joseph Addison and Richard Steele. He refers to these authors as 'middle class'—despite the fact that both gentlemen were educated at Oxford, held government offices, became members of parliament, and amassed enough wealth that the women who are the subject of this book would have viewed them as rich. The obvious disclaimer so often heard from left-leaning literary critics, 'I am not a historian,' might serve to justify the lack of concrete information about working people's lives and ideas we get in these critics' writings if only this explanation did not sit so oddly with powerful Marxist pleas for remembering ('always historicize', 'only return to history', and so on). Readers of left-leaning literary critics' critical analyses who long for concrete knowledge about the groups lumped together as 'the unpropertied', 'the transgressive', 'the repressed' may be left feeling uncomfortable with these people's double disappearance—their disappearance not only from bourgeois models of democracy, but also from left-leaning literary critics' commentaries on 18th-cent. society.
[28] John J. Richetti, 'Representing an Underclass: Servants and Proletarians in Fielding and Smollett', in Felicity Nussbaum and Laura Brown, eds., *The New 18th Century: Theory, Politics, English Literature* (New York: Methuen, 1987), 88.

potentially revolutionary question than many we have been asking
is, to what extent are we as literary scholars trained to be able to
understand the literary forms and textual practices these authors
and other print workers did participate in? Modern literary scholars of the 'Augustan period' often do not consider the vast polemical and topical literature of their period as part of their job. Nor do
most do more than nod in passing at 'material production'. A
newcomer to eighteenth-century literary studies today would most
likely assume that the dominant literary form in this period was the
novel. In actual fact, however, the novel constituted less than 1.1
per cent of England's annual print production before 1730,[29] and,
as we have seen in Part II, 'the largest single category of books
produced by British publishers in the eighteenth century was in the
field of religion'.[30] Even towards the end of the eighteenth century
'the pamphlet was still the means of reaching a mass audience'.[31]
We get a different view of the chief concerns and voices of the age
when we look at forms like broadsides, pamphlets, tracts, and
newspapers than when we concentrate on relatively decorous forms
like the novel. We get a still different view when we consider the
oral environments of early printed texts, and recognize the fundamental continuity of oral and printed forms. To consider respect-
fully these widespread forms is not to deny the modern reader
'pleasure'. Rather, it is to learn to enjoy those textual pleasures
most within ordinary eighteenth-century readers' (and hearers')
financial reach. For the price of *Tom Jones*, published in six duo-
decimo volumes, a bookbinder's daughter like Ann Barnham could
purchase some 200 political ballads.[32]

[29] James Raven estimates that the proportion of all fiction (new titles and reprints)
to total book and pamphlet production was about 1.1% for 1720–9 (*A Chronological Check-List of Prose Fiction Printed in Britain and Ireland*, 10). Margaret
Doody's recent study of the novel begins boldly by admitting that 'eighteenth-
century novels caused a stir, but they were not enormously widely read. . . . no novel
is as widely read as Scripture' (*The True Story of the Novel* (New Brunswick, NJ:
Rutgers UP, 1996), 3). As this book has shown, women writers of this period who
might first occur to 20th-cent. critics as typical 'women of Grub Street' (Eliza
Haywood for instance) are more usefully seen as exceptions to the norm of pre-1730
'Grub Street' authorship, in having specialized in more 'modern' (and, in modern
terminology, more 'literary') genres like the novel.
[30] John Feather, *A History of British Publishing* (London: Routledge, 1988), 96.
[31] Feather, 'British Publishing in the Eighteenth Century', 38.
[32] Ballads cost about a penny a piece, vs. 1–3 shillings per volume for a novel.

Terry Eagleton has suggested that in eighteenth-century England 'the literary is the vanishing point of the political; its dissolution and reconstitution into polite letters'. In delimiting the genres we study according to a set of aesthetic, moral, and generic criteria not fully articulated until after this period, feminist literary critics risk becoming the unwitting captives of values disseminated in the post-revolutionary period to undergird a changing but still firmly patriarchal and patrician social order. As Margaret Ezell and others have shown, feminist critics may stand to benefit most by asking what current literary critical traditions of intelligibility and value do and do not allow us to comprehend about our subject. Broadening our angle of vision beyond expressions of gender and even women's activity as authors will challenge our assumptions about the intellectual and political roles available to English women in the revolutionary and post-revolutionary period. It will cast light on these *other* late seventeenth- and early eighteenth-century women, whose lives, like those of their better-known male and female contemporaries, were profoundly affected by, even organized around, the new commercial and political opportunities of print. A dismantling of the current division of scholarly labour in literary criticism and publishing history opens up new avenues of research which may help to answer long-standing questions concerning women, print, and politics. What did non-élite women contribute to the emergence of the early modern literary marketplace and the institutionalization of a critical political press? How did these disenfranchised and sometimes illiterate citizens mediate their sociopolitical heritage? Opportunities to elucidate the intellectual frameworks of untutored or illiterate women are especially rare, and when paradoxically such women were employed at the centre of their society's communicative network the development of new methodologies for further study seems imperative. Continued research in these subject areas will shed new light on ordinary men and women's everyday involvement in the making and transmission of the printed word, as well as in the major national political debates of the period. Finally, this book suggests, by resuscitating mainstream early modern textual genres commonly neglected today, and by learning how to appreciate contributions to the material production and circulation of those genres made by 'impolite' persons, we will begin to resuscitate concerns of early modern print culture and political debate which have been erased from the record—even once-vocal participants whose voices have been suppressed. In the words of one historian of democracy and public discourse, 'the goal of publicness might best be allowed to navigate through wilder territory'.[33]

[33] Mary Ryan, 'Gender and Public Access: Women's Politics in Nineteenth-Century America', in Calhoun, ed., *Habermas*, 286.

Bibliography

MANUSCRIPT SOURCES

Bodleian Library, Oxford
MS Rawlinson D. 832–3. Papers of Richard Roach.

British Library, London
Add. MSS 5841. Epitaph of Joan Whitrow.
Harleian MS 5995/137. Advertisement by Ann Snowden. 1704.
Harleian MS 5995/95. Advertisement by Elizabeth Mallet. N.d.

Corporation of London Record Office
SM 60. Newgate Sessions Book. Prosecution of Elinor James. 1689.

Dr Williams's Library, London
MS 186.18 (1) a–c. Papers pertaining to the Philadelphian Society.

Guildhall Library, London
MS 10,091/26. Marriage licence of Thomas James and Elinor Bank(e)s. 1662.

Friends Library, London
Dictionary of Quaker Biography. Typescript.
Meeting for Sufferings Minutes. Vols. 1–43 (1675–1831).
Morning Meeting Minutes. Vols. 1–8 (1673–1861).
Yearly Meeting Minutes. Vols. 1–14 (1672–1723).

London Public Record Office
State Papers Domestic.
  SP 29 Charles II.
  SP 31 James II.
  SP 32 William.
  SP 34 Anne.
  SP 35 George I.
  SP 36 George II.
  SP 44/77–96 Entry Books, Criminal.
  SP 44/97–145 Secretaries Letter Books.

LC 5/191, f. 100. Lord Chamberlain's Records. Warrant for Aphra Behn. 1682.

Prob. 11/515, 109. Will of Thomas James. Proved 11 May 1710.

Prob. 11/599, 194–5. Will of Delarivier Manley. Proved 28 Sept. 1724.

Prob. 11/774, 346. Will of Tace Sowle Raylton. Proved 2 Nov. 1749.

Sion College, London

For whereabouts of MSS held at Sion College until 1996, see Note on Primary Sources.

Benefactors Book.

Mr. Thomas James's Common Place Book. N.d.

5 MS vols. of Thomas James.

PRINTED PRIMARY SOURCES

Unless otherwise noted, place of publication is London for early editions.

An Address of Thanks, On Behalf of the Church of England, to Mris. [sic] *James.* 1687.

ASTELL, MARY. *A Serious Proposal To the Ladies, For the Advancement of their true and greatest Interest. By a Lover of Her Sex.* 1694.

——*Reflections Upon Marriage. The Third Edition. To which is Added a Preface, in Answer to Some Objections.* 1706.

BALLARD, GEORGE. *Memoirs of Several Ladies of Great Britain, Who Have Been Celebrated for Their Writings or Skill in the Learned Languages, Arts and Sciences.* 1752. Ed. and intro. Ruth Perry. Detroit: Wayne State UP, 1985.

BEHN, APHRA. *A Pindarick On The Death Of Our Late Sovereign With An Ancient Prophecy On His Present Majesty.* 1685.

——*To His Sacred Majesty, King James II.* 1685.

——*A Pindarick Poem On The Happy Coronation Of His Most Sacred Majesty James II And His Illustrious Consort Queen Mary.* 1685.

——*The Lucky Chance; or, An Alderman's Bargain.* 1687.

——*A Congratulatory Poem To Her Most Sacred Majesty [Mary of Modena], On The Universal Hopes Of All Loyal Persons For A Prince of Wales.* 1688.

——*A Congratulatory Poem To The King's Most Sacred Majesty, On The Happy Birth Of The Prince of Wales.* 1688.

——*A Congratulatory Poem To Her Sacred Majesty Queen Mary Upon her Arrival in England.* 1689.

——*A Pindaric Poem To The Reverend Doctor Burnet, On The Honour he did me of Enquiring after me and my Muse.* 1689.

BEHN, APHRA. *The Uncollected Verse of Aphra Behn*. Ed. Germaine Greer. Stump Cross: Stump Cross Books, 1989.

——*Love-Letters Between a Nobleman and His Sister* (1684–7). Ed. and intro. Janet Todd. Harmondsworth: Penguin, 1996.

——*The Works of Aphra Behn*. Ed. Janet Todd. Vol. i: *Poetry*. Columbus: Ohio State UP, 1992.

BESSE, J[OSEPH]. *A Collection of the Sufferings of the People called Quakers*. 2 vols. 1753.

BOSWELL, JAMES. *Life of Johnson*. Ed. R. W. Chapman. Intro. Pat Rogers. Oxford: Oxford UP, 1983.

BOYD, ELIZABETH. *The Happy Unfortunate; or the Female Page: a Novel*. 1732.

——*A Humorous Miscellany: or, Riddles for the Beaux*. 1733.

BUGG, FRANCIS. *Jezebel Withstood, and Her Daughter Anne Docwra, Publickly Reprov'd; For Her Lies and Lightness in Her Book . . . An Apostate Conscience &.* 1699.

——*The Christian Ministry . . . Distinguished*. 1699.

——*William Penn, the Pretended Quaker, Discovered to hold a Correspondence with the Jesuite's at Rome. To which is Added, A Winding-Sheet for Ann Dockwra*. 1700.

——*News from New Rome, occasioned by the Quakers challenging of Francis Bugg, whereby their errors are farther exposed*. 1701.

——*A Seasonable Caveat Against the Prevalency of Quakerism*. 1701.

BURNET, GILBERT. *A Collection of Eighteen Papers, Relating to the Affairs of Church and State, During the Reign of King James the Second*. 1689.

——*An Answer to a Paper . . . Entitled, A New Test of the Church of England's Loyalty*. In Gilbert Burnet. *A Collection of Eighteen Papers*. 1689. 45–55.

CAVENDISH, MARGARET (Duchess of Newcastle). *CCXI. sociable letters, written by the thrice noble, illustrious, and excellent princess, the Lady Marchioness of Newcastle*. 1664.

——*The Description of a New World, Called The Blazing-World. Written By the Thrice Noble, Illustrious, and Excellent Princesse, The Duchess of Newcastle*. 1668.

CHURCHILL, SARAH (Duchess of Marlborough). *An Account of the Conduct of the Dowager Duchess of Marlborough, From her first coming to Court, To the Year 1710*. 1742. Rpt. as *Memoirs of Sarah, Duchess of Marlborough, together with her Characters of her Contemporaries and her Opinions*. Ed. and Intro. William King. George Routledge and Sons, 1830. Rpt. New York: Kraus, 1969.

——*Letters of Sarah Duchess of Marlborough . . . at Madresfield Court*. John Murray, 1875.

——*Private Correspondence*. 2 vols. 1838.

CIBBER, THEOPHILUS [Robert Shiels]. *The Lives of the Poets of Great Britain and Ireland, to the Time of Dean Swift.* 1753. 5 vols. Hildesheim: Georg Olms Verlagsbuchhandlung, 1968.

DALTON, MICHAEL. *The Countrey Justice, Conteyning The Practise of the Justices of the Peace out of their Sessions.* 1618.

D'AULNOY, MARIE CATHERINE LA MOTTE, Baronne. *The Ingenious and Diverting Letters of the Lady ——'s Travels into Spain.* 2nd edn. 1692.

—— *Memoirs of the Court of England.* 1707.

DAVYS, MARY. *Familiar Letters, Betwixt a Gentleman and a Lady.* 1725.

DEFOE, DANIEL. *The Complete English Tradesman.* 2 vols. 1725–7.

—— *A Review of The Affairs of France.* 9 vols. 19 Feb. 1704–11 June 1713. Ed. A. W. Secord. 22 vols. New York: Columbia UP, 1938.

DOCWRA, ANNE. *A Looking-Glass for the Recorder and Justices of the Peace, And Grand Juries for the Town and County of Cambridge.* Cambridge, 1682.

—— *An Epistle of Love and Good Advice to My Old Friends and Fellow-Sufferers in the Late Times, The Old Royalists.* Cambridge, 1683.

—— *A Brief Discovery of the Work of the Enemy of Sion's Peace.* Cambridge, 1683.

—— *Spiritual Community, vindicated amongst people of different perswasions in some things.* N.p., 1687.

—— *An Apostate-Conscience Exposed.* 1699.

—— *The Second Part of an Apostate-Conscience Exposed: Being an Answer to a Scurrilous Pamphlet . . . by F. Bugg, intituled, Jezebel withstood.* 1700.

—— *Treatise concerning Enthusiasm, or Inspiration, of the Holy Spirit of God.* 1700.

DRYDEN, JOHN. *The Works of John Dryden.* Vol. iii. Ed. Earl Miner and Vinton A. Dearing. Berkeley: U. of California P., 1969.

DUNCOMBE, JOHN. *The Feminiad. A Poem.* 1754. Intro. Jocelyn Harris. Los Angeles: William Andrews Clark Memorial Library, 1981.

DUNTON, JOHN. *Athenian Gazette: or, Casuistical Mercury, Resolving all the Most Nice and Curious Questions Proposed by the Ingenious of Either Sex.* Vol. 11. 1693.

—— *Petticoat Government. In a Letter to the Court Ladies.* 1702.

—— *The Life and Errors of John Dunton Citizen of London.* 1705. 2 vols. Rpt. New York: Burt Franklin, 1969.

—— *Dunton's Whipping-Post: or, a Satyr upon Every Body.* 1706.

—— *King Abigail: or, The Secret Reign of the She-Favourite.* 1715.

FELL, MARGARET ASKEW. *Womens Speaking Justified, Proved and Allowed by the Scriptures.* 1666.

GENT, THOMAS. *The Life of Mr. Thomas Gent, Printer, of York; Written by Himself.* 1746. Thomas Thorpe, 1832.

The Harleian Miscellany: A Collection of Scarce, Curious, and Entertaining Pamphlets and Tracts. Ed. William Oldys and Thomas Parks. 10 vols. 1808–13.

The Hawkers New Year's Gift: To all their Worthy Masters and Mistresses. 1727.

HAYWOOD, ELIZA. *Adventures of Eovaai, Princess of Ijaveo.* Ed. and intro. Josephine Grieder. Foundations of the Novel Series. Gen. ed. Michael F. Shugrue. New York: Garland, 1972.

Historical Manuscripts Commission. *Report on the Manuscripts of the Marquess of Downshire.* 4 vols. in 5. 1924–40.

——*The Manuscripts of His Grace the Duke of Portland.* 10 vols. HMSO, 1891–1931.

HOWELL, T. B., ed. *A Complete Collection of State Trials.* 33 vols. 1816–26.

An Impartial Account of the Tryal of Francis Smith . . . as also Of the Tryal of Jane Curtis. 1680.

JAMES, ELINOR. *Mrs. James her New Answer To a Speech said to be lately made by a Noble Peer of this Realm* [Anthony Ashley Cooper]. 1681.

——*The Case between a Father and his Children. Humbly represented to the Honourable Lord Mayor and Court of Aldermen.* 1682.

——*To the Right Honourable, the Lord Mayor and Court of Aldermen, and all the rest of the Loyal Citizens.* c.1683.

——*To the Kings Most Excellent Majesty. The Humble Petition of Elinor James. Humbly sheweth, That your poor Petitioner hath always been very Zealous for your Majesties Interest.* c.1685.

——*May it please Your Most Sacred Majesty, Seriously to Consider my great Zeal and Love.* 1685 or 1686.

——*To the Honourable the Commons in Parliament Assembled. The Humble Petition of Elianor James.* c.1685.

——*Most Dear Soveraign, I Cannot but Love and Admire You.* c.1686.

——*My Lord, I thought it my bound Duty to return your Lordship Thanks.* c.1687.

——*Mrs. JAMES's Vindication of the Church of England, In An Answer to a Pamphlet Entituled, A New Test of the Church of England's Loyalty.* 1687.

——*Mrs. James's Defence of the Church of England, in a Short Answer to the Canting Address, &c. With a Word or Two Concerning a Quakers Good Advice.* 1687.

——*Mrs. James's Advice to the Citizens of London.* 1688.

——*To the Right Honourable Convention. Gentlemen, Though you have a New Name.* 1688 or 1689.

——*My Lords, I can assure your Lordships, that you are infinitely admir'd.* 1688 or 1689.

——*To the Honourable Convention. Gentlemen, You seem (for the most part of you) to be Worthy Men. c.*1688.

——*My Lords, You can't but be sensible of the great Zeal I have had for King and Kingdom. c.*1688.

——*May it please your Majesty, to accept my thanks, for your gracious Act in restoring the Charter. c.*1688 or 1689.

——*This being Your Majesty's Birth-Day, I thought no time more proper than this, to return you Thanks. c.*1689.

——*Sir, My Lord Mayor and the Aldermen his Brethren, upon Serious Consideration for the good of the City . . . c.*1690.

——*Mrs.* JAME's [sic] *Apology because of Unbelievers.* Before 1694.

——*To the Right Honourable the Lords Assembled in Parliament, I can assure Your Lordships that I am very much troubled for Sir Thomas Cook* [sic]. *c.*1695.

——*October 28th* [c.1695]. *I have been toiling . . .*

——*To the Honourable the House of Commons . . . I am very sorry.* 1696.

——*To the Right Honourable the House of Lords. My Lords, For as much as the Most High God hath guided me with a Spirit of Truth. c.*1700.

——*Mrs. James's humble Request to the Honourable House of Lords for Unity. c.*1701.

——*The petition of Elinor James to the Lords spiritual and temporal assembled in Parliament. Mar. 21, 1702.* 1702.

——*Octob. the 20th, 1702. May it please Your Lordships, Seriously to Consider what Great Things God has done for You.* 1702.

——*To the Lords spiritual and temporal. The humble desire of Elianor James, that your Lordships should not hinder the bill from passing. c.*1703.

——*May the 15th, 1705. Mrs. Elianor James's Speech to the Citizens of London, at Guild-Hall, relating to their new Choice of Parliament Men.* 1705.

——*Mrs. James's Consideration to the Lords and Commons, wherein she plainly shews, That the True Church has been, and always will be in danger . . . Dec. the 15th 1705.* 1705.

——*To the Lords Spiritual and Temporal assembled in Parliament. May it please your Lordships, I have read a Case that is before your Lordships, relating to one Dye . . .* 1706 or 1707. Rpt. in John Nichols. *Literary Anecdotes of the Eighteenth Century.* 1812–15. i. 306–7.

——*Mrs. James* [sic] *Prayer for the Queen and Parliament, and Kingdom too. c.*1710.

——*Mrs. James's Letter of Thanks to the Q——n and both Houses of Parliament, for the Deliverance of Dr. Sacheverell, March 24th, 1710.* 1710.

JAMES, ELINOR. *The Case of Mrs. Elenor James, Or, The High-Church Legacy To the Parish of St. Bennet's, Paul's Wharf. c.*1710.

——*July 1st. 1713. Mrs. James, Wisheth Health, and Happiness . . . to this Honourable House of Commons: and Humbly Intreats the Almighty to Pardon the Sins of this House.* 1713.

——*June the 25th, 1714. Mrs. James's Letter of Advice to both Houses of Parliament.* 1714.

——*September the 14th, 1714. To my Lord-Mayor and Court of Aldermen.* 1714.

——*November the 17th, 1714. This day ought never to be forgotten, being the Proclamation Day for Queen Elizabeth.* 1714.

——*Gentlemen of the South-sea company . . . Feb. the 3d, 1714/15.*

——*Good Counsel From Mrs. Eleanor James to King George.* 1715.

——*June the 9th. 1715. Mrs. James's Letter to the Jacobites and Nonjurors.* 1715.

——*September the 29th. 1715. Mrs. James's Letter to the Lord-Mayor and Court of Aldermen.* 1715.

——*Elinor James's Advice to the King and Parliament.* 1715.

——*Mrs. James's Reasons Humbly Presented to the Lords Spiritual and Temporal. Shewing Why She is not willing, that at this time there should be any Impeachments.* 1715.

——*November the 5th, 1715. Mrs. James's Thanks to the Lords and Commons for their Sincerity to King George.* 1715.

——*Mrs. James's Advice to All Printers in General. c.*1715. Rpt. in John Nichols. *Literary Anecdotes of the Eighteenth Century.* 1812–15. i. 306–7.

LACKINGTON, JAMES. *Memoirs of the First Forty-Five Years of the Life of James Lackington, The present Bookseller in Chiswell-street, Moorfields, London.* Printed for the Author, 1792.

LEAD, JANE. *The Heavenly Cloud Now Breaking. The Lord Christ's Ascension Ladder sent down.* 1681.

——*The Revelation of Revelations.* 1683.

——'To the Reader'. Preface to *Theologia Mystica, Or The Mystic Divinitie Of the Æternal Invisibles.* [By John Pordage.] 1–9.

——*The Enochian Walks with God, Found out by a Spiritual-Traveller.* 1694.

——*The Wonders of God's Creation Manifested, In the Variety of Eight Worlds: As they were made known Experimentally to the Author.* 1695.

——*The Laws of Paradise, Given forth by Wisdom to a Translated Spirit.* 1695.

——*A Fountain of Gardens, Watered by the Rivers of Divine Pleasure and Springing Up in All the Variety of Spiritual Plants.* 3 vols.; vol. 3 in 2 pts. 1696–1701.

—— *A Message to the Philadelphian Society, Whithersoever dispersed over the Whole Earth.* 1696.

—— *A Second Message to the Philadelphian Society.* 1696.

—— *The Tree of Faith: or, The Tree of Life, Springing up in the Paradise of God.* 1696.

—— *The Ark of Faith: or, A Supplement to the Tree of Faith. . . . Together with a Discovery of the New World.* 1696.

—— *A Revelation of the Everlasting Gospel-Message, Which shall never cease to be Preach'd Till the Hour of Christ's Eternal Judgment Shall Come.* 1697.

—— *A Messenger of An Universal Peace, or a Third Message to the Philadelphian Society.* 1698.

—— *The Ascent to the Mount of Vision, where many Things were shewn.* 1699.

—— *The Signs of the Times: forerunning the Kingdom of Christ and evidencing when it is come.* 1699.

—— *The Wars of David, and the Peaceable Reign of Solomon . . . Set Forth in Two Treatises.* 1700.

—— *The Heavenly Cloud Now Breaking. The Lord Christ's Ascension Ladder sent down.* 2nd edn. 1701.

—— *A Living Funeral Testimony: or, Death Overcome, and Drown'd in the Life of Christ.* 1702.

[LEE, FRANCIS.] *State of the Philadelphian Society.* 1697.

—— *Theosophical Transactions By the Philadelphian Society, Consisting of Memoirs, Conferences, Letters, Dissertations, Inquiries, &c.* 5 nos. 1697.

LUTTRELL, NARCISSUS. *A Brief Historical Relation of State Affairs from Sept. 1678 to April 1714.* 6 vols. Oxford: Oxford UP, 1857.

MANLEY, DELARIVIER. *Letters Written by Mrs. Manley.* 1696. Reissued as *A Stagecoach Journey to Exeter.* 1725.

—— *The Royal Mischief. A Tragedy.* 1696.

—— *The Secret History of Queen Zarah and the Zarazians; Being a Looking-glass for —— in the Kingdom of Albigion.* 1705.

—— *Secret Memoirs and Manners of several Persons of Quality, of Both Sexes, from the New Atalantis, An Island in the Mediteranean.* 1709.

—— *The New Atalantis.* Ed. and intro. Ros Ballaster. 1st published by Pickering and Chatto, 1991; in paperback by Penguin, 1992.

—— *Memoirs of Europe, Towards the Close of the Eighth Century, Written by Eginardus, Secretary and Favourite to Charlemagne; And done into English by the Translator of the New Atalantis.* 1710.

—— *A True Narrative of What Pass'd at the Examination of the Marquis de Guiscard, at the Cock-Pit, the 8th of March, 1710–11. His stabbing Mr. Harley, &c.* 1711.

MANLEY, DELARIVIER. *A Learned Comment on Dr. Hare's Excellent Sermon Preach'd before the Duke of Marlborough, on the Surrender of Bouchain.* 1711.

—— *The Duke of M[arlboroug]h's Vindication: In Answer to a Pamphlet Lately Publish'd call'd* [Bouchain, *or a Dialogue between the* Medley *and the* Examiner]. 1711.

—— *A True Relation of the Several Facts and Circumstances of the Intended Riot and Tumult on Queen Elizabeth's Birth-day.* 1711.

—— *The Honour and Prerogative of the Queen's Majesty Vindicated and Defended Against the Unexampled Insolences of the Author of the* Guardian, *in a Letter from a Country Whig to Mr. Steele.* 1713.

—— *A Modest Enquiry into the Reasons of the Joy Expressed by a Certain Sett of People upon the Spreading of a Report of Her Majesty's Death.* 1714.

—— *The Adventures of Rivella; or, the History of the Author of the* Atalantis. *With Secret Memoirs and Characters of several considerable Persons her Cotemporaries.* 1714.

—— et al. *The Examiner.* 1st. ser. 1710–11.

MILTON, JOHN. *Areopagitica; a Speech of Mr. John Milton for the Liberty of Unlicenc'd Printing, to the Parliament of England.* 1644.

MOXON, JOSEPH. *Mechanick Exercises On the Whole Art of Printing.* 1683–4. Ed. Herbert Davis and Harry Carter. 2nd edn. London: Oxford UP, 1962.

A New Test of the Church of Englands Loyalty. Printed for N[athaniel] T[hompson], 1687.

The New Test of the Church of England's Loyalty, Examined by the Old Test of Truth and Honesty. Printed by R.G., 1687.

NICHOLS, JOHN. *Literary Anecdotes of the Eighteenth Century.* 9 vols. London, 1812–15.

[PHILIPS, KATHERINE.] *Poems By the most deservedly Admired Mrs. Katherine Philips The matchless Orinda.* Ed. and pref. Sir Charles Cotterell. 1667.

[POLWHELE, RICHARD.] *The Unsex'd Females: A Poem, Addressed To The Author Of The Pursuits Of Literature.* 1798.

POPE, ALEXANDER. *Poems.* Ed. John Butt. New Haven: Yale UP, 1963.

PORDAGE, JOHN. *Theologia Mystica, or, The Mystic Divinite of the Aeternal Invisibles.* 1683.

POWELL, ELIZABETH. *The Charitable Mercury and Female Intelligence. Being a Weekly Collection of All the Material News, Foreign and Domestick: With Some Notes on the Same.* 7 Apr. 1716.

—— *The Orphan Reviv'd: or,* POWELL'S *Weekly Journal.* 1719–20.

RALPH, JAMES. *The Case of Authors by Profession or Trade, Stated With Regard to Booksellers, the Stage, and the Publick.* 1758.

The Rival Dutchess: or, Court Incendiary. In a Dialogue between Madam Maintenon, and Madam M [asham]. 1708.

ROACH, RICHARD. *The Great Crisis: Or, The Mystery of the Times and Seasons Unfolded.* 1725.

SEWEL, WILLIAM. *The History of the Rise, Increase, and Progress, of the Christian People Called Quakers.* 2 vols. 1722.

[SMART, CHRISTOPHER.] *The Midwife, Or The Old Woman's Magazine.* 1750–2.

SMITH, JOSEPH, ed. *Bibliotheca Anti-Quakeriana; Or, a Catalogue of Books Adverse to the Society of Friends.* 1873.

——*A Descriptive Catalogue of Friends' Books, or Books Written by Members of the Society of Friends, Commonly Called Quakers, from Their First Rise to the Present Time.* 4 vols. 1867.

A Speech Lately Made by a Noble Peer of the Realm [Anthony Ashley Cooper]. 1681.

STEELE, RICHARD. *The Guardian.* Ed. John C. Stephens. Lexington: UP of Kentucky, 1982.

——*The Tatler.* Ed. George A. Aitken. New York: Hadley and Matthews, 1899.

——and ADDISON, JOSEPH. *The Spectator.* Ed. Donald F. Bond. 5 vols. Oxford: Clarendon P., 1965.

SWIFT, JONATHAN. *The Correspondence of Jonathan Swift.* Ed. Harold Williams. 5 vols. Oxford: Clarendon P., 1963–5.

——*The Journal to Stella.* Ed. Harold Williams. 2 vols. Oxford: Clarendon P., 1948.

——*The Poems of Jonathan Swift.* Ed. Harold Williams. 3 vols. Oxford: Clarendon P., 1937; 2nd edn., rev., 1958.

——*The Complete Poems.* Ed. Pat Rogers. New Haven: Yale UP, 1983.

——*The Prose Works of Jonathan Swift.* Ed. Herbert J. Davis et al. 16 vols. Oxford: Blackwell, 1939–74.

——*Works.* Vol. xix. Ed. Sir Walter Scott. 1884.

——et al. *The Examiner.* Ed. Herbert Davis. Oxford: Basil Blackwell, 1957.

THOMAS, PATRICK, ed. *The Collected Works of Katherine Philips The Matchless Orinda.* Vol. i: *The Poems.* Stump Cross: Stump Cross Books, 1990.

TIMPERLEY, C. H. *A Dictionary of Printers and Printing, with the Progress of Literature, Ancient and Modern.* 1839.

TOMKINS, JOHN. *Piety Promoted, in a Collection of Dying Sayings of Many of the People Called Quakers.* 1701.

WALTON, CHRISTOPHER. *Notes and Materials for an Adequate Biography of the Celebrated Divine and Theosopher William Law.* 1854.

WHITROWE, JOAN. *The Humble Address of the Widow Whitrow to King William: With a Faithful Warning to the Inhabitants of England.* 1689.

WHITROWE, JOAN. *The Humble Salutation and Faithful Greeting of the Widow Whitrow to King William.* 1690.

——To Queen Mary: The Humble Salutation and Faithful Greeting of the Widow Whitrowe. With a Warning to the Rulers of the Earth. 1690.

——To King William and Queen Mary, Grace and Peace. The Widow Whitrow's Humble Thanksgiving to the Lord of Hosts . . . for the King's safe Return to England. 1692.

——The Widow Whiterow's [sic] Humble Thanksgiving for the Kings Safe Return. With an account of John Hall's vision etc. 1694.

——To the King, And Both Houses of Parliament. Say unto them, Thus saith the Lord, etc. 1696.

——Faithful Warnings, Expostulations and Exhortations, To The several Professors of Christianity in England, as well as those of the Highest as the Lowest Quality. With 'To the King, and Both Houses of Parliament' and 'Some Remarks on a Sermon, Preached on the Death of the Late Queen'. 1697.

——et al. The Work of God in a Dying Maid: Being A short Account of the Dealings of the Lord with one Susannah Whitrow. 1677.

SECONDARY SOURCES

ALKON, PAUL. 'Recent Studies in the Restoration and Eighteenth Century', *Studies in English Literature*, 29 (1989), 579–614.

AMBROSE, PAMELA M. 'The Power of the Quaker Press'. MA dissertation, School of Library, Archive and Information Studies, University College, University of London, 1981.

ANDERSON, PAUL BUNYAN. 'Delariviere Manley's Prose Fiction', *Philological Quarterly*, 13 (1934), 168–88.

——'Mistress Delariviere Manley's Biography', *Modern Philology*, 33 (1936), 261–78.

ARBER, EDWARD, ed. *The Term Catalogues, 1668–1709.* 3 vols. London, 1903–6.

——Transcript of the Registers of the Company of Stationers of London, 1554–1640 A.D. 5 vols. London: privately printed, 1875–94.

ARMSTRONG, NANCY. *Desire and Domestic Fiction: A Political History of the Novel.* New York: Oxford UP, 1987.

ATHERTON, HERBERT M. *Political Prints in the Age of Hogarth: A Study of the Ideographic Representation of Politics.* Oxford: Clarendon P., 1974.

BACKSCHEIDER, PAULA R. *Daniel Defoe: His Life.* Baltimore: The Johns Hopkins UP, 1989.

——Spectacular Politics: Theatrical Power and Mass Culture in Early Modern England. Baltimore: The Johns Hopkins UP, 1993.

BAKHTIN, MIKHAIL. *The Dialogic Imagination: Four Essays*. Trans. Caryl Emerson and Michael Holquist. Ed. Michael Holquist. Austin: U. of Texas P., 1981.

BALLASTER, ROS. *Seductive Forms: Women's Amatory Fiction from 1684 to 1740*. Oxford: Clarendon P., 1992.

—— 'Seductive Forms: Women's Amatory Fiction 1684–1740', diss., Oxford U., 1989.

—— ed. and intro. to Delarivier Manley, *The New Atalantis*. 1st published by Pickering and Chatto, 1991; in pbk. by Penguin, 1992.

BARASH, CAROL. *English Women's Poetry, 1649–1714: Politics, Community, and Linguistic Authority*. Oxford: Clarendon P., 1996.

BARKER, FRANCIS, et al., eds. *1642: Literature and Power in the Seventeenth Century*. Proceedings of the Essex Conference on the Sociology of Literature. Colchester: U. of Essex, 1981.

BELANGER, TERRY. 'Booksellers' Trade Sales, 1718–68', *Library*, 5th ser. 30 (1975), 281–302.

—— 'Publishers and Writers in Eighteenth-Century England', in Isabel Rivers, ed., *Books and their Readers in 18th-Century England*. Leicester: Leicester UP, 1982. 5–25.

BELL, MAUREEN. 'A Dictionary of Women in the London Book Trade, 1540–1730', Masters of Library Studies diss., Loughborough U. of Technology, 1983.

—— 'Elizabeth Calvert and the "Confederates"', *Publishing History*, 32 (1992), 5–49.

—— 'Hannah Allen and the Development of a Puritan Publishing Business, 1646–51', *Publishing History*, 26 (1989), 5–66.

—— ' "Her Usual Practices": The Later Career of Elizabeth Calvert, 1664–75', *Publishing History*, 35 (1994), 5–64.

—— 'Mary Westwood, Quaker Publisher', *Publishing History*, 23 (1988), 5–66.

—— 'Women and the Opposition Press after the Restoration', in John Lucas, ed., *Writing and Radicalism*. London: Longman, 1996. 39–60.

—— 'Women in the English Book Trade 1557–1700', *Leipziger Jahrbuch zur Buchgeschichte*, 6 (1996), 13–45.

—— 'Women Publishers of Puritan Literature in the Mid-seventeenth Century: Three Case Studies', diss., Loughborough U. of Technology, 1987.

—— PARFITT, GEORGE, and SHEPHERD, SIMON, eds. *A Biographical Dictionary of English Women Writers 1580–1720*. Boston: G. K. Hall and Co., 1990.

BELSEY, CATHERINE. *The Subject of Tragedy: Identity and Difference in Renaissance Drama*. London: Methuen, 1985.

BENNETT, TONY. 'Texts, Readers, Reading Formations', *Bulletin of the Midwest Modern Language Association*, 16 (1983), 3–17.

BENNETT, TONY. 'Marxism and Popular Fiction', in Peter Humm, Paul Stigant, and Peter Widdowson, eds., *Popular Fictions: Essays in Literature and History.* London: Methuen, 1986. 237–65.

BERG, CHRISTINE, and BERRY, PHILIPPA. 'Spiritual Whoredom: An Essay on Female Prophets in the Seventeenth Century', in F. Barker et al., eds., *1642: Literature and Power in the Seventeenth Century.* Colchester: U. of Essex, 1981. 37–54.

BEVERLY, JOHN. 'The Margin at the Center: On *Testimonio* (Testimonial Narrative)', *Modern Fiction Studies,* 35. 1 (Spring 1989), 11–28.

BLACK, JEREMY. *The English Press in the Eighteenth Century.* London: Croom Helm, 1987.

BLAGDEN, CYPRIAN. 'Notes on the Ballad Market in the Second Half of the Seventeenth Century', *Studies in Bibliography,* 6 (1954), 161–80.

——*The Stationers' Company: A History, 1403–1959.* London: George Allen and Unwin, 1960.

BLAIN, VIRGINIA, GRUNDY, ISOBEL, and CLEMENTS, PATRICIA, eds. *The Feminist Companion to Literature in English: Women Writers from the Middle Ages to the Present.* New Haven: Yale UP, 1990.

BLOUCH, CHRISTINE. 'Eliza Haywood and the Romance of Obscurity', *Studies in English Literature,* 31 (1991), 535–52.

BOWYER, JOHN WILSON. *The Celebrated Mrs. Centlivre.* Durham, NC: Duke UP, 1952.

BRACK, O. M., Jr., ed. *Writers, Books and Trade: An Eighteenth-Century English Miscellany for William B. Todd.* New York: AMS Press, 1994.

BRAITHWAITE, WILLIAM C. *The Beginnings of Quakerism.* 1912. 2nd edn. rev. Henry J. Cadbury. York: William Sessions, 1981.

——*The Second Period of Quakerism.* 1919. 2nd edn. prep. Henry J. Cadbury. York: William Sessions, 1979.

BROWN, PHILIP A. H. *London Publishers and Printers c.1800 to 1870.* London: British Library, 1982.

BROWNLEY, MARTINE. 'Bishop Gilbert Burnet and the Vagaries of Power', in R. P. Maccubbin and M. Hamilton-Philips, eds., *The Age of William III and Mary II.* Williamsburg, Va.: The College of William and Mary, 1989. 77–81.

BRUCE, SUSAN. 'The Flying Island and Female Anatomy: Gynaecology and Power in *Gulliver's Travels*', *Genders,* no. 2 (1988), 60–76.

CALHOUN, CRAIG, ed. *Habermas and the Public Sphere.* Cambridge, Mass.: MIT Press, 1992.

CAPP, BERNARD. *Astrology and the Popular Press: English Almanacs 1500–1800.* London: Faber and Faber, 1979.

CARROLL, JOHN, ed. *Selected Letters of Samuel Richardson.* Oxford: Clarendon P., 1964.

CASTLE, TERRY J. 'Lab'ring Bards: Birth Topoi and English Poetics 1660–1820', *Journal of English and Germanic Philology,* 78 (1979), 193–208.

CLARK, ALICE. *Working Life of Women in the Seventeenth Century.* 1919. Intro. Miranda Chaytor and Jane Lewis, London: Routledge, 1982; intro. Amy Louise Erickson, London: Routledge, 1992.

CLARK, ANNA. *The Struggle for the Breeches: Gender and the Making of the British Working Class.* Berkeley and Los Angeles: U. of California P., 1985.

COCKBURN, CYNTHIA. 'The Material of Male Power', in Terry Lovell, ed., *British Feminist Thought: A Reader.* Oxford: Basil Blackwell, 1990. 84–102.

COTTON, NANCY. 'Margaret Cavendish, Duchess of Newcastle', in Janet Todd, ed., *A Dictionary of British and American Women Writers 1660–1800.* Totowa, NJ: Rowman and Littlefield, 1987. 231–3.

CRAWFORD, PATRICIA. 'Women's Published Writings 1600–1700', in Mary Prior, ed., *Women in English Society, 1500–1800.* New York: Methuen, 1985. 211–82.

CRESSY, DAVID. *Literacy and the Social Order: Reading and Writing in Tudor and Stuart England.* Cambridge: Cambridge UP, 1980.

CRIST, TIMOTHY. 'Government Control of the Press after the Expiration of the Printing Act in 1679', *Publishing History*, 5 (1979), 49–77.

CURTIUS, ERNST ROBERT. *European Latin Literature and the Latin Middle Ages.* 1952; Princeton: Princeton UP, Bollingen Series XXXVI, 1973.

DARNTON, ROBERT. *The Great Cat Massacre and Other Episodes in French Cultural History.* New York: Random House-Vintage, 1985.

——*The Literary Underground of the Old Regime.* Cambridge, Mass.: Harvard UP, 1982.

——and ROCHE, DANIEL, eds. *Revolution in Print: The Press in France 1775–1800.* Berkeley and Los Angles: U. of California P., 1989.

DAVIDOFF, LEONORE, and HALL, CATHERINE. *Family Fortunes: Men and Women of the English Middle Class, 1780–1850.* Chicago: U. of Chicago P., 1987.

DAVIS, NATALIE ZEMON. *Fiction in the Archives: Pardon Tales and their Tellers in Sixteenth-Century France.* Stanford, Calif.: Stanford UP, 1987.

——*Society and Culture in Early Modern France.* Stanford, Calif.: Stanford UP, 1975.

——'Women in the Crafts in Sixteenth-Century Lyon', *Feminist Studies*, 8 (1982), 46–90.

DAY, ROBERT ADAMS. *Told in Letters: Epistolary Fiction before Richardson.* Ann Arbor: U. of Michigan P., 1966.

DE CERTEAU, MICHEL. *The Practice of Everyday Life.* Trans. Steven Rendall. Berkeley and Los Angeles: U. of California P., 1984.

DE HAMEL, CHRISTOPHER. *A History of Illuminated Manuscripts.* Boston: David R. Godine, 1986.

DEJEAN, JOAN. *Tender Geographies: Women and the Origins of the Novel in France.* New York: Columbia UP, 1991.

DE KREY, GARY S. 'London Radicals and Revolutionary Politics, 1675–1683', in Tim Harris et al., eds., *The Politics of Religion in Restoration England*. Oxford: Basil Blackwell, 1990. 133–62.

—— 'Political Radicalism in London after the Glorious Revolution', *Journal of Modern History*, 55 (1983), 585–617.

—— 'Revolution *redivivus*: 1688–1689 and the Radical Tradition in Seventeenth-Century London Politics', in Lois G. Schwoerer, ed., *The Revolution of 1688–1689*. Cambridge: Cambridge UP, 1992. 198–217.

DOLAN, FRANCES E. *Whores of Babylon: Catholicism, Gender, and the Law from the Gunpowder Plot to the Popish Plot*, forthcoming.

DOODY, MARGARET. *The True Story of the Novel*. New Brunswick, NJ: Rutgers UP, 1996.

DOWNIE, J. A. *Robert Harley and the Press: Propaganda and Public Opinion in the Age of Swift and Defoe*. Cambridge: Cambridge UP, 1979.

—— *To Settle the Succession of State: Literature and Politics 1678–1750*. New York: St Martin's P., 1994.

DUFFY, MAUREEN. *The Passionate Shepherdess: Aphra Behn 1640–1689*. New York: Avon, 1977.

EAGLETON, TERRY. *The Function of Criticism: From* The Spectator *to Post-structuralism*. 1984. London: New Left Books-Verso, 1987.

—— *The Rape of Clarissa: Writing, Sexuality and Class Struggle in Samuel Richardson*. Minneapolis: U. of Minnesota P., 1982.

EARLE, PETER. 'The Female Labour Market in London in the Late Seventeenth and Early Eighteenth Centuries', *Economic History Review*, 2nd ser. 42. 3 (1989), 328–53.

—— *The Making of the English Middle Class: Business, Society and Family Life in London, 1660–1730*. Berkeley and Los Angeles: U. of California P., 1989.

EAVES, T. C. DUNCAN, and KIMPEL, BEN D. 'Samuel Richardson's London Houses', *Studies in Bibliography*, 15 (1962), 135–48.

EHRENPREIS, IRVIN. *Swift: The Man, his Works, and the Age*. 3 vols. Cambridge, Mass.: Harvard UP, 1962–83.

EISENSTEIN, ELIZABETH L. *The Printing Revolution in Early Modern Europe*. Cambridge: Cambridge UP, 1983.

ELEY, GEOFF. 'Nations, Publics, and Political Cultures: Placing Habermas in the Nineteenth Century', in Craig Calhoun, ed., *Habermas and the Public Sphere*. Cambridge, Mass.: MIT Press, 1992. 289–339.

ELLIS, FRANK H., ed. *A Discourse of the Contests and Dissensions Between the Nobles and the Commons in Athens and Rome, With the Consequences they had upon both those States*. By Jonathan Swift. Oxford: Clarendon P., 1967.

——ed. *Swift vs. Mainwaring:* The Examiner *and* The Medley. Oxford: Clarendon P., 1985.

ERICKSON, AMY LOUISE. *Women and Property in Early Modern England.* London: Routledge, 1993.

——Intro. to Alice Clark, *Working Life of Women in the Seventeenth Century.* 4th edn. London: Routledge, 1992.

ERICKSON, ROBERT A. ' "The Books of Generation": Some Observations on the Style of the British Midwife Books, 1671–1764', in Paul-Gabriel Boucé, ed., *Sexuality in Eighteenth-Century Britain.* Manchester: Manchester UP, 1982. 74–94.

——*Mother Midnight: Birth, Sex, and Fate in Eighteenth-Century Fiction (Defoe, Richardson, and Sterne).* New York: AMS Press, 1986.

ESCARPIT, ROBERT. *The Sociology of Literature.* 1958. Trans. Ernest Pick. Painesville, Oh.: Lake Erie College Press, 1965.

EYRE, G. E. B. *A Transcript of the Registers of the Worshipful Company of Stationers; from 1640–1708 A.D.* 3 vols. (1913–14). Vol. iii: *1675–1708.* London: Privately printed, 1914.

EZELL, MARGARET J. M. 'The Myth of Judith Shakespeare: Creating the Canon of Women's Literature', *New Literary History*, 21 (1990), 579–92.

——*The Patriarch's Wife: Literary Evidence and the History of the Family.* Chapel Hill: U. of North Carolina P., 1987.

——*Writing Women's Literary History.* Baltimore: The Johns Hopkins UP, 1993.

FEATHER, JOHN. *A History of British Publishing.* London: Routledge, 1988.

——'The Book Trade in Politics: The Making of the Copyright Act of 1710', *Publishing History*, 8 (1980), 19–44.

——'British Publishing in the Eighteenth Century: A Preliminary Subject Analysis', *Library*, 6th ser. 8 (1986), 32–46.

——'The English Book Trade and the Law 1695–1799', *Publishing History*, 12 (1982), 51–75.

——'From Censorship to Copyright: Aspects of the Government's Role in the English Book Trade 1695–1775', in Kenneth E. Carpenter, ed., *Books and Society in History.* New York: R. R. Bowker Co., 1983. 173–98.

FEBVRE, LUCIEN, and MARTIN, HENRI-JEAN. *The Coming of the Book: The Impact of Printing 1450–1800.* Trans. David Gerard. Ed. Geoffrey Nowell-Smith and David Wootton. London: NLB-Verso, 1976.

FERGUSON, MOIRA, ed. and intro. *First Feminists: British Women Writers, 1578–1799.* Bloomington: Indiana UP, 1985.

FINCH, CASEY, and BOWEN, PETER. ' "The Tittle-Tattle of Highbury": Gossip and the Free Indirect Style in *Emma*', *Representations*, 31 (1990), 1–18.

FLETCHER, ANGUS. *Allegory: The Theory of a Symbolic Mode.* 1964. Ithaca, NY: Cornell UP, 1986.

FORD, MARGARET LANE. 'A Widow's Work: Ann Franklin of Newport, Rhode Island', *Printing History*, 12 (1990), 15–26.

FORD, WYN. 'The Problem of Literacy in Early Modern England', *History*, 78 (1993), 22–37.

FOUCAULT, MICHEL. *The History of Sexuality*, i: *An Introduction.* Trans. Robert Hurley. New York: Random House-Pantheon, 1980.

—— *Madness and Civilization: A History of Insanity in the Age of Reason.* Trans. Richard Howard. New York: Random House-Vintage, 1988.

—— 'What is an Author?', in Josué V. Harari, ed., *Textual Strategies: Perspectives in Post-structuralist Criticism.* Ithaca, NY: Cornell UP, 1979. 141–60.

FOXON, D. F. *Pope and the Early Eighteenth-Century Book Trade.* Lyell Lectures in Bibliography, 1975–6. Revised and edited by James Mclaverty. Oxford: Oxford UP, 1990.

FRASER, NANCY. 'Rethinking the Public Sphere: A Contribution to the Critique of Actually Existing Democracy', in Craig Calhoun, ed., *Habermas and the Public Sphere.* Cambridge, Mass.: MIT Press, 1992. 109–42.

FRASER, PETER. *The Intelligence of the Secretaries of State and their Monopoly of Licensed News 1660–1688.* Cambridge: Cambridge UP, 1956.

GALLAGHER, CATHERINE. 'Embracing the Absolute: The Politics of the Female Subject in Seventeenth-Century England', *Genders*, 1 (1988), 24–39.

—— *Nobody's Story: The Vanishing Acts of Women Writers in the Marketplace, 1670–1820.* Berkeley and Los Angeles: U. of California P., 1994.

—— 'Political Crimes and Fictional Alibis: The Case of Delarivier Manley', *ECS* 23 (1990), 502–21.

GARDINER, JUDITH KEGAN. 'The First English Novel: Aphra Behn's *Love Letters*, the Canon, and Women's Tastes', *Tulsa Studies in Women's Literature*, 8 (1989), 201–22.

GARDNER, JUDITH E. 'Women in the Book Trade, 1641–1700: A Preliminary Survey', *Gutenberg-Jahrbuch.* Mainz: Verlag der Gutenberg-Gesellschaft, 1978. 343–6.

GEERTZ, CLIFFORD. *The Interpretation of Cultures: Selected Essays.* New York: Basic Books, 1973.

GEORGE, M. DOROTHY. *London Life in the Eighteenth Century.* 1925. Chicago: Academy Chicago Publishers, 1984.

GOLDBERG, JONATHAN. *Writing Matter: From the Hands of the English Renaissance.* Stanford, Calif.: Stanford UP, 1990.

GOLDGAR, BERTRAND A. *Walpole and the Wits: The Relation of Politics to Literature, 1722–1742.* Lincoln: U. of Nebraska P., 1976.

GOLDSMITH, ELIZABETH C., and GOODMAN, DENA, eds. *Going Public: Women and Publishing in Early Modern France.* Ithaca, NY: Cornell UP, 1995.

GOODY, JACK, ed. and intro. *Literacy in Traditional Societies.* Cambridge: Cambridge UP, 1968.

GOREAU, ANGELINE. *Reconstructing Aphra: A Social Biography of Aphra Behn.* New York: Dial, 1980.

GOULDEN, R. J. '*Vox Populi, Vox Dei*: Charles Delafaye's Paperchase', *Book Collector*, 28 (1979), 368–90.

GREAVES, RICHARD L. 'Shattered Expectations? George Fox, the Quakers, and the Restoration State, 1660–1685', *Albion*, 24 (1992), 237–59.

——and ZALLER, ROBERT, eds. *Biographical Dictionary of British Radicals in the Seventeenth Century.* 3 vols. Brighton: Harvester P., 1982–4.

GREEN, DAVID. *Sarah, Duchess of Marlborough.* 1967; New York: Scribner, 1987.

GREEN, THOMAS ANDREW. *Verdict According to Conscience: Perspectives on the English Criminal Trial Jury, 1200–1800.* Chicago: U. of Chicago P., 1985.

GREER, GERMAINE, ed. *The Uncollected Verse of Aphra Behn.* Stump Cross: Stump Cross Books, 1989.

——HASTINGS, SUSAN, MEDOFF, JESLYN, and SANSONE, MELINDA, eds. *Kissing the Rod. An Anthology of Seventeenth-Century Women's Verse.* New York: Farrar Straus Giroux-Noonday Press, 1989.

GREG, W. W., intro. *Records of the Court of the Stationers' Company, 1576 to 1602, from Register B.* Ed. W. W. Greg and E. Boswell. London: Bibliographical Society, 1930.

GREGG, EDWARD. *Queen Anne.* Boston: Routledge and Kegan Paul, 1980.

GRUNDY, ISOBEL, and WISEMAN, SUSAN, eds. *Women, Writing, History 1640–1740.* London: B. T. Batsford, 1992.

GUSKIN, PHYLLIS J. 'The Authorship of the "Protestant Post Boy", 1711–12', *Notes and Queries*, NS 22. 11 (1975), 489–90. (Vol. 220 of continuous series.)

HABERMAS, JÜRGEN. 'Further Reflections on the Public Sphere', in Craig Calhoun, ed., *Habermas and the Public Sphere.* Cambridge, Mass.: MIT Press, 1992. 421–61.

——'Concluding Remarks', in Craig Calhoun, ed., *Habermas and the Public Sphere.* Cambridge, Mass.: MIT Press, 1992. 462–79.

——*The Structural Transformation of the Public Sphere: An Inquiry into a Category of Bourgeois Society.* Trans. Thomas Burger with the assistance of Frederick Lawrence. Intro. Thomas McCarthy. Cambridge, Mass.: MIT Press, 1989.

HAIG, ROBERT L. *The Gazetteer: 1735–1797*. Carbondale: Southern Illinois UP, 1960.

——'New Light on the King's Printing Office, 1680–1730', *Studies in Bibliography*, 8 (1956), 157–67.

HAMBURGER, PHILIP. 'The Development of the Law of Seditious Libel and the Control of the Press', *Stanford Law Review*, 37 (1984/5), 661–765.

HAMILL, FRANCES. 'Some Unconventional Women before 1800: Printers, Booksellers, and Collectors', *Papers of the Bibliographical Society of America*, 49 (1955), 300–14.

HANDOVER, P. M. *Printing in London from 1476 to Modern Times*. London: George Allen and Unwin Ltd., 1960.

HANSON, LAURENCE. *Government and the Press 1695–1763*. Oxford: Clarendon P., 1936.

HARRIS, FRANCES. 'The Electioneering of Sarah, Duchess of Marlborough', *Parliamentary History*, 2 (1983), 71–92.

——*A Passion for Government: The Life of Sarah, Duchess of Marlborough*. Oxford: Clarendon P., 1991.

HARRIS, MICHAEL. 'A Few Shillings for Small Books: The Experiences of a Flying Stationer in the 18th Century', in R. Myers and M. Harris, eds., *Spreading the Word*. Winchester: St Paul's Bibliographies, 1990. 83–108.

——'The London Newspaper Press ca. 1725–1746', diss., U. of London, 1973.

——*London Newspapers in the Age of Walpole: A Study of the Origins of the Modern English Press*. London: Associated University Presses, Inc., 1987.

——'London Printers and Newspaper Production During the First Half of the Eighteenth Century', *Printing Historical Society Journal*, 12 (1977–8), 33–51.

——'Periodicals and the Book Trade', in R. Myers and M. Harris, eds., *Development of the English Book Trade, 1700–1899*. Oxford: Oxford Polytechnic Press, 1981. 66–94.

HARRIS, TIM. *London Crowds in the Reign of Charles II: Propaganda and Politics from the Restoration until the Exclusion Crisis*. Cambridge: Cambridge UP, 1990.

——SEAWARD, PAUL, and GOLDIE, MARK, eds. *The Politics of Religion in Restoration England*. Oxford: Basil Blackwell, 1990.

HARTH, ERICA. 'The Salon Woman Goes Public . . . or Does She?', in E. C. Goldsmith and D. Goodman, eds., *Going Public*. Ithaca, NY: Cornell UP, 1995. 179–93.

HEALEY, GEORGE HARRIS, ed. *The Letters of Daniel Defoe*. 1955. Oxford: Clarendon P., 1969.

HENRY, SUSAN. 'Ann Franklin: Rhode Island's Woman Printer', in Donovan H. Bond and W. Reynolds McLeod, eds., *Newsletters to Newspapers: Eighteenth-Century Journalism.* Morgantown, W. Va.: West Virginia U., The School of Journalism, 1977. 129–43.

HILL, BRIDGET. *Women, Work, and Sexual Politics in Eighteenth-Century England.* Oxford: Basil Blackwell, 1989.

HILL, CHRISTOPHER. *The World Turned Upside Down: Radical Ideas during the English Revolution.* 1972. Harmondsworth: Penguin-Peregrine, 1985.

HIPWELL, DANIEL. 'Mary De La Riviere Manley', *Notes and Queries*, 7th ser. 8 (1889), 156–7.

HIRSCH, RUDOLF. *Printing, Selling and Reading 1450–1550.* 1967. 2nd printing Wiesbaden: Otto Harrassowitz, 1974.

HIRST, DESIRÉE. *Hidden Riches: Traditional Symbolism from the Renaissance to Blake.* New York: Barnes and Noble, 1964.

HOBBY, ELAINE. ' "Discourse so Unsavoury": Women's Published Writings of the 1650s', in I. Grundy and S. Wiseman, eds., *Women, Writing, History 1640–1740.* London: B. T. Batsford, 1992. 16–32.

——*Virtue of Necessity: English Women's Writing 1649–1688.* Ann Arbor: U. of Michigan P., 1989.

HODGSON, NORMA, and BLAGDEN, CYPRIAN, eds. *The Notebook of Thomas Bennet and Henry Clements (1686–1719): With Some Aspects of Book Trade Practice.* Oxford Bibliographical Society Publications, NS 6 (1953). Oxford: Oxford UP, 1956.

HOLMES, GEOFFREY. *Augustan England: Professions, State and Society, 1680–1730.* London: George Allen and Unwin, 1982.

——*Britain after the Glorious Revolution, 1689–1714.* New York: St Martins, 1969.

——*British Politics in the Age of Anne.* London: Hambledon P., 1987.

HORDEN, JOHN. ' "In the Savoy": John Nutt and his Family', *Publishing History*, 24 (1988), 5–26.

HORLE, CRAIG W. *The Quakers and the English Legal System 1660–1688.* Philadelphia: U. of Pennsylvania P., 1988.

HOWE, ELLIC. *A List of London Bookbinders 1648–1815.* London: The Bibliographical Society, 1950.

——*The London Compositor. Documents relating to the Wages, Working Conditions and Customs of the London Printing Trade 1785–1900.* London: The Bibliographical Society, 1947.

HUDAK, LEONA M. *Early American Women Printers and Publishers 1639–1820.* Metuchen, NJ: Scarecrow Press, 1978.

HUNT, FELICITY. 'The London Trade in the Printing and Binding of Books: An Experience in Exclusion, Dilution, and De-skilling for Women Workers', *Women's Studies International Forum*, 6 (1983), 517–24.

HUNT, FELICITY 'Opportunities Lost and Gained: Mechanization and Women's Work in the London Bookbinding and Printing Trades', in Angela V. John, ed., *Unequal Opportunities: Women's Employment in England 1800–1918*. Oxford: Basil Blackwell, 1986. 71–93.

——'Women in the Nineteenth Century Bookbinding and Printing Trades (1790–1914), with Special Reference to London', MA thesis, University of Essex, 1979.

HUNT, MARGARET R. *The Middling Sort: Commerce, Gender, and the Family in England, 1680–1780*. Berkeley and Los Angeles: U. of California P., 1996.

——'Hawkers, Bawlers, and Mercuries: Women and the London Press in the Early Enlightenment', Special Issue: 'Women and the Enlightenment', Intro. Phyllis Mack. *Women and History*, 9 (1984), 41–68.

HUNTER, J. PAUL. *Before Novels: The Cultural Contexts of Eighteenth-Century English Fiction*. New York: W. W. Norton and Co., 1990.

——' "News, and new Things": Contemporaneity and the Early English Novel', *Critical Inquiry*, 14 (1988), 493–515.

HYLAND, P. B. J. 'Liberty and Libel: Government and the Press during the Succession Crisis in Britain, 1712–1716', *English Historical Review*, 101 (1986), 863–88.

INGRASSIA, CATHERINE. *Paper Credit: Grub Street, Exchange Alley, and Feminization in the Culture of Eighteenth-Century England*, forthcoming.

JACKSON, WILLIAM A., ed. *Records of the Court of the Stationers' Company, 1602 to 1640*. London: Bibliographical Society, 1957.

JACOB, MARGARET C. 'The Mental Landscape of the Public Sphere: A European Perspective', *ECS* 28 (1994), 95–113.

JAMESON, FREDRIC. 'Religion and Ideology', in F. Barker et al., eds., *1642: Literature and Power in the Seventeenth Century*. Colchester: U. of Essex, 1981. 315–36.

KEEBLE, N. H. *The Literary Culture of Nonconformity in Later Seventeenth-Century England*. Athens: U. of Georgia P., 1987.

KENYON, J. P. *Revolution Principles: The Politics of Party, 1689–1720*. 1977. Rpt. New York: Cambridge UP, 1990.

KERNAN, ALVIN. *Samuel Johnson and the Impact of Print*. Princeton: Princeton UP, 1989.

KING, KATHRYN. *Jane Barker's Imagined Communities: Religion, Politics, Medicine, and the Literary Tradition*, forthcoming.

KING, KATIE. 'Bibliography and a Feminist Apparatus of Literary Production', *TEXT 5: Transactions of the Society for Textual Scholarship* (1991), 91–103.

KITE, NATHAN. *Antiquarian Researches among the Early Printers and Publishers of Friends' Books*. Manchester: John Harrison, 1844.

KLEIN, LAWRENCE E. 'Gender and the Public/Private Distinction in the Eighteenth Century: Some Questions about Evidence and Analytical Procedure', *ECS* 29 (1995), 97–109.

—— 'Gender, Conversation and the Public Sphere in Early Eighteenth-Century England', in Judith Still and Michael Worton, eds., *Textuality and Sexuality: Reading Theories and Practices*. Manchester: Manchester UP, 1993. 100–15.

—— 'Property and Politeness in the Early Whig Moralists: The Case of the *Spectator*', in John Brewer and Susan Staves, eds., *Early Modern Conceptions of Property*. London: Routledge, 1995. 221–33.

—— *Shaftesbury and the Culture of Politeness: Moral Discourse and Cultural Politics in Early Eighteenth-Century England*. Cambridge: Cambridge UP, 1994.

KÖSTER, PATRICIA, ed. and intro. *The Novels of Mary Delariviere Manley 1705–1714*. 2 vols. Gainesville, Fla.: Scholars' Facsimiles and Reprints, 1971.

LANDES, JOAN B. *Women and the Public Sphere in the Age of the French Revolution*. Ithaca, NY: Cornell UP, 1988.

LANDRY, DONNA. *The Muses of Resistance: Laboring-Class Women's Poetry in Britain, 1739–1796*. Cambridge: Cambridge UP, 1990.

LANGFORD, PAUL. *A Polite and Commercial People: England 1727–1783*. Oxford: Oxford UP, 1989.

LASLETT, PETER. *The World We Have Lost*. London: Methuen, 1965.

LAUGERO, GREG. 'Publicity, Gender, and Genre: A Review Essay', *ECS* 28 (1995), 429–38.

LITTLEBOY, ANNA L. 'Devonshire House Reference Library', *Journal of the Friends' Historical Society*, 18. 1, 3 (1921), 1–16 and 66–80.

LOCKWOOD, THOMAS. 'Eliza Haywood in 1749: *Dalinda, and her Pamphlet on the Pretender*', *Notes and Queries*, NS 234. 4 (1989), 475–7.

LORD, GEORGE DE F., et al., eds. *Poems on Affairs of State: Augustan Satirical Verse, 1660–1714*. 7 vols. New Haven: Yale UP, 1963–75.

MACCARTHY, B. G. *Women Writers: Their Contribution to the English Novel 1621–1744*. Oxford: B. H. Blackwell, 1946.

MACCUBBIN, ROBERT P., and HAMILTON-PHILLIPS, MARTHA, eds. *The Age of William III and Mary II: Power, Politics and Patronage 1688–1702*. Williamsburg, Va.: The College of William and Mary, 1989.

McDOWELL, PAULA JOANNE. 'Consuming Women: The Life of the "Literary Lady" as Popular Culture in Eighteenth-Century England', *Genre*, 26 (Summer/Fall 1993), 219–52.

—— 'Tace Sowle', in James K. Bracken and Joel Silver, eds., *The British Literary Book Trade, 1475–1700*. Columbia, SC: Bruccoli Clark Layman, 1996. 249–57.

McDowell, Paula Joanne. 'The Women of Grub Street: Gender, Press and Politics in the London Literary Marketplace 1688–1730', diss., Stanford U., 1991.

McEntee, Ann Marie. ' "The [Un]Civill Sisterhood of Oranges and Lemons": Female Petitioners and Demonstrators, 1642–1653', in James Holstun, ed., *Pamphlet Wars: Prose in the English Revolution*. London: Frank Cass, 1992. 92–111.

McEwen, Gilbert D. *The Oracle of the Coffee House: John Dunton's Athenian Mercury*. San Marino, Calif.: Huntington Library, 1972.

Mack, Maynard. *Alexander Pope: A Life*. New York: W. W. Norton and Co., 1985.

Mack, Phyllis. 'Gender and Spirituality in Early English Quakerism, 1650–1665', in Elisabeth Potts Brown and Susan Mosher Stuard, eds., *Witnesses for Change: Quaker Women over Three Centuries*. New Brunswick, NJ: Rutgers UP, 1989. 31–68.

—— *Visionary Women: Ecstatic Prophecy in Seventeenth-Century England*. Berkeley and Los Angeles: U. of California P., 1992.

—— 'Women as Prophets during the English Civil War', *Feminist Studies*, 8 (1982), 19–45.

McKenzie, D. F. *The London Book Trade in the Later Seventeenth Century*. Sandars Lectures, Cambridge, 1976.

—— 'Printers of the Mind: Some Notes on Bibliographical Theories and Printing-House Practices', *Studies in Bibliography*, 22 (1969), 1–75.

—— *Stationers' Company Apprentices 1641–1700*. Oxford: Oxford Bibliographical Society Publications, NS 17 (1974).

—— *Stationers' Company Apprentices 1701–1800*. Oxford: Oxford Bibliographical Society Publications, NS 19 (1978).

McKeon, Michael. 'Historicizing Patriarchy: The Emergence of Gender Difference in England, 1660–1760', *ECS* 28 (1995), 295–322.

—— 'Politics of Discourses and the Rise of the Aesthetic in Seventeenth-Century England', in K. Sharpe and S. N. Zwicker, eds., *The Politics of Discourse*. Berkeley and Los Angeles: U. of California P., 1987. 35–51.

McKerrow, R. B. *An Introduction to Bibliography for Literary Students*. Oxford: Clarendon P., 1928.

McKillop, Alan Dugald. *Samuel Richardson: Printer and Novelist*. 1936. Rpt. Hamden, Conn.: Shoe String P., 1960.

—— 'Supplementary Notes on Samuel Richardson as a Printer', *Studies in Bibliography*, 12 (1959), 214–18.

MacLean, Gerald, ed. and intro. *Culture and Society in the Stuart Restoration: Literature, Drama, History*. Cambridge: Cambridge UP, 1995.

McLeod, Glenda K. 'Madame d'Aulnoy: Writer of Fantasy', in Katharina M. Wilson and Frank J. Warnke, eds., *Women Writers of the Seventeenth Century*. Athens, Ga.: U. of Georgia P., 1989. 91–118.

MCWHIR, ANNE. 'Elizabeth Thomas and the Two Corinnas: Giving the Woman Writer a Bad Name', *English Literary History*, 62 (1995), 105–19.

MARX, KARL. *Capital: A Critique of Political Economy*. Vol. iii. Trans. David Fernbach. Harmondsworth: Penguin, 1981.

MAXTED, IAN. *The British Book Trades, 1710–1777: An Index of Masters and Apprentices Recorded in the Inland Revenue Registers at the Public Record Office, Kew*. Exeter: Ian Maxted, 1983.

——*The London Book Trades, 1735–1775: A Checklist of Members in Trade Directories and in Musgrave's 'Obituary'*. Exeter: J. Maxted, 1984.

——*The London Book Trades 1775–1800: A Preliminary Checklist of Members*. Folkestone: William Dawson and Sons Ltd., 1977.

MEDOFF, JESLYN. 'The Daughters of Behn and the Problem of Reputation', in Isobel Grundy and Susan Wiseman, eds., *Women, Writing, History 1640–1740*. London: B. T. Batsford, 1992. 33–54.

MEEHAN, JOHANNA, ed. *Feminists Read Habermas: Gendering the Subject of Discourse*. New York: Routledge, 1995.

MITCHELL, C. J. 'Women in the Eighteenth-Century Book Trades', in O. M. Brack, ed., *Writers, Books and Trade*. New York: AMS Press, 1994. 25–75.

MONOD, PAUL KLÉBER. *Jacobitism and the English People 1688–1788*. Cambridge: Cambridge UP, 1989.

MORGAN, FIDELIS. *A Woman of No Character: An Autobiography of Mrs. Manley*. London: Faber and Faber, 1986.

MORGAN, WILLIAM THOMAS. *English Political Parties and Leaders in the Reign of Queen Anne*. New Haven, Conn.: Yale UP, 1920.

MORRISON, PAUL G. *Index of Printers, Publishers and Booksellers in Donald Wing's Short-Title Catalogue . . . 1641–1700*. Charlottesville, Va.: U. of Virginia P. for the Bibliographical Society of America, 1955.

MORTIMER, R. S. 'Biographical Notices of Printers and Publishers of Friends' Books up to 1750', *Journal of Documentation*, 3 (1947), 107–25.

——'The First Century of Quaker Printers', *Journal of the Friends' Historical Society*, 40 (1948), 37–49.

MUIR, PERCY H. 'English Imprints after 1640', *Library*, 4th ser. 14 (1933–4), 157–77.

MYERS, ROBIN, and HARRIS, MICHAEL, eds. *Aspects of Printing from 1600*. Oxford: Oxford Polytechnic Press/Publishing Pathways Series, 1987.

————*Author/Publisher Relations during the Eighteenth and Nineteenth Centuries*. Oxford: Oxford Polytechnic Press/Publishing Pathways Series, 1983.

MYERS, ROBIN, and HARRIS, MICHAEL, eds. *Development of the English Book Trade, 1700–1899*. Oxford: Oxford Polytechnic Press/Publishing Pathways Series, 1981.

——— *Economics of the British Booktrade, 1605–1939*. Cambridge: Chadwyck-Healey, 1985.

——— eds. *Spreading the Word: The Distribution Networks of Print 1550–1850*. Winchester: St Paul's Bibliographies, 1990.

NEEDHAM, GWENDOLYN B. 'Mary de la Rivière Manley, Tory Defender', *Huntington Library Quarterly*, 12 (1948–9), 253–88.

NUSSBAUM, FELICITY. 'Introduction: The Politics of Difference', *ECS* 23 (1990), 375–86.

O'MALLEY, THOMAS. ' "Defying the Powers and Tempering the Spirit": A Review of Quaker Control over their Publications 1672–1689', *Journal of Ecclesiastical History*, 33 (1982), 72–88.

—— 'The Press and Quakerism 1653–1659', *Journal of the Friends' Historical Society*, 54 (1979), 169–84.

ONG, WALTER J. *Orality and Literacy: The Technologizing of the Word*. London: Methuen, 1982.

ORGEL, STEPHEN. *The Illusion of Power: Political Theater in the English Renaissance*. Berkeley and Los Angeles: U. of California P., 1975.

PARKS, STEPHEN. *John Dunton and the English Book Trade: A Study of his Career with a Checklist of his Publications*. New York: Garland, 1976.

PATEMAN, CAROLE. *The Disorder of Women: Democracy, Feminism and Political Theory*. Stanford, Calif.: Stanford UP, 1989.

—— *The Sexual Contract*. Stanford, Calif.: Stanford UP, 1988.

PATEY, DOUGLAS. 'The Eighteenth Century Invents the Canon', *Modern Language Studies*, 18 (1988), 17–37.

PATTERSON, ANNABEL. *Censorship and Interpretation: The Conditions of Writing and Reading in Early Modern England*. Madison: Wisconsin UP, 1984.

—— *Fables of Power: Aesopian Writing and Political History*. Durham, NC: Duke UP, 1991.

PAULSON, RONALD. *Popular and Polite Art in the Age of Hogarth and Fielding*. Notre Dame, Ind.: U. of Notre Dame P., 1979.

PERRY, RUTH. *The Celebrated Mary Astell: An Early English Feminist*. Chicago: U. of Chicago P., 1986.

—— 'Elinor James', in J. Todd, ed., *A Dictionary of British and American Women Writers 1660–1800*. Totowa, NJ: Rowman and Littlefield, 1987. 177–8.

—— 'Mary Astell', in J. Todd, ed., *A Dictionary of British and American Women Writers 1660–1800*. Totowa, NJ: Rowman and Littlefield, 1987. 32–4.

——'Mary Astell and the Feminist Critique of Possessive Individualism', *ECS* 23 (1990), 444–57.

PINCUS, STEVE. '"Coffee Politicians Does Create": Coffeehouses and Restoration Political Culture', *Journal of Modern History*, 67 (1995), 807–34.

PLANT, MARJORIE. *The English Book Trade: An Economic History of the Making and Sale of Books.* 1939. London: George Allen and Unwin, Ltd., 1974.

PLOMER, HENRY R. *A Dictionary of the Printers and Booksellers who were at Work in England, Scotland, and Ireland from 1668 to 1725.* Oxford: Oxford Bibliographical Society, 1922.

——BUSHNELL, G. H., and DIX, E. R. McC. *A Dictionary of the Printers and Booksellers who were at Work in England, Scotland, and Ireland from 1726–1775.* Oxford: Oxford Bibliographical Society, 1932.

PLUMB, J. H. *The Growth of Political Stability in England, 1675–1725.* Boston: Houghton Mifflin, 1967.

POCOCK, J. G. A. *Virtue, Commerce and History: Essays on Political Thought and History, Chiefly in the Eighteenth Century.* Cambridge: Cambridge UP, 1985.

POLLARD, A. W., and REDGRAVE, G. R., comps. *A Short-Title Catalogue of Books Printed in England, Scotland, and Ireland and of English Books Printed Abroad 1475–1640.* Vol. iii: *A Printers and Publishers Index, Other Indexes and Appendices, Cumulative Addenda and Corrigenda.* By Katharine F. Pantzer. With a Chronological Index by Philip R. Rider. London: The Bibliographical Society, 1991.

POLLARD, GRAHAM. 'The Company of Stationers before 1557', *Library*, 4th ser. 18 (1938), 1–38.

——'The Early Constitution of the Stationers' Company', *Library*, 4th ser. 18 (1938), 235–60.

PORTER, ROY. *English Society in the Eighteenth Century.* 1982. Rev. edn. Harmondsworth: Penguin, 1990.

PRESTON, THOMAS R. 'Biblical Criticism, Literature, and the Eighteenth-Century Reader', in I. Rivers, ed., *Books and their Readers in 18th-Century England.* Leicester: Leicester UP, 1982. 97–126.

PRIOR, MARY, ed. *Women in English Society, 1500–1800.* New York: Methuen, 1985.

PURKISS, DIANNE. 'Producing the Voice, Consuming the Body: Women Prophets of the Seventeenth Century', in Isobel Grundy and Susan Wiseman, eds., *Women, Writing, History 1640–1740.* London: B. T. Batsford, 1992. 139–58.

RAVEN, JAMES. *A Chronological Check-List of Prose Fiction Printed in Britain and Ireland.* Newark: U. of Delaware P., 1987.

——*Judging New Wealth: Popular Publishing and Responses to Commerce in England, 1750–1800.* Oxford: Clarendon P., 1992.

RAVEN, JAMES. 'Serial Advertisement in 18th-Century Britain and Ireland', in Robin Myers and Michael Harris, eds., *Serials and their Readers 1620–1914*. Winchester: St Paul's Bibliographies, 1993. 103–22.

REAY, BARRY. *The Quakers and the English Revolution*. Foreword by Christopher Hill. London: Temple Smith, 1985.

RICHETTI, JOHN J. *Popular Fiction before Richardson: Narrative Patterns 1700–1739*. 1969. Rpt. Oxford: Clarendon P., 1992.

——'Representing an Underclass: Servants and Proletarians in Fielding and Smollett', in Felicity Nussbaum and Laura Brown, eds., *The New 18th Century: Theory, Politics, English Literature*. New York: Methuen, 1987. 84–98.

RILEY, DENISE. *'Am I That Name?': Feminism and the Category of 'Women' in History*. Minneapolis: U. of Minnesota P., 1988.

RIVERS, ISABEL, ed. *Books and their Readers in Eighteenth-Century England*. Leicester: Leicester UP and St Martin's UP, 1982.

ROGERS, PAT. 'Books, Readers, and Patrons', in Boris Ford, ed., *The New Pelican Guide to English Literature*. Vol. iv: *From Dryden to Johnson*. Harmondsworth: Penguin-Pelican, 1982. 214–27.

——*Grub Street: Studies in a Subculture*. London: Methuen, 1972.

ROSE, MARK. *Authors and Owners: The Invention of Copyright*. Cambridge, Mass.: Harvard UP, 1993.

ROSS, TREVOR. 'The Emergence of "Literature": Making and Reading the English Canon in the Eighteenth Century', *English Literary History*, 63 (1996), 397–422.

ROSTENBERG, LEONA. *Literary, Political, Scientific, Religious and Legal Publishing, Printing, and Bookselling in England, 1551–1700: Twelve Studies*. 2 vols. New York: Burt Franklin, 1965.

——'Robert Stephens, Messenger of the Press: An Episode in 17th-Century Censorship', *Papers of the Bibliographical Society of America*, 49 (1955), 131–52.

ROWLANDS, MARIE B. 'Recusant Women 1560–1640', in M. Prior, ed., *Women in English Society, 1500–1800*. New York: Methuen, 1985. 149–80.

RYAN, MARY. 'Gender and Public Access: Women's Politics in Nineteenth-Century America', in Craig Calhoun, ed., *Habermas and the Public Sphere*. Cambridge, Mass.: MIT Press, 1992. 259–88.

SALE, WILLIAM MERRITT. *Samuel Richardson: A Bibliographical Record of His Literary Career with Historical Notes*. 1936. Rpt. Hamden, Conn.: Archon Books, 1968.

——*Samuel Richardson: Master Printer*. Ithaca, NY: Cornell UP, 1950.

SCHNELLER, BEVERLY. 'Mary Cooper, Eighteenth-Century London Bookseller, 1743 to 1761', Ph.D. diss., The Catholic University of America, 1987.

—— 'Using Newspaper Advertisements to Study the Book Trade: A Year in the Life of Mary Cooper', in O. M. Brack, ed., *Writers, Books and Trade*. New York: AMS Press, 1994. 123–43.

SCHOFIELD, R. S. 'The Measurement of Literacy in Pre-industrial England', in J. Goody, ed., *Literacy in Traditional Societies*. Cambridge: Cambridge UP, 1968. 310–25.

SCHULMAN, MARK. 'Gender and Typographic Culture: Beginning to Unravel the 500-Year Mystery', in Cheris Kramarae, ed., *Technology and Women's Voices: Keeping in Touch*. New York: Routledge and Kegan Paul, 1988. 98–115.

SCHWOERER, LOIS G. 'Propaganda in the Revolution of 1688–89', *American Historical Review*, 82 (1977), 843–74.

—— 'Women and the Glorious Revolution', *Albion*, 18 (1986), 195–218.

—— ed. *The Revolution of 1688–1689: Changing Perspectives*. Cambridge: Cambridge UP, 1992.

SCOTT, JOAN W. 'Deconstructing Equality–Versus–Difference: Or, the Uses of Post-structuralist Theory for Feminism', *Feminist Studies*, 14 (1988), 33–50.

SCOTT, JONATHAN. 'England's Troubles: Exhuming the Popish Plot', in T. Harris, P. Seaward, and M. Goldie, eds., *The Politics of Religion in Restoration England*. Oxford: Basil Blackwell, 1990. 107–31.

SHARPE, KEVIN, and ZWICKER, STEVEN N., eds. *Politics of Discourse: The Literature and History of Seventeenth-Century England*. Berkeley and Los Angeles: U. of California P., 1987.

SHEEHAN, W. J. 'Finding Solace in Eighteenth-Century Newgate', in J. S. Cockburn, ed., *Crime in England 1550–1800*. Princeton: Princeton UP, 1977. 229–45.

SHEPARD, LESLIE. *The History of Street Literature*. Detroit: Singing Tree Press, 1973.

SHERIDAN, GERALDINE. 'Women in the Booktrade in Eighteenth-Century France', *British Journal for Eighteenth-Century Studies*, 15 (1992), 51–69.

SHEVELOW, KATHRYN. *Women and Print Culture: The Construction of Femininity in the Early Periodical*. London: Routledge, 1989.

SMITH, CATHERINE F. 'Jane Lead: The Feminist Mind and Art of a Seventeenth-Century Protestant Mystic', in Rosemary Ruether and Eleanor McLaughlin, eds., *Women of Spirit: Female Leadership in the Jewish and Christian Traditions*. New York: Simon and Schuster, 1979. 183–203.

—— 'Jane Lead: Mysticism and the Woman Cloathed with the Sun', in Sandra M. Gilbert and Susan Gubar, eds., *Shakespeare's Sisters: Feminist Essays on Women Poets*. Bloomington: Indiana UP, 1979. 3–18.

SMITH, CATHERINE F. 'Jane Lead's Wisdom: Women and Prophecy in Seventeenth-Century England', in Jan Wojcik and Raymond-Jean Frontain, eds., *Poetic Prophecy in Western Literature*. Rutherford, NJ: Fairleigh Dickinson UP, 1984. 55–63.

——'*Three Guineas*: Virginia Woolf's Prophecy', in Jane Marcus, ed., *Virginia Woolf and Bloomsbury: A Centenary Celebration*. Bloomington: Indiana UP, 1987. 225–41.

SMITH, HILDA L., and CARDINALE, SUSAN, comps. *Women and the Literature of the Seventeenth Century: An Annotated Bibliography Based on Wing's Short-Title Catalogue*. New York: Greenwood Press, 1990.

SNELL, K. D. M. *Annals of the Labouring Poor: Social Change and Agrarian England, 1660–1900*. Cambridge: Cambridge UP, 1985.

SNYDER, HENRY L. 'Daniel Defoe, the Duchess of Marlborough, and the *Advice to the Electors of Great Britain*', *Huntington Library Quarterly*, 29 (1965–6), 53–62.

——'The Reports of a Press Spy for Robert Harley: New Bibliographical Data for the Reign of Queen Anne', *Library*, 5th ser. 22 (1967), 326–45.

SPACKS, PATRICIA MEYER. *Gossip*. Chicago: U. of Chicago P., 1986.

SPECK, W. A. *Stability and Strife: England 1714–1760*. Cambridge, Mass.: Harvard UP, 1977.

——'William—and Mary?', in Lois G. Schwoerer, ed., *The Revolution of 1688–1689: Changing Perspectives*. Cambridge: Cambridge UP, 1992. 131–46.

SPENCER, JANE. *The Rise of the Woman Novelist: From Aphra Behn to Jane Austen*. Oxford: Basil Blackwell, 1986.

SPERLE, JOANNE MAGNANI. 'God's Healing Angel: A Biography of Jane Ward Lead', diss., Kent State U., 1985.

SPUFFORD, MARGARET. *Small Books and Pleasant Histories: Popular Fiction and its Readership in Seventeenth-Century England*. Cambridge: Cambridge UP, 1981.

STANTON, JUDITH PHILLIPS. 'Statistical Profile of Women Writing in English from 1660 to 1800', in Frederick M. Keener and Susan E. Lorsch, eds., *Eighteenth-Century Women and the Arts*. Westport, Conn.: Greenwood Press, 1988. 247–54.

STAVES, SUSAN. *Players' Scepters: Fictions of Authority in the Restoration*. Lincoln: U. of Nebraska P., 1979.

STEINEN, KARL VON DEN. 'The Discovery of Women in Eighteenth-Century Political Life', in Barbara Kanner, ed., *The Women of England from Anglo-Saxon Times to the Present*. Hamden, Conn.: Archon Books, 1979. 229–58.

STEPHENS, FREDERICK GEORGE. *Catalogue of Political and Personal Satires Preserved in the Department of Prints and Drawings in the British*

Museum. Vol. ii: *1689–1733*. London: British Museum Publications, 1978.

STEVENS, DAVID HARRISON. *Party Politics and English Journalism, 1702–1742*. Chicago: U. of Chicago Libraries, 1916.

STRAUS, RALPH. *The Unspeakable Curll*. New York: Robert M. McBride and Co., 1928.

STRUM, ARTHUR. 'A Bibliography of the Concept *Öffentlichkeit*', *New German Critique*, 61 (1994), 161–202.

SUTHERLAND, JAMES. *The Restoration Newspaper and its Development*. New York: Cambridge UP, 1986.

—— 'The Circulation of Newspapers and Literary Periodicals, 1700–30', *Library*, 4th ser. 15 (1934–5), 110–24.

SUTHERLAND, JOHN. 'Publishing History: A Hole at the Centre of Literary Sociology', *Critical Inquiry*, 14 (1988), 574–89.

SUTTON, JOHN L. 'The Source of Mrs. Manley's Preface to *Queen Zarah*', *Modern Philology*, 82 (1984), 167–72.

TERRY, RICHARD, MILLER, THOMAS P., and SISKIN, CLIFFORD. Forum on 'Literature, Aesthetics and Canonicity in the Eighteenth Century', *Eighteenth-Century Life*, 21 (1997), 80–107.

THOMAS, DONALD. *A Long Time Burning: The History of Literary Censorship in England*. New York: A. Praeger, Publishers, 1969.

THOMAS, KEITH. *Religion and the Decline of Magic*. New York: Scribners, 1971.

—— 'Women and the Civil War Sects', *Past and Present*, 13 (1958), 42–62.

—— 'The Meaning of Literacy in Early Modern England', in Gerd Baumann, ed., *The Written Word: Literacy in Transition*. Oxford: Clarendon P., 1986. 97–131.

THOMPSON, E. P. 'The Crime of Anonymity', in Douglas Hay et al., eds., *Albion's Fatal Tree: Crime and Society in Eighteenth-Century England*. New York: Random House-Pantheon, 1975. 255–344.

—— *Customs in Common: Studies in Traditional Popular Culture*. New York: The New Press, 1993.

—— 'Eighteenth-Century English Society: Class Struggle without Class?', *Social History*, 3 (1978), 133–64.

—— 'The Moral Economy of the English Crowd in the Eighteenth Century', *Past and Present*, 50 (1971), 76–136.

—— 'Time, Work-Discipline and Industrial Capitalism', *Past and Present*, 38 (1967), 56–97.

THUNE, NILS. *The Behmenists and the Philadelphians*. Uppsala: Almquist and Wiksells, 1948.

TODD, BARBARA J. 'The Remarrying Widow: A Stereotype Reconsidered', in M. Prior, ed., *Women in English Society, 1500–1800*. New York: Methuen, 1985. 54–92.

TODD, JANET. 'Marketing the Self: Mary Carleton, Miss F and Susannah Gunning', *Studies in Voltaire and the Eighteenth Century*, 217 (1983), 95–106.

—— *The Sign of Angellica: Women, Writing and Fiction, 1660–1800*. New York: Columbia UP, 1989.

——ed. *A Dictionary of British and American Women Writers 1660–1800*. Totowa, NJ: Rowman and Littlefield, 1987.

——ed. *The Works of Aphra Behn*. Vol. i: *Poetry*. Columbus: Ohio State UP, 1992.

TREADWELL, MICHAEL. 'The Burleighs: Facts and Problems', *Bibliographical Newsletter*, 1 (1973), 8–11.

—— 'A Further Report from Harley's Press Spy', *Library*, 6th ser. 2 (1980), 216–18.

—— 'London Printers and Printing Houses in 1705', *Publishing History*, 7 (1980), 5–44.

—— 'London Trade Publishers 1675–1750', *Library*, 6th ser. 4 (1982), 99–134.

—— 'A New List of English Master Printers *c.*1686', *Library*, 6th ser. 4 (1982), 57–61.

—— 'Swift's Relations with the London Book Trade to 1714', in R. Myers and M. Harris, eds., *Author/Publisher Relations during the Eighteenth and Nineteenth Centuries*. Oxford: Oxford Polytechnic Press, 1983. 1–36.

TRESIDDER, GEORGE A. 'Coronation Day Celebrations in English Towns, 1685–1821: Élite Hegemony and Local Relations on a Ceremonial Occasion', *British Journal for Eighteenth-Century Studies*, 15 (1992), 1–16.

TREVELYAN, GEORGE MACAULAY. *England under Queen Anne*. Vol. iii: *The Peace and the Protestant Succession*. London: Longmans, Green and Co., 1934.

——ed. *Select Documents for Queen Anne's Reign*. Cambridge: Cambridge UP, 1929.

UNDERDOWN, D. E. 'The Taming of the Scold: The Enforcement of Patriarchal Authority in Early Modern England', in Anthony Fletcher and John Stevenson, eds., *Order and Disorder in Early Modern England*. Cambridge: Cambridge UP, 1985. 116–36.

WALKER, D. P. *The Decline of Hell: Seventeenth-Century Discussions of Eternal Torment*. Chicago: U. of Chicago P., 1964.

WATT, IAN. *The Rise of the Novel: Studies in Defoe, Richardson, and Fielding*. Berkeley and Los Angeles: U. of California P., 1957.

WATT, TESSA. *Cheap Print and Popular Piety 1550–1640*. Cambridge: Cambridge UP, 1991.

WEEKS, ANDREW. *Boehme: An Intellectual Biography of the Seventeenth-Century Philosopher and Mystic*. Albany: State U. of New York P., 1991.

WEIL, RACHEL J. '"If I did say so, I lyed": Elizabeth Cellier and the Construction of Credibility in the Popish Plot Crisis', in Susan D. Amussen and Mark A. Kishlansky, eds., *Political Culture and Cultural Politics in Early Modern England: Essays Presented to David Underdown*. Manchester: Manchester UP, 1995. 189–209.

——'The Politics of Legitimacy: Women and the Warming-Pan Scandal', in Lois G. Schwoerer, ed., *The Revolution of 1688–1689*. Cambridge: Cambridge UP, 1992. 65–82.

——'Sexual Ideology and Political Propaganda in England, 1680–1714', Ph.D. diss., Princeton U., 1991.

WELLEK, RENÉ. 'What is Literature?', in Paul Hernadi, ed., *What is Literature?* Bloomington: Indiana UP, 1978.

WHICHER, GEORGE FRISBIE. *The Life and Romances of Mrs. Eliza Haywood*. New York: Columbia UP, 1915.

WILES, R. M. *Serial Publication in England before 1750*. Cambridge: Cambridge UP, 1957.

WILKINS, WILLIAM WALKER, ed. *Political Ballads of the Seventeenth and Eighteenth Centuries*. 2 vols. London: Longmans, 1860.

WILLIAMS, ETHYN MORGAN. 'Women Preachers in the Civil War', *Journal of Modern History*, 1 (1929), 561–9.

WILLIAMS, RAYMOND. *Keywords*. 1976. Rev. edn. 1983. New York: Oxford UP, 1985.

——*Marxism and Literature*. Oxford: Oxford UP, 1977.

——*The Sociology of Culture*. New York: Schocken Books, 1982.

——'The Writer: Commitment and Alignment', *Marxism Today* (1980), 24–6.

WING, DONALD. *Short-Title Catalogue of Books Printed in England, Scotland, Ireland, Wales, and British America, and of English Books Printed in Other Countries 1641–1700*. 3 vols. New York: Index Committee of the Modern Language Association of America, 1972.

WOODCOCK, GEORGE. *The Incomparable Aphra*. London: T. V. Boardman and Co., 1948.

WRIGHT, LUELLA M. *The Literary Life of the Early Friends 1650–1725*. New York: Columbia UP, 1932.

WURZBACH, NATASCHA. *The Rise of the English Street Ballad, 1550–1650*. 1981. Trans. Gayna Walls. Cambridge: Cambridge UP, 1990.

WYLIE, CHARLES. 'Mrs. Manley', *Notes and Queries*, 2nd ser. 72 (1857), 392–3.

YATES, FRANCES A. *Astraea: The Imperial Theme in the Sixteenth Century*. London: Routledge and Kegan Paul, 1975.

ZARET, DAVID. 'Religion, Science, and Printing in the Public Spheres in Seventeenth-Century England', in Craig Calhoun, ed., *Habermas and the Public Sphere*. Cambridge, Mass.: MIT Press, 1992. 212–35.

ZWICKER, STEVEN N. *Lines of Authority: Politics and English Literary Culture, 1649–1689*. Ithaca, NY: Cornell UP, 1993.

——'Lines of Authority: Politics and Literary Culture in the Restoration', in K. Sharpe and S. N. Zwicker, eds., *Politics of Discourse*. Berkeley and Los Angeles: U. of California P., 1987. 230–70.

Index

Taylor-made Jackpot

– sheep, horses, cats & dogs

by

Daphne Joyce Barnes-Phillips, MA (Ed), BA (Hons)

Copyright details

Spring Gardens

Publications

Dedication

This book is dedicated
to the memory of
my cousin,
Barbara Robinson,
who was happily married
to Jack Taylor
for half a century.

It is also dedicated to those
of each of their families
whose lives
overlapped their's.

Finally, it is dedicated to
all their ancestors
whose lives shaped their's;
and to their descendants,
that they may truly appreciate
what they have inherited
from them both.

Daphne Barnes-Phillips

Acknowledgements to:

Peter Bean, who supplied the modern-day Chile and Tierra del Fuego photographs, taken on his holiday there in February 2007.

Tim Berners-Lee, without whose invention of the World Wide Web, this would have been a much smaller book!

Pam Coles, who has helped with Family History research.

Joy Cuthbertson and Elaine Fowler, who typed Jack's spoken memories and thoughts before emailing them to me.

Sidney Gold, who has always been prepared to help with research whenever we have encountered him at Reading Central Library.

The Staff of Berkshire Records Office for maintaining the records of the Reading Green Girls' School.

The Staff of Reading Central Library for maintaining the collection of Reading Street Directories, maps and newspapers.

Jack Taylor, who gave us access to as many of his and Barbara's photograph albums as he could locate.

All the staff, past and present, who helped Jack through fifty years with Taylor's Racing Service.

As usual, it is my husband, Jim Barnes-Phillips, who has helped the most in this book's production. However, this time he has had to help more with research than has been the case with previous books as there has been a tremendous amount to discover. He has photographed scenes, scanned in photographs from original albums; presented all of them in an appropriate way; designed the cover; and generally been a great support since I embarked upon this project.

The Racecard

FAMILY TREES

Jack TAYLOR's Pedigree

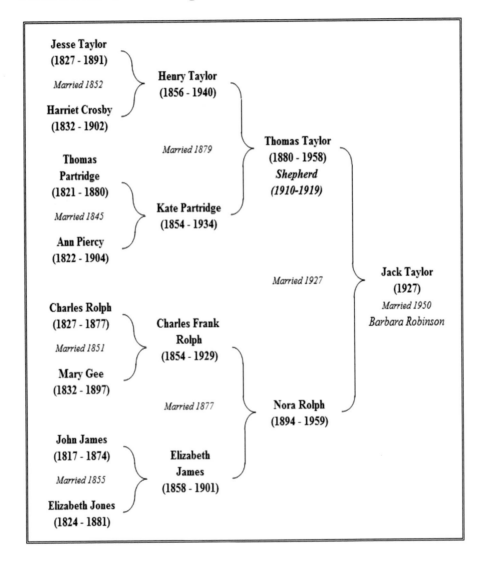

Barbara ROBINSON's Pedigree

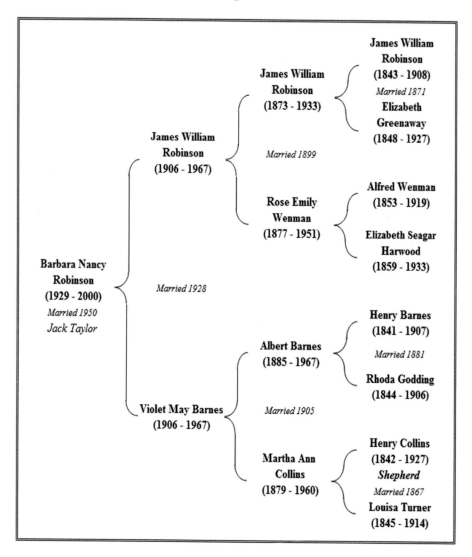

James William Robinson (1843 - 1908)
Married 1871
Elizabeth Greenaway (1848 - 1927)

James William Robinson (1873 - 1933)

Married 1899

James William Robinson (1906 - 1967)

Alfred Wenman (1853 - 1919)

Rose Emily Wenman (1877 - 1951)

Elizabeth Seagar Harwood (1859 - 1933)

Barbara Nancy Robinson (1929 - 2000)
Married 1950
Jack Taylor

Married 1928

Henry Barnes (1841 - 1907)

Albert Barnes (1885 - 1967)

Married 1881

Rhoda Godding (1844 - 1906)

Violet May Barnes (1906 - 1967)

Married 1905

Henry Collins (1842 - 1927)
Shepherd
Married 1867

Martha Ann Collins (1879 - 1960)

Louisa Turner (1845 - 1914)

Responding to a request

After a decade of writing books whose themes I had chosen, this is the first I have written as the result of a request. Yet surprisingly, it fits in superbly well with some of my previous ones as Jack Taylor, like me, spent his childhood in South Reading so knew *The Top of Whitley* area well. He attended weekly film shows at Whitley Hall Methodist Church, collected bets from under a rock in the rockery near the entrance to the Tank Recreation Ground in Whitley Street and he and my cousin, Barbara Robinson, married at Christ Church, where my parents, her parents and our grandparents had also married. Living in Surrey Road, Reading, throughout his childhood, he also knew Len Cook to whom *A Whiff of Whitley* was dedicated.

As well as being one of Barbara and Jack's bridesmaids when I was six years old, I was also an attendant with Barbara at her sister Pat's wedding to Roy Foster a decade later. Their parents, Violet and Jim Robinson were my Aunt and Uncle since Violet was the only sister of my father, Albert Edward Barnes (known as Eddie or Ted).

Like me, both Barbara and Jack had attended George Palmer School in Basingstoke Road, Reading – Barbara the Senior Girls, Jack the Infants, Juniors and Central Schools and myself the Infants and Juniors. Barbara's mother, my father and their siblings, our Uncles Wilf and Les, had also been pupils there, although her mother had started at Christchurch School. However, it was not until I started to organise Palmer School reunions from November 2003 that I discovered that Jack had attended the School, 'though almost two decades prior to me, so he received his entire schooling there whereas I completed mine at Kendrick Girls' School.

Unfortunately, Barbara had died by the time the reunions started but Jack has attended almost as many as I have during the past decade. The first three reunions in 2003/4 were held in the original buildings in Basingstoke Road prior to Jim and I producing *George Palmer School in photographs*. Since 2004, the reunions have been held in the newly-built George Palmer Primary School, whose address is now 70 Northumberland Avenue, although on the same site as the original buildings. There, *So many Hearts make a School* was launched in celebration of the centenary of the George Palmer Schools in

October 2007 and *This is our School* for the bi-centenary of its predecessor, The Reading British School, Southampton Street, in June 2011.

Despite our similar backgrounds, we have naturally had many experiences where there was no overlap and, as a result, Jack probably knew very little about the theme of Reading's twinning links as described in my *Hands of Friendship* book, while I knew very little about Tierra del Fuego, sheep farming, horse or greyhound racing prior to embarking on this project.

It was, in fact, his father, Tom's experiences as a shepherd in Tierra del Fuego from 1910 and about his returning to Reading and setting up a Back Street Bookie business around 1920 that Jack initially asked me to write. However, early on in my research, I realised that both his and Barbara's backgrounds had many similarities in that her (and my) maternal Great Grandfather, Henry Collins, had also been a shepherd for part of the time that Tom Taylor was. There were, 'though, major differences between his experience and that of Jack's father in that Henry spent his entire life in Berkshire and remained a shepherd, having been born in Childrey and christened there on 24th July, 1842. He even spent his childhood on a farm as his father, Thomas Collins, was described as a farmer of 253 acres at the time of the 1851 census when his address was *Warren Farm* as it had been at the time of the 1841 census. Incidentally, although Childrey was in Berkshire in Thomas and Henry Collins' time, the 1974 reorganisation of county boundaries means that it is now in Oxfordshire.

Jack's grandfather, Henry Taylor, also had connections with farming, being variously described as an agricultural labourer, dairyman, farmer and purveyor of milk though Tom himself was only to remain a shepherd for around a decade, admittedly in a more inhospitable terrain than Henry Collins experienced.

One interesting observation that came to me while researching for this book was how much easier it is, in the days of the internet, to obtain pedigrees for Barbara and Jack's horses and greyhounds than for their respective families!

Jack's signature "From Jack and all the animals", which he has used on cards, letters and presents since Barbara's death, is an apt summary of both his and her families and their lives together. He even used the expression to close his introduction to the Barbara Taylor Memorial Meeting held at Reading Greyhound Stadium in 2001. I have therefore written *Taylor-made Jackpot* using Jack's words and memories whenever possible but have incorporated my research to provide a better understanding of the lives of our ancestors, especially in Chile and Childrey, in the 19th and 20th centuries.

Although black and white photographs are interspersed throughout the text for continuity, there are two eight-page Colour Photo Insert sections (after pages 32 and 128) showing some more recent full colour photographs as well. Every effort has been made to contact Copyright Holders and acknowledgement has been given where we have been successful, but it is inevitable that, after this time distance, some are beyond tracing.

Daphne Barnes-Phillips

Jack and Barbara with *Caribbean Prince* at Warwick in 1994

I.   Tom's starting gate

I knew that my father, Thomas Taylor, had been born in 1880 – when there were no cars or aeroplanes. That meant that the first census information to be gleaned about him would be from the *1881 census*, which is freely available on the *FamilySearch* website. As can be seen below, Thomas had been born in Reading and was four months old on Census day – 3rd April that year. He was living with his father, Henry; mother, Kate, and uncle George in Southcot (which is now spelt Southcote) Lane. His father and uncle were Agricultural Labourers. Although Uncle George is termed a lodger, the fact that he and Kate both have the unusual "Bix, Oxford" as their birthplace would imply that they were either related or had known each other from childhood.

Name	Relation	Marital Status	Gender	Age	Birthplace	Occupation
Henry TAYLOR	Head	M	Male	25	Leckhampstead, Berkshire, England	Ag Laborer
Kate TAYLOR	Wife	M	Female	27	Bix, Oxford, England	
Thomas TAYLOR	Son		Male	4m	Reading, Berkshire, England	
George PARTRIDGE	Lodger	U	Male	17	Bix, Oxford, England	Ag Laborer

Dwelling	Southcot Lane
Census Place	Reading St. Mary, Berkshire, England
Family History Library Film	1341316
Public Records Office Reference	RG11
Piece / Folio	1304 / 8
Page Number	9

Searching the *FreeBMD* website for Henry and Kate's marriage found support for that theory as not only did it show that Henry Taylor married Kate Partridge in 1879 but that the marriage had taken place in Henley Registration District. Bix, Oxfordshire is situated in that District and would tie up with the fact that weddings tended to be held where the bride's parents lived.

Marriages Jun 1879				
PARTRIDGE	Kate	Henley	3a	837
Taylor	Henry	Henley	3a	837

11

The mention of *Jun 1879* refers to the second quarter of that year and means that their marriage had been registered some time between April and June.

Thomas' birth certificate shows that he had been born on 4th December 1880 in Southcot Lane and his birth had been registered on 31st December that year. His father, Henry, is recorded as being a *laborer* then and his mother's name is given as *Kate Taylor, formerly Partridge*. Although the family continued living in *Southcot Lane, Reading St. Mary, Berkshire* in 1881, Tom's father had been born in another part of the county – Leckhamstead – in 1856, so perhaps it was employment prospects that had led Henry to Reading.

Certainly, by the time of the *1889 Smith's Reading Street Directory*, Henry Taylor had moved his family to 65 Waldeck Street. That would seem to have been around the time that the houses in Waldeck Street were being built as the *1888 MacCauley's Reading Directory* only records even numbers from 2 – 50 on the right-hand side of the street and numbers 1 – 11 inclusive on the left, with the only Taylor being a William Taylor at no. 3. Since there is no mention of Waldeck Street in the *Smith's Directory* of *1884* and only of numbers 2 (Mrs Hummerson), 4 (Alfred Brereton) and 6 (George Hensler) in the *1885, 1886 & 1887* versions, it would be safe to assume that many of the houses were built around 1887. That year was Queen Victoria's Golden Jubilee and would account for the fact that, in the *1889 Smith's*, houses after no. 74 are shown in Victoria Terrace and those after no. 49 in Jubilee Terrace, with a Conservative Club recorded at no. 9.

Henry had become a milkman by 1888. Interestingly, fifteen of the Heads of Households living in Waldeck Street at that time worked "at H. & P." [Huntley and Palmers Biscuit Factory] and three "at H. B. & S." [Huntley, Bourne and Stevens Tin Manufactory]. J. Deane at no. 66 was designated "captain Salvation Army" and the South Reading Conservative Club was then at numbers 1 – 7.

According to Dave Tug on www.iguides.org, under the heading: "The history of Milk Delivery in the UK", the British milkman first appeared in the 1860s, when the new railway network began to bring fresh milk direct from the farm. Loaded into churns, milk was delivered by the milkman from door to door on a three-wheeled hand cart or milk pram, such as the one shown on the next page, although the company here is a London one – AGJ Cook of Emmertons

Model Dairy, East Ham. Two deliveries were made every morning. In 1869, the price of milk varied as to whether it was regular (4d. a quart) or for babies (5d. a quart, which is approximately equal to 2p. for 2 pints). Bottled milk began to appear from 1880 and pasteurisation was introduced in 1890. In the 1890s, some families had their own milk churns sealed in the dairy before delivery. Thus, it would seem that Henry had chosen a comparatively modern job for the time

It is not clear what happened next as, although the *1889 Smith's Directory* still showed Henry at 65 Waldeck Street, the *1889 – 90 Kelly's Directory* shows numbers 2 – 132 and 11 – 117 with the entry for the latter as:

117   Taylor Henry, dairyman

Either renumbering had taken place or, more likely, Henry had been waiting for no. 117 to be built as it was an end of terrace house with more ground and therefore had room for a stable for the horses – a very necessary feature as milk floats were drawn by horses in those days.

A dairy is a business established for the harvesting of animal milk – mostly from cows or goats, but also from buffalo, sheep, horses or camels – for human consumption. It is typically located on a dedicated dairy farm or section of a multi-purpose farm that is concerned with the harvesting of milk.

117 Waldeck Street overlooked Poultons Banks and I recall my father telling me that he kept rabbits in the stables. By then, he had three sisters – Annie Elizabeth (pictured with him here), Alice Maud and Blanche Victoria (who had been born in 1883, 1886 and early in 1888 respectively) so he was probably relieved when his first brother – William Henry – arrived on the scene in 1889!

13

By the time of the 1891 census, Henry and Kate's three eldest children – Thomas (10), Annie (7) and five-year-old Alice – were described as scholars while their father was termed a self-employed Milk Dairyman. The household was living at 117 Waldeck Street, Reading and was item 52 on the Schedule:

Name & Surname	R	C	Age	Occupation	E	Where born
Henry Taylor	H	M	35		Dairyman	X	Leckhampstead
Kate do [1]	W	M		37			Oxon, Bix
Thomas do	S		10		Scholar		Berks, Reading
Annie E do	D			7	do		do do
Alice Maud do	D			5	do		do do
Blanch Victoria do	D			3			do do
William Henry do	S		2				do do
Thomas Taylor	B	S	30		Carman	X	Leckhampstead

The line beneath their entry has the wording "End of Ecclesiastical Parish of Christchurch." In order to capture as much information as possible on the chart, I have only used the columns relevant to the family along with the following abbreviations:

> 2nd column   R = relation to Head of Family   S = Son
>   H = Head   D = Daughter
>   W = Wife   B = Boarder
> 3rd column   C = Condition as to Marriage
>   M = Married
>   S = Single
> 4th & 5th columns, Age last birthday, Male in 4th and Female in 5th.
> 6th, 7th & 8th columns, Profession or Occupation with Employed in 7th and Neither Employer nor Employed in 8th.

However, 65 Waldeck Street in Katesgrove in Reading St. Giles Civil Parish and the Ecclesiastical Parish of Christchurch, was shown as uninhabited in that same census, thus implying that Henry had only recently moved his family into no. 117, where they continued living throughout the 1890s.

Whereas Dad's maternal Uncle George [Partridge] had been lodging with the family in 1881, a decade later his paternal Uncle Tom (who shared his name completely, Thomas Taylor), was boarding with the family. Aged 30, he had

---

[1] This stands for ditto – much used by census takers to refer to repeated information

14

also been born at Leckhampstead, Berkshire like his brother, Henry, but he was still single. He is designated a Carman, which meant that he drove a vehicle used to transport goods. At the time of the *1881 census*, he had been living with his (and therefore Henry's) parents in their cottage at Leckhampstead as the following entry on the *FamilySearch* website shows:

Name	Relation	Marital Status	Gender	Age	Birthplace	Occupation
Jesse TAYLOR	Head	M	Male	55	Leckhampstead, Berkshire, Eng.	Ag Lab
Harriet TAYLOR	Wife	M	Female	50	Wilton, Wiltshire, England	
Thomas TAYLOR	Son	U	Male	21	Leckhampstead, Berkshire, Eng.	Ag Lab

Source Information:	
Dwelling	Cottage
Census Place	Leckhampstead, Berkshire, England
Family History Library Film	1341310
Public Records Office Reference	RG11
Piece / Folio	1272 / 9
Page Number	11

I recall Dad mentioning that he and his sisters Annie and Alice attended Katesgrove School. The School would have been a comparatively new one then as it resulted from William Forster's *1870 Elementary Education Act,* which had established a national, secular, non-charitable provision for the education of children aged 5 – 13. Reading School Board, which had been elected on 21st March 1871, had designated Katesgrove as an area most in need of school provision so had commissioned the borough architect, Joseph Morris, to design a school for 678 pupils on a sloping site formerly occupied by a villa known as Katesgrove House in 1873. Built at the bottom of the slope, Morris' school was designed to accommodate girls and infants on the ground floor and boys above, with the boys' play-ground placed at the top of an embankment and accessed via a timber bridge. Construction was undertaken by a group of contractors led by the local firm of Wheeler Bros. E. M. Brant was the first Head Mistress of Katesgrove Infants School and she commenced the School's Log Book on 14th August 1874 with:

Took charge of the school Aug 10th. Eighty-six children in attendance during the week. A half holiday on Friday on account of the school treat.   E. M. Brant

15

21st   Numbers increased by the admission of ten.

28   Numbers slightly decreased from some children being sent back to the schools from which they had come. A half holiday on Thursday in consequence of the children being absent at a Sunday School fete; school opened but no attendance marked.

In 1878, in response to worsening vandalism outside school hours, Morris was re-employed to design a caretaker's cottage for the site. When Tom, Annie and Alice were pupils in 1891, Morris was again brought in to extend and adapt the 1873 building to form a girls-only school. That was possible after the Katesgrove boys' department was moved wholesale to a new school at the top of the embankment. This Central Boys' School [2] was built by Winter & Fitt of Reading from 1890 – 1892 to designs by William Ravenscroft and also accommodated boys transferred from other schools in the borough.

I imagine that Tom, Annie, Alice and their parents remembered 31st August 1891 for some time afterwards as it was designated a holiday to commemorate the introduction of free education for everyone in Britain. *1880 Elementary Education Act* had insisted on compulsory school attendance for 5 – 10 year olds but it wasn't free. It was to be 1893 before *School Attendance Act* raised the age of exemption to 11. Prior to that, the *1819 Factory Act* had stated that no child under 9 could be employed and 9 – 16 year olds could only work 12 hours a day. That was probably why Dad had been excused school until 10.30 a.m. each day on account of his father's milk-round business when he helped him with deliveries in Castle Crescent and nearby roads. Grandad used to take him to horse auctions behind Friar Street to buy horses for the milk round.

The School Staff as at 23rd November 1891 were:

Miss Sarah Jane Martindale	–	principal teacher	
Miss Annie Budd	–	certificated assistant	
Miss Sarah Eliza Norton	–	ditto	
Miss Annie Nation	–	assistant	
Miss Grace Rain	–	do	
Henrietta Jane Howes	–	pupil teacher	4th year
May Louisa Wicks	–	,, ,,	3rd year
Mabel Annie Higwell	–	,, ,,	2nd ,,

---

[2] Morris' 1873 school is known, in 2012, as the Henry Building, and the former Central Boys' School as the Dorothy Building.

However, there had been virtually a complete change of staff since the Report six years earlier around the time when Dad probably started at the School – 23rd November 1885. Then the School Staff were detailed as:

Miss E. A. Edwards	– Principal Certificated Teacher
Miss Eliza White	– Certificated Assistant
Miss A. V. P. Attwood [3]	– Assistant
Miss A. M. Seward	– Pupil Teacher 4th year
Miss Grace Rain	– do 2nd year.

Only the youngest Pupil Teacher, Grace Rain, had remained on the School Staff, having progressed from being a Pupil Teacher to an Assistant in the intervening years.

When, he was 11, Dad left Katesgrove School and worked initially for a Butcher, who used to say to him, "Say please and thank you, Taylor – it doesn't cost anything". Both Annie and Alice would have been affected by the *1893 Education Act* and not been able to leave school until they were 11 while the two younger ones would have had to stay at school until they were 12 as the school leaving age was raised to that in 1899.

When he was 15-years-old, Tom put his age on and joined The Oxfordshire Light Infantry. Originally The Oxfordshire Militia, the regiment was transferred into The Oxfordshire Light Infantry as the 4th battalion in 1881. It was embodied during the South African War in 1900 and disembodied in mid-1901. So there you are, he was in the army at 15, as this photograph shows – how about that! In those days, things were different. I do not know how long he served in the regiment and how he was able to demob himself but he had obviously done so before the time of 1901 census.

---

[3] Annie Victoria Patti Attwood's progression from paid Monitress in 1878 to Candidate to Pupil Teacher Years 1 – 3 at Reading British School is documented on pages 142, 146, 148, 154, 158/9 in Daphne Barnes-Phillips' (2011) *This is our School*

By 1901, 20-year-old Thomas was working as a Brewer's Labourer. Dad had told me that he had worked in the wine and spirit departments of Simonds Brewery (one of Reading's well-known 3Bs – Beer, Biscuits and Bulbs). As well as showing Henry, Kate, Thomas, Blanche and William as ten years older, the entry for 117 Waldeck Street showed that the family had grown to include Fred (9) and Arthur George (6), while Annie (17) and Alice (15) had gone into "service", so were no longer living at home. Henry was termed as working on his own account, being a Purveyor of Milk.

Name/surname	R	C	Age		Occupation	Emp.	Where born
Henry Taylor	H	M	45		Purveyor of milk	Own acc	Leckhampstead
Kate do	W	M		47			Oxon, Bix
Thomas do	S	S	20		Brewer's labour	Worker	Berks, Reading
Blanche V. do	D	S		13			do do
William H. do	S	S	12				do do
Fred do	S		9				do do
Arthur G. do	S		6				do do

Annie was a nursemaid at Cothill School, Marcham, Abingdon while Alice was housemaid at "Oxendale", Caversham, Oxfordshire, the home of Thomas G. Chivers (47), a hay and corn merchant who worked on his own account, and his wife Florence A (41). Their family – Florence (21), Ethel (19), Cyril (15) and Leslie (9) also had Bertha Wheeler (24) working as a cook for them.

Ten years later (1911), Annie had moved on and was the first-named among the servants of an Army Captain on retired pay, William Chevins Hunter (40, born in Calcutta, India) and his wife of 13 years, Marion Elizabeth (42, born in Londonderry), who lived in the 12-roomed Deanfarm, Wellington College Sta. with their children, Mabel (13) and Jessie Rachel (9 months). Annie (27) was detailed as born in Southcote in Reading, Berkshire, and the other servants were: a cook, Kate Harmer (29); parlourmaid, Catherine Brooks (23, born Stanford); and housemaid, Maude Mary Doran (23, born York).

Simonds brewery had opened in Broad Street in 1785, being founded by William Blackall Simonds (although his father had had a brewing arm of his malting business from as early as 1760). The Brewery was one of the new industries that were growing up to replace the cloth industry, which had ceased by the end of the 18th century, according to Tim Lambert in his *A Brief History of Reading, Berkshire, England*. By the 1790s, Sir John Soane had been commissioned to design a new brewery complex in Seven Bridges Street

18

[and it was to remain in the later-renamed Bridge Street until 1978]. By the 1880s, Simonds was the largest brewery in Reading and, by 1938 (well after the time that Tom was working there), it was producing just over 1% of all beer brewed in England and Wales.

It was an arm injury that caused Tom to leave Simonds. While running down Poulton's Banks (which stretched from Waldeck Street to Elgar Road), he had his arm pulled out of joint, when the Keeper grabbed him. When Simonds heard about this, they sacked him and that led to his going to South America.

Established 1880.

Shipping and Emigration Offices.

G. R. SMITH,
Passenger
— and —
Tourist Agent,

**58, KING'S RD.,
READING.**

(Under Board of Trade Warrant).

PASSENGERS BOOKED TO ALL PARTS OF THE WORLD

By any Steamship Lines. Plans of all Royal Mail and other Passenger Steamships submitted to Clients and Berths promptly secured. Baggage despatched—Everything arranged. Inquiries invited.

EMIGRATION. G. R. SMITH is the sole Emigration Agent for this District, recognised by the Governments of

CANADA, NEW ZEALAND, AUSTRALIAN COLONIES, SOUTH AFRICAN COLONIES.

RHODESIA—The coming Colony.

☞ Full particulars, with descriptive pamphlets of Colonies and cost of passages (including assisted passages to Australia and New Zealand—free passages for Domestics to Queensland) can be obtained by applying as above.

In the first decade of the 20th century, there was much talk of emigration to all parts of the World, especially to the British Colonies, so Tom was probably well aware of posters such as the one here, which was published in the *1909 Smith's Directory of Reading*. Maybe, he even booked his passage to South America from that very SHIPPING, PASSENGER & TOURIST AGENT based at 58 King's Road, as, under the *Professions and Trade* section on page 474 of the *1907 Smith's*, is the entry:

SMITH G.R. 58 King's road – to Canada, United States, Australia, the Cape, India, Mediterranean, Egypt, and all parts of the World. SOLE local Agent for the leading Royal Mail lines and Steam Ship Companies, under Board of Trade Warrant. Passengers booked to all parts of the World.

It is possible that it was his mother's side of the family that had enabled Dad to go to Tierra del Fuego as among the names on La Sociedad Explotadora de Tierra del Fuego (S.E.T.F.)'s first monthly ledger of accounts for Ultima Esperanza in 1906 were: Partridge, J. and Partridge, Tom. The list included the names of employees and casual workers, in addition to former owners, suppliers and service providers (both individuals and businesses).

How J & Tom Partridge would have come to travel to Chile is pure conjecture as I do not recall being told. However, the S.E.T.F. website has helped with locating the whereabouts of Dad and his cousin through its list of those who donated to the "Magellan Times" World War I Fund. That newspaper had only been founded a few months before the outbreak of the Great War in August 1914. Its target readership was the predominantly British-owned and/ or British-managed sheep ranches, and ranch operators were exhorted to raise contributions among their employees in addition to the Funds raised directly in Punta Arenas. Among five Taylor entries are three with relevant initials:

Taylor, A.	Gente Grande (x 2)
Taylor, A.	Philip Bay (x 2)
Taylor, T.	Philip Bay (x 2)

The 2 denotes that they will each have made two separate contributions to the Fund. Since I have a photo of Dad and his cousin Arthur taken in Punta Arenas, I think it is likely that they were both living at Philip Bay and, if that is the case, then the following Farming Notes of 1898 from the National Library of New Zealand might well be relevant:

> It is reported, says 'Cold Storage', that two companies have been formed recently for farming sheep in Chilian Tierra del Fuego. One company takes its title from the country, and the other is called the Phillip Bay Sheep Farming Company, Limited. The Waldrons of Newbury, Hungerford and Ramsbury are largely interested in both companies. The capital of the Tierra del Fuego Company is £50,000 in shares of £10 and that of the Phillip Bay Company £30,000 in shares of the same denomination.

The three towns mentioned are of course all in the west of Berkshire and reasonably close to Leckhamstead where Grandad Taylor was born. In 1898, Sociedad Explotadora de Tierra del Fuego had a valuation of £1,560,000 while Waldron and Wood's ranch, Punta Delgada, was valued at £1,500,000. Tierra del Fuego Sheep Management Company's valuation was £590,000 and Phillip Bay Sheep Farming & Co.'s was £325,000.

20

II.   Estancias bigger than Britain's biggest counties

Although it has not been possible to ascertain exactly when my father sailed for South America, I recall him telling me that he travelled from Liverpool in 1910 and he felt really sorry for those who had to travel steerage (the cheapest form of travel) as they were pretty well out in the open all the time. Certainly, I could find no reference to him in the 1911 British census – the only Thomas Taylor in Reading then had been born in Berks, Theale, so was not him.

My grandparents, who had been married 32 years, only had two of their seven children remaining with them in their 4-roomed house at 117 Waldeck Street:

Surname	Forename	Born	Place of birth	Occupation in 1911
Taylor	Kate	1855	Oxon Bix	Wife
Taylor	Henry	1856	Berks Leckhampstead	Dairy Man
Taylor	William Henry	1889	Berks Reading	Helping Father Dairy
Taylor	Arthur George	1895	Berks Reading	Worker Cycle Works

Aunt Blanche had gone "into service" like her sisters, being the first-named of three servants of solicitor, Charles Gyningham Field (60, born Wallingford); his wife of 30 years, Blanche Emma (née Simpson, 64 born Glossop, Derbyshire) and two of their four children – Lilian (26) and Gwendolen (21) at 15-roomed Denmark House, Southcote Road. She was their cook, working with: parlourmaid, Annie Florence Violet Duffield (22) and housemaid, Kate Cornell (27). Charles Field had already been Mayor of Reading 1893/94 and was to be so again 1912/13 and 1913/14, then President of Berks., Bucks., & Oxfordshire Incorporated Law Society 1914/15 and, in 1926, he became one of the first Life Members of the Council of University College, Reading.

Uncle Fred was also "in service" by then, but in an even bigger house – the 22-roomed Merrow Croft in Guildford – the home of Herbert Pike Pease (43), Unionist Member of Parliament for Darlington since 1898, who had been Party Whip 1906 – 1910; his wife Alice Mortimer (40) and four of their five children: Margaret Alice (15), Ruth Evelyn (10), Phyllis Helen (6) and Ronald Arthur (2). Among their ten servants, who were listed before the family in the census, was 20-year-old footman "Frederick" – not "Fred" as he had been christened. I recall having been told that he worked in a posh house where he wore a bowler hat. His brother Tom seems to have travelled to South America by 1911. This is confirmed by the appearance of his name among the *British Consular Registrations at Punta Arenas, Chile: 1911 – 1920* as:

Taylor, Thomas   1880   Eng.

The only other documentation relating to that period of Dad's life details his return on 12th October 1919 to Liverpool from La Plata on the *R.M.S.P. Deseado* so it would seem that he was in Chile from at least 1911 until 1919, possibly in, or near, Punta Arenas for some, or all, of that time and working as a shepherd, so let us consider what his life would have been like there.

Few nations are shaped by their physical limits quite like Chile. Folklore has it that: "When God created the world, he had a handful of everything left – mountains, deserts, lakes, glaciers – and he put it all in his pocket. But there was a hole in that pocket and, as he walked across heaven, it all trickled out and the long trail it made on the earth was Chile", which is 2,800 miles in length, yet on average just 109 miles wide (only 265 miles across at its thickest point), having the Andes Mountains on the east and the Pacific Ocean to the west. The north is a desert wasteland; the middle grassy and fertile and the southern tip (where Cape Horn jabs at Antartica) is a frost-glazed outpost.

Chile gained independence in 1810, has a population of 17 million and its national animal is the condor. The opening lines of its National Anthem are:

Puro Chile, es tu cielo azulado
Puras brisas te cruzan tambien

Pure Chile, your sky is blue
Pure breezes cross you too

Punta Arenas, which means "Sandy Point" in English, is the capital of Chile's southernmost region – Magellanes and Antartica Chilena. Founded 18th December 1848, it was indisputably the world's southernmost city, being on the north shore of the Strait of Magellan. However, during the 20th century, new settlements, such as Ushuaia and Rio Grande in Argentine Tierra del Fuego, have grown up further south.

22

Tom's journey to Punta Arenas (see map opposite) probably followed the 1904 South Atlantic route: **Liverpool**, La Pallice (La Rochelle's port), Corunna, Vigo, Lisbon, Recife, Salvador, Rio de Janeiro, Montevideo, Buenos Aires, Port Stanley (Falklands), **Punta Arenas** (and would then have continued to Coronel, Talcahuano and Valparaiso).   By the time he was travelling to Tierra del Fuego around 1910, it was apparent that traffic patterns to South America were changing with the opening of new railways, and construction of the Panama Canal (which opened in 1915).

Perhaps it was the influence of those real-life outlaws, Butch Cassidy and the Sundance Kid, who took a South American getaway in Patagonia in 1901, when things got too "hot" for them in the American West, that inspired Dad to go there as indeed I have always been intrigued by cowboy films.   It is said that the wide open spaces, big skies, jagged peaks and barren plains of Patagonia reminded them of the land they had left behind.   They changed their names and became legitimate ranchers, but soon the law was on their trail again and they had to flee hastily, returning to their old bank-robbing ways.

Patagonia, the southern-most region of South America, is a wild and rugged land of mountains, glaciers, fjords, deserts and plateaux, which are home to

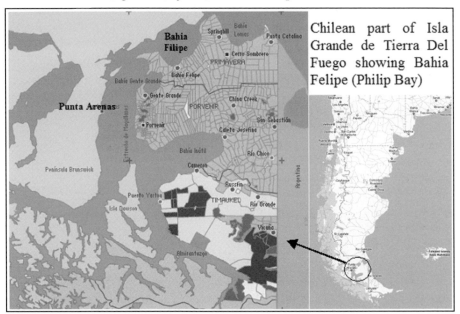

Chilean part of Isla Grande de Tierra Del Fuego showing Bahia Felipe (Philip Bay)

23

more than seven million sheep. Most of it is in Argentina and consists mainly of arid, lonesome desert but the rest lies to the west of the Andes in Chile, which is wet and green, with valleys and forests and it would seem to be there that Dad found himself. As it is the Southern Hemisphere, the seasons are reversed, with the mildest weather generally from November until March.

I do not know how much of Chile Dad would have had chance to visit but, in a country 36 times the size of Wales and with a demanding job to perform, it is likely that his travelling outside of work commitments would have been somewhat restricted, possibly to the Tierra del Fuego area.

The thing I most remember from the tales Dad told me about his time in South America was that, when he arrived in Tierra del Fuego, he had to ride 100 miles on horseback to his Settlement at Philip Bay. Since he'd never ridden a horse before, he was in bed for nearly a week afterwards! Horses were relatively cheap to buy and eventually he had seven – one for each day as they could only work for one day a week. He also had sheep dogs but they were expensive. I recall having a picture of him on horseback with his dogs, rifle and side arms and wearing a big Stetson, but unfortunately, through the years, I've lost it, which is sad. We'll therefore have to settle for two modern photos on page 1 of Colour Photo Insert, showing gauchos on horseback rounding up sheep with the help of dogs. They were taken by Peter Bean at Rio Penitentes between Puerto Natales and Punta Arenas during his holiday there in February 2007. However, this black and white one should whet your appetite for them as it shows very little has changed during the century since Tom was there:

I still have a photo which I believe shows typical living accommodation on an estancia with possibly members of Dad's boss' family in the foreground:

Dad and the other shepherds would no doubt have spent much of their time camping, or in huts, since the size of the grazing areas would have meant that they could not return to more permanent accommodation very often.

Life was tough – Tom had to ride the line fence for miles, dig sheep out of rivers when they fell in and sometimes scoff snow when he was thirsty. Obviously, he had to protect the sheep as well. The culpeo (a South American species of wild dog) has been found to be responsible for 60% of the predator losses in Patagonia but cougars and jaguars also prey regularly on livestock and are recognised as widespread potential enemies of sheep. Although canids, such as the Maned Wolf and foxes of the genus Pseudalopex, have been blamed for sheep deaths in South America, no evidence for a statistically significant amount of predation has ever been presented.

There was no law or proper medical help but Dad had a rifle and side arms as everyone did there. When a colleague was ill with appendicitis, he took him to the docks to go over to the mainland to be operated on. As the boat's siren sounded on its approach, his colleague heard it and died – a tough life to be sure.

Everyone spoke Spanish in Tierra del Fuego, which incidentally means "Land of Fire", so Tom learnt it while he was there and came to speak it like a native, soon becoming fluent in that language. I recall him speaking to me in

25

Spanish when I was a child. Another of his photos I still have shows bales of wool being loaded onto horse-drawn carts to be taken to the docks for shipping to other parts of the World:

Sheep were introduced to the Chilean part of Patagonia from the Falkland Islands in 1865 and, between about 1890 and 1940, the Magallanes Region became one of the world's most important sheep-raising areas, with one company, Sociedad Explotadora de Tierra del Fuego, controlling over 10,000 square kilometres in southern Chile and Argentina, according to *Wikipedia*.

The start of war in 1914 didn't seem to make any difference to those living in South America. Although, there were obviously many nationalities sheep farming in Tierra Del Fuego – including both Germans and English – they didn't start attacking each other. They just carried on sheep farming. In Great Britain all unmarried males (or widowers without dependent children) who were between the ages of 19 and 41 on 15th August 1915 and ordinarily resident there, were expected to enlist, unless in an exempt category.

Dad's favourite youngest brother, Arthur, had volunteered for the war, like his brothers, Bill and Fred, before the Military Service Act of 27th January 1916 brought conscription into play for the first time in the war. He had six week's training and was then sent to France as a Private in the Royal Berkshire Regiment. There he was killed by a grenade whilst in a bomb crater – it was truly a terrible war. It is likely that he was killed in August 1916 during the Battle of the Somme (which lasted from 1st July until November that year) as the only Arthur G. Taylor mentioned died on 18th August, according to the records available from the Commonwealth War Graves Commission:

26

Casualty Details

Name:	TAYLOR, ARTHUR GEORGE
Initials:	A G
Nationality:	United Kingdom
Rank:	Private
Regiment/Service:	Royal Berkshire Regiment
Unit Text:	8th Bn.
Date of Death:	18/08/1916
Service No:	21754
Casualty Type:	Commonwealth War Dead
Grave/Memorial Ref:	Pier and Face 11 D.
Memorial:	**THIEPVAL MEMORIAL**

Fortunately, Tom's other brothers fared better as both Bill and Fred returned from the conflict to continue helping their father in the dairy. I even recall that in the 1930s and later, Uncle Bill received cigarettes from an Army officer with whom he'd kept in touch since the end of the War.

During those war years, Tom was the sole witness to a tragedy that occurred. He was on a cliff top looking down at the Straights of Magellan, when he saw a little boat going along flat out with everything working. A great big ship then came into view. Catching up with the little boat, it blew it to pieces, then turned around and hurried back from whence it came.

Argentina remained neutral during World War I, although often helped the allies with food and supplies. From about 1900, Argentina had begun to identify with Europe and the United States rather than with the rest of Latin America. It had emerged as one of the leading nations in South America, its economy being based on cattle and grain production due to the mild and moist climate in the region and excellent soil. Argentinean beef became world famous and the expression "rich as Argentineans" was well-known in Europe. During that time, the British invested heavily in building railways in South America and also the first subway. In 1916, the Radicals, led by Hipólito Yrigoyen, won control of the government. With their emphasis on fair elections and democratic institutions, they supported Argentina's expanding middle class as well as the elites previously excluded from power.

A weekly publication, *Wilemans Brazilian Review,* included a section entitled "The Week's Official War News" so Tom would have been able to keep up to date with the state of the war in Europe from both sides. The publication may even have been responsible for him and Arthur choosing the *R.M.S.P. Deseado* for their return to Liverpool as this advertisement on the front of the Tuesday 18th July 1916 edition shows that ship sailing for Europe on 21st July and again on 29th September that year.

Wileman's Brazilian Review

A JOURNAL OF TRADE AND FINANCE
PUBLISHED WEEKLY TO CATCH BRITISH MAILS

| VOL. 3 | | RIO DE JANEIRO, TUESDAY, July 18th, 1916 | | N. 29 |

R. M. S. P. THE ROYAL MAIL STEAM PACKET COMPANY

P. S. N. C. THE PACIFIC STEAM NAVIGATION COMPANY

Frequent service of mail steamers between Brazil, Europe, The River Plate and Pacific Ports All steamers fitted with Marconi system of wireless telegraphy.

Regular service of cargo boats to and from all the principal British ports, also serving France, Spain and Portugal.

Cabines de luxe -- Staterooms with bath-room, etc., also a large number of Single berth Cabins

SAILINGS FOR EUROPE

DESEADO	21st July		DRINA	8th September
ORTEGA	22nd „		AMAZON	20th „
DARRO	30th August		DESEADO	20th „
ORITA	16th „		ORONSA	3rd October
DESNA	11th „		DARRO	6th „
ARAGUAYA	28th „		DESNA	13th „
DEMERARA	1st September		ARAGUAYA	25th „

FOR FURTHER PARTICULARS, APPLY TO

THE ROYAL MAIL STEAM PACKET COMPANY

⊛ 53 and 55, Avenida Rio Branco, 53 and 55 ⊛

Tel. OMARIUS — RIO — P. O. B. 21
TELEPHONE No. 1109 NORTE.

SÃO PAULO RUA QUITANDA (Corner of Rua São Bento)   SANTOS RUA 15 DE NOVEMBRO 190.

The Pacific Steam Navigation Company (PSNCo) was in 1873 the largest steamship company in the world but political unrest and competition from other shipping lines meant that it found itself in financial difficulties. Chile went to war with Peru and Bolivia in 1879 and that, coupled with the continued deterioration of conditions in the original PSNCo trade area, led to a joint venture with Orient Line marketed as Orient-Pacific Line. Collaboration was necessary with PSNCo's main competitor, Royal Mail and the larger company acquired PSNCo in 1900.

Although it has not been possible to ascertain exactly where in Chile Dad worked as a shepherd from 1911 – 1919, it would seem that the writings of George and Jennie Saunder could well throw some light on the life he would have experienced there. They lived at Estancia Cerro Castillo, Ultima Esperanza from 1949 to 1965. That farm was about 300 km [186.4 miles] north of Punta Arenas and in comparison with the majority of ranches in the region, the living conditions were very good, due to a favourable micro-climate, high wind-breaks (which protected the house and gardens) and the logistical support provided by a large corporation. In January 1971, George wrote a Ranch Manager's Report in which he described his 40 years working with the same Company – Sociedad Explotadora de Tierra del Fuego – in different parts of Patagonia, i.e. Chile and the Island of Tierra Del Fuego, on large sheep farms, which each had anything from 90,000 to 160,000 Corriedale [4] sheep. Those farms all ran one sheep per two acres with all classes of sheep kept separate in their age groups and only being retained for five shearings. Rams were imported from Australia and New Zealand to maintain a good standard of wool. Cross bred Shorthorn/Hereford cattle were also kept on those farms, but only about 600 to 1,000 on each one.

Although George's experiences would have started a decade or so after Tom had returned to England, shepherding techniques changed slowly so many of those described by George will no doubt have been shared by Tom. I knew

from Dad that all herding of sheep was done on horseback and that each shepherd's troop was made up of six horses but had not appreciated that that meant that an average farm needed 500 to 600 horses. The animals were similar to an Irish hacking horse and were bred and tamed on the farm. Dogs were also used to help with the herding, each shepherd having six dogs. That meant that on some farms there could be 180 to 200 dogs belonging to the shepherds.

---

[4] an in-bred half-breed with Merino on dam's side and English Lincoln longwool on sire's. The name Corriedale was chosen in 1902. The New Zealand Sheep Breeders Association began publishing Corriedale pedigrees in 1911, but it was 1924 before a flock book was published by Corriedale Sheep Society of New Zealand

The sheep were out of doors all the year round, and the only time they were under cover was during shearing, when they could spend some hours in the shearing shed in their stalls, or even overnight, awaiting their turn to be shorn. That usually took place in December and January after the hoggets [young sheep from about 9 to 18 months until they cut two teeth], either wether [castrated males] or ewe, had been heavily culled.

To have sufficient dry sheep for one day's shearing, the shearing sheds were capable of holding 3,000 to 5,000 sheep as 26 to 36 shearers could shear that number a day, depending on whether the sheep were rams, hoggets, young or old ewes. Once the sheep had been shorn, they were put out in the open immediately to go to their pastures in the high country for the summer. George commented that:

The Corriedale sheep has such an abundance of wool growth on the head and face, this causes it to become "wool blind" as we say, and it is necessary to shear the head and face twice a year in April and in the Spring – September – especially the ewes before lambing. Most of this work is carried out where the sheep are in their paddocks, with a portable shearing machine, with four shearers and four catchers, and there are permanent pens situated at strategic points, and also portable pens are used for this work. A total of approximately 3,000 to 3,500 sheep can be shorn per day.

This form of working is to avoid driving the sheep long distances to return to the main shearing shed for this operation. Only the sheep which are near the shearing shed are brought to it to have their head and face shorn.

The April "head and face" shearing coincided with the bringing down to their Winter Pasture in the low country. The high country could not be used in the winter months because it could become covered with snow, which could drift upwards of ten feet or more when the wind blows. It also suffers from hard frosts, ice, and shortage of water. Being similar to the weather in the north of

30

Scotland, snow and hard frosts are experienced in winter, with some rain and drying winds in the spring and summer. On average, the rainfall is only about 12 inches per annum so, if there is no good snowfall in the winter, the drying winds in spring and summer can lead to a lack of moisture. Water-holes, lakes, streams and rivers can get very low in water, with some drying out completely. The moisture is particularly needed to enable the growth of new grass in spring. Large areas of land have low hills, some quite high mountain ranges and there is also the pampa country, which is completely flat.

The weather affects these areas differently as there is not a great deal of forest or trees to give protection and the pampa just has a few stunted bushes here and there plus one or two small zones covered with a low bush called *Mata Negro*. The valleys in the hilly areas give the animals protection from the wind and cold. At times in spring and summer, the dust raised by the strong winds can be very trying and unpleasant for them, especially when there are hurricane force winds, as a dust storm can then develop.

Snow drifts can cause roads to become closed and make travelling very difficult. Sheep are never hand-fed, even during such bad weather, as it would be an impossible task with such large flocks of sheep, so it is very much the "survival of the fittest". They are usually dipped as a precaution against scab and tic once a year – in April – before they go to their winter camps and George summarised:

Foot rot is rare in this part of the world as the majority of pastures are dry, and it is only on very odd occasions, where animals have been in swampy land, that it may occur.
As a matter of fact sheep in Patagonia seem to have very few of the usual sheep diseases which are prevalent in other parts of the world where sheep are reared in large numbers.
The rams are put to the ewes in May to lamb during the first days of October. There is only one lambing per year in Patagonia as the weather is too severe to make it possible to have two lambings. This is the earliest time for lambing as in August and September the weather is still too cold, with hard frosts, sometimes snow, and no green grass for feed. Again the ewes lamb in their very large paddocks and there are so many lambs being born at one time that the weak ones just die, as it would be impossible to hand feed when dealing with such large numbers.
At lambing time, a shepherd looks after approximately 3,000 to 5,000 ewes, and owing to the great distances to be covered to do this work he travels around on

31

horseback. These shepherds live in shanties away from the main Settlement to be near their work. Some of these shanties may be as much as 10 to 40 miles from the main Settlement. As many as 3 shepherds may live in one shanty at lambing time to cope with the work. A farm may have 50,000 to 60,000 breeding ewes. As the weather is so variable here it can affect very much indeed the lambing percentage. The average for lambs runs between 85% and a 100% in good years. According to the number of young lambs there is, you are able to work out how many old ewes, wethers, and lambs that you have for disposal to be sold for meat.

Lamb marking took place at the end of November, and could occupy a period of 14 to 21 days according to the size of the farm. Tom had been made cook for about a year when the cook at the Settlement left so it was good to discover from George the difference that would have made to him:

Years ago, the Squad which consists of approximately 30 men, including a cook, and 9 shepherds, lived under canvas, and changed camp every other day. All this was achieved by using horses and horse-carts for transportation of personnel, hats, iron standards, sledge hammers, to enlarge the entrances to the permanent pens, in the large paddocks, for the shutting in of the ewes and lambs, which were in flocks of 2,000 to 2,500 ewes with their lambs.
The first day's work commenced at 3.30 hrs. and usually finished about 15.00 hrs. This type of working has now altered since mechanical transport became available, and the men and materials for making portable pens etc. are taken every day from the main Settlement in one large lorry, and the cook with his kitchen etc. in a smaller one. By this means it is now possible to mark the same number of lambs, but dealing with them in smaller flocks, averaging 500 to 1,000 ewes and lambs per pen. This also avoids driving the ewes and lambs for long distances, and one does not get so many lambs losing their mothers.
The ewes are shorn last at shearing in January, and the lambs are then weaned from them.

It's the sheer scale of the operations that would surprise anyone from Britain. As George's wife, Jennie, commented:

I had so much to learn when I arrived in Chile, to live on a Sheep Farm in Patagonia. It was very different from life in Darlington, Co. Durham ... I arrived in Punta Arenas on 3 May 1946, sailing south from Valparaiso ...
My husband, George, had worked for forty years with the sheep farming company Ganadera de Tierra del Fuego [SETF], on large sheep farms with anything from 90,000 to 160,000 Corriedale sheep and Shorthorn cattle. He had managed 'estancias' bigger than the biggest counties in the British Isles, and his pioneering

These **Patagonian Gauchos** still look after their sheep in 2007 as my father would have done in the 1910s — photographs courtesy of Peter Bean (page 24)

Colour Insert Page 1

George Palmer Schools site where I was educated from 1931 to 1941 (Page 63)

1936 Morris 8 (Page 66)   1936/38 six cylinder **Rover** (Page 66)

Mayor's **Armstrong Siddeley** (Page 66)   **1927 Austin 7** (Page 68)

Colour Insert Page 2

Barbara and I started married life in Grovelands Road, Spencers Wood
at a house called "**Byways**" (Page 79)

Sheep still graze at Childrey as this photograph taken from the wall surrounding
St. Mary's churchyard, in 2005, shows (Page 90)

Colour Insert Page 3

I ran three **London Marathons** as well as several of the **Reading Half Marathons** and I really enjoyed every footstep of the entire events (Page 104)

Dysons Wood as viewed from the rear garden at "High Thatch" (Page 107)

Barbara wrote in July 1976: This is "*Jenny*" after one of her wins at Doncaster
with "me" and the "boy who leads her round the Paddock" (Page 112)

Jenny Splendid leading the way to her first win of the 1977 season in the
Downtown Handicap at Salisbury on 23ʳᵈ June (Page 113-4)

Colour Insert Page 5

Avondale Princess clears a fence on her way to her win in the Green Norton
Novices' Hurdle at Towcester on 25th March 1982 (page 119)
Courtesy of Bernard Parkin of Woodmancote — Photographer of Racehorses

Avondale Princess being congratulated by Barbara afterwards (page 119)

Neville Thomas James Taylor married **Lynn Joyce Clarke** on
Saturday 28th February 1981. They held their **reception** at
the White Hart Hotel at Sonning. (Page 122)

Misty for Me after her win at Nottingham in the
Starting Gate Two-Year-Old Maiden Stakes on 28th June 1982 (Page 123)

Colour Insert Page 7

"Hi De Hi" star, **Felix Bowness,** who performed the opening ceremony of our
Abingdon Shop in 1990, is seen here with Joy Cuthbertson and myself (Page 129)

April Daisy

Some of **Barbara's
Greyhounds** that raced
at Reading Stadium
between 1993 and 1999.
They are referred to on
page 130.

Inspired

Exchange Express

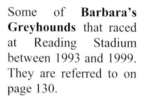

Flight Command

This is Krystal

Colour Insert Page 8

work in land reseeding attracted people from all over the world. The fact that we were not blessed with children left me free to help him in some aspects of his work – for example, I did all the typing of his information reports to the Directors of the Company, and all the planning of the year-round work on the farm.

We lived at Estancia Cerro Castillo from 1949 to 1965. This was the Company's show farm ... and we had to look after and entertain visitors who were sent by the Company ... The majority of them came from the Food and Agriculture Organization (FAO) ... The Manager's house had four double bedrooms for visitors, and we often had a "full house". Naturally, I had a large staff to help me run the house efficiently. Feeding the visitors was a full time job, as they came throughout the summer months, and some even came during the winter.

Before Tom left South America, he had a photo taken of himself with his cousin Arthur in a studio in Punta Arenas. The date – 6th August, 1919 – has been handwritten on the back of it

and that initially seemed to conflict with the passenger list of the *Deseado* which detailed their arrival date at Liverpool as 12th October 1918. Further research showed that someone must have set up the wrong year on the date-stamp on the Ship's Passenger List.

The *R.M.S.P. Deseado* had been launched by Harland & Wolff, Belfast on 26th October 1911 for the Royal Mail Steam Packet Company Steamship Line services to the West Indies and South America. Its maiden voyage from Liverpool to the River Plate had started on 5th July 1912 and it had accommodation for 98 first, 37 second and 800 third (steerage) class passengers. All R.M.S.P.Co. vessels had buff-coloured funnels from 1900 – 1972 whereas they had had black ones from 1841 – 1899. Weighing 11,475 tons, the *Deseado* was named after the city, Puerto Deseado in Patagonia in the Santa Cruz Province of Argentina. The fishing port was originally called Port Desire by the privateer, Thomas Cavendish, after the name of his 120-ton flagship which he sailed into the Deseado River estuary on 17th December 1586, accompanied by the 40-ton *Hugh Gallant* and the 60-ton *Content*. The

Deseado [5] had remained in service during the war due to its vital frozen meat carrying capacity and, on 19th January 1917, she had been attacked in heavy seas in the Bay of Biscay by four surfaced U-Boats. However, the weather prevented them from manning their guns, so she escaped.

In the period immediately following World War I, relations between capital and labour were strained throughout the whole of Southern Patagonia. For instance, in Chile, there was a confrontation at the Puerto Bories freezing works during January 1919, with eight fatalities. Thanks to the intervention of the Red Cross, worse was averted but it could have been that event that made Tom and Arthur consider returning to England.

---

[5] it was eventually scrapped in 1934 although there was to be Deseado (2) weighing 9,641 tons, built in 1942 & scrapped in 1968, and another vessel renamed Deseado (3)

Only five British 3rd Class passengers had boarded the *Deseado* at La Plata, Buenos Aires on that particular 1919 sailing. La Plata, which means "The silver", was purpose-built as the provincial capital of Buenos Aires after the city of the same name was federalized in 1880. Among the five listed as embarking there was passenger no. 125 – a 38-year-old shepherd, Thomas Taylor, whose country of last permanent residence was given as Chile, while his address in England was recorded as TIERRO DEL. BASINGSTOKE ROAD. READING. BERKS. The only other person whose previous place of residence was Chile was passenger no. 124, 21-year-old Arthur Taylor, a labourer, whose address in England was given as 43 UPPER CROWN STREET. READING. BERKS. so that would seem to confirm that they were travelling together. In those days, you were considered adult when you reached the age of 12 so Arthur could easily have travelled there with his cousin Tom in 1911 when he was 14 and worked on the same estancia as him but as a labourer.

Dad had told me that a distant relative had paid his passage for him and that his cousin Arthur had been with him in Tierra del Fuego but whether it was Arthur's parents or other relatives who paid Tom's passage, we may never be able to discover after this time lapse. Tom had been offered more money to stay in Tierra del Fuego but he felt that he had had enough of sheep farming although he had not decided what he wanted to do when he returned to Reading.

While he had been away, his father had moved his Dairyman business from 117 Waldeck Street to Basingstoke Road – the building that housed the dairy can still be seen behind that house in this modern-day photograph. The move probably happened in 1914 as the *1913 Smith's Directory* lists under DAIRYMEN on page 417:

Taylor, Henry 117 Waldeck st.

However, by the *1915 Smiths*, Henry's private and business address was shown to have moved to Basingstoke Road next to:

255 Court, George
Taylor, Henry dairyman, Tierra del.

The fact that there was no number for the property could imply that it was very much on the outskirts of Reading at that time. The address provides us with evidence that Tom's stay in Tierra del Fuego was considered noteworthy enough within his family to consider it as a name for the new family home. However, they may not have understood the full name since it is only the first two words that ever seem to have been used on official documents. Tom's address on the already mentioned passenger list of the *R.M.S.P. Deseado* (shown in the picture below in her wartime camouflage) gives it thus, as do the Reading Street Directories. Ancestry.co.uk even mis-transcribed the address as "Tierradsle" on Fred's 1915 enlistment papers.

By the time of *1917 Kelly's Directory*, Grandad Taylor is termed a farmer:

Taylor, Henry, farmer

However, in the *1918 Smith's* that reverts to:

Taylor, Henry, dairyman, Tierra del.

36

which ties up completely with the entry for 12 October 1919 for the arrival at Liverpool of Thomas Taylor on the *R.M.S.P. Deseado*. Since that would have been almost a year after the signing of the Armistice of the Great War at the eleventh hour of the eleventh day of the eleventh month – 11 a.m. on 11th November 1918, the vessel would no doubt have reverted from the camouflaged version to more like the earlier photo of the *R.M.S.P. Deseado* (page 34) during that year. Arriving in Liverpool a year after the end of the 1914 – 1918 Great War, I assume that Tom and his cousin Arthur returned to Reading by train.

Dad's siblings had started to marry while he was in South America. Alice Maud married Thomas William Partridge in the summer of 1911 in Reading:

Marriages Sep 1911				
Partridge	Thomas W	Reading	2c	803
Taylor	Alice M	Reading	2c	803

However, it seems that her husband died early in 1917 so, when she died in 1920, aged just 34, she was buried in the grave that her parents had bought for themselves in Reading Cemetery but, when the wording was engraved on it, her married surname was not included:

Also ALICE MAUD daughter died Feb 28th 1920 aged 34.

As so often happens in wartime, those who are in steady relationships prefer to marry in case anything should happen to them during such unsettled times. Aunt Blanche seems to have been the first to set the ball rolling as she married William E. Almond in the second quarter of 1915. They were to live in the

Basingstoke Road opposite the Four Horseshoes pub and I came to know him affectionately as Uncle "Nut"! He always gave me 2/- whenever I saw him – a sizeable sum in the 1930s [indeed, as my pocket money was 1/- in 1950s].

This view of the Four Horse Shoes Public House in Basingstoke Road was taken in 1905 and shows how rural the area was at that time.

23-year-old Uncle Fred had received Notice of Call-up for War Service from the Army in 1915 and, on 24th June, he swore the Oath of Allegiance to King George V in front of a Magistrate or Attesting Officer and was given the Regimental Number 103152. On 28th, he was assigned to 35th Divisional Signal Corps. At the time he was a Tram Driver (horse-drawn in those days) and his address was given as: Tierra del, Basingstoke Road (or Tierradsle, Basingston Road, according to *Ancestry*'s transcription of his service record!).

Uncle Bill married Ada Alice Griffin (who preferred to be called Alice and was a similar age to Bill) towards the end of that same year so Dad had missed both Blanche's and Bill's weddings. He had also missed the births of his nephew, Henry W. T. towards the end of the following year, and his niece, Elsa K. in the second quarter of 1918 [She was to die aged 39 in Westminster early in 1958]. Inbetween those two births, Uncle Fred too had taken the plunge and married Sarah E. Paget towards the end of 1917.

38

III. From gambolling to gambling

When he returned from being a shepherd in Chile, Tom found that beer was still 2d. a pint as it had been when he left England. However, other things had changed. During the 1914 – 1918 War, his sisters had been taking care of the milk deliveries, pushing a cart around, after his brothers had enlisted for war service in 1915. Deliveries had dropped from three [for breakfast, lunch-time pudding and afternoon tea] to two during war time but reverted to three a day, as it had been from the 1900s, as things returned to normal afterwards. It must be remembered that very few people had any form of refrigeration in their homes until well after World War II.

Milk cans, which were oval with brass lids, held a quart of milk and were left on doorsteps or brought to the cart to be refilled, using a half-pint scoop. They would then be kept in people's larders (or pantries) which had light wire covers to keep flies out. When glass milk bottles started to be used in the 1920s, their cardboard lids became a hit with subsequent generations of children who used them to make woollen pompoms to adorn scarves and hats.

Tom's youngest brother, Arthur, had made the supreme sacrifice during the war as had many others of his generation and people were considering what form memorials to those who had died should take. Eventually, his name would be on The Thiepval Memorial among those of 73,357 British and South African personnel, who fell on the Somme between July 1916 and 20th March 1918 and had no known grave. That was to be the largest British War Memorial in the world but it was not to be completed until 31st July 1932.

However, as well as the larger memorials, local communities wanted to be reminded of those they had known personally and so it was that Whitley Hall Methodist Church produced a Roll of Honour containing 116 names of those who had seen active service during the 1914 – 1918 conflict. Thirty-one of them are marked with a cross to denote that they were wounded while twelve are also underlined to denote that they were either killed in action or died of their wounds, Arthur (A. G. Taylor) being among them 'though he was one of the few not to have his regiment recorded by his name:

W. Adnams	Reg'd Brill	Walter Brill	Thos H. Cooper
Harold Cooper	A. W. Eames	Reg Edginton	Ern't Filewood
Wilfred Allen	Thos Porter	A. G. Taylor	Joss W. Wells

The Roll of Honour remained on the rear wall of Whitley Hall Church until that building was sold to a Hindu community and became a Hindu Temple in November 1997 when the Roll was given to Christ Church in Christchurch Road, along with a similar one produced for the 1939 – 1945 War. It was the most obvious place for them to find a home as both congregations had met round the War Memorial in Christ Church's grounds since it was erected in 1920 at the instigation of them both.

Interestingly, Barbara's grandfather – A. Barnes of Berks R.H.A. [Royal Horse Artillery] pictured here – is also on the First World War Roll of Honour, being one of the fortunate ones who was neither killed nor wounded.

Dad found that his surviving brothers, Bill and Fred, had returned from war service and were helping their father run the milk business. However, Henry had bought 287 Basingstoke Road (near Buckland Road) while Tom was away, naming it "Tierra del Fuego". The house for the dairy was only half built at that stage and, as his father was short of funds, Tom helped him out and finished building it while deciding what he would do next.

Towards the end of 1920, Bill and Alice's third child was born so Blanche Alice Maud was the first of Dad's nieces to be born after his return. Four-year-old brother Henry and two-year-old sister Elsa seemed pleased with their sister and, in the summer of 1925, the three of them welcomed Arthur Robert, who was to be known as Bob.

Eventually, Tom bumped into an old friend of his who was taking bets and seemed to be doing rather well at bookmaking so he decided to follow suit and start a Bookmaking business in 1920. A Bookmaker is a person or organization that takes bets on sporting and other events at agreed upon odds. At that time, "Bookies", as they are colloquially called, focused betting on professional sports, especially horse racing, but eventually a wider range of bets on topics, such as political elections and even novelty items such as whether there would be a white Christmas, could be placed with most bookmakers. In fact, a punter in the early 1960s had a £10 wager with William Hill that a man would walk on the moon before 1st January 1970. When Neil Armstrong did so on 21st July 1969, the gambler won £10,000.

By adjusting the odds in his favour, or by having a point spread, the book-maker aims to guarantee a profit by achieving a "balanced book", either by getting an equal number of bets for each outcome, or (when he is offering odds) by getting the amounts wagered on each outcome to reflect those odds. When a large bet comes in, a bookmaker can try to lay off the risk by buying bets from other bookmakers. He does not generally attempt to make money from the bets themselves, but rather to profit from the event regardless of the outcome. His working methods are similar to that of an actuary, who does a similar balancing of financial outcomes of events for the insurance industry.

Although the first betting shops appeared in London in 1815 (and there were soon 400 of them), the *1853 Act for the Suppression of Betting Houses* put bookies legally out of business for almost 108 years. However, it did not prevent hundreds of backstreet ones flourishing until the 1960s.

Tom was one of those. He can be seen smoking his pipe in this photo, which was taken on 23rd August 1926 at the start of a day trip in a charabanc. The

driver, just behind him to his left was his brother-in-law William Almond, who drove for Jarvis' Garage in Christchurch Road. Initially, Dad had the top room in the dairy along Basingstoke Road as his office for the bookmaking and his brothers collected bets during their milk rounds so that was a good beginning. Soon he had other such "runners" all over Reading. So what was a Bookies Runner? As Joe Bosher describes on "Friends of Beamish" website:

> In those days one way of making extra money was to be a bookies runner. Taking bets scribbled on the back of cigarette packets, or what ever came to hand, and running to the officially registered bookie was highly illegal with dire consequences if caught.

The first legislation that affected Dad was the result of the British Parliament's *Finance Act of 1926*. In 1923, a House of Commons Committee had been appointed to report on the introduction of a Betting Tax. It recommended the imposition of a duty on bets and betting as a means of raising revenue. The scheme of the legislation was to charge excise duties on betting and on certificates that bookmakers were required to take out in respect of their businesses. Each year, they were required to pay an annual duty of £10 for a "bookmaker's certificate" and a separate £10 for an "entry certificate", which had to be taken out for betting premises used by a bookmaker.

From 1ˢᵗ November 1926 to 15ᵗʰ April 1929, betting duty had to be paid on every bet made with a bookmaker at 32% (later 2%) of the amount staked. The lower stake of 2% applied to a bet made on the racecourse on the day of a horse race with a bookmaker on the course by a person on the course. The betting duty was payable by the bookmaker with whom the bet was made, and he had to issue to the backer at the time of making it a "revenue ticket" denoting that the duty had been paid. However, those tickets did not need to be issued by a bookmaker who had arranged with the commissioners of Inland Revenue to furnish returns of all bets made with him and had given security for the payment of the duty.

Any person found accepting a bet without issuing a revenue ticket, or failing to produce a bookmaker's certificate when lawfully required, could be arrested without a warrant and the Courts could order him to be disqualified from holding a bookmaker's certificate for any period it considered fit, although he could apply after three months for the removal of the disqualification. Keeping or using any betting premises for which a proper entry certificate was not in force, or carrying on business as a bookmaker without a proper certificate, carried such penalties.

Betting Not Legalized

When these proposals were first put before Parliament they met with much opposition. Bookmakers were apprehensive that the tax would diminish betting whereas those with religious, moral or social objections feared that, by being taxed, betting would be recognized by the State as being legal. The latter apprehensions were addressed by a clause providing that nothing in the provisions was to render lawful any betting in any manner or place in which it was at the commencement of the act unlawful. Therefore, illegal betting, as in the case of street betting, remained illegal. Bets were not made recoverable at law by the payment of the duty.

In July 1927, the Chancellor of the Exchequer stated in the House of Commons that, in the eight months to the end of June 1927, the tax had yielded about £1,750,000. An alteration made by the *Finance Act of 1927* was the extension of the 2% duty, which, in 1926, applied only to bets on horse races, or to bets made on the ground on any sporting event. On 1st October 1928, the tax on racecourse bets was reduced to 1%, and, from 32% to 2%, on those made with a bookmaker.

The decision to abolish the tax in 1929 was due to the admitted difficulties of administration, the number of evasions owing to the large volume of betting which still passed through the hands of unrecognized street bookmakers, and dissatisfaction with the returns. However, the £10 bookmakers' licence duty was retained and a new duty of £40 a year was imposed in respect of every telephone installed in bookmakers' offices. A tax of 1% was also imposed on stakes laid with a totalizator.

Winston Churchill was Chancellor of the Exchequer at the time and the tax meant that Government Officials visited those who were operating as bookies but, as Dad commented: "In those days, they had to give it up as a bad job – I leave you to draw your own conclusions!!!"

Henry had continued in charge of the milk business during the 1920s. Although he was aged 70 in 1926, that year's *Kelly's Directory* has for him:
287 Basingstoke Road Taylor, Henry, Dairyman.
It is not until the *1929 Kelly's Street Directory*, that he seemed to be taking things easier as, in the *Commercial section* on page 406, is the entry:
Taylor H. & Son, dairymen, 287 Basingstoke rd.

43

Also on page 13 under Basingstoke rd. is:

287 Taylor H. & Son, dairymen,

so he would seem to have been handing over more control to Uncle Bill by then. It is that year's Directory that makes us realise that Dad has moved from Basingstoke Road, as Surrey Road has the following entry on page 161:

43 Taylor Thos

Uncle Fred is close by at: 49 Taylor Fred

Basingstoke Road with Surrey Road off to the right.

As well as his successful work life, my father's social life had been going pretty well in the 1920s. He had found himself courting two ladies. One was a cook at Nettlebed and the other was Nora Rolph, who worked at Huntley, Bourne & Stevens. It was she that he married and I was their only child.

Nora, who had been born in Reading in 1894, was living with her family in the St. Giles parish on 31st March 1901. Her paternal Uncle John and Aunt Julia were also living in that area at that time – at 17 Queen's Cottages off Sidmouth Street. They had James Withers (25), who had been born in Wokingham and was working as a barman, boarding with them. John Rolph (41) was her father's younger brother, having been born in Little Hinton, Wiltshire as her father had been and is described as Manager of Hotel Stores. His wife – Julia (35) had been born in Ivor, Middlesex.

1901 must have been a pretty bad year for 7-year-old Nora and her immediate family as the only other ROLPHs recorded as living in Berkshire St. Giles at that time were as shown in the last three columns in the following chart:

BMD Date of birth	BMD Forenames	1901 Age	1901 Forename	1901 Place of birth
Mar 1854	Charles Frank	47	Charles F.	(Wilts Little
Sep 1884	Margaret Martha	(17)	Maggie	Berks Hunton)
Dec 1888	Laura Alice	12	Laura	do Reading
Jun 1891	Gwen Ruth	(7)	Gwen	do do
Dec 1893	Norah	7	Nora	do do
Sep 1896	Violet Emily	4	Violet	do do
Mar 1901	Lilian Eva	5 weeks	Eva	do do

Since there is some discrepancy between names, dates and places of birth given then (indicated in brackets) as opposed to details from *FreeBMD* site under Rolph, Reading volume 2c, the latter are quoted in the first two columns. Charles and Maggie's places of birth – Wilts, Little Hinton and Berks, Reading – run into each other, and Maggie and Gwen were 16 and 9!

As there is no mother's name given, yet the youngest daughter – Eva – had been born in February 1901, it would seem likely that her mother died that year, possibly during, or as a result of, childbirth, as borne out by *FreeBMD*:

Deaths Mar 1901				
Rolph	Elizabeth	43	Reading	2c	270

Since the only mention of a profession or occupation in that census is for Charles F. Rolph, who is described as a Tradesman's groom, I imagine that 16-year-old Maggie was expected to look after Laura (12); Gwen (9); Nora (7); Violet (4) and baby Eva as the school leaving age was 13 from 1899.

Mum's parents – Charles Rolph and Elizabeth James – had married in 1877:

Marriages Dec 1877				
James	Elizabeth	Reading	2c	825
ROLPH	Charles Frank	Reading	2c	825

Their birthplaces – Little Hinton, which is five miles east of Swindon, for her father and Dolgelly in the county of Merionethshire, Wales for her mother – have various mistranscriptions. In the 1881 census, they were given as:

45

Name	Relation	Marital Status	Gender	Age	Birthplace	Occupation
Charles F. ROLPH	Head	M	Male	27	Little Hindon, Wiltshire, England	Groom
Elizabeth ROLPH	Wife	M	Female	24	Merioneth Dolgellau, Wales	
Elizabeth E. ROLPH	Dau		Female	1	Taplow, Buckingham England	

Dwelling	The Green
Census Place	Passenham, Northampton, England
Family History Library Film	1341370
Public Records Office Reference	RG11
Piece / Folio	1537 / 64
Page Number	8

By 1891, they had three children as Margaret Martha and Laura Alice had joined Elizabeth Mary Ellen, and the family had moved to 218 Kings Road, on the corner of Montague Street in the Reading St. Giles area – next door to "The Berkshire" public house which was run by a widow, Eliza Higgs:

Forename	Age	Place of birth
Charles Frank Rolph	37	Wilts, Little Hinton
Elizabeth Do	34	Dolgelly, North Wales, Merion.
Elizabeth Mary Ellen Do	11	Taplow B
Margaret Martha Do	6	Berks, Reading
Laura Alice Do	2	Do , Reading

Charles was again shown as a Groom but page 164 of the *1888 Reading Street Directory* details him as a caretaker at a Tea Store at 218 Kings Road:

220   Pearce Charles, wireworker, Victoria Wire Works
        here is Montague Street
        Salmon J. S. & Son, tea stores
218   Rolph Frank, caretaker
216   Higgs Mrs. E., *Berkshire Inn*
        here is Victoria Street

Charles and Elizabeth's first-born seemed not to have been at the family home for the 1901 census and, since she would have been 21 then, she could either have been "in service" or married as those were the main options open to girls of her class at that time. Amazingly, it was consulting the Green Girls'

46

School records that led to a better understanding of what had happened to her. I recalled that my mother had been a pupil at that Reading school and, sure enough, in its MINUTE BOOK from 1901, her election was recorded on p. 41:

A meeting of the governing body was held at the School House Russell Street on Saturday the 29th September 1906 at 3 o'clock.
Present:-   The Rev. R. W. Carew Hunt, vicar of St. Giles: Chairman.
             The Rev. W. Neville, St. Mary's,
             The Rev. R. P. Newhouse, St. Lawrence's,
             Mrs Friend, Mrs Neville, Mrs Walters and the Clerk.
Election. The testimonials of 6 girls were examined and the candidates and their mothers were interviewed and the following girls were elected:-
Elsie Emily Wiggins,   born 18th December 1893   – Standard 5
Ethel May Lay,   born 19th July 1894   – Standard 5
Norah Rolph,   born   – Standard 6
Edith Emery,   born 16th January 1894   – Standard 5
The first three were elected to come in at once and Emery to come either in March next or sooner if there should be a vacancy. In the case of Norah Rolph where her father had married again and both her father and stepmother were very undesirable persons, it appears that a sister of the Candidate, namely Mrs Wheeler of 14 Elgar Road was willing to take the girl during holidays and to look after her and an undertaking was read which had been signed by the girls father, Charles Frank Rolph, dated August 27th last, giving his consent that the girl should on no occasion return to her step-mother but during the holidays should make her home with Mrs Wheeler. The girl's election was made conditional on her not going back to her stepmother.

In those days, school children could only be promoted to the next Standard (class or form, nowadays) when they had shown competence in the work of the previous one so the fact that Nora was already in Standard 6 showed that she had progressed to a higher Standard than her fellow candidates.

As well as telling us that Nora's father had remarried, the account detailing her election to the Green Girls' School implies that one of her sisters was also married by 1906. Consulting *Smith's Reading Street Directory for 1906 – 1909* showed that a James Wheeler lived at 14 Elgar Road. The *FreeBMD* website showed that it was her eldest sister, Elizabeth, who had married him around the time of her mother's death:

Marriages Mar 1901				
Rolph	Elizabeth	Reading	2c	505
Wheeler	James	Reading	2c	505

In fact, entry 246 in the 1901 census shows widower Charles Frank Rolph as a tradesman's groom living in four rooms at 134 Elgar Road – a bay-fronted terrace house – with Maggie, Laura, Gwen, Nora, Violet and 5-week-old Eva, then entry 247 shows 23-year-old James Wheeler (breadmaker at the biscuit factory) and his 21-year-old wife, Lizzie, are also living at 134 Elgar Road but in two further rooms. There are thirteen houses "To let empty" near them – numbers 114 to 130 inclusive and also 136, 138, 150 and 154 so perhaps the area was newly-built. At 82 Elgar Road lived breadmaker Francis William Knott (36); his wife Mary Jane (35) and their children Alice (13, also a breadmaker at the biscuit factory), Ernest (8), Frank (5), Frederick (4) and 5-month-old Sidney Gilbert. Francis died in the summer of 1901, aged 37, and, by the following summer, his widow had married Mum's father:

Marriages Sep 1902				
Knott	Mary Jane	Reading	2c	790
Rolph	Charles Frank	Reading	2c	790

The Governors' Minute of Nora's election confirmed our thoughts that the Green Girls' School was a boarding establishment and, on page 37 of the Minute Book, there was a copy of the type of announcement that appeared annually in *Berkshire Chronicle* and *Reading Observer* as well as on Church doors. The clerk reported in 1905 that that year's notice had been placed:

NOTICES.

READING GREEN GIRLS' SCHOOL.

AN ELECTION of CANDIDATES to fill VACANCIES will take place at the SCHOOL HOUSE, RUSSELL STREET on FRIDAY, September 29th, 1905 at three o'clock.
Names, with Certificates of Birth and baptism are required to be left with the Matron, on or before WEDNESDAY, September 27th. Candidates must be between 12 and 13 years of age, and have passed the Fourth Standard, and their parents must have resided in Reading for the six years preceding the day of election.

W. C. BLANDY
1, Friar Street, Reading
Clerk to the Trustees.

Following Nora's acceptance in 1906, we gain some idea of the size of the School when the Clerk reported, on 23rd March 1907, that there were 22 girls, one of whom was then about to leave, and that the financial position of the

48

school funds would hardly warrant the vacancy being filled up unless in the case of an exceptional candidate. A month later, on 26th April, he stated that P.G. Hatcher had withdrawn his girl from the school so numbers were down to 20. That meeting had been specially called for the purpose of hearing complaints chiefly about the quality and cooking of the food and the alleged harsh treatment of the girls by Miss Russell, the assistant matron. P.G. Hatcher, Mrs Hatcher, Mr. & Mrs Bernard, Mr. Law and Mrs Sayer were interviewed, and Miss Russell and matron, Miss Bunce, were also examined. The Committee came to the conclusion that there was very little foundation for the complaints but in certain details they promised the complainants that attention would be paid to what they had said, and the Chairman admonished Miss Russell to be as gentle as possible, consistent with discipline, and not to treat the girls as untrustworthy.

Another incident occurred soon after Nora had been at the school a year. Although she might well not have known about it until Grace Goddard was reprimanded by the Chairman before the School soon after the Matron had reported on 11th November 1907 that she (who had come into the School in March 1904) had, after endeavouring to make other girls say they were the thieves, confessed that she had stolen some towelling.

A year after the parents' complaints, the Governors had to consider the resignations of Matron and Assistant Matron on 10th March 1908 as the latter had accepted a post in a School in Abingdon under the Berks Education Committee. Miss Bunce, who had been Matron for 17 years, wrote that, owing to ill health, she could not undertake to continue the work with a stranger so the Committee accepted both resignations as from April 7th. As a result, the advertisement below appeared. This gives us more of an idea of the type of school and its location.

READING GREEN GIRLS' SCHOOL

The posts of Matron and Assistant Matron will be vacant at Easter. The School is a Church of England School whose special aim is training girls for domestic service. Knowledge of domestic training and needlework indispensible. Matron must be certificated. The School is situated at 38 Russell Street, Reading where from 20 to 24 girls (ages 12 to 16) are boarded. The salary offered is £50 for Matron and £20 for Assistant Matron with board and lodging. Further information etc…

Three Candidates were interviewed for the post of Matron on 26th March 1908 and Miss Mary Fairbairn – aged 34 – was elected to the post. The other two applicants were Miss Ella Etherington (aged 30) and Miss E. A. Edgar (41). 65 Candidates applied for the post of Assistant Matron and three candidates were short listed for interview on 4th April 1908, when 35-year-old Miss M. Birchmore was appointed. The other shortlisted candidates were Miss J. Childs – aged 41 and Miss Mary Frisk – aged 37.

The Green Girls School was the nearer of the three storey buildings in this modern-day photo. The narrow building between it and the white one was a "scattered home".

The Green Girls' School, initially called Girls' Charity School, resulted from the Collection begun on St. Thomas' Day 1779 at St. Mary's Church. The vicar, Charles Sturges, realised that, although a Sermon entitled "A Persuasive to Charity", set up by the Will of John West Esqr. late of Walbrook in London dated 9th January 1719, had been annually preached since then, no regular collection had been taken in favour of any charity as was usual in such cases.

The School originated in St. Mary's Butts on Michaelmas Day 1782 [6], when one pound one shilling was paid to a widow of St. Mary's Parish, Mrs

---

[6] 29th September is the Feast of St Michael the Archangel and was one of the Quarter Days when accounts had to be settled

50

Leggatt, to provide for the Charity Girls. She was appointed to have the care of the children for one year initially with the assistance of her daughter, Sarah, wife of William Cowdery of the same Parish, upon the following terms viz:

That she shall have the Care and Superintendence of the Six Children from Michaelmas 1782 to Michaelmas 1783 paying all Expenses whatsoever of Schooling except the Rent of the House and the clothing of the said children And that she is to receive the following Sums for the following articles in such proportions as shall be judged proper.

For boarding herself and six children at the rate of 18d pr week	46	16	0
For the use of her furniture of various kinds	3	4	0
For a Gown not exceeding	1	0	0
For Coals, Candles and Washing	5	0	0
For Schooling and Care of Children		10	0

It removed to 54 – 56 Broad Street in 1790, and it was 4th June 1852 before Jane Leggett was elected to replace her Aunt, Mrs Jane Leggett. The imposing bay-fronted castellated building had the words "Reading Girls' School Supported by Public Charity" across the front. The next major change occurred at the close of 1884 when:

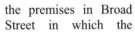

the premises in Broad Street in which the School had been carried on since 1792 were let on a building lease for 99 years for 100£ per annum school rent and the school was transferred to Russell House, Russell Street (late the residence of Rev. B. S. Edwards from whom it was bought for 1200£). At the same time Miss Jane Leggett resigned the post of Mistress to which she had been elected on June 4th 1852 and was succeeded by Mrs Kenerstone, late mistress of "The Blue School" at Sherbourne, Dorset. The Girls slept at their own homes on Friday Jan: 2nd 1885 and met at Russell House at 5.45 p.m. on Saturday Jan: 3rd. At 6 p.m. they were assembled in the Dining Hall, to the number of 20 (one having not been allowed to return to the School on account of her health) by the new Mistress Mrs Kenerstone.

The vicar of St. Mary's (the Rev. Canon Garry), in a short service, asked the blessing of Almighty God, on the School in its new home. At that service there were present: Mrs Wells, Governess for St. Lawrence parish, & Mrs H B Blandy, governess for St. Giles, who had kindly assisted in preparing the house & furniture for the reception of the girls.

The Governing Body is as follows:

Trustees　}　The Rev. Canon Garry, vicar of St. Mary's

　　　　　}　The Rev. J. M. Guilding, vicar of St. Lawrence

　　　　　}　The Rev. Cecil F. J. Bourke, vicar of St. Giles

Treasurer　Charles Stephens esq. (High Sheriff of Berks 1884 – 85)

At that time, the girls wore hats, white shawls and long green dresses covered by long white aprons tied at the waist. On 4th July 1885, it was resolved that:

the age of admittance to the School should be 12 and that no girl be admitted who is more than 12 years and 6 months at the time of election, also that the age of leaving should be 16.

Mrs Kenerstone only stayed in post until 6th January 1891 and Miss Rosa Bunce, mistress of St. Lawrence Girls' School, replaced her at a salary of 45£ on 2nd March. On 29th September that year, the School Rules were revised to:

1. Each Girl after her admittance into the School is expected to conform to all rules and failing to do so, her case will be reported to the Visiting Governor.
2. Parents or Guardians shall be allowed to see their children on the last Saturday of each month from 2 to 4 and on no other day. No children can be admitted on any account.
3. The committee will provide an outfit not exceeding £2 in value for each girl on leaving the School if her conduct in the School has been good & if she accepts the situation provided for her by the School.
4. Any girl who leaves the school before the expiration of her years from her admission, with special permission, will forfeit her claim to an outfit.
5. Should any girl not remain in the situation provided for her and give up the work for which she has been trained in the School, without a satisfactory reason, she will be required to return her outfit to the Committee.

The borough of Reading: Charities, A History of the County of Berkshire stated on pages 378 – 384 in Volume 3 that:

The Girls' Green school was originally founded by public subscriptions for girls bona fide resident in the three parishes of St. Giles, St. Lawrence and St. Mary. A sum of £3,394 18s. 8d. consols is held by the official trustees in trust for this school, arising from certain benefactions, producing £84 17s. 4d. yearly. This school also benefits from one-third share of the municipal educational charities, which in 1910 amounted to £31 16s. 5d.

52

[By the time I was a pupil at Kendrick Girls' School (1955 – 1962), it was possible to obtain grants from the Green Girls' Foundation as the headmistress, Miss Joan Atkinson encouraged my parents to apply for one for the G.C.E. "A" level French course, which I attended at Lycee Michelet in Paris from 13th to 25th April 1962. The Green Girls' School had ceased in 1924 but the Green Girls' Foundation was formed in 1929 to distribute the remaining money for educational purposes and still does so today, having been registered with the Charity Commission in September 1962.]

17-year-old Nora had left the Green Girls' School by 1911 and was "in service" as a housemaid for Archibald Simmons James (84) and his wife of 17 years – Mary Ann Gull (formerly Johnson, 70) at "The Hollies", 103 London Road, Reading – an eight-room private house where Mrs J. H. Johnson lived prior to her marriage to Archibald. They were a couple with a private income who had owned Dicker's Farm, Bramley Road, Silchester (part of the Duke of Wellington's estate) from 1905 until 1910. As well as Nora, they had a cook, Clara Taylor (58), living with them. Her place of birth interestingly had "Broad Street" recorded after "Berkshire, Reading" and Nora's similarly had "Green Town"! Since the entry was in Archibald's writing, perhaps it was to remind him that Clara had come from Green Girls' School when it was in Broad Street. Nora's surname was recorded as "Rolfe" and, as mentioned previously, her position as their Housemaid would have been found for her by the school. However, Archibald James died, aged 85, towards the end of 1913 and Mary Ann in 1922 aged 81 so I do not know when she would have ceased working for them but I do know that Mum was, at one time, "in service" with a doctor in Wokingham and I remember her telling me that she had to get up early to blacken the fire grates when she worked there.

The only other member of Nora's family whose surname was spelt "Rolfe" in the 1911 Reading Census was 10-year-old Eva who had been adopted by Charles Wheeler (29) and his wife, Mary Annie (31, née Gleed) whom he had married in 1907. They were living in 5 rooms at 29 Elgar Road with their own children – Emily Rhona (3) and Stanley George (1), and Charles was working as a tin solderer at Huntley Boorne & Stevens Tin Box Makers. Their elder sister – Gwendoline Ruth (19) – was also "in service" but in a 9-roomed house – 23 Alexandra Road. Her employers were the journalist, Charles Henry (40) and Evelyn Maud (38) Slaughter, whose son, Jack Etheridge Slaughter (5) lived with them.

53

The sister between Nora and Eva in age – Vie (14) – is, like Nora described as a domestic servant but she is shown as an inmate in a "Scattered Home" at 40 Russell Street (next door to Green Girls' School, see photo on page 50) where Harry Rolph (6) – the product of her father's 2nd marriage – was also living. The "Scattered Homes" system – devised in 1893 – placed small groups of children under the care of a foster-parent. The children attended local Board Schools so that they mixed with other children in the local neighbourhood and the homes were chosen so that no more than 30 attended any one school. Interestingly, Sidney George Knott, the youngest of Mary Jane's children by Francis Knott, was in a "Children's Home" at 75 South Street at that time.

The *1908 Children's Act* had given local authorities new powers to keep poor children out of the Workhouse so perhaps Vie, Harry and Sidney should be grateful for its implementation as the main features of the system were:

> It ensures that no children over the age of three ever enter the Workhouse. It is applicable to ALL children, not to "Orphan and Deserted" only.
> It provides Homes for the children approximating as closely as possible to the conditions of working-class life.

However, why were the children in scattered homes and a Children's Home? The main clue seems to be that their father, Charles (57), is an inmate at 344 Oxford Road and his occupation described as "Formerly Livery Stableman". Further investigation showed that address was Reading's Workhouse in 1911, the first inmates having been admitted in 1867. A new infirmary was added in 1892 and in 1909–11, a new board room, administrative block and master's house were built, as well as an additional infirmary block for up to 150 aged and convalescent patients. It could be that that is why my Grandad Rolph was there as I recall Mum telling me that he was kicked by a horse while he was working as a groom and had to have a plate fixed in his head. I don't know when the injury occurred but there were very few options available for those who were unable to work at that time since Old Age Pension was not introduced until 1909 and Unemployment and Health Insurances until 1911.

Two further sisters had married in Reading in summer 1908. Maggie married Walter John Tugwell and Laura Alice, Harry Elias Sibley. It would be the 1920s before the next Rolph weddings were to occur. Vie married Arthur H. Wise in 1925, around 18 months before my parents' wedding, and finally Eva married William E. Hart towards the end of 1927. Only Aunt Gwen remained single and she lived with Aunt Vie and Uncle Arthur in Southampton Street.

54

IV. Schooldays and my wider education

My paternal grandparents, Henry and Kate Taylor, celebrated their Golden Wedding in the summer of 1929 and this family photograph was taken as a momento of the occasion. They are obviously in a central position with four of their surviving children also in the middle row and Fred in central position in the back row so they and their children are shown in capital letters in the description. Arthur George had died on active service in 1916 and Alice Maud on 28th February 1920, aged 34. The photo was taken outside the dairy at "Tierra del Fuego", 287 Basingstoke Road, Reading:

Back row: Ada **Alice** Griffin (Bill's wife); Nora Rolph (Tom's wife); Harry B. Old (Annie's husband); FRED; Sarah Elizabeth Paget (Fred's wife); William Almond (Blanche's husband)

Middle row: WILLIAM HENRY (**BILL**); ANNIE ELIZABETH; HENRY; KATE; THOMAS (**TOM**); BLANCHE VICTORIA

Front row: Henry W.T. (**Sonner**, 12); Elsa Kate (10); Arthur R. (**Bob**, 4) – all Bill's children; **Reg**inald A. H. (9, Fred's elder son); Blanche A. M. (8, Bill's younger daughter); Harold G. (6, Fred's younger son).

[Maiden surnames have been mentioned for sons' wives and names emboldened where preferred names are not those given as first names]

I was only two years old at the time the photo was taken, having been born on 1st May 1927 so the youngest person in the photo is Bob. I gather that Aunt Gwen was looking after me that day as she often did, being Mum's unmarried sister. Here's another photo taken at the dairy, possibly on the same occasion

as Dad, Annie's husband, Grandad, Uncle Fred and Uncle Bill are wearing the same suits, although here four of them are wearing carnation button-holes.

During my childhood, I lived with my parents, Tom and Nora, at 43 Surrey Road, Reading, which they had named "Patagonia" continuing the South American theme of house names. The houses in that street were mostly two-storey compact terraced houses with bay windows and small front gardens where people knew their neighbours and chatted over the back garden wall or fence. At that time, the toilet was outside. There was also an alleyway behind the back garden walls which separated the gardens from the playground of George Palmer School. That was the nearest school to Surrey Road so I

56

naturally started in the Infants' Department there in 1931. The fact that our garden backed onto its play-ground was very handy for being given drinks at breaktime. I recall my cousin Harold's Mum handing him sandwiches through the railings. It was also handy for going home at lunchtime as can be seen from this aerial view of Basingstoke Road which shows Surrey Road and the school on the far right – just in front of the trees. Our house was the last one of the terrace in front of the School, at the edge of this photograph:

The photo shows how much less built-up the area from Elgar Road (the first road off on the left of the photo) with Winchester Road opposite, was. The next roads on the left – Rowley Road and Shenstone Road have less houses than nowadays and Bourne Avenue had not been started then.

The School had two similar-sized buildings, differentiated only by a bell tower on the one nearest Basingstoke Road. Between the two was a smaller one – the Domestic Centre. The Manual Instruction Centre is just out of view.

57

Milking the Punters

Lunchtime was of course a very busy time for the placing of bets. Since we were unofficially a Betting Shop from the 1920s up to 1960, our house (43 Surrey Road – see right) was packed with punters at that time of day. You couldn't move for them – they were all in there, reading the papers, writing their bets out and doing whatever else needed to be done, despite it being a small terraced house. It was like that until Betting Shops were established in 1961.

When I was young, I used to go around collecting bets from various agents all over the place. At the top of Whitley Hill, where the Tank (then a brick playground for children, but formerly a reservoir) was, I would go through the entrance near the park keeper's hut in Whitley Street. Either side of the driveway, there was a rockery but I knew that on the right under a particular rock I would find the park attendant's big bag of bets. After moving the rock, I would take the bag of

bets (along with the money, which was underneath), home to Dad. As I said, the house was always full of punters. I grew up in that environment, which was great.

Around 1932/33, Freddie King, a friend who was a bit older than me, used to take me once a week to see silent movies. I think it was Thursdays when we used to walk up a side passageway by Whitley Hall Methodist Church (see sketch on next page) to go and see the silent films.

Down near the screen on the right was the guy with the piano who used to play the necessary music and we all used to shout out: "Look out behind you!" to the cowboy with the big hat when somebody was coming up behind

him. I really enjoyed going there every week to see the silent movies. For me that really was the good old days in the early 1930s. That old pianist down the bottom could really knock it out!

You'll see from this recent caricature by Webb (2008) how much of a lasting impression those cowboy films had on me 75 years later!

Grandma Taylor died, aged 81, on 16th August 1934 and was buried in the graveyard at the Cemetery Junction – as shown on next page. She and Henry had been married 55 years but, as I was only seven at the time, my memories of them both are somewhat sketchy. Grandad survived her by five and a half years, dying 25th January 1940, aged 84.

59

Grandad Taylor was still a dairyman in the 1930s [7]. Electric vehicles, such as the three-wheeled "Bush Pony" began to replace horse-drawn milk carts from the 1930s though the latter were still a common sight until the 1950s.

I do recall Uncle Bill having a three-wheeled van to deliver the milk before the days when milk bottles became common. In those days, three scoops of milk was drawn from a churn.

The butcher and the baker also came round with a horse and cart. Although many people now buy their milk in polythene bottles from their local Supermarket, the traditional glass milk bottle is still in demand as it can be reused up to ten times. Infrared scanning introduced in the 1990s has ensured that they are always spotlessly clean now.

In 1935 the job of the milkman was praised in Jazzman Fats Waller's recording of "My Very Good Friend the Milkman" and, in 1971, Benny Hill's "Emie, the Fastest Milkman in the West" made it to number one in the charts.

---

[7] Entry in *1932 Kelly's Directory*: 287 Basingstoke Road Taylor, Henry, Dairyman

My Mum was very good at making toffee and she used to look after all the kids. She used to make toffee apples and give them to all the children around the various roads near where we lived – Lincoln, Winchester, Basingstoke as well as Surrey. When I meet blokes from those days who are now quite old, they still remember my Mum and the free toffee apples, how about that! Dad used to joke that his brother Fred's wife was handy with the needle whereas his wife was handy with the soldering iron (on account of her having worked at Huntley Bourne & Stevens!). Here I am with my parents around that time:

In the '30s & '40s, if my Dad had a very good day he used to take his runners down to West Street to Eighteen & Cox and buy them haddock, plaice or other fish and give it all to them as a present. He knew that if he gave them something like that, then they would take it home but, if he gave them money, they might go up the pub. He had a lot of runners all over the place, good people, and he did very well with them. As I said, the house used to be packed with punters at lunchtimes and we were very busy in that respect.

Tricks were played on us and other bookmakers by those who would put bets on late through our letter box, swearing they had put them through early. Dad had a piece of wood made to fill up the letterbox with a brass plate on the back, which was inserted into the letterbox onto two threaded shafts and screwed up with two wing nuts. At the time of the first race, this unit was fitted and you couldn't get a fag paper through the letterbox.

I remember as a young boy going up to Whitley Street to get an orange box to build a rabbit hutch one Saturday, when Ray Seymour, a good friend, though somewhat older than me, asked if I was going to the Savoy Cinema as it was opening that morning in Basingstoke Road near its junction with Buckland Road. Obviously I changed my mind and instead went to the Savoy with Ray on 20th March 1936. Unfortunately, the screen didn't work so we were given a bag of sweets each and told to return the next Saturday free of charge.

Ray was really expert with home-made four wheel trolleys, the front two wheels on a bar with a bolt in the centre to allow steering with a rope attached to each end. He took me up Bourne Avenue one day and rode the trolley down the very steep incline. He obtained quite a speed into Hagley Road then turned sharp left into Rowley Road. Giving me a go, I managed to turn the trolley over and bore the scars for a long time – good old days in the 1930s to be sure.

I later discovered that Ray died 25th June 1945 – one of just two mentioned on Whitley Hall's Roll of Honour as killed during World War II, Stanley Kybird being the other. Raymond Ernest George Seymour had been a sergeant and a flight engineer in the Royal Air Force Volunteer Reserve 199 Squadron.

About a year before I was to sit the Eleven-Plus examination, I recall Mum being very upset as the sister to whom she seemed most attached – Eva – had died. She had married William E Hart less than a year after my parents had married and their first child, Jean M. (a redhead) was born in Reading just over a year later – at the beginning of 1929. Their second child Terence had been born in Hammersmith in the spring of 1937 and it was later that same year that Aunt Eva died. Aunt Maggie, another of Mum's sisters, who lived at 56 Hemdean Road with her husband, Walter J. Tugwell, and kept a sweet shop at 25 Prospect Street, Caversham, stepped in and brought up cousin Jean, paying for her to attend Hemdean House School. Aunt Maggie and Uncle Wallie previously lived above the confectioners' shop on the east side of Prospect Street as the *1927 Kelly's Directory* indicates. Going from Church Street to Peppard Hill:

1. King, Rev. Gurnos B.A., B.D (Baptist)
3. COLEBROOK & CO. LTD, butchers, fishmongers & poulterers. Tel no 484
3. Brown, Fredk. Geo.
5. READING CO-OPERATIVE SOCIETY LTD. butchers
Here is North street
7. Gale, Frank & Son, cycle agents
9. British & Argentine Meat Co. Limited
11. Jackson E. & Sons Ltd. tailors. See advert.
13. Caversham Post Office (Miss Margaret Smith, sub-postmistress)
15. Millard, William, tobacconist
17. Cook, Frederick Charles, boot repairer
19. Jackson, George Hy. confr.
21. Salvation Army Hall
23. Creed, Mrs G. greengrocer
25. Tugwell, Mrs M. M. confr.
25. Tugwell, Walter J.

This photo shows a flock of sheep being driven down Priest Hill into Hemdean Road on its way to the Market in Reading in the 1950s, so would no doubt have been a familiar sight to cousin Jean and Aunt Maggie in the 1930s/1940s.

Although I had been awarded a Central School place in the Eleven-Plus examination, that only entailed moving to a different part of the George Palmer site in September 1938 as, in those days, one could complete one's whole education from Infant through Junior through Secondary on the same site – see page 2 of the Colour Photo Insert. Classes were around 45 or so in size in those days and my position was always in the bottom half! I even managed to miss the examination owing to a leg injury in the second term of 1939 when I'd been absent for almost a third of the total attendances (57 out of 186)! I'd been cycling down from Spencers Wood to Three Mile Cross when I came off my bike and ended up in a ditch, breaking my leg in the fall.

As well as the examination, I therefore missed the taking of the large school photo that year. However, you can see my Class Masters throughout the three

63

years – Messrs F. Wright (Year I – 1938/9), A. F. Manning B.Sc. (Year II – 1939/40) and Alexander (Year III – 1940/1) with Mr. E. Elam, the Head Master and Messrs Colyer, Everest and Hawker as they appeared on the 1935 George Palmer Central School photo before they'd met me!:

From left, along with their nicknames, are: "Bonzo" Colyer, "Frick" Manning, "Fido" Wright, "Beaky" Alexander, "Dolly" Everest, "Charlie" Hawker, Elam.

It was good to give 94-year-old "Bonzo" Colyer a lift to the George Palmer School reunion on 23rd April 2004 when he was the oldest former member of staff present at the third and final reunion in the original buildings. Allen Roy Colyer had been born towards the end of 1909 in Dartford, Kent but was still very upright and the only real sign of ageing was his hearing. He still had all his own teeth when he died peacefully at home, aged 98, on 30th November 2007. He had suffered a broken hip during a fall at home early in September then a broken leg while in hospital. Only a year before, 'though, he had still been able to shop in Marks & Spencer with his wife of 50 years, Joan.

Seeing the photo again reminded me that "Frick" Manning taught Algebra and used to box me round the ears if he didn't like what I was doing when he came up behind me. I didn't like "Fido" Wright. "Charlie" Hawker taught carpentry and the Headmaster Elam gave me the following testimonial when I left on 25th July 1941:

> Jack Taylor has been a pupil here for the past three years. I believe him to be honest, truthful and of good general character.

I don't suppose Ethelbert E. Elam, as I later discovered his name was, knew about my exploits outside school time or would have approved had he done so. Since he had taught on that school site for 41 years and was headmaster of the Central School from 1925 until his retirement in 1948, he would probably have had no recollection of me had he heard about the betting shops that were growing up around Reading in the 1960s before his death in 1967.

64

V. JACKPOT 1st Leg – Looking after the Classics

Grandad Taylor died on 25th January 1940, aged 84, leaving Uncle Bill and Uncle Fred in charge of the dairy at 287 Basingstoke Road. *Kelly's 1942 Trades Directory* lists them under Dairymen and Cowkeepers:

> Taylor W.H. and F., 287 Basingstoke Road

I was beginning to think about my future prospects at that stage as I was due to leave school the year after he died. After ten years at George Palmer School – three of which had been in the Central Department – I left in 1941 at the age of 14. My father wanted me to be a mechanic so I went to work as a Trainee Mechanic at Reading Garage in Cork Street, just off the Oxford Road (now under the Broad Street Mall which opened in 1971). Soon after I joined, the boss, Mr. Middleton, said to me as I was going out one day: "Your half day is Wednesday, Taylor." I asked the other mechanic what that meant and he said: "That means you work all day Saturday, mate."

We were being paid nine shillings a week (45p.) so, after we'd been there some little time, I headed off, taking a bunch of guys – chaps named Newman and Wiggins and a guy named Andy – up to the office to see the boss. We went through the show rooms and up the stairs to the office and I knocked at his door. "Yes, who is it?" At my reply: "It's Jack Taylor", he said: "Come on in", so we all went in and he said: "What do you want?" "Please sir, we've come to request a rise in pay", I replied. He pushed his seat back from his desk, came round, looking angry and we ran out of the door, down the stairs into the show room. When we got there, he leaned over the banisters and shouted down: "You'll have to be working a bloody sight harder than you are now before you come up to me for more money." Running past a Rolls Royce, nine shillings a week seemed such a contrast!

In about 1942, while I was at Reading Garage, the Blacksmith, George Biddall, was knocking a pin out of an axle, because it had to have new king pins. I was holding the punch and, when he missed with his sledge hammer, he hit the big finger on my left hand and split it open. Now, in those days, the Oxford Road end of Broad Street was like a little village and, if you hurt yourself, you went to Bells, the wholesale tobacconist, in Broad Street. There, Mr. Bell used to look after us lads and stitch us up. Opposite Bells was Cumbers, the butchers, which had green vans with yellow writing, which were serviced at Reading Garage. Didn't they stink when they came in! Next to

Cumbers, Woolworths (the threepenny and sixpenny store) came into being.

Since it was wartime when I worked at Reading Garage from 1941 – 1945, petrol wasn't very good then so we used to decarbonise the 1936 Morris 8s, clean the valves and grind them in then refit them and mark them with blue marker to make sure they were sealing all right. We had to clean out the plugs, pipes and carburettor, readjust the tappets, put the head back on then put it all together. We would then take the little Morris 8 with three forward gears and one reverse up the Bath Road to test it. You could push the throttle through the floor boards and, if you could do 60 m.p.h up the Bath Road, you knew that you'd done a very good decarbonise and head end service because you couldn't get any more than 60 miles per hour out of those Morris 8s.

Now Dr. Berry from Upper Shinfield had two beautiful cars which I was lucky enough to look after. They were Rovers – a red one and a black one. I think they were either 1936 or 1938, straight 6 cars, each one having six cylinders with two SU Carburettors. I used to take those SU carburettors to bits, clean them with metal polish, oil them with cycle oil and put them back together. Each SU carburettor looked after three cylinders and it was no good having the front three pulling faster than the back three as that would mean that they were pulling against one another. I used to have to tune them and get them just right. When you sat in those cars, you could smell the leather so I loved looking after them. They had solid chassis and were wonderful cars and very cheap – in the hundreds of pounds to buy at that time.

Another vehicle I used to look after when I worked at Reading Garage in Cork Street was the Mayor's Armstrong Siddeley. The Mayor, Councillor McIlroy, used to leave two big overshoes, which he obviously used for his gardening, in the car, which always stank of cigar smoke. It was the only car which had a preselect epicyclic gearbox, which meant that you put the lever on the steering wheel to the gear you wanted and then pumped the clutch, which took up that gear. See page 2 of the Colour Photo Insert to view those cars.

The Senior Mechanic, George Westwood, described the gearbox's workings to me when we had one stripped down. It had star and planet wheels and a brakeband for each gear. When the lever was preselected and the clutch punched, that particular brakeband was applied (there being brakebands for each forward gear and one for reverse). That movement activated the star and planet wheels to the gear required to propel the car forward or in reverse. However, if the epicyclic gearbox was a bit out of order when you pumped the clutch, it used to come up twice as far as it should do and it would near enough crack your knee on the steering wheel, which was not good! However, I soon became reasonably proficient with it.

On one occasion after I'd got my Driving Licence, I had to drive from Reading Garage, past The Grenadier then further down the Basingstoke Road to Strangs Farm. During that whole journey from leaving Cork Street to reaching the farm, I never passed another car. In those days there weren't many vehicles about and mine was the only one on the road.

I haven't mentioned anything about World War II up to this point as Reading had a relatively easy time at the beginning of the war but 10th February 1943 was to change that. I was in the Central Cinema in Friar Street [where the Novotel Hotel is now], watching *Bambi*. Suddenly, there was a hell of a noise, which shook the cinema and rocked the upstairs long balconies so much that you thought they were going to fall down. The projectionist lost control and "Bambi" ended up being shown on the side wall instead of on the main screen. We knew that bombs had been dropped and an announcement over the loud speakers told us: "Don't leave the cinema as Friar Street is being machine gunned." We therefore stayed put for a while.

When we did venture outside, we could see dummies, dresses and other shop items scattered in the middle of the road. The area, where "The People's Pantry" was (that's where Marks and Spencers is today) opposite the Town Hall, was all roped off. Unfortunately, it had been full of people having dinner when the bombs were dropped. I had been there many times as you got a very cheap Shepherd's Pie dinner and a starter and a dessert for virtually nothing.

As well as Friar Street, we found that Broad Street had also been bombed near Heelas (now John Lewis) and there was debris everywhere. Going down towards the Forbury Gardens, there used to be a little café on the left and I noticed that there were machine gun bullet holes in that building when I went round there. It was a terrible mess everywhere and I felt so relieved that I had been so close to the action but spared the horrendous consequences that some had to face as 41 were killed and over a hundred were injured that day.

I bought my first car in 1944. In the front garden of a house near the Cemetery Junction, as you go out of Reading on the left, I spotted a 1927 Austin 7 – like the one on page 2 of the Colour Photo Insert. I bought it for twelve pounds and ten shillings, took it to my good friend Derek Hatton's garage in Surrey Road where I stripped it down to the bare chassis and rebuilt it. We then had lots and lots of fun with that old car. When we could get petrol, we went all over the place in it and it was really, really great fun.

I continued helping my Dad during this time. He had runners all over the place. In the 1930s and 1940s, bets were always settled in ink with a circle around the returns. I remember on one occasion, a well-dressed smart gentleman copied exactly the bet and the amount (say £3-2-6) that my father would have put with a ring round but with different horses written on his slip making it worth a lot more money. When my Dad gave him the returns, he flicked his hand and said: "Now this is wrong, Tom". He was a clever con artist but my Dad realised what he was up to and, being built like a tank, had a good old row and a go at this guy and the bloke left without my father paying him. Being a big thick-set guy with a hairy chest, and, after ten year's sheep farming, he was not going to have the wool pulled over his eyes by anyone. So, after that, he got red, blue, black, purple and all sorts of inks and put them in a bottle. Shaking them up, he mixed them all together and, from then on, he settled the bets with them, saying: "Now let's see them copy THAT!"

Not all honey in Jamaica – my Army Adventures

It was my call-up into the Army that called a stop (for the time being!) to my helping my Dad with bookmaking, collecting the bags of bets, etc. The dreaded buff envelope dropped through the letter box in 1945! I had been called up into the Army. Before that, I had been a dispatch rider in the Air Training Corps so it was not entirely unexpected. I had wanted to join the

Corps so that I would be given a motorbike. I had a BSA 350 and we used to

go roaring about all over the place. In fact, a long long time ago, I rode past "High Thatch" and up through the woods, which was good fun. On one occasion, we went up in a twin engine Dominie plane with a Canadian pilot. He was a bit of a joker and decided to give us a very rough flight just to teach us what it was all about.

I must admit that, like Jimmy Savile, I had the choice of joining the Army or becoming a Bevin Boy and working down the Mine. Initially, I was sent to Bodmin in Cornwall in December 1945 for six weeks' training. It was freezing cold in January 1946 and, being in a Nissan Hut on the top of a hill with a straw palliasse and a coke stove for warmth, was not a good set-up! The old Sergeant had us screaming at dummies during bayonet practice then he would yell at us: "The only good Germans are dead ones" (what a joke!). Following that six weeks' initial training, I was nine stone nothing.

That's me, second from the right in the back row of the photo. I was then sent to Meeanee Army Barracks at Colchester for a further twelve weeks' training. There, I had a Sergeant-Major, fresh back from Burma, who was a complete lunatic. I fell out with him big time so he locked me in the cells. My knife, fork and bootlaces were taken away and I was left with a spoon, wooden bed and wooden pillow. After a week of such treatment, I was before the Commanding Officer for sentence. I managed to talk my way out of it, the case was dismissed and I was released back to my platoon.

A rifle shooting contest between all the platoons proved a turning point in my relationship with the Sergeant Major. I scored a bull's-eye every shot and was awarded a Crossed Rifles badge to indicate I was a marksman. Our platoon won the competition for the entire army barracks and, as I had helped him win the tournament, the Sergeant-major called me "Jack" after that and looked after me. I was his friend though I still didn't feel very friendly towards him! One day when I was having a shower, he said: "Hurry up, Jack, you'll be late" and I thought: "Clear off, Sir, you put me in the cells and I don't like you", but anyway he liked me after that.

When I was at Meeanee Army Barracks, I noticed that the boxers in the Boxing Team had steak and chips in the evening. Since the rest of us never had anything like that to eat at any time, I joined the Boxing Team! I managed pretty well until we had a Boxing Competition. I had to take on this guy, who came up to me and said: "Jack, I don't like to tell you but I'm a professional boxer". He even showed me photos of himself boxing professionally and I had to take him on! Well, that was no good to me. Anyway, we went in the ring and the fight started. It went alright at first then, all of a sudden, I couldn't see him. Just as I was thinking: "Where is he?", bang! aw! he caught me such a good one! I carried on but I got well pounded and, after that, I didn't want the steak and chips! I left the Boxing Team! That's the way it is in the Army, you can be an amateur and suddenly you're fighting a professional! That's just the way it goes.

We had to complete an assault course while at Colchester. I got to a river where a rope called the "swinging tit" was thrown to you to swing across. I couldn't reach the bank and was hanging on in the middle of the river with all my kit on. The sergeant was throwing thunder flashes around me telling me they were grenades and asking what I was going to do, so I let go of the rope, fell in the river and crawled out. At the end of the course, we had to fire five rounds in quick succession. They stopped me firing and put a steel ramrod up my rifle barrel. A long tube of mud came out because I had been in the river!

On another occasion we were firing Piat anti-tank guns at a disused tank. There is a shaft with a cartridge on which fires the shell which has a detonator on the end to penetrate the tank. Someone told me that, if the cartridge didn't explode, the shell would fall out of the end and blow me up. We had to fire five shells each at the tank in training. The officer could see I was nervous so, when we finished and there were still about twenty shells left, he made me fire them – happy days! After Colchester, I was sent to Civilian Billets at Kettering, Northamptonshire for a Mechanic's course. That was where my time working in a garage came in useful and I finished second overall.

On returning to Meeanie Barracks, Colchester, Jimmy Serrill and I were told we were going to Jamaica as bren gun carrier drivers. I had never even seen a bren gun carrier in my life but that's how it was! In June 1946, I was posted to Jamaica so, whereas my father had his passage paid for him by a distant relative to work in South America, it was the Government that gave me my chance to work abroad! We went on the 5000-ton "Jamaica Producer", a ship that took cars there and brought back bananas. There were only about twenty of us as we were going to reinforce numbers for the 8th Suffolk regiment.

The only way you could travel on that boat was First Class, so we had a fortnight of luxury ahead of us, with a stateroom steward, a bar steward and so on. It was great to be travelling in style – not as a 3rd class passenger as Dad had done! The officer of the Green Howards who was in charge of us said that, if we behaved ourselves, he would leave us alone. He was a nice guy but some idiot found a pair of handcuffs, did himself up with them then couldn't get out of them, so we had to report in after that – not good!

Our quartermaster at the Army Barracks had kitted us out for deepest Africa with topees [pith helmets worn for protection against sun and heat], shorts, whiskey jackets, etc. as those going in the 1920s had worn. When we arrived in Jamaica, we were dressed in our African gear but the soldiers already there were driving around in ordinary hats with light shirts and shorts. Our clothing was a joke to everyone so it was soon taken away and replaced with more appropriate gear.

For my bren gun carrier, I had a crew of three – navigator, mortar gunner and a bren gunner. Quite rightly, they all wanted to be the driver but I had been sent to do that job and things soon settled down. The main drink in Jamaica was rum and coke so I soon got used to that drink. The best rums there were the *Sugar Loaf* and *Three Daggers* but, unfortunately, it's not possible to get them in the UK.

A "not very nice" incident happened in Jamaica. If you were late back at night, you

were put in the cells. On one occasion, I'd had rather a lot to drink and I was banged up with another guy. Now he was laid out in a comfortable place where I wanted to be, so I banged his legs. He sat up and I gave him a good hiding. That went on for the best part of the night and I really beat him up. So we stood to attention in the morning when the Provo Sergeant came in and he said: "You can go, Taylor!" However, he said to the other chap: "The guy whose head you bashed with the spade is still in hospital, you can't go!" It was then that I thought: "Oh my goodness, and I've been beating him about all night". I was really glad to get out of there and lose sight of that bloke, I can tell you! So there you are. I was only a teenager but they are naughty sometimes!

I was stationed at Up Park Camp in Kingston. There, we were allowed out until midnight but I had arranged a loose rail in the perimeter so, if I didn't book out through the Military Police in the Guard House, I could come back when I liked. We had a Prisoner of War Camp which was full of mainly Germans – Merchant Navy guys who were interned when war broke out. They often escaped to go to Kingston Town, but they always came back.

After about a year, the 8th Suffolk Regiment [8] had completed their tour of duty and were replaced by the 2nd Gloucesters, which had returned from Germany in October 1946 but, within a few months, had been stationed in Bermuda & Jamaica. Following the post-war reduction in the size of the Army and the introduction of National Service, the decision was made to reorganise the 1st and 2nd Battalions of the Gloucestershire Regiment into 1st Battalion, the Gloucestershire Regiment, which took place in a ceremony on 21st September 1948 in Jamaica.

---

[8] formed April 1940, it became a training Battalion, seeing no active service. In 1946 it sailed for the West Indies to garrison Jamaica and Bermuda but was disbanded a year later.

73

I was no longer in Jamaica, nor even in the Army, when that happened as I had left that Caribbean island in May 1948 and the Army in August that year. I had had to join the 2nd Gloucestershire Regiment because my group or demob number was too high to go home but I did manage to transfer to their Motor Transport section as a mechanic. That was very good as it enabled me to drive on various missions, transporting newly-arrived wives and others to their homes or other places. I then went all over the island – up the mountains to Newcastle, Roaring River (pictured on the previous page), Moneague, Montego Bay, etc. Newcastle was in the North and considerably cooler than Kingston so the soldiers took their wives there when they first arrived in Jamaica to acclimatise them to the temperature.

However, it wasn't all honey as it were in Jamaica. When the Police went on strike, we had to police Kingston – the town etc. There was a bomb in a bus on one occasion and, after that, I had to sit in the back of the bus making sure things were all right. We had to ride around for a while in that manner to make sure nothing went wrong.

One claim to fame during my time in Jamaica occurred when I shot somebody. Let me explain. An Officer was watching us while we were on the range firing sten guns. Now, when your sten gun jams, the routine is to cock the gun, remove the magazines and squeeze the trigger. Well I cocked the gun, and removed the magazine. The bullet was lying sideways in there. I squeezed the trigger, it went off with an almighty bang and the bullet shot the Officer though the knee cap so they bundled him away. As I'd carried out the correct procedure, it wasn't my fault but he was the only guy I shot whilst in Jamaica, that Officer. It was a bit of a let down but it couldn't be helped!

Also, I've done guards at the Governor's Mansion, which is an all-night guard in stockinged feet. You just went around all the bedrooms and balconies etc. with no shoes on just to make sure the Governor was safe.

I did have one very unpleasant task to perform. A Bren gun carrier had turned over and a young soldier tried to get out and was cut in half from the left shoulder to the right hip. I had a mobile workshop at the time and I took the cable over to secure the carrier to turn it back. That was when I saw him face down, with curly golden hair – a sight I'll never forget.

74

I was quite a good photographer and my photos appeared in *The Daily Gleaner* [9], which is the main daily newspaper for Kingston, so that's one

claim to fame I had. I used to take some very good action shots with the Bren gun carriers but here is one of me just cleaning one.

While I'd been abroad, I'd been really sad to hear that Aunt Gwen had died in Reading towards the end of 1947. She was only 56 and used to look after me when I was small as she remained single. She was a lovely lady who lived with another of Mum's sisters, Aunt Vie, and her husband, Uncle Arthur, in Southampton Street and I missed her greatly.

When my tour of duty was over in May 1948, I returned home on another 5000-ton ship, the "Bayan" – see photo on next page. It went round the island loading bananas all day and night for several days. The boat was bouncing about all over the place when I arrived on it, but it soon became steady when loaded with bananas. A Danish soldier taught me how to play chess on the way home.

---

9 Now called *The Gleaner*, was established in 1834

I had various jobs when I came out of the Army and returned home in August, 1948. When my father was busy, he would get me to pack up whatever job I had taken on and stay and help him. However, in the winter or whenever the betting business was quiet, I used to go and get a job – different ones, whatever was available at the time. It was a bit like that – sometimes I was working, sometimes I wasn't!

One of the jobs I had was in a foundry, making moulds. I was the only bookmaker there so I did very well. Since the men didn't have the money available, they used to place credit bets and, on Pay Day, my man used to go round and collect the cash from them. My very good friend Freddie Much, who had books for selling fridges, vacuum cleaners and things like that, which he sold "on tick", also needed to collect his money on Pay Day. However, I used to send my man round early to collect mine and, by the time Freddie went round, the men didn't have any money left, so he struggled.

I can also recall that, even though betting was illegal then, people would queue from Aunt Blanche's terraced house in Basingstoke Road all the way along to the middle of the next terrace on Grand National Day to place their bets with her. Those were the good old days!

VI. JACKPOT 2ⁿᵈ Leg – Marriage to Barbara Robinson

While settling back into civvy life, I was introduced to Barbara Robinson by Wilf Barker. She was going out with a decorator at the time and her mother, Violet, wanted him as her son-in-law. Neither Vie nor Wilf liked the fact that Barb and I got on so well together. Here is a photo of her taken in the front garden of her parents' home:

Barbara Nancy Robinson and I married on Saturday 2ⁿᵈ September 1950 at Christ Church, Reading. The report that appeared in the following Friday's *Berkshire Chronicle* contained the following description after the details of our parents' names and addresses:

> Given away by her father the bride wore a gown of dull crepe, with embroidered veil and head-dress of orange blossom. Her bouquet was of dark red carnations. She was attended by Miss Eileen Sharpe (friend), Miss Margaret Morris (cousin of the bride), Miss Maureen Barnes (cousin of the bride), Miss Wendy Robinson (sister of the bride), Miss Daphne Barnes (cousin of the bride) and Miss Sandra West (friend). The best man was Mr. Aubrey Wren (friend of the bridegroom). A reception was held at St. Barnabas' Hall, Elm Road, Reading. The honeymoon is being spent at Southend.

From the left are: Maureen Barnes, Eileen Sharpe, Aubrey Wren, Jack Taylor, Barbara Taylor (née Robinson), Jim Robinson, Margaret Morris, Wendy Robinson. The youngest bridesmaids in the front are: Sandra West and Daphne Barnes.

Although Barb's sister is named Wendy in that description, she preferred her second name of Patricia so was known as Pat. Eileen was a neighbour of Barbara's, and Barb and I used to baby-sit for Sandra, who lived next door to Uncle Les and Auntie Doris. Uncle Wilf was also holidaying at Southend with Ismay Beasley while Barb and I were on our honeymoon. Ismay was a similar age to us, having been born in the summer of 1928 and she and Wilf (who was 17 years older) were to marry three years later, on 22nd July 1953, at Whitley Hall Methodist Church, that being his second marriage.

Barb's parents were Violet May (née Barnes) and James William Robinson of 34 Linden Road, Reading. Jim's father and grandfather were all blessed with the names James William Robinson, as so often happened in that era. The 1881 census shows that his father James (aged 8) and his siblings had been born in Woodley (as had his grandparents) but had recently moved to Sonning.

78

Name	Relation	Marital Status	Gender	Age	Birthplace	Occupation
James ROBINSON	Head	M	Male	38	Woodley, Berkshire.	Railway Lab.
Elizabeth ROBINSON	Wife	M	Female	34	Woodley, Berkshire.	
James ROBINSON	Son		Male	8	Woodley, Berkshire.	Scholar
Albert ROBINSON	Son		Male	6	Woodley, Berkshire.	Scholar
John ROBINSON	Son		Male	3	Woodley, Berkshire.	

Source Information:	
Dwelling	Headley
Census Place	Sonning, Berkshire, England
Family History Library Film	1341319
Public Records Office Reference	RG11
Piece / Folio	1313 / 20
Page Number	33

Barb and I were both in our early twenties when we married. We started married life in Grovelands Road, Spencers Wood at a house called "Byways" – see page 3 of Colour Photo Insert. My father had had the bungalow built when I was young. He told me that he could have bought most of the houses in Milman Road for £100 each but he realised that, although he could charge rents of half a crown (two shillings and six pence, written as 2/6) for each, the properties would soon need work doing on them so his expenditure could have been colossal. He therefore decided to have a house (which he named "The Canberra") built on what was originally the football pitch at Spencers Wood. Later, his builder, Mr. Yeo, suggested building him a bungalow next door. "I can knock it up for you for £300", he said. That was the time of the Great Depression so Mr. Yeo would have been glad to be employed. Tom thought that it would be a good investment so he rented out both properties while he was living in Surrey Road. However, "By-ways" was empty around the time of our marriage, so Barb and I started our married life and, in fact, spent twenty very happy years there.

Barbara turned out to be very good at settling bets so she used to help my Dad more than I did, especially when I had another job. From 1949 till 1958, when my Dad died, Barbara used to help him and she could knock out bets faster than anybody. When there was night racing, we used to go in really early in the morning – about 6 a.m. – get all the results, knock all the night racing bets out so that all the agents had them for first thing in the morning and, as I said, Barbara was excellent – very fast.

This is probably the best time for me to tell you more about Barbara's family. Her parents had married on 15th September 1928 and this photograph of that day was taken at Violet's parents' home – 10 Long Barn Lane, Reading.

Violet May Barnes was the first-born on 7th May 1906 of Albert Barnes and Martha Ann (née Collins) – both seated in the above photograph. She turned out to be their only daughter as she was followed by Albert Edward (Eddie, later Ted) on 6th September 1908; Wilfred Henry (Wilf) on 14th September 1911; and Leslie John (Les) on 1st August 1914 – all wearing caps for the wedding photo. Violet had been born in Chaddleworth, like her father, while Eddie had been born in Brightwalton; Wilf in Thatcham (when the family were living in Harts Hill Cottages near there at the time of the 1911 census); and Les at Long Barn Lane, Reading.

Eddie (far right), who had celebrated his 20th birthday on 6th September, was already courting Rose Alice Richens, who had celebrated her 17th birthday on the 11th. She is the bridesmaid seated next to the bridegroom, Jim Robinson (also born in 1906 but in Reading).

Rose and Eddie were to marry exactly five years later on 16th September 1933, and, by the time of that wedding, Violet and Jim's daughter, Barbara was old enough to be a flower girl – a natural choice as they often baby-sat for her then and looked after her as she grew up, their own family not arriving until much later (Daphne Joyce in 1944 and Alan Edward Victor in 1945):

She had been born on Christmas Eve 1929 so was 3¾ when the photo was taken and hence the youngest bridesmaid. To the right of the photo is Rose's sister, Violet May Richens, who was to marry Thomas W. Allaway later that year. The best man was Eddie's brother, Wilf, who was to marry the other bridesmaid, Beatrice M. Smith, towards the end of 1936.

This photo shows Barb when younger but already showing an interest in animals!

In the extended family photo, on the next page, she is 3rd from the left in the front row – with her maternal grandmother, Martha Ann (Annie) Barnes (née Collins), next to

her. Her mother, Violet, is 6th from the left in the middle row, with her Uncle Wilf next to her, and her father, Jim, is 2nd from right in the back row. Incidentally, there are two Violet Mays in the photo as Rose's sister also had that name! The wedding had been held at Christ Church, Reading but the photo was taken in Whitley Wood Recreation Ground.

One couple pictured had already celebrated their Ruby Wedding Anniversary

and were to go on to have 75 happy years together before Albert Herbert Collyer died, aged 98, in January 1968. He is to the far right in the middle row and Mary Ann, his wife, is four places to his right in that row. They were Rose Richens' maternal grandparents. Amazingly, Albert had been gored by a bull when he was 65 and had spent virtually a year in hospital but he had continued working, albeit at lighter gardening duties, until he was 88. Mary Ann was to die the same year as Rose – in 1972.

Les was born after the family moved to Long Barn Lane, Reading although then the address was known as 15 Long Barn Cottages, Basingstoke Road (formerly Ayres Farm). In 1908, there had been just four occupied houses in Long Barn Lane and one of those had Albert's half-sister, Rosa, and her husband Edward Huntley, living in it. By 1911, their house had been numbered 13 and eight properties were occupied.

Bert and Annie, and their young children – Vie, Eddie and Wilf – had moved into 15 Long Barn Cottages by 1913 and, as well as the eight occupied properties there, there were also four in Long Barn Lane itself, according to that year's *Smiths Street Directory*. The George Palmer Girls' School Attendance Register, which was started on 3rd October 1907 when the pupils transferred from the Reading British School in Southampton Street to the newly-built G.P.G.S., shows that Violet was given the admission number of 639 when she was transferred from George Palmer Infants on 21st April 1914. However, her address is given as 13 Long Barn Cottages then. As well as confirming her date of birth as 7th May 1906, that record shows that she left school on 23rd July 1920 on account of her age and went into Domestic Service or "into service" as the expression was in those days.

Interestingly, another pupil who was transferred from the Infants' to the Girls' School on 21st April 1914 – Winefred Alder (no. 637) – lived at 3 Long Barn Cottages. She was a little younger than Violet, having been born 13th February 1907. However, on 22nd June 1915, Winefred left the neighbourhood and transferred to Weston Road School, Southall. That proved to be a short-lived move as she was readmitted to G.P.G.S. on 18th January 1916 and stayed there until she too left on account of her age and went into Domestic Service but on 6th April 1921. Whether she and Violet were friends we do not know but it is likely that they would at least have known each other and may even have walked to and from school together, possibly with their Mums pushing younger siblings in prams.

A Berkshire shepherd

Although Violet's mother, "Annie" Barnes had been living in Long Barn Lane, Reading since 1912, she had been born Martha Ann Collins in Watchfield, Berkshire on 29th November 1879. Her father, Henry Collins, was a shepherd who had married Louisa Turner in 1867. Henry and Louisa had both been born in Childrey, Berkshire [Now Oxfordshire following reorganisation of local government from April 1974] as had their first four children – Henry, Mirah, William Thomas and John. The next two – Charles and George – were born in Harwell and their seventh – Martha Ann – was the only one born in Watchfield. The family was living at Stowell, Childrey in 1881, where Kate was born a year later (followed by Beatrice Mary in 1884 and Albert in 1888 – both in Sparsholt) so the layout of the 1879 map on the next page would have been familiar to them:

83

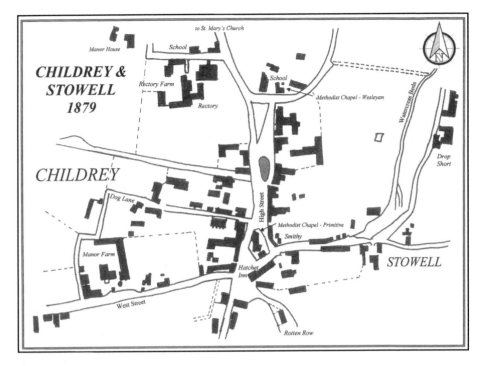

CHILDREY & STOWELL 1879

CHILDREY

STOWELL

Reeling off the names of their ten children brings to mind Daphne du Maurier's comment about her grandfather George (Kicky) on page 3 of her book "Gerald":

> The children were a great delight to him, appearing regularly every year like the lambs and the first snowdrops.

Hopefully those sentiments applied equally to Henry. Gerald was born 26th March 1873, so was of a similar age to Annie.

No doubt 10-year-old Mirah was delighted to have a sister after five brothers! It's possible that being only the second girl out of seven children was how Annie came to be named Martha Ann after her father's mother, Martha, with whom he was very close. Henry lost his father, Thomas, when he was only nine years old in August 1851, just after the census details shown opposite and, by the time of the 1861 census, he was living with his mother in very different circumstances to those in which they had lived prior to his father's death as we shall see later, but let's start by looking at Thomas' life.

84

Henry's father, Thomas Collins, had been born in Stanford-in-the-Vale, Berkshire and was baptised there on 22nd March 1789. When he married Martha Frogley on 16th December 1835, he was a widower and they both marked the Marriage Certificate with a cross, as he and Elizabeth Hicks had done on 10th August 1815. Two children from his first marriage: 25-year-old George (born 21st November 1815 and christened on the 27th) and 20-year-old Charles (actually born 31st March 1817 and christened on 12th April) were still living with him in Childrey in 1841 according to that year's Census returns, where he was described as a "Yeoman" [10], living at Warren Farm.

Martha (who had been born in Churchill, Oxfordshire in 1810 and christened there on 26th June) was only five years older than the elder of her two stepsons although both are recorded as being age 25 in the 1841 Childrey Census! She had in fact married when she was 25 and had three children of her own by 1841: five-year-old Elizabeth, William [christened 19th August 1838] and Martha [christened 19th July 1840]. Also in the household on the day of the 1841 census was Thomas' brother, John Collins [a 40-year-old agricultural labourer, who had been christened 14th September 1800 in Stanford] and two servants – 15-year-olds Charles Bush and Elizabeth Tripp.

The family was still living at Warren Farm when the 1851 Census was taken but, by then, Thomas was described as "a farmer with 253 acres employing 4 labourers". His age is again given as about 50 – the same age as a decade before! but the fact that he and Martha both seem to have been illiterate – we already know they signed their marriage certificate with a cross – may have meant that they were also not that interested in their ages either! [I recall that my grandmother (their granddaughter, Annie) only discovered her actual date of birth when she had to apply for her birth certificate much later in life – until then she had been celebrating two days early on 27th November!]

George (31), whose occupation is given as farmer's son, is the only offspring of Thomas' first marriage still living at Warren Farm as Charles (drill man agric.) had married Jane Parrott in 1847 and they had Mary Ann (2) and a baby, Richard Walter by 1851. Even Elizabeth, the first-born of Thomas' second marriage, had also left home, being already in service in Faringdon. However, Thomas and Martha (41)'s family had increased and Henry (8),

---

[10] a small landowner who farmed his own fields

Emma (6), Thomas (3) and Jane (1) had joined William (12) and Martha (10). This chart has incorporated Christening Records into the 1851 Census details:

Name	Age	Occupation	Birthplace	Birth date	Christening	Rel
Thomas	c50	Farmer of c 253 acres of	Stanford	1789	22Mar1789	H
Martha	41	land, emp 4 laborers	Churchill, Oxon	1810	26Jun1810	W
George	30	Farmer's son	Childrey	21Nov1815	27Nov1815	S
William	12	Chr 452	Childrey	1838	19Aug1838	S
Martha	10	Chr 489	Childrey	11Jun1840	19Jul1840	D
Henry	8	Chr 529	Childrey	1842	24Jul1842	S
Emma	6	Chr 593	Childrey	8Jul1845	3Aug1845	D
Thomas	3	Chr 637	Childrey	1847	10Oct1847	S
Jane	1	Chr 675	Childrey	1850	10Feb1850	D

To clarify connections between **Thomas and Martha** (née Frogley)'s family and their son **Henry and Louisa** (née Turner)'s family I have created this partial Family Tree leading to Barb's grandmother – **Martha Ann Collins**:

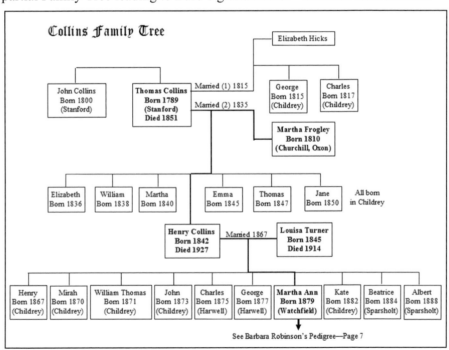

86

Thomas (62) died soon after that Census and was buried at Childrey on 21st August 1851, soon after Henry's 9th birthday. The family's lifestyle seems to have been reasonably comfortable before his death but the 1861 Census paints a rather different picture as only Henry is shown to be living with his 50-year-old widowed mother, Martha, who is described as an "agricultural labourer". Interestingly, Henry's age is given as 12 and his occupation as "shepherd boy", although the enumerator has ringed 12 and crossed through "boy"!

The discrepancy in Henry's age seems to have been rectified by the time of the 1871 Census, where it is shown as 28. He had married Louisa Turner in 1867 and she, aged 24, was termed an "agricultural labourer's wife". Their son, Harry (4), was a "scholar" and they also had a year-old daughter, Mirah. Henry's 61-year-old widowed mother was still living in Childrey but employed as a "farm servant" – what a contrast when 20 years earlier, she had two 15-year-old servants living in at Warren Farm with her and her family. By 1881, she was lodging with another widow of similar age to herself and no occupation – Sarah Herns, who was born in Letcomb Regis – just nine buildings away (three empty) from Henry and his family in Stowell, Childrey:

Name	Relation	Marital Status	Gender	Age	Birthplace	Occupation
Henry COLLINS	Head	M	Male	38	Childrey, Berkshire	Shepherd
Louisa COLLINS	Wife	M	Female	36	Childrey, Berkshire	Shepherds Wife
Henry	Son		Male	15	Childrey	Farm Servant
Mirah	Daur		Female	11	Childrey	Scholar
Thomas	Son		Male	9	Childrey	Scholar
John	Son		Male	8	Childrey	Scholar
Charles	Son		Male	5	Harwell	Scholar
George	Son		Male	3	Harwell	
Martha	Daur		Female	1	Watchfield	

Source Information – 1881 census:	
Dwelling	Stowell
Census Place	Childrey, Berkshire, England
Family History Library Film	1341313
Public Records Office Reference	RG11
Piece / Folio	1288 / 42
Page Number	16

87

Although Henry's family was living in Childrey where he and Louisa and their first four children had been born, a shepherd's life meant moving around. The births of their sons, Charles and George, at Harwell indicates that the family had been living there from 1874 – 1878 but by the time of Annie's birth, they were either living temporarily in Watchfield or her mother had been visiting someone there. Perhaps that job just hadn't worked out for Henry, which is why the family were back in Childrey by the time of the 1881 census. Their eighth child, Kate, was born there in 1882 and christened on 13th April. However, the family had moved to Sparsholt by the time their youngest daughter, Beatrice Mary, and youngest son, Albert, were born on 7th August 1884 and in the third quarter of 1887 respectively. None of the villages mentioned is very far from the other as can be seen on the following map of the west Berkshire Downs area. Sparsholt is barely a mile to the west of Childrey and there would have been many properties available for renting if no tied cottages were available:

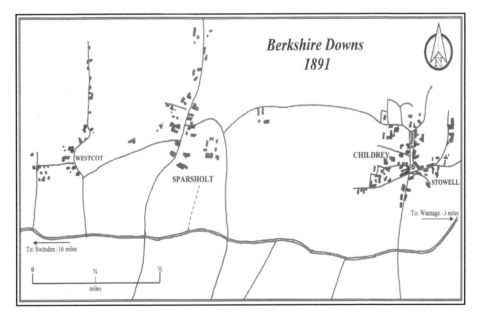

By 1901, Henry's occupation had been clarified from "shepherd" in 1881 and 1891 to "shepherd on farm". Initially after his marriage, he had been termed an "agricultural labourer" in the 1871 census, having been described contentiously as a "shepherd boy" in the 1861 census.

Henry's mother, Martha Collins, died, aged 75, in mid-1887 in Childrey. The births of Henry and Louisa's ten children show that the family had at least five house moves in around twenty years even if they were all within a small portion of west Berkshire so what was the life of a shepherd like in Berkshire from the time when Henry was first a shepherd boy in the 1950s until he became, and remained, a shepherd for the whole of his working life? After all, my father, Tom Taylor, was single when he was a shepherd in Chile and did not try to combine such a job with raising a family.

As a shepherd on the Berkshire Downs, spending his entire working life living within ten miles or so of East Ilsley, Henry would doubtless have attended the celebrated Sheep Fairs held there, as commemorated by the plaque shown here:

For over a thousand years, such Fairs were an integral part of English country life and the East Ilsley Sheep Fairs were a major attraction, being the second largest in Great Britain after London's Smithfield Market. In the 1880s, around 20,000 sheep changed hands there in a single day.

Countryside communities depended on such Fairs for survival as they were the only way that farmers could trade their produce and livestock on a large scale. As well as being very important economically, they were also important socially as they gave remote village communities opportunity to gather together in one place. Labourers could find work at Hiring Fairs, which were also called Mop or Statute Fairs. Those looking for work would come from far and wide, each wearing a symbol of their trade. As an example, a shepherd would wear a skein of wool pinned to his lapel, or a servant girl might carry a broom so that employers could see at a glance what their skills were. Fairs were also a rare opportunity for hard-working villagers to have fun and socialise, so there was plenty of music, dancing, food, drink and entertainment on offer.

The biggest Country Fairs were like a mixture of a Market, a Travelling Circus of music and entertainment, a Job Centre and a huge party. In Victorian England, they were massive events, with the biggest ones attracting crowds of up to 40,000 people. Such big crowds, all carrying money, provided rich pickings for thieves and it was said that the only way to hang on to your wallet was to sew it into the lining of your clothes. Fairs were a serious business for farmers, who would come to sell their produce. Anything from farm animals to cheese, meat, milk, hops and barley for making beer could be traded at the Fair. Other traders, selling wares such as cloth, jewellery, medicines, leather and household goods, would come from miles around.

The East Ilsley Sheep Fair continued throughout Henry's lifetime but ceased in 1934 only to be resurrected forty years later – in 1974 – as more of a village Fete held on the first Sunday in June from 12.30 to 4.30 p.m. in Pen Meadow, High Street, East Ilsley. To this day, Childrey remains a sheep-rearing area as the photograph on page 3 of the Colour Photo Insert shows. The sheep shown in the photo were grazing in the field next to St. Mary's Churchyard when Daphne and Jim visited the area in 2005.

In Berkshire, Henry would have found that there were less predators to be concerned about than my father would have encountered in Patagonia as the only wild animals that are a tangible threat to lambs here are the red fox and predatory birds, such as the Hooded Crow. However, *Wikipedia* states that domestic dogs are the biggest threat to adult sheep in the UK.

According to the British Wool Marketing Board, there are more than sixty breeds of sheep in Britain – more than in any other country. Their wool differs depending on where they live – whether it be on hills or lower land. They are kept in the UK primarily for their meat value and are easier to look after than many other farm animals as they eat grass and mostly live outdoors, protected from rain, snow and wind by their fleece.

British breeds produce mostly coarser quality wool which is ideally suited to products such as carpets, tweeds and knitting yarns. Selective breeding has eliminated the hair and kemp – a fibre unsuitable for dyeing – from the natural coat of the sheep.

I was rather more fortunate than Henry Collins as I did not lose my father until 9th May 1958, just after my 31st birthday. Here he is with Barbara and my mother in the 1950s.

While I was growing up, in the 1930s I recall that, on Good Friday each year, Dad would hire a car for thirty shillings as, of course, we did not own a car in those days. No one in Surrey Road did – posh Mr. Wren had a motorbike and sidecar but it was pushbikes for everyone else! There was no racing on Good Friday (or on Sundays) so that was why that day was chosen. Dad would hire the car and driver from Mr. Ives and off we'd go to the seaside. The car was of the wind-up variety – starting handle! – and petrol was 10d. a gallon (4p. in today's currency). Each year, he'd have me standing up in the back of the car to see how much I'd grown during the year and whether I could touch the roof.

Since I was an only child I had been able to take over Dad's book-making business completely. In fact, I carried on the agents and the 'phone business and then, when betting shops came about, I opened one at Elgar Road and had the legalised Betting Shop business, as well as my runners and 'phone business. That meant that I was quite busy and doing well. Looking back, those really were the "Good Old Days" before all the extra taxes came in and spoilt the betting business to a large degree. It was good in the old days, very good. We enjoyed it and I was bought up on it.

As he died in 1958, my father never saw betting shops. He was recorded as a "retired Commission Agent" of 43 Surrey Road on his death certificate. Like me, he had carcinoma of the prostrate but, at that time, there were less treatment options available so he eventually drifted into a coma. I had been able to stay with him in the Nursing Home at 85 Tilehurst Road and was with him when he passed away, aged 77. I was glad to have been with him then.

Unfortunately, when my Mum died just eight months later, I wasn't with her. She was only 65 when she died on 12th January 1959 and I was just 'phoned and told that she had gone. I would have liked to have had the opportunity to be with her when she left, but it didn't work out like that.

As you can imagine, 1958/9 was a very sad time for me, and Barbara was to

lose her parents within an even shorter time of each other less than ten years later.

But with all this looking back at Barb's ancestry, I've forgotten to tell you about the next generation. Our only son, Neville Thomas James, was born 11th November 1951 at his maternal grandparents' home. He was a great delight to us and to both sets of grandparents, as these holiday snaps taken at Bognor Regis Caravan Park show.

VII. JACKPOT 3rd Leg – Backstreet betting to legalised bookmaking

Neville grew quickly and Barb was soon to comment that he was nearly as tall as she was. Little did she know at that stage that he'd soon be head and shoulders taller than both of us!

The 1960s were to see many changes in the betting industry. The new Betting and Gaming Act aimed to do away with archaic, restrictive and often inconsistent laws on gambling and it was on 1st September 1960 that the Government gave the go-ahead for Betting Shops to open for business from 1st May the following year. From 1st January 1961, gambling for small sums was to be legal for games of skill such as Bridge, and Public Houses were to be allowed to introduce slot machines. As the Daily Telegraph newspaper's leader writer pointed out at the time:

> Weekly bridge clubs, meeting in the local hotel, will no longer have to settle up in the bus shelter

As you can imagine, Harold Macmillan's Conservative Government hoped that legalising Betting Shops would take gambling off the streets and so end the practice of bookmakers sending "runners" to collect from punters. Tough measures were enacted and anyone who wanted to place a legal bet on the horses had to demonstrate that they had enough credit to set up an account with a bookmaker and do all their dealings by telephone on credit. The Archbishop of Canterbury, Dr. Geoffrey Fisher, welcomed the move as a way of bringing the gambling habits of the country under greater Government control and, in fact, a large and respectable industry did grow out of that.

A timetable for the reforms was set out by the Home Secretary, Richard Austen (R.A.B.) Butler so, from October 1960, Licensing Committees were to be set up to consider applications from bookmakers from March 1961. Then, from 1st May, approved bookmakers were to be issued with licences and permits from the Racecourse Betting Control Board. Those would allow them to take bets at "tote odds", or totalizator, when the total amount staked – after tax and administrative costs are deducted – is divided among the winners.

93

Higher penalties for illegal street betting were to be introduced six months later so, naturally, I was keen to be one of the first to have a Betting Shop in Reading. My first was at 79 Elgar Road. Before I had it, it was a bread and cake shop, known as a corner shop, as it was at the end of a terrace of houses – a very usual design at the time before Supermarkets had developed. Mr. Marsh, a lovely man who owned Todds' Lino Shop in Mill Lane, let me have the shop and flat on a lease. Two local brothers had the shop initially but changed their minds about it so that was lucky for me.

I then applied to the Court for a licence. Colonel Angus was the Licensing Committee Secretary and the Magistrates took a lot of notice of him. Before they granted me a licence, the entire committee turned up at the shop, together with Colonel Angus. He needed to know where the blackboard, tills, writing desks, phones, and everything else was going. I explained it all to him and he appeared satisfied. At the next meeting, I was granted the betting office licence. That made me one of the first in Reading – along with Mr. Lusted, Mr. Sullivan and Dick Brunton. I then managed to get Rick Smith, a friend and shop-fitter, to turn the bakery into a Betting Shop for me and he proved very good at doing that.

My sister-in-law, Pat, who had married Roy Foster at Christ Church on 17th December 1960, came to work for me in the shop. Barbara and Daphne had been her bridal attendants along with Sandra West and Doreen Foster, with, from left: Daphne wearing lemon, Barb pink, Doreen blue and Sandra lilac.

94

Pat and Roy moved into the flat above the Betting Shop and that worked out very well all round. As there weren't many Betting Shops in those days, 79 Elgar Road used to be packed during racing and, in fact, it's been like that ever since. We were doing very well at that time because I still had my runners around Reading, also my phone business, as well as the Betting Shop. Incidentally, Barbara was the positive one who pushed me into purchasing 79 Elgar Road. We were in a pub at Three Mile Cross when she persuaded me to go ahead. Throughout our marriage she was very shrewd and wise over matters in life and she was a great help to me.

I had lots of adventures at 79 Elgar Road, to be sure. One of my phone customers used to phone up and have £50 x £50 and £50 win doubles. He used to like a drink – don't we all! He'd repeat this bet several times a day and phone up in the evening to see how he'd done. That was a lot of money in those early days!! At one period I had quite a few dog punters in who were very very shrewd indeed. They asked me for early prices and I would work out my odds then go out the front and up the steps to the board where the next dog sheet was displayed before early prices from Extel were shown. They watched me like hawks and if they thought I'd made a mistake, they would charge up to the counter to get their bets on – good old happy days to be sure. 79 Elgar Road was only a small shop but it was packed on Saturdays and you just could not move in there, very busy indeed.

I had John Rolt working for me part time at 79. He turned out to be one of the best Betting Shop managers and settlers in the business. He and his brother Alan were fantastic managers, who gave me 70 years service between them. You couldn't have found better managers in the country so, when John retired, I gave him Calcot Golf Club membership as Alan was already a member.

Betting Shops opened at a rate of a hundred a week throughout the country after 1st May 1961 and, by the end of that year, ten thousand had been set up so you can see why I changed from the betting system used by my father for 37 years to the new system. Through the years, we expanded to have a very nice group of Betting Shops in Reading and the South.

About a thousand casinos also opened in Britain in the first five years from 1961. Two more Gaming Acts – in 1963 and 1968 – introduced licences for other forms of gaming but loopholes in the law allowed almost anyone to open a casino and, as a result, many of them became a cover for criminal activity.

Ironically, Ladbrokes' boss, Cyril Stein, was slow to catch on to High Street shops, preferring to take punts from well-off clients who had legal phone accounts before the 1961 law change. However, in 1963, an executive persuaded him to open a shop in London's Oxford Street as a trial. When he saw how much cash had been made in one day, Cyril declared: "This is the future" and Ladbrokes opened shops across the land.

In the early 1960s, a guy, who seemed in a bad way, limped into my shop. We were busy at the time with agents, telephone calls and generally the shop was busy. He handed the staff at the counter a dog-eared printed card, which he asked them to give me. My cousin Jean was working with me at the time and said: "This poor man can hardly walk, Jack". The card read: "Yea though I have given my health and strength to my country in the war, I have no regrets, but if you can see your way clear to help me, I will be forever grateful". I said: "Give him a fiver". When the staff gave it to him, he touched his cap, said: "Thanks Guv", and trotted out without any limp at all!!

In the early days, we had absolutely no security – no cameras to record the bets being on time or late after the race. It was a very "hairy" time for bookmakers throughout the industry. The good thing about those times was that everything was very cheap – Extel for the commentary and results; rent; wages £7 0s. 0d. a week and so on – it was much better than today!

By 1964, I was ready for a second shop. My shop-fitter, Rick Smith, owned 120 Henley Road, Caversham and offered it to me for a Betting Shop. However, he then changed his mind and offered it to a rival bookmaker. It took my sister-in-law Pat, who lived in Elgar Road as did Rick, along with my wife Barbara, who knew him well, to persuade him to let me have the shop. When we went to court for a licence, H. & V. York, who had two shops in Lower Caversham, objected. Mr. John Kirk of F.S.P, my solicitors, managed to overcome their objections and I got the licence. Well done, Mr. Kirk!

Despite changing his mind about the sale, Rick Smith still shop-fitted 120 Henley Road for me and did a good job of it. Once again it was a very busy shop but, with no security at that stage, it was a bit difficult to control. Having cameras installed to record bets and times was a great help to me. The customers at 120 were very good to deal with – reasonably quiet and very fair in their dealings with us bookmakers.

120 Henley Road comprised two shops – a betting shop and a hardware shop – with a flat above the two and, eventually, I managed to purchase the freehold. (Hooray!) As time went by, I built a double-storey office with a kitchen sink unit, toilet and so forth at the perimeter of my land which was helpful to my maintenance man-cum-builder, Brian Norman, who used the building as his base and stores. His wife, Sue had worked for me from the mid-1970s at 120 and, a couple of years later, when televisions were first allowed in Betting Shops, Brian installed them in each shop for me as he is a qualified electrician. My shop in Coronation Square was the first one in the town to have televisions as they were allowed in Theale but not in Reading. I had doubled the size of the 120 Henley Road Shop and refurbished it to a high standard, which was very helpful to me. Now though the hardware shop is a sandwich bar selling bread, cakes and hot pies. Brian, who worked for me for 35 years until I sold the shops in 2010, managed to find another job – not easy when you're 63. He's standing behind me in the photo of the opening of my last betting shop on page 13 of the Colour Photo Insert.

But I'm racing ahead as my third shop was at 542 Northumberland Avenue (where the Avenue joins Whitley Wood Road). Eric, who worked for Mr. Lambeth, the owner of the newsagents and adjoining garage building, told me that the garage unit was available to let as a Betting Office so I visited Mr. Lambeth and agreed a deal with him. I then had to obtain planning permission, which was not easy as, although the Planning Officer at the time was ok, he thought I was "spreading my wings" a bit too soon. However he was a nice guy and, in the end, he gave me the necessary permission.

Applying for a Betting Office licence caused further problems. At that time, I belonged to the Reading Bookmakers' Association, which met annually (or more often if necessary) at the Southcote Hotel. We had a very long table there, which seated approximately forty of us with the Chairman, Bert Eatwell, at the top end with his Secretary, John Horwood. Someone had asked the Association to object to my application, so Bert had to go into the witness box on their behalf and oppose it. However, when the Chairman of the Licensing Bench asked him for his personal opinion of the application, Bert threw his arms out wide and in a loud voice said: "Your honour, I think it's a perfect position for a Betting Shop". The Licence was duly granted and I can remember the first day there as John Rolt was on holiday and my cousin Jean phoned to say: "Please send me help. I just can't cope." Amazingly, it still remains the best Betting Shop in that area. What a great guy Bert was!!! He had a Betting Shop in Oxford Road, Reading almost opposite the then Battle Hospital (no longer there, it has been replaced by a development of houses and flats and also a Tesco Store with petrol pumps).

Another bookmaker who was a great help to me in the early days of Betting Shops was Derek Adey. He was an on-the-course bookmaker with a credit business and he always allowed me to bet with no limit after explaining the pitfalls and how it had been with agents before shops were legalised. Derek was also a low-handicap golfer at Calcot Park where I was a member and he was very supportive there as well.

It was interesting how we acquired our Betting Shop at No. 32 Coronation Square on the Southcote Estate at Reading. Originally the local Library until the Council built a new one, it was offered to potential clients to submit sealed bids. The Council, through the local newspaper, had asked for bids for the rent to be submitted to them. Barbara convinced me that I should offer  twice the normal rent, which I did. We were the highest bidders and that is how we were successful in acquiring that unit. This modern photograph shows that shop in its post-Taylor's Racing Service livery.

My next shop, at 7 Meadway Precinct, Tilehurst, was not far from Coronation Square. It was already a Betting Shop owned by Mr. John Pegly, a most influential man at that time. He was very energetic and attended parades in London to demonstrate against the unfair taxes on bookmakers – he did work hard. For some time, I tried to persuade him to let me have the shop and eventually I did manage to buy it from him.

Before Betting Shops started in 1961, the system was so much better. We had runners all around Reading and bets were collected on a daily basis. At night, they were settled by the family – Tom, Barbara and myself – and the punters were paid out the following day. At dinner time, our house was full of punters and customers putting their bets on – those were good times. Things were better then for bookies because overheads were so much lower than they are today. When we opened the shops, we had a service called Extel which supplied oral commentaries and gave betting shows and results. The cost was minimal compared to today's charges – you could pay for Extel from your petty cash. There was only one drawback with Extel installations and that was "the man with the hammer". If you wanted an extra speaker fitted, this man came round and would attack the wall with his hammer, usually just after you had recently redecorated – happy days!!

However, betting shops in 1961 had to have blacked-out windows, no publicity outside and spartan facilities inside, much as this shot of the interior of our 178 Oxford Road shop shows:

In more recent times, television pictures were introduced to Betting Shops by Satellite Information Services (S.I.S.), so that was the end of Extel. Naturally, S.I.S. proved to be a more expensive service! In later years, TURF T.V. came on the scene. This was an additional service which took over the best of the race tracks in the country by out-bidding S.I.S. for them. In order to compete, we had to take not just one service but two, which put up our costs even more. Our fight became not against punters but against expenses – a very difficult time.

However, by the late 1960s, I knew that I was on a winning formula with the betting shops and it was about that time that Barb began buying greyhounds. Her first purchase was a dog called *Peter's Magic*, which she bought at the sales at Hackney Wick Stadium. She had him with John Sherry, a dog trainer at Reading. I'll never forget the day *Peter's Magic* won at 20 – 1. Mr. Sherry (an Irishman) came up to Barbara, doffed his trilby hat and said: "Mrs Taylor, nobody was more surprised than me with the race". I sometimes wonder!

Her second greyhound was *Saskatchuan*, an excellent dog who was always winning by a good distance at halfway and then we had to pray he could hang

on 'til the finish. In the end, it was discovered that he had a "dicky" heart and that was the reason for his strange running pattern.

Pat Witchels (second left), who worked for Mr. Sherry, looking after the dogs, became a good friend to Barbara and myself. We had other greyhounds with Mr. Sherry but stopped greyhound racing for a while when he finished training. However, we started up again later with Bob Gilling (far left). He owns Ryehurst Kennels at Binfield and was appointed secretary of the Greyhound Breeders Forum in 1973. He remained a Director of the former British Greyhound Racing Board (B.G.R.B.) until its replacement with the Greyhound Board of Great Britain (G.B.G.B.) on 1st January 2009, but is still secretary of the Greyhound Breeders' Forum.

Here is a list of Barbara's greyhounds with as much information as possible about them. "Brindle" is sometimes described as "tiger-striped" although the brindle pattern is more subtle than that of a tiger. The streaks of colour are usually darker than the base coat which is often tawny or grey. The last eight greyhounds in the list were all bred by Barb from the same litter – the offspring of *Trade Exchange* and *Miss Sophie* – so are denoted with * here:

Barbara's Greyhounds	Sex	Coat Colour	Date Born	Races	1st	2nd
Peter's Magic	M		1968/69			
Saskatchewan	M		1968/69			
Bright Boy	M		Jan. 1980		17	
Marine Damsel	F		July 1980		7	
Ryehurst Tango			Nov. 1980		18	
Muskerry Lana	F	Black	1987		2	
Walkers Hill	M	Fawn	July 1990		7	
Ryehurst Silk	F	Black/White	April 1991		4	
Ryehurst Rapture	F	Black/White	April 1991			
Drive On Boy	M	Brindle	Nov. 1991		12	
Trade Exchange	M	Brindle	Nov. 1992	1	1	
Ploverfield Ace	M	Black/White	May 1993		13	
Miss Sophie	F	White/Brindle	Sept. 1994	44	14	4
April Daisy	F	Fawn/White	April 1996	84	15	13
Princess Tahnee	F	Black/White	April 1996	74	13	11
Tian Shan	F	Brindle	Aug. 1996	96	17	19
Xenas Gold *	F	Brindle	Oct. 1999	91	16	19
Exchange Express *	M	Brindle	Oct. 1999	119	21	15
Flight Command *	M	Brindle	Oct. 1999	30	8	4
Inspired *	M	Brindle	Oct. 1999	89	16	11
This Is Krystal *	F	Brindle	Oct. 1999	22	6	6
I'm Chantell *	F	Brindle	Oct. 1999	60	8	5
Sultan Prince *	M	Brindle	Oct. 1999	18	4	2
Stock Exchange *	M	Brindle	Oct. 1999	111	19	12

Four family funerals within a year

Barbara's maternal grandfather, Albert Barnes, died in Battle Hospital on 18th April 1967, having been in Ipsden Ward there since early March. He had been a widower since 1960, when Annie died on Valentine's Day. This photo shows them during their Golden Wedding celebrations on 7th January 1955. By that time, he had been retired for five years, having previously worked for G. R. Jackson Ltd. of Oxford Road for 42 years.

Bert's funeral service was held at Whitley Hall Methodist Church at 2.30 p.m. on 24th April followed at Henley Road Crematorium by cremation then everyone returned to Ted and Rose's house – 232 Basingstoke Road – where many of the arrangements had been agreed with Violet and Jim, Wilf and Les, who had all called in several times between their father's death and funeral. He had continued to live across the road from 232 at their family home – 10 Long Barn Lane, having many of his meals with them after Annie's death or having them taken across to him.

1967 was to prove a trying year for Barb as both her parents were also in poor health. Her mother's breast cancer had spread and she died of a brain tumour at her home – 34 Linden Road – on 8th September. She had seemed a little better the evening before when Ted and Daphne visited with Wilf, Doris, Fred and Ethel. The first two had walked there but Wilf gave them a lift home. On the 3rd, when Rose and Daphne had visited her in the afternoon, she hadn't recognised them.

Daphne's brother, Alan, who had been working in a warehouse in Toronto, Canada during his long vacation from Manchester University, arrived back in England on 13th September just in time to attend his Auntie Violet's funeral service at 2 p.m. at Christ Church and 2.40 p.m. at Henley Road Cemetery that day. He had been away for three months, having flown to New York from Heathrow on 19th June. However, he'd left himself time to spend some of the money he had earned when he left Toronto on 18th August and travelled round America by Greyhound buses, which he used as hotels, sleeping on them. Alan trained to be a Civil Engineer and, like me, ended up running his own business – Alan Barnes Consulting Engineers of Swallowfield.

The Pekinese dog pictured here with Violet died of old age at "High Thatch" following her death. I had bought Ching for her from a doctor who lived off Tilehurst Road, Southcote. He had come running up to me when I visited so I gave him to her for a Christmas present.

Barb's father was being treated for heart trouble while nursing Violet and was taken into Sidmouth Ward in the Royal Berkshire Hospital on 9th October, just a month after her death. He died there on 21st, when a nurse couldn't feel a pulse while doing a routine check. When Ted and Daphne had visited him in that ward on Friday 13th October, his sisters and brothers – Rose, Beat, Bill and the youngest, Bert (born 1922 so just 7 years older than Barbara) – were all there too. Like Vie's, Jim's funeral was held at Christ Church followed by 3 p.m. at Henley Road Cemetery. I had given Ted, Daphne and Alan a lift from Linden Road and, as we crossed Duke Street Bridge, Daphne spotted her head-teacher at St. Crispin's School, Wokingham – Eric Bancroft. She had felt embarrassed at having to ask him for time off for the third funeral in six months, having only started teaching there in September 1966. However, he had been most sympathetic as he had had a similar occurrence within his own family.

Uncle Wilf gave Daphne and Alan a lift back to 232 Basingstoke Road

afterwards. Many family members had observed that Jim had died of a broken heart – not wishing to live without his beloved wife by his side. The photo shows them in happier times on holiday.

Violet's brother, Wilf, had had to go out of the bedroom while visiting her and admitted to Rose, Eddie and Daphne that he didn't think that he'd make old bones. Sure enough, he died suddenly not long afterwards. While riding his bicycle, he suffered a heart attack and, even though it happened close to the Royal Berkshire Hospital, he died before reaching there.

It was around the time of those family bereavements, when I was about 40, that I started running. I ran three London marathons, really enjoying every footstep of the entire event – it's fantastic. I also ran lots of half marathons through the years. Unfortunately, I recently had to have my knees replaced – the right one in February 2005 – so had to stop running. I suppose I wore them out with too much running but I really enjoyed the London Marathons. You can see photos of me competing in the 1993 London Marathon and in a Reading Half Marathon on page 4 of the Colour Photo Insert.

We all used to help each other out on the way round and at other times. As an example, one of the trainers I had at the Butts Shopping Centre gym in Oxford Road near Broad Street (now called the Broad Street Mall), suggested that it would be better if I did three miles steady and one mile fast. I followed his advice in a half marathon and did a wonderful time so I tried it again for the London Marathon – three miles steady and one mile fast. I was ok for about twenty miles then my legs stopped working. I had to join the queue for the First Aid lady. When she said: "Where does it hurt, Dear?", I didn't answer so she supplied her own answer: "It hurts everywhere doesn't it, Dear?" I nodded, so she gave me the painkilling spray all over then said: "What are you going to do now?" When I said: "I'm going to finish it", she replied: "You are brave, my Dear!" I managed to jog along the last six miles and finish. In fact, I always finished the London event, whatever happened.

It used to be that when you got to the other side of London Bridge and went through the tape, your medal was put on you and you had this fantastic feeling – it was great! On one of the early occasions, when I was given my silver space blanket and my bag of goodies, my grandson Craig (who was very young at the time) took them both, so that was that – I lost them, he had them!

VIII. JACKPOT 4th Leg – Moving on

In 1970, a new Gaming Act put far greater restrictions on all gaming, including bingo and slot machines, which were then subject to licence and placed under the control of the Gaming Board which answered directly to the Home Office. Gambling had become a major industry worth billions.

I soon had 90 people working for me. That proved a turning point and, as I was doing so well, I started a private pension scheme with Dentons for my family.

Barbara and I had lived at "Byways", Grovelands Road, Spencers Wood since 1950. My father had had that built and rented it out, along with the house next door, prior to our marriage. We were very happy there but, in the 1970s, we had started to look at other properties. One that we went to see was a modern style house with a balcony near Pangbourne, but Barbara would not buy it as she feared that the cats might fall off the balcony into the swimming pool.

A house at Chalkhouse Green called "High Thatch" came up for auction so I decided to go along to the Auction to attempt to buy it. I can remember being in the kitchen at "Byways" and Barb saying: "You'll never get it, you won't

get it." The Auction took place at The Great Western Hotel near Reading Station under the auctioneer, Dickie Vanderpump, who was there with his Secretary, Joy Cuthbertson. She later agreed to work for me when he packed up and in fact continued doing so for 35 years or more.

As we were going upstairs in the hotel, I looked around. Everyone seemed to have a copy of the brochure for "High Thatch" and I thought: "I've got no chance here!" When the bidding for "High Thatch" started, everyone was seated. There was a guy behind me with his wife and kids and, when I bid twenty five grand [£25,000] say, I could hear him saying at the back "dib, dib, dib, whisper, whisper" and then he'd put in another bid. I decided that the only way to knock him out was to put my bid in the second he'd put one in so the bidding was with him all the time. As a result, as soon as he went: "twenty six", I went: "twenty seven". He went: "twenty eight", so I retaliated with "twenty nine". To his "thirty", I went: "thirty two". At that, he packed up and I think I knocked it out for thirty two grand.

In the early 1970s, Barb and I moved to "High Thatch". It was quite a nice property set in two acres of land with various outbuildings. Inside there were four bedrooms, a lounge, dining room, study and large kitchen. I was lucky to buy when I did – not only "High Thatch" but also two properties in Oxford Road. I managed to buy the freehold of a Chemist's shop at no. 180 for . . . wait for it, six grand . . . when the Chemist died! I had previously bought the Betting Shop at No. 178 Oxford Road from my good friend George Salter who had it on a lease. I later purchased the freehold for £10,000 from the guy who owned the Dolls' Hospital in St. Mary's Butts. That meant that I bought the two properties for sixteen

106

grand, made one big Betting Shop of them and it became quite successful. Properties were a lot cheaper in those days!

I've made it sound as if "High Thatch" was ready for us to move into straight-away but that was not the case. It needed redecorating from top to bottom and Brian Launchbury, a great friend, who also worked for me, helped me achieve that. Brian was a great help throughout the years as well as being a very good friend and, now that he's gone, I miss him very much. We redecorated every inch of the big place before Barbara moved from Spencers Wood. There was a lot needed doing, especially to the thatched roof, because the birds had pecked through it into the loft and there were heaps of droppings in there but Brian and I did a good job.

When we first moved to "High Thatch", Barbara was most upset at the amount of shooting that seemed to be happening in Dyson's Wood, which was just across the lane at the bottom of our garden. For a view of Dyson's Wood from the back of "High Thatch", see page 4 of the Colour Photo Insert. Being an animal lover, she was determined that the shooting of the wildlife should stop and, when the four sections of Dyson's Wood came up for auction in 1984, she managed to buy all twenty acres. Sealed bids were requested and she was very cute with them. As a result of buying all four sections of Dyson's Wood, we were able to turn it into an Animal Sanctuary so that no-one could shoot the badgers, deer, foxes and other animals that are there. We discovered that the badger sett in Dyson's Wood was 100 years old when we moved to "High Thatch" so, in 2012, it's quite a bit older than that! I'm obviously concerned about the proposal to cull badgers because of the risk of the transmission of bovine tuberculosis (T.B.) and hope that nothing naughty is to be done against them.

We've obviously had our problems over the years with those who do not share Barb's and my views on animals. As you can imagine, after we made Dyson's Wood into an Animal Sanctuary and the animals could not be shot, the rabbits were coming out of the Wood at night and eating the crops on the land belonging to Cane End Farm, which adjoined it, sort of "Up your's! You can't shoot us, we're in a Sanctuary". I therefore received a letter which I forwarded to my Solicitor, John Kirk. His reply to the complainant included: "I think it's very novel you saying that they are the Taylor's rabbits as, strictly speaking, they are wild rabbits." Eventually, the Ministry of Agriculture and

107

Fish came along and said that I really ought to put my fence down a foot below ground to restrict the rabbits accessing the Farm. They said that that would mean erecting badger flaps in it, as it's not legal to restrict badgers. However, before the badger flaps could be inserted, we found that the badgers had dug through all the stones and rocks and all the rest of it and made their own routes under the wire so we didn't need to provide badger flaps for them after all. Badgers are very strong animals – very strong indeed. Dyson's Wood continues to be an Animal Sanctuary to this day.

One instance of hard times in the Betting Industry was experienced during 1974 when a 3-Day Week was introduced by the Conservative Government as one of several measures to conserve electricity. Its production had been severely limited by industrial action on the part of coal miners. From 1st January until 7th March 1974, commercial users of electricity were limited to three specified consecutive days' consumption each week and prohibited from working longer hours on those days. Services deemed essential (e.g. hospitals, supermarkets and newspaper prints) were exempt and television companies were required to cease broadcasting at 10.30 p.m. during the crisis to conserve electricity. On the three days when we were not allowed to use electricity in the shops, we used car batteries to give the race commentaries, gas lamps for lighting and calor gas heaters to warm up the shops.

OK, so everyone in Britain was affected by the 3-Day Week but there were some things that just happened to bookies. To confirm that bets had not been placed after racing had started, clock bags were used. These were leather bags which, when closed, set the time on a clock. A fellow bookmaker had a runner at the greyhound meetings and the bets in his clock bag were very often big winners. The bookmaker was so worried about these big wins that he had developed leg ulcers. Eventually he discovered that the clock was a 12 hour clock and the runner was closing it at seven o'clock in the morning after the dog meeting, not seven o'clock in the evening before racing started! What a simple crooked deal that was!

Soon after moving to "High Thatch", I took up horse riding. It must have been around 1975 and the horse's name was *Bellamy* – good old *Bellamy*! I had ridden before at Palmers' Riding Stables so knew the basics of riding but Heather Rolinson, the farmer's daughter, taught me how to jump fences. I could then complete the cross country event at the Black Horse, jumping all

108

the fences, 'though I never achieved a 1st or 2nd place in it. We used to race flat out across the open fields, which are now Caversham Heath Golf Course. Leaning forward and hanging onto the mane of old *Bellamy*, all I could hear was the wind whistling through my ears. I really enjoyed horse riding, even 'though I fell off a lot, and continued until I had my new knees fitted in 2000.

Another sport I enjoy is golf and I've played a lot in both Ireland and Scotland as well as nearer home. However, I particularly enjoyed playing on the Dunes Golf Course in Las Vegas in the 1980s when you were called to the first tee as if you were a professional. It was rather special to hear your name being announced over the loudspeaker. I recall that, after Uncle Les' funeral on 30th April 1982, Barb and I paid the deposit for us two, Neville, Lyn and Craig, to visit Las Vegas the following September. While there, Neville and I partnered a croupier and a bouncer from the casinos. The latter got quite angry when the guys behind us fired too close. They even fired some of their balls onto our green whilst we were putting about a third of the way round. The bouncer fired one off the green announcing: "I've got rid of that one!" However, they fired some more and then got in their buggy and went roaring back the wrong way. Neville and I followed until Neville said: "Why are we going this way?" When I replied that the bouncer was going back to give them a good hiding, Neville instantly turned back and went the way we should have gone! That was a bit hairy in Vegas! Here's me teeing off in Portugal:

Neville and I were members of Calcot Golf Course as were my managers. During the 1980s until 1997, we were in a society in Reading – The Curzon

Club. Each year Neville and I used to win the Curzon Club "Pairs Competition" and I've still got the prizes we won in my cabinet at home. We also played once a year against our Bank Manager and Accountant – sometimes at Calcot and some-times at their course. They were good times which we enjoyed very much.

I have been able to enjoy both those activities because I gave up smoking when I was 45 and this is how it happened. I had to go into hospital for an operation. Neville drove me there and, as I got out of the car, I stubbed out the cigarette I'd been smoking. As I walked into the hospital everything seemed white except for the great big lady, dressed all in black, who was obviously the matron. She said: "You can smoke if you want to" but I looked around and thought: "I don't want to smoke here". When my anaesthetist came in and said: "You're a smoker, are you?", I said: "Yes". "How many do you smoke? 60 a day?", he asked. I was actually smoking 20 a day and thought: "I don't know, I don't need this".

I had smoked from the age of 12 but that was the last cigarette I ever smoked! When I came out of hospital, I went to the Smoker's Forum, off the Kings Road. It was a Council affair and, each Monday, when my family went to see the Speedway, they dropped me off there. The technique was to hypnotise us, showing nasty films of operations and, each time we attended, we had to blow into a machine to see if our lungs were getting stronger. The group was a great help to me. When you first joined, you had to sit in a big circle and tell them your name and why you were there. Everybody had to do that as we were all in the same boat, all trying to stop smoking. I am convinced that part of the reason I am still alive today is that I have not smoked a cigarette between the ages of 45 and 84. Of course, when I first started smoking, nobody realised there was anything wrong with it. I remember my Uncle Arthur who saw me smoking just as I was going in the Army saying: "Well, if you don't do anything worse than that, you won't come to any harm", because smoking wasn't considered a bad thing in those days.

Barbara's Racehorses and the fun we had with them

In the early seventies, Barbara had begun to take an interest in racehorses. Around the time of our Silver Wedding in 1975, she and I went to a Jumps Meeting somewhere down South [Fontwell Park]. There was a "selling race" on 18th November and a horse named *Comic* won. I asked if she wanted to

buy that horse but she preferred another in the same race – *Hello Sailor*. Johnnie Haine, who had been a very good Jumps Jockey, was the trainer of that horse so we found him at the racecourse and asked what the chances were of buying *Hello Sailor* (pictured here on that occasion in the previous owner's colours and below in Barbara's colours). He said he would ask the owner, who lived in Devon.

A. Davies agreed to sell *Hello Sailor* to me on 3rd December 1975 so he first raced in Barbara's colours on 12th January 1976 at Windsor and that was the start of

Barbara's outstanding career as a Racehorse Owner, even though he only finished 11th out of 14 runners on that occasion.

A Splendid Month – September 1979

Johnnie became a very close friend of ours from then on. He had a yearling called *Jenny Splendid*, which he had been trying to sell to Barb for a thousand pounds. Then, one night when I was alone in the house, the telephone rang at about 3.00 a.m. I jumped out of bed to answer it. It was Johnnie! "What about this little filly?", he said. I replied: "Go on John – we'll have her". What a marvellous decision that proved to be in 1976, as *Jenny Splendid* went on to win lots of races for Barb, so how's that for luck!

Jenny Splendid's first race under Barb's colours on 14th June 1976 at Nottingham in the five-furlongs *Plumtree Maiden Stakes* gave no indication of her future success as she finished 7th with the comment:

> "Jenny Splendid never troubled leaders"!

However, less than a month later, *Jenny Splendid* achieved her first win and the photo on page 5 of the Colour Photo Insert shows Barbara congratulating her. In her usual modest way, Barb had written on the back of the photograph: 'This is "Jenny" after one of her wins at Doncaster with "me" and the boy who leads her round the Paddock.'

Us bookies were naturally happy with this success as she came in at 20 – 1. The 8th July 1976 *Doncaster Report* of Johnnie's first success as a Flat trainer stated:

> Jump jockey Johnny Haine had his first success as a Flat trainer when Jenny Splendid made all and trotted up by five lengths from Jane's Girl in the Huddersfield Maiden Auction Stakes.
> Jenny Splendid, who cost 580 guineas at the Newmarket Sales, provided Mrs Barbara Taylor, wife of a Reading bookmaker, with her first success as an owner.
> Said Haine, who plans to continue as a jump jockey, "This is only my third runner on the Flat and it is great getting off the mark for the season in your first year as a trainer. I only have a handful of horses on the Flat, and I bought Jenny Splendid with jumping in mind."

Jenny Splendid won again on 2nd August at Wolverhampton in the *Bradmore Nursery Handicap Stakes* where the photo-finish opposite shows her just ahead of *Armelle*:

That was followed by a second place at York a month later; a third at Leicester on 20th September; and her third win was at Nottingham on 28th as described here:

> Jenny Splendid toyed with the opposition and made a mockery of her handicap mark.
> Ives settled the filly in the early stages before taking the John Splendid filly to the front with over three furlongs to go and Jenny Splendid stormed clear to beat runner-up Sequioa by eight lengths.
> Jenny Splendid relished the easier underfoot conditions and I remember her sire winning the Ayr Gold Cup on soft going in 1967.
> John Haine trains Jenny Splendid at Hardwicke for Mrs Barbara Taylor.
> The former National Hunt Jockey apparently went to Newmarket last year to purchase a jumper and came back with Jenny Splendid, who cost 500gns, and White Tower who ran at Goodwood yesterday.

Jenny Splendid rounded off the 1976 season with a first at Newmarket on 15th October and a third at the same course two weeks later (30th), having achieved four wins, a second and two third places out of her first nine races under Barbara's colours. During the 1977 Flat Racing season, she had eleven outings and continued her winning ways at Salisbury (23rd June) – see Page 5 of Colour Photo Insert; Newmarket (6th July) and York (8th October). In 1978, she took part in just five events, producing three thirds, a second and finally a win on 30th October at Newmarket.

Barb's Uncle Ted and his daughter, Daphne Barnes, were to see the first of those events when *Jenny Splendid* finished third in the 4 p.m. *Brightwalton Stakes* at Newbury Races on 15th July 1978. Morlands Brewery, for which Ted had worked for 47 years until it closed its operations in Queens Road, Reading in 1970 to concentrate on its Abingdon site, sponsored the *Morlands Brewery Trophy* race annually. Past and present employees could apply for two complimentary tickets each per year [tickets for Tatersall's enclosure were £3 then, having been just 25 shillings 11 years earlier on 22nd July 1967] and sometimes it was possible to obtain further tickets. Thus it was that, on that occasion, Jim Phillips [who had been going out with Daphne since February 1977] drove the two of them plus Ted's friend from schooldays, Len Seymour and his wife Gladys to the event then onto a meal; a walk around Abingdon, enjoying the river, Abbey and converted gaol; and finally the *Spread Eagle* at East Hagbourne, which was still being run by Mollie & Ben.

Ted had seen in that morning's paper that *Jenny Splendid* was in the 4 p.m. *Brightwalton Stakes* so naturally Daphne thought it would be a good opportunity to film her performance with her cine camera. Consequently, they were most disappointed, after filming *Jenny Splendid* being exercised, to realise that we were not there with the other owners and also in the winners' enclosure when the horse finished third. Ted had backed the winners on the first and last races at that meeting so had finished about evens.

You can tell how good *Jenny Splendid* was if I tell you that she went to Cagnes-sur-Mer on the Cote d'Azur in the South of France in February 1979, all expenses paid – transport, entry, everything – because she was a good horse and they wanted her down there. By then, she was recorded as having had seven wins, a second and a third. However, such results may not always be what they seem as that sheet showed Jenny winning on 28th September 1976 at Ascot but there was no race meeting there that day because she was actually winning at Nottingham!

Neville, Peter and myself drove down in Neville's BMW. We stayed at auberges on the way – that's bed and breakfast in a French residence. We saw the race and had a fantastic time there. Unfortunately the horse didn't win but she did make the places and we came back home in the same manner. As I say, it was an all-expenses paid holiday for *Jenny* – that's getting her down there, bringing her home, entering the race, everything! It was all paid for by Cagnes-sur-Mer racecourse. That was a great time and those auberges, although they didn't look very great when we moved in, when the table was laid for meals, the food was fantastic. It was a great experience.

Her first race there was on 13th February when she finished 13th then, on 27th, she improved to 12th. However, she was back to form for her third race on 6th March when she finished 4th. Polizzi was the jockey for the first and third races while Young had ridden her for the middle event. Having to spend time in quarantine on her return from all that travelling, *Jenny Splendid* didn't race again until September 1979 but her four races during twenty days that month could be considered the pinnacle of her career as she achieved three wins and a second place, thus making her Barbara's best-performing horse ever. The events were: Haydock Park on the 8th; Salisbury on the 13th and Ayr on the 22nd then her last race was recorded in *Racing Post*:

ASCOT – 29th September, 1979
3.5 CAVENDISH CAPE SOUTH AFRICAN SHERRY HANDICAP STAKES of £14,260; 1st £9,169 2nd £2, 752 3rd £1,326 4th £613 rated 35 plus. Edward Cavendish and Sons Ltd gave £10,000. Seven furlongs.

1st **HOUSE GUARD**, ch c Home Guard – Botany Bess, by Right Royal V
(K Sasi), 4 – 9 – 8   ...L Piggott   1   (10)
2nd **JENNY SPLENDID**, br m John Splendid – Gay Maria
(Mrs. B. Taylor), 5 – 7 – 13 (6lb ex)   ...R. Fox   2   (2)

14 RAN, Off 3.10

Betting: while *Jenny Splendid* fluctuated from 7 – 1 to 10 – 1 before ending form at 9 – 1.
Closeup: 2. *Jenny Splendid* led, drifted right last two furlongs, caught near line.

By the time of that last race at Ascot on 29th September, she had competed in 28 events, being placed in 18 of them – ten firsts, two seconds and six thirds. As you can see, it was only the performance of Britain's top jockey, Lester Piggott, on *House Guard* that prevented her from rounding off her career with four wins out of four events.

115

After such a successful racing career, Barbara decided to breed from *Jenny Splendid* and, as a result, she produced *Shelly Marie* (1982, sired by *Gunner B*), *Shari Louise* (1983, sired by *Radetzky*), *Samantha Josephine* (1986, sired by *Vaigly Great*) and *Seto City* (1989, sired by *Lidhame*). All of those subsequently raced under Barbara's colours. However, one of her progeny, *Jenny's Call* (1988, sired by *Petong*), which only seems to have raced once on 5th October 1990 (under Lady Harrison's colours) when she finished 7th out of 10, did produce *Jenny*'s granddaughter, *Shannon's Dream* (1996, sired by *Anshan*).

We had lots of fun and really great times with Johnnie Haine whilst he was a trainer and, afterwards, he still helped us with the horses. He looked after them when they were not in training and also those that had finished racing altogether. He also helped us buy in stock. Barbara had several other trainers after he finished, including Matt McCourt, Graham McCourt, Richard Hanson, Rex Carter, Jackie Retter and Stan Mellor.

Stan was the first jockey to ride a thousand winners and we were honoured to have a copy of his book, which lists them all. I remember being with him at Brighton in the early 1970s before the Arabs became really involved in horseracing. One of the horses being led around the parade ring had a u-shaped c area which was bent. I commented: "That horse doesn't look good", and Stan replied: "I know. The Arabs have just paid £700,000 or so for it and I wouldn't give £75". It had a big jockey with muscular shoulders on its back and I observed: "He looks a bit overweight for that poor horse". Stan told me that he was the sheik's main bodyguard and was being given the ride as a present. Now that was the way some nationalities worked in the early days but they obviously learned their lessons as the years went by and now they are top people in horse-racing, having done ever so well. However, in those days it was a different world – when a horse they'd paid a lot of money for could be given to the sheik's bodyguard as a present. What a scenario!

Barb's third horse was *Lok Yee*, whom we bought through Rex Carter. That horse's owner, who lived just up the road from Rex, used to say that he was scraping a living from 250 acres! Rex and his wife (who had played tennis at Wimbledon) lived on the East Coast on a 1,000-acre estate, the house being approached by a half-mile drive. Their son looked after a further 1,000 acres thus making a total of 2,000 acres in their ownership. Rex trained for multi-millionaire (£100 million in 2005) Peter Greenall of Peter Greenall Breweries, who was also company director of the De Vere Hotel chain and a former high sheriff of Cheshire. Despite that, Peter was a champion amateur rider, who used to ride for Barbara.

We would be plied with drinks when we visited the Carters and Barb, who was a teetotaller throughout her life, drank half of my drink so that I wouldn't be drunk while driving home. *Lok Yee* buggered his leg up so wasn't able to better his initial potential of a first and a third in his first five races from February to September 1978. Rex used to make his own all-weather gallops and Barb also bought her fourth horse from him. *Gerards Cross* achieved three third places between 30th September and 27th October 'though Rex used to comment that when he was hit, he'd stop.

Having retired from being a public trainer in 1987, Rex died at the age of 85 in 2001. Based first near Norwich then close to Swaffham in Norfolk, he rode point-to-point winners both before and after World War II and took out a permit to train in 1948. His obituary in the *Racing Post* of 30th April 2001 summarised his achievements as:

> His best winners included Paddy's Peril, who won seven races in the 1983/84 season, Tar Knight and Rare Pleasure, but he felt the best horse he ever trained was Redbin, who won 13 races.
>
> In many of his hurdle wins Redbin was partnered by Des Briscoe, who later became Carter's head lad, and those who won on the horse over fences included Peter Greenall (now Aintree chairman Lord Daresbury), Steve Smith Eccles, Ian Watkinson and Andy Turnell.
>
> Carter owned many of his winners including Redbin, but others for whom he trained included Lois Duffey (who later won the Grand National with Mr. Frisk), Colin Bothway and David Minton.

The Rex Carter Memorial Chase is held annually at Fakenham in mid-May.

In 1978, I was nominated to join the Victoria Sporting Club in Edgware Road, London. Attending a meeting with many top bookmakers, I was interviewed before being accepted. Jack Swift broke the ice by saying: "I'll have a brandy with you anytime, Jack". I also drank occasionally with the original Joe Coral (born Joseph Kagarlitsky in Warsaw, Poland on 11th December 1904, he died 16th December 1996). Unfortunately, I had Brian Launchbury with me on one of those occasions and, as he was prone to elaborate on any happenings, no-one believed that he really had drunk with Joe Coral!

In the late 1960s and early '70s, Barbara and I had a caravan, which we kept at Brean Down Caravan Park in Somerset. The site, which leads onto the beach, is near Weston-super-Mare and was owned by two ex-Army Captains. Naturally, we always kept the caravan in first class order. One year, the site owners sent us a very nice letter saying: "We do hope you're going to change your caravan this year."

Obviously, we returned to the site and spoke with the Site Manager, a small plain-spoken Yorkshireman and asked him what the letter meant. He said: "Buy a new caravan or get off the site". That was quite upsetting as we really liked the area and the holidays we had spent there. As a result, we started to look around Brean and saw a bungalow for sale in Warren Road. The guy wanted thirteen grand for it, so I decided to buy it, along with a cooker with a fan which I spotted there. However, he said that he wanted a fiver for the cooker so I said: "Let the cooker be part of the house". When he persisted: "No, I want a fiver", I turned around, walked up the passage to go and, as  I turned right, he shouted: "All right, you can have the cooker", so I nearly didn't buy the place for the sake of the cost of a cooker!

Buying the bungalow for thirteen grand, I rebuilt it, turning it into a nice big house, as seen above. The garden goes straight down to the beach and the sea and it's lovely. My reasoning at the time was: "I've got a freehold property, I won't get a letter saying I hope you are going to change!" Since I no longer needed the caravan, I gave it to my cousin, Jean, who had been a great help to me in looking after the Betting Shops while working for me. She put the caravan on a site somewhere inland a bit.

The name of the bungalow was "Avondale", which we continued to use and which gave us the name for our next horse – *Avondale Princess*.

IX. JACKPOT 5th Leg – Following in Jenny's Hoofprints

Before we look at the performance of *Avondale Princess*, here is a Racing Summary of the first eighteen race horses during the time they were competing in Barbara's colours from late in 1975:

RACE HORSES Name	Year Born	Ownership/Raced First	Last	Races	Placings 1st	2nd	3rd	Tot
Hello Sailor	1972	03/12/75	22/08/77	13	1	2	-	3
Jenny Splendid	1974	14/06/76	29/09/79	33	11	3	6	20
Lok Yee	1973	25/02/78	29/09/78	5	1	-	1	2
Gerards Cross	1974	30/09/78	27/10/78	4	-	-	3	3
Avondale Princess	1978	08/03/82	24/03/83	14	7	1	2	10
Misty for Me	1980	28/06/82	13/08/82	8	3	1	2	6
Shelley Marie	1982	16/10/84	23/10/84	2	1	-	1	2
Kashill	1978	11/03/85	17/12/85	5	2	-	1	3
Shari Louise	1983	30/04/85	27/05/85	5	2	-	2	4
Cindie Girl	1982	09/08/85	20/12/86	5	3	1	1	5
Hachimitsu	1983	02/08/86	16/12/88	8	1	-	1	2
Saint Malo	1982	12/09/87	12/09/87	1	1	-	-	1
Samantha Josephine	1986	23/04/88	08/07/88	5	-	1	1	2
Shayama	1986	16/04/88	02/08/88	2	-	-	-	0
Karri	1985	22/08/88	22/09/88	2	-	-	-	0
Tami	1985	28/09/88	04/11/91	9	-	-	-	0
Ty-Shan Bay	1984	28/12/88	20/02/89	2	-	-	-	0
Brazilian Boy	1985	10/07/89	18/11/89	5	-	-	-	0
18 Race Horses								
Totals:		15 Years		128	33	9	21	63

As can be seen from the chart, *Avondale Princess* was born in 1978 and raced for Barbara for twelve months from March 1982. During that period, she competed in fourteen races, achieving seven wins, one second place and two thirds. She actually achieved what *Jenny Splendid* narrowly missed out on in that she gained four wins in succession in 1982 – Windsor on 8th March; Towcester on 25th March (see photos on page 6 of Colour Photo Insert) and again there on 4th April; and Taunton on 8th April.

119

The following account in *The Sporting Life* on 10th April 1982 for the *Pitminster Four-year-old Novices' Hurdle* at the latter states:

TAUNTON - April 8th 1982 – 5:00 Pitminster Four-year-old Novices' Hurdle of £900; 1St £552, 2nd £152, 3rd £72. Two Miles

1st   AVONDALE PRINCESS
2nd   CORNISH GRANITE
3rd   BANKNOTE

Winner bred by N D Hodge and trained by M McCourt at Letcombe Regis, Oxon.

Paul Leach, who took Lorna's place on Mr Jerry, was fancied to land a double for the stable on Cornish Granite in the second division of the novices' hurdle, but the 15 – 8 favourite was completely outclassed by Avondale Princess, who cruised home to complete her hat-trick.

In the 1982/3 season, she had a further three wins, one second and two third places. Her win at Stratford on 23rd October was reported in the *Racing Post*:

STRATFORD - October 23, 1982 - 4:15 BenRaad Gas Heater – Four-Year-Old Handicap Hurdle; four-year-olds which, before October 3, had been placed first, second, third or fourth in a hurdle (2m) – Value of race £2,600, winner £1,800, second £500, third £240. (Off 4 – 47) 11 ran.

1St   **AVONDALE PRINCESS,** b f by the Brianstan – Roseanne by St Paddy - (Mrs B Taylor), 11 – 1   K Whyte 1   S.P.   11 – 8 (fav)
2nd   BOLD ILLUSION
3rd   PALENTINE

Winner trained by M. McCourt at Wantage.

Another jockey to impress was Kevin Whyte who brought Avondale Princess home an easy winner of the Benraad Gas Heater Four-Year-Old Handicap Hurdle.

Avondale Princess who recently finished third in the Free handicap Hurdle at Chepstow, can expect little mercy from the handicapper after this success.

Whyte's handling of Rathgorman earned attention last season and Alnwick trainer Andy Scott was singing his praise at Carlisle on Friday after he had won on On Leave.

He is a member of the Michael Dickinson Stable and the Harewood trainer not only has a stable full of equine talent but also a wealth of highly skilled young jockeys.

After her triumph at Ascot on 13th April 1983 in the *Trillium Handicap Hurdle*, the following appeared:

ASCOT - April 13th 1983 - 2:00 Trillium Handicap Hurdle of £5,532; 1st £3,436.80, 2nd £2,028.40, 3rd £493.20, 4th £225.60. Two miles. 14 ran.

1st	AVONDALE PRINCESS - M McCourt 5-11-3	G McCourt	13-2
2nd	LULAV - D Nicholson 5-11-7	P Scudamore	14-1
3rd	GARFUNKLE - P Mitchell 4-11-1	R G Hughes	12-1

Winner bred by N D Hodge and trained by M McCourt at Wantage, Oxon

Matt McCourt has an ambitious target mapped out for Avondale Princess who shrugged off a 4 lb penalty in the Trillium Handicap Hurdle.
The trainer intends running Avondale Princess in the £25,000 added Tia-Maria Handicap Hurdle at Haydock on May 2, despite the fact that his mare has just 8 st 13 lb in the long handicap and the weights are unlikely to rise.
Avondale Princess is still a maiden on the Flat – Willie Carson advised connections to keep her to hurdles after finishing unplaced on the mare at Warwick last year – but she loves jumping and McCourt has placed her to win six times for Reading owner, Barbara Taylor.
Matt's son, Graham McCourt, equalling his previous best of 30 winners achieved five years ago, sent Avondale Princess ahead at the second last and with Lulav and Garfunkle untidy at the final flight she stormed clear to win by four lengths and a neck.

Matt McCourt's ambitious plans for *Avondale Princess* were in fact thwarted because, although the Haydock Park Race Card for 2nd May confirmed that she was indeed in the running order for the *Tia-Maria Handicap Hurdle*, this newspaper account from 3rd May explains why no result could be found for that event:

Wet week for Racing

Rain is threatening to devastate this week's racing in Britain, and there's no comfort from the weather men, who predict more to come.
Yesterday's original total of 10 meetings was halved when Haydock, Newcastle and Southwell joined the casualty list. The fixtures at Warwick and Towcester were abandoned on Sunday.

Letcombe Regis, near Wantage, where Matt McCourt trained *Avondale Princess*, is in fact just one and a half miles as the crow flies from Childrey, where Barbara's great grandfather, Henry Collins, was a shepherd.

121

Neville marries Lynn Clarke

Our only child, Neville Thomas James Taylor married Lynn Joyce Clarke of 43 Crisp Road, Henley at Reading Register Office, Castle Hill on Saturday 28th February 1981 at 10.45 a.m. Barb's sister, Pat Foster, had been amazed to realise that she had seen Jim Barnes-Phillips only the day before as he was "the chap from Burroughs who had mended the machine" at Reading Warehouses, Tadley, where she was the Accounts Manager! The main room at the Register Office only had spaces for thirty guests, the bride and groom and two registrars, so two men had to stand throughout the proceedings. Fortunately, it had stopped raining by the time the newly-wed couple emerged for photographs and remained sunny for the rest of the day – nice enough for brothers Ted and Les Barnes to walk along the river with Daphne and Jim Barnes-Phillips and Doris after the sit-down three course meal.

That was because Lynn and Neville's reception was held at the White Hart at Sonning [which combined with The Red House in 1989 to become The Great House] – see photo on Page 7 of the Colour Photo Insert. It lasted until around 4 p.m. but there was also a disco at Emmer Green from 7.30 p.m. That gave Barbara and I chance to go to Reading Greyhound Stadium to watch one of our dogs race during the evening. The dog finished second as a result of a photo finish. Neville also commented during the evening event that a horse had come up at 66 – 1 [*Balmers Combe* during the 3.45 at Kempton Park] that day so that had paid for their wedding! Lynn's parents and her sister, Debbie (who was 8 on Christmas Day) left at the same time as Daphne and Jim, who were giving Neville's Great Uncles Ted and Les a lift – Great Aunt Doris had decided against going to the evening "do".

Soon after the Freddie Laker Airline collapse [5th February 1982], Barb and I bought "Jingle's Farm", which is situated near the New Mill Restaurant at Eversley. It had belonged to the chap who produced the brochures for the Airline and, as he had not been paid and needed money for his divorce, he'd decided to sell. The main attraction for us was that the property had plenty of stabling. Being sold with the stables and a gardener, we decided to stable our horses there. We bought it fully furnished – the furniture being from Harrods – and most of it is now at "Avondale". However, I had bad vibes about a Medieval Chest, which had carvings of devils and such-like evil things, and I wanted to sell it. I felt that it would bring bad luck if I kept it. Refusing an antique dealer's offer of £1,000 for the Chest, I did agree to sell it to him

when he upped that to £1,500 the following day. "Jingle's Farm" (left) had a fountain in the front garden. However, we didn't ever move there as Barb decided that it would not be good for the cats. As a result, we sold it around 1985. Five years or so later, I bought "Hawthorn Paddocks" at Stoke Row near Henley-on-Thames to stable the horses, and kept that until recently when I sold it to a Baroness who lived at Ipsden. Her bid was the highest, it being a sealed bids process.

At the same time as Barbara was racing *Avondale Princess* over the jumps, she bought *Misty for Me*, for the flat race season and she proved to be equally successful eventually. Her first three races under Barbara's colours provided just a single third place but her winning streak showed through on 28th June at Nottingham – see page 7 of the Colour Photo Insert:

NOTTINGHAM – 28th June, 1982 5.0 STARTING GATE Two-Year-Old MAIDEN STAKES of £1,300; 1st £897 2nd £247 3rd £117.
Fillies. Five furlongs. 10 ran.
    1st MISTY FOR ME gr f Roan Rocket-Rana, by Welsh Pageant
      (Mrs B. Taylor), 8-11 R. Cochrane   1   (7) . . .
Winner bred by Mrs J.S. Lightbrown; trained by M. McCourt at Letcombe Regis, Oxon.
Betting: *Misty for Me* was in demand at 5 – 1 and 9 – 2, touching 4 – 1, including office business.
Closeup: 1. Misty for me chased leaders, led distance, quickened clear

---

A second place at Chepstow on 6th July was followed a fortnight later by a win in the *Weston Stakes* at Wolverhampton and, at the end of the month, by a win at Goodwood on 30th July 1982:

123

GOODWOOD 30th July 1982 - 3.35 RALPH HUBBARD MEMORIAL

GOODWOOD 30th July 1982 - 3.35 RALPH HUBBARD MEMORIAL NURSERY HANDICAP STAKES of £7,032; 1st £4,510.80 2nd £1,346.40 3rd £643.20 4th £281.60. Five furlongs. 10 ran.

1st MISTY FOR ME gr f Roan Rocket-Rana, by Welsh Pageant (Mrs B. Taylor), 10-0 (7 lb. ex.) R. Cochrane 1 (6) . . .

Winner bred by Mrs J.S. Lightbrown; trained by M. McCourt at Letcombe Regis, Oxon.

Betting: Misty for Me returned from 3 – 1 to 7 – 2, touching 4 – 1 before closing at 7 – 2, including wagers of £3,500 – £1,000 each way and £2,800 – £800

STARTING PRICE: 7 – 2 for MISTY FOR ME

The following article gives some idea of the reasons for *Misty for Me*'s initial slowness in producing a win:

Ray plays it cool on Misty for Me

MISTY FOR ME put up a smart performance to win the Ralph Hubbard Memorial Nursery under top weight.

She started 7 – 2 favourite but at halfway had plenty to do with the field spread across the course.

But Indian Lady wandered in front and it was not until approaching the final furlong that the winner saw daylight.

Accidental

Under Ray Cochrane she made good progress to join issue with the leaders and showed an impressive turn of foot to spring clear close home, reaching the line two lengths clear of Indian Lady.

The stewards announced an inquiry, shortly followed by the news that it did not concern the winner.

They found that Indian Lady had impeded her rivals in the final quarter mile but judged the infringement accidental and demoted her to fourth.

This is a first Goodwood winner for Matt McCourt, who trains Misty for Me for Mrs Barbara Taylor. "She wanted me to buy a grey filly and I paid 4,600 gns for her", he said.

McCourt explained that he had fancied Misty for Me on her debut at Newbury in the spring but she banged her head on the stalls and came back covered in blood.

"It has taken her quite a long time to get her confidence back", he said.

"She is pretty useful and has gone on improving all the time. She will run in the St. Hugh's Stakes at Newbury next month.

"I thought it was a good performance for a two-year-old under 10 st. I was worried two furlongs out when she had it all to do."

Yet another viewpoint on the race was:
Misty for me scorches in – Goodwood, 30th July 1982
By Captain Heath (Jim Stanford)

. . . But the most exciting runners on view at a far-from-glorious Goodwood, where the heavens started weeping midway through the programme, were the two-year-olds Dunbeath and Misty for Me . . . .

Misty for Me, a 4,600-guinea bargain buy by Matt McCourt for Mrs Barbara Taylor, who wanted a grey yearling, is certainly one of the fastest and most tenacious two-year-olds around.

Despite the steadier of 10 st, she literally hacked up in the Ralph Hubbard Memorial Nursery, though she was badly hampered by runner-up Indian Lady.

McCourt now plans to move her up in the class, and she takes on high-class fillies first in the St. Hugh's Stakes at Newbury.

Indian Lady was inevitably disqualified from second place after swerving antics had not only affected the winner, but almost took Lester Piggott's mount, Key Ring, into the Silver Ring.

What a pity that this filly's tremendous speed is not allied to good steering . . .

The season finished for her at Newbury on 13th August with a third place in the *St. Hugh's Stakes*. *Misty for me* was a really great animal. Barbara was offered 80 grand for her by a guy from Australia who had the football coupons. I can't recall his name now [Kerry Packer] but we didn't sell her to him. Instead, we kept her, eventually selling her for a brood mare because she had broken blood vessels in her lungs so was not suitable for racing but was all right for a brood mare. We took her to Newmarket where we sold her for about 25 grand so that was a good deal.

By that time, *Jenny Splendid*'s foals were starting to be born. The second one, *Shari Louise* (1983, sired by *Radetzky*), turned out to be the most successful of them as the following articles show that she had two wins and two thirds within a month from 30th April 1985. The first win was:

NOTTINGHAM – 30th April, 1985 - 2.0 CINDERHILL MAIDEN FILLIES' STAKES of £1,160; 1st £796, 2nd £296, 3rd £100, two year olds.
Five furlongs. Going good to firm. 13 ran.
1st SHARI LOUISE br f Radetzky – Jenny Splendid, by John Splendid
    (Mrs B. Taylor), 8 – 11 R. Wernham   1   (4) . . .
Winner bred by Owner; trained by M. McCourt at Letcombe Regis, Oxon.
Starting prices: 6 – 4 Shari Louise: opened 5 – 4, touched 7 – 4. Bets of £3,500 – £2,000 twice, £1,400 – £800 and £700 – £400.
CLOSE-UP: 1. Shari Louise, well placed, led over one out just held on.

That was followed by thirds at Windsor in the evening meeting on 13th May, and during the first race of the day at Newbury five days later. She was then to pull off another win at Chepstow on 27th May:

CHEPSTOW – 27th May, 1985 - 3.40   BADMINGTON STAKES (2-Y-O fillies) of £1,956; 1st £1,354.20, 2nd £376.20, 3rd £180.60. Five furlongs.
1st SHARI LOUISE br f Radetzky – Jenny Splendid, by John Splendid (Mrs B. Taylor), 8 – 11 R. Wernham   1   (4) . . .
Winner bred by Mrs B Taylor; trained by M. McCourt at Letcombe Regis, nr. Wantage, Oxon. Time: 1m. 2.9s.
CLOSE-UP
1. Shari Louise made all, held on well under pressure.

As well as buying horses to race, Barbara also supported other organisations, such as Bransby Home of Rest for Horses in Lincolnshire where she adopted *Fi-Fi*, a grey mare and *Blackie*, a 3-year-old Shetland pony. Her love of all creatures great and small is reflected in this Certificate of Adoption from the Cotswold Wild Life Park in Burford, Oxfordshire dated 29th August 1986 showing that she adopted a meerkat and a red squirrel that year.

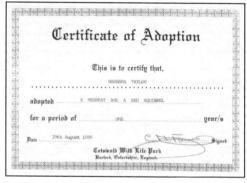

126

Our cats, being with us all the time and especially sharing our times of relaxation, rarely feature in our photo albums but this photograph of the litter – *Miranda, Bonnie, Clyde* and *Sophie* – was taken on 23rd December 1987 and certainly shows their endearing ways. When we went to see them, we had intended buying two kittens so Barb said: "Well which two are we going to have?" Obviously, I had to say: "We'll have all four" as it was impossible to choose between them. Their owner gave us the photo which she told us had appeared on the front page of the Reading Evening Post:

The last of Barb's maternal uncles died in 1988 – Uncle Ted (Albert Edward,

pictured right) – suffered a stroke at home on 22nd and another while in Minster Ward at Battle Hospital on 24th and died in a single ward there on 28th February. Uncle Les (left), seen with Barbara at Neville and Lynn's wedding, predeceased him on 27th April 1982.

Over the years, I did have some periods of very good luck. I bought my shop at Mill Street, Eynsham (right) off Percy Lewis, an affable bookmaker, who was the long-time trainer of Oxford University's Boxing Club, having been former world class professional featherweight himself (1952 & 1953 Amateur Boxing 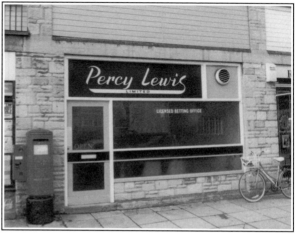 Association Featherweight Champion, who competed in the 1952 Olympics in Helsinki and who, like Henry Cooper, was managed by Jim Wicks). I also bought a shop in Oxford from him. Now, as the Oxford lease approached its

 end, they wanted me out. I didn't want to go so they offered me a shop in Cowley Road for 40 grand (which was very cheap) to entice me to go. I therefore bought it and had it as a Betting Shop. A few years later, Ladbrokes who were around the corner but weren't doing terribly great at the time, offered me forty grand to close it. So there you are, I had a lovely freehold there for nothing – forty grand I paid for it and Ladbrokes gave me forty grand to close it!

Three of **Barbara's Race Horses** remain with me
in retirement at "High Thatch" (Page 131)

Greyfriars Bobby

Nanquidno

Gushka

Doris Barnes, Daphne Barnes-Phillips, Barbara, and Pat Foster at a family get-
together on 9th July 1995 to celebrate **Barb's Aunt Doris' 80th birthday** (Page 133)

Colour Insert Page 9

After advertising was allowed on the exterior of Betting Shops, this design was chosen for the outside of the **T.R.S. shop at Cheapside**, **Reading** (Page 133)

One of three murals by P.J. Devenall (1977) retrieved from the interiors of T.R.S. Shops and now gracing the wall of my Snooker Room at "High Thatch" (Page 134)

Colour Insert Page 10

Cindie Girl—mother of *Where's Miranda*
(Page 140)

Thumbs Up I who had 11 placings in
18 races in Barb's Colours (Page 134)

Daphne & Jim took me to lunch for **my
75th birthday** in their ex-George Best
Rolls Royce Silver Shadow (Page 142)

Aunt Doris passed away on
17th December 2003 in Bracknell
aged 88 years (Page 144)

"High Thatch", showing the extensions made to the house and gardens (Page 145)

Rear view of **"High Thatch"** taken at my 80th Birthday Party on 29th April 2007 (Page 152)

Colour Insert Page 12

Reading Football Club player Glen Little opening **Basingstoke Road Shop** in 2006
(Pages 97 and 147)

Trophies to be presented at the **Barbara Taylor Memorial Meeting** at
Reading Greyhound Stadium in November 2001 (Page 141)

Colour Insert Page 13

Snooker Room at High Thatch with Stream and Putting Green — 2011 (Page 152)

I've got a lovely **Snooker Table** – really old with beautiful legs (Page 155)

Colour Insert Page 14

Tom created this little **Summer House** for me in the back garden at "High Thatch". It has a splendid view up the valley. (Page 152)

This is that **splendid view** with the Ponies' Stable behind the fence (Page 152)

Colour Insert Page 15

Jo Jo and *Goldie* — the two Shetland Ponies that we bought in 1994 (Page 156)

Goldie and *Jo Jo* are still with me at "High Thatch" (Page 156)

Clyde studies the Racing Form in the *Daily Mail* while I hold the picture of his **grandfather** taken in 1987 (Page 156)

Colour Insert Page 16

X. JACKPOT Final Leg – Hi De Hi for new Taylor shop

Taylor's Racing Service expanded into Abingdon, Oxfordshire in 1990 when we opened a licensed betting office in Reynolds Way towards the end of that year. The popular *Hi De Hi* star, Felix Bowness, performed the opening ceremony after arriving, jockey style, on a horse, in keeping with the character he portrayed in the programme. He was welcomed by myself (managing director), Mike Collins (general manager), Andy Barr (branch manager) and his assistant, Gill Fletcher. The photograph on page 8 of the Colour Photo Insert shows Joy Cuthbertson, my most efficient secretary for around 35 years, and myself being entertained by Felix, who lived in Woodley and only died 13th September 2009, aged 87.

The artistic shop window designs were by B. Heinz Barth (pictured with Barb outside the Oxford shop opposite) and the interior, furnished in the usual T.R.S. red, was revealed after Felix cut the tape. He was in good form, freely entertaining the crowd of punters and giving them tips for the afternoon's card. Placing his £100 charity bet on *One For The Pot* at £50 each way, Felix produced £93.75 for his favourite charity, the Injured Jockey's Fund. He was kept busy signing autographs and chatting with the punters as the champagne flowed and everyone took advantage of the special bets and offers which were available that day.

As mentioned earlier, Barbara first experimented with Greyhound Racing in the late 1960s when she bought *Peter's Magic* and *Saskatchuan*. She then bought three greyhounds in 1980 – *Bright Boy* on 5th January; *Marine Damsel* on 16th July and *Ryehurst Tango* on 20th November. She raced them for a few seasons with *Bright Boy* achieving seventeen firsts and *Ryehurst Tango*, eighteen. However, she had much less success with her next four dogs (including twins, *Ryehurst Silk* and *Ryehurst Rapture*) so it was not until November 1991, when she bought *Drive On Boy*, that she again experienced success as he had twelve firsts in his racing career.

Interestingly, at the first meeting we attended for *Peter's Magic* in around 1968/9, I saw people who owed me money. Naturally, I turned to Barb to tell her they were there, but when I looked in their direction again, none of them were to be seen – they had all disappeared!

Trade Exchange, born 15th November 1992, first raced for her on 1st February 1994, when he won. In fact, that was his first and only race as he was put out to stud and fathered 423 offspring from January 1997 until February 2000! The best two of his offspring were both bitches, who each won 34 races in the course of their careers – *Polo* (born September 1997 also had 17 second places) and *Mansa* (born in May 1998 achieved 40 second places). In Greyhound Racing, it is only the first and second places that count whereas for horses it can be the first four places.

Mansa's mother was *Mi Minka* and her maternal grandfather was *I'm Slippy*. If you think that *Trade Exchange's* offspring tally of 423 was impressive then you'll be amazed to realise that *I'm Slippy* sired 2,943 between 1981 and 1994. As a comparison, the most prolific dog recorded – *Top Honcho* – sired 10,292 offspring between August 1996 and July 2010. *I'm Slippy* only raced five times, achieving four first places and one second – all in 1983.

In May 1993, Barb brought a black and white dog, *Ploverfield Ace*, which had thirteen firsts. He was joined in September 1994 by *Miss Sophie*, who did one better with fourteen. Three bitches were purchased in 1996 – twins *April Daisy* (pictured on page 8 of the Colour Photo Insert) and *Princess Tahnee* in April – and *Tian Shan* in August. All three had successful careers, winning a total of 45 races between them and I still have *April Daisy's* ashes.

When any of the greyhounds needed to rest or recuperate from injury, we took them to a house near the crossroads at Tidmarsh. There, a Reading trainer, who had done naughty things, lived in one half and Rex Harrison in the other.

After a gap of nearly three years, Barbara decided to keep the first of *Miss Sophie*'s three litters of five dogs and three bitches sired by *Trade Exchange*. They were born on 15th October 1999 but, alas, Barb did not live to see any of them competing as it was between June 2001 and March 2002 that they took part in their first races. Four of the litter proved to be quite successful with *Xena's Gold* and *Inspired* both achieving 16 first places and *Stock Exchange* 19, but it was *Exchange Express* who proved to be her most successful dog with 21 first and 15 second places from 119 outings in a four year racing career. The other 4 of the litter – bitches, *This is Krystal* and *I'm Chantell* and dogs, *Flight Command* and *Sultan Prince* were somewhat less successful with 26 firsts between the 4 of them. You can see a full list of Barb's greyhounds on page 101 and photos of four of them on page 8 of the Colour Photo Insert.

Miss Sophie's second litter born in 2002 included a brindle bitch, who was named *Hachimitsu*, which takes me back to the remainder of Barb's race horses since three of them were offspring of her horse *Hachimitsu* – *Princess Shawnee* by *Ilium*, *Hi Kiki* by *Rambo Dancer* and *Fyresdal Rocky* by *Rock Hopper*. They appear in the following chart, which is a continuation of the 1975 – 1989 Racing Summary given on page 119. It shows those 22 who raced in Barb's colours from then until the end of 2000:

RACEHORSES Name	Year Born	Ownership/Raced First	Last	Placings Races	1st	2nd	3rd	Tot
Greyfriars Bobby	1986	14/12/89	01/02/94	10	1	2	-	3
Akroteri Bay	1984	29/06/90	09/10/90	1	-	-	-	0
Kalogy	1987	29/11/90	05/02/94	8	1	1	3	5
Cruise Lady	1986	12/04/91	12/04/91	1	-	-	-	0
Seto City	1989	03/08/91	23/09/91	5	-	1	-	1
Musical Lyrics	1988	28/05/91	26/10/92	10	-	1	-	1
Allyfair	1985	30/07/91	31/05/93	17	0	2	5	7
Gushka	1987	27/05/93	08/02/94	4	-	-	-	0
Princess Shawnee	1990	17/05/93	29/06/93	2	-	-	-	0
Caribbean Prince	1988	29/09/93	26/04/97	10	1	3	-	4
Hi Kiki	1991	15/10/93	29/09/95	12	-	-	2	2
Sabaki River	1994	06/12/93	05/02/96	6	1	-	-	1
Nanquidno	1990	01/08/94	20/10/94	2	1	-	1	2
Nornax Lad	1988	10/03/95	05/08/97	14	2	2	1	5
Thumbs Up I	1986	04/07/96	29/04/98	18	4	4	3	11
Where's Miranda	1992	20/11/96	25/01/00	15	1	1	-	2
Orphan Spa	1991	28/05/97	22/10/99	15	1	2	-	3
Fyresdal Rocky	1995	13/08/98	31/08/98	2	-	-	-	0
Shannon's Dream	1996	18/10/98	25/11/00	4	-	-	-	0
Direct Deal	1996	22/03/00	25/11/00	8	1	-	1	2
Hawaiian Youth	1988	25/05/00	25/11/00	3	-	1	-	1
Tampico	1997	13/10/00	25/11/00	2	-	-	-	0
Totals: 22 horses		11 Years		169	14	20	16	50
Overall Totals:		26 Years		297	47	29	37	113

Greyfriars Bobby, *Gushka* and *Nanquidno* remained with me at "High Thatch" and were photographed there on 30th October 2011 – see page 9 of the Colour Photo Insert.

131

Greyfriar's Bobby (a chestnut gelding born in 1986) started racing in April 1989 in the colours of Bernard Bates. Barbara took over ownership from December 1989 until 1st February 1994. The horse first raced for her at Wincanton on 8th February 1990 where he was pulled up before the finish. He didn't achieve any placings until 9th January 1992 when he finished 2nd at Wincanton and that course was the scene of his first (and only) win just a month later. On 19th March 1992 at Exeter, he achieved another second place. These three results proved to be the pinnacle of his racing career as he competed in eight further events before retiring in December 1994 – three of those for Barbara and the final five under David Fisher, who took over ownership on 1st February 1994.

In retirement, he has been stabled at "High Thatch" along with *Gushka*, a brown gelding born 15th June 1987, who has always belonged to Barbara but was never a successful racing horse – his best place being 12th out of 17 in his first outing on 27th May 1993 at Hereford. He was initially trained by Jacqueline Retter and latterly by Matt McCourt.

There are eight stables at "High Thatch", so also stabled there is the chestnut mare, *Nanquidno*, whom Barb bought on 1st August 1994. She was born 7th May 1990 and started racing in 1993. She had achieved five seconds out of sixteen races before she joined us. She was then to finish third at Newton Abbot on 4th October, followed by a win in the *K.J. Pike & Sons Mares Only Novices' Hurdle* exactly two weeks later at Wincanton. That proved to be her first and only win as she retired straight afterwards. Heather looks after her, *Guska* and *Greyfriar's Bobby* now.

Allyfair, a grey mare, was born 1985, and had an inauspicious start to her racing career as she fell on only her second outing under the ownership of Barb's good friend, Kathy Stuart, who sold her to Barbara at the end of July 1991 in preparation for the 1991/2 Jump Season when she raced eight times and achieved four consecutive third places. The following season, she was entered in nine races with her best result being a second at Hereford on 3rd April 1993.

Kathy of Ottery St. Mary had horses in a similar mode to Barbara – *Orphan Spa* was another of her's that Barb bought – and she used to look after Barb's horses for her. She still owns horses as the following article, which appeared in the Friday, 20th February 2009 *Point to Point News*, shows:

> Richard Barber landed a double with 4 year old Benarchat (2m 4f Maiden) and Thisthatandtother (Countryside Alliance Novice Riders). The former made an impressive debut as he quickened eight lengths clear of pacesetter Ashclyst under Rachael Green. Ottery St. Mary-based Kathy Stuart, joint owner with Julie Derham, was on holiday in Thailand, but her daughter, Chantal, quickly telephoned with the good news. Ashclyst, who was conceding 21 lbs to the winner, ran a fine race in defeat.

1994 saw the inception of The National Lottery. Since then, gambling has become not only legal but also a small contributor to the British economy. This is quite a contrast to its previous status as regulated yet illegal when licences were required but no debts arising from gambling could be enforced through the courts. New gambling websites on the Internet nowadays allow punters to gamble 24 hours a day internationally.

There was a family get-together on 9th July 1995 to celebrate Barb's Aunt Doris' 80th birthday as she had been born 5th July 1915. Her elder daughter, Maureen, had organised the celebration at her home in Lordswood, Silchester and we were blessed with a beautifully sunny day and temperatures of 32 degrees centigrade as can be seen in the photo on page 9 of the Colour Photo Insert of Doris, Daphne, Barbara and Pat taken in Maureen and Ray's garden.

From 1st January 1995, it had become legal to open betting shops on a Sunday and, from May of that year, their windows no longer had to be obscured. I had chosen vibrant designs for the exteriors of my premises as can be seen in the photo of the outside of the one at Cheapside in Reading on page 10 of the Colour Photo Insert. I had already commissioned artist, P.J. Devenall, to paint Horse Racing Murals for the interiors of some of my shops in 1977. I still have three of those murals on the walls of my Snooker Room at "High Thatch", one of which is reproduced on page 10 of the Colour Photo Insert.

Other changes introduced in 1995, were the possibility of displaying lists of "odds" and also details of bets available within. A wider range of refreshments, including sandwiches and snacks, were also permitted (as can be seen in this photo) and there was no longer any limit imposed on the size of

T.V.s displayed in the branches. From 1996, shops were allowed to sell racing-related publications – such as books, newspapers and magazines – as well as scratch cards other than for the National Lottery. During 1997, it became legal to advertise the location of betting shops in newspapers and telephone directories.

One of the few horses Barb owned whose lifetime earnings ran into six figures (circa £110,000) was *Thumbs Up I*, who was a brown gelding, born 8th May 1986 – see page 11 of Colour Photo Insert. He had 48 outings in his seven year racing career – the last 18 of which were in Barbara's colours. Barb bought him on 4th July 1996 from Michael Buckley and immediately moved him to G. M. McCourt's stables. During his career with Barbara, he had four wins, four seconds and three third placings. His first win for her – the ninth of his career – was at Haydock Park on 20th November 1996 with champion jockey, Richard Dunwoody, in the saddle. In February and March

1997, he had consecutive wins at Huntingdon and Exeter and his final win was just a couple of months before retirement at Huntingdon on 7th March 1998. However, fame did not faze Barb at all. I can remember being at a party with her after she had won a lot of money. She was supposed to be celebrating but she suddenly announced: "I must get home to feed the guinea pigs" so we both left!

I've been a supporter of Reading Football Club for a long time. In approximately 1958, I managed to buy three seats (for Barb, Neville and myself) in the Centre Stand at Elm Park (right) – on the half way line but far enough back to be out of the rain. I had those three seats until Elm Park closed on 3rd May 1998, having been Reading F.C.'s home ground for over a hundred years – since 5th September 1896. When the replacement Madejski Stadium opened for its first match on 22nd August 1998,  the Taylor family had purchased three similar seats on its halfway line, so we've been supporting the Club for more than half a century. The new Stadium, which had cost £50 million to build, had its official opening on 10th September that year.

In October 1998, Barb and I were sad to hear of the sudden death of Johnnie Haine at his home in Crudwell, Wiltshire on the 8th. He was only 55, having been born the son of a farmer in Chipping Sodbury, Gloucestershire on 30th December 1942. By the age of eight, he was riding with the Duke of Beaufort's hunt and had won more than a hundred first prizes in gymkhanas, juvenile jumping and showing classes. He rode his first winner as a jockey on *Misconception* at Bath in 1958 but, after 30+ successes on the Flat, he turned his attention to the National Hunt. *Buona Notte* gave him his first major jumps success at Cheltenham in 1963 and he was inconsolable when the horse was killed in the 1965 *Great Yorkshire Chase* at Doncaster. That was the time when he achieved his best position in the Table of Champion Jockeys – 5th with 51 winners in 1964/5, according to *Racing Post* of 16th October 1998.

Johnnie's experience of Flat-racing led him to prefer to ride a waiting race. He said that he modelled his style on the Australian jockey, "Scobie" Breasley [1914 – 2006], commenting: "He's my idol. I hate going to the front too soon and try to ride my races as if they were Flat races – after all, the obstacles are only incidental." That approach got him into trouble with the Jockey Club, which warned him off for three months between October 1968 and January 1969 for "deliberately making no effort to win a steeplechase".

However, his riding career continued to flourish, even when he took up training at Haresfield, Gloucestershire in 1975, and combined that role with his more established one of jockey for a year. Enjoying success in that sphere as well, notably with *Jenny Splendid*, who won ten [eleven] races on the Flat, he focused on training after 1976 and eventually retired in 1980, when he failed to match his achievements in the saddle. As Stan Mellor recalled: "He was a brilliant jockey and wonderfully stylish. I wasn't stylish at all and he would take the mickey out of me."

Johnnie had married three times – firstly and thirdly to Sue Williams who was the sister of Stan Mellor's wife, Elaine. It was his second marriage – to Tom Jones' daughter, Diana – that produced his son George and daughter Penny.

Our good friend Stella Dalton died the following year. We had had lots of great holidays with her and Arthur. When Arthur decided to clear out the loft at their home in Eastmoor Park, Harpenden after her death in 1999, he came across the accounts of his progress as a Lance Corporal through the invasion of Europe during World War II from D. Day [6th June 1944] to V.E. Day [5th May 1945]. Up 'til then, his war service had been spent in England. Being a Civil Servant, who worked at the National Physical Laboratories in Teddington, he had been called up in 1941 and became a radio operator with 120 Field Regiment, Royal Artillery. When he was demobbed in 1946, he returned to his job at the National Physical Laboratory.

His notes had been written in pencil and posted to Stella, who then circulated them among family members. Amazingly, all the pieces seemed to be there so his family, including son Richard, helped him decipher the original notes and transcribe them onto a computer and, in 2004, sixty years after the event, when he was 94, a 100-page book of his memoirs was published.

XI. Crossing the finishing line

Barbara had many very good horses and, when I lost her in 2000, she had owned at least forty, and still had thirty at that time. She was very shrewd and managed her estate of horses very well. As we had been doing well at the bookmaking, most of the horses were racehorses 'though some were brood mares and some foals. We had great times with all of them, winning some fantastic races at Goodwood and other meetings. Here is a summary of the achievements of those who took part in the Jumps Meetings:

GB Jumps Statistical Summary

Season	Wins	Runs	%	2nd	3rd	4th	Win Prize	Total Prize	£1 Stake
1988-89	0	7	—	0	0	1	£0	£0	-7
1989-90	0	3	—	0	0	0	£0	£0	-3
1990-91	0	4	—	0	0	0	£0	£0	-4
1991-92	2	18	11	2	5	3	£3,468	£5,933	-7
1992-93	0	15	—	2	1	2	£0	£2,678	-15
1993-94	1	11	9	3	1	1	£2,532	£4,926	-3
1994-95	2	8	25	0	1	0	£6,950	£7,404	2
1995-96	0	3	—	0	0	0	£0	£0	-3
1996-97	3	14	21	4	3	2	£13,711	£24,351	-2.13
1997-98	1	19	5	1	0	4	£3,770	£6,039	-16.8
1998-99	1	11	9	2	1	0	£2,574	£4,468	-4
1999-00	1	6	17	0	0	1	£2,651	£2,886	15
2000-01	0	6	—	1	1	0	£0	£994	-6
Totals:	**11**	**125**	**97**	**15**	**13**	**14**	**£35,656**	**£59,679**	

Barbara's death was very sudden as she died of a heart attack on Saturday, 25th November 2000. At her funeral service at St. John the Baptist Church at Kidmore End on Tuesday 5th December, the Rector, The Revd. Graham Foulis-Brown spoke of the fact that we had bought Dyson's Wood so that it could become an animal sanctuary. The wreath I had chosen for Barb's coffin was in her racing colours – pink with a black horse on it. There were so many floral tributes that it was difficult to take them all in but one that caught my eye was a beautiful white bunny holding a carrot.

Our grandson, Craig, who had only started studying Human Biology at Staffordshire University, Stoke-on-Trent that term, was a great comfort to me during the service. The only reason I was able to do the Appreciation of Barb's Life without breaking down was that I had practised every day leading up to the service and Craig had

helped me to finally succeed in doing it. After all, I had known Barb for 52 years and we had been married for 50 so I wanted to pay tribute to her, and particularly to her love of animals, which guided everything she did.

It rained quite heavily for the interment in the nearby Kidmore End Cemetery and while we were in the New Inn. We did not know it then but two of those present that day were to die themselves within a year or so of Barb's death – her cousin Maureen and Maureen's brother-in-law, John Beasley (her sister, Chris' husband). John died on 12th September 2001 – the day following the "Twin Towers" collapse. Maureen who had spoken that day of the headaches she had been experiencing and wondered if her use of a mobile phone was exacerbating the problem, found herself in hospital the night of Barbara's funeral. However, she was soon to discover that a brain tumour was the cause and she died on 6th January 2002 in St. Michael's Hospice. She had chosen a non-religious service at the Furze Bush Hotel, Ball Hill, Newbury followed by burial at an ecological burial place, Acorn Ridge, which had had just three previous burials, having only been granted planning permission the previous year.

One of the racehorses that Barb owned when she died was *Where's Miranda*. Her details are included here as they show that complete records from birth to death are maintained for race horses. However, the records are less precise about the owner's details as the implication is that Barbara died on 28th December 2000 whereas it was actually on 25th November that year:

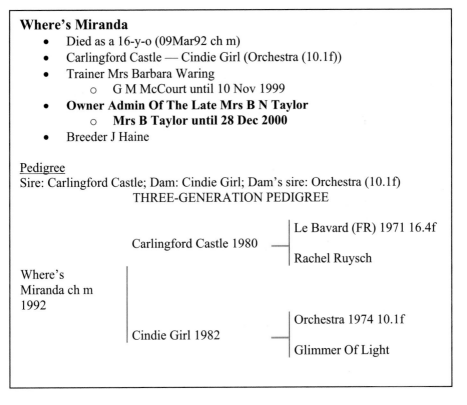

Where's Miranda
- Died as a 16-y-o (09Mar92 ch m)
- Carlingford Castle — Cindie Girl (Orchestra (10.1f))
- Trainer Mrs Barbara Waring
  - G M McCourt until 10 Nov 1999
- **Owner Admin Of The Late Mrs B N Taylor**
  - **Mrs B Taylor until 28 Dec 2000**
- Breeder J Haine

Pedigree
Sire: Carlingford Castle; Dam: Cindie Girl; Dam's sire: Orchestra (10.1f)
THREE-GENERATION PEDIGREE

		Le Bavard (FR) 1971 16.4f
	Carlingford Castle 1980	
		Rachel Ruysch
Where's Miranda ch m 1992		
		Orchestra 1974 10.1f
	Cindie Girl 1982	
		Glimmer Of Light

Race Record

Jumps placings: 420/855564/89/1694/

Lifetime Record	Starts	Wins	2nd	3rd	Winnings	Earnings
NHF	4	0	1	0	£0	£351
Hurdle	11	1	0	0	£2,651	£2,886
Rules Races	15	1	1	0	£2,651	£3,237

It has not been possible to record the full names of the jockeys in the following chart of Race Results for *Where's Miranda*, so initials have been used according to the key shown beneath it:

139

RACE RESULTS for *Where's Miranda* during Barbara's ownership:

DATE	CONDITIONS	JOC	WGT	RACE OUTCOME
25Jan00	Fon 20Gd C4NvH 3K	EH	11-3	4/15 (18L Hillview Lizzie 11-3) 50/1
08Jan00	Hay 22Sft C3NvH 3K	SW	10-12	9/16 (73L Solway Breeze 10-12) 100/1
02Dec99	Wcn 22Gd C4NvHcH 2K	PH	10-7	6/11 (34L Take Control 11-10) 14/1
15Nov99	Lei 21GS C4NvHcH 2K	EH	10-2	1/9 (nk Woodland Nymph 11-10) 20/1
18Feb99	Tau 25GS C4HcH 2K	EH	10-1	9/15 (90L Plaid Maid 10-4) 33/1
28Jan99	Hun 22Sft C4HcH 2K	RS	9-11	8/19 (36L Cathedral Belle 11-11) 40/1
25Apr98	Wor 24GS C4NvHcH 2K	WM	10-0	4/11 (23L Golden Film 10-0) 10/1
14Apr98	Exe 18Sft C4NvHcH 2K	RH	9-12	6/11 (42L Sunrise Special 10-4) 12/1
05Mar98	Tau 20GS C3NvH 2K	DM	10-11	5/14 (33L Final Hand 11-2) 9/1
09Feb98	Fon 19Gd C4NvH 2K	DM	10-9	5/16 (32L Red Curate 11-0) 20/1
10Dec97	Lei 16Sft C4NvH 2K	DB	10-7	5/10 (37L Be Brave 10-7) 16/1
19Nov97	Her 17Sft C6NHF 1K	XA	10-9	8/16 (33L Latin Mistress 11-2) 12/1
04Feb97	War 16GF C6MdNHF1K	RS	11-3	11/22 (40L Erintante 10-9) 8/1
24Jan97	Fol 18Sft C6NHF 1K	RH	10-11	2/12 (3L Tara Gale 10-11) 7/4F
20Nov96	Her 17GS C6NHF 1K	RH	10-7	4/13(3½L Melstock Meggie10-11) 20/1

Key for Jockeys

EH = E Husband; SW = S Wynne; PH = P Holley; RS = R Studholme;
WM = W Marston; RH = R Hobson; DM = DJ Moffatt; DB = D Bridgwater;
XA = X Aizpuru;

Where's Miranda was the offspring of another of Barb's horses, *Cindie Girl*, by *Carlingford Castle* – see page 11 of Colour Photo Insert. Her best placings were a second in her second outing on 24th January 1997 at Folkestone and a win at Leicester on 15th November 1999 just a couple of months before she retired from racing.

The third to last horse that Barb bought was a brown gelding *Direct Deal* which had been born 3rd March 1996. That horse, of American parentage, was bought from Maktoum Al Maktoum on 22nd March 2000. During the 2000 Flat Race Season, he rewarded her with a win on 17th July at Windsor and a 3rd place at Fontwell on 25th August. He went on to have one further win on 21st July 2001 under the ownership of the "Administrators of the late Mrs B. N. Taylor". In the 2001 Budget, Chancellor Gordon Brown announced that betting duty would be abolished before 1st January 2002 and, sure enough, on 10th October, it was replaced by Gross Profits Tax on bookmakers.

Exactly a year after Barb died, I sponsored a whole evening's greyhound racing at Reading Stadium, Bennet Road in her memory. The *Barbara Taylor Memorial Meeting* was held on Saturday 24th November 2001 (see page 13 of Colour Photo Insert) and it seemed most appropriate to name the fourteen races after her race horses or cats so the shortest race – of 275 m. at the beginning of the evening was The 'Avondale Princess' Dash at 7 p.m. The longest races of 660 m. were the tenth and twelfth – The 'Kalogy' and 'Bonnie' Stayers Trophies respectively – while all the others were simply called Trophy events, like the last – The 'Clyde' Trophy. Only one of those had a double title – The 'Jenny Splendid/Johnnie Haine' Trophy. The programme had this foreword:

THE BARBARA TAYLOR
MEMORIAL MEETING

I was very privileged to have
52 wonderful years with Barbara.

During all this time she looked after
and loved her animals;
as a racehorse owner and breeder
she enjoyed reasonable success
and always, whenever possible,
looked after her horses
to the very end of their lives.
She also had greyhounds
which gave her lots of pleasure.

It is a great honour for me
to be able to sponsor this meeting
on Barbara's behalf
and all who knew her will know
she would have liked this meeting
to put a little back into greyhound racing.

HAVE A GREAT EVENING'S RACING HERE
AT SMALLMEAD.
THANKS A LOT FOR YOUR SUPPORT.

JACK AND ALL THE ANIMALS.

The winners of the fourteen races are shown here:

Race Time	Name of Race	Dist in m	Winner (+ race no)
19.00	The 'Avondale Princess' Dash	275	Millgan Flick (1)
19.17	The 'Cindy Girl' Trophy	465	April Charm (3)
19.35	The 'Blacky' Trophy	465	Legal Gift (4)
19.51	The 'Sophie' Trophy	465	Roof Top Lass (1)
20.07	The 'Misty for Me' Trophy.	465	Hedsor Storm (3)
20.22	The 'Miranda' Trophy	465	Janus (2)
20.37	The 'Lok Yee' Trophy	465	Minnies Flower (3)
20.53	The 'Hello Sailor' Trophy.	465	Monterey Peg (4)
21.08	The 'Orphan Spa' Trophy	465	Murrin Survivor (1)
21.23	The 'Kalogy' Stayers Trophy	660	Telpete (4)
21.39	The 'Jenny Splendid/Johnnie Haine' Tr.	465	Monterey Sean (6)
21.54	The 'Bonnie' Stayers Trophy	660	Giglis Hurricane (2)
22.10	The 'Thumbs Up' Trophy.	465	Graceville Star (4)
22.25	The 'Clyde' Trophy.	465	Neat Rocket (3)

For my 75th birthday, I had my first ride in a Rolls Royce – it was Daphne and Jim's Silver Shadow, originally owned by the famous footballer, George Best – see page 11 of the Colour Photo Insert. They took me to the "Grouse and Claret" where Daphne's brother, Alan, his wife, Jan, and their son, Simon, joined us for Sunday lunch. I'd shown Daphne and Jim the extension that I'd recently had built and which was due for completion by Christmas that year before we drove to the meal. Daphne asked about what she thought was a swimming pool on the patio – it was actually the fish pond but then it is for koi and they are pretty big! I had also shown them the guinea pigs, pheasant, pigeons and rabbits and pointed out the trees that Barbara had planted when we moved to "High Thatch" thirty years before.

It was at that meal that I saw Daphne's first book – "The Top of Whitley", which she had launched along with a poetry anthology "A Whiff of Whitley" just over a month before – on 17th March 2002 – at 3 p.m. at Reading Girls' School [formerly Southlands School but originally George Palmer Girls' School before its move in April 1960]. She and Jim had given me a copy of "The Top of Whitley" for my birthday and, when they realised that I knew Len Cook, as he'd lived in Surrey Road when I did, they gave me a copy of the latter as well, since it is dedicated to him and contains some of his work.

Talking of cars, I have been attracted to Mercedes cars since about 1970 and have owned one continuously since then. My latest came about in a most unusual way. About 2002/3, my General Manager, Gordon Southcote, was driving my then Mercedes when a chap came along on a motorbike and bashed into the back of us so we all pulled into a side road. The bike rider, whom I believe was from Australia, had just bought the motorbike, which had big panniers. Anyway, he agreed to pay for the damage, so we went to Rivervale, the Mercedes specialist, where their salesman, Mike Burgess, always looks after me. The idea was to get the rear lamp mended, for which £360 was quoted. Mike though had other ideas. He said: "Jack, I've got a V12 out the front, completely loaded with every extra you can imagine."

It was certainly a lovely car, having been owned by the Managing Director of Mercedes UK, and had only done 10,000 miles. I therefore offered him mine and a certain amount of money for the V12 but he said: "I've got to go upstairs and see my boss". I thought that was strange as I'd always understood that he was his own boss but he reappeared, saying: "Oh no, he wants more". By the way, I'd been out in the car. What a performer! just over 4 seconds from 0 to 60! It had every extra you could think of – TV, heated electric seats with four different massage positions, air conditioning – it had everything! Anyway I said: "No, that's too dear! I can't afford it."

I thought that would be the end of the story but, while I was having a back massage at my gymnasium in Caversham, my mobile rang. It was Mike Burgess agreeing to my price for the V12! Jane, who was massaging me, was surprised to hear that I'd bought a V12 during the treatment. I've still got it now, nine years later. It's a beautiful car and has only done 50,000 miles. I was lucky to get it for a small fraction of the price it was when new, so I was well pleased with that! So that's the story of how breaking a rear light led me to fork out for a new car. Isn't life strange!

143

In 2003, Daphne organised a George Palmer School reunion so I helped out on 28th November, getting former pupils to sign her Visitors' Book as we had both attended the Infants and Junior Schools on that site while I had completed my schooling there at Palmer Central. Daphne wanted to build up and maintain contact with former pupils, staff and governors as we knew then that there were plans to demolish the original 1907 buildings and replace them with just one smaller Primary School and a housing development.

Even though the original 1907 buildings were indeed demolished in 2004 and replaced by a smaller school with a lift, the reunions continued because Daphne and Jim produced a booklet entitled "George Palmer School in photographs" and here you can see the year 6 leavers with some of the former pupils, who sponsored the books for them, in 2005. In the front row, you can see from the left: Christine Smith (née Masterman), who is just a day younger than Daphne, then myself, Jack Taylor, and Barb's cousins – Alan Barnes and his sister, Daphne Barnes-Phillips (née Barnes). The photo was taken by Jim.

The reunions have become an annual occurrence since 2004, having been incorporated into the Leavers' Assembly when the year 6 pupils put on a dramatisation for their parents and for former pupils. The Head, Ann Snowdon, has described the presentations as a tradition of the new school.

The family were to meet up again at Barb's Aunt Doris' funeral at Reading Crematorium and afterwards at the Grosvenor in Caversham on 23rd December 2003. She was 88 when she died on 17th in Bracknell and her younger daughter, Chris, and family were due to go on holiday on Boxing Day so it was good that the service could be arranged at short notice and they did not have to rearrange those plans. The photo of her on Page 11 of the Colour Photo Insert was taken at her 80th Birthday Party in 1995.

It was during 2003 that I'd had some of the trees felled in the front garden to open it up and have an illuminated fountain as a centrepiece – see page 12 of the Colour Photo Insert. For my annual New Year's Eve party, I had Christmas lights in the trees. The extension had given me a much larger lounge, which had a Christmas tree in the bay window and, in the smaller room next to it, which is entered through an arch rather than a door, a three-piece Jazz Band played my favourite music. I'd also had a conservatory erected off the kitchen, overlooking the fish pond. The garage was set up for the smokers. Some of Barb's guinea pigs were still alive then in their heated shed and I'd put two of the five bedrooms out of bounds so that the cats could have some peace and quiet.

Neville retired from Taylor's Racing Service in February 2004 so I found myself running the Business by myself again. That was the year that I was first diagnosed with high blood pressure but tablets soon sorted the problem and I kept a check on it using the same wrist monitor that Barbara had used.

Our grandson, Craig, was the first in our little family to go to University so I am very proud of him and the fact that he went on to achieve his Masters Degree. He is also a great runner as can be seen in a cutting from 6th October 2004 edition of *Post Midweek Sports Special* under the title:

Craig shatters personal best in Belgium.

Craig Taylor, the Reading Athletics and Reading Roadrunners star, enjoyed international success this week.
The 23-year-old had a very good race in Belgium at the weekend when he competed in the inaugural Coastal Half Marathon that ran from Nieuwpoort to Oostende.
He finished in fifth place with 73 mins 51 secs, just over a minute outside a place in the first three.
The race, with a field of 1,200 runners from all over Europe, was won in 70:33.
And Taylor's run was a staggering nine-minute improvement on his personal best

145

at Henley when he recorded 83 minutes.

His time was one of the fastest by a runner from Reading over the half marathon distance in recent times, with the exception of Sam Aldridge, also a member of Reading AC.

A large part of the picturesque course ran along the beach front and the race was part of the Belgian Coast in Action weekend with a number of running events on Saturday, including a full marathon and a relay, and walking and cycling events on Sunday.

Craig is a post graduate student studying for a Masters at Staffordshire University He is hoping for a repeat of this fine run in the Reading Half Marathon in March 2005.

His father, our son, Neville, also runs. He was a great manager, knowing all about racing and betting. There was nothing he didn't know about it and, like his Mum, he was very shrewd indeed. He stayed with me all his working career but has now retired, having done a great job whilst he worked for me. I am very proud of both him and Craig, I must say – very proud indeed.

At the end of 2004, I had seventeen Betting Shops and was going to Court on 4th January 2005 to apply for change of use for Meadway Post Office to a Betting Shop to become the eighteenth. I was to have my right knee replaced on 2nd February and it was then that I realised that I would have to pack up running and horse riding, because falling off occasionally when jumping the fences would have put too much pressure on the new knees. The surgeon said to me: "Come on in, young Jack. Unlimited walking is possible but no running" so, unfortunately, I had to pack up horse riding as well.

I still had twelve of Barbara's horses at that time but didn't race them as they were her particular interest – not mine. You could liken us to the chefs, Fanny and Johnnie Cradock. Fanny first appeared on TV in 1955 and was termed "the original celebrity chef" in the femailMAGAZINE section of 9th February 2012 Daily Mail. I was like Johnnie for Fanny Cradock in that I used to enjoy going along to the races accompanying Barb but had no wish to keep going after she died. Obviously, I have always made sure that the horses that remained were well looked after, stabling some of them at "High Thatch" in the winter and grazing them at my nearby farm in the summer.

There was also one surviving guinea pig then. However, to make sure that it did not feel lonely, I arranged for piped music to be played into its heated

146

room. Although, Barbara used to seek a double replacement when one of our small animals died, I decided, after her death, that I would not follow that principle anymore although I would obviously continue to look after any remaining ones throughout their natural lives for her sake.

I had thought it would be similar with the greyhounds, having instituted the Barbara Taylor Memorial Trophy (BTMT in the chart below), which was first presented on 23rd November 2002, following the success of the Memorial Meeting the previous year. It was then presented annually towards the end of November – except in 2004 when The Barbara Taylor Memorial Trophy (TBTMT) was presented on 4th December. All the races were held at Reading Stadium until it closed in 2007, and the distance was 465/509 [which means 465 metres or 509 yards] for each race. The 2003 event was for Puppies (P).

Trophy Name	Date	Heat	Grade	Winner	Time
BTMT	24NOV2007	4	A4	Tonetta Balboa	28.73
BTM Final	25NOV2006	10	A6	Horetown Graphic	28.97
BTMT–Heat 1	18NOV2006	5	A6	Dunbolg Ebony	29.23
BTMT–Heat 2	18NOV2006	6	A6	Horetown Graphic	28.76
BTMT FINAL	26NOV2005	7	A6	Hedsor Issy	29.24
TBTMT	4DEC2004	5	P1	Hedsor Kim	28.82
TBTMPT	22NOV2003	6	P1	Carly Armani	29.15
TBTMT	23NOV2002	7	A8	Sherwood Amaze	28.97

In October 2004, the Government introduced a Gambling Bill designed to tighten rules for betting on the Internet and lift restrictions on the number of casinos. However, gambling debts were unenforceable under English law until the Gambling Act of 2006. Trusted legal Bookmakers are members of the Independent Betting Adjudication Service (I.B.A.S.), an industry standard organisation to settle disputes.

At the end of 2005, I had 18 Betting Shops, five down from its peak of 23, although I was going to Court to obtain permission for two more on 2nd January 2006. One of those was at 441 Basingstoke Road, Reading and my long-standing support of Reading Football Club was rewarded when one of its players, Glen Little, agreed to open it, as can be seen on page 13 of the Colour Photo Insert. This was my second Betting Shop in Basingstoke Road, the other being closer to town at No. 55 (now Best & Less Supermarket).

That was in the row of shops between Surrey Road, where I lived as a child and George Palmer School. My friend, Derek Hatton, lived in the flat above it with his parents and two sisters in the 1940s when we rebuilt my first car in his garage at the Basingstoke Road end of Surrey Road (see page 68).

The Head Office of Taylor's Racing Service Ltd. was at 180a Oxford Road, Reading. Other branches in the Reading area in 2006 were:

178 – 180 Oxford Road	79 Elgar Road
542 Northumberland Avenue	481 Northumberland Avenue
55 Basingstoke Road	43 Wokingham Road
32 Coronation Square, Southcote	7 Meadway Precinct, Tilehurst
143 The Meadway, Tilehurst	120 Henley Road, Caversham

Those outside the Reading area were:

11 London Road, Newbury	5 Reynolds Way, Abingdon
41 Mill Street, Eynsham	27 Brindley Avenue, High Wycombe
38 St Luke's Road, Old Windsor	92 High Street, Colliers Wood
189 London Road, Romford	188 Hornchurch Road, Hornchurch

As mentioned earlier, the offspring of the greyhounds, *Miss Sophie* and *Trade Exchange*, did not start racing until after Barbara had died so I was able to witness their successes up until July 2005 when the last (and most successful) of them, *Exchange Express*, retired from racing. A month earlier, I had decided to continue with Greyhound Racing so bought a black bitch and named her *Miranda* after our horse *Where's Miranda*. She started racing in September 2006 and competed in 109 events, rewarding me with 14 firsts and 15 seconds.

Jack's Greyhounds	Sex	Coat Colour	Date Born	Races	1st	2nd
Miranda	F	Black	June 2005	109	14	15
Newgrange Byway	M	Blue	Oct. 2006	78	16	19
Spelathon	F	Black	Oct. 2006	96	19	27
Taylor	M	Brindle	Sept. 2007	96	19	19

Soon after *Miranda* started racing, I bought a dog and a bitch from the same litter, the dog being *Newgrange Byway* and the bitch *Spelathon* (pictured right). Both were born in Ireland and raced for me from 2008 – 2011. *Newgrange Byway* achieved 16 first and 19 second places while *Spelathon* was my most successful greyhound with 19 first and 27 second places.

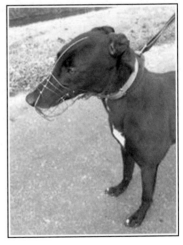

My latest greyhound gave me a chance for some personal indulgence so I named him *Taylor*. Another Irish dog born in September 2007, he took part in 96 races between June 2009 and October 2011, having an equal number of firsts and seconds – 19 of each.

"All work and no play would have made Jack a dull boy", as the saying goes, so I have made sure that I have had some memorable holidays. One fantastic experience was the Carnival in Rio de Janeiro, South America in 2006. Different floats kept coming through for 24 hours – all day and all night. My companion wanted to leave about 4.30 in the middle of the night so we left then 'though I was still transfixed. How they do it, I will never know – all those floats are out of this world! I also went up into the mountains to see the big statue of Christ with outstretched arms looking out over it all and found that really interesting as well.

However, I was perturbed by the numbers of young streetwise children, who come up with their little briefcases and suitcases trying to sell you things when you were eating near the beach. It seems that, at night, the Police try to catch them and, when they do, they shoot them. That seems accepted practice that the young lads should be shot at night but those who don't get caught, go into the hills and join the various mob gangs there. Those gangs do deals with the Police, leaving Carnival alone and, in return, the Police do them favours.

We were warned by an American guy whom we'd asked to take our photo on Rio de Janeiro beach: "Don't give your camera to anybody else to take a photo because they will run away with it!" One of our guys went out on his own at night to stroll along the front there and he got well and truly mugged. He wasn't too injured physically but everything he had was taken – rings, wallet, watch – the lot, so that brought it home to us that you've got to be so careful in such places.

Another incredible experience of a very different kind was in 2008, when I went to the very North of Norway by boat. It was as far North as you can get and, when we arrived, we saw a great big dome. Some TV people came up to me and asked why I had gone there. Naturally, I replied that I had always wanted to go to the very North, so they interviewed me.

A competition had taken place on our boat journey there and the prize seemed to be that a guy, dressed to look like Neptune, put a handful of ice down each of the winners' backs, inside their shirt! He was supposed to have come out of the sea and had all sorts of bells on him. When you consider, that it was about 30 degrees below freezing, I was really pleased not to have won a prize!

The highlight of the holiday, 'though, happened early one Saturday morning when we went with huskies right across the Northern slopes of Norway. It was still 30 degrees or so below zero but we were well wrapped up. Soon after we started off, my companion tipped the sled over and I went face down in about four feet of snow, so I said: "I'm not riding with you anymore!" The Norwegian lady let me drive her sled with the huskies by myself using the various brake pedals at my feet.

So off we went until we came to an area of solid ice. I was up on the back of the sled when the Norwegian lady said that we had to turn around. As she turned the sled rather sharply, bang, I was down in the snow again, up to my eyeballs in thick snow. When I got up, she said to me: "You have to fall out three times before you're a qualified ski driver!" I thought: "I've had enough of this", so I sat in the sled and let her drive.

At one point, when we came to a very steep hill (which must have been about 800 or 1,000 yards down), she asked: "Do you want to go down fast or slow?" When I said: "Slow", she explained that the huskies are taught to perform their bodily functions whilst they are pulling the sleds. It's therefore possible to see it happening if they need to go to number 2 while they are running!

Coming to a frozen river about 30 or 40 yards across, we were told that Russia was on the other side. The Norwegians were measuring air quality as it came over from Russia because it was felt that the Russians were not fussy about the air from their factories. If anything went wrong, they were going to set off the alarms. Although there did not appear to be any guards on the Russian side of the river, we were told that they were watching it by satellite and would have soon jumped on anyone who attempted to cross.

We carried on for about twenty miles in total then stopped, kennelled the dogs, went into the forest, lit a fire and had a good meal there – toasted sausages, bread and potato wraps – before re-harnessing the dogs and driving the twenty miles back. Was I glad to get back after we'd finished the second twenty miles! Back at the kennels there were two giant white dogs, whose job was to protect the huskies because there were a lot of bears around. When bears get hungry, they come into the kennel area so the dogs are needed to keep them out.

On the journey back to our hotel by car, the Norwegian lady recounted tales of some of the terrible things done by Adolf Hitler during World War II. She said that, when the Russians were beating the Germans back through Northern Norway, the latter were burning down all the wooden buildings as they retreated, leaving a scorched earth scenario behind.

As I have already mentioned, I have made several changes to "High Thatch" and its grounds since Barbara died. As a result it is now a big house with five bedrooms; three bathrooms (two en-suite and a family bathroom); a granny flat with a granny kitchen; a gymnasium; a sauna; a big snooker room with a bar; extra bathrooms and toilets; a sun house; an office; stables, etc.

Andrew Thompson, who prefers to be called "Tom", came to work for me around nine years ago and he's proved a very good all-rounder. By the end of 2004, he'd built the snooker room, with a full-sized bar at one end in a Scandinavian-style wooden building. Outside he created a pond with a waterfall and a bridge lit by rows of lights; then a stream to a second pond in the front garden – see page 14 of the Colour Photo Insert. In fact, he rebuilt the garden all round – front and back. The patio across the rear of the house – see photo on page 12 of the Colour Photo Insert – and round all the outbuildings was finished off with a koi pond within it, then he built a lovely wall adjoining the patio with a centrepiece for plants.

He went on to convert the garage, building a gymnasium and a shower and converting a sauna from a Shetland stable, with accommodation above, doing all the interior work. Another example of his workmanship is the summer-house built partway down the sloping back garden in such a position as to have a fantastic view of the valley as can be seen in the photographs on page 15 of the Colour Photo Insert. It was in the process of construction at the time of my 80th birthday party on 29th April 2007. There were four horses stabled at "High Thatch" then and ten more at Stoke Row. Zoe had decorated the house and patio in Barb's (pink and grey) and my (red, white and black) racing colours on that occasion and I had the usual Jazz Group playing.

Tom also built a lovely big office for Joy Cuthbertson (who was with me for around 35 years, being a very good secretary indeed and a great help to me). He has transformed the place!

Reading Greyhound Stadium was to hold its last meeting at Bennet Road on Saturday 18th October 2008. Dog Racing had been held there on Tuesday, Thursday and

Saturday evenings since 1975 with Speedway on Mondays and Fridays. The photo on the previous page shows me presenting a prize in the 1990s.

Previously, Dog Racing had been held in Oxford Road, Tilehurst and,

 following the closure of the Bennet Road site, Swindon has become the nearest track to Reading. That was too far away for me to travel to see them so I gave my greyhounds to Bob Gilling their trainer, seen here (left) with Pat Witchels, myself and Barb.

The Greyhound Owners', Breeders' and Trainers' Association (GOBATA) website's tweet on 14th March 2011 headed "Gilling cites poor prize money and recession for downward dive" shows that he is still Secretary of the Breeders' Forum after more than 30 years:

"PRIZEMONEY remains stagnant; there is still a them and us 'relationship' between owners and promoters; throw in the soaring cost of living, and therein are just three reasons why greyhound racing is currently in decline."
So says Bob Gilling, who recently marked his 30th year as secretary of the Greyhound Breeders' Forum and whose views are shared by many people in the sport. Yet, despite the troubled times greyhound racing is experiencing, Gilling remains as keen and as committed as he ever was.

"It is sad the way the game has gone", he says, "and there are a number of other reasons to blame. Folk cite the recession but it is the same for any business, everyone is finding it tough out there but greyhound racing is unquestionably suffering more than most."

2010s – Time to sell

It was only in the present decade that I thought it was time to have a rest so, at the age of 83, I sold the Betting Shops to the *Tote*. After taking over on 19th July 2010, it sold them on to *Bet Fred* a year later, in July 2011. I've kept the freeholds and rent out the shops and flats above so still have an income from those. On 24th May 2011, there had been a raid at T.R.S. in The Meadway when a man wielding a lump of wood failed to snatch a bag of money.

At one time there were over 15,000 Betting Shops in the United Kingdom. Now, through consolidation, there are about 8,500. *William Hill* is the Market Leader and there are three other major "high street" bookmakers: *Ladbrokes*, *Coral* and state-owned *ToteSport*. *BetFred* is among the bookmakers that are rapidly emerging in terms of turnover and event sponsorship along with *Sky Bet*, *Bet 24*, *Victor Chandler*, *Stan James*, *Sportingbet*, *Mansion* and *Bet365*.

In the U.K., on-track bookies still mark up the odds on boards beside the race course and use tic-tac or mobile telephones to communicate the odds between their staff and to other bookies. However, improved TV coverage and modernisation of the Bookmaking Laws have led to an increase in online and high street gambling.

I also decided to sell "Hawthorn Paddocks", the 17.1 acre private equestrian establishment at Kit Lane, Stoke Row in 2010. Planning permission for

Change of Use of Barn from Agricultural to purposes incidental to the keeping of Horses (including stabling) had been granted in August 2006 subject to the usual conditions.

As well as the Bookmaking, another long-standing interest of mine ceased in 2010. Roy Loader started the Friendly Football League in 1965 and ran it for 45 years. I helped him whenever I could throughout that time, doing various promotions, sponsoring Shields, *Jack Taylor* Trophies and other things and really enjoyed those 45 years. Towards the end, I sponsored the entire League when the chap, who had been doing it, had to drop out. Roy's ill-health and the lack of teams caused the League to finish in 2010 but I consider it to have been the best League in Reading for Sunday football. Neville played in it and Taylor's Racing Service had both a team and a reserve team in it.

However, some interests continue as I still play golf every Tuesday with a great bunch of guys, who are all retired. I refer to them as *The Summer Wine Gang* on account of their age. Bob was a Building Society Office Manager; John had a very good job with Legal and General and Robert was a Company representative, who spent a lot of time abroad. We have a great time playing golf if the weather is good but, if it is bad, especially during the winter months, we play snooker in my snooker room at "High Thatch". I've got a lovely table – really old with beautiful legs – which I bought down at the coast somewhere. The big slabs that go in there before you put the felt on means that it weighs a ton or two, so I had to have supports put in the snooker room floor for it – see page 14 of the Colour Photo Insert.

Although I have had prostrate cancer for about fifteen years and have had an operation, radiotherapy and recently chemotherapy, I have been well looked after by my oncologist, Dr. Rogers; before him, Jane Barrett; and, before her, my surgeon, Mr. Malone. The Oncology Department at the top of Castle Hill in Reading are very good to me, so I'm still going strong at 84 years of age, thanks to all those who help me. Although I've been feeling very tired during the chemotherapy treatments, which happened every three weeks, I am doing ok. I feel fortunate that my cancer was discovered quite early as it is possible to survive these things if they are caught early enough nowadays. I was lucky that mine was discovered early as it has given me a longer life than my father, who died of prostrate cancer when he was seventy-seven.

155

I have had some really good people working for me over the years, especially Joy Cuthbertson, who was my secretary for 35 years or so. Currently, it is Elaine who cleans the house, looks after me and is my secretary in 2012. She is also very good indeed with computers so I am doing very well, being very well looked after.

At the end of October 2011, I still had three of Barbara's race horses paddocked at "High Thatch" – *Greyfriar's Bobby*, *Gushka* and *Nanquidno*, whom I've mentioned already. There are also two Shetland ponies, *Goldie* and *Jo Jo* – see page 16 of Colour Photo Insert. *Red Cedars' Jo Jo* (the full breed name given by breeder, Mrs S. Freeman) is a black and white colt born on 4th June 1994 to the black 36" Dam, *Georgia of Southfieldgate*, and sired by the 32" skewbald, *Foxley's Firefox*, with pedigree stretching back to great-great grandparents.

I have five cats – the brothers, *Bonnie* and *Clyde*, *Miranda*, *Mollie* and *Nelson*. *Mollie* is the most distinctive as she has a bump on her head and can bring her tail right over her head. They come and go as they please, having the run of the whole house and grounds, often settling on the beds, but they do like to lie on the Daily Mail while I am trying to read it! – see page 16 of the Colour Photo Insert. In case you're wondering why I haven't any greyhounds at "High Thatch", they are trained to kill small animals, so are not good with cats.

Recently, while having the concrete dug up at the side of "High Thatch", newts were found so, naturally, work has had to cease until their natural life span has enabled them to move on.

Although I have always enjoyed the company of animals, I could never have guessed that they would play such a large part in my life and lead to the successful career that I have been fortunate enough to enjoy during an era when we, as a nation, no longer seem to have much time to spend with them now that we do not need their services as much as our forebears did.

List of Principal Sources

Primary Sources

Daphne Barnes' Diaries – handwritten

1967: 24 April   : Albert Barnes' funeral
1967: 13 September : Violet Robinson (née Barnes)'s funeral
1967: 26 October : James Robinson's funeral
1978: 15 July   : Jenny Splendid finished 3rd at Newbury

Daphne Barnes-Phillips' Diaries – handwritten

1981: 28 February   : Neville and Lynn's Wedding
1982: 30 April   : Leslie John Barnes' funeral
1988: 4 March   : Albert Edward Barnes' funeral
1995: 9 July   : Doris Barnes' 80th Birthday
2000: 5 December : Barbara Taylor (née Robinson)'s funeral
2002: 16 January   : Maureen Brown (née Barnes)'s funeral
2002: 17 March+5 May : Book launch and Jack's 75th Birthday lunch
2003: 28 November : First George Palmer School reunion
2003: 23+31 December : Doris Barnes' funeral & Jack's Open House
2004: 31 December : New Year's Eve Open House
2005: 31 December : New Year's Eve Open House
2007: 29 April   : Jack's 80th Birthday party

The History of our Family – Barnes-Phillips – handwritten

Wife's Parents' Family : Barnes side

George Palmer Girls' Sch., Reading Attendance Registers – handwritten

3 October 1907 – 13 April 1915 and 13 April 1915 – 23 April 1934

Green Girls School, Reading Minute Book 1840 – handwritten

1885: 3 January, 4 July : Transfer to Russell Street, admission age
1891: 29 September : School rules revised

Green Girls School, Reading Minute Book 1901 – handwritten

1905: 29 September : Election of Girls (page 37)
1906: 29 September : Election of Norah Rolph (page 41)

Katesgrove Infants' School Log Book – handwritten

1874: 14 August   : E. M. Brant's taking charge of School (p.1)
1885: 23 November : School Staff (page 335)
1891: 23 November : School Staff (page 473)

Secondary Sources

Books, Booklets or Articles

Barnes-Phillips, D J (2011) : *This is our School* – a celebration of the bicentenary of the Reading British School, Southampton Street 1811 – 2011

Du Maurier, Daphne (1934) : *Gerald* (page 3)

The borough of Reading Charities (1923) : *A History of the County of Berkshire: Volume 3* (pages 378 – 384)

Encyclopaedia Britannica : Betting tax; Betting not legalized

Leadbeater, Chris : *Independent* Traveller Sat 8 October, 2011, p. 4

Racing Diary 2006 : Taylor's Racing Service Ltd.

Census CDs

: Berkshire 1891
: Berkshire 1901

Newspapers

Berkshire Chronicle
1950:   8 September : *Wedding Taylor/Robinson*

Daily Mail
2012:   9 February : *Who knew? Fanny Cradock*

Herts Advertiser:
2004:   11 June : *One man's D-Day memories*

Racing Post
1982:   23 October : *BenRaad Gas heater 4-year-old Handicap Hurdle*
1998:   16 October : *Johnny Haine*
2001:   30 April : *Rex Carter*

The Sporting Life
1982:   10 April : *Pitminster Four-year-old Novices' Hurdle*

The Sun
2011:   28 April : *50 on the nose* by John Kay (Chief Reporter)

Reading Street Directories

Kelly	: 1889/90
	: 1913, 1917, 1926, 1927, 1929, 1932, 1936, 1942
MacCauley	: 1888
Smith	: 1884, 1885, 1886, 1887, 1889, 1892,
	: 1906, 1907, 1908, 1909, 1913, 1914, 1915, 1916,
	: 1917, 1918, 1921
Steven	: 1893

Websites

2.france-galop.com	: *Race Record for Jenny Splendid*
ancestry.co.uk	: *Daphne Barnes-Phillips' Family Tree*
ancestry.com	: *Arrival of Deseado at Liverpool*
freeBMD	: *Births, Marriages and Deaths*
Commonwealth War	
Graves Commission	: *World War I & II deaths*
David Nash Ford	: *Royal Berkshire History – Simonds*
english Heritage	: *Katesgrove Board School*
familySearch	: *1881 Census*
Friends of Beamish	: *What Did Grandad Do in the Coalhouse?*
Genes Reunited	: *1841 – 1911 censuses*
gobata.co.uk	: *Greyhound Owners' Breeders' & Trainers' Assoc.*
greyhound-data.com	: *Statistics for greyhounds from January 2002*
iguides.org	: *The history of Milk Delivery in the UK* (Dave Tug)
Lambert, Tim	: *A Brief History of Reading, Berkshire, England*
Lummis, Eric	: *The History of The Suffolk Regiment*:
News.google.com	
/newspapers	: Glasgow Herald *Horse Racing Results*
Scattered Homes	: www.workhouses.org.uk/sheffield
S.E.T.F.	: *La Sociedad Explotadora de Tierra del Fuego*
Soldiers of	
Gloucestershire	: *Time Line 1925 – 1950*
thegoodgamblingguide	: *Biographies of William Hill, Joe Coral*
thisisDorset.co.uk	: Friday, February 20, 2009 *Point to Point News*
tierradelfuegochile.cl	: *ocupasciontierradelfuego* – map
Tom Wick's blog	: *Buenos Aries Argentina Travel Guide*
Wikipedia	: Definitions of *Agriculture in Chile, Bookmaker,*
	: *Domestic Sheep Predation, Puerto Deseado*

If you have enjoyed reading **Taylor-made Jackpot**, we are sure you will also appreciate the following books by Daphne Barnes-Phillips:

	**This is our School – Reading British School, 1811-2011** Built in two months in 1810; considered unsuitable accommodation for a Board School in 1902; this building still stands in Southampton Street, Reading two centuries after it started life as Reading Lancasterian School on 8th January, 1811. In *This is our School*, Daphne brings us tales of educational life in Reading in the 19th century, through the characters involved in it, including George Palmer MP, who was its secretary for 50 years. Fully illustrated with black and white photographs. 208 pages. **Price £9.95** ISBN 978 1 897715 12 9
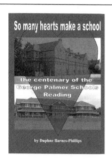	**So many hearts make a school** Daphne, who was born and raised just a quarter of a mile from George Palmer Infant and Junior Schools, recalls her own memories, and also those of 50 other pupils and staff across the 100 years that are celebrated in this book. Hours of research at the Berkshire Records Office, Reading Library and on-line showed up facts and figures previously unknown to most pupils and staff throughout the century. Fully illustrated with black and white photographs. 240 pages. **Price £12.95** ISBN 978 1 897715 07 2
	**George Palmer School in photographs – 1907 to 2004** A photographic record of events in the life of George Palmer School, Reading, in its original buildings from 1907 to 2004. Fully illustrated with black and white photographs. 40 pages. **Price £4.95** ISBN 978 1 897715 16 1
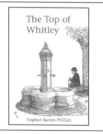	**The Top of Whitley – A study of the Spring Gardens area of Reading** The Spring Gardens area of Reading may only be about half a mile square, but *The Top of Whitley* uncovers its history over a 160-year period, with reminiscences from twenty people who played, worked, lived or were educated there. Fully illustrated with black and white photographs. 160 pages. **Price £8.95** ISBN 978 1 897715 01 3

All books are available from: Corridor Press, 19 Portland Avenue, Exmouth, Devon, EX8 2BS – email: *corridorpress@yahoo.co.uk* or phone: 01395 263494. All Prices include postage & packing within UK. Please make cheques payable to "Corridor Press".